Sea Change at Annapolis

Sea Change
at Annapolis

* * * * * * * * * * * * * * * * * * *

The United States
Naval Academy,
1949–2000

H. MICHAEL GELFAND

Foreword by Senator John McCain

The University of
North Carolina Press
Chapel Hill

© 2006 The University of North Carolina Press
All rights reserved

Designed by Kimberly Bryant
Set in Quadraat by Keystone Typesetting, Inc.
Manufactured in the United States of America

The paper in this book meets the guidelines for
permanence and durability of the Committee on
Production Guidelines for Book Longevity of the
Council on Library Resources.

Library of Congress Cataloging-in-Publication Data
Gelfand, H. Michael.
Sea change at Annapolis : the United States Naval
Academy, 1949–2000 / H. Michael Gelfand ; Foreword by
Senator John McCain.
p. cm.
Includes bibliographical references and index.
ISBN-13: 978-0-8078-3047-5 (cloth: alk. paper)
ISBN-10: 0-8078-3047-X (cloth: alk. paper)
1. United States Naval Academy—History—20th century.
I. Title.
V415.L1G45   2006
359.0071′173—dc22

                                    2006013100

10 09 08 07 06   5 4 3 2 1

★ ★ ★ ★ ★ ★ ★ ★ ★ ★ ★ ★ ★ ★ ★ ★ ★ ★ ★

For my parents,
Elayne Phyllis Jaffee Gelfand
and
Gerald Gelfand

Contents

Map and Illustrations

Tables

Foreword

In 1845, Secretary of the Navy George Bancroft set out to create an academy that would provide the United States with a naval officer corps unmatched by any seafaring nation. Bancroft envisioned these officers as men whose sense of duty, honor, loyalty, and character would be unparalleled.

This guiding spirit of the Naval Academy remains unchanged to this day; the Academy serves as both the repository of the Navy's core values and the benchmark of its unflagging moral and military leadership to this great nation. It stands as the very soul of the United States Navy.

In this history of the last fifty years of the Naval Academy, Dr. Gelfand explores both the events and people that have shaped the Academy's midshipmen and the future of the Navy. He adeptly discusses the Academy's attempts to continually transform itself in the recognition that "change is inevitable and forthcoming."

Change at an institution as large as the Academy takes both dedication and patience. The analysis offered regarding the inclusion of minorities and women into the Brigade of Midshipmen provides a critical examination of areas in which Annapolis will continue to improve. As Dr. Gelfand writes in his concluding remarks, administrators have "fulfilled their charge and obligation to lead the Academy through fundamental alterations in the institution's culture." This change will continue as long as dedicated sailors and marines administer and attend Annapolis.

Since its inception, Annapolis has endeavored to train the best and brightest in America. The Academy is in a position to bring together midshipmen from every economic background, race, religion, and region of our country. These students are drawn to the Academy to pursue academic excellence, athletic prowess, and military service. The Academy is able to take all these students and develop within them the ideal that strength of character is a goal above all others. It is in this way that the Academy is able to strengthen not only the Navy but society as a whole.

A man I love and admire, Vice Admiral William P. Lawrence, once said that the Academy "must graduate special persons—officers who will place the interests of the country and the welfare and safety of their subordinates above their own."

The values and mission of the Naval Academy have never been more imperative than today. The threat posed by global terror demands that our armed forces be guided by the best of the best, sailors and marines who will carry the torch of American values wherever they are needed. We can only succeed in building a free world if our men and women in uniform conduct themselves with a level of honor and integrity that shines through the walls of dishonor and hypocrisy inherent in tyrannical governments. Theodore Roosevelt once said, "To educate a person in mind and not in morals is to educate a menace to society."

It is my belief that any institution of higher education can produce students who demonstrate excellence in academics or athletics; it takes amazing dedication to graduate students who possess excellence of character as well. These timeless ideals—duty, honor, loyalty, and strength of character—that the Naval Academy engenders are critical if we are to help develop citizens capable of the highest responsibilities in both military and civilian life. Annapolis will continue to serve as the mental, moral, and physical training ground for America's present and future leaders.

As a graduate of the Naval Academy, I have experienced firsthand the dedication of faculty, coaches, and students to the ideals of the Navy. The values I learned in my plebe summer and internalized during my time at Annapolis have stayed with me throughout my life. They have served as an ever-present polestar, showing and occasionally reminding me of the path of honor through the darkness.

God grants us all the privilege of having our character tested. The tests come frequently, as often in peace as in war, as often in private as in public.

It is my great pleasure that others will now be able to understand the rich history and unique mission of the Academy and the service it provides to this great nation.

This text adds a critical volume to the literature about the Navy and Annapolis itself. I would like to thank Dr. Gelfand for his efforts in creating a wonderfully engaging and accessible history of this treasured institution.

Senator John McCain

Preface

    This book examines challenges to the Naval Academy's culture and traditions, from both inside and outside the Academy's walls, between 1949 and 2000. The manner in which the Naval Academy has responded to these challenges disproves the common claim that the Academy is "a hundred and sixty years of tradition unmarred by progress."[1] Rather, events at Annapolis reflect the transformation of American culture and society at large in the post–World War II era. As television arose as a popular form of entertainment, the Naval Academy responded by using it for recruitment. While African Americans fought for and achieved greater acceptance and integration in American society, USNA took steps to increase minority enrollment in the Brigade of Midshipmen. When students across the country began to challenge in loco parentis policies, USNA's students similarly began to protest rigid regulations at the Academy. And as Congress created laws that mandated non-discrimination, the Naval Academy prepared for and admitted female midshipmen.

  The British military historian John Keegan was correct when, in 1995, he noted the exceptionality of the Naval Academy. Keegan wrote that "only at Annapolis, the naval cadet academy, cramped in its sylvan Ivy League setting on the banks of the Chesapeake, have the American armed forces managed to combine the liberal arts ideal with the rigours of training for the service life."[2] To a large extent, the liberal arts facet of the Academy's culture derives from the historically equal balance that Academy administrators have maintained between civilian and officer faculty, unlike at West Point and the Air Force Academy, where faculty members are almost exclusively military officers. USNA is also unique because it is located in a southern state's capital, because it prepares officers for two related but separate branches of the military (the U.S. Navy and the U.S. Marine Corps), and because its students live under a distinctive Honor Concept and in a single expansive dormitory. Finally, the Academy's short, thirty-five-mile distance from both Baltimore, Maryland, and Washington, D.C., places it in close proximity to major newspapers and governmental and military leaders and makes the institution a popular destination for those leaders along with journalists, foreign dignitaries, and tourists.

The five decades after World War II encompassed tremendous change and increased opportunities for most groups in the United States largely because the federal government, through the executive, judicial, and legislative branches, set out to foster a more equitable society for its citizens. And yet in the early twenty-first century, it remains clear that the democratic ideals and promise behind the American participation in World War II have not come to complete fruition. African Americans and other non-white groups continue to experience discrimination and de facto segregation, living in the economic and social margins of American society. Religious fundamentalists have found greater voice in the United States by supporting conservative and Republican Party candidates and politicians and seek an increased role for Christianity in governmental affairs and public life. Women, in spite of tremendous advances in most aspects of life in the United States, are still, through the constraints of gender bias, working to achieve equity with men. And students are still living within, and on occasion challenging, universities' in loco parentis regulations, which were designed to control students' behavior and activities on campus.

One common argument used to explain the imperfect and incomplete improvement in the status of these groups has been that the government is incapable of legislating morality. But what about forums in which the government *can* legislate morality? In the case of race, for example, the federal government chose to crack segregation in two spheres, the military and public education. No observer or student of either public schools or the armed forces would argue that success has been complete in these efforts. However, changes in the military and public education have been considerably successful since President Truman formally integrated the military by executive order in 1948 and since the Supreme Court found segregated public school education to be unconstitutional six years later. Persistent white supremacist legal wrangling and the creation of private white-only academies aside, many school districts in the United States chose to comply with the Court's order. And in the case of the military, any officer or enlisted person who desired to remain in good standing with the armed services had no choice but to follow the order of his or her Commander in Chief.

As a result, a federal institution that is both military and educational in form offers an opportunity to examine how such an institution has changed culturally along with American society between 1949 and 2000. I chose to examine the United States Naval Academy (USNA) at Annapolis, Maryland, which is one of the nation's five federal service academies and one of its three military academies. The Naval Academy has prepared professional military leaders since its founding in Annapolis in 1845. As the most revered source of officers for the Navy, for the Marine Corps since 1887, and for the Air Force between 1949 and 1963, the Naval Academy is both a prominent engineering-oriented institution of higher education and a prestigious military organization.[3] Receiving its funding from the United States government, the Naval Academy promotes both federal and broader American societal goals as it fulfills its education and training mission.

The Naval Academy is an institution heavily laden with traditions, and this book utilizes culture as a vehicle to study and analyze the transformation of events at Annapolis. I draw on two theorists in order to understand cultural change. Anthropologist Marshall Sahlins argues that a group's culture "is the legacy of their ancestral tradition, transmitted in the distinctive concepts of their language, and adapted to their specific life conditions."[4] Historian Lawrence Levine notes that "culture is not a fixed condition but a process: the product of interaction between past and present. Its toughness and resiliency are determined not by a culture's ability to withstand change, which indeed may be a sign of stagnation, but by its ability to react creatively and responsively to the realities of a new situation."[5] Furthermore, two historians offer an understanding of culture and change over time in the context of higher education. Historian Lawrence Cremin has suggested that "educational institutions . . . always confront novelty" through one of three approaches: self-adaptation to change, alliance with change, or resistance to change.[6] Renaissance scholar and Yale University president A. Bartlett Giamatti considers the place of institutions of higher education within their nations, describing universities as "deeply conventional and yet future oriented," functioning "as the culture's place to generate and test and disseminate new knowledge, and [as] the medium whereby a people remember who they are and where they came from."[7] Although there are slight differences in the nature of these definitions, the four perspectives constitute a summary of the term "culture" and help to describe how the Naval Academy has dealt with challenges that the

American public, Congress, federal courts, the military, and the Academy's own administration, staff, and midshipmen have posed to it. Furthermore, these definitions help us to understand and interpret the transformations that have taken place at the Naval Academy in the second half of the twentieth century.

Several generations of USNA midshipmen, in reciting the statement that follows each day's announcements (a task performed by freshmen), have told upperclassmen that "time, tide, and formation wait for no one." In thus encouraging their peers to keep track of the hour, these midshipmen also underscore the need to keep abreast of coming change. Indeed, I accept that change is inevitable and I argue that each of the developments that I describe in the following chapters has, after a period of concern and adjustment, led the Naval Academy to more closely align with and reflect the democratic principles and ideals of the United States. I agree with Thomas Jefferson's insistence that "laws and institutions must go hand in hand with the progress of the human mind. As that becomes more developed, more enlightened, as new discoveries are made, new truths disclosed and manners and opinions change with the change of circumstances, institutions must advance also, and keep pace with the times."[8] I also find truth in the words of the celebrated novelist of the American West Wallace Stegner, who wrote that "no society is healthy without both the will to create anew and the will to save the best of the old: it is not the triumph of either tendency, but the constant, elastic tension between the two that should be called our great tradition. In this society we may confidently count on the will to change. It is one of the strengths of our civilization, and as I have already said, history lines up in support of the rebel."[9] Indeed, the topical studies that follow not only outline transformations but are also largely the stories of men and women who define the term *rebel*.

Like Jefferson and Stegner, many members of the Naval Academy community have contemplated the concepts of change and continuity. Some leaders and midshipmen have clung to the status quo, preferring to observe more conservative, comfortable, and accepted practices and viewpoints. However inevitable change may be, the Naval Academy environment, like that of its parent culture, the United States Navy, is not always one that is conducive to rapid transformation. Retired USNA academic board secretary and dean of admissions Robert McNitt notes, "The Navy is a very conservative and prudent organization [because] we deal with ships that last for 20 or 30 years. We deal with elements that can do you in in a hurry if you make a mistake, so seamen and naval officers have always been unwilling to move rapidly until they've proven that something works. Even then they're sometimes very slow to make a change."[10] However, progressive trends have not been unknown at USNA, and some military leaders and midshipmen have been more open-minded toward change. On occasion, some Navy officers have counseled midshipmen not to fear original ideas, new practices, and novel approaches to leadership. For example, during his address to the graduating class of 1956, chairman of the joint chiefs of staff and alumnus Arthur Radford told the assembled midshipmen,

> The key words I emphasize are "tradition" and "progress." At first glance, you may think these words are incompatible. But I can tell you they are not. They go together, and each complements the other. For the readiness of the man is gauged, in part at least, by his flexible and timely adjustment to the new and novel, without sacrifice of principle or abandonment of standards. You need never feel that you would be untrue to the classes who sailed before you if you sail courses different from ours. . . . No one can deny the need for progress. There is always a place for change. It is an inescapable law of life.[11]

The manners in which administrators, officers, alumni, midshipmen, faculty, and community members reacted when faced with such issues as change and progress constitute the core of this study.

Although it contains references to earlier time periods, this manuscript focuses on changes and developments at the Naval Academy during the Cold War and post–Cold War eras, beginning in 1949. That year, Superintendent James Holloway successfully defended the existence of independent service academies, including USNA, against governmental proposals to unify them into one generalized academy.[12] In the same year, a number of notable programmatic changes began for both the Academy and its midshipmen: company officers began to teach a formal, structured leadership course; the scope of athletics expanded when USNA teams began to use commercial aviation in order to reach distant competitors; USNA began joint training of midshipmen with West Point cadets; an Academy-oriented radio station, WRNV, started operations; and administrators began to consider the Sponsor Program, a support network for midshipmen in the Annapolis community. Furthermore, the year's graduates were the first post–World War II class prepared to graduate in the typical four-year cycle rather than an expedited wartime three-year course and were the first USNA graduates who could choose to enter the U.S. Air Force.

However, 1949 was also extremely significant because the impact of larger trends in American society had major implications for the institution's future. Midshipman Wesley Brown became, in June, the first African American to graduate from USNA, and midshipman candidate John Cruzat, an African American, completed the course of study at the Naval Academy's preparatory school in Newport, Rhode Island. Takeshi Yoshihara, a member of the class of 1953, became only the second Asian American to enter Annapolis when he took the Midshipman's Oath in the summer of 1949. Later in the year, Genevieve Waselewski became the first woman to seek admission to USNA. Finally, near the end of 1949, a group of midshipmen met to discuss the preliminary plans for what became an institutional hallmark, the Naval Academy's Honor Concept. These events set the stage for the dramatic changes that transformed the Academy's culture over the course of the next five decades.

I present this study in eight chapters. In Chapter One, I portray the midshipmen's lives and activities within the institutional culture of the Academy. Beginning with an overview of the Naval Academy's history from its founding in 1845 through the year 1949, Chapter One includes a description of USNA's setting, campus, architecture, and physical development. Buildings and monuments throughout the campus serve to remind midshipmen of the institution's history, Naval and Marine Corps achievements, and the accomplishments of its graduates. The chapter outlines the complex USNA administrative organization—with emphasis on the academic revolution that was a backdrop for other significant changes in the post-1949 period—and describes midshipman life from the admission process through graduation.

Chapter Two describes the experiences of minority midshipmen and follows the origins of organized recruiting efforts, including specialized recruiting activities involving midshipmen and private citizens, radio programs, the celebrated television series *Men of Annapolis*, and dramatic films that served the dual function of entertainment and advertisement. The chapter then examines midshipmen who were members of a variety of minority groups at USNA before 1965. What happened to early African American, Jewish, Asian American, and American Indian midshipmen illustrate the ways in which institutional treatment of these men mirrored racial and religious sentiment in the nation.

Chapter Three describes the drive to recruit minority midshipmen and the continuing problems with racism at USNA. The chapter begins with a look at the Kennedy and Johnson White Houses' observations of the dearth of minority students at the Naval Academy and Johnson's efforts to convince USNA leaders to take steps to increase their minority enrollment. When the Academy created its Candidate Guidance Office in 1970 as the center for recruiting efforts, it established a Minority Candidate section to seek minority midshipmen and began utilizing the Naval Academy Preparatory School to funnel minority group members into Annapolis. The chapter follows recruiting developments and reveals the experiences of a variety of minority midshipmen in recent decades. Although a higher number of minority students presently attend USNA, the numbers have reached a plateau, recruiting efforts have not changed dramatically since the 1970s, and some minority midshipmen still encounter racism.

Chapter Four looks at the role of religion and the tensions that religious observance have caused at USNA. Beginning in the nineteenth century, the Naval Academy required its midshipmen to attend religious services. In 1970, just as their civilian counterparts protested on university campuses, midshipmen joined with a West Point cadet in suing the Academies to end obligatory chapel attendance. The chapter examines the development of mandatory attendance and early discussions of the policy's legitimacy, including a detailed account of cadet efforts to terminate required chapel at West Point. This chapter then describes the courtroom debates and proceedings that pitted high-ranking Naval and Defense Department officials against midshipmen, cadets, and their ACLU attorneys. After reviewing a federal appeals court's decision to end the practice in 1973, the chapter concludes by examining the beliefs of several administrators about the fate of mandatory chapel attendance.

Chapter Five describes women's earliest presence at Annapolis. Although not permitted to be midshipmen, women have had a variety of roles in the Academy community. The chapter then follows a number of young women as they attempted to seek admission to the Academy. While male midshipmen continued to see women as the objects of their longing and desires, federal judges, Naval leaders, and the U.S. Congress debated the possibility of allowing women to attend USNA. As Gloria Steinem predicted in a 1972 speech to midshipmen, the federal government did eventually allow women to attend the Naval Academy. Chapter Five follows these legal proceedings and describes the Academy's preparations for the arrival of its first female midshipmen.

Chapter Six begins with the entry of three women to the Naval Academy Preparatory School in 1976. The hostility of their male colleagues was a foreshadowing of what lay in store at Annapolis. Once the women were plebes, they faced difficulties with their uniforms, the media, Academy officers and faculty, alumni, and male midshipmen. Chapter Six follows the women of the class of 1980 from their arrival at USNA through their graduation, and, utilizing interviews with the women, shows the pressures they faced until their commencement day. Shocking, emotional, and disturbing, the experiences of the first female midshipmen at USNA symbolize the challenges women faced in American society as they attempted to enter institutions firmly ensconced in masculinity.

Chapter Seven looks at both the progress and the continuing difficulties for women who graduated after the class of 1980. Although over twenty years have passed and much of the open hostility toward women has subsided, women remain on the fringes of acceptance within the Brigade of Midshipmen. Derogatory comments and remarks have not disappeared, women's uniforms continue to cause them uneasiness, and extensive numbers of female midshipmen face eating disorders. However, the chapter demonstrates that women's sports have provided female midshipmen with a supportive community and that women have succeeded in every academic, athletic, and leadership pursuit at USNA.

Chapter Eight presents a series of episodes in which midshipmen reacted to both administrative attempts to tighten control over their lives and to national and international events and trends. In 1949, within two years of the executive and legislative branches taking steps to ascertain the loyalty of government employees, midshipmen William Lawrence and H. Ross Perot took the first steps to create an honor concept. Members of the class of 1952—annoyed by changes in their designated free time—carried out a protest during their graduation parade, and members of the class of 1970—similarly upset with administrative changes in their designated free time—staged a sit-in on the superintendent's lawn in the fall of 1968. The next year, editors of the Academy's humor magazine, the LOG, became embroiled in a free-speech dispute with Maine senator Margaret Chase Smith. At the same time, midshipmen sporting wigs during their off-campus activities brought attention to their desire to assimilate with their civilian peers in a decidedly anti-military era. The plight of prisoners of war in North Vietnam frustrated two midshipmen who began what became a national letter-writing campaign to bring attention to the issue in 1970. Finally, in 1982, a midshipman created an action group that has continued to provide community service to Annapolis.

Historians have given the modern Naval Academy some attention, beginning with John Lovell's 1979 study of the nation's military academies, *Neither Athens Nor Sparta?: The American Service Academies in Transition*, which provided a frank look at developments and trends at USNA until that date. Sixteen years later, Jack Sweetman and Thomas Cutler presented *The U.S. Naval Academy: An Illustrated History*, a descriptive and pictorial overview of the institution's history. In 1998 and 1999, two insightful works appeared. The first was Sharon Hanley Disher's *First Class: Women Join the Ranks at the Naval Academy*, a valuable work that offered the earliest account of the experiences of the Academy's first female midshipmen. The second was retired admiral Randolph King's thorough and comprehensive timeline of USNA history, found in the 1999 USNA Alumni Association's *Register of Alumni*. Recently, two historians have published focused studies on USNA. In 2004, Todd Forney published *The Midshipman Culture and Educational Reform: The U.S. Naval Academy 1946–1976*, which examined and retold the story of USNA's academic transformation as covered in Charles Sheppard's 1974 dissertation, "An Analysis of Curriculum Changes at the United States Naval Academy During the Period 1959 Through 1974." Robert Schneller's insightful 2005 *Breaking the Color Barrier: The U.S. Naval Academy's First Black Midshipmen and the Struggle for Racial Equality* looks at the experiences of African Americans at USNA until 1949. Finally, journalist David Lispky's 2003 study of the U.S. Military Academy, *Absolutely American: Four Years At West Point*, addresses many issues of relevance to the contemporary experience of midshipmen at USNA. In this book, I look at all of these issues in a broad and comprehensive context to examine and analyze how they and other subjects impacted the Naval Academy's culture between 1949 and 2000.

Even today, the topics that I outline in this book continue to draw attention. Just as Americans are still grappling with racial equality and the enlisted military forces become more varied ethnically and racially, USNA makes continued attempts to recruit increasing numbers of minorities. Furthermore, in 2005 USNA received its first African American commandant and announced plans for a new field house to be named for Wesley Brown, the first African American to graduate from the Academy. While the citizenry debates the proper role of religion in American life and government, and in spite of a federal court case banning mandatory religious activity at the military academies, USNA chaplains continue to lead lunchtime prayers in the meal hall. Although the Naval Academy decided to alter its alma mater by removing references to men in 2004, female midshipmen still confront discrimination and harassment as their counterparts at the Air Force Academy have witnessed large-scale attempts to cover up rapes and sexual assault in Colorado Springs. And, just as youth culture has long questioned authority, midshipmen continue to critically assess their relationship with the Academy's administration and officers. This study, which provides a cultural analysis of the transformation of an institution of higher education, not only sheds light on events and changes at the United States Naval Academy but also offers a novel perspective on the developing fulfillment of democratic ideals in the United States.

Acknowledgments

The community of people who have facilitated the creation of this book is vast, and I thank everyone who has supported me and had faith in this project.

Leonard Dinnerstein, Kevin Gosner, and Tom Holm served as mentors and advisors to this project from its origins. Each has provided counsel, meals, support, and encouragement and has offered me friendship; none will ever comprehend the depth of my appreciation for their humanity, devotion, understanding, and example. Leonard and Myra Dinnerstein warmly entertained me countless times at their home to give keen advice, creative solutions, kind words, and emotional support. Kevin Gosner always gave me refuge in the ocean of calm that is his office, and always assured me that I was on the right path. Tom Holm never ceased to show his compassion for, and confidence in, me and this project, always welcoming me with his hearty laugh. Michael Schaller provided superb advice and guidance on many aspects of this project.

Paul Green, Charles Hudson, and Marty Tagg have provided me with personal and professional guidance. Each has had an indelible impact upon me, and I am humbled to have them as my gurus. Charles Hudson provided me with the intellectual framework for this study. John Bodnar, Vincent Davis, George Herring, Ben Holt, John Inscoe, Randolph King, Diane Miller, Mike Nassr, Peter Randrup, Leonard Sapera, Paul Stillwell, and Robert Timberg helped me to develop the parameters for this book.

I extend special appreciation to Admiral Charles Larson, who graciously permitted me to conduct research at the Naval Academy. I would also like to thank the former superintendents, commandants, and administrators who offered invaluable guidance, including Charles Buchanan, Julian Burke, James Calvert, Robert Coogan, Marcy Dupre, Leon Edney, D. K. Forbes, Randolph

King, Samuel Locklear, Robert McNitt, William Miller, Gary Roughead, John Ryan, Richard Werking, and James Winnefeld.

The leaders and staff of the Naval Academy Preparatory School welcomed me in Newport. Thanks to Steven Arendt, Richard Black, Bonnie Boiani, and the faculty and students at NAPS.

The Naval Academy's Nimitz Library staff answered questions, guided me toward sources, looked up countless pieces of information during and after my time at USNA, permitted me to have lending privileges, and sponsored me during my time at USNA. Thanks to Lillian Blake, Larry Clemens, Madeleine Copp, Howard Cropper, John Cummings, Katherine Dickson, Ruth Hennessy, Donna Hurley, Leanne Kelley, John Martin, Bill McQuaide, Patti Patterson, Josephine Perkins, Tim Syzek, and Barbara Yoakum. I owe a huge debt to Barbara Breeden and Barbara Manvel, who from my first day at USNA have treated me as if I were part of their families. How fortunate I am that Barbara Manvel answered the phone at Nimitz when I first called in 1996.

Members of the USNA Archives and Special Collections staff provided access to the source material upon which much of this book is based. Thanks to Mary Rose Catalfamo, Alice Creighton, Gary LaValley, and Beverly Lyall for uncovering so much material for me and laboring on my behalf.

At the Naval Academy, I benefited from the guidance and ideas of Nancy Arbuthnot, Lisa Bozzelli, Doug Brattebo, George Breeden, Leslie Burnett, Edward Carroll, Shannon French, J. D. Fulp, Brian Goodrow, Mark Harper, Ed Peery, Margie and Randolph King, T. S. Michael, Donald Montgomery, and Dave Smalley.

I would like to thank sincerely all of the members of the USNA community, including administrators, officers, faculty members, coaches, alumni, midshipmen, staff and workers, and townspeople who, in formal and informal settings alike, helped me understand numerous dimensions of the Naval Academy. Many of them consented to the interviews that support the stories found in this book and these identities are known only to them and me. I would like to thank all of the groups with whom I interacted, including the Admissions Board; the Midshipmen Black Studies Club; the Character Development Department; the classes of 1952, 1970, 1972, 1999, 2000, 2001, 2002, and 2003; the Leadership, Ethics, and Law Department; the LOG magazine staff; the men's crew team and coaches; the Seventh Company; the Oregon Parents Club; and the WRNV radio station staff. Attorney Warren Kaplan in Washington and alumni Bradley Nemeth and Michael Oliver in San Diego shared insightful recollections when I visited with them numerous times.

I owe a special debt to the courageous women of the class of 1980 who inspired me and allowed me to spend time with them. I especially want to thank Janice Buxbaum, Tina Marie D'Ercole, Stefanie Goebel, Sharon Hanley Disher, and Elizabeth Sternaman for teaching me so much and for welcoming me into their community. Thanks, too, to Beth Patridge for sharing a moving speech she wrote, the title of which I have adopted for Chapter Six.

Among the Annapolis and West Point alumni who generously granted me access to their personal papers and collections are Sherman Alexander, John Bodnar, Richard Denfeld, Marcy Dupre, Tina Marie D'Ercole, Randolph King, Michael Nassr, James Reeve, Rick Rubel, James Troutman, Lucian Truscott IV, David Vaught, and Takeshi Yoshihara.

Thanks to Sherman Alexander, Tina Marie D'Ercole, Daniel Ellison, and Rick Rubel for sharing photographs from their personal collections that accompany this book. Beverly Lyall of the USNA Archives, Jennifer Wallace of the U.S. Naval Institute, and H. Wright of the U.S. Navy Visual News located institutional photographs, and Hugh Hefner and David Schmit of Playboy Enterprises generously granted permission and gave assistance in reprinting an item from *Playboy* magazine. In Tucson, Miguel Argueta prepared my portrait for this book.

Institutional archivists provided access to valuable source material. Thanks to Hill Goodspeed, Emil Buehler Library, National Museum of Naval Aviation, Pensacola; Mike Parrish, Lyndon B. Johnson Presidential Library, Austin; Angie Stockwell, Margaret Chase Smith Library, Skowhegan; Sheilah Biles and Debbie McKeon-Pogue, U.S. Military Academy Special Collections Library, West Point; Robert Schneller, U.S. Naval Historical Center, Washington; Ruth Dickstein, University of Arizona Library, Tucson; and Dorinda Hartmann, Wisconsin Historical Society Center for Film and Theater Studies, Madison. I also thank staff members at the Federal Records Center, Suitland; National Archives Film Center, College Park; U.S. Court of Appeals, District of Columbia; U.S. District Court, District of Columbia; U.S. Marine Corps Historical Center, Washington; and especially the independent scholars and oral historians Paul Stillwell and Susan Sweeney, Annapolis.

I have been fortunate to be part of communities at five history departments. Thanks to Joseph Berrigan, Will Holmes, Charles Hudson, John Inscoe, William McFeely, Ann Nadeau, Robert Pratt, Phinizy Spalding, and Lester Stephens at the University of Georgia; Hilary Aquino, Michelle Berry, Alexsis Blake, Richard Cosgrove, Leonard Dinnerstein, Alison Futrell, Juan Garcia, Kevin Gosner, Jack Marietta, David Ortiz, Jadwiga Pieper, Michael Schaller, Laura Tabili, Gina Wasson, and Donna Watson at the University of Arizona; Karin Enloe, Kyle Longley, Suzanne Rios, Scott Stabler, Noel Stowe, Francinne

Valcour, and Norma Villa at Arizona State University; Robert Artigiani, Randy Balano, Lori Bogle, Mary DeCredico, Ann Quartararo, William Roberts, and Craig Symonds at the U.S. Naval Academy; and Sidney Bland, Jane Crockett, Jessica Davidson, David Dillard, Michael Gubser and Elisa Oh, Steven Guerrier, Daniel Kerr and Tatiana Belenkaya, Amy Larrabee, Sonja Lovell, Alison Sandman, and William Van Norman at James Madison University. Thanks also to my students at Arizona, Arizona State, and James Madison who have shown interest in, and asked compelling questions about, this book.

I extend my appreciation to Nancy Henkle of the University of Arizona for awarding me a grant for the equipment used for my interviews.

I have benefited from the suggestions and close readings of various portions and versions of this book by Sherman Alexander, Michael Anderson, Barbara Atwood, Edward Carroll, Catherine Clinton, Croom Coward, Julie Dinnerstein, Leonard Dinnerstein, Myra Dinnerstein, Marcy Dupre, Edwin Ebbert, Jean Ebbert, Leon Edney, Daniel Ellison, J. D. Fulp, Kevin Gosner, Tom Holm, Warren Kaplan, Colby Kavanagh, Kay Kavanagh, Randolph King, Michael Nassr, Jay Sanders, Michael Schaller, Nancy Shunfenthal, Jane Slaughter, Geoffrey Smith, Paul Stillwell, Craig Symonds, James Troutman, Lucian Truscott IV, and Richard Werking. Thanks also to the members of my Tucson discussion group for their comments, ideas, and friendship: Sharon Bailey Glasco, Michael Crawford, Jodie Kredier, Jerry Pierce, Laura Shelton, and Meghan Winchell.

I would also like to thank everyone at the University of North Carolina Press who labored and assisted me in bringing this book to completion. Charles Grench has been an advocate, enthusiastic supporter, and insightful commentator, and Brian Frazelle, Amanda McMillan, Ron Maner, Katy O'Brien, Ellen Bush, and Kathy Ketterman all helped guide me through the publication process. They made this process a pleasure.

I also extend my appreciation to John McCain for his personal kindness to me and for his generosity in preparing the Foreword to this book. Thanks, too, to Senator McCain's Tucson, Phoenix, and Washington office staffs for their assistance.

One of my greatest fortunes is to have many close friends, and for their support I would like to thank David and Pat Armstrong, J. P. Benedict, Jeff Darling, Romeel Dave, Julie Dinnerstein, Jean Ebbert, Blake Espy, Becky and Marc Galvin, Don and Marsha Garczewski, Rick Goddard, Nicholas Gudovic, Stan Hare, Michael Hetke, Richard and Susan Hetke, Phil Higdon, Connie Hudson, Harold and Simone Hyams, Kay and Colby Kavanagh, John and Kay Lloyd, Doug Lusko, Charlotte and George Marshall, Carol Messer, Bruce and

Carolyn Newhouse, James Northam, Ben Pearson, Will Percy, Andy and Tina Petersen, Nick Ravden, Ann and Bill Romano, Adam Ross, Jay and Sallie Sanders, Beth Savage, Lori Tagg, Susan Frances Barrow Tate, Conner Watts, Chris Wisbrock, Mark Witzel, Ilene and Russell Wong, and Marian and William Zerman.

Croom and Sandy Coward opened their hearts and Annapolis home to me as if I were one of the dozens of midshipmen they sponsor. They offered meals, invaluable advice, guidance, connections, support, and, most of all, friendship from the beginning to the conclusion of this project.

I am incredibly indebted to Leon Edney, who sponsored me at USNA and served as my advisor, mentor, and friend. He has provided opportunities and possibilities for my research and experiences that made this project feasible and a labor of love, and he and his wife Margon have looked after me at every stage of this project from Annapolis to Coronado. This book would not have been possible without them.

Special thanks go to the Dizzia Family, who made this project possible. Phyllis Dizzia provided me with much of the means to conduct my research. Neil and Betty Dizzia graciously allowed me to live with them while I was at Annapolis. Their encouragement and love was without end.

Nancy Shunfenthal has been the most faithful friend I could hope to have. She has advised me on every aspect of this book, listened to my arguments and ideas, and always responded with the clearest insights. Her sense of humor kept me and this project on track.

I extend my sincere thanks to my closest friends and family members who have done the most to sustain me, listen to me, guide me, and laugh with me: Miguel Argueta, Neal and Laura Armstrong, Jack and Terry Barker, Charles and Nancy Belin, John and Shawn Belin, Heather and Joe DeGaetano, Sam Espy, Shannon French and Doug Brattebo, Marti Gelfand, P. Gelfand, Jarita Holbrook, Eric Peterson, Ben Powell, Brian Raphel, Diane Vanderbeck, Michael Wong, and Matthew Wood.

Finally, I thank my parents, Elayne and Gerald Gelfand, who have stood by me and supported me in so many ways. They have always shown me encouragement, devotion, and love, and have always known exactly when I needed a smile, a hug, and a laugh. I love them very much.

Academic buildings	1	Michelson Hall	2
Alumni Hall	2	Mitscher Hall	2
Bancroft Hall	3	Naval Academy Cemetery	2
Memorial Hall	3a	Naval Academy Museum	2
Rotunda	3b	Nimitz Hall	2
Smoke Hall	3c	Old Naval Academy Guard Houses	2
Tecumseh Court	3d	Power Plant Smokestack Site	2
Wing 1	3e	Ricketts Hall	2
Wing 2	3f	Rickover Hall	2
Wing 3	3g	Robert Crown Sailing Center	3
Wing 4	3h	St. Anne's Church	3
Wing 5	3i	St. John's College	3
Wing 6	3j	Stribling Walk	3
Wing 7	3k	Superintendent's House	3
Wing 8	3l	Uriah P. Levy Center and Jewish Chapel	3
Bishop Field	4	USS *Delaware* / Tamamend / Tecumseh Statue	3
Carvel Hall Site	5	USS *Maine* Foremast	3
Chapel	6	Ward Hall	3
Chauvenet Hall	7	Wesley Brown Field House	3
Dahlgren Hall	8	Worden Field Officers' Houses	4
Downtown Annapolis	9	Worden Field Parade Ground	4
Fort Severn Site	10		
Glenn Warner Soccer Facility	11		
Greenbury Point	12		
Halsey Field House	13		
Herndon Monument	14		
Ho Chi Minh Trail	15		
Hubbard Hall	16		
King Hall	17		
Lejeune Hall	18		
Luce Hall	19		
Maryland State House	20		

Navy Academy Bridge
Forrest Sherman Field
Hospital Point
15
23
Dorsey Creek
25
2
16
41
24
Worden Field
4
40
College Creek
32

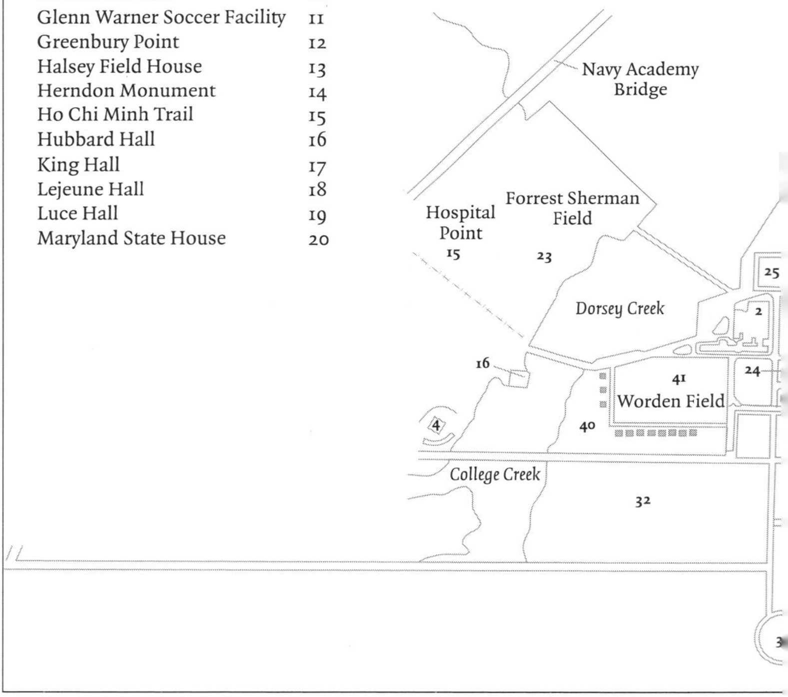

The United States Naval Academy

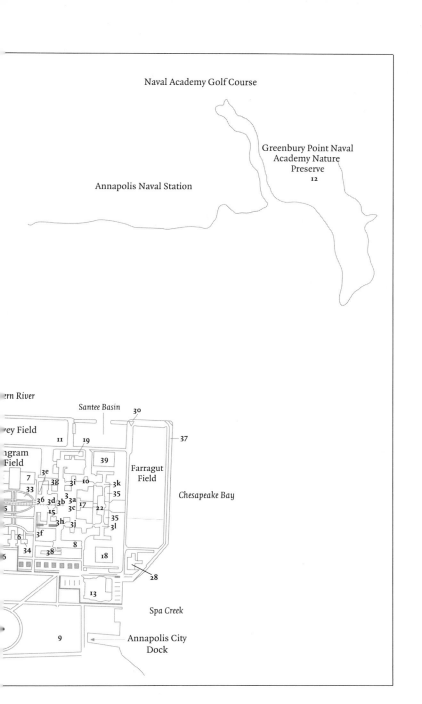

Naval Academy Golf Course

Greenbury Point Naval
Academy Nature
Preserve
12

Annapolis Naval Station

ern River

Santee Basin   30

vey Field   11   19   37

ıgram
Field   39
7   3e
3g   3i   10   3k
33   35
36 3d 3b 3   3a
15   3c 17   22   35
3h   3j   3l
6   3f
34   38   8
18
28

13

Spa Creek

9   Annapolis City
Dock

Chesapeake Bay

Farragut
Field

Sea Change at Annapolis*

1

An Introduction to the United States Naval Academy

★ ★ ★ ★ ★ ★ ★ ★ ★ ★ ★ ★ ★ ★ ★ ★ ★ ★ ★ ★

Formal military education in the United States originated in the creation of the United States Military Academy at West Point, New York, in 1802.[1] President George Washington advocated the establishment of a formal military school in 1790, the same year that Miami tribal leaders led the defeat of the U.S. Army. After the Miami overpowered the Army a second time the next year, the government enlisted Anthony Wayne, who trained the men serving under him and delivered the United States its long-awaited victory over the Miami in 1795. Washington understood that many national leaders feared a standing army, yet he continued to call for a center for army training in 1796. His support was crucial for the creation of West Point, where the U.S. Army began to educate its future officers. West Point superintendent Sylvanus Thayer, who led the Military Academy from 1817 to 1833, organized the institution in a manner that later served as a model for the Naval Academy.

Thayer's plan included guidelines for discipline, pedagogy, lifestyle, and coursework. As historian Lawrence Cremin has described it, "The system of discipline had been strictly hierarchical, involving a commandant of cadets, with responsibility under the superintendent for discipline and training, who was assisted by a group of subordinate military officers, who were in turn responsible for a corps of cadets with its own cadet officers, mostly first- and second-classmen." In the classroom, the cadets recited from their lessons each day and received moral and professional military training, although their courses centered around engineering.

Just before the founding of West Point, President John Adams suggested creating an institution for the education of Naval leaders.[2] He received little support initially, as the Navy already made provisions to educate young men, called midshipmen, aboard its ships. But in 1815, the Navy decided to establish a school on land at the Charlestown Navy Yard near Boston, and by 1839 the Navy was overseeing similar schools at Norfolk, New York City, and Philadelphia. These schools, however, were small, one-year programs and did not represent a centralized, consistent approach to Naval education. New Jersey senator and former secretary of the Navy Samuel Southard authored a bill in 1836 "to establish a Naval Academy for the improvement and instruction of the midshipmen and other officers in the Navy of the United States." Simultaneously, the Navy was taking steps to increase the number of teachers aboard its ships, indicating a continued disagreement as to whether formal Naval education should be conducted aboard a ship or in a classroom.

Challenging circumstances, which had sparked the creation of West Point, also helped resolve the dispute over the forum for formal Naval education.[3] In 1842, midshipman Philip Spencer devised a plan to kill the officers of his ship, the Navy brig *Somers*, and lead its crew into Caribbean piracy. Learning of the planned mutiny, the ship's captain, Alexander Mackenzie, ordered Spencer and two cronies to die by hanging. This mutiny might have gone unnoted, but Philip Spencer was the son of John Spencer, then the secretary of war. The elder Spencer charged Mackenzie with murder, but the captain was later cleared of the crime. The events, however, brought the issue of Naval education to the forefront of public attention.

Among those considering a comprehensive instructional program was a teacher at the Naval Asylum School in Philadelphia, William Chauvenet, who believed that Navy officers would benefit from formalized education in a centralized location, particularly due to the complexity of the Navy's newest technology, steam ships. He presented the idea of a two-year program for that purpose in 1843. Chauvenet's proposal for a new Naval school caught the attention of the incoming secretary of the Navy, George Bancroft, in May 1845.[4] Bancroft had been concerned about the *Somers* incident, and wrote to Chauvenet to inquire about his idea and his work at the Navy's school in Philadelphia. When the overseeing board of the school met in June, Bancroft addressed them in a formal letter and won their support for his new school. He then chose Fort Severn, a small Maryland fort at the junction of the Severn River and the Chesapeake Bay, to house the school. The Army had constructed the fort in 1808 to protect the town and harbor of Annapolis; the installation consisted of a small roundhouse and ten related buildings. In an August 1845 letter to Navy commander Franklin Buchanan, whom Bancroft chose to head the new school, the Navy secretary indicated that the president and war department had approved the fort's transfer to the Navy.

Bancroft, Buchanan, Chauvenet, and Naval Asylum School instructor Samuel Marcy, in creating their plan for the Naval School at Annapolis, studied West Point and modeled their own school after it.[5] Named as the first superintendent, Buchanan presided over all aspects of the two-year school, including its personnel. Bancroft wanted Navy leaders to do as much of the instruction as possible, although several of the earliest faculty members were civilians. An academic board, comprised of faculty members, would judge the midshipmen's performance, while an external board of visitors would make recommendations on the school's operation to the secretary of the Navy. Midshipmen would spend time in Annapolis, as well as aboard ships, and they would be graded on their classroom recitations. Fundamentally, this plan has remained the organizational form of the institution ever since. On 10 October 1845, the Naval School at Annapolis officially opened with fifty-six midshipmen.

For the first fifteen years of its operation, the Naval School developed physically and organizationally.[6] The Academic Board in 1849 created academic departments, a numerical grading scale, and midshipman rankings. Formal marching became a requirement, and the board extended the amount of time a midshipman would spend at the school from two to four years. The Navy added an executive officer to the school's leadership, called the commandant, to oversee tactical and seamanship training. Emphasizing these changes, the Naval School adopted its new name, the United States Naval Academy, on 1 July 1850. In spite of the addition of twenty-seven new buildings and structures on the campus by 1861, the Naval Academy abandoned Annapolis at the outbreak of the Civil War. The Navy reestablished the Academy at Fort Adams, outside of Newport, Rhode Island, in 1861. When conditions at the fort did not prove conducive to proper training, the Academy moved again to a residential area of Newport, where it remained until returning to Annapolis at the conclusion of the war in 1865.

Superintendent David Porter and Commandant Stephen Luce developed the Academy in the years after the Civil War.[7] By 1869, the two men had brought athletics, graduation celebrations, class rings, attention to honor in behavior and personal affairs, and twelve additional buildings to the Naval Academy. A Marine guard had been present at the Academy since 1851, but in 1865 the Navy assigned a permanent detachment of Marines to Annapolis to assist midshipmen in military training. Much of the remainder of the nineteenth century, as historian Lance Buhl has noted, saw a lull in the activities of the U.S. Navy because Congress did not seek to maintain a large or powerful Navy.[8] Such sentiments began to change after 1890, when alumnus Alfred Thayer Mahan published The Influence of Sea Power Upon History, 1660–1783, which began as a series of lectures at the Naval War College while he was its president.[9] Not only did the Navy itself benefit from the popularity of Mahan's work, which reviewed the dominance of past seafaring nations, but the Naval Academy began a major transformation. While Theodore Roosevelt touted Mahan's ideas as a reason to expand the nation's Navy, and in particular to bring it into the age of battleship superiority, the Naval Academy's Board of Visitors was realizing the limitations of the Academy's physical plant. Although the Spanish-American War temporarily halted ideas for expansion, the war also proved to the nation the value of its Navy. For the first time, Congress appropriated liberal funding for the Naval Academy, while allowing for considerations of the replacement of the Academy's older buildings with a vast new campus.

This new emphasis on the Naval Academy also brought two of the Navy's current technologies to the midshipmen.[10] The Navy stationed a submarine at the Academy for the first time in 1900 and established an airfield at Greenbury Point, a peninsula across the Severn River from the campus. The Academy, because of the midshipmen's exposure to these technologies, played a prominent role in the First World War. In addition to its own graduates, the Academy set up a separate training program, the U.S. Naval Reserve Officers' Force. Between July 1917 and January 1919, the Academy trained over 2,500 men—many of whom were college students hailing from across the nation—as Naval officers. After the war, the Academy's academic, athletic, and physical training programs all expanded in depth and size. The Association of American Universities, recognizing these developments, accredited the Naval Academy in 1930.

Although many midshipmen completed their Academy training early to fight in the Civil War, the Spanish-American War, and World War I, the naval requirements of World War II brought an unprecedented need for officers.[11] As was the case with the First World War, the Academy again trained reserve officers. By the end of the war, over 3,300 men had completed what the Navy called V-5 and V-7 officer educations. As for the Academy's own midshipmen, its 1941 graduates finished four months ahead of schedule, its class of 1942 graduated a semester early, and subsequent classes spent three, rather than four, years in Annapolis. The intensified, expedited program required midshipmen to attend summer classes. Academy administrators maintained athletics, which they saw as crucial for training, but abandoned other extra-curricular activities. Wartime expedition ended with the class of 1948, half of which graduated in 1947 and half on the normal four-year schedule. The class of 1949, therefore, became the first class since the beginning of the war to understand that they would be at the Naval Academy for four years. During the years immediately following World War II, Naval Academy leaders introduced emphases on aviation, submarine, and weapons technology and leadership training, all of which would develop further in the Naval Academy curriculum in subsequent decades.

The Naval Academy's central campus, at coordinates 38°58'.8 North, 76°29'.3 West, is located three blocks from the Maryland State House, two blocks from the Annapolis City Dock, twenty-five miles south of Baltimore, and thirty miles east of Washington, D.C.[12] The main section contains midshipmen and officer housing, athletic facilities, and classroom, laboratory, and administrative buildings. Much of the 338 acres consists of landfill on the Severn River and the Chesapeake Bay. The USNA campus also includes three noncontiguous sections located throughout the Annapolis area. The Naval Academy's football team plays in the Navy–Marine Corps Memorial Stadium, located 1.5 miles northwest of the central campus. Across the Dorsey Creek from the main campus is Hospital Point, which encompasses officer and enlisted housing, athletic fields and buildings, facilities management, a medical center, and the Naval Academy Cemetery. The fourth section of USNA, Greenbury Point, lies across the Severn River from the central Academy on a peninsula in the Chesapeake Bay. It is the site of the original 1649 Annapolis-area English settlement and now contains the Naval Academy Golf Course, an elementary school, and a large nature preserve. The Academy also utilizes facilities in the adjacent Annapolis Naval Station, a small base supporting USNA operations. Lastly, there was a fifth section of USNA from 1918 until 1998 near Gambrills, Maryland, eighteen miles northwest of Annapolis. There, the Naval Academy operated a dairy farm in order to supply its own milk and dairy products.

Referred to as the "Yard," the Naval Academy's main campus began as Fort Severn.[13] The Navy expanded the Academy in 1868 and 1869 to include most of the area east of King George Street and added numerous facilities to the Academy's physical plant. By 1895, when President Grover Cleveland ordered the Academy's Board of Visitors to examine USNA's physical plant, the campus comprised fifty-five buildings and facilities. Finding the physical plant to be insufficient, the board recommended a new building scheme, as well as land purchases and landfilling, in order to increase and improve the Academy grounds. Robert Thompson, a Board of Visitors member and Academy alumnus, wrote to New York architect Ernest Flagg in 1896 and asked him to draw a rendering for a new campus.

The next year, Flagg responded with a stunning vision for the Academy.[14]

After calling for landfills along the Severn River and Spa Creek, Flagg adjusted the east/west axis of the Academy campus to conform to the northwest/southeast layout of the city of Annapolis. Flagg based his plan on a quadrangle, the four sides of which would consist of a group of academic buildings, a large dormitory with an attached armory and boat house, a chapel flanked by an administration building and a home for the Academy superintendent, and a boat basin. To give unity to the design, Flagg designed all of the buildings in the Beaux-Arts architectural style. After the Board of Visitors accepted the plan, construction of the new campus began in 1899 and lasted until 1913. Flagg's plans led to the destruction of nearly the entire old Academy. A cemetery across Dorsey Creek remained, as did a substantial green area in the center of the grounds, two guard houses at the Maryland Avenue gate to USNA, and the eleven houses lining the parade ground, Worden Field. In spite of several modifications to Flagg's intended specifications, the overall composition was an impressive one.[15]

Two of Flagg's buildings were, and remain, crucial elements of his plan. Much like Thomas Jefferson and Benjamin Latrobe's design for the University of Virginia in Charlottesville, Flagg's placed a dominant, domed building at one end of the quadrangle to unify the composition.[16] Instead of Jefferson and Latrobe's library, however, Flagg devised a 210-foot-tall chapel and placed it on the highest location of the Academy grounds. One observer of Flagg's plans for the chapel noted that "although all of the [new Naval Academy] structures are of impressive size and architecture, the great height of the chapel and its dimensions will make it one of the most imposing religious edifices in the United States when it is completed." Construction concluded in 1908, and, fulfilling Flagg's desire to have the chapel serve as a monument to John Paul Jones, the father of the American Navy, the Navy entombed Jones in an Invalides-like crypt beneath the chapel in 1913. The Academy has modified the chapel's appearance twice, replacing its terra-cotta dome with the current copper one in 1928 and expanding the chapel's seating capacity by creating a nave projecting toward the Severn River in 1940. Popular as the site of many alumni weddings, as well as serving as the venue for religious services and funerals of alumni and midshipmen who pass away while at USNA, the chapel is likely the most popular and inspirational building for midshipmen, alumni, and tourists.

The second exceptional building that Flagg designed is the dormitory Bancroft Hall.[17] Named for the noted historian, secretary of the Navy, and USNA founder George Bancroft, the building's first midshipmen residents moved into its rooms in 1904. Bancroft Hall initially consisted of two wings with

This photograph of the Naval Academy, taken between 1919 and 1940, shows much of Ernest Flagg's original design for the campus. Bancroft Hall, in the foreground, includes today's Wings Three and Five, right, and Wings Four and Six, left. The chapel, at left, had yet to have its nave extended. The academic buildings—Sampson, Mahan, and Maury Halls—are in the background. USNA has since increased its grounds through landfilling on the Chesapeake Bay, foreground, the Severn River, at right, and the Dorsey Creek, background. Most of the buildings that USNA has added in subsequent decades reflect Flagg's Beaux Arts style: grey walls with green or black mansard roofs. (U.S. Naval Institute Photograph Archive)

courtyards, now Wings Three and Four, connected to a central space containing an elaborate entrance, a mess hall, and a ceremonial area called Memorial Hall. Contained in Memorial Hall are highly inspirational and moving paintings, displays, and plaques commemorating deceased midshipmen and describing remarkable events and courageous acts in Navy and Marine Corps history. Since the construction of Bancroft Hall, USNA leaders have seen community-promotion benefits in housing the entire Brigade of Midshipmen —the formal name for the population of midshipmen enrolled in USNA—in the building. As a result, when more housing space has been needed, the Academy has added new wings to the dormitory: Wings Five and Six in 1919,

Wings One and Two in 1941, and Wings Seven and Eight between 1959 and 1961. Now encompassing 33 acres of floor space, 4.8 miles of hallways, and 1,873 dormitory rooms, Bancroft Hall's immense size makes it the largest dormitory in the world. For modernization purposes, the Academy began a complete, eight-year, wing-by-wing restoration of the building in 1994, costing over $251,000,000.

As Bancroft Hall is the center of midshipmen's life at the Naval Academy, the building contains facilities that more properly resemble those in a city than in a dormitory.[18] The building has its own post office and zip code, and contains two chapels and chaplains' offices. There are also medical facilities, a dental clinic, barber shops, laundry facilities, a small visitors' center, a banquet facility, meeting rooms, a weight room, squash courts, administrative offices, a small restaurant, a 55,000-square-foot store, and offices for extracurricular activities. Bancroft Hall also includes the midshipmen's ward room, called King Hall. Containing kitchen spaces and enough seating to hold the entire Brigade of Midshipmen at once, King Hall covers 65,000 square feet of space. One USNA writer commented that "although Bancroft Hall may seem a cold, imposing granite dormitory to the casual observer, it means a great deal more to those who spend four years of their lives in it."

Since the reconstruction of USNA under Ernest Flagg, the Academy has improved its physical plant by adding fifteen buildings and eight athletic facilities, most of which match, in modified styles and designs, Flagg's original design.[19] Among these is Mitscher Hall, which began as a library but later became a chaplain's center. In September 2005, administrators dedicated a large addition to Mitscher Hall, named the Uriah P. Levy Center and Jewish Chapel. USNA also constructed three large academic buildings, Michelson and Chauvenet Halls in 1968 and Rickover Hall, the major engineering facility, in 1975. Nimitz Hall, a library complex and academic facility, also opened in 1975, and Alumni Hall, an arena designed for Brigade-wide assemblies and sporting events, opened in 1988. Prominent athletic facilities include the Navy–Marine Corps Memorial Stadium for football, Lejeune Hall for swimming and wrestling, the Robert Crown Sailing Center, Bishop Field for baseball, the Glenn Warner Soccer Facility, and Hubbard Hall, the Academy's crew house. Almost all of these buildings memorialize prominent Navy and Marine Corps leaders.

References to Navy and Marine Corps history can be found throughout the Yard, serving as prominent reminders to midshipmen of the history of their institution and of the military service of generations of their predecessors.[20] Hundreds of graduates are buried in the Naval Academy Cemetery, and their names adorn streets on the USNA campus.[21] The Naval Academy Museum and Bancroft Hall's Memorial Hall contain physical artifacts of the Navy and Marine Corps's past achievements and activities.[22] Throughout the corridors of Bancroft Hall and Luce Hall, plaques with the names of Medal of Honor recipients adorn the walls, in some cases giving detail of distinguished service in battle.[23] The Academy has also placed monuments to battles, wars, ships, and submarines, alliances with foreign nations, and notable figures around the grounds.[24] Some of the monuments, such as the foremast of the USS *Maine*, commemorate tragedies; others have become part of Naval Academy culture.[25] For example, midshipmen paint "Tecumseh," the figurehead of the USS *Delaware* and actually a bust of the Delaware chief Tamemand, before sporting events and in past decades threw pennies at the monument to "help" them pass exams.[26] The most prominent memorial at the Naval Academy, however, is the Herndon Monument. A twenty-one-foot-tall granite obelisk, Herndon is the center of the plebe year–ending ceremony in which the plebes form a human pyramid to climb the monument—which seniors grease with lard in advance—to replace its crowning plebe cap with a midshipman's cover.[27] These monuments, along with the distinctive buildings and well-kept grounds, help to create a unique setting and serve as what anthropologist Pierre Nora has called a "Lieu de Memoire," a physical manifestation of intended remembrance of the past through "material, symbolic, and functional" means.[28] The monuments also combine to make the Naval Academy one of the most popular tourist destinations in the Washington/Baltimore metropolitan area.[29]

Although the basic goal of the Naval Academy has always been the training and education of future leaders for the Navy and Marine Corps, Superintendent James Holloway Jr. and the Naval Academy's Academic Board created a mission statement for the institution in 1947.[30] That statement read, "Through study and practical instruction to provide the midshipmen with a basic education and knowledge of the naval profession; to develop them morally, mentally, and physically; and by precept and example to indoctrinate them with the highest ideals of duty, honor, and loyalty; in order that the naval service may be provided with graduates who are capable junior officers in whom have been developed the capacity and foundation for future development in mind and character leading toward a readiness to assume the highest responsibilities of citizenship and government."[31]

Seeking to emphasize the military's desire to develop career officers, Superintendent Charles Melson and his Academic Board wrote a new mission statement in 1960: "To develop midshipmen morally, mentally, and physically and to imbue them with the highest ideals of duty, honor, and loyalty in order to provide graduates who are dedicated to a career of naval service and have potential for future development in mind and character to assume the highest responsibilities of command, citizenship, and government."[32] Shortly after his leadership in Annapolis began, Superintendent James Calvert discovered that few members of the Naval Academy community knew anything about the mission statement beyond it being "complicated." As a result, Calvert reworded the mission in 1971 to read, "To prepare young men morally, mentally, and physically to be professional officers in the naval service." USNA leaders changed the words "young men" to "midshipmen" after the arrival of female midshipmen in 1976, and in 1987, Secretary of the Navy James Webb returned the mission statement to its 1960 wording, which remains the current statement.

The federal government exercises control of the Naval Academy through different branches and agencies, whose actions will be discussed in detail in this and subsequent chapters.[33] Among the federal authorities who influence the Naval Academy is the president, who appoints the secretaries of defense and of the Navy and the chief of Naval operations, who exercise power over policies and leadership at Annapolis. For example, Secretary of Defense Robert McNamara was interested in systems analysis and Secretary of the Navy John Lehman had a strong interest in liberal arts; both took steps to emphasize these areas at USNA. The president also appoints Board of Visitors members, including senators and representatives. Congress has ultimate control over the Academy's budget and has the authority to create and change laws with consequences for the Naval Academy. As a part of its investigative responsibilities, the General Accounting Office has conducted studies of issues and events at Annapolis and recommended procedural changes. Federal courts, too, have made rulings that have changed and altered Naval Academy policies and traditions. Among the nongovernmental actors influencing Annapolis are the media, accrediting associations, and private consultants commissioned to study specific issues.

The organization with the greatest impact on the Naval Academy is the U.S. Navy.[34] Until 1971, USNA fell under the Navy's Bureau of Naval Personnel. The Bureau provided both the funding and overall management for USNA, although, as Superintendent William Smedberg III later explained, "Frankly, the Naval Academy for most of its life . . . had very little priority from the rest of the Navy." Frequently, it was the relationships between Academy superintendents and Navy leaders, many of whom were USNA graduates, that secured the Academy's needs. In 1971, the Navy transferred supervision of the Academy to the newly instituted position of Chief of Naval Education and Training (CNET). Superintendent William Mack, who led USNA between 1972 and 1975, later recalled that the move "created a bureaucratic, financial nightmare" because the Academy then had to compete with the Navy's Reserve Officer Training Corps (NROTC) and Officers Candidate Schools (OCS). By 1975, Navy leaders began to recognize this problem. The following year, chief of Naval operations and USNA graduate James Holloway III took the Academy out of the purview of CNET and gave his own office direct control and oversight over it and its superintendent, a relationship that continues today. Both the chief of Naval operations and the commandant of the Marine Corps maintain ultimate responsibilities for the officers who serve at the Naval Academy.

A second organization with significant oversight over the Academy is the Board of Visitors (BOV). The BOV is charged under Title X of the U.S. Code with the mission "to inquire into the state of morale and discipline, the curriculum, instruction, physical equipment, fiscal affairs, academic methods, and other matters relating to the Academy that the board decides to consider."[35] The board's fifteen members, including six presidential appointees and nine congressional appointees, report any findings and decisions to the president of the United States in an annual report.[36] Since the Middle States Association of Colleges and Secondary Schools recommended changes to the BOV in 1966, the board has also included professional educators and successful alumni in addition to politicians.[37] Each semester, USNA invites members of the BOV to a meeting in Annapolis.[38] Although some superintendents and members of Congress have pointed out the lack of involvement on the part of the BOV, the board—particularly through the appointment of special committees—has produced significant studies and has supported various advancements in the Academy's development.[39]

At the top of the Naval Academy organizational hierarchy is the superintendent, a position similar to that of a university president.[40] The superintendent is responsible for overseeing the external relations and internal affairs of USNA. Superintendent Draper Kauffman noted that the office requires its holder to be "initiator, creator, inheritor, consensus-seeker, persuader, educator, and mediator [in order to] enable the Academy to keep pace with a highly complex, ever-changing industrial society." Superintendents also deal with the media outlets in Washington and Baltimore, often resulting in national coverage of events at USNA. From the end of World War II until the late 1960s, most superintendents served for a period of two years. Since 1968, however, reflecting a preference for leadership continuity, most superintendents have held the office for three or four years. A similar trend has been the shift from lower ranking, younger admirals to higher ranking, more experienced senior admirals filling the position.

Each of the twenty-one superintendents since 1949 has been a Naval Academy alumnus and has had his own distinctive approach, leadership style, and goals.[41] William Smedberg was particularly concerned about making the Academy environment a midshipmen-oriented one, while James Holloway Jr. and James Calvert favored academics.[42] Calvert created, for example, the Forrestal Lecture Series, named for former secretary of the Navy and secretary of defense James Forrestal, as a means of enhancing "the education, awareness, and appreciation of the Brigade of Midshipmen in the social, political, and cultural aspects of their nation and the world."[43] Others, like Harry Hill and John Davidson, were athletic fans.[44] Charles Kirkpatrick won widespread admiration and respect from the midshipmen, who referred to him as "Uncle Charlie," due to his inspirational speeches.[45] Charles Larson, who twice served as superintendent, returned for his second tour in 1994 with a desire to encourage ethics and respect among the midshipmen.[46]

The USNA superintendent oversees what has become, since 1949, an increasingly complex bureaucracy.[47] There are currently eight governing divisions within the Academy. Although this structure has changed slightly over the past fifty years, the fundamental activities have remained the same. Among the divisions are the Executive Department, which includes Judge Advocate General's Corps officers and Public Affairs, and the Management Division, responsible for computer services and internal research. The Operations Department addresses personnel, fire and security, and medical and dental services, and another division, the Naval Station Annapolis, provides USNA with additional support functions, including Marine guards and maintenance of the Academy's practice ships. The remaining four divisions, Admissions, Academics, the Commandant, and Athletics, all oversee the education and training of midshipmen from the time the students are candidates until their graduation. Between 1994 and 2000, there was a ninth division, Character Development, which in 2000 was incorporated into the Office of the Commandant.

The dean of admissions and the Office of Admissions supervise all aspects of the recruiting and application processes for prospective candidates to the Naval Academy.[48] Among the biggest selling points of USNA are the guaranteed job after graduation and the free tuition, room, board, medical and dental coverage, and monthly pay that midshipmen receive. Furthermore, as historian John Lovell has noted, the "aura of romance" and the "feeling of being part of [an institution that is] special" are significant influences on candidates. In order to qualify for admission, candidates must meet USNA's scholastic, medical, and physical requirements and then obtain a nomination to the Academy.

The Office of Candidate Guidance works to guide potential midshipmen through their applications and nominations.[49] Fixed numbers of nominations are available to enlisted personnel of the Reserve and Regular Navy and Marine Corps, NROTC and Junior ROTC, children of deceased or disabled veterans, children of prisoners of war or military personnel missing in action, children of Medal of Honor recipients, and candidates from foreign nations. Children of active or retired military personnel qualify for nominations from the president of the United States, and about 4–6 percent of each entering class consists of children of USNA alumni. However, the majority of candidates seek nominations from the vice president or from members of Congress, each of whom is permitted "five constituents attending [USNA] at any one time." This system allows for a geographical distribution of midshipmen from across the United States and creates a "democratizing" effect for midshipmen because, as one USNA administrator explained, the admissions process "is a melting pot where young [people] of all types start from scratch together. No fraternities, no money influences, no other tangibles differentiate. . . . Individual merit controls." At any one time, there may also be one midshipman each from U.S. territories Puerto Rico, American Samoa, and the Northern Marianas Islands, two midshipmen from Guam, and two from the Virgin Islands. Each year, the Academy also admits several candidates from foreign nations. The admissions process is, by design, a difficult one in which candidates must display their perseverance.

Until 1971, the Bureau of Personnel, Naval Academy Admissions Branch, in Washington, D.C., supervised admissions at USNA.[50] That year, Superintendent James Calvert successfully lobbied the Navy to allow the Academy to oversee its admissions directly. Commander Ronald Campbell became the first dean of admissions in 1971, and a complex network of participants has assisted every dean since then. In addition to the admissions counselors and staff in Annapolis, USNA has roughly a dozen admissions officers throughout the United States. The dean also coordinates the Blue and Gold program, created in 1962.[51] Consisting of approximately 1,750 retired military personnel, called Blue and Gold officers, the program provides counseling to candidates and helps to ensure that applicants will qualify for admission. Several midshipmen also participate every year in Operation Information, a program begun in 1955 in which midshipmen return to high schools in their hometowns to spread information about USNA.[52] Similarly, the admissions staff annually brings dozens of high school educators and guidance counselors to Annapolis for briefings about the application process.[53] The Admissions Office also has three programs that bring prospective candidates to the Academy. One program pairs candidates with midshipman hosts for a day, while a second program offers candidates a week of training at USNA during the summer.[54] A third program consists of engineering and science summer seminars, during which high school juniors visit and study at USNA.[55] These activities provide students considering the Naval Academy a practical, insightful look at the lifestyle of midshipmen.[56]

Finally, the dean of admissions oversees and is a member of the Admissions Board.[57] Beginning in 1959, under the leadership of Dean William Shields, the board has typically consisted of sixteen to eighteen people, including the directors and faculty members from each of the four academic divisions, Commandant staff members, and admissions officers. As they will eventually interact with most if not all of the candidates who will become midshipmen, the board members have a vested interest in assuring the highest possible quality of the applicants. Shields encouraged the individual members to study all aspects of individual candidates and to speak with the applicants' coaches and teachers and sometimes with the applicants themselves. Board members assemble weekly for an all-day meeting to discuss the candidates and make decisions about the applicants' qualifications for entry or suitability for preparatory programs for later admissions. Although, as several board members have explained, the process is intense, time-consuming, and potentially frustrating, it provides a group consensus and gives each member a direct contribution to the excellence and diversity of the Brigade of Midshipmen.

Shields also established in 1959 the means by which the Admissions Board would evaluate candidates.[58] Prior to this, candidates had to meet mental and physical requirements and pass the Academy's own entrance exam. In 1946, USNA began to require Educational Testing Services examinations, and after 1958 the College Entrance Examination Board. Shields and the members of his board created the "whole man" concept of evaluating candidates. As Superintendent Charles Melson described it, the "whole man" or "candidate multiple" concept considered candidates' high school records, academic performance, letters of recommendation, athletics, extracurricular activities, and, for the first time, scores on the Scholastic Aptitude Test (SAT), in an attempt to evaluate candidates' "leadership qualities, motivation, and aptitude for service." Former dean of admissions Robert McNitt noted that the board "looks behind each record for indications of curiosity, resolution, leadership, and something you don't very often see in high school students: tough-minded, independent thinking." McNitt also recalled alumnus and Admiral Arleigh Burke's reasoning as to why variety in USNA's applicant pool is vital. Burke stated that "you could run this place for ten midshipmen if you knew who would become your good leaders. You depend on diversity of input. You bring them along as best you can, and out of this through a lifetime of service will be those that have the toughness to survive and become good leaders." All of these considerations combine to form a candidate multiple, today called the "whole person multiple," upon which the Admissions Board ultimately judges each applicant.

In addition to acceptance or rejection, the Admissions Board exercises two other options that permit candidates to improve their qualifications if they do not fulfill entry standards. One is entry into the Naval Academy Preparatory School (NAPS), located in Newport, Rhode Island, since 1974.[59] In 1919, when the Navy established NAPS, the school was co-located in San Diego, California and Newport, Rhode Island; Norfolk, Virginia was later added. In 1943, the schools were merged at Bainbridge, Maryland, where NAPS remained until 1949. From 1949 until 1951, NAPS returned to Newport, and then returned to Bainbridge in 1951, where it remained until 1974. Traditionally USNA's means of preparing promising enlisted personnel for Annapolis, NAPS has increasingly been turned to by the Admissions Board as an option for civilian applicants. The second option is a Naval Academy Foundation (NAF) Scholarship, which provides finances for private preparatory school enrollment to high school students who are not accepted to USNA or NAPS. Up to a quarter of the students to whom NAF gives scholarships may be athletes.[60] Once it has made a decision, the Admissions Board informs the successful candidates of their appointment to the Naval Academy.[61]

The superintendent also oversees the Academic Department, which includes the Naval Academy's faculty. Since the Academy's inception, the faculty has consisted of varying but nearly equal percentages of civilian and military professors.[62] Civilian faculty help to bring deep academic knowledge from their fields, while military officers bring practical, professional experience from the Navy and the Marine Corps.[63] As Superintendent Charles Larson explained, "This unique concept among service academies has proven its worth by providing for continuity in the curriculum, and the academic expertise required for advanced classes."[64] The Academy has bridged the inherent division between the two groups of faculty by establishing a number of different groups, including the Civilian Faculty Affairs Committee in the 1950s and an Academic Council and Faculty Forum in 1965 in which such issues as academic freedom are discussed, and by renaming the officers' club as the

Officers' and Faculty Club.[65] Academy officials have also transformed the quality of the faculty since 1949. Cooperating with the Board of Visitors, superintendents successfully worked to require civilian faculty to possess Ph.D.s or terminal degrees in their fields and to insist that military faculty have master's degrees, both trends in American universities during this period.[66] Administrators have implemented other programs to boost the quality of faculty, including distinguished chaired professorships; the William P. Clements Jr. Award for outstanding military faculty; Permanent Military Professors, a program in which military faculty earn Ph.D.s and return as long-term USNA faculty; and the Midshipmen for a Day program, which allows faculty to spend an entire day shadowing midshipmen, helping the faculty to better understand the midshipmen's lives.[67] Superintendent James Calvert allowed civilian faculty to serve for the first time as department chairs during his 1968–72 term in the office.[68] Faculty members, who are generally teaching-oriented, also offer extensive out-of-classroom instruction, called "EI" or "extra instruction," to midshipmen.[69]

Many of the events in this book occurred as the Naval Academy underwent one of its most dramatic transformations, what has become known as the "Academic Revolution." That process, described in extensive detail in Charles Shepherd's dissertation "An Analysis of Curricular Changes at the United States Naval Academy" and again in Todd Forney's *The Midshipman Culture and Educational Reform*, got underway in 1959 when the Academy began to reassess the Academic Department. That year, the Navy asked Rensselaer Polytechnic Institute president Richard Folsom to examine USNA academics and to chair a curriculum study group.[70] Folsom's findings sparked a number of significant changes that altered the Academic Department's structure and operations over the following decade, the most profound of which was the dismantling of the standard "lock-step" curriculum that had characterized the education and training at USNA before 1959: all midshipmen took the exact same course of study, with choice of foreign language being the sole decision they could make.[71] Although some leaders felt that "lock-step" provided discipline because midshipmen learned by rote memorization, marched to class, and knew precisely what courses and information for which they would be responsible, other Navy leaders and Academy professors understood that the system had drawbacks.[72] As Superintendent William Smedberg later recalled about his tenure from 1956 to 1958, a standard curriculum held little intellectual challenge for superior students and was illogical for students who had mastered the same material in previous preparatory or college work.[73] Some military leaders were further concerned that the increase in technological knowledge after World War II, within the bounds of "lock-step," put a tremendous burden of knowledge on already time-constrained midshipmen.[74]

Folsom concluded that the "lock-step" program confined midshipmen's academic education to the equivalent of only three of their four years at USNA, with the remaining year's worth of courses focusing on professional training.[75] Knowing that increasing percentages of USNA graduates were getting advanced technical training, Folsom argued that the Academy had to make its academic program more flexible in order to get its graduates on a par with those of other prominent engineering colleges. While he spoke to a long-term argument about whether the Naval Academy's purpose was education, technical training, or some hybrid including both, Folsom convinced Navy and Naval Academy leaders that some modification of the "lock-step" program was in order.[76] Several departments were already offering accelerated studies to small numbers of advanced midshipmen.[77] After Folsom's 1959 report, however, administrators began allowing midshipmen who entered USNA to take "validating" examinations to place out of required courses and permitting qualified midshipmen to take "overload" courses.[78] Both of these changes allowed midshipmen who were in the higher academic rankings of their classes to begin to work toward minors in elective disciplines.[79] Because the end of "lock-step" made the traditional marching to class impractical, Superintendent John Davidson eliminated the practice.[80] Alumni, as Davidson later recalled, were displeased and "thought the place had really gone to hell—no more military bearing or anything."[81]

The Folsom Report led to a number of other developments, among which was the adoption of a civilian academic dean to head the Academic Division.[82] Traditionally, a Navy officer served as secretary of the Academic Board, acting as the superintendent's academic aide and much as a civilian college dean, responsible for overseeing faculty and the operations of the academic departments. In 1962, several Navy leaders, with the urging of alumnus and nuclear advocate Admiral Hyman Rickover, decided that a civilian dean would improve the educational quality and continuity of the institution. The following year, Academic Board secretary Robert McNitt contacted A. Bernard Drought, the dean of engineering at Marquette University, to come temporarily to the Naval Academy as the first civilian academic dean. In 1964, Drought became the full-time academic dean, a position which replaced the secretary of the Academic Board. After receiving recommendations from the superintendent and chief of Naval operations, the secretary of the Navy is now responsible for appointing the academic dean.

Another development was the restructuring of the entire Academic Division.[83] Instead of the secretary of the Academic Board supervising the Academy's twelve academic departments, Superintendent Charles Melson placed the departments into one of three groups, Naval Science, Social Sciences, and Science and Engineering, with a director in charge of each. These directors reported to Drought, who also altered the basic curriculum to reflect changing technology. The composition of the Academic Board, responsible for assessing the academic status of midshipmen and determining whether academically deficient midshipmen could remain at USNA, also changed from including all of the department heads to just the three division directors. USNA also established a permanent curriculum review board and began to grade midshipmen with a "quality point rating system" of letter grades that conformed to the system used by most other colleges and universities.

The final significant academic change at USNA was the move toward academic majors, which, as Naval Academy historian and librarian W. W. Jeffries suggested, was the "follow-up development from the validation and electives program."[84] In 1964, the Academy further chipped away at "lock-step" by reducing the core curriculum from all to just 85 percent of classes, leaving the remaining 15 percent for electives. The number of courses had gone from 40 in 1959 to 210 by 1965.[85] With faculty suggestions in mind, Superintendent James Calvert again reorganized the Academic Division in 1970.[86] He broadened the number of academic divisions to five and the number of departments to eighteen.[87] Historian Charles Sheppard comments that Calvert's actions reflected trends in American higher education and military education during the era: the "rapid growth of new knowledge, evolving conceptions of the purposes of higher education, developments in technology and the military-industrial complex, and the demand by students for relevancy in the curriculum."[88] Calvert also ceased all vestiges of "lock-step" and created a true majors program with a core engineering curriculum; members of the class of 1971 became the first to graduate with one of twenty-four majors.[89] Among the midshipmen who experienced the change from "lock-step" to majors, opinions varied from support to disagreement, as is typical of most changes.[90] By the mid-1970s, Superintendent Kinnaird McKee, who believed that Calvert had created too many majors, reduced the number, and today midshipmen have their choice of nineteen majors.[91]

The Naval Academy has, since 1949, made a number of other additions to the academics program that have improved its quality. Superintendent William Smedberg created the Superintendent's List, similar to a civilian university's dean's list, in 1956.[92] A decade later, Superintendent Draper Kauffman devised the program that eventually became the Voluntary Graduate Education

Program, whereby as many as twenty senior midshipmen could begin working on graduate degrees during their final year at Annapolis.[93] Midshipmen now choose from a greatly expanded group of elective courses, and for the most academically superior midshipmen, Secretary of the Academic Board Robert McNitt and Superintendent Charles Kirkpatrick created the Trident Scholars Program in 1963.[94] Midshipmen in the program pursue individual research projects that have, in some cases, led to technological advances for the Academy and Navy and are similar to master's degree–level undertakings. In order to assist midshipmen and faculty with their research projects, USNA opened its large, modern library facility, named for Fleet Admiral Chester Nimitz, in 1972, and obtained high-technology laboratories and computer and engineering equipment.[95] In 1983, USNA ended the long-standing practice of Saturday classes, and for midshipmen with academic difficulties, Superintendent Virgil Hill Jr. opened an academic center with tutors and academic advisors in 1989.[96] In spite of occasional expressions of disapproval by detractors, there is, as Academic Dean William Miller stated, "no question that the academic quality [of USNA] has changed dramatically."[97]

The seventh USNA division that the superintendent oversees is the Office of the Commandant.[98] The commandant, usually a senior Navy captain or a junior-level admiral, oversees both the provision of food and supplies and the military, professional, and leadership development of midshipmen, as well as their religious, ethical, and physical education. The responsibilities of the commandant also include sitting on boards that assess midshipmen who seek leadership positions, who are academically deficient and face dismissal, or who are in potential violation of the Academy's Honor Concept (discussed in Chapter Eight). Most commandants since 1949 have served two- or three-year terms, all but one have been USNA graduates, and like superintendents, all have had different leadership styles. Some commandants have also developed goals for their time as the "commanding officer" of Bancroft Hall. Six commandants, Charles Buchanan (1952–54), Robert Coogan (1969–71), D. K. Forbes (1973–76), James Winnefeld (1976–78), Leon Edney (1981–84), and Samuel Locklear (1999–2001), openly sought to increase midshipmen's accountability and responsibility, while Sheldon Kinney (1964–67) emphasized military excellence.

The varying approaches brought by these commandants to rules, regulations, and the liberty of midshipmen have been deeply cyclical—to the point that commandants who were believed, by midshipmen, officers, faculty, and other administrators, to have been strict were predictably preceded and followed by commandants who were more flexible.[99] Perhaps the most liberal commandant was Jack Darby, who, during his brief term between 1978 and 1979, loosened regulations so dramatically that plebes could consume alcohol and date. Leon Edney's active involvement in the lives of midshipmen, including his participation in features in the Academy's humor magazine and his morning public address announcements in Bancroft Hall, was notable, but the most celebrated commandant was Robert Coogan (1969–71). Coogan later described his approach to his position by explaining that "my primary goal was communication with the midshipmen. I wanted to know exactly where they were coming from." The class of 1970, with appreciation for such an open, caring attitude, named commandant Coogan its "Man of the Year" and referred to him in their yearbook as "one helluva guy for the Brigade to follow."

The commandant supervises a number of different activities at the Naval Academy. One is the Midshipmen's Store, a large facility in Bancroft Hall in which midshipmen may purchase clothing, books, food, and entertainment items; another is the Academy's mess hall, in which midshipmen consume 11,000 meals each day.[100] Marines, assigned to USNA and under the direction of the commandant, help the midshipmen to learn military bearing, formations, and marching, all of which are means of developing discipline and represent the most overtly military aspect of life at Annapolis.[101] USNA's Division of Professional Development, and its Leadership/Ethics/Law and Seamanship/Navigation departments supervise the professional preparation of midshipmen. Military officers have primary responsibility for managing the professional and leadership development of midshipmen, through a series of courses and specialized training activities, many of which take place during the summers between academic years at USNA.[102] Ethics education, addressed in courses taught by both military and civilian faculty, first developed in the early 1970s but blossomed during the second term of Superintendent Charles Larson between 1994 and 1998.[103] Another group of officers associated with ethics education are the chaplains, whose official role at USNA includes providing religious services, pastoral care, and advice to midshipmen.[104] Finally, the commandant supervises the Physical Education Department. As wrestling coach Ed Peery explained, "Physical education is a core part of this institution," and all midshipmen engage in daily physical activities. If they are not members of varsity teams, midshipmen participate in intramural or club sports.[105] All midshipmen must also pass the physical readiness test, consisting of running, sit-ups, and push-ups, each semester.[106]

Because participation in athletics is such a key component of the Naval Academy, the Superintendent's remaining responsibility is over the Athletic

Director (AD).[107] Concerned by the short duration of the terms of officers filling the position, Superintendent James Calvert sought greater continuity by setting the precedent for either a non-rotating or a civilian AD. The AD works in coordination with the Naval Academy Athletic Association (NAAA), an organization that, since 1881, has supplied funds for USNA sports. Furthermore, NAAA arranges team schedules, provides coaches, staff, and supplies, and sponsors teams when they travel to play opponents. USNA teams fall under the jurisdiction of the National Collegiate Athletic Association, an organization that Annapolis leaders helped to create, and played in two conferences before joining the Patriot League in 1991.

The physical development aspect of the Academy's mission requires the participation of all midshipmen in sports. Also promoting a second military goal—teamwork—athletics is one of the most notable aspects of life at Annapolis.[108] The Academy currently has eight women's varsity sports, eighteen men's sports, and three co-ed teams.[109] USNA has had a number of notable athletes, including Heisman trophy winners Joe Bellino and Roger Staubach and basketball great David Robinson, but its most notable team remains the Olympic-gold-winning 1952 crew team.[110] Since 1973, the Academy has awarded the Admiral James Calvert Coaches Award to a graduating varsity-letter winner to recognize that individual's contributions to Navy athletics, and since 1980 the Vice Admiral William P. Lawrence Sword for Personal Excellence in Women's Athletics.[111] Midshipmen have also generally tended to be extremely supportive of the athletes in their midst.[112] In response to some midshipmen's complaints about USNA giving athletes preferential treatment and exempting them from typical responsibilities, Commandant Leon Edney gave team captains leadership responsibilities.[113] Many coaches, too, strive to be role models and work to encourage leadership, determination, and the acceptance of challenges in their team members.[114] For example, some coaches deliberately schedule competitions against notably stronger university teams as a means of building character and mental strength.[115] Because of the intensity of athletics and the long hours shared practicing, competing, and traveling with other midshipmen, teammates tend to develop friendships and bonds with one another and with coaches that are similar to those of best friends or roommates.[116]

Two annual athletic events have become recognized components of Naval Academy tradition: the annual Naval Academy–St. John's croquet match and the Army-Navy football game. In order to promote positive relations with students at Annapolis's St. John's College, midshipmen and the college's students have engaged in a yearly croquet match since 1982.[117] In the fight for croquet's Annapolis Cup, the St. John's team had by 1999 earned a 15–3 record against the Navy team, traditionally made up of members of USNA's 28th Company. The Army-Navy game has taken on meaning as both the symbol of friendly competition with cadets at West Point and as the source for the mantra plebes use walking at "double-time" (a fast-paced walk) through the corridors of Bancroft Hall.[118] The game's spirit has led to a tradition of pranks, which has included cadets stealing the arrows from Tecumseh and inciting a riotous food fight in King Hall just before the 1978 game.[119] Spirited midshipmen have hoisted huge "BEAT ARMY" banners on large memorials in Washington, D.C., and USNA Flying Club members have covered the West Point campus with "BEAT ARMY"–embossed ping pong balls from the air.[120] The kidnapping of mascots, midshipmen, and cadets was common enough to lead to a 1992 memorandum of agreement to avoid future recurrences.[121] Even military leaders have been involved with the competition: Army general and chairman of the Joint Chiefs of Staff Colin Powell wrote to USNA superintendent Thomas Lynch in 1993, "Please convey our best wishes to the midshipmen for a successful academic year and an outstanding football season. That is, of course, with the exception of the 4 December game! GO ARMY-BEAT NAVY!"[122] After the 2005 game, Navy led the series with fifty wins over Army's forty-nine victories. The two teams have tied seven times.[123]

The commandant, in addition to the aforementioned responsibilities of the office, oversees the Brigade of Midshipmen. The size of the Brigade has, since 1949, fluctuated between 3,200 and 4,700 midshipmen.[124] Organizationally, the primary unit within the Brigade is the company.[125] The number of companies has varied; in 1950, Commandant Robert Pirie reduced the thirty-six companies to twenty-four for greater administrative efficiency. A decade later, Commandant Charles Minter returned the Brigade to thirty-six companies as a means of decreasing the individual responsibilities of company officers, but Commandant W. T. R. Bogle lowered the number to thirty companies in 1996, reflecting a slight decrease in the Brigade's size. The current thirty companies are organized into six battalions of five companies, and into two regiments of fifteen companies. Each company is further divided into three platoons, and each platoon includes three squads. Commandant Sheldon Kinney created the squad system during his 1964–67 term, replacing the traditional system of assigning seniors to look after plebes. Squads are the smallest unit within the Brigade and company, and squad leaders, who are senior midshipmen, serve as leaders, advisors, and trainers to the midshipmen in the squad. Each company has a company commander, also a senior midshipman. In 1990, USNA administrators partially reestablished a more formal relationship between seniors, or first classmen, and plebes, in which the seniors provide counseling, advice, and guidance.

The Brigade of Midshipmen has both an officer and a midshipmen military structure. Navy and Marine Corps officers oversee each battalion and company, and these company officers serve simultaneously as a link between the administration and the company and as supervisors of the company's midshipmen and activities.[126] Some commandants, like Robert Coogan, have gone out of their way to search for highly successful Navy and Marine officers to serve as company officers because they frequently become role models and inspire midshipmen to decide on their own career path. For example, many members of the USNA community believe that the Marine Corps sends top quality officers to USNA in order to inspire midshipmen to choose the Marines. In 1995, Superintendent Charles Larson also began to assign an enlisted person, either a chief petty officer or a gunnery sergeant, as "an extra set of ears and eyes for the chain of command to correct and inspire midshipmen" in each of the companies.[127] The Brigade itself also has a formal military leadership structure called the "striper" organization (in reference to shoulder board and sleeve markings) that oversees midshipmen activities and reports to the commandant.[128] Because midshipmen at USNA are junior officers, the Brigade leadership structure reflects the Navy's overall organization. Each semester, a panel of the commandant and other officers selects the senior midshipmen who will serve in striper billets. The highest ranking midshipman position is the Brigade commander, also known as the "six-striper" or "midshipman captain." Below the Brigade commander, in a military structure mimicking that of a Navy vessel, is a series of six "five-stripers," seventeen "four-stripers," and ninety-eight "three-stripers" who have leadership and operational responsibilities in the Brigade organization. Nearly all other senior midshipmen hold two-stripe or one-stripe leadership positions.

As the primary unit of organization within the Brigade, the company has significance for each midshipman.[129] Every company is assigned its own living area in Bancroft Hall and maintains a company ward room serving as a meeting, study, and entertainment space. Companies also utilize "dining-ins," or formal dinners, and the decoration of the walls and bulletin boards within their company area as means of expressing humor, inspiration, and unity among company mates.[130] Midshipmen choose roommates, in previous decades called "wives," from within their companies. As one midshipman keenly observed,

A roommate is a necessary piece of equipment for survival at Navy, whether it is having someone to drag you out of the rack for reveille bell or console you over a "Dear John" letter. . . . A roommate is a symbiotic support system. The relationship between good roommates is like ying and yang; they complement each other's strengths and weaknesses. . . . The support a roommate provides ranges from physically lending a hand to being a source of motivation, entertainment, or even competition. . . . The support provided by a roommate is rarely equaled in life outside the Academy. One classmate of mine remarked that a roommate is the closest thing a midshipman has to a wife. Frequently roommates serve as confidants and best friends.[131]

Company mates share tables in King Hall during meals and work together in perfecting their military bearing and marching. Each company's yearly activities focus around the Color Company Competition, a comprehensive comparative assessment of the company members' academic, professional, and athletic achievements. Among the privileges of each year's Color Company winner is the opportunity to lead the Brigade in the subsequent academic year's parades, carrying the "colors," or flags, and to choose the Color Girl, the host of the final parade each year.

Aside from their companies and company mates, midshipmen have two external support networks: sponsor parents and parents' clubs. Future superintendent William Smedberg III devised the sponsor program while he was a faculty member in 1949.[132] Smedberg wanted plebes to have an officer or civilian "to whom [the plebe] could go for academic advice, occasional relaxation in a home, or just a change from the severe atmosphere in Bancroft Hall."[133] Smedberg's idea led to serious discussion at USNA, as the administration feared interference with the training of midshipmen.[134] Smedberg, however, enacted the idea when he became superintendent in 1956.[135] In the subsequent decades, the sponsor program has proved to be one of the most helpful relationships and pleasant aspects of many midshipmen's time at USNA; many sponsors have continued to help their midshipmen beyond their plebe years.[136] Sponsors have included a wide variety of Naval Academy and Annapolis community members.[137] Parents' clubs have their roots in 1950, when Superintendent Harry Hill invited midshipmen's parents to Annapolis to acquaint them with life at USNA.[138] Twenty-three years later, the Blue and Gold officer program formalized the relationship between parents and the Academy by creating a parents' club in the San Francisco Bay area.[139] Presently, over seventy parents' clubs in the United States and overseas work to transmit information about USNA and midshipman life to parents. The clubs meet regularly to share news and events about the Academy and function as a support group for midshipmen and their families.[140] Parents also visit USNA annually for an open-house weekend.[141]

Another group with which midshipmen have strong interaction is alumni. Alumni have served in capacities including administrators, Blue and Gold officers, Admissions and Candidate Guidance officers, company officers, military and civilian faculty, assessors of particular institutional problems, Naval Academy Alumni Association and Naval Academy Foundation leaders, sponsor parents, and coaches.[142] Administrators have frequently tried to have alumni, as officers and particularly those who had distinguished combat experiences, return to USNA to inspire the midshipmen.[143] Such alumni have also been involved in what Naval Academy ethics professor Patrick Walsh has called "generational nurturing," through the use of "sea stories," or tales from the Navy, sharing of traditions, and providing perspectives on how the Academy has changed.[144] The class of 1950, for example, provided the shoulder boards for the graduates in the class of 2000 in order to symbolize "the 50-year bond between the two classes."[145] Other graduates maintain relations with USNA through the Naval Academy Alumni Association.[146] Alumni have an especially deep sense of devotion and pride in their institution, as alumnus Robert Sleight described in his memoir: "Trying to analyze the whole [Naval Academy experience] many years later, I am convinced that what we learned from our books was secondary in nature. . . . It is what we absorbed that was important. The quickening of the pulses as we marched to the martial music of the band remains with me today. Just walking through the Yard touched me with an intangible feeling that shall make me forever a Navy man."[147]

Because of their typical love for the Naval Academy and the praise for its traditions, however, alumni can also be a source of tension, especially for Academy administrators to whom alumni complain about changing traditions and supposedly declining standards.[148] Alumni tend to claim that they had a much harder time at USNA, particularly during plebe summer, than current midshipmen, but as Superintendent Draper Kauffman once told alumni who made such comments, USNA "has been going to hell to my own and my father's personal knowledge since at least 1904." Other alumni have criticized the Academy for changing too slowly. Perhaps the most visible public critic of the Naval Academy was alumnus and nuclear Navy leader Hyman Rickover, who between 1959 and the 1976 testified before Congress and the USNA community on what he considered the Naval Academy's failure to modernize.[149] A second major critic, alumnus and author James Webb, noted for his diatribes against the presence of women at the Academy, will be discussed in Chapter Six. Because of their various roles and relations to the Naval Academy, Annapolis alumni have had a striking degree of influence over, and involvement in, the institution after their graduations.

Alumni of the Naval Academy almost always remember their Induction Day (I-Day), the beginning of their lives as midshipmen.[150] The day usually begins at 6:00 A.M. with the processing of the young people admitted into the Academy, and includes vision and blood tests, weighing, and receipt of nametags. The next step is the regulation haircut, perhaps the most symbolic step in the transformation from civilian to military life that inductees experience. For example, in order to prepare for his haircut and show his excitement about becoming a plebe, midshipman Sean Doyle deliberately grew his hair for five months and arrived for his I-Day with blue and gold beads in his braided hair. Naval Academy employees then fit the inductees with their plebe summer uniforms, which include white cotton "white works" uniforms with "dixie cup" hats. Plebes also receive "P.E. gear": blue athletic shorts, "blue rim" t-shirts, and athletic shoes—a physical activity uniform they wear for the rest of their time as midshipmen. Upperclass midshipmen, called plebe detailers, then instruct the inductees on how to wear their uniforms and how to salute. After further medical and dental examinations, the inductees and midshipmen enter Bancroft Hall and review basic marching techniques and meal etiquette. The inductees begin reading their personal copy of *Reef Points*, the official guide for plebes. Later in the evening, often with parents, families, and friends watching, the superintendent administers the Oath of Office for Midshipman Candidates in a ceremony that USNA administrators have historically held either in Bancroft Hall's Memorial Hall or in Tecumseh Court. After officially becoming plebes, the new midshipmen have thirty minutes to meet with their loved ones before entering Bancroft Hall for the continuation of their plebe summer.

The first major task of plebe summer for most plebes is finding their rooms in Bancroft Hall.[151] In the course of attempting to figure out the numbering system of rooms, many plebes hear for the first time the yelling and questioning by upperclass midshipmen that makes up part of the plebes' training during their first year at USNA. One alumnus recalled that "it took me two hours to find my room, and every time a plebe detailer saw me, they made me do pushups." For six weeks, plebe detailers instruct the plebes in military indoctrination, training in athletics, seamanship, sailing, first aid, meal etiquette, computers, and small arms.[152] Physical education faculty also lead plebes through the morning exercises called the Physical Excellence Program, or PEP.[153] Academy leaders also arrange academic advising and inspirational lectures by distinguished military leaders and, since its opening in 1994, a thought-provoking trip to the United States Holocaust Museum in Washington, D.C.[154] Many plebes also spend considerable time memorizing extensive tracts of *Reef Points*, which detailers frequently require them to recite flawlessly.[155] *Reef Points* and the plebe detailers also teach the plebes Navy and Naval Academy slang, the words to the USNA alma mater, "Navy Blue and Gold," and, as journalist and alumnus Robert Timberg has written, "the six verbal responses to . . . seniors: Yes, sir, No, sir, Aye aye, sir, I'll find out, sir, No excuse, sir, or the right answer to any question . . ."[156]

Superintendent William Smedberg described the point of plebe summer activities, which strive to integrate the plebes into the Naval Academy environment: "You have to learn to follow instantaneously, to take orders, [and] carry them out."[157] Plebe summer is a mental challenge for some young midshipmen, a physical challenge for others, and a "game" for a few. One midshipman, for example, remembered that the frequent sit-ups "beat the shit out of me, to be honest." Not all plebes adjust to the Academy environment, and some decide that the Annapolis lifestyle is not for them; from 1986 to 1992, for example, 4.2 percent of the male plebes and 7.3 percent of the female plebes resigned during the plebe summer. The parents of those plebes who remain gather in Annapolis at the end of plebe summer, and as Superintendent Smedberg observed, they remark "that they've never seen their [children] look better, act better, or seem more physically fit." Chief of Naval Personnel Michael Boorda commented in 1990 that "at the end of plebe summer, individuals are perhaps more motivated, disciplined, and military than at any other time in their four years" at USNA.

The plebe experience continues with the start of the new academic year and the return of the upperclassmen from their summer training activities. Although the upperclass call the first day back at USNA "Brigade Reform Day," plebes refer to it as "Hell Night."[158] Throughout the 1990s, the day began, for shock value, with the blasting of the rock group Guns-N-Roses's tune "Welcome To The Jungle" throughout Bancroft Hall. Plebe year is difficult by design. As Superintendent William Smedberg told plebes in 1956, "For a very few of you, a trying period will follow, but for most of you—those who can keep their sense of humor and refrain from indicating inner resentment or annoyance—plebe year will bother you very little. The system is designed to test plebes to see whether or not they can take it. Every graduate of the Naval Academy, including Fleet Admiral [Ernest] King, Fleet Admiral [William] Halsey, Fleet Admiral [Chester] Nimitz, your Commandant and myself, have gone through this same irritating, trying year and have been better men for it."[159] Principally, plebe year is about academics and about indoctrination in all of the information required to become successful midshipmen and junior officers.[160] The academics for plebe year consist primarily of required courses in calculus, chemistry, leadership, literature, history, naval science, and government, and plebes choose their majors before the year is complete. Discipline is a major focus of the indoctrination process during the plebe year. As a result, plebes are required to maintain their rooms in a spotless, organized condition ready for inspection, to "sound off," or announce themselves, in the presence of upperclassmen, and to run down the center of hallways (a practice called "chopping"), instead of walking, whenever they are in Bancroft Hall. Plebes also memorize and announce "chow calls" (recitations of the details of meals), lists of midshipmen officers on duty, and events of the day, and they meet regularly to sing the USNA alma mater and design billboards in the company areas.

Upperclassmen use a variety of means to impart lessons, leading some midshipmen, alumni, and observers to question those methods and the value of what may be called "hazing."[161] As alumnus John McCain, a member of the Class of 1958, described:

> We were expected to brace up, sit or stand at rigid attention with our chins tucked into our neck, whenever upperclassmen came into our view. Our physical appearance was expected to conform to a code with rules so numerous, esoteric, and pointless that I thought them absurd. We were commanded to perform dozens of menial tasks a day, each one intended to be more demeaning than the last, and made all the more so by a heap of verbal abuse that would accompany it. We were ordered to supply encyclopedias of obscure information to any silly son of a bitch who asked a question. When we did not know an answer, which of course, our interrogators hoped would be the case, we were made to suffer some further humiliation as punishment for our ignorance.[162]

Frequently, such demanding recitations of information take place at the table during meals.[163] Just three years after McCain's graduation, then–chief of Naval personnel William Smedberg remarked that "plebes should be brought up strictly—for one purpose and one purpose alone—to help them develop into better officers. Silly—sophomoric requirements to memorize lengthy chunks of ridiculous material do not help plebes—or anybody else—to become better officers. It merely interferes with their opportunity to get their work done for the next day's classes. . . . Yet from reports I continue to receive . . . firstclassmen are still permitting plebes to be brought up as if they were pledges in a fraternity house."[164]

Veiled and clear references to, and accusations of, plebe hazing are common throughout Naval Academy history. Introduced as a practice during the pre–Civil War era, hazing caused a number of incidents and scandals throughout the remainder of the nineteenth and twentieth centuries and has been one of the most repugnant of USNA traditions.[165] Since 1950, Naval Academy officials have suggested and claimed that hazing has disappeared, but incidents have continued to be identified and reported as recently as 1992.[166] At least seven superintendents and commandants have taken steps to reform the indoctrination process and reduce the occurrence of hazing.[167] Among these measures are Superintendents Draper Kauffman, James Calvert, and Charles Larson's promoting of professionalism between upperclassmen and plebes and Superintendents Virgil Hill and John Ryan's "hands off plebes" rule.[168] Superintendent Smedberg lucidly noted in 1957 that "hazing problems periodically will recur. . . . I would be the last person to infer that our rules and regulations concerning hazing are perfectly observed. They are not. We do have some abuses of authority by upperclassmen. And, in dealing with a large group of rigorous young men, I am not quite sure that we shall ever achieve perfection in this regard."[169] As Smedberg predicted, the elimination of hazing has been unachievable because of the impossibility of monitoring activities in Bancroft Hall at every moment of every day. Other administrative officials have come to similar conclusions as Smedberg, and have rightfully utilized regulations and the chain of command to eliminate the likelihood of hazing behaviors and to ensure that plebes receive enough sleep, study time, and food. Some commandants have, on occasion, even gone so far as to help plebes by granting privileges such as dating, listening to music, and consuming alcohol.[170]

Even without the threat of serious hazing, plebe year is a difficult one for all midshipmen.[171] Plebes who find it difficult to meet standards garner particular attention from upperclassmen, who have recently referred to such plebes as "shitscreens." Individual upperclassmen may also demand to see specific plebes on a daily basis for what are called "come arounds"; for example, a first classman required one plebe who had difficulty in tying a knot in neckties to report with three perfectly tied neckties each night of the plebe year. Other upperclassmen take a more lighthearted approach to their interactions with plebes, promising "carry-on" (upperclass privileges) or "spooning" (friendship) for such activities as a good joke, consuming twelve or more baked apples (called "cannonballs"), off-color hijinks such as eating cicadas, and placing bets on Navy football games. Lost bets can result in consequences such as a plebe having to march outside of an academic building in a "speedo" bathing suit yelling that his class "sucks."

Plebes have had at their disposal several methods for maintaining their humor and expressing their feelings for the upperclassmen who have challenged them.[172] From 1947 until 1950, plebes published a small newspaper called the *Plebeian*, which outlined rules and regulations but also told amusing and inspirational stories. When there are one hundred days remaining before the graduation of the senior class, midshipmen have traditionally celebrated "Hundredth Night" in which seniors and plebes change places and the plebes have the chance to abuse those who have abused them. In the 1990s, "Hundredth Night" became "Hundreds Night," a general night of liberty. Plebes may also attempt to perform a "Wildman," throwing some food, beverage, or combination of both at an upperclassman during a meal; a plebe succeeds only if he or she is able to exit King Hall and make it to their room before the victim catches them. First classmen return such antics by greasing the Herndon Monument that the plebes climb prior to the end of each academic year, a ceremony that, while messy and exhausting, has come to symbolize the official end of the plebe year experience.

At the conclusion of their plebe year, the new third classmen (called the 3/C or "youngsters") go to sea for the first time as midshipmen.[173] As Superintendent Kinnaird McKee explained, "Summer training for midshipmen . . . is intended to reinforce and complement professional knowledge acquired in the classroom." Third class midshipmen have traditionally gone aboard Navy vessels in the fleet for their 3/C summer. In more recent decades, third classmen have gone on cruises aboard the Academy's Yard Patrol craft, 108-foot ships used for teaching seamanship and navigation. These tours travel to ports on the Atlantic seaboard, and midshipmen have the opportunity to interact with enlisted personnel in a ship environment. Some third classmen serve as leaders of the summer seminars for prospective candidates, and all 3/C either sail aboard USNA sailboats or participate in Naval Tactical Training, which includes exposure to SEAL, Marine, and joint operation training. The return to Annapolis and the sight of the Naval Academy chapel, even more than the Herndon Ceremony, has been the traditional end of the plebe year and the beginning of the 3/C year.

As the third class academic year gets under way, administrators decide whether or not to "shotgun" the new third classmen to companies different than those in which the former plebes had spent their first year at USNA.[174]

The justification for such a step is that the members of the 3/C can get a new start with a company whose members did not witness plebes' performance or give particular plebes a tough time, and that the members can expand the scope of midshipmen they will know and their exposure to different leadership styles. However, distancing company mates can also serve to cut off established bonds and to diminish company spirit. Whether they do or do not remain in their original company, third classmen face a difficult academic year with basic major courses and required courses in mathematics, naval engineering, ethics, navigation, history, and physics. Superintendent Draper Kauffman later recalled his youngster year "was an absolutely dead year. . . . the only time that I was in the Navy that I had no motivation." Kauffman's experience was not unique: youngsters face a tough academic schedule, are no longer the focus of attention in the Brigade, and have few leadership responsibilities. Furthermore, they must decide whether or not they will remain midshipmen, with no further cost or obligation to them, until graduation. Some 3/C midshipmen just "hunker down" and work at making themselves a positive example for the new plebes. But, as one such midshipman explained, "There were many hours of personal debate, and I had applications for other colleges ready, but my decision to stay was a real turning point in my life at USNA."

The new second classmen (2/C) spend the summer between their sophomore and junior years getting a firsthand look at the various activities of the Navy and Marine Corps.[175] The 2/C midshipmen participate in Marine maneuvers in Quantico, Virginia, and in aviation and submarine activities in Florida before joining the crews of Navy ships around the world for one month. These activities allow midshipmen the opportunity to observe shipboard activities and to interact more extensively with officers and enlisted personnel. Such experiences help to mold the midshipmen's ideas about their eventual choice of service communities, and the midshipmen tend to return to USNA with a deeper commitment to their careers.

The 2/C academic year includes courses in majors as well as requirements in electrical engineering, weapons, leadership, and tactics.[176] Some midshipmen spend the fall semester of their 2/C year as exchange midshipmen at other service academies, a program with its roots in World War II–era exchange weekends with West Point designed to foster better relations with, and understanding of, the other services.[177] The program has run continuously since 1949 with the exception of the years 1972 through 1975.[178] For those who remain in Annapolis, much time is spent on the training of plebes.[179] The 2/C year ends ceremonially with the Ring Dance, a symbolic "marrying" of the midshipmen to the Naval service in which midshipmen dip their class rings into a container of water from all ends of the earth and officially become seniors.[180] The class ring also becomes a formal symbol of the link between the individual midshipmen, their class, and the Academy itself.[181]

Shortly after the Ring Dance, senior midshipmen begin their lives as first classmen (1/C).[182] They begin the summer before their senior year as junior officers attached to Navy or Marine units to utilize their skills and also to be involved with units of the type in which they hope to serve after graduation. Frequently, these tours go to destinations around the world. Back in Annapolis, 1/C take courses related to their majors, weapons, and law. Much of their time is spent in direct leadership of the Brigade and on the training of plebes. The 1/C also go through the service selection process. Utilizing the experiences they have had interacting with the various Navy and Marine communities during the academic years and summer training periods, the midshipmen select their top choices for their career specialties. After interviews with officers stationed at the Academy, and sometimes with Navy leaders in Washington, the midshipmen find out their career paths early in the spring semester of their 1/C year. Nuclear Navy leader Hyman Rickover conducted the most notorious of these interviews, frequently barking harsh questions at the midshipmen in an attempt to identify the most capable of the 1/C.[183] Up to 16.6 percent of each class can enter the Marine Corps, and the remainder, with the exception of a small number of midshipmen who choose to transfer to other services, enter the Navy. Between 1949 and 1963, a quarter of the graduating class could also choose the Air Force as an option in order to satisfy the needs of that fledgling service.

First classmen also spend their fourth and final year engaged in a variety of activities that have been a part of their lives as midshipmen. All members of the Brigade abide by the Academy's Honor Concept, live under a series of rules and regulations, and participate in extracurricular activities. The Honor Concept is one of the deepest aspects of USNA culture and one of the defining characteristics of Annapolis.[184] Reading in part that "a midshipman will not cheat, lie, steal, or tolerate anyone who does," the Naval Academy Honor Concept is not a monolithic list of punishable infractions, but is a flexible tool designed to allow midshipmen to learn how to assess, evaluate, and deal with other midshipmen's infractions.[185] As historian Jean Ebbert has explained, "The Naval Academy midshipman has the option of using whatever means of persuasion he or she can muster to convince the erring midshipman of the folly of his ways. If personal counseling and pressure can make the errant midshipman stop his dishonorable behavior and make the proper restitutions, the matter can rest there. The observing midshipman is obligated to report the miscreant only when other measures of persuasion fail to mend the matter."[186] In 1994, after a copy of an electrical engineering test was stolen and 125 midshipmen ended up with knowledge of the exam's contents, Superintendents Thomas Lynch and Charles Larson expanded midshipmen's consideration of the Honor Concept by implementing monthly Honor Education Programs and Integrity and Character Development seminars.[187]

USNA rules and regulations—which cover most aspects of midshipmen's lives and activities, including uniforms, room standards, behavior, automobile policies, alcohol, and drugs—outline the types of punishments that midshipmen will receive for various violations.[188] Midshipmen have historically been upset by rules dictating the amount and duration of their liberty away from the Academy and about changes in regulations that decrease their freedoms and privileges.[189] As one observer noted, "There are so many rules [at USNA] that it is impossible for even the most conscientious midshipman to follow them all—leaving individuals to decide for themselves what the 'real' rules are. If everything is important, nothing is."[190] Furthermore, the regulation-dominated environment causes some midshipmen to adopt the philosophy that "you rate what you skate," meaning that they will push the limits if not ignore rules altogether through a variety of actions, including pranks, that symbolize a defiance of authority.[191] Others allow cynicism to fester and adopt a culture of loathing for the Academy.[192] For example, midshipmen commonly detest the long hours in preparation for and the exercise of marching. As Robert Timberg has commented, "Over the years, the phrase 'I hate this fucking place' has become the equivalent of a secret handshake between Annapolis men. It's so common that the actual words are superfluous. Usually you just say IHTFP."[193]

Extracurricular activities (ECAs) serve, in part, as an outlet for such feelings and also represent the diversity in midshipmen's interests and backgrounds.[194] There are currently over seventy ECAs involving a range of academic, athletic, community service, ethnic, musical, professional, publication, recreational, religious, theatrical, and Brigade support activities.[195] Some organizations, like the Glee Club and the Gospel Choir, serve as public relations and recruiting tools, whereas others, like the Brigade Activities Committee, help to raise spirits and pride within the Academy itself.[196] Several other activities are geared toward midshipmen, including WRNV, the Naval Academy's radio station. Run by midshipmen since 1949 and currently on 89.7 FM, the station airs music, covers athletic matches, and features midshipmen who share often humorous and irreverent commentary about life at Annapolis.[197] Irreverence also became the standard for the LOG, which began as a news, sports, and information publication in 1909 but had transformed into a satirical humor magazine by 1968.[198] The most enduring LOG feature was the "Salty Sam" column, in which an anonymous midshipman posed as a crusty sailor who recounts incidents of questionable judgment and debauchery among the Academy's midshipmen, faculty, and officers. Academy officials quashed the LOG in 2000 after deciding that the magazine had become disrespectful, and for a short time midshipmen maintained the publication online. Finally, although it is not an official ECA, midshipmen enjoyed the entertainment of the Eighth Wing Players from the early 1980s until 2000.[199] An informal combination of talent show and mockery of USNA, the Eighth Wing Players was described by one midshipman as "the best satire on Academy life there is to be found," until it, too, was terminated because of its disrespectfulness.

These humorous activities, in addition to the hard work and challenges during four years at Annapolis, occupy the thoughts of the first classmen as they approach their graduation ceremony. Until the superintendency of William Lawrence, graduation ceremonies took place in June and the final week of activities at USNA was referred to as "June Week." Under Lawrence, the graduation was moved to May and the week has henceforth been known as "Commissioning Week."[200] The seniors watch the plebes climb the Herndon Monument and then see the 2/C attend their Ring Dance. The entire Brigade marches in the Color Parade, the final dress parade of their four years, after which 1/C traditionally jump into the Severn River, fountains, or from the high dive into the Lejeune Hall swimming pool.[201] The next day, first classmen and their families and friends assemble for the commencement ceremonies, held in the past in Dahlgren Hall or Halsey Field House, but since the 1960s in the Navy–Marine Corps stadium.[202] Among the most unusual graduation events, a reflection of McCarthyism, was the secretary of the Navy's decision to interview three members of the class of 1954 prior to the ceremony in order to ensure that they and their parents were not "subversives" due to their own or their parents' associations with socialist unions or communist nations.[203] In more recent years, graduation onlookers have watched the Blue Angels Demonstration Squadron perform a fly-by, or low-altitude passage, over the stadium.[204] Notable Americans serve as graduation speakers and then as distributors of diplomas.[205] By tradition, the final midshipman to receive his or her diploma, due to having the lowest standing in the class, is called the "Anchor Man."[206] A high-ranking officer from the Navy reads the oath of office for midshipmen entering that service, and a high-ranking Marine then swears in the midshipmen entering the Corps. After the underclassmen offer a cheer for the graduates, and the graduates return a cheer for the rest of the Brigade, the new ensigns and second lieutenants toss their hats into the air and receive their first salutes, the official end of their Naval Academy experience.[207] In the pages of the Academy annual, the *Lucky Bag*, the midshipmen and their experiences are immortalized for them, their classmates, and future generations of the Brigade.[208]

The Higher Ideals of Democracy

Race and Recruiting through 1964

★ ★

As the dawn broke on the morning of 1 January 1955, the rain that had drenched New Orleans for several days finally ended. The Gulf sun dried the city that Saturday, and football fans from across the nation tuned their television sets to ABC affiliates for the 12:45 kickoff of the 1955 Sugar Bowl. Although the University of Mississippi Rebels entered the game as the favorite, Navy scored a touchdown on the opening kick, a feat it repeated when the second half of the game began. The midshipmen, whom coach Eddie Erdelatz called his "Team of Desire," later scored a third time, never allowing the Rebels to gain a single point.[1] Mississippi's coach, John Vaught, told reporters that "we met a fine team on a peak day. Navy was great in every way." The 82 thousand fans present at the game were listening, as were approximately 65 million television viewers throughout the United States. Naval Academy recruiting, then in its infancy, blossomed dramatically as USNA leaders realized the benefits of television exposure to the American public. This chapter examines the growth and development of Naval Academy recruiting, as well as the attendance of minority midshipmen, through 1964, the year White House officials began to pay attention to minority enrollment at USNA.

Among those present at the Sugar Bowl was the Academy's superintendent, Walter Boone. In 1954, Boone had begun work on a plan to raise awareness of USNA among the nation's male youth.[2] His action was likely motivated by three causes. Although the Korean War had brought an increase in interest in admissions to Annapolis as a refuge from combat, the number of applicants waned after the war's conclusion. Secondly, Boone did not feel that the Academy was attracting enough young men with the highest qualifications for entry. Lastly, attrition rates in the 1950s rose beyond those of former years. Among the classes of 1950 through 1954, 23.4 percent of entering midshipmen did not graduate. By the fall of 1954, attrition had already claimed 31.4 percent of the class of 1955 and 29.2 percent of the class of 1956. Boone conceived of a program in which midshipmen would return to their hometowns during vacations and speak to local high school students and youth groups as a means of raising awareness of, interest in, and applications to the Naval Academy.

The dramatic climb after the Sugar Bowl in the number of letters from young men interested in attending the Academy had a strong impact on the thinking of Boone and other administrators contemplating recruiting plans.[3] Prior to the Sugar Bowl appearance, the Academy relied primarily on individual prospective candidates contacting the Academy or their congressmen to demonstrate a desire to attend USNA. Interested high school students learned of the Naval Academy from news sources, books, family, friends, and alumni, or from the more than twenty dramatic Hollywood films that featured the Naval Academy and its midshipmen as part of their story lines.[4] Movie theater news films, including those of Metro-Goldwyn-Mayer News, Movie Tone News, Paramount News, and Warner Brothers News, frequently covered Naval Academy events such as June Week and graduation ceremonies. Army-Navy games and USNA basketball games appeared on television as early as 1947, but it was the extensive Sugar Bowl viewership that truly led USNA administrators to take note of the power of television. The ensuing decades brought still more methods of recruitment and expanding goals, reflecting both the changes in American society and transformations at the Naval Academy.

Superintendent Boone devised his plan, known as "Operation Information" ("Op Info"), which became fully functional during the 1955–56 academic year under his successor, Rear Admiral William R. Smedberg III.[5] As Smedberg explained, the Academy chose approximately one hundred midshipmen, each of whom displayed academic achievement and public speaking skills, as volunteers for the program. During winter and summer leaves, these midshipmen returned to their hometowns and arranged speaking engagements; when feasible, they also arranged radio or television interviews, appearances, and announcements. As the LOG noted in 1957, midshipmen who participated in Operation Information had the benefit of nearly an extra week of Christmas leave. "Never has this entered [a midshipman's] mind," LOG writers quipped, "as a reason for applying for Op Info." Whether cynical or not, midshipmen understood that the Naval Academy was profiting from Operation Information in numerous ways. 1958 Brigade administrative officer Robert McFarlane noted about his speech in Gainesville, Texas, that his efforts were useful for even those young Texans who would not qualify for the Academy. McFarlane wrote, "I believe [USNA] can benefit from keeping people informed on how their money is being used and talking to some of the representatives of an institution maintained by their taxes." McFarlane gave a typical Op Info speech in Gainseville, describing the purpose of the Naval Academy, life and activities at Annapolis, career opportunities after commissioning, and admission procedures. McFarlane and other Op Info participants succeeded in keeping the public informed about the Naval Academy and in telling prospective candidates useful knowledge about "what they will be up against" if they became midshipmen.

Boone and other Academy officials understood the popularity of television and theaters in providing comedy, drama, and sports entertainment to the public in the 1950s.[6] In 1955 USNA and the Pentagon approved the release of a motion picture about life at the Academy, the first such film since the 1930s. Entitled An Annapolis Story, the film focused on two brothers during their years at the Academy and their early Navy careers. Historian Lawrence Suid describes the film as "a cut-and-paste movie created with a few location shots of the Academy" and reiterates a contemporary film critic's observation that An Annapolis Story was "wholesome" and patriotic but not realistic. Recognizing this, Superintendent Boone quickly agreed when a television production company approached him in the fall of 1955 about creating a program with USNA as its subject.

John Sinn, president of California's F. W. Ziv Radio and Television Syndication Companies (ZIV), wanted to demonstrate in the proposed series "the youthful virility, drive, action, conflict, and enthusiasm that exists at Annapolis."[7] Although some USNA officers had objected to "selling the Naval Academy with corn flakes," the Academy and ZIV signed a memorandum of agreement on 9 December 1955 for the television series, to be entitled Men of Annapolis. USNA and ZIV agreed to produce thirty-nine half-hour television episodes. ZIV gave to the Academy the ultimate right of approval of all scripts and story content and agreed to have a Naval Academy graduate on the sets to ensure the authenticity of all visual and narrative details. Although ZIV planned to do some of the filming at Annapolis, the company promised to interfere as little as possible with life at the Academy. And while the federal government would incur no costs for its role in the series, the Naval Academy insisted that ZIV not allow alcohol or tobacco companies to advertise during the series' commercial spots. ZIV's Richard Dorso served as the company's representative and the program's creative director, and Superintendent Boone chose Admiral Charles Erck, a USNA graduate, and Eugene Starbecker, who had worked on *An Annapolis Story*, as advisors. Ultimately, public information officers Marcy Dupre and A. G. Esch handled *Men of Annapolis* issues at the Academy, and USNA alumnus Sherman Alexander served as a technical advisor at the ZIV studios.

From the beginning, the entire Naval Academy community was involved in the creation of the television series.[8] USNA had two separate committees to assist ZIV with the program. One group, whose goal was to devise ideas for stories, consisted of midshipmen, including the Brigade commander and company officers. A second group, including the commandant and other officers, also provided ideas, but in addition worked to authenticate the story lines and details. On 14 January 1956, A. G. Esch sent Dorso a twelve-page report with sixty-six ideas representing "the compilation of the thoughts of many, many officers, professors, and midshipmen here." Public Information Officer Marcy Dupre later recalled that the involvement of so many people, including alumni, "not only made my job easier but I firmly believe that the result reflected the extra effort."

The two groups' first forty-four suggestions represent themes that the commentators thought would be essential to an understanding of USNA, beginning with the admissions process.[9] The groups also sought to provide a description of the essential components to a Naval Academy education: academics, plebe year training, athletics, physical training, leadership and character development, and professional training and development. The biggest emphasis among these ideas, however, was on those personal characteristics that the Naval Academy itself saw as crucial for midshipmen: personal honor, motivation, discipline, determination, hard work, a "can-do" attitude, teamwork, pride in the Navy uniform, and an understanding of the equality of all midshipmen, regardless of their backgrounds. These ideals became the themes of *Men of Annapolis* episodes. The producers addressed admissions in two episodes, "Underfire" and "The Clash"; the former explained how enlisted personnel could enter the Naval Academy, whereas the latter promoted the concept that any young man, even the son of an Italian immigrant fisherman, could qualify for entry to USNA. "Breakaway" addressed the challenges of plebe summer and the value of humor, whereas several other episodes explored the value of confidence to success at USNA. Midshipmen's teamwork appeared in scripts about football, soccer, and the Color Company Competition. The producers also wove academic and professional training issues—such as steam power, ship steering and navigation, and life-saving skills—into the series. Similarly, the Navy's various technological and warfare communities appeared in a number of episodes, providing a portrait of the varied yet unified branches of the service.

Esch's report also contained specific recommendations for story lines.[10] Although few of those proposed stories resulted in actual episodes, various elements of the original suggestions frequently coalesced into scripts. Proposals about a graduate who had difficulty in climbing a rope and about a midshipman who knowingly entered USNA with an unacceptable contact lens led to Episode Eight, entitled "Blinding Light." In that story, a midshipman who could not pass a rope-climbing test forged a passing score, went through an Honor Committee hearing, and was expelled from the Academy. Suggestions about portraying the relationship between seniors and plebes and about describing "the typical introvert midshipmen" who searched for romance combined to form the third episode: in "Mail Call," two seniors convinced an unconfident young plebe to write to a famous model. Further ideas on portraying the "personal contrast between two midshipmen" and a scenario in which a midshipman prevailed over a previous academic problem only to save a distressed ship in the end resulted in two episodes, "The Challenge" and "Hot Steam," respectively.

ZIV began to film the episodes of *Men of Annapolis* in the spring of 1956, by which point Boone's successor, William Smedberg, had become the superintendent. ZIV filmed outdoor and some indoor scenes at the Naval Academy and recorded other supplemental interior scenes at the ZIV studios in Hollywood.[11] After the completion of the first episode, Sinn wrote to Smedberg that "it is difficult for me to tell you in a letter how much I appreciate the courtesy and cooperation which you and your staff extended to our people. . . . All of us here are most enthusiastic about the project."[12] Members of the Naval Academy community remained engaged and excited as the filming progressed. Although ZIV supplied actors, the Academy's Public Affairs Office coordinated the use of midshipmen as extras.[13] Some midshipmen apparently took their acting roles seriously. A *LOG* comic showed two midshipmen observing a third midshipman walking with verve; the caption read, "Don't mind him— he's just trying to get those ZIV TV boys to notice him."[14] With such widespread involvement, there was much excitement when ZIV screened the first episode in the Mahan Hall auditorium on 1 June 1956.[15]

After the screening that evening, Naval Academy administrators held a cocktail party at Carvel Hall, a nearby hotel and social gathering spot in Annapolis.[16] Admiral Smedberg began to receive feedback during the celebration, and a week later, he wrote to Richard Dorso with his comments

In 1956 and 1957, F. W. Ziv Radio and Television Syndication Companies filmed the television series *Men of Annapolis* on the USNA campus and in Hollywood. This photograph depicts the filming of a 1957 episode entitled "The Star." In the episode, a midshipman becomes a soccer star but works hard as an individual and not a team player. Here, he attempts to win over the team captain's girlfriend before he realizes the value of teamwork. Popular with the American public, *Men of Annapolis* served to educate citizens about USNA and inspired many young men to pursue an education at the Academy. (Courtesy of Sherman G. Alexander)

and observations. The Superintendent felt that the episode, entitled "Counter Flood," was "too severe, too dramatic, [and] that it could have been softened in some areas." The story described a midshipman named Bill who found that his military professor's expectations were too high. However, with hard work, Bill achieved a perfect classroom presentation, thereby pleasing the officer. Smedberg felt, for example, that the commander in the episode could have shaken Bill's hand rather than saluting him. Yet Smedberg had confidence in the product and the effort, and he told Dorso, "I think that the story told in the pilot film will have a tremendous impact on its viewers. It is certainly dramatic and points up the fact that our instructors are not merely referees between the textbook and the grades assigned. All of us here feel that . . . we will be telling the Naval Academy story well indeed."

Given the emphasis on honor and proper behavior in Men of Annapolis, it is ironic that one of the most difficult challenges arising from the series originated with the actors portraying midshipmen. The Naval Academy supplied the actors with midshipmen uniforms for their scenes around the Yard. On 25 October 1956, after a Navy home football game, several actors appeared at Carvel Hall and became intoxicated and disorderly while they wore midshipmen uniforms.[17] Members of the class of 1957, who were also present, immediately observed what they believed to be a drunken group of their colleagues and confronted the men. Upon realizing that the perpetrators were actors, the midshipmen were "shocked almost to disbelief" and feared a smearing of the reputation of their class. Timothy Keating, the midshipman who reported the incident to USNA administrators, was particularly concerned that townspeople and alumni, who witnessed the drunken actors, would not have "the impression that our class has exceptional leadership abilities." Superintendent Smedberg decided that, thereafter, actors would wear uniforms only during the actual filming of episodes.

Men of Annapolis premiered on Pittsburgh, Pennsylvania, television station KDKA on 7 January 1957, and began its national syndication on WTOP in Washington, D.C., a month later.[18] Television stations broadcast the thirty-nine episodes during the remainder of 1957 and into 1958, with thirteen repeated episodes after the originals aired.[19] The Naval Academy then linked the television series with its Operation Information campaign. When midshipmen returned to their hometowns for Op Info activities, USNA lobbied local television stations to allow the midshipmen to appear during commercial breaks. In a letter to station managers, the Academy wrote that "the midshipman's visit is an ideal opportunity to use MEN OF ANNAPOLIS posters, streamers, photo blow-ups and other displays, as well as special announcements telling the community of the visit as well as your show."[20] The immediate impact was astounding, as the *New York Times* reported in the spring of 1957. In the first six days of March that year, "The number of inquiries about entrance at Annapolis equaled the number received during [all of] March in 1956."[21] The combination of the Sugar Bowl, Op Info, an advertising pamphlet sent to high schools nationwide, and *Men of Annapolis* doubled the number of applicants in 1957 over that of the previous two years.[22]

By the summer of 1957, the Naval Academy was assessing the success of *Men of Annapolis*.[23] USNA conducted several opinion surveys among the plebes. One survey showed that while most of the plebes had seen the series and thought it was "good," the majority also felt that "it was not very true to the life of a midshipman." A large number of plebes reported that *Men of Annapolis* had not influenced their decision to enter the Academy. A second survey led an officer in charge of plebe detail to conclude that "out of 194 plebes who were asked the direct question 'did this program influence your decision to enter the Naval Academy?', only three replied in the affirmative." The officer noted that criticism of the series centered around several complaints; it was seen as "unrealistic," "corny," and "too much Hollywood." It seems reasonable to conclude that the television series, which began after these particular young men had made their decision to attend the Naval Academy, would not have been a tremendous influence on them.

Richard Dorso's desire to extend the production beyond the original thirty-nine episodes may have precipitated these surveys.[24] Dorso likely understood the popularity of the television medium and knew that by 1957 40 million American homes had televisions. He informed Smedberg that *Variety* magazine had placed the series among the top ten syndicated television programs in five major markets that summer. Smedberg, however, was skeptical. He felt, in part, that there were no remaining realistic story lines. For example, two of the last episodes, "Rescue at Sea" and "The Runaway," did not take place at the Academy. The superintendent's staff rated the quality of thirty-nine episodes and found only one to be "outstanding," four to be "excellent," and ten to be "good"; the remaining twenty-four episodes were only "fair" or "poor." Taking these factors into consideration, and aware of the plebe surveys and comments from others in the Naval Academy community who disliked the "tone and story lines," Smedberg indicated his feeling that "the series should not be renewed." He did acknowledge, though, that *Men of Annapolis* was playing a role in promoting and advertising the Academy. Sherman Alexander, moreover, has since discovered that the series had a substantial impact on the successive classes whose members saw the series as elementary, middle, and high school students. In an informal survey of 140 graduates from the classes of 1962 through 1969, Alexander found that 95 percent of the respondents "were positively influenced to attend the Naval Academy by *Men of Annapolis*." His findings affirm what Secretary of the Navy Thomas Gates realized when, in the fall of 1958, he recognized ZIV with a certificate reading, "For outstanding service to the Department of the Navy in the fields of public information, morale, and recruiting. As producer of the television series 'Men of Annapolis,' ZIV Television has brought to nearly fifty million viewers each week an accurate picture of the life and training of midshipmen at the United States Naval Academy. The quality of the programs —with the stress on standards of morality and the values of honor as they are stressed at the Naval Academy—has promoted nationwide understanding of the purposes, ideals, and achievements of the Navy."[25]

The Naval Academy's appearances in popular media did not end with the series, however.[26] The USNA football team beat Rice in the Cotton Bowl in 1958, the Naval Academy Glee Club appeared on the popular *Pat Boone Show* in 1959, and the football team lost by a touchdown in the 1961 Orange Bowl. Smedberg later noted that the televised football bowl appearances led to "a tremendous burst of requests" for information about the Academy. A Baltimore radio station began producing a thirty-minute radio program about the Naval Academy in 1959, featuring interviews and musical performances; the program also aired on a Richmond, Virginia, radio station. Radio had been a medium for public information about USNA in the Annapolis area in the 1940s with programs entitled *Naval Academy Soundings* (1947), *Who's Here at the Naval Academy* (1948), and *Navy Hour* (1949). Midshipmen had even produced their own national radio program, *Welcome Aboard*, in 1950. In 1960, Annapolis got another radio transmission, *The Naval Academy Hour*.

That same year, USNA appeared in two recruiting films, the Navy's *Five Steps to the Brigade* and the Academy's own production, *Ring of Valor*.[27] Superintendent Charles Melson argued that the film *An Annapolis Story* had become outdated for recruiting purposes. Melson's predecessor, William Smedberg, was serving at the time as the chief of Naval personnel, and he secured funds, a narrator, and a technical advisor for *Ring of Valor*. Filming took place during the spring and summer of 1960. Centering on the achievement of wearing a Naval Academy ring, the film gave an overview of all the steps and requirements of midshipmen from their entry as plebes until graduation. The film also contrasted the Academy's traditions, like mandatory chapel services, with its modern facilities, including chemistry laboratories and flow tanks.

The next major step in the development of Naval Academy recruiting took place in the summer of 1962 when the Bureau of Naval Personnel created the Blue and Gold program, a system of admissions advisors.[28] In concept, Blue and Gold may have had its roots in 1932 when football coach Rip Miller set up his "bird dog" recruiting system. Miller, a former football star under University of Notre Dame coach Knute Rockne, utilized forty civilian contacts who identified prospective Naval Academy candidates who showed skills in athletics and academics. Named for USNA's school colors, Blue and Gold consisted initially of thirty-three reserve officers responsible for spreading information about the Academy in areas away from Annapolis. By 1973, Dean of Admissions Robert McNitt had expanded the program to over 1,500 "local citizens and members of the Naval Reserve [who] counsel, recruit, and assist young men throughout the country." Currently, Blue and Gold officers are located in every state and frequently play a role in interviewing and interacting with prospective candidates.

At the height of the civil rights movement, amid discussions about the 1964 Civil Rights Act, President Lyndon Johnson noted the low number of African American midshipmen at Annapolis. The next stage in Naval Academy recruiting was about to begin. Prior to Johnson's observation, issues of race and ethnicity were not, apparently, frequent topics of administrative discussion. As Superintendent James Holloway indicated in a 1948 letter, "The official records of midshipmen kept here at the Naval Academy do not include data on racial origin or extraction."[29] However, Academy officials had in fact been keeping informal notes on non-white midshipmen since at least 1944.[30] The 1952 McCarran-Walter Act, which made minimal changes in American immigration policy, and the 1954 Brown v. Board of Education case, the first major chip in the block of segregation in education in the United States, had a big enough impact on USNA that administrators began to pay closer attention to racial and ethnic characteristics of its midshipmen.[31] By 1959, Naval Academy records included notes on the race and ethnicity of its midshipmen, classifying them as "Negro," "Mongolian," "Malayan," "American Indian," and "Caucasian."[32]

The Naval Academy never experienced a formalized integration, nor was there ever deliberate recruiting of "minority," meaning non–"White Anglo Saxon Protestant," applicants prior to the 1960s. Members of various ethnic, racial, and religious groups began attending the Naval Academy as early as the nineteenth century, sometimes unnoted by contemporaneous members of the Academy community. How these individual midshipmen chose to identify themselves is unclear.[33] It is reasonable to assume that some individuals may have deliberately identified their racial or ethnic identity in such a way as they found politically expedient in particular time periods and under particular circumstances. For example, an African American midshipman with light skin may have had serious reasons not to identify himself as black. Catholic midshipmen were likely present at USNA from its earliest years, when anti-Catholic sentiment in the United States was especially strong (although no specific instances of anti-Catholic actions at USNA are known).[34] Midshipmen of Hispanic descent likely attended the Academy early in the twentieth century, but it is unknown whether they would have self-identified as such prior to the Census Bureau's use of the term "Hispanic" in the 1970s.[35] Horacio Rivero, a native of Puerto Rico and a member of the class of 1931, may have been the first Hispanic midshipman, and by the end of the 1950s, five other Puerto Rican natives had been in the Brigade of Midshipmen.[36] The Naval Academy Preparatory School had a Hispanic-American midshipman candidate by 1963.[37]

American Indian, Native Alaskan, and Native Hawaiian midshipmen are equally difficult to trace in Naval Academy history. Midshipmen of partial American Indian descent graduated as early as the 1890s. Peter Fullwinder, who was likely of Indian background, graduated in 1894, but USNA currently lists Joseph Clark, class of 1918, as its first American Indian graduate.[38] Clark's heritage appears, however, to have eluded Naval Academy officials when he was a midshipmen, although it was known by 1980 when the Navy named a frigate as the USS Clark.[39] As another American Indian graduate noted, "To the best of my knowledge, [the Naval Academy] had no interest in my Indian background."[40] An examination of photographs and biographical texts in the Lucky Bag (the Naval Academy annual) of the 413 men with congressional nominations from the state of Oklahoma—a state with a substantial Indian population—revealed thirty-seven graduates from the classes of 1913 through 1962 who may have been American Indians.[41] However, since Lucky Bag biographies are often ironic or playful in nature, it is impossible to know whether or not a nickname like "Chief" or "Red," or a statement such as "[He spent] much of his wampum on one specific squaw" is or is not an indication of American Indian heritage.[42] As historian Tom Holm has pointed out, such indications could simply be examples of whites making use of particular ideas about Native peoples.[43] A similar study of the fifty-four midshipmen with congressional nominations from Alaska in the graduating classes between 1915 and 1965 led to no conclusion about the entry or graduation of any Native Alaskans, although one newspaper source suggests that the first Native Alaskan midshipman arrived in Annapolis in 1970.[44] Hawaii has sent midshipmen to the Naval Academy since 1905, but the class of 1934's Gordon Chung-

Hoon, of mixed ethnic ancestry, appears to have been the first Native Hawaiian graduate of USNA.[45] By 1965, approximately eleven Native Hawaiian midshipmen had attended the Naval Academy.[46]

Gordon Chung-Hoon is also the first known Asian American midshipman, but Asians of non-American citizenry had attended classes at Annapolis before him.[47] In 1868, the U.S. Congress approved a measure allowing Japanese students to attend American colleges as a part of the Japanese government's desire to modernize.[48] As a result, seventeen Japanese men were midshipmen between 1869 and 1906, and Matsumura Junzo was the first to graduate, with the class of 1873. Filipino citizens also began to attend the Naval Academy before Chung-Hoon.[49] The 1916 Jones Act, which affirmed the U.S. commitment to granting independence to the then-territory of the Philippines, allowed for a maximum of four Filipino midshipmen to be enrolled at USNA at any given time. The first Filipino citizens to enter the Academy arrived in 1919, and by 1959 twenty-four had graduated from USNA and returned to their country to serve in its armed forces. Americans of Filipino descent continued to work at USNA as mess attendants into the 1970s.[50]

The second Asian American midshipman, Takeshi Yoshihara, arrived as a plebe at the Naval Academy in 1949.[51] Yoshihara grew up in Renton, Washington, and spent the years before his high school education at the Minioka Japanese Internment Center in Idaho. During World War II, Michael Masaoka, the public relations representative of the Japanese American Citizens League, lobbied members of the U.S. Congress to nominate Japanese Americans to the Naval Academy. He believed that active involvement of Japanese Americans in the armed forces was the most effective means of proving their patriotism toward the United States. Congressman Thor Tollefson (R-Wash.) allowed Yoshihara to take a competitive examination to earn a nomination to USNA, and Yoshihara succeeded. Even though he was the only Japanese-American to attend the Academy during World War II, Yoshihara recalled that "I never felt any discrimination from other students there." At least a dozen other Asian Americans were midshipmen and graduates of the Naval Academy by 1959.

Two minority groups did experience discrimination at the Naval Academy. Jewish midshipmen, whose presence at USNA dates to the nineteenth century, made up the first group. Adolph Marix, in the class of 1868, was the first Jewish graduate of USNA.[52] Although Jewish midshipmen were allowed to attend religious services in Annapolis synagogues beginning in 1938, they were not provided a place to pray at the Academy until 1975 and did not have a Jewish chaplain until 1987.[53] Four Naval Academy buildings bear the names of Jewish Americans: Michelson Hall, after physicist and alumnus Albert Michelson, Rickover Hall, after nuclear power proponent and class of 1921 member Admiral Hyman Rickover, the Robert Crown Sailing Center, after the former president of the U.S. Navy League, and the Uriah P. Levy Center and Jewish Chapel, after the famed nineteenth-century Navy leader.[54]

Yet the anti-Semitism that was common in American culture appeared at the Naval Academy as well.[55] Much speculation has surrounded, for example, the experiences of Hyman Rickover.[56] Although his biographers, Norman Polmar and Thomas Allen, conclude that Rickover "probably did not suffer because he was Jewish," other members of the USNA community had differing assessments. One alumnus recalled that Rickover once told him that "no one gave me a break because I was a Jew," and believed that other midshipmen "did not make Rickover's life at the Academy easy." Another alumnus argued that Rickover "absolutely" faced anti-Semitism as a midshipman and that he "spent the next thirty five years getting even with the Academy for it," a reference to the Admiral's tirades against USNA before Congress. However, it was a member of the class of 1922 who faced a more disturbing anti-Semitic experience at the Naval Academy.

During the tenure of the class of 1922, one of the two midshipmen vying for the top slot in the class, Leonard Kaplan, was Jewish.[57] The other midshipman, Jerauld Olmsted, a Protestant, was the editor of the class's *Lucky Bag* and designed a layout that placed roommates side by side on each page. Kaplan, however, lived "in coventry," meaning that other midshipmen refused to live with him and suggesting that they also refused to speak to him. Olmsted placed beside Kaplan a caricature of a large-nosed, unshaven midshipman and twisted Kaplan's autobiography, replacing words in Kaplan's sentences with unseemly details and mentioning "Zion" three times. As the final insult, Olmsted contracted with the *Lucky Bag* publisher to place Kaplan's page at the end of the graduating class and to perforate the page to allow for easy removal. As Olmsted explained, "During the spring of 1921, a number of the class approached me in the corridors or came to the office and stated that they did not care to send a book containing Midshipman Kaplan's picture home, in view of the fact that this man had been kept in coventry for the three years that were nearly completed. I refused to accede to the viewpoint that no mention be made of him, but, when so many men spoke to me on the subject, I agreed to fix the page so that those wishing to do so might remove it without damaging the book."[58] Kaplan appeared nowhere else in the book, including the index of graduates, so if one tore Kaplan's page out of the book, there would be no indication that he graduated in the class.

Olmsted attempted to defend himself, arguing that when the class changed their sentiments toward Kaplan, he, as editor, wrote to the publisher and requested that the page not be perforated. However, the publisher stated that the production process had already begun, and the 1922 *Lucky Bag* appeared, as planned, with Kaplan, the caricature, and the altered biography on a perforated page. Olmsted and Kaplan graduated first and second in the class, respectively, and after the yearbook appeared, administrators conducted an investigation in which Olmsted claimed that "I have no reason for trying to spite [Kaplan], if anyone could consider that such a poor means would be used to do it." Olmsted died of polio the next year, and his classmates erected a large plaque to memorialize him on an upper-story wall of Dahlgren Hall. Ironically, the plaque reads, in part, that "intellect placed him one in class standing. Character and disposition enthroned him in our hearts." Kaplan achieved notable careers in the Navy and in the private sector, and in 1984, after his death, his estate created an annual award for the midshipman graduating second in the graduating class. It was not until the creation of the Kaplan Award that the USNA Alumni Association created an award for the first graduating member of each class.

The second group of people to face discrimination at the Naval Academy, and the subject of Lyndon Johnson's 1965 inquiry, were African Americans, a group with a considerably long history at Annapolis. As in the pre-desegregation Navy itself, African Americans served as mess attendants, servants, and cleaning staff at the Naval Academy as early as the 1860s.[59] As a part of the wave of Radical Republicanism that swept the states of the South after the Civil War, three African American young men sought and won appointments to USNA. The first man was James Conyers, who became a midshipman in 1872.[60] Recalling Conyers's arrival, Midshipman Robley Evans later recalled that "the place was in an uproar at once. . . . When I reached my own quarters, my dining-room boy, a small copper-coloured imp, with his eyes sticking out of his head, said to me, 'My Lord, Mr. Evans, a nigger done enter the Naval Academy!' " In spite of the protective efforts of some midshipmen, other midshipmen hazed Conyers extensively, including assaulting him and in one incident forcing him, wearing almost no clothing, to climb a tree during a cold winter night and imitate a barking dog. After his classroom work suffered, the Academy expelled him for academic deficiency in 1873. That year, Alonzo McClennan became the second African American to enter USNA as a midshipman.[61] Hazing and excess attention resulted after the news spread that he was African American, a fact that his light complexion at first disguised. Such pressure and his faltering academic work caused McClennan what he called "a depression that cannot be described or explained," and he resigned in 1874. Henry Baker, the third African American midshipman, arrived at USNA later in 1874.[62] Baker, too, was a victim of hazing and had such serious academic trouble that the Academy forced him to repeat his plebe year. A mess hall scuffle, in which he used an "opprobrious epithet" against a midshipman "who had hit Baker's leg with a chair as he sat down to dinner," led to Baker's dismissal during the fall of 1875. Pressure continued after the secretary of the Navy reinstated Baker, leading him to later resign permanently from USNA.

African Americans are largely absent from the Academy's historical record for the following six decades. Sentiments in that time period were not favorable toward African Americans in the United States or at the Naval Academy, which in 1899 chose a black man for its mascot in the annual Army-Navy game.[63] Other blacks continued to work at USNA, and one Academy official speculated that some African Americans of a light complexion might even have graduated without incident.[64] Between 1896 and 1937, congressmen including Oscar DePriest (R-Ill.), Joseph Gavagan (D-N.Y.), Arthur Mitchell (D-Ill.), William Shattuc (R-Ohio), and George White (R-Ill.), gave twelve African American men nominations to Annapolis, but all twelve failed or did not take the Academy's entrance examinations.[65] That these nominations were made at all was due to the work of Civil War veterans and, later, the growth of African American political strength in New York City, Chicago, and St. Louis.[66]

Chicago congressman Arthur Mitchell became the first representative to get African American candidates to Annapolis in the twentieth century. White midshipmen gave James Johnson, who arrived at Annapolis on 15 June 1936, an especially hard time by acknowledging Johnson only to insult him or to assign him difficult and time-consuming tasks.[67] Superintendent William Mack, a senior midshipman when Johnson arrived, recalled that other first classmen "put [Johnson] on report and various other things to harass him frequently," concluding that Johnson "had not gotten a fair deal." As a result, Johnson was tardy for formations and became deficient in his academics, and the Academy dismissed him on 18 February 1937. Another alumnus, Bruce Hayden, later recalled that "from my limited contact with him, [Johnson] seemed like a very decent guy, a smart one, a thoroughly patient one who knew exactly what was happening to him, but who did his best to survive nonetheless. He had more guts than the 200 or 300 of us who knew what was going on but didn't speak out." These comments reflect, as alumnus Norman Meyer later recalled, "the attitudes and prejudices that were passed down at Annapolis from one generation to the next."[68] Mitchell subsequently nominated George Trivers, who became a midshipman in 1937.[69] Trivers remained at USNA for three weeks before resigning, explaining that he was not "prepared for the hazing and the isolation, of not being able to talk to anyone and to get help." When called to explain the blatant prejudice against Johnson and Trivers, USNA officials insisted that the racism "has been that of individuals. In no case has there been any concerted discrimination on the part of the regiment or the officers attached to the Academy."[70] A Navy investigator claimed that "in both cases the authorities have bent over backwards to see that the Negro midshipmen had fair and impartial treatment, and in neither case were the midshipmen involved 'ousted.' One resigned for personal reasons and the other merely failed to meet the required standards, as do many others."[71] Seven other African American young men earned nominations from congressmen but failed to achieve admission to the Naval Academy between 1938 and 1944.[72]

At the same time that blacks seeking to become midshipmen were experiencing these difficulties, African Americans in Annapolis still lived in a racially segregated environment.[73] Many local African Americans held steward positions at USNA, but a small number were successful in achieving fairly high positions within the Naval Academy's civilian workforce. By the 1940s, five African American men served as messengers to the superintendent, overseers of the mess hall, mess hall menu designers, and payroll supervisors. These and other black employees formed their own social organization, the Blue and Gold Club. Whether or not they interacted with the black Navy enlisted men stationed at USNA during the Second World War is unknown. Local taxi driver James Hicks amassed such extensive knowledge of the Academy and its grounds that he gave tours to local schoolchildren. Another man who offered Academy tours was perhaps the most recognized African American in the Naval Academy community, Marcellus Gabriel Hall. From the 1910s until 1965, Hall worked as a host at Carvel Hall. Academy officials considered Hall to be "an institution himself."

Another African American man who had a dramatic impact on the institution was Congressman Adam Clayton Powell Jr. (D-N.Y.), who, in the spring of 1945, nominated Howard University student Wesley Brown to the Naval Academy.[74] Brown recalled that "the prospect of being the first Black to graduate from the Naval Academy appealed to me." Brown's entry to the Naval Academy in June 1945 predated President Harry Truman's 1948 military desegregation order and the *Brown v. Board of Education* case. However, the successful role of African Americans in World War II, in addition to the support of a powerful Harlem congressman, provided Brown with the seeds of success.

Wesley Brown, like other plebes, faced many challenges.[75] However, due to his skin color, Brown's challenges were of a more extreme degree. His

Prior to 1949, when Wesley Brown became the first African American midshipman to graduate from the Naval Academy, African Americans at USNA were likely to be employees such as stewards, reflecting policies of the U.S. Navy and of a segregated Maryland. Here, two African American stewards serve a meal to midshipmen during a formal company "dining out." It was not until the late 1960s and 1970s that significant numbers of African Americans began to arrive at the Naval Academy as midshipmen. The presence of an Asian American midshipman, at left, dates this image to after 1949, the year that Takeshi Yoshihara became the second Asian American to attend USNA. (U.S. Naval Institute Photograph Archive)

decision to disregard racial comments, both spoken and unspoken, likely helped him when other midshipmen would get up and move if he sat near them during various activities, including chapel. "That didn't bother me," he recalled, "because I figured the other guy's got a problem." More difficult to ignore were instances in which other midshipmen granted him questionable violations, deliberately disorganized his room, and performed sloppily while Brown was leading his colleagues, all in attempts to provide him with demerits. Brown consciously chose not to have a roommate because, as he explained, "I just didn't feel that I wanted to have someone else try to bear my burdens." Yet a number of midshipmen befriended him and served as a support network, including future president James Carter, a fellow USNA cross-country team member, and two upperclass Jewish midshipmen, Stan Schiller and Howard Weiss. Both men might themselves have understood the meaning of being a minority in a larger, white, Protestant environment; Weiss in particular was concerned about rumors of a past black midshipman being tied to a buoy in the Chesapeake Bay and wanted to help Brown avoid a similar fate. With time, and in particular after the plebe year ended, other midshipmen—especially those with whom he interacted frequently—began showing Brown signs of acceptance. A company mate from Louisiana, for instance, told Brown that "I have the advantage of seeing you every day. I know what you're up to, and I know how things are coming. But the other guy over there who's never seen you—all he knows is you're here, and he doesn't like the idea of you being here. And if I were over there, I might be the same way." Another company-mate, future USNA superintendent William Lawrence, remembered that Brown "was very popular in our company. . . . You know, I never saw any indication of any racial prejudice or anything toward Wes Brown in my company. . . . He was well accepted and liked and everything."

Brown's support network did not end with other midshipmen.[76] Members of the African American community in Annapolis would applaud Brown while he marched in town. "I guess I represented to them," Brown later noted, "at least a chance." Black stewards in the Academy's mess hall also supported Brown by bringing him extra pies and cakes at meals, and he recalled their glances while he was a plebe; Brown remembered that "sometimes I was just [sitting with no chair], or would just be sitting there, I could see one of the stewards in the galley area there—I could just see the tears coming down his eyes, you know. And I felt sorrier for him than I did for me. In fact, I felt, 'Gee, this guy doesn't understand at all. I just hope one of these guys doesn't come out and cock the guy [making me sit with no chair].' "[77] Officers constituted a third source of support. One, his battalion officer, indicated that Brown could inform him at any point at which the midshipman felt he was the center of discrimination. Other supportive officers, about whom Brown was unaware at the time he was a midshipman, were in the USNA administration. Superintendent Aubrey Fitch and Commandant Stuart Ingersoll assigned a military professor and the Brigade commander to ensure Brown's safety and fair treatment. Finally, Adam Clayton Powell intervened in a manner that he, but not Brown, thought useful. As the congressman described:

After Wesley Brown had been at Annapolis several months, I wrote a letter to Secretary of the Navy James Forrestal. . . . In the letter, I complained that there were "forces at work at the Naval Academy that are about to put Wesley Brown out." Jim Forrestal was so disturbed by my message that . . . he personally went to Annapolis and investigated. He then wrote to me that he found no complaints being made by . . . Midshipman Brown, nor by his family, and that everyone else he talked with said Brown was getting along fine. This I knew. I had deliberately fabricated that letter in order to make sure nothing would happen to Wesley Brown.[78]

Powell's action undermined Brown's attempt to stay out of the media, and was quelled only when Brown's mother denied the allegations in the *Washington Post*. Wesley Brown succeeded in speaking to the media only upon his June 1949 graduation, when he told reporters that "I feel it is unfortunate that the American people have not managed to accept an individual on the basis of his ability and not regard a person as an oddity because of his color. My class standing shows that around here I am an average 'Joe.' " The Navy, which sent Brown to speak with black audiences in Chicago to highlight awareness of the Academy among African American youth, apparently did not agree with Brown's modest self-assessment.

During the sixteen years between Brown's graduation and Lyndon Johnson's inquiry about African American midshipmen, Naval Academy administrators gave only slight attention to the issue of race.[79] The graduating classes in this time period included twenty-six African Americans and a small number of members of other minority groups.[80] Extant Academy records also note that midshipmen of "American Indian," "Malayan," "Mongolian," and "Polynesian" descent, as well as men of mixed ancestry, received nominations to, attended, and graduated from Annapolis, although records do not explain these terms.[81] In spite of Takeshi Yoshihara, Wesley Brown, and others breaking barriers, non-white midshipmen likely continued to face stereotypes and prejudice as evidenced by cartoons seen in USNA publications like the LOG.[82] Superintendent William Smedberg hinted, in 1956, at difficulty in finding sponsor parents for non-white midshipmen, and indicated that he and his wife were willing to serve as sponsors for such midshipmen.[83] USNA athletes were beginning to face all-black teams as opponents, and administrators were learning that increasing sensitivity to issues involving race was becoming a necessity.[84] Department of Defense leaders suggested to Smedberg, for example, that he lower USNA entry requirements to increase the enrollment of non-whites, an action Smedberg refused to take.[85] With his approval, however, a small number of black officers visited predominantly black high schools as a means of generating interest in Annapolis, but symbolic of the Navy's poor relations with the nation's black communities, students booed some of those officers.

Some citizens raised attention to racial issues at USNA in 1959 in a letter charging discrimination when, after a USNA football game, they saw two African American midshipmen in the back of a company formation.[86] Administrators tasked one of the two midshipmen in question, Mack Johnson, to respond. Johnson replied to the letter-writers that his presence at the rear of the company was "due to height, or maybe I should say lack of height," since companies line up in height order from tallest to shortest. "In closing," Johnson remarked, "I must state my true opinion that if more of the nation's institutions adhered to and promoted the higher ideals of democracy as does the U.S. Naval Academy, we as a nation would more fully realize those principles upon which our great government was founded. I am proud to be an integral part of such an institution maintaining such high standards and principles as does the U.S. Naval Academy."[87] The Naval Academy's commitment to those high ideals of democracy was, in 1964 and 1965, about to come under close examination.

3

The Right Thing to Do

Race and Recruiting since 1964

★ ★ ★ ★ ★ ★ ★ ★ ★ ★ ★ ★ ★ ★ ★ ★ ★ ★ ★

In his first speech as United States attorney general, Robert F. Kennedy indicated in 1961 his intention to enforce federal court and Supreme Court rulings on school desegregation.[1] Later that year, when his brother, John F. Kennedy, spoke at the Naval Academy's graduation ceremony, the president "noted that there were practically no black faces in the graduating class." Robert Kennedy shared the same observation in 1964 with Charles Minter, who served as the Naval Academy's commandant and superintendent that year, arguing that the number of African American midshipmen should reflect the number of blacks in American society as a whole. Neither Kennedy ever proposed or implemented any specific policy to that end. As Minter later recalled of his leadership of USNA, "There was no effort made certainly to keep [blacks] out of the Naval Academy. On the other hand, we didn't feel any sense of obligation to go out and try to enlist a larger number than we had." By the summer of 1965, as Minter's term as superintendent was coming to a close, White House involvement in the number of African Americans at Annapolis was about to become much deeper. This chapter traces that involvement and the resultant focusing of recruiting efforts toward increasing minority enrollment through 1975. It then examines subsequent developments in recruiting, diversity, and the experiences of minority midshipmen at the Naval Academy.

A White House special counsel, Clifford Alexander Jr., noticed an Associated Press ticker item describing the low number of African American midshipmen, and sent the piece and a brief note to Lee White, the White House's top civil rights aide, on 21 July 1965.[2] Alexander and White wrote a memorandum for President Lyndon Johnson nine days later, suggesting that "you may wish to jack up the Navy with a memo." Shortly thereafter, Johnson sent a letter to Secretary of the Navy Paul Nitze that "it has come to my attention that at present there are nine Negroes in the 4,100-man student body at the Naval Academy. I think this figure clearly indicates that there is some hesitancy on the part of qualified young Negroes to seek out an appointment or apply for admission to Annapolis. I would appreciate your letting me know of any ways you feel we might encourage Negroes to apply for and obtain admittance to the Academy."[3] On 3 August, Roy Wilkins, the executive director of the National Association for the Advancement of Colored People (NAACP), visited the White House for a meeting about an upcoming conference on the implementation of civil rights laws.[4] Wilkins, who served as Johnson's primary advisor on civil rights, mentioned the Annapolis statistics to the president, who, Wilkins later noted, "looked back at me in disbelief." In speaking with reporters later that day, the NAACP chief noted that he was not charging the Academy with discrimination, but suggested that the statistics "look a little suspicious." Press secretary Bill Moyers also told the media that just after Wilkins' departure from the White House, Johnson ordered an investigation. It is unclear whether the president was deliberately feigning ignorance in front of Wilkins or if he and Wilkins were preparing some official White House action before making his plans known to the media.

Only two days later, Secretary Nitze sent a memorandum to the president outlining recruiting efforts that the Navy, but not the Naval Academy, had been making since 1962. These efforts consisted of contacting the administrators of high schools and colleges with high percentages of African American students, leaders of black organizations, and journalists in the African American media.[5] Nitze stated his belief that young black men who were qualified for admission to USNA faced many other options for their career paths, but indicated his intention to work with civil rights leaders and members of Congress to seek a solution. Clifford Alexander "wasn't very satisfied" with Nitze's memo, and by the end of August Johnson asked for further information because of his concern that "so much needs to be done."

These proceedings were concurrent with the congressional passage of the 1965 Voting Rights Act, and historians agree that Johnson was serious when he said that civil rights reform was "my personal priority."[6] He directed Nitze and Secretary of Defense Robert McNamara to discuss the issue of African American midshipmen with the Academy's new superintendent, Draper Kauffman, who began his term in June 1965. Kauffman later related that he had previously given "this problem no thought whatsoever," but with deliberate speed and the understanding that the president wanted action, he began to ponder methods of resolution.[7] The Naval Academy took a significant step in hiring its first black faculty member, chemistry professor Samuel Massie, who began teaching classes at Annapolis in 1966.[8] But to gain a better sense of the issue of black enrollment, Kauffman began by opening a dialogue with the nine African American midshipmen currently enrolled at the Academy. Those young men "had to do a lot of educating of their white Superintendent," he later recalled, "frequently to my chagrin, and even more frequently to their amusement."[9]

However, Minter and Kauffman perceived the growing importance of more generalized recruiting activities during their administrations.[10] Both men understood the need to take action on admissions; the Academy had suffered a 10 percent drop in applications in 1965 alone. The service commitment that graduating midshipmen owed to the Navy or the Marine Corps had gone from four to five years, and the other military academies were expanding their incoming classes. The growing war in Vietnam and the resultant antiwar movement, which was developing by 1965, fostered an era of antimilitary sentiment in the United States. Colleges were offering greater scholarship opportunities for lower income students, and Kauffman perceived a "fast growing gap between the discipline [at USNA] and the increased permissiveness [of American society]." As a result, the two superintendents devised a number of notable activities geared toward increased integration and recruiting. Minter and Kauffman worked to double the number of Blue and Gold officers, expanded the Operation Information program, and began a letter-writing campaign aimed at highly successful high school students. Kauffman also took high-ranking midshipmen with him to off-campus meetings, later noting that "midshipmen were the finest advertising we had," and brought high school guidance counselors to USNA to familiarize them with the Academy's offerings. Kauffman arranged for national television coverage of the USNA Choir and USNA Glee Club, and the Academy created a sixteen-page information insert, which included photographs of black midshipmen, in a Sunday *New York Times* edition in October 1965.

Administrators developed two films designed to promote USNA and advertise the Academy to prospective candidates, African Americans among them. The first was an updated version of 1960's *Ring of Valor*.[11] In addition to new narration, creators added numerous references to the nation's burgeoning space program and spliced in a brief scene of black midshipmen in Bancroft Hall's rotunda. The original scenes of African American barbers, mess attendants, and cooks remained. The second film, also completed in 1966, was called *Mark*.[12] Lacking dialogue but with a musical score performed by flute, the film featured a seven-year-old boy following a group of midshipmen as they marched to St. Anne's Church, a prominent downtown Annapolis landmark. The boy then ran all over the Academy grounds, ultimately ending up in Bancroft Hall's Tecumseh Court, where the Brigade and Superintendent Kauffman greeted him. In the final sequence, as the boy followed the midshipmen from St. Anne's Church back to the Academy, two African American midshipmen finally acknowledged the boy with smiles. Both films, of short duration, could be used for Operation Information and other recruiting activities.[13]

Kauffman understood that two films, with slight inclusion of African American midshipmen, were not going to go far toward promoting interest in the Academy among black high school students. He believed that there were, in addition to the general challenges facing USNA at the time, four reasons why those students did not show great interest in attending USNA.[14] First, because black children did not usually swim during childhood, most African American midshipmen ended up participating in the "sub squad," mandatory regular swimming practice for midshipmen unable to meet Academy swimming standards. Second, Kauffman thought that "blacks did not like the idea of being in such confined spaces with whites." Third, the 1919 Navy regulation that had allowed African Americans to serve only as stewards did little to promote positive relations between the Navy or the Naval Academy and the black community, with which USNA had virtually no contact. In 1965, the highest-ranking black officer in the Navy was only a captain, whereas African Americans had reached the flag rank in the other services. Finally, Kauffman viewed the Navy as a symbol of white snobbery.

To address the issue of African American recruiting, Kauffman kept the black midshipmen at USNA as an advisory group.[15] One of those midshipmen, Charles Bolden, had an aunt who owned a black radio network in Georgia, North Carolina, and South Carolina. With the assistance of the Midshipmen Radio Club, USNA created thirteen thirty-minute descriptions of the life of black midshipmen at USNA that the radio stations then broadcast. The Academy also publicized the fact that Bolden was the president of the class of 1968 and that another African American midshipman, Tony Watson, was the class of 1970's leader. The six black midshipmen who were upperclassmen agreed to speak at selected high schools as part of Operation Information during their vacations and to speak with journalists from the black media. Additionally, the Academy communicated with a thousand African American National Merit Scholars across the country, and the Board of Visitors and the chief of Naval personnel instructed Navy recruiters to "encourage young men from racial minority groups to seek admission" to USNA. Congressional changes to the admissions system for candidates in 1964 gave the secretary of the Navy power to appoint 150 men who were congressmen's alternative choices for nominations to USNA, and Navy personnel discussed the issue of appointments for African American men with members of Congress. In 1966, USNA coaches first began to recruit black athletes, a move facilitated by the NCAA championship of the predominantly black Texas Western College basketball team that year as well as the coaches' desire for qualified, talented athletes.

What were the results of these efforts? At the end of 1967, acting–secretary of the Navy Charles Baird reported to President Johnson that "twelve Negroes entered the Academy in 1966, and another twelve in 1967."[16] There were, Baird wrote, "twenty-six Negro midshipmen attending the Academy, in contrast to the nine who were enrolled in 1965." The Navy wanted to ensure that standards for admission were not lowered in this quest to increase non-white enrollment. Baird included in his report admissions statistics on "minority group candidates" who would become plebes in the summer of 1968. Ultimately, twelve of those men would graduate from Annapolis. White House staff continued to report the Academy's activities and accomplishments to President Johnson throughout Superintendent Kauffman's administration. The Board of Visitors noted its satisfaction with USNA efforts, and Johnson, who never made another inquiry about African Americans at Annapolis, was apparently pleased as well. Kauffman later speculated that Johnson knew that recruiting and admitting a large number of young black men was "impossible," but that Johnson "was very successful in shaking the very dickens out of us." The Nixon White House continued, in a much more passive manner, to monitor the Naval Academy's efforts toward diversification among its midshipmen.

James Calvert, who became superintendent in the summer of 1968, agreed with Kauffman's assessments of the problems behind low minority presence in the Brigade of Midshipmen and shared his predecessor's commitment to increasing the number of non-white midshipmen at USNA.[17] Calvert believed that "through no fault of their own," African American youth had inadequate high school preparation that would qualify them for Annapolis. Reflecting on his administration's efforts, Calvert later recalled a conversation with a white midshipman who could not understand the commitment USNA officials were making to black midshipman. The young man asked, "If I were having trouble with calculus, would you give me so much help and attention?" Revealing his philosophy, Superintendent Calvert answered, "Absolutely not. We have deprived these people for two hundred years of an adequate education, and even today, their education is not what it ought to be. We're trying to help."

TABLE 1. Minority Admissions Statistics, 1968

Prospective Candidates Contacted	787
Selected for Further Consideration	595
Declined or Failed to Complete Testing	332
Not Physically Qualified	52
Not Scholastically Qualified	113
Encouraged to Seek Nominations	77
Received Nominations to Date	23

Sources: Charles Baird to the President, 26 Dec. 1967, LBJ, White House Central Files Subject File, ND 15-8, 1968, Box 190; "Negro Gains at Naval Academy Cited," EC, 14 Jan. 1968, 2.

Calvert's four years at Annapolis included four significant steps toward increasing non-white enrollment.[18] In 1970 Calvert created the Office of Recruitment and Candidate Guidance, under the leadership of Captain Kenneth Haynes, as a division of the Admissions Department. The office consisted of six sections: Administration, Nominations and Appointments, Congressional Liaison, Special Projects, Information, and Minority Candidates. The Minority Candidates section itself had six components, which included Minority Affiliate and Blue and Gold Recruiting, Media Relations, Naval Recruiting Liaison, National Merit Scholars, Navy Junior ROTC, and Minority Projects. Calvert was aware that the Navy had few minority officers and only two African American Blue and Gold officers. To promote more effective recruiting of non-whites, therefore, Calvert took a second notable step by appointing an African American lieutenant, Kenneth Johnson, to serve as chief of the Minority Candidates section in the fall of 1970. Johnson, an ROTC graduate of Iowa State University, immediately identified USNA's service commitment, the Navy's "lily-white" image, and racial tensions and incidents aboard Navy ships as recruiting challenges for the Academy. As he implemented USNA Minority Candidates policies and traveled widely, Johnson told high school students that "we have problems in the Navy just as we do in the rest of the country. The same people who are in the Navy causing problems were out there as civilians causing the same kinds of problems."

In 1968, Chief of Naval Personnel Charles Duncan devised a third step toward minority recruitment, an educational program in which the Navy would provide non-white men with courses prescribed for individual deficiencies— as well as training in study and time management skills—as a means of preparing the men for the Navy's officer procurement programs.[19] The next year, the Navy established a school for this purpose in Bainbridge, Maryland, called the Broadened Opportunity for Officer Selection and Training Program (or BOOST), with twenty-five students. BOOST moved to San Diego in 1971, and then to Newport, Rhode Island, where it has been since 1974. Entrants to BOOST consist almost exclusively of enlisted sailors and Marines who applied, and were turned down, for the Navy's ROTC program (chiefly for academic reasons) but who showed potential for being exemplary officers. A small number of students enter as civilians. BOOST has fifteen faculty members who teach courses in English, mathematics, chemistry, and physics over the two years that students spend in the program. However, BOOST has never been as successful for the Naval Academy as it has been for the Navy as a whole. The Navy does not require BOOST students to meet USNA entrance requirements regarding age, marriage, and parental status; furthermore, the BOOST student body, more recently focused on "disadvantaged" sailors and Marines, has typically consisted of only 50 to 75 percent minorities. In a typical current class of 275 students, generally between five and ten BOOST graduates will move on to Annapolis.

A fourth step, years in the making, centered on the Naval Academy–sponsored preparation of candidates to meet USNA entry requirements. Schools that coached young men to pass Naval Academy entrance examinations operated in the nineteenth and early twentieth centuries.[20] The Naval Academy Foundation, which today produces about eighty midshipmen each year, began sponsoring athletes and other high school students at private college preparatory schools around the United States in 1944.[21] However, the American Civil Liberties Union (ACLU) reported in 1955 that the twenty-three preparatory schools with which the Naval Academy then had agreements were not, largely, open to admitting African American students.[22] The ACLU noted that "only six headmasters . . . replied that he would enroll a Negro student. From seven schools there was no reply. Of the other ten, four definitely stated that they would accept no Negro student. Others said their rosters were now full but held out no hope for another year. Another recommended a correspondence course from the school."[23] This lack of access to private preparatory schools, the ACLU concluded, was a prominent cause of the dearth of African American midshipmen.[24] Naval Academy administrators took no specific actions as a result of the ACLU's findings.

In 1965, however, the Board of Visitors remarked that the Naval Academy's own Preparatory School (NAPS) was a "ready-made avenue" for bringing non-white candidates to Annapolis.[25] The Navy had created NAPS in 1915 after the U.S. Congress passed legislation allowing men from the enlisted ranks who showed leadership potential to improve upon their educational backgrounds and meet USNA's entry requirements. For men needing less time toward that goal, the Navy created a short-duration Naval Academy Preparatory Course (NAPC) in 1919, but the two programs finally merged in 1974 in Newport, Rhode Island. By that time, USNA administrators had begun to use NAPS as a preparatory school for young men who were not previously enlisted in the military, but who upon entry to NAPS joined the Naval Reserve. Superintendent Kinnaird McKee explained in 1976 how NAPS functioned to help the Naval Academy prepare highly desirable applicants, stating that "the Admissions Board identifies candidates throughout the year who have outstanding leadership potential but who are not successful in competing for an appointment and who could benefit from a year [of educational development] at NAPS. Among these candidates will be minority members and athletes who show promise of becoming excellent midshipmen and officers."[26] While minority candidates helped to make NAPS and USNA more representative of the American population, administrators sought talented athletes largely because of their propensity for leadership skills. Superintendent Calvert believed that no Ivy League college spent "more time, money, and effort on athletic recruiting than the Naval Academy." For most of its history, NAPS fell under the purview of the Navy's chief of personnel or chief of education and training command, with the Naval Academy having oversight of the curriculum only. However, in 1990, the Navy transferred NAPS to the full control of the USNA superintendent, ensuring stable funding, coordination with USNA academic programs, and supply of equipment.

Overseeing NAPS is a commanding officer, usually a Navy captain, under whom are a Marine executive officer, a civilian academic dean, and an athletic director.[27] NAPS offers courses in English, mathematics, chemistry, physics, and information technology, and also has athletic and military programs. Its staff has included civilian and military faculty members who teach the academic courses and military personnel, some of whom are USNA alumni, who work on the military training of midshipman candidates (Napsters) at NAPS. Faculty and staff have, like Napsters, become more diverse. NAPS had its first black military faculty member in 1967, and in 1972 had both the first female military faculty member and first black athletic coach. Naval Academy midshipmen have indoctrination responsibilities when the Napsters arrive to begin the prep school program. Midshipman candidates, upon successful completion of the NAPS program and with recommendation from the commanding officer of NAPS, become eligible for entry to Annapolis.

With the Board of Visitors' suggestion in mind, USNA and Navy officials began in 1969 to utilize NAPS as a tool in the quest to increase minority enrollment at Annapolis.[28] The change in NAPS was immediate and dramatic. The NAPS class of 1970, with 203 graduates, included twenty-nine minority graduates, more than the combined total of the previous six classes. Among the twenty-nine were twenty-three African Americans, five Hispanics, and one Asian American. It is not surprising, therefore, that Superintendent William Mack could report in 1973 that "the Naval Academy looks upon NAPS as the mainstay of its minority recruiting program." In 1976, Navy officials calculated that NAPS graduates accounted for 40 percent of non-white admissions at USNA. USNA leaders and midshipmen have acknowledged the benefits of the bonding that Napsters experience at Newport. Not only does the NAPS experience create close friendships among the NAPS graduates, but, as Superintendent Kinnaird McKee noted, it has been successful in "providing highly motivated candidates who strengthen the commitment of the entire entering class." Although the percentage of Napsters who were previously enlisted has steadily declined, subsequent mission and significance statements frequently refer to the prominent role NAPS plays in bringing disadvantaged and underrepresented groups into the Brigade of Midshipmen.

With these four developments in recruiting and increasing diversity under way at Annapolis, Superintendent William Mack took office in the summer of 1972. Mack understood the importance of these changes and was anxious to continue the efforts in accordance with the chief of Naval operations, Elmo Zumwalt, who had taken that position in 1970.[29] Through policy directives, called "Z-Grams," such as his 1970 Z-Gram 66, Zumwalt had expressed his desire to "throw overboard once and for all the Navy's silent but real and persistent discrimination against minorities—not only blacks, the chief victims, but Puerto Ricans, American Indians, Chicanos, Filipinos, orientals, and, indeed, women as well—in recruiting, in training, in job assignments, [and] in promotions."[30] General Leonard Chapman took similar steps in the Marine Corps.[31] Tying Zumwalt's policy together with that of Superintendent Mack, Minority Candidate Advisor Johnson told the media in 1973 that "it is more important that [the Navy] changes things here [at USNA] than any place else. The people who run the Navy, by and large, are Naval Academy graduates."[32]

Superintendent Mack both continued and built upon the policies of Calvert and Kauffman. To increase interest in USNA, he invited five hundred high school students to Annapolis for a five-day seminar during which they learned about the Naval Academy's lifestyle, research facilities, and academics programs.[33] After the seminar's immediate success, Mack called his idea "one of the finest recruiting tools we have." Mack understood the growing opportunities that qualified young black high school students had to seek any number of higher education paths as well as the persistently negative reputation the Navy had in the black community. Believing that exposure to, and communication with, those communities was crucial, Mack arranged for the assignment of nine of the twenty-one black graduates of the class of 1975 to recruiting commands around the nation. They, like Johnson, would work as advisors to potential black candidates, speak with students and guidance counselors in predominantly black high schools, and develop links with community leaders. Furthermore, Mack utilized black media resources, collaborated with the Navy's recruiting staff on advertising endeavors, increased efforts of Blue and Gold officers, and housed Hispanic recruits with local Hispanic families to assist in the recruits' mastery of the English language. Mack and his administrators also oversaw the creation of Naval Academy catalogs that would appeal to young people, including non-white, music-oriented applicants who might not be enthusiastic about activities like the Vietnam War. The photographs in the 1972–73 catalog, for example, include as many midshipmen playing guitars as holding rifles, as well as thirteen representations of African American, Hispanic, and Asian American midshipmen and faculty. One photograph even featured midshipmen playing with a dog. All of these efforts led to a substantial increase in the number of minority midshipmen. While the classes of 1970 through 1974 included sixteen black midshipmen, the classes of 1975 through 1979 included seventy-five.

In addition to attempts to bring more minorities to the Naval Academy, Superintendents Calvert and Mack and their administrators also took steps to show support for the non-white midshipmen and personnel at USNA. Calvert's term included a number of challenging issues for the Academy, including the 1968 assassination of Martin Luther King Jr. For several days, Marines surrounded the Academy's grounds and Calvert canceled midshipmen's liberty beyond the immediate area, presumably in response to the riots and violence that broke out across the nation.[34] "Tea Fights," the Academy's traditional dances in which midshipmen and women from local colleges were randomly matched up as partners, led to negative attention for USNA in 1969.[35] That year, a plebe told a *New York Times* reporter that he and other black midshipmen met their dates at the door (meaning that they had chosen their own dates), thereby avoiding the possibility of being matched with white women.[36] Calvert told inquiring politicians that all midshipmen, not just African Americans, had the option of meeting "a special young lady" at the door.[37] Just months later, black enlisted personnel at the Academy staged a "sit-down" at Ricketts Hall and demanded that Calvert investigate charges of racially biased behavior against them. The men threatened to destroy the building due to disproportionately harsh punishments they allegedly received compared with their white counterparts, as well as having curtains in their doorways instead of doors like white enlisted men.[38] As per the men's request, Calvert led an investigation and defused the situation.

Calvert and Mack took further steps, including bringing Terrance Lewis, a black offensive line coach, to Annapolis in 1972.[39] Calvert also oversaw the introduction of courses on black literature and history. To educate the entire Academy community on issues related to race and social movements, Calvert instituted a Human Relations Council in 1972. Mack furthered this effort with the implementation of the 1973 training course, "The Professional Officer and the Human Person," which covered such topics as race relations, cultural heritage, and drug awareness. Mack also invited Student Nonviolent Coordinating Committee leader Julian Bond as a Forrestal Lecturer in 1972, and Bond forthrightly told the Brigade of Midshipmen that many American citizens had the "unreconstructed mentality . . . that the American social agenda does not include those at the bottom of the ladder." Calvert and Mack's steps in recruiting and improving awareness of non-white midshipmen did not, however, entirely please all military leaders. Nuclear Navy chief Hyman Rickover decried USNA efforts before an Academy audience, asking, "What are we? Not an athletic institution or minority institution!" Similarly, Marine General Victor Krulak, in commenting on the various activities at USNA, told Mack that "there is no obligation levied upon you whatsoever to try and make the Naval Academy into a black or brown institution just to correct a longstanding wrong. Rather, I would feel it your obligation to try and run a school that is intellectually and morally 'monochromatic' with malice toward none, and I believe you are doing it."

How "morally monochromatic" had the Naval Academy become between Wesley Brown's graduation in 1949 and the end of Mack's term as superintendent in the summer of 1975?[40] USNA historian John Bodnar looked at Naval Academy slang terms found in *Reef Points* and discovered that while some terms, like "chico," a reference to Filipino mess workers, disappeared by 1946, other terms such as "moke," used to describe black mess attendants, and "Spanish athlete," denoting a poorly skilled athlete, persisted. Midshipmen called foreign languages "Dago" until 1968, and in 1971 *Reef Points* included the term "MOC," a revival of "moke," but then meaning a midshipman who cleaned up a corridor in Bancroft Hall. When residents of a wealthy subdivision in Annapolis refused to rent their properties to black midshipmen for

June Week festivities, Superintendent Kauffman did not hesitate to threaten the residents, many of whom were government employees, with media attention. In 1972, Commandant Max Morris informed the class of 1973 that he expected them to show leadership in educating the Brigade on why "symbols [such as] confederate flags, black liberation flags, swastikas, and [certain] pictures are extremely abrasive to many midshipmen of certain cultural, racial, or religious backgrounds." Morris noted that he shared those midshipmen's concerns, but the fact that his successor, Commandant D. K. Forbes, sent the exact same letter to the class of 1974 indicates that the symbols had not disappeared.

The experiences of midshipmen demonstrate that racist attitudes, perceptions, symbols, and comments persisted between 1949 and 1975.[41] About a black classmate, Edward Sechrest, class of 1956 member William Flight remembered that "he was acknowledged by whites as so sharp and so unique he didn't have a problem at all." Over a decade later, Cory Bailey similarly noted white surprise at high-performing black midshipmen. He remembered that one of his fitness reports read, "Although Mr. Bailey is black, he does well." Kenneth Dunn, a plebe in 1969, recounted an example of overt racism when, on his first day at USNA, "my plebe summer roommate, a guy from a Northern state, said, 'Hey, I've never roomed with a Nigger before.' " When upperclass midshipmen told a black plebe to recount news stories, the plebe described features from *Ebony*, *Jet*, and a religious publication called *Muhammad Speaks*, thereby obtaining upperclass scorn. He further mentioned that "as the academic year started, I quickly came to find out why I was always being called out at a distance. Although we all wore the same uniform, my dark skin made me an easy target. You see, I was the only black in my company, so at any given distance, the upperclass would call me by name even when I had my back to them. I was therefore constantly called around to [demonstrate] my knowledge of *Reef Points*."[42] Another alumnus vividly recalled white midshipmen dressing Tecumseh up as a Klansman, an action that nearly led to racial violence. Several alumni noted the less overt, but equally bothersome and frequent, comments about black midshipmen entering USNA with vastly lower standards and not being able to swim. "For me," explained another alumnus, "I was never included socially with any of my white peers. The Naval Academy, for me, was a completely isolating experience."

However, by 1966 a number of developments demonstrate that progress was taking place toward integration and community within the Brigade of Midshipmen.[43] That year, seven midshipmen, including one African American and one Asian American, joined to form a musical group, The Outriggers.

During this period, LOG editors gradually moved away from cartoons mocking black workers and toward accepting black midshipmen as equals. For example, Eileen Baltimore became the first black woman to grace the pages of the LOG, and in 1975 area college women chose a black midshipman for the first centerfold of the annual "Femmes Issue" of the LOG; USNA running back Cleveland Cooper appeared in a series of revealing and provocative photographs. Much bolder was a 1969 article in which midshipman C. E. Riles explained how he and other black midshipmen faced the duality of being members of a group culturally unique from whites while also being part of the Naval Academy. Perhaps rhetorically, he asked, "Do you know a Black Midshipman? I mean do you know, really know the man—not just seeing him everyday, and saying hi, but trying to understand him?" Unquestionably the most enduring action from this period, however, was when in 1974 seven black midshipmen learned of black history celebrations at West Point and Colorado Springs and decided to have a similar activity at Annapolis. Their action resulted in the creation of the Midshipmen Black Studies Club, which has sponsored cultural and historical activities, lectures, and, with the early help of a local woman who served as a social director, dances and social gatherings.

The recruiting programs and policies that Naval Academy administrators created prior to 1975 have shown success in increasing interest in USNA and have remained the basis for recruiting efforts ever since.[44] Subsequent superintendents have modified some programs, like Blue and Gold and Operation Information, to better integrate the Academy's efforts to increase the minority population of the Brigade of Midshipmen. Administrators expanded the Blue and Gold program to Puerto Rico and encouraged Blue and Gold officers to seek promising non-white youth in their recruiting areas. Midshipmen who are members of various ethnic and racial groups participate in Operation Information as a means of demonstrating, in person, possibilities for minorities at USNA. In the spring semester of 1990, for example, the group of midshipmen who gave speeches and appeared on television and radio or in newspapers included sixteen African Americans, thirteen Hispanics, one Asian American, and ten whites. The Director of Candidate Guidance concluded that year that "Operation Information is our most cost-effective recruiting program." USNA also continued to use catalogs as a method of informing prospective candidates about the Academy's requirements and lifestyle. The 1977–78 catalog, for example, included a photo of an African American midshipmen stating that "any brother coming off the streets who wants to make an eventual contribution to Blackness could do a lot worse than to

DO YOU KNOW HIM?

By C. E. RILES '71

This article is an attempt to show the Black Midshipman and a few of his problems. It is also an attempt to show not only my feelings, but those of the majority of the Black upperclass Midshipmen at the Academy.

All Mids have things in common. We're all in the military and volunteers to become officers in Navy or Marine Corps. We have pretty much the same goals. We're known and respected everywhere just by the uniform we wear and manners we display. We are all, Black and white, bound together by the specific rules and regulations set down by the Brigade such as our Honor Concept, but the things in common do come to an end.

Other than the difference in complexion, there are other differences between the white and the Negro Midshipman. Our cultural backgrounds are as different as night and day. Very few whites, here, have grown up in the same social context as the Blacks. Many whites have seen it but only at a distance. Our languages are also quite different. We all speak English, however, the slangs, colloquialisms, and pronunciations in some cases are entirely different. The Black Midshipman must play a dual role. He must be a Black man and a Midshipman. By this, I mean we must not lose sight of what is happening with our people on the outside. We can not forget that we are Black also. We must maintain the respect of the rest of our race or we will lose the home from whence we came. We must have pride in ourselves and our heritage. On the other hand, we are Midshipmen at the United States Naval Academy. We "should" uphold the branch of the service we have entered and

its tradition. We "should" follow the rules and regulations of the system. And most of all we must be proud of both. A person who is not proud of what he is as far as race, creed, or nationality is concerned is a "sorry" individual.

Do you know a Black Midshipman? I mean do you know, really know the man?—not just seeing him everyday, and saying hi, but trying to understand him.

Understanding is the main problem. Very few whites understand the Black man. Some act too nice to try to cover up an opinion which is negatively prejudiced or to "really show the world" that he's trying to give a deprived person help. Most whites have had very little or no real contact with Blacks, but still will make generalizations about the attitudes and ways of all Blacks and will consider themselves experts. The funny thing is that these whites don't realize most Blacks have seen people like him all their lives and are not fooled.

With rationalization, much of what I've written can be put into reverse and said about the Blacks. No one group's way is right. To satisfy the most in each group a compromise must be reached.

A Fourth class summed up the opinions of all of us concerned with how we made it here. This fourth class saw a picture of a little Cuban boy on a plane with other refugees bound for Miami. The little boy was crying and very sad. The boy was heading for freedom and he was crying. The article stated that the boy was crying for his friends back on the island, and the fact that they could have been on the plane except there wasn't anymore room.

By the time midshipman C. E. Riles penned this article in 1969, African Americans had become an increasing presence within the Brigade of Midshipmen. USNA began formal minority recruiting efforts in 1970, leading to larger numbers of African Americans at Annapolis. Riles asked, "Do you know a Black Midshipman? I mean do you know, really know the man?—not just seeing him everyday, and saying hi, but trying to understand him." This article represents one of the few public discussions of African Americans' feelings at USNA and is just as pertinent thirty-seven years later. (U.S. Naval Academy Archives) come here." By the late 1990s, however, the Office of Recruitment and Candidate Guidance put such specific references to racial and ethnic groups only in specialized recruiting brochures.

Newport, Rhode Island, home of the Naval Academy Preparatory School and BOOST, remains an important component of USNA minority midshipmen recruitment.[45] Minorities accounted for an average of 41 percent of the graduating classes between 1986 and 1996, which averaged 265 graduates a year. NAPS administrators and teachers have gone to great lengths, such as helping non-English speakers learn the language and helping midshipman-candidates to succeed in their program. One administrator "refused to discharge anyone until they had exhausted every avenue to succeed," while another spent his lunch hour eating with midshipman-candidates with deficiencies and discussing the students' problems and possible means for improvement. Although skeptics have accused NAPS of being an "athlete factory" for the Naval Academy in the past decade, NAPS has been a valuable experience for those midshipmen who attended the school. Some midshipmen benefit from the academic strengthening and military discipline, but for all midshipman candidates NAPS can further serve as a mechanism for interacting with people unfamiliar to them. As one African American midshipman later noted, "NAPS was the place where I got to mesh with different people than I'd ever met before. I even learned to like [recording artist] Jimmy Buffett." Superintendent Charles Larson concluded in 1996 that "NAPS is truly a success story and its importance in preparing candidates for the Academy cannot be underestimated."

As has been the case since the 1950s, Academy administrators have also utilized technology to advance awareness of Annapolis among the American public. Since the late 1990s, the Candidate Guidance office has made videocassettes, CD-ROMs, and an internet Web site available to prospective candidates.[46] However, the older technologies of film and television have continued to have a role in advertising the Naval Academy. Most prominent among television communications is the annual Army-Navy football game which, in spite of the generally lackluster success of the two academies' teams, has become a staple of college football tradition.[47] Although Academy administrators have not created or produced any television series or films as they did in past decades, USNA has appeared prominently in several notable productions. The lead character of the detective-oriented 1980 to 1988 television series *Magnum P.I.* was a Naval Academy graduate, a detail often noted.[48] Brief imagery of USNA symbols was a part of the celebrated 1986 film *Top Gun* in a scene in which "Maverick," a Navy pilot, mourns the death of his radar interceptor officer "Goose," a USNA alumnus. Teamed with the successful *Patriot Games*, a 1992 film version of a Tom Clancy novel in which a Naval Academy history professor becomes embroiled in combating Irish terrorism, *Top Gun* helped bring about tremendous interest in USNA among the nation's youth.[49] Although the popular television series *JAG*, which ran between 1995 and 2005, centered on legal drama, its story lines frequently included references to and characters—including the lead, "Harmon Rabb"—from the Naval Academy.[50] In 2005, production began on a boxing-centered film about the Academy entitled *Annapolis*. Musician Jimmy Buffett even featured the Naval Academy in his popular 1983 song, "We Are the People Our Parents Warned Us About."[51]

Whether through its own recruiting efforts or through the indirect attention in various forms of public media, the Naval Academy has succeeded in reaching its goal of raising the number of minority midshipman-candidates at NAPS and midshipmen at Annapolis.[52] Statistics on graduates of NAPS from 1976 to 1996, shown in the Appendix, demonstrate the dramatic rise in minority populations there. Graduating classes at NAPS have typically included 250 members. In 1970, 1.3 percent of the graduating class was minority, but by 1976 that percentage had risen to 21.3 and by 1986 it was 42.8. The 1991 graduating class had the highest minority representation ever, 50 percent. The dates at which different groups achieved consistently high numbers varied, but the 1970s were the crucial years for three groups. African Americans graduated in double digits beginning in 1970, a feat matched by Hispanic Americans in 1976 and Asian Americans in 1979. Women, a group discussed in later chapters, first attended NAPS in 1976 and reached significant numbers only with the graduating class of 1987.

Statistics on minority midshipmen at USNA show a much less dramatic increase and greater consistency among the graduating classes between 1980 and 2000.[53] Entering and graduating women are the only group to change substantially in proportion during this period, as demonstrated in the tables in the Appendix; when minority statistics are calculated without those for women, overall numbers are stable. African Americans, American Indians, Asian Americans, and Pacific Islanders have, as groups, entered and graduated with remarkably consistent numbers and percentages. American Indian attrition rates, due to the minute number of American Indians who attend USNA, can fluctuate greatly if even one such midshipman fails to graduate. Beginning with the class of 1984, Hispanic Americans have also attended and graduated with consistent numbers and percentages through the year 2000. Attrition percentages for minorities as a whole for all of the classes between

1980 and 2000, including or excluding women, are 29.9 percent, compared with 23.5 percent for the classes as a whole.

USNA minority statistics correspond to findings at other institutions of higher education.[54] Analyst Daryl Smith has argued that many minority students "experience culture shock by being in an environment where dominant values, expectations, or experiences may be very different from their own and may be implicitly or explicitly devalued. . . . While poor academic preparation and socio-economic status may be a barrier to matriculation, evidence is growing that the poor quality of minority students' life on campus and their sense of isolation, alienation, and lack of support are more serious factors in attrition."[55] Other studies have demonstrated, as psychologist Marilyn Ross has written, that African American students in particular experience "feelings of alienation, sensed hostility, racial discrimination, and lack of integration" on largely white college campuses. Smith further notes that American Indian students accustomed to indirect eye contact and quiet behavior are disadvantaged in college environments where "argument, assertiveness, and directness" are seen as proof of a student's ability.

Four reports on minority midshipmen, prepared between 1989 and 1997, concluded that Smith's and Ross's arguments were true at the Naval Academy. A superintendent's panel found in 1989 that USNA officials could be highly proactive both in identifying midshipmen as early as their entry as plebes who would be "at risk" for academic problems and challenges and in working to provide those midshipmen with needed academic support.[56] The report also suggested hiring a civilian minority affairs program coordinator and a computer analyst to assess methods of communication in order to interact with minority midshipmen. This report led to Superintendent Virgil Hill's creation of an academic center to address such issues. In 1992, The General Accounting Office (GAO) told Congress that it had found that African American midshipmen receive worse treatment than anyone at USNA (and as a result have the worst performance records) and that traditional white male attitudes of the Navy contributed to problems for non-white midshipmen.[57] All non-white midshipmen, GAO concluded, suffered from stress as part of small-numbered minority groups, due to white stereotyping and a lack of a sense of belonging within the Brigade.

Two other reports provided greater insight into the challenges minority midshipmen were facing in the mid-1990s. The 1996 Superintendent's Minority Midshipmen Study Group (MMSG) praised Hill's academic center, but stated that USNA officials needed to do more to show support for minority plebes and encourage more non-white midshipmen to seek leadership positions on the Brigade of Midshipmen staff.[58] MMSG, a group that Superintendent Ronald Marryott created in 1988, was particularly concerned about the lack of non-white officers at USNA, and suggested increasing their number and visibility to reflect both the general population and the possibilities for success in the Navy and Marine Corps. The report also showed the MMSG's desire to resolve minority midshipmen's poor swimming skills and subsequent time in remedial pool training, while recommending that USNA hire a civilian minority recruiter for continuity in admissions efforts. Finally, MMSG stressed the importance of institutional support for the Midshipmen Black Studies Club, which continued to help African American midshipmen and was a tool the administration could utilize for problem shooting and resolution. The Board of Visitors published an assessment of USNA the next year and reiterated the fact that minority graduation rates, academic standing, and military performance grades were lower than average.[59] Among its observations, the BOV noted that "of 33 Academy officers holding the rank of Navy Captain or Marine Corps Colonel, none—including the chair of the Minority Midshipman Study Group—is a minority group member." Two of the BOV's findings were even more disturbing than the conclusions in earlier studies. Increased minority recruiting efforts were translating into white midshipmen's belief that USNA was lowering standards for some segments of the Brigade, and while few white midshipmen believed so, 47 percent of African American midshipmen indicated that they considered "racial prejudice a serious problem at the Academy."

Racism, as in American society as a whole, has not disappeared at Annapolis, and it is apparent that white midshipmen are bringing their earlier beliefs about race to the Naval Academy.[60] Blatant examples of racist acts have included four midshipmen dressing as Klansmen in 1976 and a football banner the next year reading "Homecoming 1977: Open Season On All Indians." LOG readers complained of racist references in the humor magazine's articles and cartoons since the early 1980s, and Commandant Samuel Locklear, calling the LOG "a vehicle for gross cynicism, laced with overt sexism and racism," decided to quash the publication in 2000. The Lucky Bag has also contained biographical statements that, while attempting to prove that race is inconsequential, indicate that race was still on people's minds. One graduate's entry read, "He's intelligent. He's handsome. Musically gifted. Athletically inclined. And he's black (Oh God, quick run [and] get the officer in charge)." Another biographer noted about a classmate, "A minority, yes, but one would never guess this by her self-confidence, big voice, and high stature in the Brigade."

Classmates stated that another graduate could be described in one word: "No, it's not wetback, but class."

As ironically supportive as these statements might appear, minority midshipmen in the classes of 1999, 2000, and 2001 have had experiences that are neither humorous nor supportive.[61] Many minorities at the Academy agree that race is an issue that, as one midshipman pointed out, causes "bad stress. I mean really bad stress." As non-white individuals have pointed out in the past, they have a tendency to stand out in any circumstance or setting at USNA. Among those circumstances are plebe summer and plebe year, during which bigoted upperclassmen can exhibit behaviors and impose atypically harsh punishments under the guise of discipline or training. Many midshipmen have overheard racist comments around the Academy, and in particular in Bancroft Hall, while others have endured repeated comments and questions such as "Hey, did you ever meet an Eskimo?," "What kind of last name is that, anyway?," and "You don't look white to me." One minority midshipman expressed frustration with the Academy's efforts to eliminate such negative stereotyping: "Relying on a childish dramatic video to make a statement on the illogical nature of racism is just not good enough," he commented.

Two ways that minority members of the Brigade have responded to the racism they perceive seem especially bothersome to their white counterparts.[62] One is the tendency, particularly among African American midshipmen, to sit as a segregated group in classrooms, in King Hall, and at other public events and venues. In part, such a decision may be due to the constant stares, comments, and apparent shock that whites display when friends of different races do anything together or when minorities play on predominantly white sports teams. Furthermore, as Superintendent William Lawrence discovered after he deliberately tried to integrate midshipmen at a dinner engagement, there is "a natural inclination of [minorities] to do things together . . . [and] you had to allow [them] to do things together." A second action is the participation of many minority midshipmen in ethnically and racially dominated extracurricular activities, including the Chinese American, Filipino American, and Japanese American Clubs, the Korean Midshipmen Club, and the Latin American Studies Club. Another largely minority group is the Gospel Choir, an organization which travels around the nation and goes a long way toward advertising the existence of minority midshipmen at USNA. The largest organization, however, is the Midshipmen Black Studies Club (MBSC), which remains today the cohesive center of community for African American midshipmen. White midshipmen often question the existence of such a group and seem resentful that they do not have a similar society. Being members of the majority, they seem unaware of the overwhelming sense of support, positive attitudes, and belonging that MBSC provides through its meetings, celebrations, and lectures. As one African American midshipmen confided, "White midshipmen definitely do not understand black midshipmen the way black midshipmen do."

For the purpose of recruiting, Naval Academy officials have tried to make progress in developing a better working relationship with minority candidates and communities and with USNA's own non-white alumni.[63] In part, Candidate Guidance incorporated its minority goals into its larger recruiting efforts, which became increasingly crucial as applications to the Academy declined from 16,000 in 1990 to 10,000 in 2000. Recruiting activities have included bringing high school students to USNA for summer seminars and holding two annual informational briefings called "Center of Influence Visits" for high school guidance counselors. USNA first began to involve its own alumni in these efforts in 1981 when it invited Hispanic civilians and military officers to Annapolis to discuss recruiting strategies. Eight years later, Candidate Guidance contacted thirty-two African American alumni to assist in spreading information about USNA where they resided. The Office of Admissions merged these ideas in 1998 by creating the annual Minority Alumni Conference, an opportunity for the admissions staff to discuss with a wider group of alumni how they could "communicate the exceptional opportunities USNA offers to young men and women in their communities." As a part of its Web site, USNA has occasionally included a page entitled "Minority Alumni Profiles" on which it provides biographical information on a number of notable African American graduates. Candidate Guidance also has young minority alumni who serve in the Navy and Marine Corps on its staff as recruiters in large urban areas around the United States.

The placement of those recruiters indicates, however, that the Naval Academy's philosophy in minority recruiting has not, curiously, changed a great deal in the past four decades. Recruiters continue to focus their efforts on inner-city, heavily minority-populated high schools.[64] The Naval Academy's first chief of the Minority Candidates Section, Kenneth Johnson, suggested in 1987 that recruiters needed to look at non-white young adults from rural and suburban areas, yet this has still not happened.[65] Furthermore, low American Indian enrollment could be remedied by actively recruiting on Indian reservations and pueblos. A second issue is that some administrators continue to believe that there is a finite number, usually cited as about a thousand, of African American high school graduates in the United States who can meet the entrance standards of all of the best colleges, USNA included, annually.[66]

This number may have been legitimate when Academy officials began thinking about minority enrollment in the mid-1960s, but it is presumptuous to believe that the figure still holds true after nearly forty years of social and educational advances for minority groups in the United States. As a former White House official who helped bring the low number of minorities at USNA to Lyndon Johnson's attention in 1965 stated recently, "If administrators still say there are only a thousand blacks qualified, that simply means they are not willing to work on it. The kids are obviously out there."[67] Superintendent Thomas Lynch noted in 1992 that poor relations with minority communities continued to plague USNA, and former superintendent Charles Larson recently voiced his belief that USNA can increase minority enrollment by developing interest in children while they are in middle school.[68] These ideas about broadening the dimensions and locations of recruiting efforts effectively offer USNA the opportunity to increase its applicant pool, if not its total minority enrollment, to levels proportional to minority populations in the nation—as Robert Kennedy suggested in 1964.[69]

For minority midshipmen at the Naval Academy, substantial achievements, particularly for African Americans, have occurred. Several African Americans have served as Brigade commander, the first of whom, Mason Reddix, held the position in 1976, the same year as the first African American color girl, Stephanie McManus.[70] Perhaps the most famous alumnus of the late twentieth century is an African American, basketball star David Robinson.[71] Although the number of minority officials at USNA has remained low, African Americans have held chaplain positions and have served as high in the administration as commandant.[72] And while not itself planning celebrations for the events, the USNA administration has marked the annual African American, American Indian, and Asian–Pacific Islander Heritage Months by scheduling announcements and press articles and has brought prominent minority speakers like Colin Powell and Andrew Young to USNA as Forrestal Lecturers.[73] Even the city of Annapolis, which clung tightly to segregation practices long after its 1966 legal desegregation, brought recognition to minorities in 1999 by erecting a statue and memorial plaque to Kunte Kinte, a fictitious slave who landed at Annapolis.[74]

Finally, a wide variety of minority group members have shown moral leadership as role models, as advisors, and as part of a support system for minority midshipmen.[75] Included in these ranks are minority sponsor parents like Lillie Mae Chase, who was a sponsor mother to several generations of African American midshipmen; professors who assign readings, like August Wilson's *Fences*, that deal with racial issues; faculty, administrators, and staff members, some of whom themselves are minorities, who offer encouragement to midshipmen; King Hall and USNA cleaning staff members, who are largely African American and provide inspirational support much as they did when Wesley Brown was at Annapolis; non-minority military officers and faculty who show unbounded support for minority midshipmen; and alumni, like Charles Bolden, Wesley Brown, and Takeshi Yoshihara, who broke personal and military barriers and proved their physical and mental capabilities.[76] USNA took a major step toward recognizing such individuals by deciding to name its new major athletic facility the Wesley Brown Field House in 2005. Like American society, the Naval Academy has work remaining before it has established full representation and participation of minorities and fostered true racial neutrality in its community. However, the Academy's achievements to date, along with administrative efforts to bring larger numbers of minorities to the Brigade of Midshipmen and the recent adoption of the precept that "diversity is strength," indicate that the Naval Academy is working toward historian John Hope Franklin's charge that "we need to do everything possible to emphasize the positive qualities that all of us have . . . which we must utilize if we are to solve the problem of the color line in the twenty-first century."[77] As Dean of Admissions Dave Vetter stated in 1998, "The Naval Academy is a national institution and we believe it should be demographically and ethnically representative of the society it serves. We note that about 35 percent of our enlisted forces are minorities. These young people need and deserve good minority officer role models, and the Naval Academy is institutionally committed to providing them. It is the right thing to do!"[78]

The Spiritual Ball Game

Anderson v. Laird *and the End of* *Mandatory Chapel Attendance*

★ ★

Underneath the vast dome of the United States
Naval Academy Chapel, with its carvings of the unified races of humankind,
Senior Chaplain John J. O'Connor delivered his usual Catholic mass to the assembled midshipmen, officers, and guests on the morning of Sunday, 7 January 1973.[1] However, as O'Connor and his Protestant counterparts looked up
from their prayer books and into the long nave of the chapel, with winter
sunlight shining through the small stained-glass and monumental clear-glass
windows, they for the first time did not see hordes of midshipmen before
them.[2] Instead, they noted many open, unoccupied seats among the chapel's
pews. Just five days earlier, the Academy announced its compliance with a
federal appeals court's decision that USNA's ninety-seven-year-old requirement of mandatory chapel attendance was a violation of the Constitution. Remarkably, it was a group of midshipmen—influenced by the social changes of
the mid-1960s as well as student challenges to university regulations through
in loco parentis court cases—who had raised the issue in the judicial system by
joining with a West Point cadet in suing the Naval Academy to end the practice
of compulsory chapel.[3] These midshipmen, like many of their civilian college
counterparts of the era, challenged established institutional customs and, in
the process, succeeded in bringing about a major transformation in the culture and traditions of the Naval Academy.

"No culture," the noted literary figure T. S. Eliot wrote in 1948, "has
appeared or developed except together with a religion." This argument holds
true broadly in respect to American culture and more narrowly in respect to
the Naval Academy.[4] The role of religion at the Academy dates to 1850, when
administrators established regulations that, for the first time, mandated devo-
tional contemplation by requiring midshipmen to spend fifteen minutes in

prayer each morning.[5] In 1855, USNA altered those regulations to further require that midshipmen attend Sunday religious services at the Naval Academy chapel. Between 1863 and 1876, modified Academy regulations "suggested," but did not require, attendance at the chapel. Academy leaders restored the chapel requirement in 1876 and repeated the rule in the regulations of 1887, 1902, and 1906.

Chaplains in the Naval Academy's chapel conducted only non-denominational services, with a slant toward Episcopalian traditions, for most of USNA's early history.[6] Beginning in 1913, USNA allowed midshipmen with written permission from their parents to attend the services of other denominations, including Catholic masses, in Annapolis instead of at the Naval Academy chapel.[7] In 1938, Academy chaplains permitted Jewish midshipmen to attend services, on Sundays, at a local synagogue, and in 1947 the Navy began to assign Catholic chaplains to the Academy.[8] Administrators repeated the 1906 and 1913 policies in the 1928 regulations, and at an unknown date the Academy also began to require parents of midshipmen under twenty-one years of age to grant permission for their son to change the denomination of the service he attended. Switches in religion could occur only at the beginning of an academic year and had to reflect, in the opinion of Naval Academy chaplains, the midshipman's intention to affiliate with the new house of worship.[9] If a midshipman wished to transfer from an Annapolis church to the Naval Academy chapel, however, no waiting period or parental contact was required.[10] Punishments for not attending religious services included reprimands, demerits, marching, confinement to quarters, and, potentially, expulsion.[11] Chapel attendance had become a firmly ingrained aspect of midshipmen life by 1908, the year of the completion of the massive chapel in the center of the Academy's campus.

The prominent role of religion at the Naval Academy first came under question during the Supreme Court tenure of Chief Justice Fred Vinson, between 1946 and 1953. A supporter of the New Deal as a congressman, Vinson brought a concern for civil liberties issues to the high court.[12] As legal historian C. Herman Pritchett has noted, the Vinson Court "encouraged suitors to come to it with . . . a variety and profusion of civil liberties problems," among which was religious freedom.[13] In 1946, the American Civil Liberties Union first questioned mandatory chapel attendance at USNA, asking what role religion played at Annapolis.[14] The inquiry came at the same time as the Supreme Court's religious freedom decision in *Everson v. Board of Education*. In his majority opinion in that case, Justice Hugo Black argued,

The "establishment of religion" clause of the First Amendment means at least this: Neither a state nor the federal government can set up a church. . . . Neither can force nor influence a person to go to or to remain away from church against his will or force him to profess a belief or disbelief in any religion. No person can be punished for entertaining or professing religious beliefs or disbeliefs, for church attendance or non-attendance. . . . In the words of Jefferson, the clause against establishment of religion by law was intended to erect "a wall of separation between church and state."[15]

Naval Academy superintendent Aubrey Fitch apparently understood the context of the *Everson* case and its relation to the ACLU inquiry, and he replied to the organization. Because religious services constituted an "essential" part of training at USNA, Fitch explained, the chapel requirement aided the "molding of character" and, therefore, was "not in violation of the religious freedom guaranteed by the Constitution."[16]

When the Supreme Court decided the *Illinois ex rel. McCollum v. Board of Education* case in 1948, the justices discussed the Naval Academy's chapel services. Justice Black was especially concerned with "tax-supported public school buildings used for the dissemination of religious doctrines" and found that religious leaders giving lessons in faith in public schools was a violation of the Constitution's Establishment Clause.[17] In his dissent in the case, Justice Stanley Reed used the Naval Academy and Military Academy chapels as examples of churches receiving state aid in the form of no taxation.[18] Soon after this case, citizens began writing to the Naval Academy to complain about mandatory chapel attendance. One writer told Academy officials that the Constitution prevented them from forcing their "inmates to attend church at any time."[19]

The ACLU again contacted the Naval Academy in 1955, perhaps inspired by the Supreme Court's 1952 action in *Zorach v. Clauson*.[20] In that case, Justice William Douglas had stated that the federal government "may not make a religious observance compulsory. It may not coerce anyone to attend church, to observe a religious holiday, or to take religious instruction."[21] Much of the public understood this case and *Illinois ex rel. McCollum*, and a concerned citizen wrote to the Academy citing the cases and arguing that compulsory chapel attendance was a constitutional violation.[22] In 1956, Academy superintendent William Smedberg told another inquiring citizen that the requirement for chapel was in place as "part of the whole education of a midshipman as a future Naval officer who will be responsible to those under him in seeing that their complete welfare is provided for."[23]

In 1957, Curtis Crawford, a minister who headed the Annapolis Unitarian Fellowship, began lobbying Smedberg to end mandatory chapel attendance.[24] At about this time, Smedberg ended the Sunday morning formations that took place before the midshipmen marched to chapel services, hoping to give the midshipmen a chance to relax because they had to march together to classes every day of the week except for Sunday.[25] The chapel issue may have come up in the annual superintendents' meetings—which Smedberg devised as a forum for discussions by the superintendents of the Naval, Military, Air Force, and Coast Guard Academies—because later that year West Point issued a statement on chapel services with which Naval Academy leaders would have agreed: "The United States Military Academy accepts responsibility for the total development of a cadet: mental, physical, moral, and spiritual. In recognition of this responsibility, the fact that biblical faith is the foundation stone of honor and integrity, and the necessity for every officer to have a first hand knowledge of one of the three great religious traditions of our country, the Academy requires all cadets to attend Protestant, Catholic, or Jewish chapel on Sunday."[26] As in the case of the Naval Academy, the chapels at the Military, Coast Guard, and Air Force Academies occupy symbolically prominent places on campus. The West Point chapel is a large gothic building on the side of a hill overlooking the Hudson River; the Coast Guard chapel is crowned with a lighthouse beacon and sits on the highest point in the city of New London, Connecticut; and the Air Force Academy chapel is both the centerpiece of the Colorado Springs campus and one of the most recognizable and celebrated designs of the major American architectural firm Skidmore Owings and Merrill. After Reverend Crawford received no satisfaction for his efforts with Superintendent Smedberg, he then unsuccessfully lobbied Smedberg's successor, Superintendent Charles Melson.[27] Crawford succeeded only in convincing the *New York Times* to cover the story and to print his contention that mandatory chapel represented "a serious and unjustified offense against freedom of conscience."[28]

The academies began paying closer attention to Supreme Court decisions in the early 1960s. Under Chief Justice Earl Warren's leadership, the high court showed an activist support for civil liberties.[29] The 1961 cases of *Dixon v. Alabama State Board of Education* and *Braunfield v. Brown*, 1962's *Engle v. Vitale*, and the 1963 case *Abington School District v. Schempp* all dealt with religious freedom and confirmed the Supreme Court's desire to keep a firm separation between church and state.[30] James Kelly, the Naval Academy's senior chaplain, appeared to understand the nature of these cases. He told Commandant Charles Minter, "I really hate to say it, but I'm afraid if [mandatory chapel] is ever challenged in the courts, we're probably going to lose."[31]

Beyond the Naval Academy, military leaders were also aware of the Court's opinions and their significance. Navy chaplain Roland Faulk pursued a policy of non-mandatory chapel attendance for Navy recruits in his assignments at training centers, causing William Smedberg, then the chief of Naval personnel, to order a Navy-wide examination of the issue.[32] The Army's judge advocate general declared, in June 1963, that if the issue of mandatory chapel at West Point were to be raised in a court, the practice would be found unconstitutional on the basis of violating the First Amendment.[33] In a February 1964 issue of *Newsweek*, an Air Force Academy cadet told the magazine that mandatory chapel there existed "primarily as a show for the Academy visitors" and that he found "atheism more attractive than trying to put God in my life in such a hollow way."[34]

The next month, in a memorandum on compulsory chapel at the service academies, Army lawyer R. Tenney Johnson examined whether the service could justify the practice. While admitting difficulty and uncertainty, Johnson stated that four components could be used to defend mandatory chapel: attendance was an integral part of training; a military academy was a small community and would not threaten the Establishment Clause; presence at a service academy was voluntary; and the chapel requirement was simply to attend, not to profess or accept a particular religious ideology. Johnson concluded his paper by stating that "the ultimate decision [on mandatory chapel attendance] should be based on the needs of the Academy in the proper accomplishment of its mission."[35] The undersecretary of the Army, Paul Igantius, agreed with Johnson on the "absolutely fundamental" role of chapel in education and training, concluding, "I see no reason why the Services should yield to the pressures of a few citizens and change [such] time tested regulations."[36]

As these discussions were taking place, the role of religion became a major topic of consideration in the Naval Academy's expansion plans. USNA hired architect John Warneke to design a much-needed classroom building.[37] After an uproar developed in the Annapolis community over the original plan to construct the building on the site of three blocks of historic structures, Warneke, with the input of Academy officials and professors, planned to place the new building on USNA land then used for tennis courts.[38] Almost immediately, an unanticipated commotion developed among Naval Academy alumni who realized that Warneke's proposal would block the scenic view of the Severn River from the Naval Academy chapel and the traditionally inspirational view of the chapel for midshipmen on ships and boats on the water.[39] Two versions of what happened next exist. Then–secretary of the Academic Board Robert McNitt remembered that Superintendent Charles Kirkpatrick "stood on the steps of the Chapel, looked across the Yard, and made his decision. Make two buildings."[40] Charles Minter, who was then the commandant, later recalled, "I will never forget [Warneke] telling us that the one thing that needed to be done was to retain a view of the water from the Chapel steps to keep the character of the Naval Academy. Therefore, he designed a split building so that, as you look down from the Chapel steps . . . you look to the Severn."[41] Warneke's classroom buildings were completed in 1968.[42]

Midshipmen, however, were not always so serious about chapel, and at times they showed a forthright sense of humor about it. In the early twentieth century, the chapel was the scene of a traditional ceremony, "Sob Sunday." Held just prior to graduation ceremonies, "Sob Sunday" involved underclassmen bringing handkerchiefs to the chapel, feigning sadness at the imminent departure of the seniors, and singing the hymn "God Be With You 'Till We Meet Again." In 1920, the underclassmen brought towels and sponges and made a large spectacle; as one writer recalled, the ceremony had "an unusually moist ending."[43] Mandatory chapel may have inspired class of 1958 member and future Mamas and Papas frontman John Phillips to write the group's popular song, "California Dreamin'." Naval Academy legend claims that Phillips's lyrics, "Stopped into a church / I passed along the way / Well I got down on my knees / And I pretend to pray / You know the preacher likes the cold / He knows I'm gonna stay / California Dreamin' / On such a winter's day," were the result of his experiences with mandatory chapel at USNA. (As it turned out, Phillips did not stay; he never graduated.)[44] One of the Academy's mascots, a small dog named Dodo, frequently attended chapel services in the late 1960s. His presence inspired one of the chaplains to design for him a blanket reading "BITE ARMY," a takeoff on the popular Naval Academy phrase, "Beat Army."[45] The LOG, USNA's humor magazine, featured a spoof of the board game "Monopoly" in 1966. One of the prized properties for sale was "Sleepy Hollow," the area of the Naval Academy chapel in which tired midshipmen could find an unobserved pew on which to nap.[46]

Yet, the chapel and mandatory services there began to strike several midshipmen as a problem. Three midshipmen asked Superintendent Draper Kauffman, who served as the head of the Academy from 1965 until 1968, to be excused from mandatory chapel. Kauffman complied and set up a course on Sunday mornings for the three. A professor taught the midshipmen religious history and required a passing grade to continue their exemption from chapel services. Kauffman later noted that he chose the hardest faculty member at USNA to teach the class, and only one of the three midshipmen could pass the course. No other midshipmen again asked him to be excused.[47]

At West Point, five cadets also began to question mandatory attendance at chapel services during the 1960s. Their actions would have a profound effect on events at the Naval Academy. At the Military Academy, mandatory chapel services had been in effect since 1821.[48] One cadet challenged mandatory chapel by becoming responsible for typing the weekly chapel attendance roster and covering up his absence from required services. Eventually, administrators caught on to his actions, and subjected the cadet to punishments that ultimately led to his resignation from West Point.[49] In 1967, Cadet Robert Leslie, a sophomore, made a request to two officers to be excused from attending chapel.[50] One of those officers told Leslie that regulations required cadets to attend Sunday services and that those regulations were in place to maintain the proper "public image" of the Military Academy. The only choices for chapel attendance at West Point were among the large non-denominational Protestant, Catholic, and Jewish chapel services. Wishing to avoid Protestant services, Leslie became a "volunteer Jew" and began to attend those services. During his junior year, Leslie again attempted to be excused from mandatory chapel. In May of 1968, he and Cadet Lucian Truscott IV spoke with their regimental commander, Alexander Haig, and called mandatory chapel a "mockery." The two cadets told Haig that they wanted to file a complaint with the Academy's inspector general, to which Haig responded that there might be "some kind of boomerang effect" if the men proceeded with their request.

During the week prior to Labor Day 1968, when West Point cadets reassembled for the new academic year, Leslie made a startling discovery. While studying budgetary forms, Leslie learned that all cadets were making a mandatory donation of $6.50 to the chapel each semester. He told Truscott and Cadet David Vaught about the donations, which, unbeknownst to them, they had been making for three years. They shared their findings with a fourth cadet, Richard Swick. Leslie and Truscott articulated their concerns in a statement they called "The Hotbed Sheet," outlining the constitutional, legal, and moral reasons they found mandatory chapel abhorrent. They concluded the document by stating that "it is a paradox that the officers here at the Academy support the requirement for mandatory chapel, a flagrant violation of the very Constitution they have sworn to support, to such an extent it reflects upon the integrity of these officers."

While taking a constitutional law course, the men became familiar with Captain Wynne Morriss. A young Harvard Law School graduate, Morriss was drafted into the Army and assigned to the law faculty at West Point.[51] He also served as the legal assistance officer at the Military Academy, a position that allowed him confidential interaction with the cadets. Morriss understood the implications of cadets raising a legal issue of this nature, and he began to advise the men in October 1968 on steps to take, legalities of the chapel issue, and keeping records of their chapel-related transactions with officers in the chain of command. Even after West Point administrators ordered him not to advise or interact with Leslie, Swick, Truscott, or Vaught, Morriss continued to do so as the legal assistance officer.

The four cadets decided that they might have more success with their goals if they centered solely on the less-charged issue of mandatory chapel donation. On 5 September 1968, Truscott penned a short letter to the West Point treasurer asking that the donation no longer be taken from his cadet account.[52] Several days later, Vaught wrote a similar letter. The Military Academy returned the letters and asked the cadets to clarify their reasoning, so Truscott and Leslie visited the treasurer and asked for a refund of their previous donations. They still received no satisfaction.[53] It had become clear that the administration was concerned about their actions. West Point leaders ordered other cadets to report any information about the issue that Leslie, Swick, Truscott, and Vaught might reveal in the course of conversation. Vaught and Truscott then began feeding information to other cadets to keep the administration confused about their actions and intentions.

By the beginning of October 1968, Truscott still had no response from the administration about his request to discontinue mandatory chapel donations. The four cadets decided to send letters requesting that they be permanently excused from mandatory chapel attendance. During the evening of 29 October 1968, the men met with the new regimental commander, Marion Ross. Ross had replaced Haig, who had become the deputy commandant. As Truscott explained, Haig told Ross to have a meeting with the four men and "scare the living piss out of them." Leslie, Swick, Truscott, and Vaught, while standing at attention in the back of Ross's office, informed him that they wanted to file a complaint with the inspector general to end mandatory chapel attendance and donations. Ross asked why they did not just resign from West Point and indicated that his secretary, who had stayed late and was ready with a typewriter and resignation forms, was on hand to expedite that process. From Truscott's written transcript of the events, the conversation continued:

ROSS: "You came here voluntarily and agreed to abide by the regulations."
TRUSCOTT: "I haven't broken any regulations, Sir. I go to chapel. I have never skipped chapel."
SWICK: "I pay attention to sermons, but I see most guys sleeping and inattentive—can you see them from where you sit, Sir?"

ROSS: "No, I sit in front and can see very little from my point of view."

ROSS (TO SWICK AND VAUGHT): "You might not graduate on June 4th."

SWICK: "I may not be alive on June 4th, Sir."

LESLIE: "That sounds like a threat, Sir."

ROSS: "No, I am just stating a fact. I think you ought to resign."

SWICK: "Why should I give up a career I've worked three years to get, Sir?"

ROSS: "I could care less what you do with your career, Mr. Swick."

TRUSCOTT: "What is done with other people who want to change things? Are they asked to resign and threatened with separation, Sir?"

ROSS: "I am not threatening anyone."

LESLIE: "Do you think we get satisfaction out of getting discriminated against and time taken out of our day, Sir?"

ROSS: "You are troublemakers."

SWICK: "We are not troublemakers. If we were, we would have had this in court a long time ago and we could still have it in court in two days, Sir."

ROSS: "Yes, and if you did you could face charges."

SWICK: "What do you mean, sIr?"

LESLIE: "I don't understand, Sir."

ROSS: "We will courtmartial you."

LESLIE: "For what, Sir?"

ROSS: "I don't know, but I am sure we can think of something."

VAUGHT: "Sir, you mean you would arbitrarily do this?"

ROSS: "Yes, it's been done before and we will be do it again."

LESLIE: "Sir, you would trump up false charges and arbitrarily courtmartial and separate us for a perfectly legal lawsuit?"

ROSS: "Yes."

TRUSCOTT: "Sir, if you are doing that, would that be in keeping with the Cadet Prayer and with your duty as a sworn officer to uphold the Constitution?"

ROSS: "Yes, I don't give a damn if it is in conflict, and neither does anyone else around here, and it won't be any skin off of our asses. I seriously doubt if any of you will graduate."[54]

The conversation then ended, and the four cadets returned to their quarters.

Because Haig and Ross believed Truscott was a leader of the other men, which by Truscott's later admission he was not, they began a series of discussions with him the next day. These meetings continued until the middle of November 1968. Truscott was attempting to get Haig and Ross to pass his requests up the chain of command, but Haig refused and kept the papers on his desk. During their final meeting, on 17 November, Haig indicated that he would not send the letters up to his superiors and was returning the requests to the cadets. Truscott responded by asking Haig if he was aware that refusal to send papers up the chain was an offense punishable with fines and a prison term. Truscott recalled that "Haig went ballistic," pounded his finger into Truscott's chest, and called the cadet "a little fucking son of a bitch."

On 14 November, West Point refused the requests of several cadets, including Vaught, "to attend services of their own faith" rather than the services in the West Point chapel.[55] Knowing this and aware of Truscott's last meeting with Haig, Vaught submitted an action request up the chain of command on 21 November 1968. He asked the Army's inspector general for a cessation to mandatory chapel attendance, calling the practice unconstitutional and "discriminatory to cadets of various religions, and . . . harmful to my moral development."[56] Vaught also argued for the end of mandatory donations. When he returned from the winter holidays, Vaught received a brief letter from the Army's deputy chief of staff indicating that compulsory chapel attendance would continue, but that mandatory chapel donations would cease.[57] The money they had "donated" was returned to them.

Vaught, Truscott, Swick, and Leslie now understood that their fight to end mandatory chapel attendance had come to an end. Truscott later recalled that "we were tired of being yelled at." The men concentrated, rather, on marching off demerits accumulated for infractions caused by other cadets who were sympathetic to the administration. Such infractions resulted from others messing up papers on the four cadets' desks, searching their rooms until something punishable could be found, and stealing required footwear. Clearly the West Point administration had not forgotten about Leslie, Swick, Truscott, and Vaught. In a May 1969 speech to the junior class, Commandant Bernard Rogers told the cadets that the chapel policy would not change while he was in charge. During that year's June Week, the celebratory week leading up to graduation, the Military Academy's superintendent, Major General Samuel Koster, referred to the four men as "troublemakers" and warned other cadets about them. Vaught recalled that Koster made these remarks "because we didn't stand for the same things [the other cadets] did, and we would lead them astray."[58]

Two months after Leslie, Swick, Truscott, and Vaught graduated from West Point, the mandatory chapel attendance issue reappeared at the Naval Academy. Thomas Travis, a junior, raised the topic with an Academy chaplain.[59] The chaplain responded that a change in the policy was "unlikely," but that Travis could work on it. During the fall of 1969, Travis also discussed the issue with a professor in the English/History/Government Department, Major Constantine Albans, who had served as a secretary for the April 1969 annual conference of the service academies' superintendents. Among the decisions made that year was a statement about mandatory chapel attendance: "It is the consensus of the four Superintendents that the purpose of regular attendance at religious services is to instill a sense of respect for religion as a factor in the daily lives and activities of the vast majority of mankind. It is therefore . . . [our] policy that cadets and midshipmen will attend regularly scheduled religious services. It is understood that intelligent provisions must be made for bona fide cases where attendance would be in conflict with sincerely-held convictions of individual cadets or midshipmen."[60] Travis followed Albans's advice, and on 19 November 1969 submitted to Academy commandant Robert Coogan a request to be excused from chapel services.[61] Two days later, Travis sent an alternative chapel attendance plan to the Brigade Communications Organization, which Coogan created in July 1969 to help inform the administration about midshipmen's ideas for policy changes.[62] Travis proposed allowing those midshipmen who wished to continue to attend Sunday chapel services to do so. Midshipmen who did not wish to participate would attend a course that would cover philosophies of various religions, the organization of religious services, and the study of ethics.[63] As Travis's plan made its way up the chain of command, midshipmen leaders above him supported his proposed policy. One midshipman indicated that "this is a question that is going to continue to arise. It's a serious problem and something should be done."[64] A few days later, during the Thanksgiving recess, Travis and another midshipman, Nicholas Enna, met with Lawrence Speiser, the director of the Washington, D.C., office of the ACLU.[65]

Toward the end of November, two other midshipmen in the 23rd Company, David Osborn and his roommate Mark Cooper, found out that Travis and Enna were attempting to eliminate required chapel. The four men continued to discuss the topic into the month of December. Unknown to them, the Academy's chaplains were discussing Travis's proposal.[66] The senior chaplain, Robert McComas, told one of the Brigade leaders that he disagreed with Travis's contention that the chapel requirement "inhibits natural growth toward religious maturity."[67] Rather, McComas argued, the midshipmen needed to be exposed to worship, an experience that the classroom environment could not adequately replicate. Midshipman Enna, meanwhile, decided he would not attend services at the Naval Academy chapel.[68] The Academy, he argued, "placed me in the position of violating the dictates of my conscience." The Academy awarded him fifty demerits and ten hours of marching as punishment for violating regulations.

On 2 December 1969, Speiser wrote to the secretaries of the Navy, Army, and Air Force arguing that the chapel requirement was unconstitutional.[69] Instead of the silence he received in response to a letter he sent ten months earlier, Speiser heard from the Department of Defense that a "review" of the chapel subject, presumably the superintendents' conference, concluded that there was no need for a change in policy. At the end of December, Speiser wrote letters to the "newspapers" of the Naval, Military, and Air Force Academies. His purpose was to inform the midshipmen and cadets that the ACLU was "planning to file suit" and to solicit young men willing to participate in the case. "Our sole interest," Speiser wrote, "is to protect the constitutional rights of individuals." Speiser mistakenly sent the Annapolis letter to the editor of the *Beacon*, a publication that gave news to Naval Academy staff and employees. The *Beacon* forwarded the letter to D. A. Ellison, editor of the LOG. Intending to support the administration on the chapel issue, Ellison refused to print Speiser's letter. The ACLU letter likewise never appeared in print at West Point or Colorado Springs.

Upon returning to Annapolis for the spring semester of 1970, Midshipman Travis learned that the Academy had quashed his proposed alternate plan because the chaplains did not support the idea.[70] On 12 January 1970, the Commandant wrote Travis and told him that his request, from two months earlier, to be excused from chapel would necessitate a detailed explanation. Travis replied to the Commandant with a long letter, giving an explanation of his agnosticism. His discomfort was with "formal worship," not religion. During a meeting with his company officer four days later, Travis indicated that he had no intention of being a plaintiff in any developing ACLU lawsuit, although he had discussed such a possibility with a USNA faculty member.

On 14 January, Speiser called Cadet Michael Anderson at West Point to mention that the ACLU anticipated just such a suit.[71] Although he was a year behind Leslie, Swick, Truscott, and Vaught, Anderson had observed the four men's attempts within the Military Academy's chain of command. While Anderson was a student in the constitutional law class at West Point, he "couldn't help noticing the conflict between the mandatory chapel policy and the . . . establishment of religion clause . . . and the oath that all officers and cadets take to 'uphold the Constitution.'" After Speiser mentioned the possibility of court actions to end required chapel, Anderson met with a law professor (likely Wynne Morriss, who had advised the four 1969 graduates) to discuss the ramifications of such a step. About their meeting, Anderson later recalled that "his advice was that [pursuing a fight against the chapel policy] would ruin my military career and I should be very careful. He did nothing to encourage me, and I think he was truly concerned that someone so young would screw themselves permanently. Still, he didn't make much of a defense for the policy and it was clear to me that he knew it was unconstitutional. He showed me two sheets of paper, one of which was the official policy of the academies [that] described the in loco parentis argument. The second sheet was an insider poop sheet . . . and it was, in my view, very incriminating. . . . It was a sort of 'how to baffle 'em with bullshit' piece."[72] Morriss made sure that Anderson had the opportunity to read the documents and to understand their contents.

The nineteenth of January, 1970, was a significant day at Annapolis and West Point. Midshipmen Osborn and Cooper, along with their colleagues Jeffrey Gossett and two other midshipmen, met with their company officer, James Simms.[73] Prior to the meeting, Speiser mailed the men forms giving the ACLU authorization to represent them in a court case.[74] They immediately presented the forms to the Naval Academy's legal officer, who informed the midshipmen that they had a legal right to be involved with any court proceedings. When the four showed Simms the forms, he became angry, and according to Osborn, he told the midshipmen that they were "fools" for becoming "involved with the Communist-oriented ACLU." The company officer recalled the events differently, stating that he wanted to impress upon the midshipmen that the ACLU cared only about the case and not about them as individuals. At the Military Academy, Michael Anderson informed his company officer that he had decided to proceed as a plaintiff with the ACLU.

The ACLU filed the case on the morning of 20 January 1970 in the Federal District Court in Washington, D.C.[75] The plaintiffs to the lawsuit were Cadet Anderson and Midshipmen Cooper, Enna, Gossett, Osborn, James Bradley, and Gary Currey, who represented students at their academies.[76] Although no Air Force Academy cadets were plaintiffs, the class action nature of the case covered them as well.[77] In the initial complaint to District Judge Howard Corcoran, the ACLU argued that military regulations requiring midshipmen and cadets at the academies to attend weekly services represented an establishment of religion and violated the young men's free exercise of religion under the First Amendment. As proof of the injury, the ACLU stated that compulsory chapel attendance represented a religious test under Section 3 of Article VI of the Constitution.[78] Furthermore, the ACLU indicated that the

Naval Academy was punishing Enna with demerits for not attending chapel services, thereby damaging his class standing. Speiser and his co-counsel, Warren Kaplan, pointed out that some of the plaintiffs did "profess to religious beliefs" and explained that it "is not the availability of religious services, but only the compulsory nature thereof which plaintiffs challenge."[79]

Two days later, Speiser and Kaplan submitted a brief to Judge Corcoran outlining the Supreme Court decisions relevant to their argument. In addition to *Everson v. Board of Education*, *Zorach v. Clauson*, *Braunfield v. Brown*, and *Engle v. Vitale*, they presented two other religious freedom cases with pertinence to mandatory chapel attendance.[80] First, Speiser and Kaplan quoted Justice Owen Roberts's 1940 majority statement in *Cantwell v. State of Connecticut* in which Roberts stated that the Constitution "forestalls compulsion by law of the acceptance of any creed or the practice of any form of worship" and guarantees "the freedom of conscience and the freedom to adhere to such religious organizations or form of worship as the individual may choose."[81] Then the ACLU lawyers referred to *United States v. Ballard*, in which Justice William Douglas wrote, in reference to the framers of the Constitution, "Man's relation to his God was made no concern of the state. He was granted the right to worship as he pleased and to answer to no man for the verity of his religious views."[82]

Superintendent James Calvert, who represented defendant Secretary of Defense Melvin Laird, justified and defended mandatory chapel attendance at all of the military academies.[83] Calvert's first statement to the Court came as an affidavit on 4 February 1970. The Superintendent explained that "because a genuine sense of honor, devotion to duty, and absolute integrity are qualities demanded of an officer, and because these qualities are fostered in religious principles and traditions, the Naval Academy requires midshipmen to attend Chapel services." Carefully pointing out that the Academy was not forcing midshipmen to pray or "profess a belief or disbelief in any religion," Calvert stated that the practice existed for the moral development of midshipmen and to give them an understanding of the religious beliefs of the men they would lead and the foreign citizens with whom they would later interact as officers.

Military leaders understood that the argument for maintaining compulsory chapel would have to be based on non-religious motivations if it were to survive the constitutional separation of church and state. Yet not all military leaders and their lawyers agreed with the practice, including William Mack, a Navy officer then serving as the deputy assistant secretary of defense for manpower and reserve affairs.[84] Mack recalled that his civilian superior, Roger Kelley, assigned him the task of writing the Department of Defense (DOD)'s defenses for the case. "I said I didn't like [mandatory chapel] much," Mack recounted, and that "I could dream up some arguments all right, but I didn't believe it, it shouldn't be compulsory. That caused consternation in the ranks." Columnist Jack Anderson similarly wrote that "the DOD has assigned some of its best lawyers to fight the case. But some of the younger members of the legal staff believe the midshipmen are right and the Pentagon wrong. Those young lawyers drafted a strong memo, declaring that the DOD did not have a legal leg to stand on. The senior attorneys were so horrified over their underlings' dissenting opinion that they classified the memo and locked it up.[85] The Department of Defense continued to delineate its views in an argument based upon custom when it asked the U.S. Court of Appeals for the District of Columbia on 6 February to dismiss the case. The DOD lawyers and the Washington U.S. attorney cited "the long-standing policy of our courts not to become involved in matters of military disciplines" and the "long tradition" of mandatory chapel attendance at the academies" as reasons for the irrelevance of the case.[86] The appeals court was not convinced.

Even before Judge Corcoran began the trial on Monday, 9 February, public knowledge of the case had expanded. Michael Anderson wrote an anonymous letter to the editor of Playboy magazine describing the West Point punishments for not attending chapel.[87] Anderson suggested that any cadet involved with the court case "would almost certainly be blacklisted by the senior officers."[88] The day before the trial started, the Reverend Billy Graham delivered the sermon at the Sunday Protestant service at the Naval Academy chapel.[89] Graham believed the case was part of a move to exclude chaplains from the military and openly gave his support to the continuance of compulsory chapel. The reverend enthusiastically told the gathered midshipmen and members of the public that "I think [required chapel] is a tremendous thing. It would be the greatest possible tragedy if it were to be stopped. It is part of the discipline, part of the training. . . . We need it now more than ever before. It imparts a moral and spiritual strength." Ironically, midshipmen had to submit special chits to hear Graham speak because "the administration was expecting too many guests." A midshipman called this policy "hypocritical" given that chapel attendance was mandatory, proving to him that "the Academy is concerned with an image rather than a reality."[90]

The next day, Superintendent Calvert was first to testify.[91] In his eloquent testimony to the court, he stated that "it is a voluntary thing to be a professional officer in the Armed Forces, and it has certain implications which are not secular but which are moral and philosophical in nature." Referring to the possibility of leading distressed men in a combat situation, Calvert explained

On 8 February 1970, the day before courtroom proceedings for the *Anderson v. Laird* case began, the Reverend Billy Graham preached at the Naval Academy chapel and vocalized his support for continuing mandatory chapel attendance. Graham was an advisor to President Richard Nixon, whom a reporter later accused of trying to influence the verdict in the case. Here, Graham stands on the steps of the chapel after his sermon, accompanied by Senior Chaplain Robert McComas and Superintendent James Calvert. (U.S. Naval Academy Archives)

that "it is our effort to make sure, to the best of our ability, that our young men understand these dimensions of their command that we require" mandatory chapel. Calvert based his testimony on his own experiences as a submarine commander during World War II. Speiser and Kaplan then called four religious leaders to the stand, and, in sequence, a Baptist minister, a Jesuit priest, an Episcopal reverend, and a Jewish rabbi all testified that they and their denominations found compulsory chapel attendance objectionable.[92] The ACLU lawyers hoped to demonstrate that representatives of a variety of religious organizations and denominations would insist on the essentiality of voluntarism to religion.

Calvert again took the stand during the second day of the trial.[93] He told the court that if a midshipman were to express a legitimate explanation of how attending chapel services was counterproductive to his training as an officer, "I would permit him to take some other kind of moral and ethical training." Although he made no reference to the three midshipmen Kauffman had excused, Calvert stated that the Academy had, in the past, excused two midshipmen from chapel services. The claim referred to a Buddhist midshipman from an unknown date and a Muslim midshipman who attended around 1905.[94] One alumnus described the latter, writing that "the punishment fit the crime—he was told he would have to read the Koran and demonstrate the thoroughness of his devotion by writing a long religious essay." Calvert's testimony underscored one of the DOD's claims: the cadet and the midshipmen in the suit had not "exhausted their administrative remedy" by going through the chain of command at West Point and Annapolis.[95] To prove his point, Calvert offered the case of Midshipman Travis, whom the Commandant had in fact excused from attending chapel the exact same day that the ACLU filed the case. Travis was instead attending a Sunday morning class called "Ethics and Comparative Religion," for which Major Albans was the professor.[96]

Kaplan and Speiser understood that they faced a dilemma. The DOD was preparing a motion for dismissal on the basis of the cadet and midshipmen's failure to seek administrative remedy.[97] West Point law professor Wynne Morriss, who was following the case closely, knew that four cadets had sought administrative remedy. As one of those former cadets, David Vaught, recalled, "Morriss . . . [feared] that the plaintiffs' attorneys were going to blow a good case. Had he not stayed in touch [with me], I don't think they would have found me, or one of the other three who had pursued the administrative remedy, in time." Morriss called Vaught, who agreed to travel to Washington to meet with the ACLU lawyers. On the same morning that the DOD presented its motion, Vaught took the stand and described in compelling detail his experiences in attempting to bring an end to mandatory chapel attendance through the chain of command at West Point.

Immediately after Vaught stepped down, Michael Anderson testified that he had not sought remedy through the chain of command based on his observation of the actions of Vaught, Truscott, Leslie, and Swick. Anderson told the court that he realized that making a similar attempt would be "futile."[98] Kaplan and Speiser called David Osborn and Thomas Travis to the stand to testify about Midshipman Travis's vain attempt to resolve the issue of mandatory chapel within the Brigade Communications Organization.[99] The DOD's lawyer, Assistant U.S. Attorney Joseph Hannon, implied that Osborn should have sought administrative relief under the Uniform Code of Military Justice (UCMJ), but Osborn replied that the Academy's legal officer never pointed out such an option to him.[100] Admiral Calvert even testified that he would not have expected midshipmen to utilize the UCMJ.[101] Speiser thus argued to Judge Corcoran that "administrative remedy that is futile is no administrative remedy at all," and Corcoran agreed that administrative remedies were not available to the midshipmen and cadets.[102]

The courtroom scene in the case was remarkable in that it pitted high-ranking Navy officers against young midshipmen and cadets. Corcoran was clearly biased toward the military officers. Kaplan later remembered that "Judge Corcoran thought . . . [the plaintiffs] were a bunch of wise guy hippies." Yet the young men were articulate, intelligent, forthright, and incisive in their testimony.[103] For example, Anderson took one of the more dramatic steps in the courtroom when he took out a copy of the Cadet Prayer; when the defense objected, Anderson handed Hannon the copy and recited the prayer from memory. He recalled that "the government lawyers assumed I was just a kid being manipulated by liberal left wing Washington lawyers."[104] In fact, the lawyers were inexperienced. Speiser had never tried a case before *Anderson v. Laird*, and Kaplan was only a few years out of Harvard Law School.[105] Vaught recalled that "I, of course, was impressed by all the lawyers who took [the case] up. I had never seen before a courtroom where only . . . two barely prepared but brave, smart attorneys take on a plethora of government . . . lawyers, armed with tons of research, briefs, and all the big gun expert witnesses. I had never seen young [military officers] . . . going up against [admirals] and assistant secretaries of defense on the witness stand. . . . I was hugely impressed by our lawyers."[106]

Typifying Judge Corcoran's respect for the defense's witnesses was an exchange that took place while Admiral Calvert was on the stand. Kaplan was trying to figure out whether or not Calvert could decide himself, as the Naval Academy's superintendent, to drop the chapel requirement, and whether midshipmen understood that they could be excused from chapel services:

KAPLAN: "Do you think there is any possibility, Admiral, that when a cadet or midshipman reads the regulation which says, 'All cadets will attend chapel,' that he might get the idea that 'all' means 'all'?"

HANNON: "Objection."

KAPLAN: "Do you think midshipmen understand that they can be excused?"

CALVERT: "Many of them are aware—I would suppose most of them, I don't know—that this has been granted in the past. Certainly, it is among the folklore of the Naval Academy widely understood. . . . There are two sections to the Naval Academy regulations: one of the sections requires approval by the Secretary of the Navy, and the other one is issued by the Superintendent."

KAPLAN: "Well, under which of those sections do the compulsory chapel requirements fall?"

CALVERT: (After conferring with Hannon) "This is in Part II of the Naval Academy regulations which are issued by the Superintendent that do not require Secretary approval."

KAPLAN: "So that it would be within your power to change these regulations without seeking any higher authority if you were so disposed, is that correct?"

CALVERT: "Well, I think in the course of being reasonable, Mr. Kaplan, that any reasonable man occupying the office of Superintendent contemplating changing such a very basic regulation which affects the very heart of the way the Academy goes about its business and has for more than a century, that any Superintendent would in the reasonable conduct of his affairs discuss it with his superiors in Washington."

KAPLAN: "Well, do you mean it would be politically unwise to do it without consulting the Secretary of the Navy? Is that it?"

HANNON: "I object, your Honor."

CORCORAN: (To Kaplan) "I wouldn't ask him to characterize it. Let him answer what he would do."

KAPLAN: "Admiral, my question is: do you have authority to make the change yourself?"

HANNON: (Responding for Calvert) "The answer is yes."[107]

During testimony the next day, Midshipman Travis noted that he had deduced, from speaking with a USNA chaplain, that the Naval Academy's chapel policy was controlled from outside Annapolis, and that therefore an internal attempt to change the policy would be ineffective.[108]

Reactions at Annapolis and West Point to the midshipmen and the cadet, following the trial, varied. Anderson explained that "some cadets gave me a little bit of a hard time, but for the most part the Academy was meticulous in avoiding harassment." While Anderson felt the commandant resented him, Superintendent Koster "was very polite—even fatherly," and informed Anderson that they could speak at any time the cadet felt repercussions for his involvement in the case.[109] The Naval Academy, too, announced that it would not punish any of the litigants.[110] To make certain, however, Judge Corcoran ordered the academies to eliminate any punishments put in effect before the case.[111] Midshipmen demonstrated a variety of opinions about the involvement of their peers in the lawsuit.[112] One participant in the case recalled that he got "very little directly" from his peers in terms of reaction. The LOG magazine dealt with the issue frequently. Editor D. A. Ellison continued to show opposition to the case and wrote in an editorial, "I am yet to realize why it is necessary for a tiny fraction of the Brigade to actively pursue a course of action outside the Academy with the purpose of undermining the one tradition and practice [dedicated] toward improving the moral values of the Brigade." Another midshipman countered Ellison's point, stating that he failed "to see how an unwilling, tired, and uninterested mid is improving his morals by sitting benumbed in Chapel every Sunday." After the Academy discharged Nicholas Enna for academic deficiency, the LOG featured a cartoon called "The Chapel Seven." The drawing shows a gallows, on which one cadet and five midshipmen glance at another midshipman who has been hanged.

In spite of Hannon's contention that many midshipmen and cadets believed in the usefulness of chapel attendance, Judge Corcoran continued the class action status of the suit on 27 April 1970, thereby allowing the plaintiffs to continue representing their fellow midshipmen and cadets.[113] He also added four more plaintiffs to the case: West Point cadet Bruce Bartley and midshipmen Bernard Bandish, Stephen Gemmell, and Ted Rogers.[114] The court then heard testimony from Ray Applecrist, a Baptist minister representing the General Commission on the Chaplains for Armed Forces Personnel.[115] Chaplain Applecrist referred to a 1964 study endorsed by Protestant, Jewish, and Catholic organizations that disagreed with the compulsory nature of chapel attendance. Applecrist claimed that his organization had past difficulties in recruiting chaplains due to mandatory chapel attendance at the military academies.

Hannon then presented two of his star witnesses, the first of whom was Chairman of the Joint Chiefs of Staff Admiral Thomas Moorer.[116] Admiral Moorer's testimony contained the same line of argumentation that Admiral Calvert had made earlier on the stand. Moorer suggested that midshipmen and cadets might not realize the benefits of chapel until much later in life when they would understand it as "a very vital part of the overall leadership package." Noting that the military academies were but one source of the nation's military leaders, Moorer argued that academy graduates played a vital role in passing their experiences, chapel attendance among them, on to their OCS and ROTC counterparts who looked to academy graduates for guidance on leadership. When Kaplan asked the chairman if midshipmen would attend chapel services if they were not required, Moorer quipped, "I wouldn't make an estimate, but I'm sure some would not go. But I am sure if we did not make math class mandatory, some would not go to that either." In closing, Moorer told the court that the purpose of mandatory chapel attendance for midshipmen and cadets "is to deepen their understanding of religion, instead of their religious understanding; there is a difference. . . . They will understand the attitudes and desires [and] the needs of all men who come under their command."

Hannon also called Assistant Secretary of Defense for Manpower and Reserve Affairs Roger Kelley to the stand.[117] When Speiser was examining him, Kelley said that the chapel requirement existed for two purposes, to provide the midshipman and cadet with effective leadership skills and to instill "in him an understanding of the religious beliefs and spiritual values of other people." Speiser then asked the assistant secretary of defense why a class on religions would not better meet this goal. Kelley replied that such an approach would fail "to provide the individual students with any particular insight or understanding of the convictions held by other individuals." The two engaged in an interchange:

SPEISER: "Maybe I mistook you, but I thought you said the purpose of going to compulsory chapel was that you attain an appreciation of the religious beliefs of others. How does going to a Jewish service by a Jewish midshipman give him an appreciation of the beliefs of Protestants and Catholics?"

KELLEY: "It is all part of the same spiritual ballgame, and to the extent that attendance at one of the three is required, he develops an understanding which, otherwise, he would not have."[118]

Kelley went on to admit that midshipmen and cadets would probably learn more if they attended a variety of religious services but that constraints on time would prohibit such an alternative. He concluded by telling the court that military officers not being experts, "or even knowledgeable about the Moslem, the Mohammedan, or the Confucian religions" in no way "impaired" the ability of the officers "to understand the strongly-held religious beliefs of others."

The final witness in the case was Robert Leslie, the West Point graduate who had taken the first steps to end mandatory chapel attendance.[119] Leslie recounted the details of his experiences with Swick, Truscott, Vaught, and Haig at West Point and described a research project that he had helped another cadet, Fred Van Atta, conduct in 1968. Van Atta randomly distributed five hundred questionnaires for a psychology class and asked cadets for their opinions and habits in regard to compulsory chapel. From the 236 responses he received, Van Atta learned that many of the respondents seldom paid attention at chapel, felt that services should not be mandatory, had skipped chapel, and would attend chapel less often it services were not compulsory. Leslie deduced from the written responses to the questionnaires that many cadets "thought that the Chapel was a farce, that it was just another ceremony," and that their "general feeling was one of revulsion toward this type of religious experience." Van Atta concluded that mandatory chapel had not been beneficial and wrote that "in my opinion the study indicated that the management decision of [mandatory] chapel was bad. It caused rebellion more than acceptance and habit. In effect they killed God at West Point."

Over a month after the trial ended, Kaplan and Speiser wrote a memorandum of law to Judge Corcoran outlining the points of their case.[120] They astutely observed that the military had failed to present any of its own chaplains as witnesses during the trial. Referring to the testimony of the religious leaders the ACLU lawyers had presented, they asked, "Is it conceivable that any academy chaplain would agree that chapel policies are intended to serve a 'wholly secular purpose?' " Kaplan and Speiser argued that it was clear that some midshipmen and cadets benefited from mandatory chapel, but they cited Vaught as an example of a Southern Baptist forced to attend an essentially Episcopal service at West Point. They asked Corcoran to find that compulsory chapel violated the Free Exercise Clause in forcing service academy students to attend chapel and in requiring them to get their parents' approval for switching from Academy chapels to other churches. Likewise, they reiterated Thomas Clark's opinion in *Abington School District v. Schempp*, telling Corcoran that "a government practice which has both a secular purpose and a secular primary effect may, nevertheless, be in violation of the Establishment Clause if it involves the use of religious means to achieve secular goals, where non-religious means [such as a class on religion] would suffice." Based on these two alleged violations, the ACLU labeled mandatory chapel a religious test and "an outworn anachronism, a curious relic of a bygone era."

On 25 June 1970, Corcoran called the litigants to the Washington courtroom to indicate that he was excluding the Van Atta survey, as well as any testimony on the topic, because he did not find the survey to be "reliable."[121] Two weeks later, he approved the DOD's motion to remove Cooper and Osborn, who had resigned from USNA, and Enna and Bandish, whom USNA had discharged for academic deficiency, as plaintiffs.[122] Then, on the final day of July, Corcoran offered his opinion.[123] Although he again stated that he would not allow any of the academies to punish any of the midshipmen or cadets who had been plaintiffs, Corcoran concluded that mandatory chapel attendance did not violate the Free Exercise or Establishment Clauses of the Constitution and, therefore, he would not forbid the academies from enforcing the requirement.

Corcoran stated that he believed administrative remedies were not available to the plaintiffs. However, after hearing the testimony in the case, he determined that midshipmen and cadets could, in fact, be excused from attending chapel if they asked. He also argued that the long tradition of mandatory chapel at the academies could not be overlooked or "lightly discarded." The bulk of Corcoran's reasoning centered on what he called "the limitations which have traditionally guided the courts in dealing with matters military." He then stated that "the amount of deference given the military in matters of discipline and training should be wide" and said that because the plaintiffs had failed to present any military officers who trained future leaders and found chapel to have "negative effects," he would have to defer to the opinions of Admirals Calvert and Moorer. Furthermore, he did not find the chapel requirement to constitute a religious test, and he therefore found no violation of Article VI of the Constitution. Judge Corcoran closed by finding that he found "church or chapel attendance [to be] an integral part of the military training of the future officer corps, that its purpose is secular, and that its primary effect is purely secular."

Warren Kaplan was not surprised at Corcoran's decision, believing during the trial that the judge would uphold compulsory chapel attendance.[124] He and Speiser filed an appeal with the Court of Appeals for the District of Columbia Circuit on 7 August 1970.[125] A few weeks later, President Richard Nixon wrote a letter to Superintendent Calvert expressing his opinion that religious training was a significant part of the character and leadership training of midshipmen. Nixon stated how "pleased" he was "with the outcome of the recent suit" and congratulated Calvert on the "principal" role that the Admiral played in the case.[126] Calvert replied to Nixon, writing that "the fact that you were personally interested in the case gave all of us increased confidence and determination to do our best" and asking for the president's support in bringing the suit to the Supreme Court were the appeals court to overturn the district court decision.[127]

Was the White House involved in influencing Corcoran's verdict?[128] In 1972, journalist Robert Timberg presented, in an *Evening Capital* article, a letter dated 2 September 1970 lending credence to such an allegation. James Hughes, an Air Force general and military assistant to Nixon, wrote to General William Knowlton, then the Superintendent of West Point, saying "I just wanted you to know that I feel, perhaps erroneously, that the success we had with the chapel law suit was due to strong behind the scenes support from the President. I paid a courtesy call on Admiral Calvert and he raised the issue, and I pursued it with the Attorney General." A Navy officer remembered a meeting between Calvert and Nixon and recalled that when the meeting was over, Nixon commented that there was no way he could go on record and support mandatory chapel. The president understood, apparently, the delicacy of the DOD's position in the case. What seems more plausible than Nixon's personal intervention, therefore, is that of Alexander Haig, who by the time of the lawsuit was the military advisor to Nixon's national security advisor, Henry Kissinger. Given Haig's opinions on the issue of mandatory chapel when he was at West Point, it would seem likely that if there were a White House figure sympathetic to the DOD's position in *Anderson v. Laird*, it would be Haig.

It was not until 8 June 1971, ten months later, that the appeals court heard the case.[129] At the Naval Academy, little changed in terms of compulsory chapel requirements. As one midshipman wrote in the *Lucky Bag*, the Naval Academy's yearbook, "some of us sleep in Chapel, some of us check out the female complement, and some look into themselves."[130] The appeals court judges, David Bazelon, Harold Leventhal, and George MacKinnon, deliberated for so long that Kaplan wrote to Bazelon on 25 May 1972 to ask what he could do to expedite their decision.[131] Three weeks after Secretary of Defense Melvin Laird told midshipmen at that year's Annapolis graduation that "the way to achieve lasting peace is through hard, tough, meaningful negotiation," the court of appeals finally announced its decision.[132]

Judge Bazelon presented the majority opinion on 30 June 1972.[133] He and

Judge Leventhal constituted the majority overturning Judge Corcoran's decision. Bazelon was extremely clear in his finding, writing that "attendance at religious exercises is an activity which, under the Establishment Clause, a government may never compel." Citing *Torasco v. Watkins*, *Engle v. Vitale*, and *Abington School District v. Schempp*, Bazelon argued that worship and attendance at chapel services were "indistinguishable" and that "freedom from government imposition of religion is a core value protected by the Establishment Clause."[134] Secondly, Bazelon found that the regulations requiring mandatory chapel attendance violated the Free Exercise Clause. On this subject, Bazelon argued that "manifest restraints on the free exercise of religion can be saved from unconstitutionality only if they were enacted to serve paramount and compelling state interests, and if there are no alternative means to achieve the government's goals. . . . [It does not] appear that the ruling will have any detrimental impact on the academies' training programs. The [DOD has] made no showing that chapel attendance requirements are the best or the only means to impart to officers some familiarity with religion and its effect on our soldiers."[135]

Judge Leventhal agreed with Bazelon's finding that compulsory chapel violated the Establishment Clause, but because of that conclusion, he did not feel the need to consider whether the requirement also violated the Free Exercise Clause.[136] He criticized Roger Kelley's assertion that although midshipmen and cadets might learn more about others' religions by attending services of those religions, time constraints prohibited such an option. "Administrative convenience" might be a factor in "denying leave to different places of worship," Leventhal wrote, but that was scarcely an excuse to compel attendance at chapel services. The judge concluded that "the approach of the military officials seems permeated with a sense of tradition, which is laudable, but not a justification for disregarding First Amendment considerations."

Arguing that the First Amendment should not be the basis for consideration in the case, Judge MacKinnon dissented.[137] He found that Article I, Section 8 of the Constitution, which deals in part with the raising and maintenance of an Army and Navy, was an equally important consideration as the First Amendment. MacKinnon also believed in the principle of in loco parentis and, deferring to the military leaders in the trial, found that "some minimal *exposure to religion* . . . is an absolute necessity in the academies' program of moral and character development." He therefore concluded that if the military academies required chapel "as a *necessary* part" of their training, "such minimal regulation does not violate the First Amendment."

MacKinnon's dissent may have given hope to the Department of Justice, which, along with the Department of Defense, submitted the case to the United States Supreme Court on 27 October 1972.[138] The departments simply restated the government's earlier positions, concluding that "the danger our country faces today is the decline in spirit and morality, observable among young and old alike. The Supreme Court should not let stand a decision which would weaken the Naval Academy at the point where it now needs its greatest strength." However, the high court was not convinced. It notified the two departments on 18 December 1972 that the nine justices declined to review the case.[139] The next week, an editorial in the *New York Times* scathingly attacked the government's stand in *Anderson v. Laird* and saw the Supreme Court's action as "an enlightened judicial effort to block the abuse of religion by those who seek to increase the power of the state."[140]

The Department of Defense, ultimately, did not take long to conform to the rulings of the appeals court and the Supreme Court. On the second day of 1973, Secretary of Defense Laird wrote to the secretaries of the military's branches, directing them to alter their regulations on mandatory chapel attendance.[141] Until that day, as a midshipman noted in another letter to the editor of *Playboy* magazine, mandatory attendance continued.[142] On 8 January, Judge Corcoran ordered the defendants to change their regulations, reversing his own findings.[143] The Naval Academy's new superintendent, William Mack, told midshipmen in a memo about the high court ruling, stating that chapel attendance would henceforth not be mandatory.[144] Encouraging the midshipmen to continue to worship, Mack told them that they owed it to themselves and the men they would lead in the future "to gain an insight into the moral, ethical, and religious dimensions of leadership." Mack later recalled being "secretly overjoyed when the case was overturned and we were told to get ready for voluntary chapel. Everybody thought [ending compulsory attendance] was terrible, and I thought it was just fine."

In addition to ending mandatory chapel attendance, Naval Academy administrators also canceled the course entitled "Ethics and Comparative Religion," which the Academy originally designed for Midshipman Travis when it exempted him from attending services.[145] The Academy had been permitting other midshipmen to take the course, and its catalog told prospective candidates for entry that while USNA considered chapel attendance to be a requirement, some midshipmen "may prefer more secularly-oriented approaches." An officer had described the course, held on Sunday mornings, as an hour-long "moral and ethical uplift." Mack further explained the secular approach:

"The Morals and Ethics Discussion Group was conducted by line officers, not by chaplains, and dealt primarily with the behavioral consequences of belief and value systems which a naval officer encounters during port calls abroad and during overseas assignments. . . . The Group also dealt with the moral and ethical dimensions of leadership, but always from a practical perspective."[146] While it is unknown exactly how many midshipmen were choosing this alternative to chapel attendance, the number was sizeable enough to warrant multiple sections each Sunday.

Michael Anderson, who was then a first lieutenant in the Army serving in Alaska, wrote to the superintendents of the military academies and encouraged them to end such required classes and mandatory chapel, as the courts had ordered.[147] He then told the superintendents that "religion by subscription will serve you infinitely better than religion by conscription. The cadets and midshipmen are, I think you will find, very responsive to religion to fill their needs. . . . You have simply neglected to provide religion to fill their needs. This, gentlemen, has been your biggest failure. . . . Your religion by regulation was a theological albatross and its weight will be around your necks for some time. If you are willing to let the religious experience be open and spontaneous and free you may discover a real spiritual awakening at the Academies."[148] Was there such a spiritual reawakening? On the first Sunday after mandatory chapel ended, then–senior chaplain John J. O'Connor tabulated that 1,790 of the 3,830 midshipmen at the Naval Academy attended religious services of some type.[149]

By February 1973, O'Connor noted that attendance at the Naval Academy chapel's Protestant services had dropped by 50 percent, while its Catholic services had seen only a 10 percent decline.[150] Commandant Max Morris then created and distributed a list of twenty-eight Annapolis synagogues and churches with suggested departure times for the midshipmen to leave for those services; during a meeting with Annapolis clergymen, O'Connor discovered that an increased number of midshipmen were attending services in the city's houses of worship.[151] A Bible-distributing organization confirmed O'Connor's contention that the number of midshipman Bible study groups increased "very substantially": midshipmen requested 464 Bibles in the first two months of 1973, compared with 270 requests for the entire previous year.[152] Superintendent Mack recalled that "I followed Father O'Connor's feeling that when Chapel opened voluntarily you'd find the same number of worshipers there as before. . . . Those who went in the back of the Chapel and slept . . . now they slept in their rooms!"[153] Midshipmen joked about the issue, and the

Lucky Bag biography of Gary Currey, the only plaintiff to graduate after the case was finally resolved, made reference to the capacity of midshipmen to remain in bed. The biography stated that "he won the respect and admiration of his classmates for his efforts to establish a Sunday morning respite in white surrounding (i.e., the rack)."[154]

O'Connor was not deterred from promoting religious activities at the Academy.[155] He spurred the creation of an annual award for a midshipman who made outstanding contributions to chapel-related activities. Concerned that Jewish midshipmen did not have a place at the Academy for worship, as their Protestant and Catholic counterparts did, O'Connor succeeded in turning a room in the midshipmen's library into a Jewish prayer space. O'Connor and Superintendent Mack together created a course entitled "The Professional Officer and the Human Person," a non-credit course that emphasized such topics as religion, ethics, morals, drugs, race, and gender.[156] (However, Mack's successor, Superintendent Kinnaird McKee, did away with the class; one of his administrators explained that the course "went over like a lead balloon. It was a bomb.")

Education in ethics and leadership has continued to be a concern of USNA administrators. Superintendent William Lawrence raised the issue during his 1978–81 administration.[157] He saw religious programs, the example of military officers, guest speakers, background on Naval Academy traditions and heritage, and the Academy's unique Honor Concept as crucial contributing factors in the ethical development of midshipmen. By the 1990s, however, a series of incidents raised concern that the sorts of ethical and moral training that Naval Academy leaders believed chapel attendance had provided were no longer being fulfilled.[158] In 1990, two midshipmen broke into the Electrical Engineering Department's offices to steal their final exam, and other male midshipmen chained a female midshipman to a urinal during a playful exchange gone awry. Late in 1992, another electrical engineering final exam was compromised in an incident that ultimately implicated 133 midshipmen.

As a result of these events, the Board of Visitors created a subcommittee, with Ambassador Richard Armitage as the chair and with Admiral Calvert as a member, to investigate and make recommendations.[159] The Navy chose Admiral Charles Larson, who had been the superintendent from 1983 until 1986 and was then one of the Navy's highest ranking officers, to return to that post in 1994. Larson believed that American society had undergone substantial changes and had experienced a decrease in personal integrity and accountability among its youth. His approach to his second term involved application of many of the ideas from the Armitage Report, and he created an ethics curriculum, a Character Development Program, Integrity Development Seminars, and a Human Dignity Education Resource Program. Larson later recalled his efforts, saying "when I was growing up we got our values at home. So when I got to the Academy I knew what my values were. . . . There's a society out there right now that is [more] worried about what is legal than what is right. . . . We don't stand up and say, 'I'm going to do what is right.' I wanted to fix that."

The *Anderson v. Laird* case also brought about an increased emphasis on ethics at the U.S. Military Academy.[160] From 1982 until 2000, cadets at West Point learned about *Anderson v. Laird* in their "Constitutional and Military Law" course. One Army officer who was an instructor in the course recalled that "we got a great reaction from the cadets. . . . In my opinion, the cadets were impressed by the fact that one of their own had made it to the Supreme Court and won a victory over 'The System.'" There is no evidence that *Anderson v. Laird* has ever been taught in any capacity at the U.S. Naval Academy.

Clearly, many older Naval Academy leaders felt that the strong-arm approach to ethics, character development, and leadership could have been avoided through the maintenance of mandatory chapel attendance. Superintendent William Smedberg later said that "the required attendance at Sunday service was as much a part of the education of a naval officer as anything he got [at USNA]. It was with a tremendous amount of disgust that I viewed [the courts'] action."[161] Superintendent John Davidson agreed, insisting that "the greatest disappointment in my life came . . . when [the midshipmen] didn't have to go to Chapel. . . . I think it was a terrible mistake on the part of the Supreme Court."[162] Superintendent Charles Minter commented that mandatory chapel was "something you kind of hated to see go by the boards. . . . [Many alumni] as midshipmen really could have cared less, I think, for the service, but it left its mark though they may not have realized it at the time."[163] Superintendent Draper Kauffman commented that "I regretted very much later on when [mandatory chapel] was canceled. . . . [Even the midshipmen] who sat in Sleepy Hollow, I felt that they definitely got something out of it."[164]

Superintendent Mack continued to believe that the end of mandatory chapel was a "good contribution to Naval Academy life." He remembered being upset only by the ACLU's involvement with the case. "That was one of my regrets," Mack said, "why did we not have the moral courage to do this ourselves rather than have it forced on us by the courts."[165] Superintendent James Calvert later remarked on the benefits of compulsory chapel, arguing that "it gave the Brigade a sense of being together at something other than a football game." Yet he understood that not all midshipmen liked the practice: "You can't expect all 4,000 [of the midshipmen] to be ardent supporters of the superintendent, especially when it means they can sleep in on Sunday mornings." Recalling his involvement with *Anderson v. Laird*, Calvert said that "I gave my most influential, persuasive speeches [in the case], but it didn't do any good. The ACLU won out. . . . When you get right down to how the law read, they were right. When you get right down to what was good for the country, I was right. But the law always wins."[166]

5 The Seeds of Revolution

Women at the Naval Academy through 1976

★ ★ ★ ★ ★ ★ ★ ★ ★ ★ ★ ★ ★ ★ ★ ★ ★ ★

On Wednesday, 28 May 1980, underneath a clear, warm sky, members of the class of 1980 walked across a stage in the Navy–Marine Corps stadium and, one by one, received their Naval Academy diplomas.[1] Among the 947 graduates that day were 55 women, the first female graduates of the Academy. As West Point's deputy commandant Alexander Haig had insinuated when he argued that "you challenge mandatory chapel, and they find it unconstitutional and end it, and the next thing, there will be women in here, and then we won't have West Point any more—all we'll have is a goddamned college," the break in tradition that the *Anderson v. Laird* case on mandatory chapel attendance represented prepared the stage for the entry of women to the service academies.[2] Their presence and the events that led to their arrival less than three years after the Washington, D.C., federal court of appeals rendered mandatory chapel attendance unconstitutional represent the largest challenge yet to the traditions of the Naval Academy.[3] Laws and conceptions of masculinity had previously prevented women from serving in combat roles, thus denying them the possibility of exercising their full rights as citizens. Women's acceptance into the Brigade of Midshipmen was a significant step in getting females into combat and, therefore, helped them to fulfill their roles and responsibilities as American citizens.[4] The following three chapters address the issue of women at Annapolis. This chapter examines the roles of women at USNA prior to 1976, when women came to the Academy only as the wives of officers, as civilian and military employees, as dates, as speakers, as teachers, or as parts of pranks. It also describes changes in male midshipmen's conceptions of women and looks at the steps, many of which were unsuccessful, in getting women to the Naval Academy. Chapter Six recounts the experiences of the women in the class of 1980, and Chapter Seven demonstrates the achievements made and ongoing obstacles faced by women in subsequent classes.

Women have been involved with the Academy from its foundation in a number of roles. Among Naval Academy employees, women performed in a service capacity, working as laundresses as early as 1850 and, by the 1920s, on superintendents' staffs.[5] Women have also been present at Annapolis as the wives of officers and as girlfriends, "drags" (the USNA slang term for female dates), and objects of midshipmen's affection.[6] Such fondness for women was visible as early as 1896, when members of that class placed a poem and illustration, both entitled "Navy Girl," in their Lucky Bag.[7] Similar pictures, which resembled American artist Charles Dana Gibson's popular "Gibson's Girls," appeared in later Lucky Bags and on Naval Academy Christmas cards until the mid-1920s.[8] Beginning in 1897 and continuing to the present, graduating classes have selected a Color Girl to be the matron of their final dress parade.[9] In 1930, the wives of officers stationed at Annapolis decided to occupy themselves more actively and formed the Naval Academy Women's Club. Their goal was to maintain their cultural pursuits collectively, including musical productions and speeches, in an era of economic depression.[10] Superintendent William Smedberg later commented on such activities, explaining that "one of the greatest satisfactions of this wonderful job of mine is to observe the interest and participation of our ladies in so many of the affairs of [the Naval Academy]. That is, as it should be, a community of families with common interests."[11]

As the Women's Club's activities got under way, two young women who were not a part of that community participated in a prank at the Naval Academy that brought the institution into the media spotlight.[12] In July 1930, while some midshipmen were stationed at the Academy for aviation training, Midshipmen Miller Burgin and Lawrence Myatt permitted two female friends, Mary Eleanor Hayden and Lorette Taylor, to wear the midshipmen's "whiteworks" uniform over their clothes and eat breakfast in the USNA mess hall. One alumnus later speculated that he would not have been surprised if the women had "spent the night before in Bancroft Hall." Because such an incident broke Academy rules against women in the mess hall and was counter to the strict moral codes of the era, other midshipmen quickly realized the dimensions of the prank and the possibilities for punishment and warned Myatt and Burgin to escort the women out of the building. News of the incident spread quickly, and Commandant Charles Snyder recommended Burgin and Myatt for dismissal while punishing eighteen midshipmen who failed to report the incident. By 25 July 1930, Secretary of the Navy Charles Adams approved the dismissals of the two midshipmen, and, in spite of mass media coverage and a six-month battle waged by several congressmen to return Burgin and Myatt to USNA, President Herbert Hoover approved the dismissals in January 1931.

For the remainder of the 1930s and the 1940s, men at the Naval Academy returned to thinking of women as dates but also as contributors to the World War II effort. To encourage dating, but to simultaneously set the bounds for young women's behavior, USNA began to publish a series of "Drag Handbooks." The Academy designed these books to inform "drags" about etiquette, expectations, logistics, and dating rules while they visited Annapolis, effectively dictating the women's roles.[13] Unlikely to have consulted such handbooks were three enlisted women assigned to the Naval Academy during World War II.[14] Training Specialist Rosemary Grimes taught aviation beginning in the summer of 1944, and Training Specialists Alta Gray and Katherine Usher worked on equipment in the Department of Seamanship and Navigation in 1945. Because these women were fulfilling their roles as WAVES, the noncombat-oriented Women Accepted for Volunteer Emergency Service, administrators did not see these women as a threat to the traditional concept of men's exclusive ability to serve in combat roles.

A real threat to USNA's prevailing standards developed, however, in 1949. In a curious reflection of the events of 1930, the LOG featured in March a photo of drag Judy Agee smoking a cigarette and sporting a midshipman's uniform.[15] Administrators may have had that photograph in mind when, months later, Genevieve Waselewski became the first woman to seek admission to USNA.[16] Remarking that "this may amaze you for I am a young woman of 31," Waselewski explained her interest in attending the Academy for the sole purpose of taking some of the courses it then offered. She concluded her letter by commenting that "I am not worried it is a man's school." USNA officials, however, were quite concerned about her gender, and replied to Waselewski that "the course of instruction at the Naval Academy is designed solely for the purpose of preparing young men for a life-time military career." In the absence of a popular women's movement in American society, neither Waselewski nor any other woman challenged the officials' statement.

The opinions of Naval officials and the status of the national women's movement had not changed dramatically between 1949 and 1956 when a second woman showed interest in becoming a midshipman. Throughout the early 1950s, the LOG had featured midshipmen's musings about the Academy having female midshipmen.[17] One spread of photographs, for example, showed young women in uniform doing many of the things that midshipmen would do: inspecting plebes, standing watch, attending class, eating in the mess hall, and standing in formation.[18] Administrators were not laughing, however, when Mary Ann Bonalsky wrote her congressman in 1956 to seek admission to the Academy.[19] Bonalsky told James Tumulty (D-N.J.) that she deserved a chance to become a midshipman because "we, the girls, have equal rights with the male." Remarkably, Bonalsky composed her letter before the second wave of the national women's movement became front-page news.[20] Tumulty took Bonalsky's request seriously because, as he told the media, "there is a certain amount of logic in her stand," although he admitted that there were some "practical difficulties" in nominating Bonalsky. He contacted Secretary of the Navy Charles Thomas, who quickly announced that he would not accept any plan to allow Bonalsky to attend Annapolis, confessing that "I can't conceive of one girl over there with all of those midshipmen." Whether Thomas feared what the men might do to Bonalsky or what she might do to them is unclear. Most likely, the secretary's fears of mixing the genders in close quarters and of challenging men's role as combat warriors led to his declaration to Tumulty that the "question" of women midshipmen "would be answered in due course."

Naval Academy officials were still not prepared or willing to address such a question—or the idea of a female faculty member—when, in November 1958, Susan Johnson, a senior at Annapolis High School, "masqueraded" as a midshipman.[21] Going beyond Hayden and Taylor's sneaking into the mess hall in 1930, Johnson reflected a trend of women's increasing assertiveness during this period when she entered Bancroft Hall, stood evening meal formation in the dormitory, marched with the rest of the Brigade of Midshipmen into the mess hall, and then had dinner with a table of young men. Johnson's mother told the press that Susan's actions were "just a prank" and that "there was no question of any moral issue being involved." Although Academy administrators agreed that the incident was an "immature prank," they disciplined two midshipmen who had supplied Johnson's uniform and three midshipmen leaders who failed to report the incident immediately. The publicity surrounding the Susan Johnson case elicited attention from retired military personnel, one of whom told the Academy's commandant that "it would seem that the valuable public relations which could be achieved by this accomplishment are doomed by the unfortunate reputation the Academy has of being 'stuffy.' Many of us regard the entire incident as the kind of prank which endears today's youth to us elders. It is refreshing and delightful. It is reassuring to know that our future admirals in their youth are genuine people, willing to take the chance even in so serious a setting as that which might make or break them."[22] In reaction to the events, Johnson's father told the *New York Times* that he would exercise more control in "keeping [his daughter] home nights."

From 1958 to 1971, American society, as evidenced by the immense popularity of publications like *Esquire* and *Playboy*, became more open in its discussions of sexuality while midshipmen, like other men in American society during this era, began to openly objectify women.[23] The midshipmen's publication, the LOG, demonstrates the shift away from a reserved news publication showing women as beholden girlfriends back home to an entertainment magazine showing women as sexual objects. The LOG began to address issues that would have been scandalous at any previous point since midshipmen began the publication in 1913. Although drawings of women had appeared in the LOG as early as 1923 and the "Drag of the Week" was a long-standing feature, it was the 4 April 1958 edition, a spoof on *Esquire* Magazine, that began a new era by including a drawing of a clothed but buxom woman as the centerfold.[24] The next month, the LOG included a cartoon of a group of tourists in front of Bancroft Hall with the silhouette of a nude woman in one of the building's windows, and the Christmas 1959 issue contained the first LOG cover to feature a photo of a woman.[25] The first overt reference to sexual activity was a 1963 photograph of a woman walking in front of the two cannons that guard Tecumseh Court, the courtyard in front of Bancroft Hall. The cannons did not fire, an indication in Naval Academy lore that the woman was experienced sexually.[26]

Although the LOG never featured any nudity, the layout, font, and features of the magazine began to resemble those of *Playboy* by 1964. A cartoon that year even included, in the background, a stack of *Playboy* magazines.[27] Whether administrators were unaware of this change or simply saw it as a benign display of young men's desires is unclear. One of the LOG's famed features, a photograph section of midshipmen's girlfriends entitled "Company Cuties," began in 1965, and in 1966 Teddi Smith, an actual *Playboy* centerfold model, appeared in an advertisement on the back cover of a LOG issue.[28] Later in 1966, in spoofs of *Playboy*'s recognizable self-advertisements and novel holiday gifts, the midshipmen editors began features entitled "What Sort of Man Reads LOG" and "Gifts for Middies."[29] "The Midshipman Advisor," another takeoff on *Playboy*, began in 1968, just months before "Drag of the Week" Geri Moore appeared in the LOG in a bikini.[30] One 1969 issue of the LOG, with a woman wearing only a midshipman's blue coat on the cover, was based entirely on Hugh Hefner's magazine and featured the first African American woman to appear in the LOG.[31] An issue in March of the next year featured a photo spread of a young woman, Julie Biggs, in a room in

Bancroft Hall; for one of the photos, Biggs posed in a suggestive position on a midshipman's bed.[32] These *LOG* items may reflect an increase in sexual activity at USNA as administrators simultaneously created a new regulation stating that "midshipmen will not loiter in the cemetery with young ladies."[33] No records exist to state if a particular incident or incidents precipitated such a change, but the Naval Academy Cemetery's secluded nature has contributed to lore about sexual activity there.[34]

Yet, in spite of this atmosphere, a number of remarkable events occurred that demonstrated the increasing popularity and recognition of the developing women's movement in the United States. In a 1960 *LOG* "Femmes Issue," a long-lived annual *LOG* issue in which female friends of midshipmen took control of the editorship of one issue of the magazine, one young woman gave a curiously precise prediction for the future. Gay Ann Cornell posited that "the [1980s] will be the beginning of a big transitional period in the ways of the U.S. Naval Academy. Yes, girls (present company accepted), on to bigger and better things. . . . The U.S. Naval Academy will be changed to the U.S. Coed Naval Academy to accommodate us women. . . . Three cheers for 1980! May it bring a new way of life. At any rate, I can dream, can't I?"[35]

In 1968, the Navy assigned Captain Alma Ellis to USNA as the director of the Naval Academy Museum.[36] And in 1971, Barbara Brimmer, a seventeen-year-old woman, announced her desire to enter the Naval Academy as a midshipman.[37] Her quest, with the assistance of her senator, was similar to both Waselewski and Bonalsky's earlier failed attempts at seeking admission, but was an important step in the process of eventually gaining women entry into the service academies. On 22 September 1971, Senator Jacob Javits (R-N.Y.) wrote to the Navy to inform authorities that he was considering appointing a female nominee to the Naval Academy. Javits understood the depth of the developing women's movement and earlier in 1971 had appointed the first female page in the Senate. Consequently, when a seventeen-year-old constituent wrote to Javits to express her interest in attending Annapolis, he took the letter seriously. He learned that Brimmer was from a Navy family: her mother had served as a WAVE during World War II, and her father was a 1920 Annapolis graduate. After a fall 1971 meeting with Brimmer, Javits realized that her desire to attend USNA was genuine and that her family fully supported her quest. Javits wrote to Secretary of the Navy John Chafee for clarification of the policies concerning women who wished to attend Annapolis. The senator pointed out the ambiguity in Title X of the U.S. Code, which made no mention of gender in requirements for admission to the Naval Academy, and declared that "I take it that the term 'midshipmen' is simply a title, and is not intended to exclude women." The Navy's own policies in the Code of Federal Regulations did state, however, that "all candidates to the U.S. Naval Academy be male citizens of the United States."[38]

Douglas Plate, the deputy chief of Naval personnel, responded to Javits's inquiry and explained that congressional mandate did, indeed, prohibit the Academy from accepting women. Because the Navy understood that the Naval Academy's mission was one of preparation for officers in combat, it saw women's attendance at USNA as unnecessary.[39] Women had, indeed, served in the Navy during World War I and World War II, but the positions that they filled were never in the arena of combat.[40] As historian Cynthia Enloe has pointed out, men have traditionally "assumed" that "the military, even more than other patriarchal institutions, is a male preserve, run by men for men according to masculine ideas and relying solely on man power."[41] Plate's letter explained the Navy's justification for the continued exclusion of women from combat:

It must be recognized that the Navy's current position is a clear reflection of the Judeo-Christian traditions and concepts, relating to the status of women. These concepts contributed heavily to the elevation of that status, especially during the Age of Chivalry, until the basic attitude in our American culture became one in which women were to be protected, cherished, and spared from the rigors associated with war and life at sea.

In as much [sic] as our own Navy is designed as an instrument of war, the inclusion of women in the sea-going role has been and still is viewed as a basic contradiction to the aforementioned philosophical traditions. Congressional recognition of this concept has appeared in the law since women were first authorized to serve in the Navy. Further evidence of Congressional recognition of this concept appears in the exclusion of women in the provisions of the Selective Service Act.

The constraints already in the law would make it illogical to train women for combat service at sea and in combat aircraft. Unless across-the-board revisions to the laws relating to women in the armed forces are contemplated, including the Selective Service Act, service on combat vessels and in combat aircraft, changes to the admissions criteria for the Naval Academy would not be appropriate.[42]

In spite of these arguments, which reflected concepts of warrior traditions and seemed legalistic, chauvinistic, and ignorant of the extensive military role women played in the Second World War, Javits's determination was unfettered.[43] While USNA midshipmen continued to spend their time that fall staring at women during religious services and admiring women on homecoming floats, Javits "haggled" with Navy officials for the next four months.[44] His principal idea was to alter the USNA curriculum for women, adding a nursing program and exempting women from any training involving combat preparation. As Javits's efforts were proceeding, Congressman Jack McDonald (R-Mich.) indicated to the press that he intended to nominate University of Michigan freshman Valerie Schoen to the Naval Academy. McDonald indicated late in January 1972 that he was "impressed" by Schoen's "explanation that she was seeking the nomination because she wanted to receive the best education possible" and Schoen herself later recalled that "I did not apply to Annapolis as a women's liberationist to break down any sex barriers. I [wanted] to serve my country." Javits publicly announced his support of Brimmer several days later and noted his intention to "introduce legislation making it mandatory for the Academy to accept women" if USNA chose not to process Brimmer's application.

Javits left Secretary of the Navy Chafee in the position of figuring out what step to take next. Before Chafee could make any decision, another situation involving a woman at USNA arose. Naval officers at the Academy prevented Laraine Laudati, a young woman from Annapolis who served as a manager for the USNA swimming team, from eating dinner in the mess hall with the team. Chafee explained to Laudati that the exclusion of women from the dining area was a tradition but invited her to eat in the mess hall whenever she was at the Academy in the future. Just two months after congratulating Laudati for "single handedly [breaking] an old tradition," Chafee announced that he would not break USNA's tradition of an all-male Brigade.[45] Rather, in an attempt to compromise with Javits, Chafee declared that the Navy would open its previously all-male Navy ROTC programs to women as a source of its needed female officers.[46] Chafee seemed to carefully ignore, as historian Jeanne Holm later noted, that "the question then was one of equity [because USNA graduates] were traditionally singled out for the choice opportunities. . . . Thus, by being denied admittance to the academies, women were being denied equal opportunity for successful careers commensurate with other officers."[47]

By 1972, Congress was discussing, debating, and passing a number of proposals and acts focusing on women. Among these were Public Law 92-496, which extended Commission on Civil Rights jurisdiction over sexual harassment issues; Title IX of the Education Amendments to the 1964 Civil Rights Act, which banned gender discrimination "under any education program or activity receiving federal financial assistance"; and the Equal Rights Amendment, intended to give men and women equal rights under the United States Constitution.[48] Reflecting this increased interest in promoting women's issues, and unmoved by Chafee's ROTC policy change, Javits submitted a joint resolution in the Senate to allow women to be admitted to, and trained at, the service academies.[49] The Senate passed his resolution, but House Armed Services Committee chairman F. Edward Hebert (D-La.), an ardent adherent to the Pentagon's wishes, let the proposal die in his committee.[50]

Like the members of Congress, Naval Academy leaders were contemplating the prominence of the national women's movement. Superintendent James Calvert invited feminist leaders Gloria Steinem and Dorothy Pitman Hughes to address the midshipmen, and they spoke at USNA on 4 May 1972.[51] Steinem began her speech by remarking that "women have been much too docile and too law abiding for too long, but I think that era is about to end." She then argued that strong American "cultural training" influenced the white men who constituted the overwhelming majority of the Brigade of Midshipmen, creating a "masculine mystique." Steinem argued that men "are made to feel that their masculine identity depends on earning a lot of money, or being violent, on winning all the time, on going off to Indochina, on wearing short hair or uniforms, or beating each other up in bars, or killing small animals, or being members in good standing of the jock-ocracy. Whether they want it or not, they are taught that they can't show feeling, that they can't admit weakness." She continued, "There are very few jobs that require a penis or a vagina, and all other jobs should be open to everyone."[52] Some midshipmen reacted to these comments with laughter and by tossing the fruit that they had taken from the mess hall for evening snacks in the air and onto the stage. Steinem and Hughes believed that the midshipmen were preparing to aim the fruit at the stage where they were standing. As one alumnus recalled, "We were just yanking her chain." Steinem, in fact, enjoyed the "excitement and high spirits" of the midshipmen. She concluded by telling them that the Naval Academy would be a different place in ten years: "Some day, there will be fifty percent female cadets here and some day the mystique will have changed."

Indeed, as Steinem gave her speech, the women's movement in the United States and the efforts of Chief of Naval Operations Elmo Zumwalt were beginning to impact that "mystique."[53] Zumwalt was known in Annapolis and throughout the nation as a highly proactive leader of the U.S. Navy because of his policy decisions, termed "Z-Grams." Among his announcements was 1972's Z-Gram 116, entitled "Equal Rights and Opportunities for Women," indicating his support for women in the Navy. His attitude toward women was, in fact, so unique that federal officials told him that he would not be the military's spokesman in congressional hearings on women at the service academies. As a result of Zumwalt's policies, however, the Naval Academy Preparatory School and the Naval Academy obtained their first female officer instructors in 1972.[54] Lieutenant Georgia Clark reported from Annapolis that aside from some unusual stares in the mess hall and plebes' calling her "sir," there were no problems: "I thought they might treat me warily, and there was some curiosity, but on the whole," she noted, "nothing out of the ordinary has occurred." When reporters questioned her about the possibility of female midshipmen, however, Clark gave the apparently standard response that with other officer training routes available, there was no need for women's attendance at USNA. In 1973, the Naval Academy hired its first female civilian faculty member, economics professor Rae Jean Goodman.

Throughout 1972, discussions of the possibility of female midshipmen had not subsided. Javits told Secretary of the Navy John Warner that "traditionally, the Academy has served as the training grounds for the Navy's uniformed leadership. It seems to me that true equality for females requires that they be given the opportunity to attend the Academy and therefore aspire to that leadership. Further, I suggest that such a change in policy would be consistent with the now common conclusion of historically segregated institutions that the quality of education is improved by moving to a two-sex system."[55] That year, some male midshipmen were angered when an officer at USNA cited regulations against the presence of women during meals and insisted that three women, part of an Academy tour, leave the mess hall where they were eating with their group. "Few individuals can deny that women are being discriminated against," one midshipman wrote in the LOG, "and it casts the Naval Academy in a very poor light."[56] Other LOG writers mocked the institution's seemingly hard-line attitude on women by featuring a photograph of Superintendent Calvert hugging his wife in Tecumseh Court, accompanied by a fake report of Calvert's conduct. In violation of the rule against any "public display of affection," the report cited Calvert for allowing "a young lady to hug him."[57] However, Javits's arguments, the bad publicity resulting from the mess hall incident, and the aforementioned policy changes for female officers and faculty did not alter the Naval Academy's determination to maintain an all-male student body.

Just before Christmas of 1972, two daughters of Navy officers, Jeanne Bauer and Gail Storms, wrote to Zumwalt to indicate their interest in attending the Naval Academy and benefiting from its education.[58] Superintendent William Mack responded to the women, concluding that the Academy's mission, curriculum, and facilities, geared toward men, would make their attendance at USNA "wasteful."[59] As congressmen nominated female applicants, Academy officials' responses were little different. The Navy told Congressman Jerome Waldie (D-Calif.) that his nominee, Coralie Cross, was disqualified because she was a woman.[60] After USNA rejected Claudia Baptista, James Burke (D-Mass.), her sponsoring representative, wrote to the Navy. Burke quoted Zumwalt's Z-Gram 116 and commented that "I am amazed at how the [admission regulations barring women] have managed to survive, as it were, in a vacuum."[61] Zumwalt himself responded to Burke, indicating that he was "carefully" assessing the entire issue of women at Annapolis.[62] Navy and Academy officials also sent letters to Congressman James Corman (D-Calif.), Senator William Proxmire (D-Wisc.), and Congresswoman Patricia Schroeder (D-Colo.) explaining USNA objections to female candidates.[63] Superintendent Mack, uncertain about the fate and potential consequences of the Equal Rights Amendment and proposed changes to laws, told Schroeder that "of course we can not predict what the eventual outcome might be."[64]

But before Zumwalt could finish his assessments of potential policy changes to get women to USNA, he and Mack discovered what the next step in that quest would be. Nearly two years earlier, an undisclosed Navy official had predicted that the "issue" of women "will probably be taken up in court."[65] On 26 September 1973, that prediction came to pass.[66] Just eight months after the court of appeals decision rendering mandatory chapel at the service academies unconstitutional, the resistance to change in gender policies brought the Naval Academy into the courts again. Virginia Dondy, an attorney with the Washington, D.C., Center for Women's Policy Studies, filed suit against Secretary of Defense James Schlesinger in federal court in the nation's capital. The court actions involved two young women, Coralie Cross and Jolene Ann Schwab, who sought and were denied admission to Annapolis and the Air Force Academy, respectively. With what can be characterized as a hint of the comedic, USNA informed Cross that it based its decision on a medical exam, which determined "that you are a female." Cross's sponsoring congressmen, Jerome Waldie and Fortney Stark (D-Calif.), and Don Edwards (D-Calif.), all young, liberal, California Democrats, sought to challenge the policy of excluding women from the Naval Academy's admissions process. In the second suit, Edwards and Congressman Leo Ryan (D-Calif.) hoped to overturn the Air Force Academy's decision not to process Schwab's application. For judicial expediency, the U.S. District Court for the District of Columbia combined the cases *Waldie v. Schlesinger* and *Edwards v. Schlesinger*.

Dondy argued that the Naval Academy, in refusing to consider women for appointment, was violating the Equal Protection and Due Process Clauses of the Constitution's Fourteenth Amendment.[67] The Naval Academy and Department of Defense, however, insisted that they were upholding the "intention" of Congress because that body forbade women from serving aboard combat vessels and aircraft.[68] As a result, the defense argued, it planned to continue to prohibit women and "defend against the suit brought by Coralie S. Cross."[69] U.S. District Attorney for the District of Columbia Harold Titus Jr. suggested that the district court "lacks jurisdiction over the subject matter" since it was a congressional issue.[70] Members of Congress were not ignorant of these claims, and several chose to act on them. Early in October, Congressman Pierre S. DuPont IV (R-Del.) introduced legislation to allow women to be appointed to the service academies; the House Armed Services Committee immediately began to study the proposal.[71] Congressman Samuel Stratton (D-N.Y.) explained that the issue of women at service academies was unrelated to legislation then under consideration, and he quashed the proposal.[72] However, late in December, a powerful cast of sponsoring Senators, including William Hathaway (D-Maine), Javits, Mike Mansfield (D-Mont.), John Stennis (D-Miss.), and Strom Thurmond (R-S.C.), attached an amendment to a military pay act to allow qualified women to attend the military academies.[73] Historian Michael Sherry has argued that the reason behind these men's support was likely their belief "that imminent ratification of the Equal Rights Amendment would mandate such an outcome anyway," while historian Lance Janda has suggested that the congressmen never expected women to go to combat but believed the issue was entirely one of equality and that the limited step was therefore palatable.[74] Furthermore, as historian R. Shep Melnick has noted, "opposition to non-discrimination statutes became politically treacherous" by this time.[75] The proposal went to committee.

As 1973 concluded, Superintendent Mack, well aware of the developments in Washington, sent an end-of-the-year letter to midshipmen's parents describing a new training course, "The Professional Officer and the Human Person."[76] The Superintendent felt strongly, he said, that the class, which included discussions of discrimination and injustice, would help to create "a world in which the dignity of each person is respected for its own individual worth." Mack, uncertain of the outcome of the debate over women at the Academy, wanted to be certain that the Academy would be within the guidelines of the law, whatever it ultimately would state. He oversaw a list of potential female nominees, reserved five spaces for women in the entering class, and coordinated dates by which USNA would need to have court or congressional action for women to enter with other plebes.

At the same time, Mack responded to the affidavits in the *Waldie* and

Edwards cases by arguing that federal law prohibited women "from going to sea in combatant ships and aircraft," reflecting "societal concepts" abhorring the idea of women in combat.[77] He reasoned that "there would be little purpose for women to participate in most aspects of the professional education and training program of the Academy." Were women to be admitted, he explained, a number of difficult issues would arise. How many women would attend Annapolis, and where would they live? What would the women study? By necessity, Mack posited, USNA would have to create a second set of courses designed to train women for noncombat roles in the Navy. Such a separation would inherently be unfair, Mack argued, to other officers in the Navy since women would graduate with the Academy's name but none of "the rigorous training for which the Academy is a hallmark." "To admit women," the superintendent concluded, "is to dilute the resource and offer to the women nothing of the Academy's uniqueness."

Reviewing Admiral Mack's points, Virginia Dondy, the plaintiffs' lawyer, argued that the superintendent's opinions were grounded in "simple and pure error."[78] She repeated her allegation that USNA was discriminating against the two women "based on sex alone" and thereby depriving eligible women "of their right to attend the Academy." She noted that the Naval Academy had reserved five spots for women in its plebe classes were the law to change yet refused to process the applications of fifteen women with congressional nominations. In a long argument, Dondy explained that Academy graduates have "unquestionable advantages" in their Navy careers, and that therefore the inability of women to attend Annapolis put them at a comparative disadvantage in the Navy. In spite of Admiral Mack's statements to the contrary, Dondy stipulated that the Academy could easily accommodate a limited number of women. Finally, Dondy alerted the court that the appointing congressmen had been "injured" because constituents saw the nominations of females as "irresponsible," explaining that "their injury is not that their nominees have not been appointed, but that they have not been considered."

In June 1974, Superintendent Mack appeared in front of the House Armed Services Committee. During his remarkable testimony, he moved away from the military's hard-line opinion on women and told the representatives present his honest feeling that "in my estimation, women could serve in any role in the U.S. Navy at any time if this law were changed. They could come to the Academy; they could pass the courses in large numbers, and do all that's required of them physically, mentally, and professionally, and in any other way, and there would be little requirements for change in any course curriculum, physical facilities, or anything of that sort. If the law were changed, in my mind, women could do anything that men could do, and in some cases, perhaps even better."[79]

Clarifying his point, Mack continued that the United States "never had women serve in combat positions except perhaps in pioneer days. It would be a major policy shift for this country." Mack was frustrated because, as he later explained,

> The Congress had done [the women] an injustice. They have required that we take women into the Naval Academy and give them the same education as men and give them the same chance at promotion and so forth, yet they deny the Navy the authority to send them to sea where they were going to learn what they had to learn about the elements of their profession so they could be promoted fairly. In other words, they'd given the Navy something to do which it couldn't carry out. . . . Congress has no collective responsibility, really, just a lot of people, each one saying "yes, that's right," and when it comes time to vote they forget about this sort of thing and just blithely do something like this, putting the Superintendent of the Naval Academy in an untenable and impossible position.

The Superintendent took an unusually bold step for a Navy leader and an Academy administrator. He told the committee that "if you want us to take women in, you have to do only one thing, that is repeal the law which prevents [women] from going to sea in combatant ships and aircraft."[80] Even Dondy, as the plaintiffs' lawyer, had never asked for such a radical step.[81] Mack may have understood then the likelihood of women's eventual entry into the Academy and sought to make their ultimate integration a success.

In June 1974, district court judge Oliver Gasch began to disclose his opinions in the case.[82] He told the litigants on 14 June that the Naval and Air Force Academies existed "primarily for the purpose of training line officers" and that American laws, "as well as the customs of this country, preclude sending women into combat duty." Later that day, he rejected Dondy's request for an extension of admission dates for the nominated women, explaining that the women still had Navy ROTC as an option and that Dondy had "failed to demonstrate probability of ultimate success." Then, on 19 June 1974, he announced his formal decision. Reiterating Deputy Secretary of Defense William Clements's statement that "the primary function of the three service academies is, and always has been, to train military officers for combat duty," Gasch cited the Title X prohibitions on women aboard combat vessels and aircraft. He noted that "no attack has been made on the constitutionality" of those statutes, and he therefore upheld the exclusion of women. Gasch concluded that "the admissions policy of the Naval and Air Force Academies is reasonably related to furthering a legitimate governmental interest, the preparation of young men to assume leadership roles in combat where necessary to the defense of the nation."

The case went immediately to the U.S. District Court of Appeals in Washington, D.C., and judges spent the summer reviewing the lower court's verdict. Naval Academy officials, meanwhile, contemplated a new recruiting direction. Superintendent Mack was concerned about the all-volunteer military force (AVF), which came into effect in 1973.[83] He feared that the AVF would bring a steep decline in admissions, and he might also have understood the potential gender implications of the AVF.[84] As historian Linda Grant De Pauw has noted, "the introduction of increasingly sophisticated weapons systems made technological skill more important in recruits than their muscle mass."[85] Mack devised a plan that would have allowed graduates to pursue professional football careers after graduation, instead of joining the Navy, as a means of competing with civilian colleges for candidates.[86] Reviewing the proposal, other USNA administrators quickly realized, as one stated, that "this could be the wedge for women at the Academy" since the plan would have created a noncombat destination for male graduates.[87] The Bureau of Naval Personnel concurred with that assessment, and the Academy abandoned the idea.[88]

Hoping to influence the appeals court judges, Congressman Jerome Waldie wrote to them in November 1974 and asked them to order the academies to admit women.[89] Soon after, Judge J. Skelley Wright announced the court's decision, noting that the plaintiffs in the case sought only to have the women's applications processed.[90] "This limited approach," he reiterated, "challenged neither the traditional and statutory . . . exclusion of women from combat nor the propriety of the Academies preparing only men for these roles." Observing that there were only affidavits and no in-court testimonies, Wright argued that

a crucial element in the plaintiffs' case is the distinction between combat roles from which women are barred by policy and statute and combat *support* roles in which women may now serve. Without cross-examination, it is impossible to know exactly what the affiants mean when referring to the role of the Academies in preparing men for "combat." Likewise, when affiants declare that the purpose of the Academies is to prepare men for combat, it is unclear whether they mean it is the sole purpose, the primary purpose, or merely a purpose. Plaintiffs' case hangs on resolution of such ambiguities, and plaintiffs should have the opportunity to resolve them in court.

As a result, Wright concluded by deciding that "the judgment of the District Court is reversed and these cases are remanded for a full trial on the merits." No new trial or hearing ever took place, perhaps because the plaintiffs chose other life plans.

Members of Congress followed the *Waldie v. Schlesinger* case and its verdict, and congressional inquiries into the possibility of allowing women to enter Annapolis and the other service academies continued.[91] Governmental agencies, including the General Accounting Office and the Marine Corps, continued to present statistics proving that all Naval Academy graduates, eventually, went on to combat assignments.[92] As historian Judith Stiehm has noted, Senate and House discussions until that point, at the very least, raised congressional members' awareness of the issue of women at the service academies.[93] In April 1975, Congressman Samuel Stratton, who had earlier quashed the proposal on allowing women into the service academies, announced that he planned to submit new legislation permitting women to attend.[94] Stratton, who had long supported issues of civil rights and had served in the Navy, indicated his belief that the military should not bar women from serving in combat if they so chose. Further, he alleged that some military leaders supported him but that their superior officers prohibited them from speaking freely.[95]

The National Organization for Women (NOW) began to support Stratton's efforts.[96] Throughout 1974 and 1975, the group's leaders urged Congress to allow women into the academies. Two of NOW's national leaders, President Karen DeCrow and Legislative Vice President Ann Scott, were especially active in Washington. Both testified before the House Armed Services Committee in July 1974 in support of women's entry. DeCrow, along with leaders of other women's groups, met with President Gerald Ford and lobbied for his support as well. Pat Leeper, the chairman of the Women in the Military Committee of NOW, also asked Congress to establish dates for women's potential entry to the academies. During a speech to the Annapolis NOW chapter on 1 October 1975, Leeper described her preparation for interactions with congressmen: "The fact that my husband and father are Naval Academy graduates," she told the audience, "gave me plenty of opportunity to practice my arguments."

As Stratton indicated his new opinions, Naval Academy leaders increasingly realized the possibility that Congress might mandate the admission of women to Annapolis.[97] Just days after the congressman's press conference, the Academy, seeking to prepare for any congressional policy change, announced that it would allow several women to attend the Naval Academy Preparatory School midyear, in January 1976, to begin to prepare women for Annapolis if the law changed.[98] Superintendent Mack continued to express the Department of Defense's opinion that the Academy should remain all-male and repeated the anticipated "disastrous" effects were Congress to admit women without changing the combat exclusion law.[99] In spite of the fact that none of its twentieth-century mission statements contained the word "combat," there was an implicit understanding that midshipmen were preparing for careers in which combat training would be a part.[100] Admiral Mack affirmed that principle, as well as the Code of Federal Regulations, when he argued that "the Academy should remain an institution whose sole purpose is to train officers fully qualified for service at sea and in combat in the Navy and Marine Corps."[101]

Countering Mack's assertion, Stratton insisted the General Accounting Office's own report showed that some Academy graduates did not, initially, go into combat.[102] As a result, the congressman told his colleagues that the entry of women into the academies was an issue of "equity" and that the combat issue could be resolved at a later date.[103] "The idea of women in the service academies," Stratton charged, "is an idea whose time has come."[104] The majority of the House of Representatives agreed, and on 21 May 1975, they rejected ideas for a women-only academy and an exemption for West Point, and voted 303–96 to accept Stratton's military appropriations bill amendment and allow women to become midshipmen and cadets.[105] Such a strong vote should not have been unexpected. In the aftermath of the Watergate scandal, Nixon's resignation, and President Ford's subsequent pardon of his predecessor less than a month after assuming office, Democrats, who were liberal on most social issues and more responsive to women's issues, had won widespread victories in the congressional elections of 1974. Other military officer training programs were integrated, and opening the military academies to women seemed a better alternative to having men with potentially lower standards and capacities in the service.[106] Furthermore, the public sentiment for gender integration and the Equal Rights Amendment was high, and the lack of victory in the Vietnam War indicated that new approaches for leadership in the military were necessary.[107]

Reactions to the amendment's passage were mixed. The *New York Times* reported that President Gerald Ford wanted "to think about it a little bit" before commenting. One of the most prominent military critics of the move was retired Army general Maxwell Taylor, who told the media that the entry of women would cause the service academies to turn qualified men away. "We might be turning away another Grant or Lee or Pershing or MacArthur," Maxwell exclaimed.[108] Many alumni feared the lowering of standards to accommodate women.[109] Annapolis's *Evening Capital* reported that midshipmen raised questions about women's ability to handle the physical regimen and hazing, while expressing concern over the possibility of lowered standards, the disappearance of the "fraternity atmosphere," and the development of "morality problems."[110] Some midshipmen predicted that "the Academy's reputation will go down," and another commented that "it's just going to ruin the image of this place. If I wanted to go to a coed college, I would have gone somewhere else." While one sophomore worried about "just what the girls are going to look like," other midshipmen supported the House's decision. A number of young men remarked on women having a place in the Navy and on Annapolis being an excellent place for leadership training. As one midshipman commented on the equal citizenship of women, the "Academy education is paid for with government money, and I don't think only males should take advantage of it."

Agreeing with these, Senator William Hathaway again proposed an amendment to a 6 June 1975 military procurement bill allowing women to enter the service academies.[111] When the matter came to the Senate floor the next day, there was no debate; a simple unanimous voice vote sufficed to indicate the Senate's opinion. The Naval Academy's public affairs officer, Robert Lewis, again raised the possibility of two curriculums, one for men and one for women, "unless Congress resolves this dilemma." Six weeks later, House and Senate leaders ironed out the final issues of the defense bill for 1976. It became clear that Congress would not address the combat issue but would opt for what historian John Lovell termed "relatively radical reform in permitting women's attendance at the military academies." After four years of personal struggle and congressional and judicial activity, women had finally achieved the right to attend service academies.

Kinnaird McKee became the new superintendent on 1 August 1975, and he quickly prepared for the seemingly impending arrival of women. Although administrators, officers, and staff throughout the Academy had roles in getting USNA ready, those with primary responsibilities included the commandant, the deans of admissions and academics, and the staffs of the Candidate Guidance, Physical Education, Public Works, and Public Affairs departments.[112] Public Affairs staff identified events likely to elicit great media attention, and Commandant D. K. Forbes began to study steps necessary for the integration of women.[113] Forbes indicated that "the Naval Academy can accommodate, through internal actions, the majority of the impacts created by the admission of women."[114] Academics would not change, and admissions, professional standards, and professional training and education would require only slight modifications for women's physical differences.[115] Similarly, those differences necessitated minor alterations to physical training and athletic requirements, a topic on the minds of university administrators nationwide in 1975; that year the federal government began implementation of the Title IX educational provisions related to women's athletics and the National Collegiate Athletic Association began to consider overseeing women's sports.[116] The most significant changes, Forbes deduced, would involve devising uniforms, altering housing, obtaining female officers and staff, and procuring items for the midshipmen's store, while the Navy itself would oversee changes involving finances, legal statutes, and admissions goals and recruiting.[117] McKee's legal staff concluded that the Naval Academy itself should attempt to maintain as much control over legal and admissions procedures as possible, and the superintendent then shared all of these findings with the Navy's leadership.[118]

Academy administrators spent the rest of the summer trying to work out solutions to these issues using McKee's guiding principle that "women will be fully integrated into the Brigade and will complete the same training, education, and physical programs that their male counterparts receive."[119] "Every effort," he stated, "will be made to ensure that there are no differences other than those dictated by [physiology]."[120] Chief of Naval Operations James Holloway III, in keeping with this philosophy, wanted the women to have uniforms that were "practical, but not completely defeminizing."[121] The Academy's chief medical officer even proposed that clinic staff be permitted to dispense contraceptive devices to women and, to be fair, to the men as well.[122] Public Affairs officers, seeking to present a positive and prepared perspective to outside observers, indicated their desire to be kept abreast of "all unusual incidents" relating to female midshipmen.[123] "The Navy," historian Judith Stiehm comments, "was determined that outsiders see the integration as a 'nonevent.' "[124]

A major issue that loomed on the planning horizon was what to do about summer training for women.[125] Forbes noted that summer training for men and women would by necessity diverge based on the legal prohibitions upon women serving aboard combat vessels.[126] Summers between the academic years traditionally provided midshipmen opportunities to see the Navy's various missions and activities firsthand, and since 1851 has involved time aboard ships. Women first served in the U.S. Navy during World War I, but only as enlisted personnel performing clerical, intelligence, medical translation, and other types of work on shore. When over 81,000 women served in World War II, they did so as both officers and enlisted personnel, but they were never aboard combatant vessels. By 1975, Title X, Section 6015, of the U.S. Code permitted women aboard Navy hospital ships and transports, but as Academy officials realized, the Navy no longer had these types of vessels.

Naval Academy leaders traveled to Colorado Springs for the Interservice Academies' Conference on the Admission of Women, held 8–9 September 1975.[127] A central focus of attention at the conference was on the experiences of the U.S. Merchant Marine Academy (USMMA) in Kings Point, New York, which began admitting women in 1974. While the conference was proceeding, the U.S. Coast Guard Academy (USCGA) was integrating its first class of women at its campus in New London, Connecticut. Both USMMA and USCGA were substantively different from the Naval Academy in that their focuses were not military: the Merchant Marine falls under the Department of Commerce, and the Coast Guard, which falls under Navy control in times of war, was a division of the Department of Transportation and now falls under the Department of Homeland Security. Although all three organizations are sea-oriented governmental agencies, and Merchant Marine Academy leaders reported no problems with men and women on board vessels together, USMMA and USCGA did not have to deal with the issue of including combat training in the creation of equal treatment for women. In spite of these differences, Annapolis leaders decided they could learn from these recent precedents.

Merchant Marine Academy representatives indicated that a "positive approach" to gender integration had served them well.[128] Academic aspects remained the same, and USMMA officials noted that women there were unquestionably competitive and were "adamant about wanting to participate in physical activities." Physical trainers had replaced the men's boxing and wrestling activities with a personal defense course but found that some women voluntarily boxed. Those trainers also found that they needed to have females on their staff for the benefit of both women and men. Keeping the doors of dormitory rooms open except when cadets were dressing was successful, but USMMA officials indicated that "the women will gain substantial weight" due to the diet at their institution. Among the major problems USMMA faced was the media. Initially, there were few problems, but with time the press's attention to the integration of women caused great resentment among the male and female cadets. Coast Guard officials apparently learned from that experience and decided to keep the media's attention to a minimum; as historian Judith Stiehm described it, the entry of women at USCGA was "quiet." In summation, one conference participant from Annapolis noted that "the Merchant Marine Academy believes that the academies should not single women out as a 'problem' nor attempt to convince the cadets that their integration will be a problem. The lessons learned by the Merchant Marine Academy prove that after the male cadets observe the capability of the woman cadet this situation will resolve itself."[129]

After the conference, Academy leaders began to address specific issues requiring action for the arrival of women. Commandant Forbes assembled what became an extensive list of officers' roles and a "log of justifications or logic" behind all proposals for changes in the Academy's operations and physical plant.[130] The proposed actions ranged from setting physical standards for female candidates, securing funds for modifying some men's bathrooms for women's use in Bancroft Hall, discussing policies on pregnancy and abortions, and creating locker room space for women in the Academy's various athletic facilities.[131] Dean of Admissions Robert McNitt also began preparing accommodations plans for women at the Naval Academy Preparatory School.[132] USNA and Navy leaders tried to determine the Academy's ideal number of women for its next entering class. Considering the Navy's needs and historical attrition rates for men at the Naval Academy, administrators decided to seek an entering group of seventy-six women.[133] Lastly, reflecting ideas from the Merchant Marine Academy, Superintendent McKee suggested that the Academy create a publicity approach that was "responsive to the press but [maintained] a 'low profile' on the admission of women."[134]

The official entry of women to the service academies became a reality on the evening of 8 October 1975 when President Gerald Ford signed Congress's "Defense Appropriation Authorization Act," known as "Public Law 94-106."[135] In part, the new law read that

the Secretaries of the military departments concerned shall take such action as may be necessary and appropriate to insure that (1) female individuals shall be eligible for appointment and admission to the service academy concerned, beginning with appointment to such academy for the class beginning in calendar year 1976, and (2) the academic and other relevant standards required for appointment (admissions), training, graduation, and commissioning of female individuals shall be the same except for those minimum essential adjustments in such standards required because of physiological differences between male and female individuals.[136]

The Academy immediately released public statements affirming its efforts to integrate women. USNA actions included the assignment of women officers to both the Commandant's and the Candidate Guidance offices, but because USNA officials' policy was for company officers to have warfare specialties, female officers would not serve in that capacity.[137] The administration also created the Midshipmen's Planning Review Group for Women at the U.S. Naval Academy, which consisted of class leaders from the classes of 1977 and 1978 and provided insight and feedback on issues such as training, facilities alterations, and uniform changes.[138] At the same time, a group of three midshipmen who were management majors monitored the impending changes as a class project.[139] Navy officials also took further steps to prepare the Naval Academy Preparatory School for women.[140]

On 9 October, Commandant Forbes ordered Captain W. J. Holland Jr., the head of the Professional Development Division, to read the new press release to the Brigade of Midshipmen at the commencement of lunch that day.[141] One alumnus recalled the scene inside of the mess hall:

> In those days, the Brigade was . . . more rambunctious in general, and . . . during football season there was a lot of cheering and . . . higher incidences of what I would call bad etiquette. I remember [the press release] being read. . . . There was certainly some hooting and hollering, and the noise level was pretty high. . . . And then the Brigade was called to attention for a prayer, and that quieted everybody down, and then "Seats," and then when you had "Seats," there was an ensuing discussion about it around all the tables. This is a pretty fundamental change in the way we do business around here. There were those who were vehemently against it, there were those who reserved their opinion for later, there were those who were oblivious to it. . . . There wasn't a pep rally, there wasn't a protest, there wasn't a food fight.[142]

The midshipmen needed, perhaps, some time to consider the substantive change that was about to take place. Within weeks, Captain Holland reported that the midshipmen involved with the Planning Review Group were "interested, enthusiastic, [and] favorably disposed to giving the women more than a 'fair break.' "[143] The LOG offered a wider variety of opinions. One midshipman writer, who had visited the State University of New York's Maritime College in New York City after the 1975 integration of women there, was extremely positive and argued that the women at Annapolis, like those at the Maritime College, wanted "to be treated like everyone else. They don't want any special privileges, they don't want to be mothered, and they don't want to be the objects of everyone's attention."[144] Another LOG writer lamented the end of "colorful expressions" in Bancroft Hall, believed local men with poor eyesight would be the most excited about the arrival of women, and predicted that the LOG magazine would be "the last bastion of male chauvinism."[145] Lastly, the LOG featured an interview with *Patton* actor George C. Scott, who lamented the arrival of women; Scott told the midshipmen that women coming to USNA "is tragic. . . . It will no doubt change, if not destroy, the image and idea that has been associated with all of the academies. It's really a shame."[146]

Internal investigations into midshipmen's ideas on the arrival of women yielded findings that did not differ substantially from what appeared in the LOG. Two informal surveys of midshipmen indicated that 72 to 80 percent of the male midshipmen did not believe women should be allowed into the Naval Academy, chiefly for reasons related to perceptions of lowered standards, women's incapacity for meeting Academy missions, and women's inability to serve in combat.[147] Such sentiments are not surprising among a student body composed of generally conservative young men who chose to prepare to be professional military officers at a prominent military institution.[148] As legal scholar Lucinda Peach has noted, military trainees are often "able to prove their masculinity by exhibiting aggression and other 'macho' characteristics." The mere "presence" of women in a military environment is, Peach argues, enough to challenge men's masculinity.[149] Furthermore, as alumna Tina Marie D'Ercole observed, part of the difficulty of the Naval Academy's gender integration was that it would be the first time many men dealt with women who were not relatives or girlfriends.[150]

Male midshipmen expressed a variety of opinions in the Academy's surveys.[151] One suggested that having female midshipmen was not cost-effective for USNA because women's athletic feats were comparable to fourteen-year-old boys' physical achievements. While some midshipmen reported that they and their peers were serious about their desire to make the transition a success and that they were prepared for the "challenge," others were more frank and humorous about their feelings. One young man was upset over not being allowed to "[wear] bathrobes all the time" in Bancroft Hall, and another remarked that "women belong here about as much as men belong in a brassiere factory." One midshipman, however, seemed particularly excited about the arrival of women. He exclaimed, "I want one for a roommate."

As 1975 came to a close, USNA administrators informed midshipmen about their plans for changes to life at USNA.[152] Academy leaders were especially determined to maintain solid communications with everyone at the Naval Academy, including members of the class of 1977 who were to be the midshipmen leaders when females became plebes.[153] The secretary of the

Navy's Advisory Board on Education and Training occasionally offered advice on the integration process.[154] Furthermore, to assist themselves with their planning, Academy leaders read management and psychology journals and participated in professional psychology conferences.[155] USNA leaders ultimately decided to hire a professional consultant on women. As Captain Holland noted, "I am now convinced that male officers of the backgrounds and experiences of those assigned the Brigade are utterly unprepared mentally and emotionally to lead women. Our base of experience as husbands, lovers, fathers, and brothers is totally inadequate because of its narrow base and scope. If we are to guide and assist the women as we do the men, some significant education and training is required."[156] Administrators chose Edith Seashore, a consultant who specialized in training and educating women in organizations, to help with the continued goal of assuring everyone inside and outside the Academy's walls that the institution was stable and that "nothing is going to change except the plumbing."[157] Seashore kept abreast of topics related to women in the military by attending meetings with, and leading tours for, the members of the Defense Advisory Committee on Women in the Service (DACOWITS), a thirty-member civilian group that advised the secretary of defense on issues relating to female servicewomen.[158] Seashore also gave courses to help prepare midshipmen and officers for women in their midst and established open communications with midshipmen to monitor the integration process.[159]

By the end of 1975, administrators were still plotting their strategies for obtaining women and integrating them into the Bancroft Hall environment. Over six hundred women had shown interest in becoming midshipmen, and Navy leaders slightly readjusted their numerical goal, based on Navy needs and speculated attrition, to eighty women for the class of 1980.[160] Administrators decided, therefore, that twenty-seven of the Brigade's thirty-six companies would have women, translating to three women in each of those companies.[161] Seashore helped develop the plan to have women from adjoining companies live in neighboring rooms as a means of providing "peer reinforcement and support," a concept behind the decision to have all women in a company assigned to the same squad.[162] Administrators decided to locate women's rooms in well-traveled areas of Bancroft Hall, clustered near bathrooms hastily changed to be of use to women, and to house none of the women on the building's "notorious" fourth deck, which officers noted was "extremely difficult to control/patrol" because of the floor's "relative isolation and inaccessibility."[163] Inside the dormitory, men were to knock on women's doors when closed, and doors would be kept open whenever men and women were together in a room.[164] Academy officials modified conduct regulations to prohibit the hanging of naked "girlie" pictures in rooms, dating between plebes and upperclassmen, flirting and solicitation of physical activities, and sexual activity.[165] They also reiterated the prohibition on public displays of affection. Lastly, the common practice of wearing "skivvies and slippers" as evening attire in Bancroft Hall ceased.[166]

Superintendent McKee spent the remaining days of 1975 addressing issues related to law, public relations, and communication with female applicants. With his Judge Advocate General officers, he gave further contemplation to having women on board ships for summer cruises and whether the congressional mandate on women implied that women must receive sea training (which would supersede the prohibition of women on combat vessels).[167] McKee appeared on television during halftime of the 1975 Army-Navy football game to explain the significant changes about to occur at USNA and to remind the public that the Academy was seeking women.[168] To the women who were applying, he included with the USNA catalogs sent to them a pamphlet in which Academy leaders wrote, "We're planning to change very little at the Naval Academy next year. Because, first and last, like all the rest, you'll be a *midshipman*. But it'll probably take a little getting used to. For all of us. We're looking forward to it."[169] Starting with resistance to the idea of women at Annapolis, impelled by changing attitudes toward women, sparked by the women's movement and legislative changes, the Naval Academy reluctantly responded and prepared to have female midshipmen in its ranks. In January 1976, the first Annapolis-bound women entered the Naval Academy Preparatory School. They and their female classmates at the Naval Academy were about to find out that the most challenging aspects of the struggle to integrate women into the Annapolis were yet to come. As historian John Lovell noted a short time later, "What is notable about Annapolis . . . is not the mere presence of attitudes of *machismo* among midshipmen, but rather the extent to which these attitudes were fostered by nearly all facets of the Academy environment."[170]

6

Revolutionary Change at Evolutionary Speed

Women in the Class of 1980

★ ★ ★ ★ ★ ★ ★ ★ ★ ★ ★ ★ ★ ★ ★ ★ ★ ★ ★

When three women, Janice Buxbaum, Amber Hernandez, and Lynn Vostbury, arrived at the Naval Academy Preparatory School (NAPS) in Newport, Rhode Island, in January 1976, they became the first female Napsters in the school's history.[1] Women's experiences at NAPS served as a forecast for what would later take place at Annapolis. The women attempted to integrate with the men, for example by shoveling snow along with their male colleagues, but this goal was thwarted by a regimental commander who ordered the men to treat the women "as if they were his daughters." As a result, men at the school began ignoring the women. Montel Williams, an African American midshipman-candidate who would later host a syndicated television talk show, felt that the silence was wrong, and he eventually spoke to and ate meals with the women.[2] His Caucasian colleague, Ron Rockwell, soon joined him. Janice Buxbaum recalled that other men then ignored Rockwell and Williams as well, although with time more men spoke with the women. Most, however, continued to say nothing to the women or made comments about females being out of place there. NAPS's yearbook later reported that "the first few days were chaotic ones, marked by complete confusion," but according to Buxbaum the first few months were, overall, "not too bad." This chapter follows the stories of these three women at NAPS and the first group of eighty-one women at the Naval Academy, exploring their experiences as midshipmen as well as the Academy's reaction to them.

Although Buxbaum told the media that women "fit in well" and that "the men are very helpful," life for the women at NAPS was in reality stressful as Buxbaum realized that she and the other women were "guinea pigs." Men were increasingly resentful that the women had arrived in January, thereby missing half of the NAPS school year. When women received the required nominations for USNA and some men did not, it reinforced the idea that women were stealing men's places at Annapolis. Negative comments then became increasingly common, and pranks, some potentially dangerous, began. When some of the midshipman-candidates discovered that one of the women was dating an African American colleague, they entered her room, stuffed a female uniform with paper, and then set it on fire. Buxbaum recalled that the incident was the first time she realized that "an individual woman's actions were going to turn into 'women's actions.'" The women, facing rising flames in the room, were forced to escape out of the window.

As fewer men got nominations, their frustration led to a second attack on the women. A group of men stabbed a female uniform, covered it with ketchup to resemble blood, and then hung it from the ceiling in a woman's room. Buxbaum became increasingly concerned, and she consulted a Preparatory School administrator. The officer informed her that Navy leaders had ordered him to "see what happened with no controls over the men," but as a result of the fire and the effigy hanging, he realized that he would have to take some protective steps. He dismissed ten men linked to the incidents.

Meanwhile, at Annapolis, Kinnaird McKee wrote to midshipmen, faculty, and staff in February to update them on administrative actions he and other administrators had taken during the first six months of 1976 to make the final arrangements for the arrival of women.[3] One topic McKee did not mention, but about which he and other administrators became aware, was a study of the 1969 integration of women at Yale University. As the *Wall Street Journal* reported, the study indicated that "to win acceptance from their male classmates, the Yale women affected masculine mannerisms: lower voices, athletic walks, and profane language."[4] As a result, Academy administrators began to consider how similar circumstances would play out in Annapolis.

Administrators' considerations centered on the question of how to support the femininity of female midshipmen while at the same time being certain that it did not stand in the way of women fulfilling their requirements as midshipmen. In April, the commandant ended the four-year-old custom of having a homecoming queen to avoid the "fixation on 'good looks.'"[5] Yet administrators displayed a somewhat inconsistent attitude by suggesting, in a report on the integration of women, that USNA could end the tradition of acquiring cheerleaders from outside of the Academy if female midshipmen with "a good appearance" were to come to USNA.[6] How female midshipmen should look became a pressing issue. In its Midshipmen Regulations, USNA officials ruled, for example, that women had to wear bathing suit tops while sunbathing and could have hair down to the tops of their uniforms' collars.[7]

The Academy even established a beauty salon for hairstyling.[8] USNA leaders sought "an attractive uniform that looked both sharp and 'feminine,'" as Elizabeth Lutes Hillman demonstrates in her study of service academy uniforms for women.[9] For the sake of efficiency, the women's uniforms mirrored both the male midshipmen's uniforms and the Navy's fleet uniforms for women, with a purse allowed for the carrying of "sanitary articles."[10] Hillman notes, too, that USNA "feminized" only the dress white uniforms; working blues, working whites, and full dress blues were the same for men and women.[11] Furthermore, women were allowed to wear "conservative cosmetics," including "moderate makeup and lipstick, faint eyeshadow, and light rouge . . . appropriate if generally unnoticeable in appearance."[12]

Officers also assessed plans dealing with athletics, maternity, and support for women. Conversations with sports experts at other institutions, studies of professional articles, and precedents at the Merchant Marine Academy led USNA athletics officials to decide not to allow women to participate in boxing, football, lacrosse, rugby, and wrestling.[13] One athletic coach explained a common concern: "What if women got hit in the breasts?" Instead of those sports, women participated in a self-defense course. Athletic officials ultimately substituted the flexed arm hang for pull-ups in the midshipmen's physical aptitude exam for women and also added an extra minute for them to run the Academy's obstacle course. Swimming requirements, however, were the same for women and men. After extensive and heated discussions about how to handle issues of paternity and maternity, Superintendent McKee decided that "each case will be examined on an individual basis" by the superintendent.[14] Administrators wanted to assist women by arranging sponsor parents for them in the Annapolis community. Acknowledging that women "will lack peer support more than the men," Captain Holland sought non-faculty and staff as sponsors to avoid the appearance of preferential treatment of the women.[15] Chaplains, also wanting to help women, replaced the word "man" in the Midshipman's Prayer.[16] Finally, in an apparent appeasement of midshipmen's complaints, Commandant Forbes allowed bathrobe wearing in Bancroft Hall to continue with the stipulation that "when wearing the bathrobe, it will be closed and proper underwear shall be worn."[17]

From the beginning of the plans for integrating women into the U.S. Naval Academy, officials knew that they wanted female officers on board in order to assist administrators and the female midshipmen.[18] Not only could female officers serve as advisors and role models for the young women, but they could also identify unanticipated problems and solutions for administrators. By the summer of 1976, Commandant Forbes had concluded that younger female officers were going to be "more utilitarian" for the Academy. Older female officers, he felt, were "obstructive . . . based on their own difficult experiences as junior officers in an unaccepting environment which existed ten or more years ago." Administrators pondered, then rejected, the idea of having female officers present at any time that male officers were counseling women midshipmen. The Academy decided not to permit women to serve as company officers because the combat exclusion prohibited them from having warfare specialties in the Navy and Marine Corps. Forbes did, however, expect to utilize female officers at USNA as a source of feedback on how the integration process progressed. In May 1976, he formed the Women Officers' Advisory Group, which would report directly to him.

Over six months earlier, the Academy's first female officer, Susan Stevens, arrived to serve as an assistant company officer.[19] Some of her colleagues found her to be "a pro" but demonstrated concern that she was too often singled out on account of her gender. One officer was irked that other officers, and even administrators, frequently swore, and then apologized, in front of her. When speaking with a male midshipman interviewing her for the LOG, Stevens was evenhanded in her responses. She warned about stereotyping the women who would soon be midshipmen. Some, Stevens posited, would take "kidding" without offense, and some would be upset: "It all depends on the individual," she insisted. "They aren't all going to be bionic women. . . . There will be a few super ones, some below average ones, and some right in the middle. That's the way it should be." Finally, when asked whether women seeking admission to Annapolis should have their heads examined, Stevens responded, "Let me put it this way. I think that anyone who comes here has to be a particularly motivated individual."

Early in 1976, however, it was unclear whether the Naval Academy could meet its goal of eighty qualified women for its first integrated class. Admissions Dean Robert McNitt reported in February that among the three hundred women with congressional nominations, only thirteen "were fully qualified primary candidates [who were] principals or top competitors among men and women in a district or state."[20] USNA officials worked diligently to increase the applicant pool substantially, and the next month they announced the names of the first seven women who would become midshipmen.[21] McNitt continued to select female candidates, and by April he informed the eighty-one women whose applications the Naval Academy accepted that they were members of the class of 1980.[22] The dean and Navy leaders had decided to select the women "on the same basis as men since they would be expected to undergo the same program at the Academy."[23] Blue and Gold officer ranks began to include women, and a variety of people, including admirals and alumni who had decidedly mixed emotions about women at USNA, began to write letters of recommendation for the young women.[24] One admiral, a 1921 graduate, wrote a letter on behalf of a female applicant that expressed the same unsettled yet pragmatic attitude to women entering USNA that administrators adopted. "Well, you jerks," the admiral wrote, "I can't believe you went and let women in our institution. You really screwed it up this time. I can't believe you did this, but if you're going to let them in there, I think you ought to let this one in."[25]

Female applicants were remarkably similar to men in their reasons for choosing to attend Annapolis.[26] Some of the women were daughters of USNA graduates or were from military families and therefore had early knowledge of, or familiarity with, the Academy. Other women joined because they were patriotic and wanted to serve their country. Lastly, some of the women were aware of the Naval Academy's reputation and wanted to take advantage of the educational opportunities and possibilities for a military career. Women were not, as some scholars have alleged, seeking to attend USNA simply to be "pioneers."[27] Rather, they were choosing to attend Annapolis for the same reasons as men.

As the admissions letters addressed to women went out and the inevitable change drew closer, male sentiments at the Naval Academy were still decidedly mixed. One of the LOG's comic strips, a spoof of Garry Trudeau's work entitled "Doonesbanana," addressed the men's ambivalent feelings. In one installment, a commentary on the notion that women would steal men's slots at the Academy, a female plebe arrives at USNA with an astronaut's helmet. When an officer questions her about the helmet, the plebe replies that her uncle "said all of us girls at the Academy would be taking up space."[28] In a second installment, an enthusiastic senior exclaims, "I can't wait to get a hold of my first plebe. Boy, I'll make a man of him!" Frightened, the midshipman discovers that his plebe is a woman.[29] Some Naval Academy administrators shared and understood such feelings.[30] As Edith Seashore, the Academy's advisor on women's integration, later commented, "Some male officers were not for the change. But their jobs depended on it, so any disagreement was kept to themselves."[31] Those officers, for instance, led an orientation for women in May 1976, sent special instructions to all of the women on "grooming and clothing," and worked out preparations for the anticipated "intense news media interest" that would accompany the women to Annapolis.[32] In reviewing the preparation process, Dean McNitt concluded that "the Naval Academy went about the entire approach with good faith and good will."[33]

After President Gerald Ford signed a defense appropriation bill on 8 October 1975 that included stipulations for women's entry into service academies, Naval Academy officials realized that the possibility of women coming to Annapolis would soon be a reality. Among the many reasons given by those who opposed this change was that women, who could not serve in combat, would waste valuable spaces at USNA that men, who could serve in combat, would ordinarily fill. One midshipman, a cartoonist for the LOG, captured this sentiment in this 9 May 1976 spoof of Garry Trudeau's famed "Doonesbury" comic strip. (U.S. Naval Academy Archives)

When the eighty-one women arrived for Induction Day on Tuesday, 6 July 1976, there were twelve television crews and 113 media representatives waiting to record the event.[34] In spite of the warnings from Merchant Marine Academy officials, USNA did little to minimize the press's intervention in what alumnae Sharon Hanley Disher labeled "the end of 131 years of tradition." No activity that day seemed off limits to the cameras: millions of newspaper readers around the world, for example, saw the image of one female midshipman's inoculations. Many male inductees were not pleased with the special attention the media gave their female counterparts, contributing to a sense of difference within the class that would last all four years. Naval Academy officials believed that the press coverage was "excessive" but were pleased that the reports, which appeared on the CBS and ABC evening news programs, were "evenhanded." The class of 1980's I-Day created the same reactions among the women as it has typically for all plebes: excitement, fear, sadness at saying goodbye to family members, and mental preparation for the experiences to come. The new commandant, James Winnefeld, was present, as was Dean McNitt, who, as was his custom, was on hand to greet many of the men and women. A compassionate leader, he remembered that he "looked at the women's arrival as a parent would. I felt responsible for helping them since I had been involved in choosing them."

Beyond the media, the most immediate issue the female plebes faced was that they seemed to stand out from their male counterparts.[35] When townspeople, tourists, and members of the press saw the women, they would point, as if at a curious sight, and ask, "Do you think she's one of them?" Ill-fitting plebe uniforms, generally called "white works" uniforms, further prevented women from blending in with their 1,218 male classmates. Upon receiving the uniforms, the women realized that their white outfits were tailored for men. One female midshipman recalled her squad leader who, frustrated over the ill-fit for women, ended up stapling her uniform to give it a proper appearance. A few women had difficulty carrying their suitcases into Bancroft Hall, causing squad leaders to order the male plebes to assist the women. Although the point was to give a lesson about helping their shipmates, some men got the immediate impression that the women were unprepared. Once inside the building, the women faced the same dilemma as most plebes: finding their rooms. But once they were finally in their rooms, as one woman recalled, she and her roommates said, "We made it this far. We can do the rest."

Perhaps the woman who most stood out both from the men and from her fellow female midshipmen was Janie Mines, the only African American woman in the class of 1980.[36] Uniforms presented Mines a particular problem: the Naval Academy had acquired only beige-colored panty hose, which she was forced to wear until USNA could obtain more appropriately toned stockings. Her female classmates speculated that Mines had to be having a particularly challenging and lonely plebe year. Mines later described her experiences in an article about the refuge and solace she found in a small chapel in Bancroft Hall, recounting that

on a hot July day in 1976, I was in the first class of women to enter the Naval Academy. I don't think any of us expected the greeting we received. To say that we were not welcome would be a huge understatement. We had intruded upon one of the last bastions of male sanctity. Over the years, I have come to understand, and even sympathize, with my male peers, but being a

19-year old African American female, the only one in the class, sympathy was not what I felt at the time. . . . My plebe year at the Academy was a difficult time. On a good day, I was referred to as a "double insult." The other women did not know quite what to make of me and they had their own problems. The feeling of isolation was unbearable at times.[37]

Academy officials did feel compelled to deal with certain issues affecting women. They began by sending midshipmen trainers to plebes' rooms to demonstrate the proper folding and storage of clothes. However, this necessitated the young men having to show the women how to fold their underwear and brassieres, an awkward situation that left the men flustered and the women laughing.[38] Captain Holland led a discussion about how women's menstrual cycles might be thrown off due to the rigors and stresses of plebe summer, following which the women watched feminine hygiene films that were thirty years old.[39] One of the films focused on the rumor than the use of tampons would deprive women of their virginity; as one woman remembered, "We were absolutely on the floor because we hadn't even heard that rumor. We didn't come from a generation that worried about that sort of thing."[40] A related issue was what women would do about storing their personal products. Although officials intended that women would carry purses for that reason, this was impractical, particularly given the athletic nature of plebe summer. As a result, Academy tailors sewed small pockets into the women's pants.[41]

Women faced further obstacles during plebe summer. They had earlier become aware of the presence of a female officer, Lieutenant Sue Stevens, who had modeled female uniforms for photographs in admissions publications. When the women actually met Stevens, they believed that she was "squared away," but they also understood that she was not going to be a good role model. Her method of dealing with the female plebes was to distance herself from them, thereby avoiding the impression of favoritism.[42] The uniforms Stevens modeled had problems, including skirts and shoes that made marching difficult.[43] As an officer reported, "The original black oxford uniform shoe had a 1 ½ inch heel. That fact, plus in a few cases, a poor initial fitting, caused blisters and sore ankles after the intensive drill training began."[44] Even after cobblers modified the heels to only one inch, walking problems persisted.[45] One woman was even forced to wear men's shoes because her feet were too large for the shoes the Academy had acquired for women.[46] Elizabeth Lutes Hillman explains that the problem was, primarily, the fault of administrators' "presumptions about appropriate footwear for women."[47] Another problem was, as Commandant Winnefeld explained, that some of the women were physically unprepared for the rigors of plebe summer's physical training.[48] One alumna cited the absence of proper physical preparation in her high school for the lack of strength and physical coordination that became obvious during plebe summer; however, she felt comforted that several men had not mastered all of the activities either.[49] Furthermore, since women and men lived next to one another during the summer, one woman remembered that a degree of bonding occurred between the male and female plebes in her company.[50]

The most significant event of the women's plebe summer, however, was what the women now refer to as the "Plebe Summer Mutiny."[51] Janice Buxbaum felt that her female classmates were distanced physically from one another, and that they might all benefit from a meeting to discuss their common experiences. She left notes for all of the other women to meet at a specified time and location and also mentioned her plan to a female officer. On the morning of the meeting, the officer of the deck informed her that her planned meeting "broke rules" against unlawful gatherings, but the gathering took place anyway. For three quarters of an hour, about fifty-five of the eighty-one women shared their stories in a room in Mitscher Hall. Buxbaum recalled that "ninety percent of the complaints were about women being the 'shitscreen,'" a USNA term for plebes who gain particular attention and scorn from the upper class; "this was simply because women stood out." Buxbaum explained that the remaining comments and complaints dealt with "emotional rape": male midshipmen making sexual remarks and being naked in front of the women in Bancroft Hall. She attempted to help the other women based upon her experiences at NAPS: "I tried to encourage the women to have a sense of humor, to defend themselves, and to avoid becoming friends with men who were going to talk shit behind their backs." The day after the meeting, the commandant summoned Buxbaum and warned her that the meeting could be considered a mutiny, and that she could be thrown out for "conspiracy." After she promised never to plan another meeting of the women, a serious dialogue developed between Buxbaum and Winnefeld that took the form of a weekly meeting to discuss women's issues. The women, however, never met again as a group while they were midshipmen.

By the end of plebe summer and the beginning of the 1976–77 academic year, seventy-five of the original eighty-one women remained.[52] As the upper class returned from their summer training and the fall semester got under way, women were still something of a novelty for a substantial portion of the Naval Academy community.[53] As one female midshipman later explained, "We were such an oddity and a tourist attraction" for the male midshipmen in Bancroft Hall.[54] Another woman recalled that men from around the Brigade would descend upon her company to "razz the women."[55] The male midshipmen were prone to comments about women's weight, looks, intelligence, appearance, sexual orientation, and being out of place at USNA, and they began to refer to women as "plebettes."[56] One woman posited that the men's insulting, "horrendous attitude" toward the female midshipmen was the result of consultant Edith Seashore and administrators using "overkill" when lecturing and warning the men about swearing in front of or abusing the women.[57] Or, as another woman guessed, all of the training might simply have made many of the men "indifferent" to the women's presence.[58]

There were, additionally, other sources of the men's bad attitudes. Clearly, the transition away from an all-male lifestyle changed the atmosphere with which the men had become comfortable.[59] The media's attention on the women, which continued well after the initial press coverage during Induction Day, also contributed to men's negative sentiments.[60] When a *Chicago Tribune* reporter used a female plebe's comments about being at USNA out of context, male midshipmen plastered the article all over the walls of Bancroft Hall.[61] The rest of the women learned to avoid the media from that point forward and to make only positive and vague statements, or to say "no comment," when forced to speak with journalists.[62] A third source of fuel for the male midshipmen's resentment was the Academy's own faculty, both civilian and military, who believed that women's integration was a "major social undertaking."[63] The faculty, by 1977, included twenty-eight women.[64] Some of the male faculty members were kind to the female midshipmen, even excited about their groundbreaking presence.[65] But others expressed different opinions.[66] One professor made comments about a woman's appearance in an athletic outfit, and another mentioned that women needed to be "concerned with their physical conditioning . . . [or else they] ended up looking like all the women at the Naval Academy: basketballs with arms and legs."[67] A third professor spent fifteen minutes of each class dwelling on the inability of women to box, asking repeatedly, "So it's not equal, is it?"[68] Another military officer chastised a midshipman for doing well on a quiz since she would never be able to use the information in the Navy.[69] In most cases, the professors uttered these comments in the presence of male midshipmen.

Some of those young men, however, did not see women as a problem and were willing to accept and interact with their female colleagues.[70] African American and Hispanic midshipmen, in particular, encouraged, befriended, and helped the women, likely due in part to their common association as "minorities."[71] Beginning with the class of 1980, which entered Annapolis in 1976, and in most classes since, the number of females in each entering class has been larger than the number of African Americans.[72] It was also African American midshipmen who monitored plebe activities and decided, as one alumna remembered, "when enough was enough."[73] Other men, particularly in the gender-integrated companies, were willing to be friends with the female midshipmen.[74] Maureen Foley later explained that "it was very easy to win [men] over just in a one-on-one friendship. But in groups, it was not socially acceptable to be overtly nice to the women."[75] USNA advisor Edith Seashore stated that men liked the females in their companies and seldom saw the women with whom they interacted as the "stereotype" attributed to them: the unqualified, unprepared, unsuccessful female midshipman.[76] Furthermore, researcher Kathleen Durning, who studied the women during their plebe year, discovered that "the men assigned to mixed-sex platoons or squads reported the most egalitarian attitudes. Those assigned to mixed companies, but not mixed platoons or squads, exhibited the most traditional attitudes, and all-male companies responded with intermediate attitudes."[77]

Women adapted and learned to deal with these relationship dynamics. If a female midshipman failed to meet expectations, other women developed great resentment toward her.[78] As Janice Buxbaum learned at NAPS, the men, in such situations, were prone to lump women together and so, as another female midshipman stated, one woman's actions could easily reflect poorly upon all of the women.[79] Some of the women chose to take a humorous attitude toward the men. Women quickly adapted to the frequency of seeing naked men who, while they dressed, failed to shut their doors.[80] "I would just make a joke of it," Pamela Wacek Svendsen explained. "I'd say, 'Well, there's nothing for me to see anyway.'"[81] Buxbaum coupled her humor with an "in-your-face attitude." When waist and neck zippers on women's bathing suits repeatedly rendered her unable to succeed at plebe "uniform races," during which plebes hurriedly changed from one uniform to another, Buxbaum chose to deal with the situation by arriving at one race topless. "There was never another uniform race in my company," she recalled.[82] One woman discovered that sanitary napkins were particularly useful for polishing shoes and belt buckles. But when midshipmen inspectors discovered a Brasso-covered sanitary napkin under a woman's sink, they were upset. As a result, the woman distributed sanitary napkins to the entire company for polishing purposes; Sandy Daniels remembered that "everyone had one under [their sink], so it was sort of like a major protest."[83] This episode underscored the possibility of women gaining a degree of acceptance within their own company.[84]

Some women found other means, such as athletics, through which to deal with men and garner their respect. One woman, for example, decided to exceed the men's physical standards as a means of showing the men that she was competitive.[85] The standards for women were much lower, an athletic coach explained, because "our expectations of what women could achieve were much lower."[86] Athletics turned out, however, to be a forum for women to show their talents to men, whether it was serving as a baseball manager, as one female midshipman did, or participating on a team.[87] Coach Dave Smalley, the first women's basketball coach, recalled that when the team began, there were neither uniforms nor a schedule. Most of the women had little previous experience with the sport, but with the women's persistence and Smalley's stress on basic fundamentals, the team achieved a 10–1 record against women at local colleges in its first year.[88] Sports in which men and women participated together offered opportunities for social interaction as well.[89] For example, female midshipmen who rowed crew, one of the Academy's most physically and mentally demanding sports, found time spent in Hubbard Hall, the crew boat house, to be beneficial.[90] In the boat house, one woman stated, "The guys, when they were there, kind of forgot they were midshipmen too. We could all sit around and have a kind of fraternity/sorority type deal."[91]

Dating, too, was an activity in which the female plebes interacted with male midshipmen.[92] One female midshipman explained that dating was a means by which some women could get along, and another alumna believed that dating was a quick way for women to be accepted by their male peers. In describing a midshipman that she dated as a plebe, a woman recalled that the young man was supportive of her efforts to maintain an ideal weight and a good appearance. Although some men would ostracize their peers who dated female midshipmen, such treatment did not, apparently, prohibit many of the young men from pursuing relationships. One woman calculated that all but five of the women midshipmen were dating upperclass members of the Brigade, in spite of prohibitions to the contrary. She further commented that some of her company mates would repeatedly ask her why she dated outside of the company, suggesting that they might be disappointed by their lack of interaction with her. In response, she quipped, "You jerks never ask me out."

Sexual activity was also a dimension of the interaction between some female and male midshipmen. Captain Holland had acknowledged the normality of sex between young adults but cautioned that "some limits must be placed on the time, location, and type of such activity to maintain propriety and a military professional environment."[93] The Academy set specific guidelines: there would be no sex, under penalty of discharge from USNA, anywhere on campus, and solicitation or improper behavior would result in demerits or dismissal.[94] Administrators also wanted the midshipmen to avoid "public displays of affection" while they were in uniform, but allowed handholding during liberty periods.[95] The Academy also set up courses and seminars to deal with issues involving fraternization, gender roles, and how certain behavior by women could be misunderstood as a sexual signals. The meaning of men's behavior, however, does not appear to have been the topic of much discussion.[96] Administrators' discussions and policies were continually directed at the women as if women were the problem; officials did not stop to consider that male midshipmen, faculty, and officers might be the root of gender issues at USNA. This approach likely reflected what historian Cynthia Enloe has identified as women's historical role in mending men's spirits, mentally and physically, so that men could engage in war-related activities.[97]

The extent of sexual activity that actually occurred at the Academy is difficult to gauge. A major but unsubstantiated allegation among the male midshipmen was that the women were using sex to achieve leadership positions, grades, and lessened punishments.[98] If women were using sex for a particular reason beyond normal sexual desire, some female midshipmen believed that it was more likely to be in the pursuit of acceptance within the Brigade environment.[99] Such a desire for acceptance and companionship may have contributed to a so-called "lesbian ring" that involved several female midshipmen on the basketball and volleyball teams and a female officer who served as an assistant basketball coach.[100] Female midshipmen discovered that any sexual relations they had would quickly become common knowledge.[101] For this reason, and due to fears of isolation and of greater scrutiny and attention, the women were unlikely to report any improper incidents or sexual misconduct on the part of their male colleagues.[102] While the women of 1980 were midshipmen, administrators noted five sexual misconduct cases, all of which involved alcohol.[103] Parents of subsequent female applicants, aware of the media attention to these "sex escapades," later questioned Academy officials about the prevalence of sex in Bancroft Hall.[104]

Male midshipmen boldly demonstrated their opinions of women during the 1976 football season. As a result of earlier administrative decisions, six female midshipmen joined six men on the Academy's cheerleading squad.[105] This represented the first time in USNA history that plebes led the upperclass in cheers at athletic events. Although the male cheerleaders were especially kind to the women, the remainder of the Brigade greeted and responded to the female cheerleaders with boos. One woman vividly recalled that she and other cheerleaders felt "victimized," particularly when the Brigade would yell "What's for morning meal?" and other questions normally reserved for plebes inside of Bancroft Hall.

The plebe year experiences of cheerleaders, and of the women of the class of 1980 as a whole, appeared to encourage a strong determination to succeed.[106] As a female graduate later recalled in an interview, "I got to a point where I had to finish, no matter what, no matter what happened or how terrible it was." Other women noted that they did not want to cry in front of the men or quit the Academy, thereby allowing the men to believe they were responsible for the women's reactions. This determination was evident in responses to the questionnaires researcher Kathleen Durning gave to class of 1980 midshipmen during the spring of 1977. Women made explicit their feelings that they belonged at USNA, that they should have the same career opportunities as men, and that they would perform well in combat if the Navy gave them that opportunity. Most male midshipmen, however, thought the Navy should train women elsewhere and that they themselves benefited little from having female classmates. Durning also found that the only men who seemed to accept women fully were those who were in integrated squads, platoons, and companies.

Even though they no doubt sensed these feelings, the women seemed undaunted. By the end of plebe year, one female midshipman noted a sense of satisfaction that she had finished the year and proven that women could succeed at Annapolis.[107] She and her female colleagues felt that they had earned their place at the Academy by the time their class prepared for its Herndon Monument climbing ceremony.[108] Although the purpose of the activity is to demonstrate class unity, male midshipmen failed to demonstrate a willingness to allow the women to participate fully. The men openly and symbolically defied their female classmates. When female midshipmen began to rise in the human pyramid, "there would be a hand that would all of a sudden come up and pull them down." As a woman later wrote, "We expected to be treated as plebes. When our class climbed Herndon, we expected to be accepted because, like the men, we had made it." However discouraging the ceremony might have been, the day concluded on a more positive note for one woman and her roommate. When they finished their meal at an Annapolis restaurant, a civilian patron who had noticed them paid for their dinner.[109]

That diner may have agreed with Commandant Winnefeld's statement that "I am personally very proud of our women midshipmen. They have done everything asked of them. They are pioneers who are weathering the combined rigors of plebe year and 'being the first' with grace, pluck, and even a sense of humor. There is a growing realization that the presence of women here is not going to ruin the U.S. Naval Academy, and in some ways gives it an added dimension!"[110]

Just after the conclusion of the plebe year, the female midshipmen set off on what became one of their most positive experiences at the Naval Academy, their third class summer cruise.[111] Although USNA and Navy officials had discussed possible changes to the combat laws excluding women from ships, no policy alteration resulted. Rather, the Academy decided that women, along with some men, would spend their third class cruise aboard the Academy's yard patrol crafts (YPs), cruising to various ports between Annapolis and Newport, Rhode Island. Initially, those men selected for these cruises and the women were upset because they would not be aboard fleet vessels; some midshipmen quickly labeled the YP cruise "The Love Boat." Once they were actually under way, however, almost all of the midshipmen had a positive experience as the women and men worked together, side by side. The cruises also allowed the female midshipmen to interact directly with the Navy's enlisted personnel and officers. Administrators concluded that the cruises were an exceptional success for the participating midshipmen, whose seamanship training was virtually identical to those aboard fleet vessels. For the women, it was a further step toward feeling accepted in the Brigade.

Such sentiments quickly ended, Maureen Foley later noted, "when we were back in the Bancroft Hall environment."[112] While the women may have anticipated the difficulty of their plebe experience, they had no such expectations about their youngster year.[113] The third class year is frequently a challenging one for midshipmen: they must adjust to life as a midshipman who is not a plebe, they are no longer the center of upperclass attention, they have only minor leadership roles, they have heavy academic loads, and by the end of the year, they must decide if they will commit to finishing their career at USNA.[114] Midshipmen who separate, or are separated, from USNA after their youngster year are under obligation to repay the cost of their education to the federal government; midshipmen who depart before the end of that year incur no such responsibility. While women in the class of 1980 were typical in this sense, they also faced a different dimension of difficulty as females. One woman later observed that "my impression was that the women were a lot easier to harass that second year." Because the constraints of the plebe system were no longer in effect, "it was open season" for the male midshipmen to say "I don't want you here, get out of my sight."[115]

No one sensed the harsh reality of youngster year more than the cheerleaders. Sharon Hanley Disher noted that the new academic year did little to change the male midshipmen's reactions to the female cheerleaders. "Whenever the home games turned boring," Disher has written, "the mids relentlessly turned on the cheerleaders, showering them with abuse from the stands."[116] The taunts were not tame, and included men yelling "Suck my cock!" During one home game, men took soda cans, filled only with the aluminum seal tabs for use as noisemakers, and pelted the female cheerleaders. Adding to the women's horror was the knowledge that male officers, the only persons present who could have stopped the insulting and potentially injurious attack, did nothing to end the barrage of cans. The officers merely stood and watched, leading some observers to wonder whether administrators or male midshipmen were running the Academy. The only factor preventing the women from quitting their role as cheerleaders was male athletes' personal appeals to continue their support.

Another substantial change during the 1977–78 school year was the arrival of a second class containing women. When USNA officials, believing the women would help their new colleagues, had asked the female midshipmen what they would tell the female plebes, the dominant response was "Don't come!"[117] And as the ninety new women began their lives at the Naval Academy, the women in the class of 1980 said a prayer for them and then kept their distance. Two women noted that they did not want to be "buddy-buddy" with the 1981 women because they "felt like they had to earn their place in the hierarchy." Similarly, another woman explained that "in a lot of cases it wasn't any easier [for the women in the class of 1981] because the upperclass women didn't make it any easier. There was some feeling in my class that, well, it was hard for me and nobody helped me, so these women will have to make it on their own. And that's sad . . . but I think it was sort of a natural reaction because it was so difficult for us that there was almost a resentment for the women coming in that they had it easier."[118] For two other female midshipmen, the fear "of being too protective of our fellow women" prevented them from reaching out to the plebes. Another female midshipman believed that her classmates "did not do much for the other women; we possibly made it harder on them. But we did not know how to help. We'd never been minorities before." Indeed, the tradition of Jewish midshipmen looking out for the first African American graduate, Wesley Brown, and minority midshipmen

As they had when they were plebes, women in the class of 1980 served as cheerleaders for the Brigade of Midshipmen during their third class, or sophomore, year. During football games, male midshipmen taunted and insulted the women with impunity and frequently with officers observing the antics. In this photograph, midshipman Tina Marie D'Ercole cheers during a game in the fall of 1977. (Courtesy of Tina Marie D'Ercole)

looking out for the women in the class of 1980 did not extend to the women in the class of 1981. The 1981 female midshipmen were fully aware of this situation, and as one alumna recalled, "We were pretty much out on our own." She further explained, however, that 1981's isolation led her and her classmates to feel "a responsibility to help those behind us." Later contemplating these women's experiences, Edith Seashore explained that the women in the class of 1980 were themselves "vulnerable" and concluded that their reactions to subsequent classes of women were not unusual "given the Naval Academy's strong institutional culture."

As women were aware by their third class year, that culture included some male midshipmen continually subjecting the women to a wide variety of antics ranging from seemingly harmless pranks to overtly cruel and disheartening abuses.[119] One woman described situations in which male midshipmen "set up a gal, have one guy pretend he likes her so they can go out on a date in town, and have all the other guys come along and laugh at her." Furthermore, as another female midshipman noted, "At night the 'wardens' all go home and the language gets a little 'raunchy,' and the Hall [gets] a little threatening." Male midshipmen had a particular affinity for throwing items, including pies, manicotti, and shaving cream "bombs" at the women. Women occasionally found dead rats in their mailboxes, and during meals might see pornographic drawings that men created in newly opened jars of peanut butter. Men spat upon women, and in one incident spat in a female midshipman's cover, or uniform hat. On occasions when women spoke in King Hall during meal announcements, male midshipmen would mock the women's high voices. Whenever a newspaper or magazine featured women from the class of 1980, or if men were able to take photographs of the women in compromising or embarrassing situations, the female midshipmen could expect to see their likenesses plastered on the walls of Bancroft Hall. Not long before the first women graduated, male midshipmen went to the Academy's obstacle course and painted some of the barriers and wooden structures, lowered for women, pink.

Words often spoke as loudly as these actions and could be particularly derisive.[120] Men were not shy about voicing their opinions on women's appearance, behavior, weight, and activities.[121] Such comments also appeared in the popular and satirical "Salty Sam" column of the LOG, as well as in other places in the magazine. "Salty," for example, complained about the "varsity fat squad," and John Wayne told a LOG writer that he thought that the whole concept of women at USNA was "ridiculous."[122] Male midshipmen made more explicit comments in what they called the "Hog Log," a notebook midshipmen on watch in Bancroft Hall's main office kept to record descriptions of the women, principally drags, who entered and departed the dormitory. The Hog Log's origins are unclear, but the tradition dates to at least 1970 and did not cease with the entry of women to USNA.[123] Among the terms used, verbally and in writing, for women, the term "WUBA" had the most derogatory insinuation. Originally the name of a uniform style, "Working Uniform Blue 'Alpha,'" men used "WUBA" to mean "Women with Unusually Big Asses" and "Women Used By All," references to exaggerated perceptions of women's weight and sexual promiscuity.[124]

Women's weight, aside from being a source of jokes and negative comments, was an issue of concern for the female midshipmen and for USNA administrators.[125] Edith Seashore reported in March 1977 that many of the women were gaining weight because their squad leaders insisted they eat during meals and because high-calorie food continued to dominate the meals in the mess hall. In spite of the rigorous physical and athletic regimens at Annapolis, the diet led to weight control issues for many of the women. A year later, Captain Richard Ustick revealed that weight, diet requirements, and food habits were still problems. One remedy was the creation of a "diet table" in the mess hall where lower-calorie items could be found, but because the diet table was located in a central, high-traffic area, any woman seeking food from it was subject to many male midshipmen's eyes and comments. The result of these concerns over weight and appearance in uniform, teamed with the stress of being in a male-dominated environment, was that many female midshipmen developed eating disorders.

Academy officials were not unaware of these problems.[126] Chaplains, who often serve as midshipmen's confidants, were fully aware of the pressures women faced.[127] One woman recounted a chaplain making a point about prejudice to a group of midshipmen and saying, "You know, it's just like when you guys walk in the Yard and see a woman and you say things to her like 'Get out of my Yard.'" "I almost fell on the floor," the woman explained, because "I didn't think anybody knew that except us."[128] The Academy's consultant, Edith Seashore, was also aware of these problems from her meetings with both the women and the men.[129] Women, however, seemed ambivalent about the gatherings, which usually turned in to "bitch sessions." Another woman also explained that officials "took all the [ideas we shared] in, but they didn't do anything with the information."[130]

Women found varying levels of support from officers around the Academy.[131] Commandant Winnefeld felt that female officers were important as role models, yet the female midshipmen felt that those officers, whom the

Navy had trained elsewhere, could little understand their unique situation.[132] By the fall of 1977, USNA assigned a female as a company officer, although she does not appear to have had substantial interaction with the women midshipmen. Another female officer, for example, gave advice on wearing lipstick and told the midshipmen that "you can go further with sugar than spice." Reactions and responses from male officers were decidedly mixed. Some refused to salute women, while others were completely indifferent to women's presence.[133] Winnefeld remarked that the most difficult situation he faced was with the company officers, who "were not completely behind the women." Seashore noted that company officers set the tone for the acceptance of women, and she recommended annually retraining all company officers on their roles. One officer who was highly supportive was a battalion officer who had been a POW in Vietnam; according to one female midshipman, he knew what "it was like to be set aside, to be picked on, to be persecuted. It helped out a lot that he was there."[134]

In August 1978, another POW from the Vietnam War, Admiral William Lawrence, assumed the leadership of the Naval Academy. Although Lawrence believed that Superintendent McKee was "really trying to make [the integration of women] work," he also noticed early in his own term as superintendent that, in his words, "there was subtle harassment of women. And it manifest itself in a lot of ways."[135] In addition to continuing Seashore's consultations, Lawrence gave Captain Richard Ustick, the head of Professional Development at USNA, the unofficial title of Dean of Women as an indication of his determination to see a smooth integration of women into the Brigade. Ustick, among other responsibilities, followed developments and achievements of women in the Navy in order to inform the female midshipmen about any potential changes to their career paths or legal status. Next, Superintendent Lawrence addressed each of the classes at the Academy and told them he would not tolerate undignified behavior toward the women; specifically, he addressed the issue of men who treated women well on an individual basis but harshly while with other men. In a meeting with midshipmen, he told the young men that "anybody that does something in a group that they wouldn't do individually is the ultimate coward as far as I am concerned."

Lawrence showed great interest in women's sports, which was quite apparent to the midshipmen.[136] As a female crew team member later told Superintendent Lawrence, "It always meant *so* much to me, as well as the team, when you would take the time to show a personal interest in our rowing success. Seeing you at the finish line was an incentive to pull a little harder." Lawrence began presenting an annual prize sword, in his name, to a female midshipman for "personal excellence" in athletics. His words on the issue provide an insight into his keen understanding of athletics and women's psychological needs; as Lawrence stated,

> I was a great advocate for establishing as many women's varsity sports as possible, because it wasn't [as] important to me that we have a great won-loss record as it was to have those sports. Because it was my perception that women here at the Academy, in an integrated living situation, professional situation, needed to have those opportunities [in which] they just inter-faced with women. And it's just the nature of the sexes. . . . I think, although you can have real good integration, they need those times when they're just with themselves. So women needed these opportunities just to be together as a group. And sports was the best mechanism for making that happen here at the Academy."[137]

It was quite clear that Lawrence was a strong supporter of women at the Naval Academy, although his personal support did little to effect real change in the male midshipmen's attitudes and behavior toward their female classmates.[138]

Women's relations with other female midshipmen continued to be complicated. Only mid-way through their plebe year, women from the class of 1980 indicated their desire for their rooms to be located well within their company areas, as opposed to Seashore's suggestion that the women live adjacent to women in neighboring companies.[139] Academy officials obliged. Roommates also presented a potential problem to many women. Because there were few female midshipmen within any one company, the women usually had no choice about with whom they would live; few opportunities existed for the resolution of personality conflicts. Dean McNitt contemplated arranging roommates in order to increase the chances for smooth living situations among the female midshipmen, but such formal interaction never fully developed. Rather, in situations of severe personality conflicts, and in cases where women quit, officials eventually allowed some women to switch companies and to room with other women.

The greatest challenge for women, however, remained their isolation and the absence of relationships between them and among the women as a group.[140] The plebe summer "mutiny" meant that the only significant female interaction took place between roommates, team members, or neighboring company-mates within Bancroft Hall. In cases where women did venture into other company areas to introduce themselves to their female colleagues, un-easiness prevailed. As one woman later explained, "I don't believe there was any camaraderie between the women in my class. . . . It was competitive and we made every effort to be accepted. . . . There was a lot of jealousy between the women." "Black midshipmen," another woman concluded, "survive because they stick together, but women did not follow them." Female midshipmen were essentially concerned for their individual acceptance among their male colleagues, and the mere presence of another woman might make the female midshipmen the subject of their male counterparts' negative attention.

One aspect of the women's preparation at USNA that improved with time was summer training.[141] During the summer of 1978, female midshipmen went for Marine training at Quantico, Virginia, and were fully integrated with male midshipmen for their experiences there. While men went for submarine training, which was still prohibited for women, some female midshipmen served aboard ships and interacted with the crews. Other women observed shore operations, and during both of these activities, women learned about the career paths that were available to them. Prior to their senior year, some women also got to participate at the Academy as plebe detailers and as trainers at NAPS. Also in 1978, Congress altered the U.S. Code's Title X provisions to allow women to serve aboard ships that were not expected to be in combat for training. USNA administrators understood the benefits of getting the women aboard Navy ships; with Navy officials, they arranged for female officers to be assigned to all vessels with women from Annapolis and for training of crews with no prior female officers in their ranks. Furthermore, Academy officials assigned women to ships, including cruisers, destroyers, and helicopter assault ships, the first women on such Navy vessels, and made certain the women would have separate berthing space from the men. The women appreciated at-sea training because it helped to reduce the differences between them and their male classmates and allowed them to interact with Navy personnel. As one female midshipman later reported, "The most rewarding experience was having a crusty old chief tell me that I'd make a 'damn fine officer.' "

As the class of 1980 neared the end of their second class year, the women anticipated that their level of acceptance within the Brigade of Midshipmen might finally be solidifying.[142] Beth Leadbetter, a member of the class of 1980, noted that regulations permitted her and her classmates to wear civilian clothes as 2/C, and that such an opportunity helped give women a greater degree of acceptance within the Brigade.[143] The women's preparations for their Ring Dance, however, once again reminded them that their status was atypical.[144] At all previous dances, the female midshipmen felt out of place in their uniforms while their male counterparts entertained civilian women in dresses. The maintenance of femininity was a difficult task at USNA, where women wore generally defeminizing uniforms, faced less-than-desirable haircuts, and avoided the time and reactions make-up would entail. As usual, women were in their uniforms for the Ring Dance, but USNA officials stated that the female midshipmen, unlike the men's dates, could not wear corsages or wear the class rings around their necks, as the dates did. One woman recalled her female classmates' reactions: "Kind of as a group, no real talking about [it], but just one by one, you'd see a gal pinning a corsage or putting the ring around their neck. One by one, we all started doing it, and [said], 'Now you tell me to take it off. . . . This is my Ring Dance, this is what is supposed to happen, and I'm going to do it.' "

By the time the ceremonies of the Ring Dance began, the female midshipmen were aware that the soon-to-graduate class of 1979 wanted to distinguish itself as the final class to be exclusively male.[145] The men of 1979 had adopted, as their motto, "Omnes Viri," the Latin term for "all male," a phrase that appears on the class members' rings. Rumors abounded about some members of the last all-male class inscribing their rings, and printing t-shirts, with the acronym "LCWBOH," meaning "Last Class With Balls On Herndon." Further attempting to emphasize the absence of women from their midst, the class of 1979 wanted to revive a tradition dormant since 1963: a class sweetheart. Shortly before the class's graduation ceremonies, Superintendent Lawrence discovered plans more obvious than t-shirts and sweethearts. "The word got back to me," he later disclosed, "that the class of '79 was contemplating, when they threw up their hats at graduation, they were going to have ping pong balls in their hats that go up—the last class with balls." Lawrence immediately addressed the class and informed them that following through with their plan would "put a stigma on your class that might take you years to overcome."[146] The Superintendent was relieved "when those hats went up at graduation. . . . I was holding my breath, but there were no ping pong balls there."

After all of the statements that the class of 1979 sought to make about its place in Naval Academy history, its *Lucky Bag* closed with a moderate statement. Editor Grant Thornton wrote that "the subject of women at the Naval Academy is a tricky one these days, and when I have dealt with it, I have tried to show that when you get right down to brass tacks, it is not the problem that the media is trying to make of it. Society changes, and so must we."[147] That other midshipmen did not share Thornton's position became vividly apparent during the fall of 1979 when the women in the class of 1980 had, at long last, become first classmen. At the end of October, Admiral Thomas Hayward, the chief of Naval operations, delivered the Forrestal Lecture.[148] Finishing his closing remarks, Hayward accepted questions from midshipmen, one of whom was female. Hoping for a statement on women in combat, she asked if the admiral perceived the need to draft men and women in the near future, to which midshipmen responded with a wave of boos. Heyward responded, "Let me duck the question . . . because I don't think we'll have to do either." The CNO shared his opinions and ideas about several other midshipmen's questions, including his disapproval of midshipmen graduating and becoming doctors and dentists; all midshipmen should be headed, he argued, in the direction of combat service. His comments elicited a question from a second woman, a member of the class of 1982, who, continuing the first woman's point, wanted to know why, then, the commissions of the women in the class of 1980 would be only in fields such as engineering, intelligence, and public relations. Because of combat restrictions, the women did not have warfare specialties and the Navy referred to them as "General Unrestricted Line Officers," or by the unfortunate acronym "GURL." Amid the midshipmen's laughter, Admiral Hayward reluctantly began to answer that there were "differences" between these fields, but then suddenly quipped, "Are you saying that women don't belong at the Naval Academy?" Pandemonium erupted in the audience, and the chief of Naval operations, unable to silence the Brigade, left the stage.

Within days, the women of the class of 1980 got a clearer indication of the sentiments toward them. Women returning to Bancroft Hall one day discovered their male colleagues attaching copies of a *Washingtonian* magazine article to the walls of the dormitory.[149] In an article he entitled "Women Can't Fight," 1968 graduate James Webb gave voice to many male alumni's opinion that women's presence at Annapolis was improper. Webb had come back to Annapolis in 1979 to spend three semesters as a teacher and writer-in-residence. After one semester, however, Webb left. During that one semester, faculty in the English Department, where Webb worked, noticed that Webb "always had midshipmen coming and going." Shortly after he left, Webb wrote the Superintendent to indicate that an article that "may appear a little controversial" was in the works.

"Women Can't Fight," however, was more than just slightly controversial.[150] Webb opened with the declaration that "it was really tough in combat in Nam," and argued that "no benefit to anyone can come from women serving in combat." Therefore, he saw no reason for women at the Naval Academy because women's "presence at institutions dedicated to the preparation of men for combat command is poisoning that preparation" and turning the military into "a test tube for social experimentation." Webb contradicted Navy leaders who, in 1976, had declared that they viewed "the admission and training of women at Annapolis as part of its mission and not as an experiment." The bulk of Webb's article was based on conversations with "hundreds" of male and female midshipmen. After a long diatribe in which he lamented the cessation of abusive plebe training, Webb claimed that the arrival of women changed USNA irreparably. Webb argued that female leaders arrived at their positions differently than the men did; that women could, at best, manage rather than lead; that the highest-ranking female had that status merely for political reasons; that sex was "commonplace in Bancroft Hall"; that the Academy was, because of the large number of men, "a horny woman's dream"; and, lastly, that reporters' remarks that the gender integration of USNA was "working" were flawed due to the shallowness of the journalists' observations. About the female midshipmen, Webb wrote, "They are for the most part delightful women, trusting and ambitious and capable in many ways, and I admire them, more for who they are than for what they are doing. . . . It would be unfair not to mention that no other group of women in the country has undergone such a prolonged regimen, however watered down."

It is doubtful that any of the women in the class of 1980 believed that their complex and difficult experience at the Naval Academy was "watered down."[151] As one female midshipman explained, "I was extremely offended because of the fact that we'd worked so hard and we were starting to make inroads, I felt, to being accepted." She and another woman saw Webb as an outsider, giving further credence and "ammunition" to those midshipmen who disliked the presence of women. The female midshipmen were outraged. One was "furious," a third woman was "disappointed," and a fourth felt "shame." A fifth woman, in reference to "that freaking article," shared her belief that "I just felt it was really more an axe to grind for him rather than a well-written substantiated article." Retired USNA professor Paul Roush was less restrained, calling the article "the single greatest purveyor of degradation and humiliation on the basis of one's gender that academy women have had to endure." Webb's arguments, ironically, completely ignored the psychological combat through which the women in the class of 1980 had lived.[152]

When Webb initially informed the superintendent about the planned article, Admiral Lawrence told Webb that the Academy could "handle it."[153] But Lawrence never suspected the article to be, as he later described it, "sensationalistic" and a "misrepresentation of the facts." Due to his great concern for the female midshipmen, Lawrence immediately understood the negative implications for the women and on the institution as a whole, a conclusion confirmed when librarians told him of the many requests for the article from male midshipmen. "It really was very demoralizing to women here," Lawrence later told an interviewer. For example, one direct impact was to help inspire the same anti-female sentiments among the underclassmen and the men in the class of 1980 that men in the earlier all-male classes had expressed. Although Lawrence wrote a rebuttal, completely supportive of female midshipman, in a later edition of the *Washingtonian*, the damage had been done. Women completed the remaining months of their Academy experience under the same stresses, criticisms, and mockery that had characterized their previous three-and-a-half years as midshipmen.

Among the lingering difficulties was the female midshipmen's feeling that when they were in positions of leadership, or asserted their leadership skills, their male colleagues did not take them seriously.[154] During their youngster year, when one female midshipman attempted to lead several plebes into the mess hall, her male company mates undermined her authority by ordering the plebes to ignore her. As the women became first classmen, Academy officials believed that some women would be leaders like men, whereas others would lead in "a female manner," and therefore administrators created several classes to address this issue. Naval Leadership 303, for example, presented midshipmen with an overview of different approaches to leadership. Such administrative actions did not, however, stop many midshipmen from later believing that the women USNA officials chose as senior leaders were in those positions for reasons of political expediency. Outside observers did not share that assessment. Board of Visitors members praised one female midshipman, a five-striper, after she addressed them. Superintendent Lawrence, too, believed that women were "performing effectively in leadership roles" during their senior year.

As the first graduation ceremony to include women approached, the media reported midshipmen's and administrators' thoughts about the occasion and the previous four years.[155] Several men in the class of 1980 confessed that they still resented the attention their female classmates received, and Edith Seashore indicated that men still differentiated between the women with whom they worked and interacted and the "other" female midshipmen to whom they were opposed. The women acknowledged their limited acceptance in the Academy environment. A female midshipman told reporters that "you still have to prove yourself to [the men] but not as much," and another woman said that "in any group of 4,300 men you're going to have some resistance and some prejudice. The big thing is that the novelty is over." The Academy gave the women specialized career counseling and, looking toward the future, a senior optimistically told the *New York Times* that "I'll be thankful when [men]

After the commandant termed the meeting that Janice Buxbaum arranged for women in the class of 1980 a "mutiny," the women never again met as a group while they were midshipmen. After their graduation ceremony on 28 May 1980, thirty-one of the fifty-five women, newly commissioned Navy ensigns, posed for this photograph at the Navy–Marine Corps Memorial Stadium.

Front row: Sandra Irwin, Rebecca Olds, Beth Leadbetter, Elizabeth Sternaman, Elizabeth Durham, Maureen Foley, Jill Hawkins, Paula Smith, Barbara Morris.

Middle row: Tina Mare D'Ercole, Nancy Burke, Pamela Wacek, Janet Kjotovsky, Cheryl Spohnholtz, Beth Lindquist, Barbara Geraghty, Karrie Kline, Barbette Henry, Marjorie Morley, Janice Buxbaum, Kathleen Henderson.

Back row: Robin Druce, Kathy Shanebrook, Claire Sebrechts, Crystal Lewis, Susan Presto, Susan Keller, Kathleen Walsh, Patricia Taylor, Lynn Ramp, Suzanne Grubbs. (Courtesy of Tina Marie D'Ercole)

find out we're really no different." Superintendent Lawrence concluded that "the integration of women has been completely successful. We see no discernible difference between men's and women's performance in any area of the Academy's program." Indeed, Lawrence noted women's proficiency in marching. Furthermore, women had statistically fewer demerits and higher conduct grades than men.

The long-anticipated Commissioning Week began on 23 May 1980, and was filled with the typical ceremonies and traditions that characterized previous graduations.[156] One event, the annual tradition of seniors jumping into pools, frightened some of the women. As one woman later explained, the usually lighthearted nature of the event involved some men "splashing us and holding us under the water. No joking around kind of stuff. Like you could tell that they were being serious." That outcome, along with the massive media onslaught, raised a degree of defensiveness, amid the thrills of finally being done, for female seniors. Just before the graduation ceremony, in the Navy–Marine Corps Memorial Stadium on 28 May, most of the fifty-five female graduates decided not to be a part of a group photograph of the women. Sharon Hanley Disher wrote that "there was no way [some women were] going to be part of this group segregating themselves from the guys the last day they would all be together. [They] didn't want that to be one of the last impressions the guys had of them." In his keynote speech, Chief of Naval Operations Hayward, aware of the novel nature of the day, told the midshipmen, officers, and families gathered that "some of you are puzzling why I haven't made a big thing about this being the first class ever to count women among its graduates. It seems to me it's about time we stop making firsts out of these young women. I am confident they're tired of it. They have met the test. . . . They have earned just as smart a salute and just as much respect as any other graduate."[157] After the speech, Elizabeth Belzer, whose class rank was 30 among the 938 seniors, was the first woman to walk across the stage and receive her diploma. After the graduates received their commissions, the women waited for the final act of their career as midshipmen: the celebratory tossing of caps into the air. But in one final statement of defiance toward their female classmates, the men waited three seconds after the women to throw their caps . Supportive of women yet tolerant of the male midshipmen, Academy officials never took those men to task for the action. The event contradicted hypotheses that men, with long-term exposure to their female classmates, would eventually tend to accept those women, and it left open the question of how successful the integration of women into the Brigade of Midshipmen really had been.

7 A New Mystique

Women at the Naval Academy since 1980

★ ★ ★ ★ ★ ★ ★ ★ ★ ★ ★ ★ ★ ★ ★ ★ ★ ★ ★

About six months after the first graduation ceremonies to include females, Superintendent William Lawrence told Kathy Slevin that "you and your fellow women in the Class of 1980 can be immensely proud of your achievements at the Academy. I know there were many frustrations and occasional unpleasantness, but you fully proved the soundness of admitting women to the Academy. Further, you made it easier for the women who followed in succeeding classes."[1] Lawrence, like other USNA officials, believed that "once the pioneer group of women graduates, the progress of integration will accelerate to an even higher level of success and become a very routine experience."[2] Captain Richard Ustick, head of USNA Professional Development, reported in 1979 that "a description of difficulties encountered by the Class of '80 is often not understood by the Class of '82, which has had an entirely different immersion in the predominantly male environment. We interpret this as a positive indication of the success of our program."[3] By that same year, women appeared in an abundance of photographs in the Academy's catalog and visitors' brochures. These illustrations made the point that women were present but, as Beth Leadbetter pointed out, they also gave the impression that "the sexes had a one-on-one ratio."[4] Although the percentages of female and male midshipmen have never reached parity, the number of women attending the Naval Academy has increased since the women of 1980 graduated. Yet, in spite of these increasing numbers of female midshipmen and the greater distance separating them from the women in the class of 1980, the experiences of recent female midshipmen demonstrate remarkable similarity to those of the first female graduates. This chapter explores those experiences and similarities.

In fact, the experiences of the second class with women during the 1980–

1981 academic year did not seem much of a departure from those of the first women at Annapolis. Wendy Lawrence, a Brigade leader, remarked that there was a marked increase in women being "the butt of some very cruel and crude jokes. . . . Hardly a day goes by," she noted, "without my hearing the word 'WUBA' and seldom is it in referring to the uniform." Lawrence saw this as an indication of lack of respect, an observation shared by F. R. Donovan, the new head of Professional Development.[5] Donovan noted a trend toward "unwarranted 'pot shots' taken at women and other minorities" on posters hung around Bancroft Hall and in the LOG and requested that in the future an officer should more closely screen the magazine "for objectionable material."[6] The officer who began to oversee the LOG was USNA's new commandant, Leon Edney, who told the LOG staff that he would not accept humor that "cut on women" or use of the term "WUBA" in the publication.[7] As the spring semester began, newspapers covered the story of a film depicting a female midshipman and four of her male counterparts engaging in sexual activities.[8] A Naval Academy calendar, which contained cartoons mocking women, also raised concerns with the public.[9] This negative publicity compounded Edney's decision to list as one of his goals for the following academic year, "Continue positive emphasis in area of Brigade attitude toward women."[10]

When Superintendent Lawrence departed USNA in the summer of 1981, his policy of considering the head of the Division of Professional Development as the Dean of Women ceased.[11] As historian Sue Guenter-Schlesinger has argued, "One problem for the notion that top leadership can influence culture is that military leadership typically lacks continuity, with usual assignment rotation patterns of less than three years. This presents a challenge for those selected leaders to strongly enforce policy against sexual harassment and inhibits them from having a lasting impact."[12] However, Edney did maintain the spirit of Ustick and Seashore's earlier calls for the administration to maintain support structures for women and "keep pressure on the [USNA] environment to make the integration effort work."[13] He later recalled, "I spent a lot of time convincing midshipmen and alumni that women belonged here." A supporter of women's athletics, he oversaw the development and implementation of a women's health care program that began in 1982. The program's first two phases covered professional and personal appearance issues, while the third phase examined dieting and weight control. The final two phases addressed weight training, physical fitness, sexual harassment, and assertiveness. Edney noted that preparatory discussions with Professional Development staff and company officers "generated many suggestions to improve the quality of life for female midshipmen," including the increased availability of personal hygiene products.

By 1984, it was clear that attitudes about women at USNA were still unresolved. On 23 February, James Webb returned to the Naval Academy to speak to the Semper Fidelis Club. His mere presence led to much discussion and joking among the male midshipmen, effectively reviving Webb's ideas in "Women Can't Fight."[14] In April, opponents of women's presence complained of double standards when USNA superintendent Charles Larson decided to grant a medical waiver to a female midshipman who, because of a diagnosed fear of heights, could not complete the requirement of jumping off of a 34-foot-high diving board into a swimming pool.[15] Weeks later, the Academy announced the resignation of a midshipman who became pregnant, and another midshipman told the *Washington Post* that "people have sex here [at USNA]."[16] Many of the scenarios predicted by skeptics opposed to women at USNA appeared to be playing out.

The situation for women at Annapolis appeared much better when Kristin Holdereid became the class of 1984's top graduate, the first woman to achieve that accomplishment at any of the military academies.[17] Earning an extremely high grade point average and accruing no demerits, Holdereid publicly addressed questions about whether women belonged at the Academy. She told the media that "there will always be some diehards who say women don't belong." In an issue of the LOG, which editors based entirely on *Playboy* and called *Playmid*, Edney's replacement, Commandant Leslie Palmer, rejected claims that there was political pressure to see female midshipmen succeed or give them top leadership roles. "On the other hand," he stated,

> I would think that because we do have women here, and we are trying desperately to have them accepted as being part of the Brigade, which by law they are supposed to be, there would be some effort to make sure they are represented in the striper organization. I think you also have to show the women that are doing well that they can be a high-ranking midshipman striper. But I don't really know what went into the selection process. I'd like to think it was on merit, and from what [I've seen] of female midshipmen who have been in striper positions, that's exactly what it is.[18]

During the next academic year, administrators repeated their intention to integrate women into the Brigade. As part of his goals for the 1984–85 school year, Larson sought to eliminate plebe/upperclass fraternization (and thus the sexual harassment and misconduct it often brought about) and to "increase Brigade-wide acceptance of women as the natural and right thing to do."[19] Palmer, following that lead, created an advisory group to warn him of potential problems to allow for appropriate resolutions; as he told another officer, "One of the first areas of examination [should be the] acceptance of women in the Navy. I consider women at the Academy in this context."[20]

Dean McNitt believed that increasing the number of women at USNA would be a benefit for female midshipmen, strengthening their participation in Academy activities and boosting their acceptance by men. When he suggested steps to that end in 1985, he noted that Annapolis had a total of 319 enrolled females, 169 fewer than West Point and 217 fewer than Colorado Springs. He believed that there were as many as thirty more women that USNA could have accepted into the class of 1985's 113 women but that the "current limitations on availability of 'meaningful' women's billets" was an impediment.[21] The Academy's new commandant, Stephen Chadwick, believed that a further hurdle was the Navy's own leadership, who might perceive an increase in admissions of women as a decrease in "prospective surface warriors and aviators."[22] Administrators heeded Dean McNitt's advice, and, as seen in the table below, the class of 1989 included 138 women. At the end of 1985, Chadwick noted that while women made up only 7 percent of the Brigade, "they tend to contribute by a greater percentage in both leadership and extracurricular roles—62 percent are in varsity athletics." Female midshipmen, he noted, "are not only holding their own, but proving themselves as individuals to their male counterparts."[23]

Features in the LOG in 1986 and 1987 showed, however, that Chadwick's assessment was, perhaps, optimistic. Although the LOG staff showed equal opportunity sexism by including a revealing photograph of midshipman Robert Monroe, a water polo player, wearing only his bathing suit, three months earlier, "Salty Sam" reported two incidents of male midshipmen watching their female counterparts shower through the windows of Bancroft Hall.[24] A Navy wife, Mary Evert, complained about the magazine's treatment of women, arguing that "The LOG personifies a sick, dated attitude shared by far too many in the Yard and in the Navy . . . about the 'place' of women at the Academy."[25] Superintendent Ronald Marryott, who succeeded Larson in 1986, apologized, explaining both the magazine's tradition at USNA and his regret that, in spite of officer oversight, "inappropriate material" occasionally made its way into print.[26]

Within a week of Marryott's 1987 expression of concern for the content of the LOG, James Webb, the author of 1979's "Women Can't Fight," was being interviewed in a congressional inquiry about his suitability for becoming the secretary of the Navy. Senators drilled Ronald Reagan's nominee about his attitudes toward women in the Navy in light of "Women Can't Fight." Webb responded that "the question is no longer should they be admitted, but how should they be trained. I believe the service academies no longer exist purely to graduate combat leaders. I accept that. It's history."[27] Webb then claimed that he was "not really sure any more" about his objection to women at the Naval Academy.[28] Three days later, the Senate approved Webb's nomination.[29] Some female graduates of the class of 1980 were infuriated by Webb's ascent to power, and several of them wrote letters to senators to dissuade them from conferring Webb.[30] On the day of Webb's swearing-in ceremony, female midshipmen covered trees in Tecumseh Court with their undergarments. As Robert Timberg later wrote, it was "a taunting declaration by the women of the brigade that they were at Annapolis to stay."[31]

In 1986, Naval Academy leaders took formal steps to study and analyze the position of women in the Annapolis environment. USNA began to participate in Corbin Seminars, annual conferences to study women in service academies that West Point and the Air Force Academy had held for several years. Late that year, Marryott convened a formal organization, the Women Midshipmen Study Group (WMSG), to assess the progress of women during their first decade at USNA.[32] The organization consisted of USNA officials, including the director of Candidate Guidance and Commander Marsha Evans, who was the Academy's first female battalion officer.[33] In November 1987, the group published its findings, based on statistics and interviews with various members of the Naval Academy community, and concluded that

> the bottom line when looking over the performance of women in the eleven years they have been part of the Brigade of Midshipmen is that they have done well in the Naval Academy's five areas of excellence: academics, military and leadership training, physical education and athletics, conduct, and honor. Their attrition rate is well below the national average, and lower than the other service academies. While problems do exist, they are being identified and addressed. The administration, faculty, and staff of the Naval Academy are committed to continue the assimilation of women midshipmen as valued, contributing members of the Brigade.[34]

Among the "problems" to which WMSG referred was the lower performance of women during their first two years at USNA. However, during their last two years, the women were outperforming men, leading to WMSG's

TABLE 2. Statistics on Female Midshipmen at USNA

Graduating Class	Women at NAPS	Women at USNA	Total at USNA	Women as % of Class	Women Graduated	Total Graduated	% of Female Attrition	% of Total Attrition
1976	3	0	1,324	0	0	832	0	37.2
1977	7	0	1,445	0	0	967	0	33.1
1978	4	0	1,522	0	0	986	0	35.2
1979	8	0	1,334	0	0	934	0	30
1980	9	81	1,294	6.25	55	947	32.1	26.9
1981	12	90	1,328	6.77	60	966	33.3	27.3
1982	unknown	96	1,364	7.03	63	1,048	34.4	23.2
1983	10	90	1,404	6.4	53	1,081	41.1	23.3
1984	14	100	1,249	8	63	1,004	37	19.6
1985	14	109	1,331	8.2	76	1,010	30.3	21.6
1986	15	97	1,333	7.27	65	1,049	33	22.9
1987	23	111	1,360	8.14	70	1,050	36.9	23.8
1988	23	113	1,366	8.32	80	1,061	29.2	22.4
1989	19	138	1,390	10.02	94	1,076	32.9	22.2
1990	22	143	1,374	10.49	98	1,008	31.5	26.6
1991	37	119	1,312	9.04	81	950	31.9	27.6
1992	34	147	1,365	10.89	96	1,027	35.6	24.1

1993	unknown	131	1,433	9.34	91	1,059	30.5	23.9
1994	34	136	1,236	11.04	101	939	25.7	24.3
1995	40	146	1,168	12.89	106	906	27.4	19.7
1996	38	170	1,284	13.71	115	921	32	23.8
1997	17	164	1,222	13.89	115	936	30.7	19.8
1998	33	191	1,214	15.82	138	804	27.4	24
1999	14	194	1,170	16.65	134	883	30.9	24.1
2000	28	200	1,223	16.5	133	947	33.8	22.6
2001	unknown	210	1,186	17.87	153	924	28.5	22.1

Sources: Cruise, 1976–81, 1983–92, 1994–96; Class Profiles, 1976–2001, ARF "Midshipmen: Class Profiles"; 1979, 1989, 1999 LB; Roland Brandquist, "Women at the Academy: Are They Measuring Up?," Shipmate, Vol. 43, No. 1, Jan./Feb. 1980, 15–18; Robert McNitt to Superintendent, 6 Mar. 1985, SR3, 1985, Box 1530-1710/34, Folder "1531/1"; Women Midshipmen Study Group, "Report to the Superintendent on the Assimilation of Women in the Brigade of Midshipmen," 1 Jul. 1990, 31, SR5, Binder 5; V. L. Hill Jr. to Blue and Gold Officers, 31 Aug. 1990, SR3, 1990, Box 1531/1-1710/5, Folder "1990"; "Plebe Summer Resignations, Percentages by Gender," 12 Aug. 1992, SR5, Box 4; Superintendent to Chief of Naval Operations, 30 Nov. 1992, SR3, 1992, Box 1000-1531, Folder "1992"; "Minority Attrition at the Naval Academy, by Percentages," 31 Jan. 1993, SR5, Box 4; Superintendent to Bureau of Naval Personnel, 31 Mar. 1996, SR3, 1996, Box 1531, Folder "1531"; Eva Janzen, "Military Women Finally Have a Place of Their Own," Trident, 6 Nov. 1998, 11; USNA Admissions Office, "United States Naval Academy History of Incoming Class Composition," 1999, HMG.

supposition that attrition before the junior year left only women "who have the ability and the will to excel." Reflecting Superintendent Lawrence's point from a decade earlier, WMSG identified as problematic the lack of a "single person, organization, or group tasked to handle women's issues." As a result of this omission, the military chain of command frequently overlooked issues of harassment and improper treatment of female midshipmen, including men's use of demeaning cadences, offensive jokes, and derogatory names. WMSG also indicated that while 2.5 percent of women, as compared with 0.2 percent of men, actually were overweight, the female midshipmen's uniforms gave the impression that more women had weight problems. Members of WMSG identified a "preoccupation" with weight among some women, including the skipping of meals and eating disorders, although the group did not believe the latter to be widespread. When WMSG observed that "overweight women are visible to everyone" and that other women "regard their overweight peers as unprofessional and are embarrassed by them," the group may have downplayed the true extent of eating disorders while at the same time providing part of an explanation for the problem.

The 1987 WMSG report gave two significant insights into women at the Naval Academy. First, the group observed that male midshipmen continued "preventing" women from reaching the top of the Herndon Monument during the plebe year-ending ceremony and that administrators failed to end the practice. Calling the persistent practice "an embarrassment" to the institution, WMSG argued that "the fact that such behavior occurs at all subverts the creation of a cohesive, team-oriented Brigade." Secondly, on the topic of athletics, WMSG noted that statistics revealed the crucial role that varsity team participation played in the success of individual female midshipmen at USNA. In this manner, female athletes at USNA were remarkably similar to their counterparts at civilian colleges.[35] As demonstrated in the table below, women who participated in sports as varsity athletes had a markedly higher retention rate than women who were non-athletes. Again echoing Superintendent Lawrence, WMSG explained that "available to women athletes are the support of coaches, officer and faculty representatives, and teammates; a hospitable place to meet regularly; respite from the routine; and the exclusive company of women." The WMSG concluded its report by suggesting a series of recommendations, including the creation of a professional organization for women to serve as a support and guidance mechanism for all female midshipmen. Other suggestions included the continued analysis of recruiting practices, uniforms, and meals; the hiring of larger numbers of female officer and civilian faculty; improved sexual harassment education for officers; and the

TABLE 3. Attrition of Female Midshipmen versus Female Varsity Athletes

Graduating Class	Attrition of Female Midshipmen, Overall	Attrition of Female Varsity Athletes
1980	32.1%	4.8%
1981	33.3%	15.4%
1982	34.4%	10.8%
1983	41.1%	27.6%
1984	37%	10.7%
1985	30.3%	5.7%
1986	33%	36.9%
1987	36.9%	15.3%
Average	35.1%	12.7%

Sources: Women Midshipmen Study Group, "The Integration of Women in the Brigade of Midshipmen," Nov. 1987, 72, SR5, Box 4.

creation of an organization of female officers to guide administrative policies for women.[36]

For several years after the publication of the 1987 WMSG report, a series of events showed some official support for women and, at the same time, an undercurrent of male midshipmen's persistent mockery and mistreatment of women. Just after the report's release, Leon Edney, then an admiral serving as the deputy chief of Naval operations for manpower, personnel, and training, reaffirmed the Navy's commitment to overcoming sexual harassment and increasing support for women.[37] Superintendent Marryott indicated the admissions department's dedication to finding female applicants who, due to their intelligence, technical and athletic inclination, active leadership, and determination, were likely to succeed at USNA.[38] Missy Cummings, a member of the class of 1988, became the first woman to serve as the editor of the LOG. Under her editorship, the magazine occasionally poked fun at women, including a brief mention of the "Hog Log."[39] But Cummings also presented a bold statement of women's sentiments in a parodic pie chart entitled, "What Female Mids Hate." Among the dozen items were "being called a midshipwoman" and "tourists saying 'Look! It's a girl one!' " Also listed were the lack of female restrooms, men's comments, uniforms, roommates, and lectures in which women felt singled out.[40] The pie chart demonstrated that the issues that confronted women in 1976 persisted in 1988.

During the 1988–89 academic year, the inappropriate actions of some male midshipmen brought negative attention to the Academy. After a football game between Navy and Yale on 1 October 1988, officials from New Haven complained that midshipmen had passed a Yale cheerleader through a crowd at the game and groped the woman.[41] That incident paled in scope compared with what happened in the March 1989 edition of the LOG.[42] LOG staff members created another Playboy parody entitled Playmid, which contained several pages of midshipmen's girlfriends in bathing suits, and a centerfold photograph of a woman wearing a bathing suit. Academy superintendent Virgil Hill Jr. felt that the LOG issue demeaned women with "sexual stereotyping" and ordered the destruction of all 5,000 copies of the magazine. However, midshipmen stole some hundred copies and one midshipman sent a copy to Playboy magazine. Editors at Playboy were struck by the Academy's actions, and in the September 1989 issue of their publication they printed several excerpts from the banned LOG magazine and noted, "The members of the Brigade, in training to uphold democratic principles, weren't even allowed to see the magazine to decide for themselves. Now they can. Destroy 5,000 copies, end up with 18,000,000 readers. That's the lesson in censorship."

Before 1989 was over, the elements of an even larger challenge took form.[43] During the traditionally prank-filled week before the Army-Navy game, Gwen Dreyer threw a snowball at two of her company-mates, John Hindinger and Tom Rossen, in their company area inside Bancroft Hall. A series of pranks between Dreyer and the men ensued, and after a short time, Hindinger and Rossen used a pair of theatrical handcuffs to chain Dreyer to a urinal in a men's restroom. Dreyer initially laughed, and as a group of midshipmen gathered to observe the activities, one midshipman photographed Dreyer and another midshipman pretended to urinate in an adjacent urinal. Dreyer's roommate, Carmen Amezcua, who first believed the incident to be "the typical rumble in the hall," then tried to convince Hindinger and Rossen to release Dreyer. Although they continued to taunt Dreyer and told Amezcua that the female midshipmen needed "to get a sense of humor," the men eventually loosened the handcuffs. Dreyer returned to her room, and some of the male midshipmen apologized for humiliating her later that evening. At the very least, this incident demonstrated that not all male midshipmen were looking out for the best interests of their female company-mates.

Superintendent Hill and Commandant Joseph Prueher investigated the incident and gave Hindinger and Rossen the punishment of demerits, restriction to the Academy for one month, and letters of reprimand. The administrators also gave six other midshipmen letters of reprimand for failing to intervene on

46

LOG magazine editors spoofed Playboy magazine in 1989, copying Hugh Hefner's publication and including a bathing-suit-clad female midshipman in the centerfold. Superintendent Virgil Hill banned distribution of the issue, entitled Playmid, for containing sexist material, but one midshipman sent a copy to Hefner. The September 1989 issue of Playboy included these images from Playmid, along with a statement about censorship and freedom of speech. (Courtesy of Hugh Hefner. Reproduced by special permission of Playboy. © 1989 by Playboy)

Dreyer's behalf. Although Hill attempted to convince her otherwise, Dreyer resigned from the Naval Academy upon hearing about what she considered to be light punishments. She enrolled at the California Polytechnic Institute, to which she had sent her Academy transcripts in November, perhaps indicating an inclination to depart prior to the urinal incident. The entire episode remained largely insular for months. In January, the new Trident calendar featured a commentary about the incident, including a photograph of two male midshipmen standing in front of a urinal with the caption, "It's always nice to have conversation pieces around."[44] Neither Hill nor Prueher had any idea how much of a conversation piece the event was about to become.

When the Academy in May 1990 announced the urinal incident, the punishments, and Dreyer's resignation, a firestorm of criticism developed immediately. After the New York Times and other newspapers published details of the story, Senators John Glenn (D-Ohio) and Sam Nunn (D-Ga.) publicly stated their opinions that Hill and Prueher were "insensitive" in their handling of the situation. Members of the Board of Visitors, who learned about the Dreyer case from the media, became angry that the administration had not told the committee about the incident earlier. Citizens, equally perturbed by the seemingly lenient punishments, wrote USNA administrators a barrage of angry letters demanding explanations. In spite of his repeated explanations that the punishments of Hindinger and Rossen were not minor and in fact were just short of separation from the Academy, Hill found himself and the Naval Academy in a whirlwind of criticism for appearing unable to maintain control at the Academy. Even when the superintendent changed USNA regulations to make such an incident a separable offense in the future, cartoonist Garry Trudeau mocked USNA in a New York Times article and members of National Organization for Women picketed outside the Academy's gates.

As 1990 progressed, criticism took the form of investigations. Deputy Chief of Naval Operations Michael Boorda, Navy Inspector General M. E. Chang, the Navy's Education Programs Branch, the USNA Board of Visitors, the reconvened Women Midshipmen Study Group, and the USNA administration itself all commenced investigations of the Naval Academy. Chang and Boorda's reports focused on Dreyer's experience in the larger context of conduct and honor issues at Annapolis, a connection that Boorda explained in a speech to midshipmen. As Boorda explained,

> The Gwen Dreyer case has lots and lots of interesting twists in it. Did she truly want to be here, or didn't she? Was there provocation, or did it look like fun? Was it just kids blowing off steam before the Army-Navy game?

And one could argue all those things until one was blue in the face, but did what happen rob the person of her dignity? And you can't argue that one very much, can you? The answer is yes, it did. And if you take my concept of honor, that's cheating and something none of us can do, and something we are all sworn not to do. . . . Women belong here. . . . [They] are part of this institution, and they are part of the Navy. . . . It is not negotiable.[45]

Chang suggested that "an alternative means of reporting a grievance should be in place," and Boorda advised the Academy to completely overhaul ethics, honor, and conduct education and processes.[46] Navy education leaders reported that USNA had few females on its administrative staff and, because of the dearth of women with graduate degrees in science, most female faculty members were in social sciences or humanities. Few female officers, Navy leaders concluded, "have regular contact with midshipmen" or were at USNA to serve as role models.[47]

The Academy's self-study, the BOV report, and the WMSG report all came to similar conclusions. Economics professor William Bowman, who chaired USNA's self-study, called the institution "the last bastion of male chauvinism in the Navy."[48] He described midshipmen wearing t-shirts with a silk-screened woman wearing boxing gloves and the caption, "She can't wrestle, but you should see her box." Discounting Marryott's earlier contention that the lives of female midshipmen would be improved through recruiting hardy women, Bowman suggested that the Academy instead focus on improving the treatment of women. Agreeing with that conclusion, the Board of Visitors was angered that the Academy's administration punished midshipmen in the Dreyer incident for poor discipline, not for sexual harassment.[49]

The BOV surveyed 1/C midshipmen and found that half believed USNA to be a "tough place for women," and 38 percent did not believe that women belonged at the Academy. The Board thus indicated that "the magnitude of the cultural barriers to the acceptance of women midshipmen" was great. Primary among those barriers, the BOV explained, was the continued prohibition of women in combat. Finally, the BOV charged itself to have a larger oversight role in the integration of women and suggested the full implementation of the WMSG's 1987 recommendations to bring about equality for women. As BOV member and Maryland senator Barbara Mikulski (D) told the media, "Equal treatment doesn't mean identical treatment."[50]

The final report was the 1990 WMSG study, which began with a review of the successes WMSG found since publishing its 1987 report.[51] The numbers of women in the Brigade had increased, and the admissions staff was following Superintendent Marryott's idea of recruiting highly motivated women. The Academy's staff now included a female psychologist and more gynecologists, and the administration was overseeing an equal opportunity training program. Furthermore, women's athletics were promoted from the NCAA's Division II to Division I, and USNA established the Women's Professional Association, which was sponsoring lectures, workshops, and field trips for women. Yet WMSG in 1990 repeated many of the same findings it had provided in 1987 and recorded the persistence of "steady, low-level sexual harassment [passing] as normal operating procedure in company areas and classrooms alike."

The 1990 WMSG argued that the only basis for substantive change would come through ongoing education about women for the entire USNA community, regular meetings and reports of the WMSG, and a zero-tolerance policy for sexual harassment. Although much of the 1990 WMSG report examines statistical data, the group devoted one section to describing the forms that harassment took at the Naval Academy. Many of the examples, such as the use of "WUBA," dirty jokes at meals, "diminutives" such as "plebette," and sexual propositions were not new. Female midshipmen also reported to the WMSG the showing of pornographic films in company wardrooms, obscene e-mail messages, and the men's term "going over to the Dark Side," a reference to Star Wars, to describe male midshipmen dating female midshipmen. The 1990 WMSG also, for the first time, reported on Academy-sanctioned activities that rose to the level of harassment. Midshipmen entitled a WRNV radio program Tales from the Dark Side, and the LOG continued its "Company Cuties" section. WMSG even cited the Color Girl ceremony as an example of the Academy perpetuating stereotypes. Lastly, WMSG noted that as the Academy cracked down on sexual harassment, USNA leaders needed to anticipate and prepare for male midshipmen's backlashes against their female colleagues.

In the midst of the fury over the urinal incident and the Navy's Tailhook scandal, Midshipman Julianne Gallina emerged as the Brigade commander for the fall semester of 1991.[52] As the first woman to hold that position, Gallina knew that in light of recent events her appointment would raise eyebrows. She told journalists that she wished the public would focus on her performance and not her gender, as the Academy's selection board members explained that they had done in choosing Gallina. Furthermore, although she anticipated negative reactions, Gallina declared, "I'm going to embrace the controversy." While she was the Brigade commander, Gallina penned an essay that the admissions staff mailed to prospective female candidates. She wrote that

I can readily say my Academy experience has been influenced by the fact that I am a woman, but I would never concede that it has made my experience more difficult. . . . Since I-Day, I have pushed myself and my peers to surpass the perceived limits of women merely by accepting the daily challenges of being a midshipman. . . . I truly doubt [if] I would have pushed my limits if I had attended any other school. I did not push these bounds merely for the sake of proving myself to others, but rather because the U.S. Naval Academy demands performance from all midshipmen. I have done the jobs I have been asked to do, and as a result, my perceived boundaries have crumbled.[53]

Underlying Gallina's words is a strong sense of similarity to other midshipmen, a point female midshipmen had been making since their arrival in Annapolis.

Was Gallina's experience, however, representative of a significant change in status for women at the Naval Academy? Interviews with eight women who graduated between 1988 and 1993 reveal experiences similar to those of previous female graduates.[54] All of the women remembered repeated comments from male midshipmen about their weight, attractiveness, supposed sexual promiscuity, intelligence, and their being out of place in a man's environment. Instantaneous Brigade knowledge of even a minor sexual interaction put women on alert, and one alumna said that she felt compelled to establish herself as "a genderless sister figure" to avoid comments. The use of the term "WUBA" and the telling of "WUBA" jokes persisted. One woman recounted attending a male midshipman's party with her roommate. "When we walked into the house," she remembered, "the place was so packed you couldn't turn around. Within two minutes, we had the place cleaned out. The comments were flying: 'Who brought those &*%$% WUBAs?,' 'Get those fat cows out of here,' etc. I didn't even know those guys. They just hated us because we were women—it was the cool thing I guess." "It was hard," she concluded, "to overlook things like that when they happened on a daily basis."

Other issues also persisted as problems for women. These included the continued lack of female role models and the fact that many female officers who were not USNA graduates could not salute properly while some singled the female midshipmen out by using their first names. As one alumna explained, male midshipmen would refer to a poor-quality female officer and would tell the women, "You'll end up that way." All of the women shared horror stories about roommates and the pressures that their small number in each company presented. "Swapping," or taking turns living with undesirable

TABLE 4. Forms of Harassment Female Midshipmen Reported in 1992

Form of Harassment	Female Midshipmen Who Experienced the Harassment Two or More Times Each Month
Derogatory comments, jokes, and nicknames	28%
Claims that USNA lowered standards for women	33%
Claims that women do not belong at USNA	19%
Offensive posters, signs, graffiti, and t-shirts	26%
Derogatory letters and messages	5%
Mocking gestures, whistles, and cat calls	15%
Exclusion from social activities	10%
Unwarranted horseplay and hijinks	6%
Unwarranted pressure for dates	4%
Unwarranted sexual advances	4%

Source: U.S. General Accounting Office, "Testimony Before the Subcommittee on Manpower and Personnel, Committee on Armed Services, U.S. Senate, Status Report on Reviews of Student Treatment, Department of Defense Service Academies," 2 June 1992, 5, SR5, Box 4.

company-mates, remained a common practice, because, as one woman explained, "The survival techniques were used to get the attention off of yourself and on to someone else. It was the only way." Pressures to look good in uniforms and to prove themselves to male midshipmen continued, contributing to the enduring presence of eating disorders. The alumnae recounted instances of anorexia, bulimia, and women charting their daily salad intakes. Three of the interviewed women were athletes, and they identified their team as a separate, female-dominated community, a source of support from other women, and a means of gaining acceptance from men. Reviewing her four years at the Naval Academy, one female graduate noted an axiom true of many female and male midshipmen: "We were all concerned about hiding weakness and appearing confident."

Throughout 1991 and 1992, Naval Academy administrators received external advice and several more reports on their institution. In 1991, the WMSG, then a subcommittee of the Board of Visitors, indicated "significant momentum and steady progress" toward the assimilation of women at USNA.[55] After a 1992 DACOWITS meeting, Superintendent Thomas Lynch, who learned of the frequency of eating disorders among female college students, began to deal with the issue. He initiated attention to food and weight problems, along with counseling and prevention, among the Academy's officers and staff.[56] The same year, the General Accounting Office (GAO) released the findings of its study of student treatment at the service academies.[57] Surveys of midshipmen at USNA determined that women commonly experienced sexism in a variety of ways, as outlined in the following chart. The GAO concluded that "sexual harassment occurs more frequently than is reported to officials."

Former USNA English professor Carol Burke expanded on the GAO's assessment in a scathing *New Republic* article, "Dames at Sea," which appeared in the summer of 1992.[58] Burke introduced readers to some of the Academy's vocabulary, including the "Hog Log" and "pig pushes," dances where midshipmen are set up with women from local colleges. Revealing another facet of USNA culture, Burke described midshipmen placing banana stickers under their uniform hats, or covers, after sexual encounters: "The Chiquita sticker signifies 'scoring' in one's room; the Dole sticker, anywhere on the grounds." She also transcribed offensive cadences, and shared "WUBA" jokes, including:

QUESTION: How are a WUBA and a bowling ball similar?
ANSWER: You pick them up, put three fingers in them, and throw them in the gutter.

QUESTION: What do you call a mid who fucks a WUBA?
ANSWER: Too lazy to beat off.

Burke was careful to point out that "in recent years officials have banned such practices," but observed that "many of [the terms and behaviors] continued unofficially in the Hall, where upperclass exercise casual intimidation and midshipmen are reluctant to incriminate one another." Academy officials were understandably concerned about the article's content and tenor and were disturbed that Burke did not accurately address the recent corrective actions they had taken after the Dreyer incident. In a letter to the *New Republic*'s editor, Superintendent Lynch invited readers and Burke "to put the past behind and visit us today, view our accomplishments, speak with our midshipmen, both male and female, and evaluate our performance."[59] Only four months later, however, Lynch was punishing four men for yet another prank: in this case the men attacked two women with pillows, causing the female midshipmen bruises and a black eye.[60]

The bad publicity over women, in combination with extensive media coverage of an incident in which over a hundred midshipmen were involved in a compromised electrical engineering final examination, prompted Lynch to create a week-long "intercessional" at the Naval Academy in 1993.[61] The program included "sensitivity training, rape awareness lectures, etiquette briefs," and military leaders' speeches. Although one midshipman, Christopher Graves, felt that parts of the "intercessional" were "banal," the program likely had its desired effect for some of the members of the Brigade. Graves indicated his outrage toward "some unscrupulous grads" who painted six cannons on the Academy's grounds pink, and he likened the incident to the painting of swastikas in terms of its impact on female midshipmen.[62] Within a month of USNA's "interecessional," Congress began to dismantle the prohibitions on women in combat, based in part on the success of women's activities in the Gulf War, the repercussions of the sexual assaults on women at the Navy's Tailhook Convention, general societal advances for women, and women's participation in a myriad of military occupations. The impact that this monumental change would have upon the Naval Academy was as yet uncertain.[63]

Among the Academy administrators attempting to advance women at USNA was Director of Candidate Guidance Asbury Coward IV, who served in that position between 1992 and 1994.[64] Coward took an activist approach to attracting women to Annapolis. His assistant, 1990 graduate Lynne Smith, was the women's advocate for the admissions board and spoke personally with most of the female applicants about their academic, athletic, and extracurricular activities. Coward devised a newsletter, which Smith oversaw, for all of the female recruits; as Smith recalled, "This was a brilliant idea because the women were friends before they even showed up. Many of them had parties before [coming to USNA] so they could meet. They walked in with a solid foundation under their feet. I think it was instrumental in their success." As Coward and his wife Croom became involved as sponsor parents to midshipmen, they realized the significance of roommate problems among female midshipmen. Thereafter, Coward and Smith set out to arrange roommates, for example by placing a woman with a strong academic record with a woman who excelled in athletics, based on the idea that the women would help each other. Upon discovering that such combinations caused competitive stresses, Croom Coward advised her husband to place women with similar strengths together. That policy, along with Smith's service as an advisor and role model to the women after they became midshipmen, was a success. As Smith later explained, "Five of the top ten graduates of the Class of 1999 were women—I think it worked!"

When Superintendent Charles Larson returned for his second term in 1994, he began to follow many of the suggestions of the 1993 "Report of the Honor

Committee to the Secretary of the Navy on Honor at the U.S. Naval Academy."[65] Known informally as "The Armitage Report," the study outlined ideas "to educate and train officers of character."[66] The resulting establishment of new ethics courses, integrity development seminars, and leadership training reassessments created an atmosphere in which issues pertaining to, and relevant for, women could be discussed more openly.[67] Larson also altered USNA's policy on pregnancy, which until 1995 required the dismissal of any midshipman who was pregnant or had caused a pregnancy.[68] Thereafter, a midshipman could reapply for admission after a year and after legal and financial arrangements no longer rendered the child a dependent of the midshipman.[69] In 1995, Larson quashed the LOG, ending its publication because he did not feel that the irreverent humor was compatible with his goals.[70] This was a significant and symbolic step that prevented the publication of disrespectful and disheartening comments about women and other members of the Naval Academy community. The next year, Larson created new "guiding principles" that warned against gossiping and spreading rumors and suggested that midshipmen "treat everyone with dignity and respect."[71] Indirectly, these dictums may have referred to the treatment of women. Later that year, Larson gave the media a positive spin after four female midshipmen reported a male counterpart, Scott Ward, for assaulting and sexually harassing them.[72] The superintendent told reporters that "we have finally created an environment that women will report what happened and trust us to take strong action."[73]

Two internal studies shed further light on the progress of women within the Brigade of Midshipmen. Superintendent Larson announced in 1996 that the results of a USNA "quality of life" survey indicated that 96 percent of the male midshipmen accepted their female colleagues, and the percentage of women who felt that their male classmates accepted them rose from 59 percent in 1990 to 95 percent in 1996.[74] These findings seemed promising, but midshipmen Daniel Bozung and Julie Gill's 1996–97 study clarified the results of the quality of life survey.[75] Based on questionnaires Bozung distributed, he and Gill concluded that male midshipmen fully accepted women on an academic level. Only 80 percent of the men, however, "felt comfortable socializing with females in groups," and those men were the most likely to be accepting of women at USNA. Professionally, however, the men were much less accepting of female midshipmen; the men perceived that women had low "physical and leadership capabilities" and that the Academy gave "special consideration [to women] in both areas." Bozung and Gill also found that the recent opening of combat billets to women had not yet fostered more positive views of female midshipmen and their futures. In a statement that could apply to all minority groups, the two midshipmen noted that

> female midshipmen tend to compete against not only their male classmates, but their female classmates as well. Although women are proud of those who bound ahead and are chosen for stripes, they alienate themselves from these achievers and the "striper stigmatism" that they ultimately receive. Females do not make it a habit to support each other; they are "clickish." When a female midshipman acquires a bad reputation among males, the women tend to ostracize her rather than taking her aside to explain the impact such a stigma has on herself and women in general at the Naval Academy. The fact remains that one female represents all females, despite their increased number at USNA.[76]

A fascinating finding that Bozung and Gill noted was "a trend in decreasingly egalitarian attitudes as midshipmen progress from fourth to first class."[77] Whether some observers are correct that young men arrive at USNA with an anti-female "cultural bias," interviews with midshipmen and alumni led to the same conclusion as Bozung and Gill's: over time, many male midshipmen become less accepting of women.[78] During a group interview with four male plebes in 1999, for example, the young men were uncertain about the meaning and intent of the question, "Do you think women belong at USNA?"[79] However, asking the same question of upperclass midshipmen led to a variety of negative responses. When asked to comment on particular women within their own companies, male midshipmen usually had only positive remarks, but many upperclassmen were still critical of what they considered to be "stereotypical" women at USNA.[80] An alumna commented that she barely recognized a male relative by the time of his graduation; "He certainly did not grow up with those sexist attitudes," she remarked.[81] While imperfect female midshipmen may garner negative attention that spread to all women, it is likely that a number of factors are more responsible for the men's attitudes. Interaction with alumni at events like football tailgaters; pressure from older midshipmen seeking to preserve anti-female attitudes; the continued popularity of James Webb, his writings, and his guest lectures at USNA; and sexism in the Navy and American culture at large all combine to influence male midshipmen's beliefs.[82]

Had female midshipmen's lives improved dramatically, as Larson alleged? Interviews with ten women in the classes of 1997–2002 indicate, as did interviews with earlier female graduates, continuities on a number of issues.[83]

Six of the ten women were varsity athletes, and all spoke at length about the positive support that time with team members provided. One woman remembered that she "was able to spend four to five hours a day and most weekends with all the girls. . . . We could pretty much talk about anything with each other. It was almost like normal college life with the team. We were like a close-knit sorority in the midst of a huge fraternity and we had a blast."[84] Other women spoke of bonding with teammates, and another female midshipmen explained that the men in her company and classes frequently commented on her success in her sport, perhaps reflecting the respect that sports garner in American society at large. Coaches and officer representatives, too, are aware of the importance of women's athletics. One officer representative recounted conversations during bus rides that covered "make-up, cute guys, and other issues 'normal' women speak about." Contemplating her experiences with female midshipmen on her team, one coach explained that "females definitely have an easier time here at the Academy being on an athletic team. They have a 'sisterhood' support group; they can share emotions, thoughts, and opinions openly without being criticized or judged. Some of the guys just do not let them 'in' as one of the group. When they are with women, [female midshipmen] feel accepted. Some guys still carry the negative attitude as if women do not belong here; other guys are great and treat the women as a contributing factor to the success of the military, as it should be!"[85] Athletic team participation is significant enough to make female athletes 60 percent more likely to graduate than their non-athletic female counterparts.[86]

At the same time, women continued to face some of the same pressures and problems as previous female midshipmen. Six women noted the continued use of "WUBA," a term which remains in common use at USNA.[87] Two women's crew team members even noted that male midshipmen referred to them as "CREWBA's," a takeoff on "WUBA." All ten women recounted male midshipmen's derogatory language and negative comments. Male midshipmen were still telling each other not to think about "darksiding," and continued proclaiming that particular activities and rooms in Bancroft Hall were "balls only." Seeking to ward off comments directed at her, one female midshipman told her company-mates that she was devoutly religious and did not appreciate foul language or discussions; "I wanted them to know that I did not want them calling me 'WUBA,' dyke, or slut." As was the case with Janice Buxbaum two decades earlier, personal assertiveness seemed effective.

Roommates and eating disorders were also continuing problems for women. Conflicts over roommates created difficulties for six of the ten women. The women in one company spent their last two years at USNA trading off an undesirable company-mate, while the female members of another company had to live with women of different classes in order to bring peace among them. One woman faced a semester of complete silence because she and her roommates so disliked one another. Seven women also spoke of the prevalence of eating disorders at the Naval Academy. After a succession of roommates with "minor food issues," one female midshipman decided to intervene in one instance because she feared for her roommate's well-being. She and other women felt that USNA did not intervene properly in severe cases of anorexia and bulimia. Meals during which female midshipmen will eat only plain lettuce, or an apple, or a container of yogurt, are not uncommon. Attempting to explain the reason for eating disorders, two women cited the pressure to "look good," the forced presence at meals even if one is not hungry, the presence of "unhealthy" foods, and the desire for personal control. As one woman stated, "for many midshipmen, especially women, eating or what they put in their bodies is the only thing they CAN control, so they CONTROL it to an excess."

Two other issues persisted as challenges for female midshipmen. Contradicting Superintendent Larson's assertion that women felt comfortable reporting sexual harassment, one alumna remembered "one girl who was raped, one sexually assaulted, and one who was sexually harassed." None of the perpetrators suffered consequences, she explained, because "there is still a perception that there will be a reprimand [against the women]. Offending one guy, even if he is a slime, just isn't worth the ostracizing that can occur." A male midshipman asked, in a 1998 Naval Institute Proceedings article, why a woman had still not reached the top of the Herndon Monument during the annual ceremony. Citing sexism, the author, Alton Stewart, expressed his dissatisfaction that women's own "classmates will not allow [the women] to reach the top," but rather pull the women off the obelisk to prevent them from achieving "the title of first woman to climb Herndon."[88] A female midshipman has commented that men who pull women off of Herndon "do not feel good about themselves," and another woman noted after the 1999 ceremony that "I didn't see quite as many getting pulled off this year." Before the class of 2003 began its Herndon Ceremony in May 2000, Commandant Samuel Locklear became the first Naval Academy administrator to intervene by threatening to expel any male midshipman whom he saw pulling a female midshipman off of the monument intentionally. For the first time in the twenty-three years of women's participation in the ceremony, men did not hinder their female classmates.

The final issue that women cited in interviews was the cost, style, and masculine appearance of their uniforms. Uniforms were also at the center of a May 1999 controversy involving the class of 2000's Ring Dance.[89] Midshipmen had, in prior years, worn uniforms, but their dates attended the junior-year ending ceremony in civilian attire. For up to a year before the event, female midshipmen in the class had contemplated whether they would wear their uniforms or formal dresses. As one woman explained, "We all rationalized it. This was our one chance to dress up and look good for these guys who have been making fun of us for three years and telling us how ugly we are, and we want to look nice. All the guys bring their pretty little girlfriends, and we just wanted to be pretty for one night." The Academy had ordered all of the women to appear at the function in their uniforms at 6:00, so anyone wanting a picture in civilian attire had to have her photograph made and then change into her uniform before that time. While some of the female midshipmen never intended to appear in their uniforms, a rainstorm and subsequent photographic delays provided other women the opportunity to remain in their formal dresses.

Ultimately, only about a dozen of the 133 women in the class appeared at the Ring Dance in uniforms. During a casual conversation with one of the women who had changed into her uniform, the wife of Commandant Gary Roughead asked where all of the female midshipmen were. The midshipman replied, "Oh, they're all here." Within a week, administrators began investigations, which extended into the summer. Influenced by the insistence of high-ranking female officers at USNA, the commandant decided that the punishment for the women would be severe and would include limits on weekend liberty, seven trash tours (walks around the Yard during which midshipmen remove any garbage they find on the Academy grounds), and thirty-five demerits. The high number of demerits gave the offending women a "C" grade in conduct, thereby lowering their class ranks and potentially eliminating their chances of attending graduate school during their senior year and participating in Trident Scholar projects. Women who had planned to pursue such goals had to apply for individual waivers from the commandant. When the women went through their service selection interviews during their senior year, military officers questioned some of the women about their decision that evening. At least one woman told the officers questioning her that she would, given similar circumstances in the future, remain in her civilian attire.

As news of the incident spread throughout the Naval Academy community, many officers, alumni, and male midshipmen were disgusted and told women, "You go to a military school, you should be wearing a uniform." Most female midshipmen, however, were unfazed by such an argument. Although they understood that they had broken a rule—failing to obey an order to appear in uniform at a particular time—and even accepted their punishments, the women were frustrated with administrators. "No one cared about all of the underage drinking that went on that night," one woman recalled. Another stated that "there were at least six male mids there who were not in their uniforms, and they were not punished." However, as the women and at least one midshipman leader acknowledged, the Academy missed out on the opportunity to assess the statement female midshipmen made that night. Furthermore, USNA officials might have considered expanding the Ring Dance activities to include an event to which midshipmen could wear formal attire instead of uniforms.

Commandant Samuel Locklear, who succeeded Roughead in 1999, arrived with the desire to stress accountability and respect among the midshipmen.[90] When several troublesome incidents arose early in his term, Locklear took steps that he believed were appropriate for maintaining respect for female midshipmen and officers. During the Eighth Wing Players performance on 2 December 1999, just before that year's Army-Navy game, Navy captain Bradford McDonald participated in a skit that mocked the personality and appearance of a female company officer. Although Locklear was not in attendance, a midshipman videotaped the skit, and shortly thereafter the commandant permanently ended the Eighth Wing Players. Administrators removed McDonald from his position, but he remained on duty at USNA. A second activity with which McDonald was involved in planning and advertising was a women's football competition between female midshipmen and cadets from West Point. Two games, which took place before the Army-Navy games in 1998 and 1999, featured male midshipmen dressed as cheerleaders while their female colleagues battled on the gridiron. Cheers were loudest when the competing women demonstrated particular verve and violence. The games ceased after the 1999 game. Finally, on 7 February 2000, Locklear permanently discontinued the publication of the LOG. The magazine had been dormant since 1995, but a female Navy officer, Mary Jo Sweeney, helped return it to print in January 1997.[91] The magazine resumed its irreverent look at USNA and its officers and administration.[92] Locklear was disturbed by an in-production volume that was to have featured a cover photograph of a large-chested woman in a Naval Academy t-shirt, description of a beer brand—Yuengling—as having a "gay" name, and references to a marijuana cook book called Cooking With Ganja.[93] As punishment, the commandant required individual character development training for the LOG's staff members.

Locklear's efforts represent another attempt at remedying some of the ongoing challenges women face at the Naval Academy.[94] Some observers and even female alumni, a number of whom have returned as officers, have noted improvements in life for women upon their return to Annapolis.[95] One of those alumnae, for example, recalled a male midshipman smiling, saluting, and greeting her while she walked, in uniform, at USNA some twenty years after her graduation. Many male midshipmen, clearly, are now supportive of their female colleagues.[96] The number of women in the Brigade has continued to increase and has even included multiple sisters from the same families attending the Academy.[97] Due to administrative policies on registration, women are seldom the only female midshipman in their classrooms, and women have graduated at the top of USNA's classes.[98] Higher numbers of female officers and female faculty, furthermore, serve to present role models for the female midshipmen. Athletic teams continue to provide an environment of support for some female midshipmen, and women's success as athletes remains a source of respect from male midshipmen.[99] A small number of women benefited from their involvement in the Joy Bright Hancock Club, a women's organization active at USNA in the late 1990s.[100] Other emboldened female midshipmen have taken possession of the term "WUBA," proudly defining it as "Women Underestimated By All."[101]

Current faculty frequently discuss the role of women in the military in classroom discussions in courses such as "Military Ethics: The Code of the Warrior" and "Naval Leadership," and in "Integrity and Character Development" seminars.[102] Even when the issues of female midshipmen and women in the military were not specifically the topic of Integrity Development Seminars (IDS) and Character Development Seminars (CDS) in 1999 and 2000, such issues came up in the course of discussions with the midshipmen present. In one instance, a reading on the military's drug policy led to a discussion of eating issues at USNA and the observation that while all the male midshipmen present had large lunches in front of them, the female midshipmen ate only apples and yogurt. In another instance, midshipmen raised the issue of fraternization in the Academy environment, and all midshipmen present were able to speak at length about sexual relations at USNA. Such discussions reveal that sexual activity at the Academy even has its own language. For example, "sinking" refers to midshipmen who wear "PE Gear" ("blue-rim" t-shirts and blue mesh shorts), in order to allow for quick undressing and dressing, and engage in activity on sinks in their rooms. "Sportfucking" refers to engaging in sexual activity in a wing of Bancroft Hall while construction staff refurbished that particular wing.

As eating disorders, roommate problems, uniforms, sexuality, and men's comments have persisted as difficulties for female midshipmen, so have a degree of institutional ambivalence and negative sentiment toward women among male midshipmen, officers, and alumni.[103] As USNA English professor Bruce Fleming noted in 2005, "Male bonding is still at the center of the Academy."[104] Although the administration oversees frequent and extensive sexual harassment and gender equity training, some midshipmen have grown resentful toward the repetitiveness and frequency of such training.[105] Female midshipmen, female officers, and women who date midshipmen continue to experience sexual harassment, and despite rules to the contrary, sexual activity between midshipmen continues at the Academy.[106]

Similarly, many of the women of the class of 1980 still bear emotional scars of their time as midshipmen. The class of 1979's continued practice of ending its monthly *Shipmate* column with "Omnes Viri" serves to regularly remind those women of their troubled experience at USNA.[107] There was no formal administrative recognition of Sharon Haney Disher's *First Class*, an account of the experiences of the women of the class of 1980, when it was published in 1998.[108] The sole commemoration of the twentieth anniversary of women's first graduation was Superintendent John Ryan's briefly noting the fact during the graduation ceremony in May 2000.[109] No prominent ceremonies or recognition took place then or for the twenty-fifth anniversary in 2005, as was the case at West Point and Colorado Springs.

After the release of the findings of a July 2000 cultural assessment that addressed the environment for women at USNA, one alumna remarked, "I found it interesting that we're still talking about women in the Brigade the same way we were twelve years ago."[110] The assessment ultimately raised the question of when the long series of studies finding similar conclusions would end and substantial improvements could be measured.[111] Prominent alumni Leon Edney and H. Ross Perot have suggested that the solution is peer pressure: midshipmen influencing one another to end sexual harassment toward women at USNA.[112] It is clear, however, as the continued popularity of James Webb and his viewpoints attest, that some men will never be convinced of the validity of women at the Naval Academy—just as some men will never accept women's advances and equality in American society as a whole.[113] One former superintendent, William Smedberg, demonstrated the complex sentiments many male alumni have harbored toward women in the Brigade of Midshipmen. In 1979, he told an interviewer, "I have quite a feeling for [the female midshipmen], and I think they're doing well. That doesn't mean that I

Among the notable traditions of the Naval Academy is the climbing of the Herndon Monument, the symbolic end of the freshman year when plebes scale the 21-foot-high granite obelisk to grab the prize, an upperclass hat. Since the first Herndon climb to include women, and in spite of administrative warnings against the practice, male midshipmen have pulled their female classmates off of the human scaffolding around the monument. Although no female midshipman has ever succeeded in grabbing the upperclass hat, women have fared better in recent years, as depicted in this photograph of the class of 2006's Herndon climb in May 2003. (Courtesy United States Navy. Photograph by Photographer's Mate 1st Class Brien Aho. U.S. Navy imagery used in illustration without endorsement expressed or implied)

approve of women being at the Naval Academy. I heartily disapprove of it. I think it's the worst thing that's happened to our military in many, many years. To try to force the idea of women and men being trained in combat together . . . is the most outrageous thing I've heard of. It couldn't possibly work, and only people who have lived in destroyers and been away for four or five months at a time can understand why it would never work."[114] Also demonstrating conflicting sentiments is former superintendent James Calvert, who has written letters of recommendation for female candidates: "The Naval Academy is a good school, but the day that women got there in 1976, it wasn't Annapolis any more. It was a different place. There is a mystique about an all-male military training program. Once women got there, that mystique was gone. Now that's hard for anybody to understand who hasn't been through it, but it's correct. But on the other hand, I'm a great believer in being a realist, and American society has changed. Therefore, I think what we have to do is make the best of it. In many ways, the Academy is a better place because of women."[115]

Although the Naval Academy has had excellent leadership, the continued difficulties that female midshipmen have faced since 1980 attest to that leadership's general ambivalence about women. A few leaders have taken active steps toward the successful integration of women, as noted, but were administrators not so generally ambivalent, it is possible that they would have intervened in clearer terms and at earlier dates to reduce or eliminate anti-female behavior and attitudes and to dramatically change events like the Herndon Ceremony.[116] Furthermore, administrators might have used an occasion like the 1999 Ring Dance to analyze the concerns of women within the institution. Clearly, life for female midshipmen at the Naval Academy has improved since 1976. However, whether past leaders were influenced by personal attitudes or whether pressure from higher military leaders, politicians, and military culture is to blame, present and future leaders have the opportunity to take more specific, concise steps to create a fully integrated, accepting atmosphere at Annapolis.

That Inescapable
Trait of Midshipmen

*The Creation of the Honor
Concept, Protests, Pranks, and
Other Remarkable Activities*

★ ★ ★ ★ ★ ★ ★ ★ ★ ★ ★ ★ ★ ★ ★ ★ ★ ★

After contemplating a topic for his senior paper
for the English/History/Government Department in January 1953, midshipman H. Ross Perot decided to examine the manner in which previous generations of midshipmen had treated the notion of honor. Perot wrote to the secretaries of surviving graduate classes and asked for their recollections of honor offenses. He discovered from the men's responses that, beyond cases in which the midshipmen treated an offending classmate in a particular manner or officials administered punishments, there was no uniform policy for dealing with midshipmen who had violated their class's conceptions of honor.[1] Midshipmen responded to honor violations in an improvised and ad hoc manner. Members of the class of 1897, for example, would refuse to speak to classmates who had acted inappropriately.[2] Conversely, in a show of support, the entire class of 1910 went "on the wagon" when Academy administrators threatened to expel one of their classmates who had consumed alcoholic beverages.[3] The responses assured Perot that his and other midshipmen's recent actions to create an Honor Concept for the Naval Academy constituted a valid step in improving the training and development of midshipmen. This chapter outlines how midshipmen have shown conviction, effervescence, and at times irreverence—what one member of the Brigade called "an inescapable trait of midshipmen"—in voicing their opinions about issues that concern them at Annapolis.[4] This chapter also examines pranks, which have likely been a part of Naval Academy culture since its founding. All of these actions have occurred within the disciplined, authoritarian, pressured environment of the Naval Academy, and they show that bold midshipmen demonstrate courage, leadership, and cunning when they choose to challenge USNA policies, make a difference within their community, or exercise their sense of humor.

The decision of the classes of 1950, 1951, 1952, and 1953 to create an Honor Concept had two roots.[5] One was Brigade Captain Charles Dobony's determination to eliminate the Academy's traditional "dope system." Because midshipmen, under the "lock-step" academic system, all took the same courses, the distribution of quiz questions throughout Bancroft Hall to assist midshipmen in later course sections succeed on examinations was ubiquitous. Dobony met with each class's president, including William Lawrence (class of 1951), James Sagerholm (class of 1952), and H. Ross Perot (class of 1953), and convinced them that any continuation of the "dope system" would "sooner or later bring discredit to the Academy."[6] The second root was the presence of Superintendent Harry Hill.[7] While Hill served as a USNA battalion officer in 1931, he unsuccessfully attempted to convince the midshipmen then at the Academy to accept an honor code to deal with what he perceived as low standards concerning honor. Hill based his opinion on the midshipmen's tradition of not "bilging," or reporting, their classmates' wrongdoings. In 1950, Hill returned to Annapolis as the superintendent and decided to rekindle his earlier goal. During a speech that December, he told the Brigade that he would support them and remove proctors from their academic examinations if the midshipmen unanimously accepted "the responsibility for maintaining a high degree of personal honor."[8] The leaders of the Brigade Executive Committee (BEC), including the class presidents and other leaders of the three upper classes, held meetings with each company in the Brigade to discuss honor. After securing unequivocal verbal support, the BEC reported to Hill during the 1950 Academy Christmas dinner that the midshipmen had accepted his challenge. Hill later noted that the declaration was "one of the greatest events in my life."[9]

During the 1951–52 academic year, midshipmen worked on organizing the means of dealing with honor violations. All four classes voted to support the BEC's efforts and Commandant Robert Pirie's suggestion that the classes create their own honor committees. The BEC outlined its functional procedures: midshipmen would report a case of "moral turpitude" to their class honor committees, which would then meet to investigate the incident and ultimately report findings to the BEC. The BEC would in turn indicate findings and recommendations to the USNA administration, although the officers decided that midshipmen should not have a role in the punishment decisions. The BEC examined the U.S. Military Academy's Honor Code to study how cadets handled honor cases there. However, the midshipmen found the West Point Code heavy-handed and punitive, amounting to a list of actions cadets could not take, a mandate that cadets report each other's violations, and an encouragement for cadets to work creatively around prescribed rules.

BEC members opted, rather, to maintain the traditional, informal nature of dealing with honor violations at USNA, and so created an Honor Concept, not an Honor Code, affirming the principle that midshipmen "will not cheat, lie, steal, or tolerate anyone who does."[10] The Academy's emphasis was, therefore, on using the Honor Concept as a means of inspiring the highest moral standards among members of the Brigade because the midshipmen themselves oversee the Concept's operation.[11] Brigade Captain William Lawrence, who led the Concept's adoption, explained that "honor is a personal quality and, as individuals differ, so do violations of honor. . . . Each case should be received and considered on its merits alone."[12] Lawrence further advocated what he called the "counseling option," which, as historian Jean Ebbert later noted, provides the Concept's flexibility: "The Naval Academy midshipman has the option of using whatever means of persuasion he or she can muster to convince the erring midshipman of the folly of his ways. If personal counseling and pressure can make the errant midshipman stop his dishonorable behavior and make the proper restitutions, the matter can rest there. The observing midshipman is obligated to report the miscreant only when other measures of persuasion fail to mend the matter."[13] After serving as the class president and later as the superintendent, and after spending nearly six years as a prisoner of war in Vietnam, Lawrence noted that the counseling option "is a great strength of our concept. The best way you learn in this world, I found, is by making mistakes."[14]

The Honor Concept has remained a prominent part of the Naval Academy's culture, and although its wording has occasionally been expanded and altered, its precepts have remained the same.[15] Although administrators have commended midshipmen for upholding the Honor Concept, it has come under scrutiny on a number of occasions.[16] Lawsuits involving midshipmen and West Point cadets dismissed for honor violations have been the precursors to procedural changes in honor cases, such as occurred after a 1965 federal court case involving a West Point cadet who claimed unfair treatment due to that Academy's Honor Code.[17] As a result, the Navy reconsidered the USNA Honor Concept and made several democratizing modifications in honor investigation procedures, including regulations requiring midshipmen to tell the accused of charges against them, giving the accused representation, and destroying files related to cases in which the accused were found innocent.[18] Subsequent superintendents worked to make the Honor Concept relevant for midshipmen.[19]

However, a series of instances of cheating and extreme misbehavior, particularly in the 1990s, warranted further investigations into the Honor Concept by the Board of Visitors, Naval Academy administrators, and Navy leaders.[20] A 1990 BOV group looking at women's issues at USNA noted that the Honor Concept was unclear and inconsistent in application, and Admiral J. Michael Boorda, the chair of a Navy review board on the Honor Concept, concluded that honor education was necessary for midshipmen throughout their four years at Annapolis.[21] Like Navy Inspector General M. E. Chang, who led a climate assessment of USNA in 1990, Boorda noted a continued problem at Annapolis: "We found that midshipmen perceive a conflict between the concept of class loyalty and commitment to the larger principles exemplified in the Honor Concept."[22] After a major cheating incident in 1993, a Secretary of the Navy Review Board looked again at honor at USNA and at allegations that the administration itself had violated the Honor Concept by giving preferential treatment to athletes during investigations. Its conclusions were far-reaching, emphasizing the importance of ethics, character development, and honor as prominent fixtures in the training of midshipmen.[23]

The Honor Concept continues to play a prominent role in the lives of midshipmen. The Brigade Executive Committee evolved by the 1970s into the Brigade Honor Committee and a system of class honor representatives, and by the 1990s the Brigade had a staff of honor officers.[24] As Commandant Stephen Chadwick noted in 1985, "The Brigade Honor [Committee] is viewed by all as a professional, yet compassionate, body striving to both educate and enforce the ideals of the Brigade."[25] However, honor violations remain a problem at the Academy, perhaps, as some observers of events at USNA have explained, because the Brigade of Midshipmen derives from an American society that some citizens believe has declined morally.[26] Also persistent is the concept of not "bilging" one's classmates. One midshipman, for example, noted recently that some of his classmates had not spoken to him for several years because he had reported another midshipman who clearly violated USNA regulations.[27] Recent efforts, like the class of 1999's reaffirmation of its commitment to the Honor Concept while their parents visited the Academy, the 1997 construction of a large photographic and historical display about the Concept in a busy area of Bancroft Hall, and continued administrative efforts to deal with violations, effectively attest to the continuing importance of the Honor Concept at the Naval Academy.[28]

Just as midshipmen were establishing the Honor Concept, another remarkable event in the history of USNA was unfolding.[29] When Vice Admiral Harry Hill replaced Rear Admiral James Holloway Jr. as the superintendent on

28 April 1950, Hill decided to eliminate freedoms for first classmen that Holloway had instated, including liberty every other weekend, the ability to keep civilian clothes in their Bancroft Hall rooms, and permission to stay up until 11:00 P.M. each night. Furthermore, Hill added more marching to the midshipmen's regimen.[30] The members of the classes of 1950 and 1951, beyond some complaints, did not respond in any notable way to these changes. However, the removal of expected liberties bothered some members of the class of 1952 as they approached their graduation.

Two class of 1952 members realized that the administration had scheduled five separate dress parades for them during their June Week, the traditional celebratory week leading up to graduation ceremonies.[31] After discussing the issue, the young men decided "to suggest a mild degree of protest over the excessive number of parades . . . and the overall way we . . . had been treated during our first class year in comparison to the classes before us." Over dinner on the eve of the Color Parade, the traditional annual and final dress parade before graduation ceremonies, the first classmen devised their plan: they would ask their classmates "in the rear ranks of our company [to] leave their shoes on the field when we marched off at the end of the Color Parade."[32] Such a prank was not entirely beyond the norm for Color Parades. In past years, a small number of graduating midshipmen had left their shoes on Worden Field, and the 24th Company, then numerically the final company in the Brigade, had adopted the tradition of carrying red lanterns.[33] Discussion of the idea, however, spread quickly through the Brigade, and many more midshipmen decided to join in the protest. One of the midshipmen who devised the idea later confided that "the creativity and inventiveness of what transpired the next day on the parade ground was not thought of by us nor anticipated."[34]

Families of first classmen arrived in Annapolis on the morning of Thursday, 5 June 1952, while the midshipmen were busy practicing for the Color Parade. By 5:00 that evening, the viewing stands on Worden Field began to fill, as did the tent set up at midfield for the Naval dignitaries who had arrived for the festivities. All eyes were fixed upon Helen Kidd, the Color Girl, as she presented the American flag and company colors to the 13th Company, the winner of the year's color competition. The assembled guests continued to watch the activities on the drill field as the twenty-four companies lined up to begin their final pass before the Navy leaders. However, instead of an orderly progression, disorder began to erupt. The *Annapolis Capital* reported that "almost every Academy company, as it passed the reviewing stands, dropped shoes, gloves, and handkerchiefs in the path of the oncoming group."[35] With the Navy's and news media's film cameras rolling, other midshipmen released balloons and displayed brightly painted swords.[36] As the following companies moved further and further astride to avoid the increasing pile of personal effects, other midshipmen began to exhibit street signs and Confederate flags. Although many members of the public laughed and rushed onto Worden Field for souvenirs, military officers, including Chief of Naval Operations William Fechteler and former chief Louis Denfeld, were not quite so amused.[37]

While midshipmen returned to Bancroft Hall, Admirals Hill, Fechteler, and Denfeld retired to the superintendent's house to contemplate the display they had just witnessed. Angered and embarrassed, the men contemplated several courses of action. Two of the potential responses were to dismiss the class of 1952 without graduation or commissioning or to delay the men's commissioning until after Navy ROTC graduates had received their commissions. However, the class of 1952 included midshipmen who had chosen the Air Force as a career path. Typically, the Navy, Marine Corps, and Air Force sent high-ranking officers to Annapolis to swear in the new ensigns and second lieutenants at the graduation ceremony.[38] However, in order to conform to the Air Force's schedule that year, Air Force second lieutenants had received their commissions two days before the Color Parade. As a result, neither option permitted a uniform punishment for the entire class. A third option was for the Academy's administrators to work on ensuring that the lower classes would not take any examples from the graduating seniors, and in the name of expediency, the admirals chose this final course and left the class of 1952 unpunished.

Other Naval Academy officers expressed great frustration with the class of 1952's actions and thereby guaranteed the fulfillment of the admirals' plan to counsel the remaining classes. One administrator noted that he was "thoroughly disgusted with the antics" at the parade, while another officer expressed his concern that "the adverse impression on the many visitors who witnessed the parade cannot help but discredit the Naval Academy in the minds of these people, their families, and their friends."[39] Having gathered suggestions from fellow officers, Commandant Charles Buchanan stated the administration's plan that "the new firstclass, at the outset of the academic year, must be appraised of the disgrace which their predecessors brought on themselves and the Naval Academy, and informed that any semblance of a recurrence will not be tolerated. In addition, a more rigid inspection by company and battalion officers, both when they fall in at the Armory and prior to entering the parade ground, must be made. The effect of the aggregate of this kind of horseplay on the final parade was so serious that future firstclassmen must be appraised that violators will not be permitted to graduate with their class the following day."[40] By the time midshipmen returned to Annapolis for the fall semester of 1952, Admiral Hill had retired but administrators had begun their quest to eliminate a possible replay of Color Parade antics. The USNA administration brought a tough, highly scrutinizing set of Marine drill sergeants to Annapolis, and Commandant Buchanan addressed the class of 1952's actions in a speech to the class of 1953:

> And who was responsible for the spectacle that occurred at the last parade last June—the Color Company parade? Actually the final responsibility was mine. . . . On the subject of the last parade . . . does it make any sense that [what] we strive for all year—namely to bring the Brigade up to peak performance June Week, should be ruined by the first class falling on its face and disgracing not only the Academy and the Brigade but themselves? Not to mention the insult to the Color Girl who was taking the review? . . . I know that Admiral Hill will carry a permanent scar in his heart as a result of the last parade as Superintendent. I know the Class of '52 immediately regretted their action—but it came too late—the deed had been done. I am giving you now, the Class of '53, as a target . . . the mission to wipe out the memory of the last June Week Parade. I am sure you want as much as I to carry out that mission.[41]

Buchanan's comments that September would not be the last that the midshipmen who witnessed the 1952 June Week Parade heard about the event. Trying to ward off any thought of creating a new tradition, the commandant reminded the seniors that he wanted proper behavior at the 1953 Color Parade. With the threat of not graduating over their heads, the class of 1953 performed flawlessly during their parade and the rest of June Week.[42] Lest the class of 1954 have any illusion of resurrecting the 1952 antics, Buchanan wasted little time in warning them, when they became first classmen, that any unusual behavior would warrant the use of "shock troops."[43] That threat worked, and the class of 1954 caused no "disgrace" to their commandant or to the retiring superintendent, C. Turner Joy. Although Captain R. T. S. Keith, who replaced Buchanan as the commandant, never mentioned the 1952 June Week to the class of 1955, the Academy's new superintendent, William Smedberg, poked that ember one last time.[44] During a 1956 Bancroft Hall radio address, Smedberg counseled the Brigade that "a first class upon its graduation can leave a wonderful impression upon the Brigade . . . or it can leave a bad taste—as did the Class of 1952 with its disgraceful final June Week Parade—which the service heard about with disbelief and disgust, and which the class will be a long time living down."[45]

As the class of 1952 moved through their careers and as decades passed, the 1952 June Week parade attained legendary status, particularly for the large number of shoes its members had left on Worden Field. Prominent mementos of the event can be found throughout the Naval Academy's campus. One of the large scoreboards in the Navy–Marine Corps stadium features the class's motto, "Tough Shoes To Fill," and includes a picture of the class logo, an anchor resting on a pair of midshipman's shoes. The motto and logo are featured prominently in the Naval Academy Alumni Association's ballroom, which the class of 1952 sponsors. The class also planted a red oak tree along Stribling Walk, one of the main pathways on the central campus green. A playful bronze plaque, which includes the Latin word for shoe, identifies the tree as a "Scarlet *Caligae* Oak"; as one class member commented, the Academy apparently "was ignorant of both Latin and botany when they approved our plaque!"[46] In order to make up for the stress they inadvertently caused for succeeding classes, 1952 graduates have also interacted with plebes during a variety of events at USNA in recent decades.[47] One alumnus has commented, "I take no pride in what occurred that day. It was merely a juvenile prank thought up by a couple of carefree, immature near-grads who didn't consider the potential consequences or realize that actions, once started, can sometimes get wildly out of hand when other carefree, fertile minds get into play."[48] However, some class of 1952 alumni enjoy their legendary distinction and believe that their June Week has become "an icon around which to rally class spirit and prove that '52 was unique among [Academy] classes."[49]

After the creation of the Honor Concept and the class of 1952's June Week Parade, the 1950s and early 1960s remained a quiet period in terms of midshipmen's activism. Pranks, however, were fairly common. As discussed in Chapter One, some of the mischief revolved around the spirited competition between midshipmen and cadets from West Point prior to the annual Army-Navy game. One alumnus recalled that there were also instances of midshipmen loaning their civilian friends uniforms so the friends could spend time inside of the Academy.[50] Members of the class of 1948, hoping to inspire classmate J. P. Tagliente to develop prowess in the swimming pool, succeeded by faking a letter to him from a Hollywood studio seeking a new "Tarzan" who could swim.[51] Alumnus John McCain has described water balloon fights and the television that he and nine other midshipmen purchased and, against USNA regulations, watched in McCain's room during the 1957–58 school year.[52] Admiral John Davidson recalled an incident from his 1960 to 1962 superintendency that involved several midshipmen who had unsatisfactory grades in their electrical engineering course. The men wired a telephone wire from an office in Ward Hall to their room in Bancroft Hall and used the telephone to support their business stenciling "GO NAVY! BEAT ARMY!" on women's panties. Davidson and his commandant, Charles Minter, decided to punish the young men lightly "because we thought the whole thing was pretty darn funny. . . . Here they were unsat in juice, and yet they could wire this whole thing at night and get away with it."[53]

This period of relative quiet and subdued pranks gave way, however, to an era of remarkable midshipman activity at Annapolis. Between 1968 and 1973, as college students across the United States were protesting on their campuses, challenging the beliefs and policies of adults, university administrators, and government officials, the Naval Academy, like other American military colleges, appeared to be a bastion of discipline and conservatism.[54] To outside observers, the brick wall surrounding the Naval Academy, as well as USNA's location in a southern state's capital, symbolized the physical and cultural separation of orderly midshipmen from most of the nation's young adults.[55] For the most part, that impression, underscored by the men's voluntary attendance at a military academy during the period of intense anti–Vietnam War sentiment, was true.[56] But it was also true that midshipmen were aware of the concerns and tactics of their civilian counterparts and were willing to modify those tactics and approaches as they addressed issues that mattered to them at the Naval Academy.[57]

About a year before six midshipmen decided to challenge the Academy's mandatory chapel policy and become plaintiffs in the *Anderson v. Laird* case, another significant occurrence reflecting events outside of the Naval Academy's walls began.[58] On a Friday evening in the fall of 1968, Academy administrators announced their decision to limit the time that the second classmen, the class of 1970, would have away from Annapolis for the Army-Navy football game in Philadelphia that season. During the 1967 Army-Navy game, some members of the class of 1969 were involved in a questionable activity, called the "'69 Coed Pep Rally" in the 1970 *Lucky Bag*, and administrators hoped to avoid a recurrence of that incident.[59] The second classmen expected to have the customary liberty on Thanksgiving Day, Thanksgiving Friday, and Saturday, the game day, and as result had arranged to spend the entire weekend in Philadelphia with their dates. The new administrative plan, supposedly based on the need for leadership at the Academy on the nights in question, would have required the men to stay at the Academy on Friday night. The class of

1970, believing they were entitled to the original liberty schedule, realized that they would have to cancel their plans with their dates. As one junior later recalled, "We were not happy."[60]

The weekend was a tense one as members of the class of 1970 contemplated their situation. Several midshipmen decided to vocalize their disagreement with administrators, and early the next week, officers indicated that administrators had revamped their earlier decision: the Academy would allow three juniors from each company to have the expected long weekend, but would require the remainder of the class to stay in Annapolis. Believing the new plan to be arbitrary, the second classmen became infuriated and decided that "either all of us would have extended liberty, or none of us would."[61] One midshipman authored a widely circulated inspirational pamphlet on the subject, and on that Thursday, a midshipman radio announcer on WRNV announced that there would be a class pep rally that evening. At 8:00 that night, midshipman Michael Oliver and his roommate looked out of their Fourth Wing room's window and noticed "all these guys running around [in Tecumseh Court] chanting, and pretty soon it was obvious what they were chanting about." Oliver and his roommate joined the other midshipmen, and shortly thereafter, the entire group walked to the superintendent's house and sat on Admiral James Calvert's lawn. The men declared that they would not end their sit-in until the administration permitted them their full liberty. Superintendent Calvert came to his door, and the assembled midshipman, about half of the class of 1970, greeted him with football songs and complaints about their dissatisfaction with the Army-Navy leave policy; they then returned to Bancroft Hall.

Midshipman Oliver's excitement about the issue, however, did not end on Admiral Calvert's lawn. Oliver returned to his room and discussed the leave policy with several company-mates. In what he later described as a "fit of energy and enthusiasm," he sat at his typewriter and began to compose an editorial commentary that, he hoped, would persuade Calvert to fully restore the juniors' liberty. With verve, Oliver included passages from his Naval leadership course's textbook in creating what he felt was a rational argument. After he read the finished product to his company-mates, the men decided to copy the statement and distribute it to all members of the class of 1970 in order to show the solidarity of the class.

Oliver later explained that during the following weekend, "The letter had a much larger readership than the second class. But that possibility had never entered our minds."[62] During Sunday night dinner in the Academy's mess hall, Brigade leaders began to question Oliver and class of 1970 vice president

Bradley Nemeth about the editorial essay and about the sit-in. Nemeth remembered that the first class leaders began an investigation that night and, in the course of individual interrogations, accused him, Oliver, and the participants in the sit-in of instigating a mutiny. The second classmen began to argue that the administration "can't fry us all" (punish the entire class), but Calvert did just that and the juniors spent the next several weekends, including the Army-Navy game weekend, restricted to the Academy's grounds.[63]

The class of 1970 succeeded in carrying out a sit-in, but failed to achieve their desired change in policy. Nemeth believes that the events "gave solidarity to the class, and provided a gel that still bonds us."[64] The midshipmen received some satisfaction, however, from the December 1968 arrival of Commandant Robert Coogan, who almost immediately set out to change the manner in which the commandant and midshipmen interact.[65] Coogan gave the midshipmen more liberty, yet increased their responsibility, because as he later recalled, "I wanted to treat the midshipmen as men and not as boys."[66] Superintendent Calvert supported this philosophy, stating that

With students on every college campus across the nation pressing demands for a greater voice and influence in the administration and operations of their schools, midshipmen at the Naval Academy are quietly exercising a degree of control and authority over the entire institution that would astonish their civilian peers. Certainly the military environment prevails; young men are being prepared for a military career. But what so many people overlook is that this means preparing young men for leadership, responsibility, and authority, and this is what life at Bancroft Hall is all about. The midshipmen run the Brigade, they plan and implement the activities at all levels and they are held accountable for their efforts. They assume responsibility for their own conduct and enforce the honor concept and the ethical values that attend. . . . [While the current mind-set of] many young people is free-wheeling, undisciplined life—not every young man finds that appealing.[67]

Coogan also rewrote midshipmen's regulations and made greater attempts to obtain high-quality company officers for USNA to increase communications and personal interaction with the midshipmen; he also wandered Bancroft Hall to observe midshipmen and directly address their problems and challenges.[68] In their *Lucky Bag*, the class of 1970, in appreciation for his efforts, thanked Coogan "for being one helluva guy for the Brigade to follow."[69]

At the same time that the *Anderson v. Laird* case on mandatory chapel began, midshipmen editors of the LOG decided to take a more daring approach to their traditionally light-hearted but reserved publication.[70] Superintendent Calvert believed that the LOG provided "humor, news, and a sense of unity to the Naval Academy," but under the 1969–70 editorship of midshipman Daniel Ellison, the magazine began to show the influence of the youth culture of that period.[71] In an October 1969 letter to the editor, midshipman Brad Harbin argued that "we as midshipmen are representatives of American youth, and not outcasts from it!"[72] Another midshipman, Mike Trent, reported after he and several classmates attended the Woodstock music festival that "one thing that the weekend proved was the Midshipmen are human and can get along with civilian college students, as long as the civilians do not know they are Midshipmen. Take away the short hair, the regulations, the drills, and taps, and a Midshipman is just another college kid."[73]

In an editorial, Ellison noted that his "generation has long advocated breaking away from the establishment, finding ourselves and doing our own thing," and in that spirit he presented the December 1969 issue, perhaps the most controversial in the magazine's six-decade history and one that sparked a series of events resembling, in small scale, the Berkeley free speech movement.[74] The cover included an illustration of Santa Claus leaving a buxom woman as a gift for a midshipman, and the interior features were especially controversial. One item was a favorable review of the film *Woodstock*, and in a pseudo–advice column a writer mocked both God and Vice President Spiro Agnew. A third article, referring to *Anderson v. Laird*, contained a midshipman's confession that, in spite of attendance at religious services, he was an atheist. Furthermore, cartoons in the issue showed a midshipman taking a hog on a date, another midshipman attacking an annoying officer with his saber, and a Marine cheerfully hanging grenades on a Christmas tree and singing, "'Tis the season to be jolly."[75] Ellison may have forgotten that over 3,000 copies of the LOG went to subscribers outside of the Academy.

About a dozen of those readers angrily forwarded their copies of that LOG issue to Senator Margaret Chase Smith (R-Maine), the ranking Republican on the Senate Armed Services Committee and an outspoken proponent of the Vietnam War.[76] Senator Smith expressed concern over these items as well as a reference in the November 1969 LOG to the Academy's social director, Mrs. M. E. Marshall, as "Old Thunderthighs."[77] After Smith's administrative assistant contacted various military officials at the Pentagon, Superintendent Calvert decided to meet with the senator in Washington in January 1970. During their meeting, Smith indicated her concerns about the LOG's contents, which she feared were indicative of an impending demonstration at Annapolis

During his 1969–70 term as editor of the *LOG*, midshipman Daniel Ellison oversaw some of the most controversial articles, cartoons, and editorials that the midshipmen's publication had ever featured, reflecting the student activism across the United States during this period. The *LOG*'s contents drew the attention of figures outside of the Academy, who began to complain about the publication to Naval officials. Ellison later explained that in this photograph from 1970 he was engaged in another potentially controversial activity, "sorting out the Company Sweethearts [midshipmen's girlfriends] section of a spring issue, always a daunting task." (Courtesy of Daniel Ellison)

similar to those on other college campuses. Calvert recalled that "at that time, everybody was sensitive about the troubles on campuses. Those were big troubles."[78] Upon his return to Annapolis, Calvert met with the *LOG*'s officer representative, Marine major Constantine Albans, and voiced the senator's concerns. Albans, an officer who was popular with midshipmen, was a combat veteran of the Korean and Vietnam Wars and taught various courses at USNA.[79] He believed that midshipmen, "like students at other colleges, want to communicate their views," and as a result did little to censor Ellison's work.[80] Commandant Robert Coogan then met with Albans and *LOG* staff members, and Coogan told the assembled men to "square away" because Senator Smith was upset.[81]

Ellison and his staff, however, continued their quest for editorial freedom. The January 1970 issue was considerably subdued, although it mentioned the issue of censorship.[82] More boldly, Ellison replied to a non-USNA reader's complaints about the "radical" nature of the December 1969 issue by explaining that "The Log is the magazine of and for the Brigade, [and] much of it is not intended for outside readers. You appear to have fallen into the normal trend of knowing what attitudes prevail at the Academy and which values we should all possess, ranging from religious, to moral, to academic, to social. . . . You paint quite a rosy picture for the way our lives should be shaped. Excuse me if I am wrong but did you ever think that shaping our lives and values might possibly be left up to us?"[83] During a February speech, Admiral Calvert told midshipmen that Senator Smith had "raked him over the coals" because of the LOG.[84] The magazine's staff apologized to Calvert and Coogan in the February issue, but Ellison included still more antics. In a mock exam, readers could choose to describe the USNA Executive Department as "incompetent," "sadistic," "sneaky," and "the Annapolis Branch of the Mickey Mouse Club." Cartoons mocked Billy Graham's recent sermon at the Naval Academy chapel and suggested that a USNA recruit, an ape, would make a good Marine.[85]

Senator Smith had apparently given up reading the LOG when the March 1970 appeared.[86] Ellison printed several provocative items, among which were a spread of photographs of a young woman in a midshipman's room and a photograph of an attractive woman who, according to the caption, knew from experience the quality of mattresses. Both Ellison and the anonymous author of the "Salty Sam" column critiqued an unnamed Washington, D.C., official who claimed to have his or her fingers on the Academy's pulse from reading the LOG. The issue also contained a cartoon that referred to the *Anderson v. Laird* case and showed six midshipmen and a West Point cadet on a gallows, representing the plaintiffs in the case. Another cartoon on the same page was midshipman W. G. Smith's drawing of an angry female senator sitting at her desk reading the LOG while papers on poverty, pollution, economic recession, and prisoners of war piled up around her.[87] There was little doubt as to whom the comic referred.[88]

For just over a month, the cartoon mocking Senator Smith garnered no particular attention. However, the drawing arose in the course of conversation at an Academy officer's social engagement on the evening of Friday, 17 April 1970. While speaking with a Navy commander and his wife, Major Albans began to criticize Senator Smith and her administrative assistant, whom Albans referred to as "arrogant, rude, presumptuous, overbearing, and

After Maine senator Margaret Chase Smith complained to USNA officials about the tone and content of articles and cartoons in the LOG, a midshipman drew this cartoon for the 13 March 1970 edition of the magazine, depicting the Senator—unnamed—sitting in her office angrily reading the LOG instead of dealing with several major issues of the period. Smith later shared her belief that a conspiracy was being waged against her at the Academy, and by the end of the school year USNA officials responded by removing the publication's officer representative and exercising tighter editorial control over the publication. (U.S. Naval Academy Archives)

vindictive," for their role in both the LOG and in politics. When later recounting the evening's events to journalist Robert Timberg, Albans noted that "existential absurdity" kicked in when the commander's wife announced that she was Margaret Chase Smith's personal secretary. Undaunted, Albans mentioned the cartoon, which the commander and his wife noted was "symptomatic of the problems of the Academy and youth in general." Albans quipped, "It's people like [you] that are wrong with the country."[89]

On Monday morning, the commander's wife shared the details of Albans's comments with Senator Smith and her administrative assistant. Smith became convinced that Albans was conspiring against her and immediately contacted the secretary of the Navy.[90] Albans simultaneously told the story to a sympathetic Superintendent Calvert and noted his willingness to resign from his position at USNA, but Calvert did not accept the offer. However, Chief of Naval Personnel C. K. Duncan and Chairman of the Joint Chiefs of Staff Thomas Moorer read the March issue the next day, and by Wednesday an "ice cold" Calvert asked for and received Albans's resignation.[91] Journalist Robert Timberg observes that Albans continued his teaching responsibilities for the semester but lost his LOG officer representative responsibilities.[92] The new officers exercised a heavy editorial hand, and although the resultant April LOG issue was completely benign, a midshipman noted that the magazine had become "the number one conversation piece of company wardrooms, academic classrooms, and interested friends!"[93]

Senator Lee Metcalf (D-Mont.), who sponsored Daniel Ellison's nomination to the Naval Academy, showed unequivocal support for the LOG's editor. Metcalf told reporters that Ellison had demonstrated "a reasoned and informed judgment beyond his years. I believe that anyone reading these [LOG] issues would commend a service academy for a healthy acceptance of opinions that differ but do not inflame."[94] The new officer representative's strict censorship continued, but in the May 1970 issue, the final LOG for the academic year and before Daniel Ellison's graduation, the editor managed to sneak one last editorial statement in amidst an assortment of advertisements. Ellison wrote,

> I had intended to write a final editorial which was to set down future goals for the LOG and the type of editorial policy which most readers would find enlightening and stimulating. I had hoped to base my remarks upon the experience I had gained from being editor for the past year. Unfortunately it has been decided that I cannot exercise my job without editing from above. My staff and I have been virtually silenced. We have published an issue to project an image rather than express thoughts and ideas. When my expressions are subject to someone's approval they are no longer my own, I cease to be an individual, and my job can be better done by a machine. My editorship has ended.[95]

After 1970, USNA administrators generally permitted LOG editors to have creative license, although they quashed the magazine three times and it is not currently published.[96] Ironically, in spite of the incident between Senator Margaret Chase Smith and the LOG, the Margaret Chase Smith Foundation created the annual USNA Margaret Chase Smith Leadership Excellence Award "to recognize and enhance the accomplishments of women . . . in leadership and ethics" in November 1999.[97]

While midshipmen waged their battle for editorial freedom, the Naval Academy found itself in the spotlight for an entirely different reason in March 1970.[98] Pauline House, the owner of the Colonial Wig Shop in downtown Annapolis, told a *New York Times* reporter that, as military personnel were doing across the nation, hundreds of midshipmen from the Academy were purchasing wigs at her boutique "so they can face their girls and hip friends [while] off duty."[99] House further revealed that the midshipmen were keeping their wigs hidden, along with their "girls and liquor," in their rooms in Bancroft Hall.[100] Whether hundreds of midshipmen had purchased wigs, as House claimed, is unknown, but the LOG first mentioned the topic in 1968 when it suggested that wigs were a popular commodity in the Brigade.[101] Midshipmen dismissed and mocked the media attention as "exaggeration," particularly in a LOG comic that spoofed the Times and subsequent Washington Post coverage of wigs at USNA.[102] Superintendent Calvert was less amused and found himself assuring retired chief of Naval operations Arleigh Burke that the newspaper accounts "represent a totally inaccurate view of the Naval Academy today" and were not "a [true] measure of what is going on [here]."[103] What was going on, it appears, was that at least some midshipmen were attempting to fit in with their civilian counterparts at a time when it was difficult for young men to be associated with the military.

A dimension of that difficulty included the increasingly large Bancroft Hall display of photographs of Academy graduates who were killed or missing in action (KIA or MIA) in Vietnam.[104] Furthermore, as a Lucky Bag writer later noted, midshipmen read "daily MIA and KIA notices . . . [before meals] in remembrance of those who had recently filled the ranks of the Brigade."[105] After the child of a prisoner of war (POW) dined with midshipmen early in the fall of 1970, two midshipmen, class of 1972 president Joe Glover and his classmate, Rick Rubel, discussed the psychological challenges that the children of MIAs and POWs faced. With the idea of showing support to those children, Glover and Rubel decided to pass a hat around the mess hall one night and quickly raised $5,000 to purchase Academy sweatshirts as Christmas gifts for them. The two midshipmen wrapped the gifts and utilized an address list of the MIAs' and POWs' families to distribute the shirts to midshipmen who lived in those areas. Over the 1970 holiday break, the midshipmen then delivered the shirts, met and interacted with the children and families, and thus created a rapport between the families and the Brigade. Rubel also sold thousands of bracelets inscribed with the names of POWs to midshipmen, their friends, and girlfriends.

However, Rubel and Glover wanted to do something more to draw attention to the POWs' situation. Glover contacted businessman and alumnus H. Ross Perot, who, after the public disclosure earlier that year of the poor treatment of POWs by their Vietnamese captors, had begun seeking various means of alleviating the men's suffering. Among the captured men was William Lawrence, with whom Perot had created the Honor Concept nearly two decades before.[106] Together, Perot and Glover devised a letter-writing campaign in October 1970. Their goal was to inform citizens of the issue, to show Ho Chi Minh the degree of public support for the POWs, and to convince North Vietnam to abide by Geneva Conventions guidelines on the treatment of prisoners. Rubel served as the Brigade's chairman for the POW campaign, and Glover penned a pamphlet entitled *How You Can Help* in which he encouraged midshipmen, West Point cadets, and the American public to write letters to Ho Chi Minh urging fair treatment of the POWs. Perot loaned the Academy a replica of a bamboo cage of the type the North Vietnamese used to imprison American captive Nick Rowe, and midshipmen set the cage up in Smoke Hall, a large meeting space in Bancroft Hall.

As letters from midshipmen, cadets, and thousands of other citizens arrived at USNA, Rubel put them in the cage and, as the stacks of letters grew higher, in piles around Smoke Hall. Rubel maintained a map of the United States in the rotunda of Bancroft Hall and placed push pins on the map as communities across the nation responded with letters. By the end of November, midshipmen had received tens of thousands of pieces of mail. Rubel, Glover, and Perot contacted Secretary of the Navy John Warner, and Warner arranged a ceremony during the halftime of the Army-Navy game in Philadelphia. Millions of American viewers watched on their televisions as a Postal Service mail truck drove the letters to a midfield podium and the midshipmen presented the letters, which were later airlifted to North Vietnam, to the POWs' wives. The women, who had been pressing the Nixon administration to do more to recognize, ensure the humane treatment of, and free their husbands, showed tremendous gratitude to Rubel and Glover.[107]

Perhaps because of the White House's inaction, USNA administrators were completely silent on the issue of the letter-writing campaign, although Commandant Coogan simultaneously banned opponents of the Vietnam War from speaking at USNA.[108] As Rubel recalled, "We wanted to help personalize the POW situation, and at the Army-Navy game we made the point. The whole process caught fire because midshipmen felt this was something they could do, not to affect the war, but to be part of the recognition [of POWs]. [Vietnam] was a strange war in that you felt bad about the people fighting and dying, and about the prisoners, but you also felt that you had a military role. It was a hard time to be a midshipman. That is why midshipmen latched on [to our project]. It was something positive and a way for us to carry the pride we felt here outside of the Academy walls." Midshipmen and the POWs' families maintained close relationships for some time, and as Rubel later concluded, "We all got a lot out of it. It was a win-win situation."[109] In April 1973, after

Upset by the growing number of Naval Academy graduates who were missing in action (MIA) or prisoners of war (POW) in Vietnam, midshipmen Joe Glover and Rick Rubel decided to draw attention to the issue. In addition to raising money for gifts for the children of MIAs and POWs, members of the class of 1972 led a public letter-writing campaign to urge Ho Chi Minh to exercise fair treatment of the POWs. Rubel, left, Glover, right, and the Brigade commander, center, held a press conference in Smoke Hall, a meeting area of Bancroft Hall, in the fall of 1970. In the background is a replica, supplied by alumnus H. Ross Perot, of the bamboo cage that North Vietnamese captors used to imprison American Nick Rowe. (Courtesy of W. Rick Rubel)

their release from North Vietnam and return to the United States, former POWs Captain Wendell Rivers, Commander James Bell, and Lieutenant Commander Edward Davis appeared at their alma mater.[110] Cheering midshipmen carried the three men around the Academy's mess hall, and as Bell later remembered, "Someone mentioned the midshipmen's letter-writing campaign. During our visit, we were royally entertained. It was a big moment during a period of a lot of big moments of my life."[111]

Although the scope of their actions might pale in comparison with those of their civilian counterparts, the midshipmen's remarkable activities at the Naval Academy between 1968 and 1973 were a direct reflection of the era's student activism and idealism. As Superintendent Calvert explained, "The period from 1968 to 1972 has literally seen a revolution in standards of conduct, grooming, personal appearance, and acceptance of authority on the part of America's youth."[112] Midshipmen demonstrated that they were indeed part of the bold youth of their generation, but they also demonstrated their persistent penchant for pranks. Just prior to the aforementioned 1970 Army-Navy game, as a USNA public works official recalled, "Midshipmen were exuberant in applying paint to various Academy structures" including the colonnade between Dahlgen Hall and Bancroft Hall's Third Wing.[113] The classes of 1969 and 1970 painted the smokestack of the Academy's old power plant, and prior to the building's demolition, the class of 1971 wrote in paint, "IF THE STACK GOES, WE GO WITH IT."[114] In 1970, midshipmen removed the contents of an officer's room and teased the officer by setting up his furniture and belongings in a restroom.[115] Midshipmen also continued older traditions: forcibly shaving the heads of first classmen slated to join the Marine Corps; "attacking" upperclass midshipmen on their birthdays and throwing them in the shower; using the cynical anagram "IHTFP," meaning "I Hate This Fucking Place," when referring to the Academy; and attempting to eat twelve "cannonballs," apples baked in pie crust, to achieve privileges.[116]

Pranks have remained a component of midshipmen's culture since 1973. A launching point for many of these activities has been the "Ho Chi Minh Trail," a system of tunnels that runs under, connects, and carries water and heat to many of the buildings on the USNA campus.[117] The Ho Chi Minh Trail allows access to buildings, and midshipmen have used it to hang banners from roofs, booby-trap classroom buildings, move static aircraft displays and cannons around the Yard, have sex on roofs, escape the Academy at night, and throw parties and surf in the wave-producing flow tank in the basement of Rickover Hall.[118] Members of the Brigade have also continued to target particular officers, in one instance filling an officer's room, from floor to ceiling, with empty aluminum cans.[119] Graduates of the class of 1974 jokingly gave their ceremony's speaker, an amused President Richard Nixon, flags, cigars, rubber chickens, windup airplanes, and live pigeons as he handed them their diplomas.[120] As always, the range of pranks has included antics related to the Army-Navy game. As demonstrated in Chapters Six and Seven, however, women became the object of many male midshipmen's cruel pranks in the months and years after their 1976 arrival. Yet in one rather touching incident, members of the class of 2000 modified the upperclass challenge to plebes that permits relaxed privileges to any fourth classmen who place their covers on the top of the Naval Academy chapel's dome: after plebe Joanna Simer died of a heart attack on 14 August 1996, her classmates scaled the chapel dome and affixed a cover in Simer's honor.[121]

Unlike pranks, however, activism has been rather infrequent among midshipmen. Since 1973, only two notable instances of bold midshipmen's actions have occurred. The first was the aforementioned decision, by many of the female midshipmen in the class of 2000, to appear at their Ring Dance in civilian attire. The second instance was midshipman Blake Bush's 1982 creation of a volunteer-coordinating organization, the Midshipmen Action Group (MAG). Bush noted that "during your four years [at the Academy], you develop close ties to Annapolis. The city becomes almost like a second home to us, and we want to do our part to make it a better place to live."[122] By the late 1980s, because of MAG's role in the community, President George H. W. Bush recognized the organization as one of his "Thousand Points of Light."[123] Midshipmen currently participate in over twenty projects and partnership organizations through MAG, which is now a popular activist organization at USNA.[124]

The occurrence of only two major instances of midshipmen's activism in thirty-three years seems to mimic the lack of activism among youth in the broader American society.[125] Yet, taken as a whole, the episodes between 1949 and 2000 prove that the U.S. Naval Academy has a unique culture that is influenced simultaneously by the institution's seriousness, its military bearing, its discipline, and by the midshipmen's creativity, energy, and youthful exuberance.[126] As Commandant Gary Roughead stated upon his 1999 departure from the Academy, "I tell everyone to keep in mind that we do not commission commanding officers out of the Academy. We commission ensigns and second lieutenants. We must be careful not to stifle great creativity in the name of discipline."[127]

Conclusion

When plebes stand in the corridors of Bancroft Hall and in the course of daily announcements recite, "Time, tide, and formation wait for no one," they are not just politely telling the upperclassmen to hurry up. They are inadvertently proclaiming a fundamental truth: change is inevitable and forthcoming. This book has outlined changes that the Naval Academy underwent between 1949 and 2000. The Academy embraced some of the changes, such as the use of television for recruitment, and has struggled with other changes, such as the full and complete integration of women within the Brigade of Midshipmen. Some members of the Academy community were convinced that changes, such as the adoption of the Honor Concept, would not only positively alter life at USNA but would become crucial components of the institution's culture. They were correct. Other members of the community argued that some changes, including the arrival of minorities and women and the end of mandatory chapel attendance, would quickly deliver the Academy "to hell in a handbasket," irretrievably ruining USNA culture for all time.[1] They were incorrect. One of the Academy's great strengths, ultimately, is its ability to adapt to changes, whether sparked by the federal government, the American public, or members of its own community, and to continue to meet its mission.

However, the Academy's adaptation to some issues has not been complete. It is quite easy to look at the current Academy recruiting and admissions process, for example, and be impressed by the intense devotion of recruiters, Admissions Board members, and Naval Academy Preparatory School staff to the goal of bringing the highest caliber youth to Annapolis. Similarly, any cursory observation of the role of USNA chaplains and their relationships with many midshipmen indicates the fundamental spirituality of those midshipmen even when attendance at religious services is not required. At the same time, it is quite apparent that issues related to gender and race have not been fully resolved. As has been the case with U.S. society at large, many Americans remain unwilling to accept the fundamental equality and capabilities of persons who are not white, Protestant, and male. It is clear that all midshipmen, due to the disciplined military tenor of the Annapolis environment, feel pressure and tension. As Superintendent James Calvert explained in 1972, that type of stress is part of the midshipmen's training and development and is deliberate.[2] But when midshipmen who are African American or female face constant racial or gender isolation five decades after the graduation of the first African American midshipman and three decades after the arrival of the first female midshipmen, it becomes clear that the Naval Academy is falling short of its own ideals and of society's democratic expectations.

The spring 2000 Forrestal Lecture by Secretary of the Navy Richard Danzig is a revealing case in point. Danzig spoke of how the Navy itself had changed over the course of the twentieth century and distributed to the Brigade a photograph of a 1949 ship's crew. The black sailors, rather than standing in ranked order as did the rest of the crew, stood behind everyone else. Danzig's point was to suggest that midshipmen should exercise moral courage in dealing with the changes they were likely to face during their careers. After Danzig's remarks, a midshipman stood and asked, "Sir, after hearing you speak about the importance of morality over discrimination of race and gender, what are your views on gays in the military, and their place in the Navy?" The midshipman touched on a subject with which the Academy has fundamentally not dealt, but Danzig responded,

> My own view about this is that it is really much more an issue for society at large than it is an issue for the military. It's a problem in the military whenever the military gets very far from society at large. We can be a little ahead of it, or a little bit behind it, in the evolution of an issue, but the military isn't essentially a testing ground for a variety of propositions about social existence. It needs to be reflective of the consensus in that society. I think the problem on the issue about gays is that society hasn't reached that consensus. It's going through a variety of kinds of transitions, and difficulties, and arguments back and forth. My own sense is that this issue will continue to do that, and that it will get resolved—as I think it should appropriately get resolved—in Congress over these years. In the end, the military itself and its viewpoints about these things shouldn't be so much a

driver of the issue as a follower of that larger societal consensus. That's my view, in a nutshell.[3]

The secretary, while formulating his comments in a forthright and well-versed manner, overlooked the fact that midshipman Wesley Brown was accepted to and attended the Naval Academy before President Harry Truman integrated the United States armed forces and graduated five years before the Supreme Court's *Brown v. Board of Education* decision and over a decade before equal opportunity legislation. Most serious social change in the United States has occurred as the direct result of action by the federal government, not society's sudden acceptance of groups previously discriminated against. Had the Navy waited for society to form a consensus on the equality of African Americans, as Danzig suggested the military should do in the case of gay Americans, ships' crews may well have remained segregated for decades.

Even when it has not been ahead of the curve in terms of bringing about substantial changes, the Naval Academy's leaders have committed to implementing changes as the federal government has mandated them. As both *Anderson v. Laird* and the integration of women into the Brigade of Midshipmen demonstrate, after a period of resistance, administrators fulfilled their charge and obligation to lead the Academy through fundamental alterations in the institution's culture. Alumnus John Bodnar has noted that

> Changes in military culture parallel changes in American culture in a curious way because the military is simultaneously one of the most conservative and most progressive cultures in America. It is conservative because those who choose to make the military a career are upholders of traditional values and are usually politically conservative. On the other hand, the military is progressive because once the Commander in Chief or Congress decides by policy or by law that any of those values need to change, the military is usually the first to implement those changes. When a significant change in social values has enough popular support to cause a change in law, the military will go through a period of upheaval in which the most progressive social values are implemented in an organization led by some of its most conservative individuals.[4]

What has happened after the "periods of upheaval," however, has been inconsistent. After the Washington, D.C., Federal Appeals Court rendered its decision in the *Anderson v. Laird* case, for example, there was little for the Academy to do other than cancel mandatory chapel attendance. Midshipmen, of their own volition, sought out religious and spiritual guidance and comfort. Yet, after the initial attempts to increase minority enrollment and to integrate female midshipmen, the Academy's administrators largely ceased to concern themselves with those issues; the various groups were at Annapolis, so what remained to be done?

This is not to suggest that USNA officials never addressed the issues of race and gender again. As specific incidents have arisen, and as USNA has complied with Navy and Defense Department sexual harassment and equal opportunity regulations, Academy leaders have in fact dealt with such topics. However, the Academy's culture, like American culture at large, remains one that permits the existence of differing personal opinions. As a result, racist and sexist attitudes, behaviors, and postures continue at the Academy in spite of training and instructional efforts to eliminate them. Unlike the USNA zero-tolerance policy on drugs, the presence of which can be physically tested, it is virtually impossible to police midshipmen's attitudes and difficult to police attitudinal-based actions in Bancroft Hall. After several years of training in character and integrity development, which has frequently focused on issues related to minorities and women, unenlightened attitudes persist. Some midshipmen have argued that the Academy's constant harping on these topics has a cumulatively detrimental impact on the midshipmen's willingness to accept the precepts being promoted.

A seemingly obvious method of demonstrating the capabilities of minorities and women would be to assign more of them to powerful high-profile positions at the Academy. However, as USNA leaders are quick to point out, the dearth of such individuals makes them highly desirable in a multitude of Navy and Marine Corps positions. Few women or minorities have served in the Academy's highest administrative positions, including superintendent, and only in June 2005 did an African American, Bruce Groom, assume the position of commandant, the second-highest rank at USNA. One remedy has been to bring successful female and minority officers to the Academy to address and interact with the midshipmen. Two cases demonstrate, however, the limits of this approach. In 1999, one of the Academy's most successful female graduates, astronaut Wendy Lawrence, returned to Annapolis to speak before a combined group of midshipmen and cadets from other service academies. Beyond the primary conferees, the remaining audience members were midshipmen whose professors had "suggested" they attend the address. Many midshipmen slept, read, or did homework, although Lawrence imparted the enlightening message that part of what helped her to achieve astronaut status was the behavior of "individuals who, along the way, did not make being female an issue for me."[5] Also in 1999, astronaut Charles Bolden, among the most accomplished minority alumni of the Naval Academy, spoke before the Midshipmen Black Studies Club for Black History Month. The audience was made up almost exclusively of minority midshipmen, and so the majority of the Brigade was not present to hear the general's counsel on an extraordinary variety of topics, including his charge to "make a difference. You can't solve the problems of the world, but you can make a difference in the world."[6] Academy administrators missed the chance to invite such notable alumni as Lawrence and Bolden to deliver its prestigious Forrestal Lecture, and the entire Brigade of Midshipmen thus lost the opportunity to learn from two highly accomplished alumni, one of whom happened to be female and another African American.

A somewhat larger group of midshipmen assembled in 1999 for an address by former Army helicopter pilot Hugh Thompson. In a moving speech, Thompson recounted how he landed his helicopter in a remote Vietnam village and, after standing up to a superior officer, brought an end to what historians now refer to as the My Lai massacre. He told the midshipmen that "the lesson I want to give to you is to do the right thing, to make the right decision. You are responsible for every decision you make."[7] Similarly, Admiral William Mack's remarks on the *Anderson v. Laird* case bear reconsideration. When asked if he regretted the involvement of the American Civil Liberties Union in the case, Admiral Mack replied that "that was one of my regrets, why did we not have the moral courage to do this ourselves rather than have it forced on us by the courts. That was terrible. That's what I was saying while I was in the Defense Department. I was told, no, we're going to [fight to keep mandatory chapel], you make the argument and we'll fight it. I said, why do you fight it, we'd be better off to do it of our own volition, but I was told to fight it so I had to fight it, not with good grace, I must admit."[8] Thompson and Mack speak to an ideal of leadership, commitment, and personal obligation: to do what is right. Not only do these accounts provide midshipmen with an ideal for their own careers, but they can serve equally as a guide for Naval Academy administrators who are in a position to utilize their leadership to create an environment in which the unequivocal acceptance of all midshipmen will prevail.

In addition to the fundamental truth of the inevitability of change, another constant is the remarkable character of the individuals who make up the Naval Academy community. As the previous chapters have shown, some of the men who have served as superintendent and commandant have done so with verve and a keen desire to set a leadership example for the midshipmen. Whether it was Harry Hill's inspirational speeches to the Brigade, Robert Coogan's willingness to listen to midshipmen, William Lawrence's supportive words during athletic practices, Leon Edney's playful dressing up as a detective during football pep rallies, or James Calvert's determination to steer the Academy through the troubled late–Vietnam War era, the Academy's administrators have frequently served as fitting role models in the Annapolis "leadership laboratory."[9] Taken as a whole, the superintendents and commandants between 1949 and 2000 represent an astonishing variety of leadership styles, talents, and approaches for leading the institution and educating and training midshipmen. The solid commitment of the entire USNA staff—including coaches, faculty, librarians, and mess hall workers—has been a vital component of the administrations' successes.

Yet it is the midshipmen themselves who remain the center of Naval Academy culture and the most notable component of the Annapolis community. Characterized by a dichotomous yin/yang of cynicism and activism, drawn to both conformity and individualism, midshipmen represent a fascinating and diverse group of youth from around the United States who opt to spend their college experience in one of the most challenging and yet inspirational environments in American higher education. They are equally comfortable strumming their guitars on the sea wall rocks as they are marching in formation on the parade ground or stroking in synchronicity in their shells on the Severn River. While the Brigade members can impress even a pundit with their exceptional military bearing and their marching, the ultimate embodiment of personal control and commitment, they also readily enjoy the sordid tales of the LOG's "Salty Sam," the melodramatic mockery of Academy life in Eighth Wing Players skits, and the quick quips of WRNV disc jockeys. These humorous actions are perhaps not surprising among midshipmen living under the rigors of Brigade life, yet they fail to reflect how the same midshipmen, while gazing from the balconies of Bancroft Hall's lighted rotunda, can find inspiration in the great Navy and Marine Corps leaders who crossed the marble floors before them or in Oliver Hazard Perry's Battle of Lake Erie flag with its emphatic message, "Don't give up the ship."

The U.S. Naval Academy's culture was transformed, along with that of American society as a whole, between 1949 and 2000. When the public began to embrace television for its entertainment, USNA used television as the forum for its recruiting. When Americans decided to permit minorities and women to play a fuller role as citizens, minorities and women came to Annapolis as midshipmen. When college students began to question governmental and institutional authority, midshipmen challenged required religious services and demonstrated activism by expressing their opinions on a variety of topics important to them. These factors fundamentally altered the Academy and its culture, but the commitment of administrators and staff to educate and train midshipmen and the midshipmen's determination to challenge themselves and to succeed have remained constant. This book has shown what the U.S. Naval Academy was in the past, described what it is today, and offers ideas about what it can become in the future as it continues to meet its mission to prepare leaders for the U.S. Navy and the U.S. Marine Corps.

Note on the Sources

Primary Source Research

The primary-source research for this book took place largely during a two-year research period at the U.S. Naval Academy from 1998 through 2000 and included three types of historical inquiry: participatory observation, oral history, and archival research. The participatory observation component involved interacting with many members of the USNA community. This included attending meetings of administrators; classes, lectures, and ceremonies; reunions and meetings of alumni groups; athletic practices and sporting events; and meetings of extracurricular activities. These events provided me with the opportunity to gain a firsthand understanding of the culture and community of the Naval Academy.

Oral history plays a prominent role in this book, and for this project I interviewed over three hundred members of the Naval Academy community. This group of people included administrators, officers, enlisted personnel, midshipmen, faculty, coaches, alumni, midshipmen's parents, USNA employees, and citizens of Annapolis. I make reference to 225 of these interviews in this book. These interviews were in one of four formats: correspondence interviews, which took place through the mail; electronic interviews, which took place via e-mail; personal interviews, which took place in person; and telephone interviews, which took place over the telephone. Most of the interviews were personal interviews. Some interviewees chose to be identified by name. In those cases, I refer to the interviews in the Notes in the following format:

Type of interview, Name of interviewee, Location of interviewee, Date of interview.

The overwhelming majority of the interviewees chose to be anonymous, and in order to protect their identities I developed a completely random number assignment system to reference those interviews. In these cases, I refer to the interviews in the following format:

Type of interview, Anonymous interviewee number.

Because of the extensive variety of members of the USNA community that I interviewed, I did not utilize one standard questionnaire form but rather adjusted my series of questions as appropriate to the individual interviewee. I have also made extensive use of written oral history source material, in particular from the extensive U.S. Naval Institute collection of published and unpublished interviews with Navy personnel.

The archival research component of the research for this project centered on National Archives and Records Administration Record Group 405, known as "Superintendents' Records," which are housed at USNA's archives in Nimitz Library. These papers constitute the institutional history of USNA and are primarily reports, correspondence, memorandums, directives, and orders. I make reference to hundreds of documents from this collection. The record group consists of five sections, each of which has a unique filing system. To reflect the organizational system of the Superintendents' Records and to facilitate references in the Notes, I broke these five sections down as follows:

Section 1, Papers through 1959
Section 2, Papers, 1960–84
Section 3, Papers, 1985–2000
Section 4, *Men of Annapolis* Papers
Section 5, Papers on Women

Complementing this extensive series of papers, and with similar contents, is USNA Archives' collection of Commandants' Records. Both USNA Archives and USNA Special Collections have reference files, reports, maps, photographs, personal and organizational papers, and books related to USNA. Nimitz Library's Electronic Resource Center also made their collection of films, recordings, and television programs available to me.

I have also utilized a number of USNA-related publications as primary source material. This includes annual Board of Visitors reports; findings and recommendations prepared by USNA's group of government-appointed advisors; *Character Quarterly*, the USNA Character Development Department's quarterly publication; *The LOG*, the midshipmen's news, humor, and entertainment magazine; *Shipmate*, the monthly magazine of the USNA Alumni

Association; and *Trident*, the official public affairs newspaper of USNA. I have also used yearbooks from USNA (*The Lucky Bag*), the Naval Academy Preparatory School (*The Cruise*), and the U.S. Military Academy (*The Howitzer*), and I make reference to *Reef Points*, the USNA plebe manual.

The archival research extended beyond USNA, however, to include a number of other institutional collections around the United States. The Lyndon B. Johnson Presidential Library supplied records related to ideas for increasing "minority" enrollment at USNA. I used the collections of the Motion Picture, Sound, and Video Collection, National Archives and Records Administration, to locate newsreel coverage of USNA graduations in the 1950s. The National Park Service's National Register of Historic Places collections outlined historical and architectural features of the USNA campus. The *Playboy* Magazine Archives located a copy of a 1989 issue of that magazine containing excerpts from a banned *LOG* magazine issue. The Margaret Chase Smith Library made available records outlining the Senator's interaction with the editors of the *LOG*. At the Washington National Records Center, I utilized U.S. Court of Appeals and U.S. District Court records to study several cases. I used several works from the U.S. Naval Historical Center and the U.S. Marine Corps Historical Center. At the Wisconsin Center for Film and Theater Research, I had access to copies of episodes of the television series *Men of Annapolis* and related archival material. Nimitz Library's Electronic Resource Center has recently acquired copies of the episodes, which can now be viewed at USNA as well.

I have also made use of the personal collections of several members of the Annapolis and West Point communities who generously offered access to their materials. These papers were related to the *Anderson v. Laird* case, the *Men of Annapolis* television series, women at USNA, Academy graduates who served in the Air Force, the class of 1952's graduation week, and USNA history in general. Several USNA professors allowed me to study research they did concerning USNA, and two West Point alumni, Lucian Truscott IV and David Vaught, provided me access to their extensive personal records on the events preceding and involving the *Anderson v. Laird* case.

Finally, the archival research included newspaper, internet, magazine, scholarly journal, and official report sources. Although I utilize articles from many newspapers, I frequently relied on the three papers in the Annapolis area: the *Annapolis Evening Capital*, the *Baltimore Sun*, and the *Washington Post*. The most important newspaper in this study, however, is the *New York Times*, which is thoroughly indexed and has covered events at USNA since World War II in detail. Internet source material was limited to items from the official Web sites of USNA, the USNA Alumni Association, and the U.S. Navy. In accordance with currently accepted procedures for internet citations, I provide the sponsoring organization, the web address, and the date on which I referenced a Web page in the Notes.

Secondary Source Research

This survey of secondary sources that influenced my ideas and upon which some of my research is based contains those works that are readily available to interested readers.

Although literature on the Naval Academy is not prolific, there are many useful works that will acquaint the reader with the institution's history and culture. Jack Sweetman and Thomas Cutler's *The U.S. Naval Academy: An Illustrated History* is an excellent starting point for the historical development of the institution. Randolph King has produced two important and detailed timelines of events that have taken place at USNA. One was published as part of the 1999 USNA Alumni Association's *Register of Alumni*, Vol. I, and the second as part of his excellent overview of sources on USNA, *The United States Naval Academy, 1845–1995: Chronology, Bibliography, and Sources of Information*. John Lovell's *Neither Athens Nor Sparta?: The American Service Academies in Transition* has remained the standard comparative work on military academies since its 1979 publication. Readers seeking visual representations of USNA should refer to Robert Stewart's *The Brigade in Review: A Year at the U.S. Naval Academy*, which has well-presented images of Annapolis as it was in 1993. Readers hoping to understand Naval Academy culture as it exists at present should refer to three books. One is Bruce Fleming's *Annapolis Autumn: Life, Death, and Literature at the U.S. Naval Academy*. Fleming describes his experiences as a professor and comments on homosexuality and homoeroticism, among many other topics, at USNA. A second work is Shannon French's *The Code of the Warrior: Exploring Warrior Values Past and Present*. French shares valuable insights into midshipmen's thinking about their training as warriors. Another is David Lipsky's fascinating work, *Absolutely American: Four Years At West Point*. Although he writes about USNA's arch-rival, Lipsky addresses a variety of topics that apply equally to Annapolis.

Several works offer more directed looks at particular aspects of USNA. James Calvert's *The Naval Profession* provides an overview of the expectations of midshipmen, while David Lebby's dissertation, "Professional Socialization of the Naval Officer: The Effect of Plebe Year at the U.S. Naval Academy," considers plebe experiences. Charles Sheppard's "An Analysis of Curriculum Changes at the United States Naval Academy During the Period 1959 Through

1974" and Todd Forney's *The Midshipman Culture and Educational Reform: The U.S. Naval Academy 1946–1976* are thorough examinations of USNA's "academic revolution." Those seeking information on the *Men of Annapolis* television series should consult Sherman Alexander's *Shipmate* articles on that topic, as well as Morleen Rouse's dissertation, "A History of the F. W. Ziv Radio and Television Syndication Companies, 1930–1960." Robert Schneller's *Breaking the Color Barrier: The U.S. Naval Academy's First Black Midshipmen and the Struggle for Racial Equality* looks at the experiences of African Americans at USNA up to and including Wesley Brown.

Readers interested in the Naval Academy's campus and architecture will find several works to be of use. Margaret and Randolph King's *The United States Naval Academy Chapel: ". . . For Those in Peril on the Sea"* is necessary reading for those who want to study USNA's most famous building, while John Keegan's *Fields of Battle: The Wars for North America* contains a vivid description of USNA's campus and place among Western military institutions. Mardges Bacon's *Ernest Flagg: Beaux Arts Architect and Urban Reformer* describes USNA's architect and his original designs for the campus. A more recent study of the campus is the 1996 *United States Naval Academy North Severn Master Plan*. For a perspective on the unique aspects of the USNA campus as it relates to other prominent university campuses in the United States, see the 1999 *University of Georgia Master Plan*.

Autobiographical works by alumni are numerous. Among those used in this text is Anne Marie Drew's *Letters from Annapolis: Midshipmen Write Home, 1848–1969*, which contains vignettes of midshipmen's experiences at the Academy. Ralph Earle's *Life at the U.S. Naval Academy* and Robley Evans's *A Sailor's Log: Recollections of Forty Years of Naval Life* include portraits of the nineteenth-century Academy. Robert Slieght's *Sixteen Hundred Men: A Personal Remembrance, USNA, 1932–1936* gives a pre–World War II glimpse of USNA, while John McCain and Mark Salter's *Faith of My Fathers: A Family Memoir* and Robert Timberg's *The Nightingale's Song* provide frank, unrestrained commentary on life at the Academy in the 1950s and 1960s. However, the single most insightful work based on recollections is Sharon Hanley Disher's *First Class: Women Join the Ranks at the Naval Academy*, which offers a semi-fictionalized account of the experiences of a large number of the Academy's first female midshipmen.

Published oral histories constitute a substantive portion of the research in this book, and the most noteworthy collection is the U.S. Naval Institute's Oral History Program, which sponsored extensive and highly detailed interviews with major Naval leaders. Many interviews are with officers who served in leadership capacities at USNA, and those which I have referenced extensively here include Julian T. Burke Jr., John F. Davidson, Roland W. Faulk, Francis D. Foley, Draper L. Kauffman, William P. Mack, Robert W. McNitt, Charles L. Melson, Charles S. Minter, and William R. Smedberg III. This remarkable resource, much of it prepared by the remarkable historian Paul Stillwell, is a treasure of information for researchers interested in a myriad of topics. The Navy's Chaplain Corps also sponsors an oral history program; interviewed chaplains who served at USNA include Henry Rotrige, Samuel Sobel, and John Zimmerman.

Literature on the Navy is quite extensive. Two valuable reference books are Bill Bearden's *The Bluejackets' Manual* and William Mack and Royal W. Connell's *Naval Ceremonies, Customs, and Traditions*. Among the historical works that impacted my interpretations of events at USNA in relation to the Navy are James George's *The U.S. Navy in the 1990s: Alternatives for Action*, Kenneth Hagan's *In Peace and War: Interpretations of American Naval History, 1775–1984* and *This People's Navy: The Making of American Sea Power*, and Frederick Hartmann's *Naval Renaissance: The U.S. Navy in the 1980s*. Norman Polmar and Thomas Allen's *Rickover* is the standard biography of one of USNA's most notable alumni and critics, and Elmo Zumwalt Jr.'s *On Watch: A Memoir* is a requirement for readers interested in the Vietnam-era Navy. In *Sailing on the Silver Screen: Hollywood and the U.S. Navy*, Lawrence Suid presents a compelling look at the Navy through the genre of film.

A number of works have influenced my commentary on culture. Such theoretical works on culture include T. S. Eliot's *Notes Toward the Definition of Culture*, Lynn Hunt's *The New Cultural History*, Lawrence Levine's *Black Culture and Black Consciousness: Afro-American Folk Thought from Slavery to Freedom*, and Marshall Sahlins's three works, *Culture and Practical Reason*, *How "Natives" Think: About Captain Cook, for Example*, and *Islands of History*. Charles Joyner's *Drums and Shadows: Survival Studies Among the Georgia Coastal Negroes* is an excellent early example of oral history focused on culture, and James Gregory's *American Exodus: The Dust Bowl Migration and Okie Culture in California* is a multi-faceted examination of group culture. Eric Hobsbawm and Terence Ranger's *The Invention of Tradition* is the standard work in the formation of group identity and traditions, and Renato Rosaldo's *Ilongot Headhunting, 1883–1974: A Study in Society and History* is a focused examination of the cyclical nature of group cultural practices. An excellent overview of the cultural development of the United States is Michael Kammen's *Mystic Chords of Memory: The Transformation of Tradition in American Culture*.

To understand the Naval Academy in relation to other institutions of higher education, I relied on Lawrence Cremin's comprehensive three-volume series, *American Education*. A. Bartlett Giamatti's *The University and the Public Interest* and his beautiful essay *Reflections on Our University* are worthwhile commentaries on higher education. I also found three works to be beneficial on student culture and activism: Alexander DeConde's *Student Activism: Town and Gown in Historical Perspective*, Ronald Fraser's *1968: A Student Generation In Revolt*, and Helen Lefkowitz-Horowitz's *Campus Life: Undergraduate Cultures from the End of the Nineteenth Century to the Present*.

My interpretation of legal issues in this book is heavily dependent upon Melvin Urofsky's comprehensive study of Supreme Court law and cases, *A March of Liberty: A Constitutional History of the United States*. I also utilized an account of the *Anderson v. Laird* case that is found in Mary Edwards Wertsch's *Military Brats: Legacies of Childhood Inside the Fortress*.

A popular genre on which I have relied is political biography and autobiography. Among the useful congressional works I have utilized are Wilbur Cross's *Samuel Stratton: A Story of Political Gumption*, Jacob Javits and Rafael Steinberg's *Javits: The Autobiography of a Public Man*, and Francis Valeo's *Mike Mansfield, Majority Leader: A Different Kind of Senate, 1961–1976*. I have also utilized four books on Margaret Chase Smith, including Alberta Gould's *Lady of the Senate: A Life of Margaret Chase Smith*, Janann Sherman's *No Place for a Woman: A Life of Senator Margaret Chase Smith*, Patricia Ward Wallace's *Politics of Conscience: A Biography of Margaret Chase Smith*, and Smith's own *Declaration of Conscience*. In regard to African American political figures and their role in getting African Americans to USNA as midshipmen, several books are informative: Wil Haygood, *King of the Cats: The Life and Times of Adam Clayton Powell Jr.*, Peggy Lamson, *The Glorious Failure: Black Congressman Robert Brown Elliott and the Reconstruction in South Carolina*, Adam Clayton Powell Jr., *Adam by Adam: The Autobiography of Adam Clayton Powell Jr.*, and Roy Wilkins and Tom Mathews, *Standing Fast: The Autobiography of Roy Wilkins*.

On the role of two prominent figures in this study, Robert Kennedy and Lyndon Johnson, I have referenced a number of works. On RFK, C. David Heymann's *RFK: A Candid Biography of Robert F. Kennedy*, James Hilty's *Robert Kennedy: Brother Protector*, Victor Navasky's *Kennedy Justice*, and Evan Thomas, *Robert Kennedy: His Life* are useful, but Arthur Schlesinger Jr.'s *Robert Kennedy and His Times* is the most insightful. On LBJ, I have referred to Michael Beschloss's *Reaching For Glory: Lyndon Johnson's Secret White House Tapes, 1964–1965*, Robert Dallek's *Flawed Giant: Lyndon Johnson and His Times, 1961–1973*, Robert Divine's *The Johnson Years, Volume Three: LBJ At Home and Abroad*, Doris Kearns,

Lyndon Johnson and the American Dream, and Jeff Shesol, Mutual Contempt: Lyndon Johnson, Robert Kennedy, and the Feud That Defined a Decade.

Literature on race and African Americans is extensive. Related to USNA, I have relied on Robert Schneller's extensive articles on Wesley Brown, on Philip Brown's A Century of Separate but Equal in Anne Arundel County and The Other Annapolis: 1900–1950, and Paul Stillwell's The Golden Thirteen: Recollections of the First Black Naval Officers. Cynthia Enloe's Ethnic Soldiers: State Security and Divided Societies is a superb theoretical work, and an excellent philosophical piece is John Hope Franklin's The Color Line: Legacy for the Twenty-First Century. The three standard works on African Americans in the U.S. military remain Richard Dalfiume's Desegregation of the Armed Forces: Fighting on Two Fronts, 1939–1953, Morris MacGregor Jr.'s Integration of the Armed Forces, 1940–1965, and Bernard Nalty's Strength for the Fight: A History of Black Americans in the Military.

Works on women at USNA have become more common. The absolute standard for anyone interested in the topic is Sharon Hanley Disher's First Class: Women Join the Ranks at the Naval Academy, a fictionalized account of actual experiences of USNA's first female midshipmen. A useful study is Carmen Neuberger's "A Comparative Study of Environmental Expectations of Female v. Male Midshipmen Entering the United States Naval Academy." Kathleen Durning's Women at the Naval Academy: The First Year of Integration discusses the same issue. Elizabeth Lutes Hillman's "Uniform Identities: Women, Gender, and Images at the United States Service Academies" covers all military academies, and although Judith Stiehm's Bring Me Men and Women: Mandated Change at the U.S. Air Force Academy does not address USNA extensively, it too looks at the gender integration of service academies. Stephen Frantzich presents an account of some of the first women who challenged gender bans on women at USNA in Citizen Democracy: Political Activists in a Cynical Age, while Missy Cummings offers a vignette of life for women after the first female midshipmen graduated in Hornet's Nest: The Experiences of One of the Navy's First Female Fighter Pilots.

The literature on women in the military and gender issues is rather broad, but I found several works particularly informative. Jean Ebbert and Marie-Beth Hall's Crossed Currents: Navy Women in a Century of Change provides the best coverage of women in the Navy as a background to women's experiences at USNA. Three broader works, Francine D'Amico and Laurie Weinstein's Gender Camouflage: Women and the U.S. Military, Mary Katzenstein and Judith Reppy's Beyond Zero Tolerance: Discrimination in Military Culture, and Linda Kerber's No Constitutional Right to Be Ladies: Women and the Obligations of Citizenship are insightful studies. E. Anthony Rotundo's American Manhood: Transformations in

Masculinity from the Revolution to the Modern Era is also useful for understanding gender issues.

Finally, I have been especially influenced by two excellent works: the collection of theoretical essays in Wallace Stegner's *The Sound of Mountain Water: The Changing American West* and the influential, synthetic U.S. history survey by Howard Zinn, *A People's History of the United States, 1492–Present*.

Statistical Appendix

TABLE 5. Minorities and Women at NAPS

NAPS Graduating Class	African Americans	Hispanic Americans	Asian Americans	Women
1966	3	0	0	0
1967	3	0	0	0
1968	4	0	0	0
1969	7	0	0	0
1970	23	5	1	0
1971	10	1	0	0
1972	15	0	4	0
1973	35	0	2	0
1974	43	5	6	0
1975	19	7	3	0
1976	33	11	9	2
1977	16	13	5	8
1978	18	5	4	4
1979	47	9	13	8
1980	46	13	12	9
1981	34	11	10	12
1982	N/A	N/A	N/A	N/A
1983	43	29	17	10
1984	42	20	3	14
1985	39	30	13	14
1986	59	23	15	15
1987	46	22	16	23
1988	37	22	15	23
1989	35	20	17	19
1990	52	21	19	22
1991	61	30	9	37
1992	61	33	4	34
1993	N/A	N/A	N/A	N/A
1994	53	16	13	29
1995	34	24	7	40
1996	20	18	3	38

Sources: *Cruise*, 1965–81, 1983–92, 1994–96; Superintendent to Chief of Naval Education and Training, 27 Sept. 1973, SR2, Sec. NC/1500, Folder "1974."

Minority Women	Total Minorities and Women	Total Graduates	Total % of Minorities and Women
0	3	225	1.3
0	3	178	1.7
0	4	120	3.3
0	7	121	5.8
0	29	203	14.3
0	11	213	5.2
0	19	194	9.8
0	37	224	16.5
0	54	286	18.9
0	29	275	10.5
0	55	258	21.3
2	42	172	24.4
0	31	246	12.6
4	77	266	28.9
6	80	239	33.5
2	67	242	27.7
N/A	N/A	N/A	N/A
10	99	259	38.2
8	79	285	27.7
10	96	272	35.3
10	112	262	42.8
12	107	255	41.9
8	97	284	34.2
6	91	254	35.8
9	114	320	35.6
19	137	274	50
11	132	294	44.9
N/A	N/A	N/A	N/A
10	110	267	41.2
17	105	225	46.7
14	89	222	40.1
14	89	222	40.1

TABLE 6. Minorities and Women Entering USNA

Graduating Class	African Americans	Hispanic Americans	Asian Americans/ Pacific Islanders	American Indians	Women
1980	65	35	44	9	81
1981	58	49	57	8	90
1982	62	42	45	4	96
1983	80	48	57	6	90
1984	57	63	50	7	100
1985	51	51	58	9	109
1986	72	63	62	6	97
1987	68	65	46	4	111
1988	61	74	44	3	113
1989	80	73	65	6	140
1990	92	76	69	11	143
1991	66	82	54	10	119
1992	71	86	49	8	149
1993	88	89	70	14	131
1994	105	100	55	10	136
1995	87	80	50	14	146
1996	96	70	53	7	169
1997	75	68	44	9	166
1998	90	89	52	13	190
1999	87	88	40	19	194
2000	71	86	53	9	201

Sources: PI, Interviewee #164; Class Profiles, 1976–2001, ARF "Midshipman: Class Profiles"; Lists of American Indian Midshipmen, ARF "Midshipmen: American Indian Midshipmen"; Superintendent to Chief of Naval Operations, 11 Jan. 1989, SR3, 1989, Box 1000–1531/2, Folder 1531; Minority Attrition Summary, 17 Jan. 1990, SR3, 1990, Box 1000–1531/1, Folder "1990"; Women Midshipmen Study Group, "Report to the Superintendent on the Assimilation of Women in the Brigade of Midshipmen," 1 July, 1990, 6, 8, 13, 31, SR5; Superintendent to Chief of Naval Operations, undated, SR3, 1990, Box 1531/1–1710/5, Folder "1990"; Superintendent to Chief of Naval Operations, 15 Oct. 1991, SR3, 1991, Box 1531–1710/2–35, Folder "1991"; "Minority Attrition at the Naval

Total Minorities	Total Minorities and Women	Total in Class	Total % of Minorities	Total % of Minorities and Women
153	234	1,294	11.8	18.7
172	262	1,328	13	19.7
153	249	1,364	11.2	18.3
191	281	1,404	13.6	20.2
169	269	1,249	13.5	21.5
203	312	1,331	15.3	23.4
203	300	1,333	15.2	22.5
183	294	1,360	13.5	21.6
182	295	1,366	13.3	21.6
224	364	1,390	16.1	26.2
248	391	1,374	18	28.5
212	331	1,319	16.1	25.1
214	363	1,358	15.8	26.7
261	392	1,400	18.6	28
270	406	1,241	21.8	32.7
231	377	1,141	20.2	33
226	395	1,242	18.2	31.8
196	362	1,187	16.5	30.5
244	434	1,214	20.1	35.7
234	428	1,170	20	36.6
219	420	1,220	18	34.4

Academy, by Percentages," 31 Jan. 1992, SR5, Box 4; Superintendent to Chief of Naval Operations, 30 Nov. 1992, SR3, 1992, Box 1000–1531, Folder "1992"; Superintendent to Bureau of Naval Personnel, 31 Mar. 1996, SR3, Box 1531, Folder "1531"; USNA Admissions Office, "United States Naval Academy History of Incoming Class Composition," 1990, HMG. Virgil Hill to Blue and Gold Officers, 31 Aug. 1990, SR3, 1990, Box 1000–1531/1, Folder "1531/1"; Northrup et al., *Black and Minority Participation in the All-Volunteer Navy and Marine Corps*, 133; John Bodnar, "Retention of Minorities at the Service Academies," HMG; "USNA History of Incoming Class Composition, HMG.

TABLE 7. Minorities and Women Graduating from USNA
Note: Numbers in parentheses are attrition rates

Graduating Class	African Americans	Hispanic Americans	Asian Americans/ Pacific Islanders	American Indians	Women
1980	48 (26.2%)	25 (28.6%)	34 (22.7%)	4 (55.6%)	55 (32.1%)
1981	38 (34.5%)	36 (26.5%)	44 (22.8%)	5 (37.5%)	60 (33.3%)
1982	39 (37.1%)	31 (26.2%)	34 (26.7%)	1 (75.0%)	63 (34.4%)
1983	50 (37.5%)	34 (29.2%)	43 (24.6%)	2 (66.7%)	53 (41.1%)
1984	39 (31.6%)	48 (23.8%)	33 (34.0%)	6 (14.3%)	63 (37.0%)
1985	38 (25.5%)	32 (37.3%)	41 (29.3%)	4 (55.6%)	76 (30.3%)
1986	46 (36.1%)	43 (31.7%)	49 (21.0%)	3 (50.0%)	65 (33.0%)
1987	36 (47.1%)	52 (20.0%)	38 (17.8%)	3 (25.0%)	70 (36.9%)
1988	39 (36.1%)	47 (36.5%)	37 (15.9%)	2 (33.3%)	80 (29.2%)
1989	60 (25.0%)	52 (28.8%)	50 (23.1%)	4 (33.3%)	94 (32.9%)
1990	63 (31.5%)	47 (38.2%)	54 (21.7%)	9 (18.2%)	98 (31.5%)
1991	39 (40.9%)	52 (36.6%)	44 (18.5%)	6 (40.0%)	81 (31.9%)
1992	45 (36.6%)	56 (34.9%)	46 (6.1%)	5 (37.5%)	96 (35.6%)
1993	57 (35.2%)	63 (29.2%)	63 (10.0%)	8 (42.9%)	91 (30.5%)
1994	71 (32.4%)	71 (29.0%)	44 (20.0%)	10 (0.0%)	101 (25.7%)
1995	66 (24.1%)	64 (20.0%)	43 (14.0%)	12 (14.2%)	106 (27.4%)
1996	59 (38.5%)	47 (32.9%)	44 (17.0%)	5 (28.6%)	115 (32.0%)
1997	54 (28.0%)	48 (29.4%)	38 (13.6%)	8 (11.1%)	115 (30.7%)
1998	60 (33.3%)	61 (31.5%)	43 (17.3%)	9 (30.8%)	138 (27.4%)
1999	59 (32.2%)	58 (34.1%)	33 (17.5%)	15 (21.1%)	134 (30.9%)
2000	52 (26.8%)	63 (26.7%)	40 (24.5%)	5 (44.4%)	134 (33.3%)

Sources: PI, Interviewee #164; Class Profiles, 1976–2001, ARF "Midshipman: Class Profiles"; Lists of American Indian Midshipmen, ARF "Midshipmen: American Indian Midshipmen"; Superintendent to Chief of Naval Operations, 11 Jan. 1989, SR3, 1989, Box 1000–1531/2, Folder 1531; Minority Attrition Summary, 17 Jan. 1990, SR3, 1990, Box 1000–1531/1, Folder "1990"; Women Midshipmen Study Group, "Report to the Superintendent on the Assimilation of Women in the Brigade of Midshipmen," 1 July, 1990, 6, 8, 13, 31, SR5; Superintendent to Chief of Naval Operations, undated, SR3, 1990, Box 1531/1–1710/5, Folder "1990"; Superintendent to Chief of Naval Operations, 15 Oct. 1991, SR3, 1991, Box 1531–1710/2–35, Folder "1991"; "Minority Attrition at the Naval

Total Minorities	Total Minorities and Women	Total in Class	Total % of Minorities	Total % of Minorities and Women
112	167	946 (26.9%)	11.8	12.9
123	183	966 (27.3%)	12.7	13.8
105	168	1,047 (23.2%)	10	12.3
129	182	1,077 (23.3%)	12	13
126	189	1,004 (19.6%)	12.5	15.1
115	191	1,044 (21.6%)	11	14.4
141	206	1,028 (22.9%)	13.7	15.5
129	199	1,036 (23.8%)	12.5	14.6
125	205	1,060 (22.4%)	11.8	15
166	260	1,082 (22.2%)	15.3	18.7
173	271	1,008 (26.6%)	17.2	19.7
141	222	955 (27.6%)	14.8	16.8
152	248	1,031 (24.1%)	14.7	18.3
191	282	1,066 (23.9%)	17.9	20.1
190	291	940 (24.3%)	20.2	23.4
185	291	916 (19.7%)	20.2	25.5
155	270	946 (23.8%)	16.4	21.7
148	263	952 (19.8%)	16.4	22.2
173	311	923 (24.0%)	18.7	25.6
165	299	888 (24.1%)	18.6	25.6
160	294	958 (21.5%)	16.7	24.1

Academy, by Percentages," 31 Jan. 1992, SR5, Box 4; Superintendent to Chief of Naval Operations, 30 Nov. 1992, SR3, 1992, Box 1000–1531, Folder "1992"; Superintendent to Bureau of Naval Personnel, 31 Mar. 1996, SR3, Box 1531, Folder "1531"; USNA Admissions Office, "United States Naval Academy History of Incoming Class Composition," 1990, HMG. Virgil Hill to Blue and Gold Officers, 31 Aug. 1990, SR3, 1990, Box 1000–1531/1, Folder "1531/1"; Northrup et al., *Black Minority Participation in the All-Volunteer Navy and Marine Corps*, 133; John Bodnar, "Retention of Minorities at the Service Academies," HMG; "USNA History of Incoming Class Composition, HMG.

TABLE 8. Superintendents and Commandants, 1949–2000

Superintendent	Term	Commandant	Term
R. Adm. James L. Holloway Jr.	1947–50	Capt. Frank T. Ward	1947–49
		Capt. Carlton R. Adams	1949
V. Adm. Harry W. Hill	1950–52	Capt. Robert B. Pirie	1949–52
V. Adm. C. Turner Joy	1952–54	R. Adm. Charles A. Buchanan	1952–54
R. Adm. Walter F. Boone	1954–56	Capt. Robert T. S. Keith	1954–56
R. Adm. William R. Smedberg III	1956–58	Capt. Allen M. Shinn	1956–58
R. Adm. Charles L. Melson	1958–60	Capt. Frederick L. Ashworth	1958
		Capt. William F. Bringle	1958–60
R. Adm. John F. Davidson	1960–62	Capt. James H. Mini	1960–61
R. Adm. Charles C. Kirkpatrick	1962–64	Capt. Charles S. Minter Jr.	1961–64
R. Adm. Charles S. Minter Jr.	1964–65	Capt. Sheldon H. Kinney	1964–67
R. Adm. Draper L. Kauffman	1965–68	Capt. Lawrence T. Heyworth Jr.	1967–69
Capt. Lawrence T. Heyworth Jr.	1968	Capt. Robert P. Coogan	1969–71
R. Adm. James F. Calvert	1968–72	Capt. Max K. Morris	1971–73
V. Adm. William P. Mack	1972–75	Capt. Donald K. Forbes	1973–76
R. Adm. Kinnaird McKee	1975–78	Capt. James A. Winnefeld	1976–78
R. Adm. William P. Lawrence	1978–81	Capt. Jack N. Darby	1978–79
		R. Adm. William McCauley	1979–81
V. Adm. Edward C. Waller	1981–83	Capt. Leon A. Edney	1981–84
R. Adm. Charles R. Larson	1983–86	Capt. Leslie N. Palmer	1984
R. Adm. Ronald F. Marryott	1986–88	Capt. Stephan K. Chadwick	1985–86
R. Adm. Virgil L. Hill Jr.	1988–91	Capt. Howard W. Habermeyer Jr.	1987–89
		Capt. Joseph W. Prueher	1989–90
R. Adm. Thomas C. Lynch	1991–94	Capt. Michael D. Haskins	1990–92
		Capt. John B. Padgett III	1992–94
Adm. Charles R. Larson	1994–98	Capt. W. T. R. Bogle	1994–97
Adm. John R. Ryan	1998–2002	R. Adm. Gary Roughead	1997–99
		R. Adm. Samuel Locklear	1999–2001

Sources: ARF "Superintendents"; ARF "Commandants."

Notes

MPSVC	Motion Picture, Sound, and Video Collection, National Archives and Records Administration, College Park, Md.
NPS/NRHP	National Park Service/National Register of Historic Places Records, Washington, D.C.
NYT	*New York Times*, newspaper, New York, N.Y.
PI	Personal interview by HMG
PMA	*Playboy* Magazine Archives, Chicago, Ill.
SC	USNA Special Collections, Annapolis, Md.
SCF	Special Collections Files, USNA Special Collections, Annapolis, Md.
Shipmate	*Shipmate*, USNA Alumni Association magazine, Annapolis, Md.
SR	Superintendents' Records, National Archives and Records Administration, Record Group 405, housed at USNA Nimitz Library, Annapolis, Md.
	SR1 Papers, through 1959
	SR2 Papers, 1960–84
	SR3 Papers, 1985–present
	SR4 *Men of Annapolis* Papers
	SR5 Papers on Women
TI	Telephone interview by HMG
Trident	*Trident*, USNA public affairs newspaper, Annapolis, Md.
USNAAW	U.S. Naval Academy Alumni Association Web site
USNAW	U.S. Naval Academy Web site
USNHCW	U.S. Naval Historical Center Web site
USNIOH	U.S. Naval Institute Oral History Collection, unpublished collections, Annapolis, Md.
OHFFG	Oral Histories with First Female Graduates of USNA
USNIP	*U.S. Naval Institute Proceedings*, journal, Annapolis, Md.
USNW	U.S. Navy Web site
WCFTR	Wisconsin Center for Film and Theater Research, film and archival collections, Wisconsin Historical Society/University of Wisconsin, Madison, Wis.
WP	*Washington Post*, newspaper, Washington, D.C.
WvS1	*Waldie v. Schlesinger* papers, U.S. District Court, Washington National Records Center, National Archives and Records Administration, Suitland, Md.
WvS2	*Waldie v. Schlesinger* papers, U.S. Court of Appeals, Washington National Records Center, National Archives and Records Administration, Suitland, Md.

Preface

1   Poyer, *The Return of Philo T. McGiffin*, 63.

2   Keegan, *Fields of Battle*, 49, 141–42.

3 Mike Nassr, "From Navy Blue to Air Force Blue: Memorial Planned For USNA Role In Building The USAF," USNAAW (<http://usna.com/News_Pubs/Publications/Shipate/2004/01/afarticle.htm>, 29 Feb. 2004).

4 Sahlins, How "Natives" Think, 12.

5 Levine, Black Culture and Black Consciousness, 5.

6 Cremin, American Education: The Colonial Experience, 266.

7 Giamatti, Reflections on Our University, 7.

8 Thomas Jefferson, "Letter to Samuel Kercheval," 12 July 1816, in Mayer, The Constitutional Thought of Thomas Jefferson, 295–96.

9 Stegner, The Sound of Mountain Water, 284–85.

10 Reminiscences of Rear Admiral Robert W. McNitt, 367–68.

11 Arthur Radford, "Graduation Day Address," 1 June 1956, 2–3, SC, William Renwick Smedberg Papers, Box 1.

12 "Talk By Vice Admiral William R. Smedberg III, USN, to the Naval Academy Alumni Association, Lawyers' Club, New York, N.Y., 12 Nov. 1962," SC, William Renwick Smedberg Papers, Box 1; Lovell, Neither Athens Nor Sparta?, 42–45; Sweetman and Cutler, The U.S. Naval Academy, 206–7.

Chapter One

1 The following discussion of the origins and setup of West Point is based on Frank Brown, "A Study of the Failure of Naval Academy Legislation Between 1800 and 1845," MFCP #200, 1953, 2–6; Sidney Forman, "Why the United States Military Academy Was Established in 1802," Military Affairs 29, no. 1 (Spring 1965): 16–17; Michael Warner, "General Josiah Harmar's Campaign Reconsidered: How the Americans Lost the Battle of Kekionga," Indiana Magazine of History 83, no. 1 (Mar. 1987): 43–64; Leroy Eid, "American Indian Military Leadership: St. Clair's 1791 Defeat," Journal of Military History 57 (January 1993): 71–88; Allen, George Washington, 497, 510; Coffman, The Old Army, 6; Cremin, American Education, 503; Kohn, Eagle and Sword, 302–3; Lovell, Neither Athens Nor Sparta?, 16–23; Prucha, The Great Father, 23; Zinn, A People's History of the United States, 87.

2 The following discussion of early Naval education is based on Senate Bill by Samuel Southard, 14 May 1836, ARF "History: Naval Schools Prior to Establishment of Naval Academy," 1; "The Founding of the Naval Academy by Bancroft and Buchanan," USNIP 61, no. 10 (Oct. 1935): 1367–68; Louis Bolander, "A Hundred Years of the Naval Academy," USNIP 72, no. 4 (Apr. 1946): 149; Speech by R. T. S. Keith to Cosmos Club, Washington, D.C., 1953, ARF "Talk by CAPT R. T. S. Keith," 2, 3; "Our First Naval School," unidentified, ARF "History: Naval Schools Prior to Establishment of Naval Academy"; Calvert, The Naval Profession, 93; Meade, ed., Reef Points 1997–1998, 89–90.

3 The following discussion of the Somers incident and Chauvenet is based on Louis Bolander, "Biographies of Founders of the Naval Academy," 1, undated, ARF "History: Biographies of Founders of the Naval Academy"; "A Way of Life: Past and

Present," LOG, vol. 45, Class of 1956 Public Distribution Issue, 10–11; Calvert, The Naval Profession, 94–96; Lovell, Neither Athens Nor Sparta?, 28–29; Meade, ed., Reef Points 1997–1998, 90; Sweetman and Cutler, The U.S. Naval Academy, 3–4, 12–13.

4 The following discussion of Bancroft and Fort Severn is based on George Bancroft to Franklin Buchanan, 7 Aug. 1845, 3, ARF "History: Establishment of Naval Academy: Letters Relating To"; Bolander, "Biographies of Founders of the Naval Academy," 1, undated, ARF "History: Biographies of Founders of the Naval Academy"; Calvert, The Naval Profession, 96; Lovell, Neither Athens Nor Sparta?, 28; Meade, ed., Reef Points 1997–1998, 90–91; Sweetman and Cutler, The U.S. Naval Academy, 15–16, 24.

5 The following description of the setup of the Naval School is based on Louis Bolander, "Biographies of Founders of the Naval Academy," 1–8, undated, ARF "History: Biographies of Founders of the Naval Academy"; "Important Events in the History of the U.S. Naval Academy," undated, ARF "History: Historical Facts," 1; Sturdy, "The Establishment of the Naval School at Annapolis," USNIP 72, no. 4 (Apr. 1946): 10; Cremin, American Education, 503; Lovell, Neither Athens Nor Sparta?, 29; Meade, ed., Reef Points 1997–1998, 91; Sheppard, "An Analysis of Curriculum Changes at the United States Naval Academy," 4; Geoffrey Smith, "An Uncertain Passage: The Bureaus Run The Navy, 1842–1861," in Hagan, ed., In Peace and War, 79–106.

6 The following discussion of the development of the Naval School is based on EI, Interviewee #33; "Important Events in the History of the U.S. Naval Academy," undated, ARF "History: Historical Facts," 1; "A Way of Life: Past and Present," LOG, vol. 45, Class of 1956 Public Distribution Issue, 10; Calvert, The Naval Profession, 97; Lovell, Neither Athens Nor Sparta?, 30–31; Meade, ed., Reef Points 1997–1998, 93–96; Sweetman and Cutler, The U.S. Naval Academy, 10, 26, 39, 63.

7 The following discussion of late-nineteenth-century developments is based on Barton Strong, "A History of the Marine Barracks, Annapolis, Maryland," MFCP #1586, 1964, 1; James Calvert, "Letter from the Superintendent," Shipmate 33, no. 8 (Jan. 1970): 4; Charles Paullin, "Beginnings of the U.S. Naval Academy," USNIP 50, no. 2 (Feb. 1924): 173; Lance Buhl, "Maintaining an American Navy, 1865–1889," in Hagan, ed., In Peace and War, 168–69; Ronald Spector, "The Triumph of Professional Ideology: The United States Navy in the 1890s," in Hagan, ed., In Peace and War, 175–77; Bacon, Ernest Flagg, 112–19; Calvert, The Naval Profession, 97–98; Lovell, Neither Athens Nor Sparta?, 31–34; Mahan, The Influence of Sea Power Upon History; Meade, ed., Reef Points 1997–1998, 97; Potter, Sea Power: A Naval History, 155, 161–63; Sweetman and Cutler, The U.S. Naval Academy, 86, 133, 135.

8 Lance Buhl, "Maintaining an American Navy, 1865–1889," in Hagan, ed., In Peace and War, 145–73.

9 Puleston, Mahan: The Life and Work of Captain Alfred Thayer Mahan, 76.

10 The following discussion of early-twentieth-century developments is based on Thomas Cutler, "Those Other Grads," Naval History 8, no. 2 (March/April 1994): 46; The Anchor Watch; Meade, ed., Reef Points 1997–1998, 101–4; Sweetman and Cutler, The U.S. Naval Academy, 172–73, 175–93; United States Naval Academy North Severn Master Plan, 50.

11 The following discussion of the 1945 to 1949 period is based on Commandant to

Superintendent, 29 Mar. 1943, SR4, Folder "Efficiency of Naval Academy," 1–2; William Rhodes, "The Class of 1921, U.S. Naval Academy," MFCP #1229, 1; 1948 *Annual Register of the U.S. Naval Academy*, 25, 1942 BOV, 12; "A Way of Life: Past and Present," *LOG*, vol. 45, Class of 1956 Public Distribution Issue, 11; Louis Bolander, "The Naval Academy in Five Wars," *USNIP* 72, no. 4 (Apr. 1946): 35–45; Thomas Cutler, "Those Other Grads," *Naval History* 8, no. 2 (March/April 1994): 47–48; Richard West, "The Superintendents of the Naval Academy," *USNIP* 71, no. 7 (July 1945): 809; Lovell, *Neither Athens Nor Sparta?*, 40–41, 46–54, 208; Sheppard, "An Analysis of Curriculum Changes at the United States Naval Academy," 129; Sweetman and Cutler, *The U.S. Naval Academy*, 63, 138.

12 The following discussion of the USNA campus is based on Unpublished Interview with William Lawrence, USNIOH, 1990, 1022; *Reminiscences of Rear Admiral Draper L. Kauffman*, 844; *Reminiscences of Vice Admiral Charles L. Melson*, 135, 267; *Reminiscences of Vice Admiral Charles S. Minter Jr.*, 481–82; *Reminiscences of Vice Admiral William R. Smedberg III*, 526–32, 563; William Smedberg, "Speech Delivered to the Historic Annapolis Foundation," Annapolis, Md., 17 May 1956, SC, William Renwick Smedberg Papers, Box 1; "Historical Sketch of the Severn River Naval Command," 1958, ARF "History: Naval Schools Prior to the Establishment of the Naval Academy"; John LaFond, "The Development of the Naval Academy Land Reclamation Project," MFCP #822, 1959, 1–18; Robert Johnson, "The Naval Academy Dairy," MFCP #867, 1966, 1–5; 1941 BOV, 5; 1945 BOV, 7; 1946 BOV, 6, 11; 1947 BOV, 4, 5; 1948 BOV, 7; 1952 BOV, 2; 1953 BOV, 2; 1954 BOV, 6, 14; 1955 BOV, 11; *United States Naval Academy North Severn Master Plan*, 45, 50; Ruby Duval, "The Naval Academy Cemetery on 'Strawberry Hill,'" *USNIP* 72, no. 4 (Apr. 1946): 74–77; Sarah Robert, "The Naval Academy as Housekeeper: Feeding and Clothing the Midshipmen," *USNIP* 72, no. 4 (Apr. 1946): 124–25; "The Man at the Helm," *LOG*, vol. 45, Class of 1956 Public Distribution Issue, 2–3; Hanson Baldwin, "Spaniards Seeking Return of '98 Ship," *NYT*, 12 Mar. 1957, 35; Hanson Baldwin, "Annapolis Aweigh," *NYT*, 8 Apr. 1957, 6; "Old Ship Leaves Navy," *NYT*, 7 Nov. 1957, 36; "Academy Expansion Stirs Annapolis Ire," *NYT*, 11 Mar. 1962, 5; "Navy to Muster Out Cows After 55 Years," *NYT*, 14 Apr. 1966, 28; Wallace Shugg, "The Navy's Real Brig," *Naval History* 7, no. 2 (Summer 1993): 20–23; Amy Argetsinger, "Out To Pasture," *WP*, 9 July 1998, 8; Amy Argetsinger, "Towers Give Way to Flowers," *WP*, 16 July 1998, Anne Arundel Section, M1, M3; Calvert, *The Naval Profession*, 99, 100, 102; Stewart, *The Brigade in Review*, 6; Sweetman and Cutler, *The U.S. Naval Academy*, 167, 172, 208.

13 The following discussion of the development of the USNA main campus is based on Map, "United States Naval Academy—To-day and Yesterday," *USNIP* 61, no. 10 (Oct. 1935): 1442; Map, "U.S. Naval Academy—1895," appendix in Donald Lathan, "Planning v. Reality: Flagg's Plan, 1899–1910," MFCP #1013, 1966; Carroll Alden, "The Changing Naval Academy: A Retrospect of 25 Years," *USNIP* 55, no. 6 (June 1929): 496; James Cheevers, "Museum Tidbits," *Yard Talk*, 1983, SCF Folder "USNA: Buildings and Grounds," 4; Bacon, *Ernest Flagg*, 113–15, 196; King and King, *The United States Naval Academy Chapel*, 4–6; Mack and Connell, *Naval Ceremonies, Customs, and Traditions*, 315; Meade, ed., *Reef Points 1997–1998*, 97; Potter, *Sea Power*, 161–63; Ron-

ald Spector, "The Triumph of Professional Ideology: The U.S. Navy in the 1890s," in Hagan, ed., *In Peace and War*, 175–76; Sweetman and Cutler, *The U.S. Naval Academy*, 84–85, 123.

14 The following discussion of Flagg and his design for USNA is based on Donald Lathan, "Planning v. Reality: Ernest Flagg's Plan, 1899–1910," MFCP #1013, 1966, 5–6; Ernest Flagg, "New Buildings for the United States Naval Academy, Annapolis, Maryland," *American Architect and Building News* 94, no. 1697 (1 July 1908): 1, 2; Map, "United States Naval Academy—To-day and Yesterday," USNIP 61, no. 10 (Oct. 1935): 1442; Ruby Duval, "The Perpetuation of History and Tradition at the U.S. Naval Academy Today," USNIP 64, no. 5 (May 1938): 669; Ruby Duval, "The Naval Academy Cemetery on 'Strawberry Hill,' " USNIP 72, no. 4 (Apr. 1946): 74–77; Bacon, *Ernest Flagg*, 133, 196; Calvert, *The Naval Profession*, 100; Earle, *Life at the U.S. Naval Academy*, 281; Sweetman and Cutler, *The U.S. Naval Academy*, 142, 144.

15 Modifications to Flagg's plan included joining Mahan, Maury, and Sampson Halls into one building; utilizing concrete construction rather than granite for the chapel; substituting granite for the intended red brick façade of Bancroft Hall; constructing Macdonough Hall as a gymnasium rather than a boat house; and not adding Flagg's lighthouse-like beacons to the boat basin.

16 The following discussion of the USNA chapel is based on Willard Browson, Superintendent's Notice, 1 June 1904, ARF "Buildings and Grounds: Chapel"; Ernest Flagg to E. B. Meader, 17 Nov. 1930, SCF Folder "USNA: Chapel, Buildings, and Grounds"; USNA Notice 5050, 3 July 1963, SR2 Sec. 5800/1, Folder "1 Jan 1968–31 Dec 1968"; Donald Lathan, "Planning v. Reality: Ernest Flagg's Plan, 1899–1910," MFCP #1013, 1966, 8; "The Chapel of the United States Naval Academy," 1969, SCF Folder "USNA: Chapel, Buildings, and Grounds," 15, 23; "U.S. Naval Academy, Annapolis, Maryland," National Historic Landmark files, NPS/NRHP; Day Willey, "The New Concrete Chapel of the United States Naval Academy, Annapolis," *Scientific American* 92, no. 5 (Feb. 1905): 101; Ernest Flagg, "New Buildings for the United States Naval Academy, Annapolis, Maryland," *American Architect and Building News* 94, no. 1697 (1 July 1908): 3, 6; "Secretary's Notes: The Cathedral of the Navy," USNIP 66, no. 12 (Dec. 1940): 1068; Sarah C. Robert, "The Naval Academy Chapel: Cathedral of the Navy," USNIP 72, no. 2 (Apr. 1946): 98–99; Wayne Marks, "A Crypt For Whom?," LOG 45, no. 1 (23 Sept. 1955): 6–7; Bacon, *Ernest Flagg*, 130; Calvert, *The Naval Profession*, 177; Cunningham, *In Pursuit of Reason*, 338, 342; Dober, *Campus Planning*, 21; Fleming, *Annapolis Autumn*, 23–25; Hamlin, *Benjamin Henry Latrobe*, 468–70; Karsten, *The Naval Aristocracy*, 29–30; Keegan, *Fields of Battle*, 141; King and King, *The Naval Academy Chapel*, 1, 3, 5–7; Lovell, *Neither Athens Nor Sparta?*, 3, 34; Stewart, *The Brigade in Review*, 66–67; Sweetman and Cutler, *The U.S. Naval Academy*, 147.

17 The following discussion of Bancroft Hall is based on EI with Beverly Lyall, Annapolis, Md., 3 May 2001; Commandant to Superintendent, 27 Apr. 1981, CR, Folder 5400/5, 1981; 1948 BOV, 6; 1949 BOV, 7; 1953 BOV, 2; 1954 BOV, 12; 1957 BOV, 7; 2000 LB, 100; Ernest Flagg, "New Buildings for the United States Naval Academy, Annapolis, Maryland," *American Architect and Building News* 94, no. 1697 (1 July 1908):

1, 2; Richard West Jr., "The Superintendents of the Naval Academy," USNIP 71, no. 7 (July 1945): 809; Earl Thompson, "The Naval Academy as an Undergraduate College," USNIP 74, no. 3 (Mar. 1948): 274; Hanson Baldwin, "84% of Naval Academy Athletes Reported Screened and Assisted," NYT, 15 June 1952, 1; "Letter from Fleet Admiral Nimitz," LOG 59, no. 5 (10 Apr. 1970): 7; Effie Coffman, "Academy Plans Expansion," EC, 10 Apr. 1987, 1; Susan Herendeen, "Bancroft Hall," EC, 10 May 1998, 41, 48; Calvert, The Naval Profession, 98–99; Fleming, Annapolis Autumn, 26; Meade, ed., Reef Points 1997–1998, 189; Stewart, The Brigade in Review, 33; John Ryan, "Pennsylvania Parents Club Remarks," Feb. 1999, USNAW (<www.usna.edu/pao/speeches/speechjr8.html>, 21 May 1999), 3; "Bancroft Hall," USNAW (<www.usna.edu/pao/virtual/map/bancroft.html>, 21 May 1999).

18 The following discussion of Bancroft Hall's contents is based on Reminiscences of Vice Admiral William R. Smedberg III, 539; John Ryan, "Pennsylvania Parents Club Remarks," Feb. 1999, USNAW (<www.usna.edu/pao/speeches/speechjr8.html>, 21 May 1999), 3; "Bancroft Hall," USNAW (<www.usna.edu/pao/virtual/map/bancroft.html>, 21 May 1999); Susan Herendeen, "Bancroft Hall," EC, 10 May 1998, 48; "Bancroft Hall: A Four Year Home," LOG, vol. 45, Class of 1956 Public Distribution Issue, 26–27; Stewart, The Brigade in Review, 6, 19.

19 The following discussion of additions to the physical plant is based on PI with Seymour Einstein, Tucson, Ariz., 15 Feb. 2002; EI with Beverly Lyall, Annapolis, Md., 11 Mar. 2002; Interview with William P. Lawrence, USNIOH, 1036; Reminiscences of Rear Admiral Draper L. Kauffman, 750–51; Reminiscences of Vice Admiral William P. Mack, 804–5; Reminiscences of Rear Admiral Robert W. McNitt, 633–34; Reminiscences of Vice Admiral Charles S. Minter Jr., 481–82, 490; PAO Announcement 4472, undated, ARF "Midshipmen: Food Preparation"; 1958 BOV, 15; 1983 LB, 43; "Armel Leftwich Visitors Center," USNAW (<www.usna.edu/pao/virtual/map/visitor.html>, 21 Dec. 2001); "The Construction of Nimitz Library," USNAW (<www.usna.edu/LibExhibits/nimconst.html>, 12 Jan. 2002); Rachel Goldberg, "Midshipmen Get New Tool for Leadership Training," USNAAAW (<www.usna.com/news_pubs/publications/Shipmate/2001/2001_07/chapel.html>, 2 Jan. 2002); Mike Nassr, "There Will Be Some Changes Made," LOG 41, no. 8 (18 Jan. 1952): 22; Wayne Weeks, "The New Look at Navy," LOG 44, no. 17 (27 May 1955): 16; Frank Rigler, "Some Thoughts on the Naming of Buildings," Shipmate 31, no. 4 (Apr. 1968): 3–4; "Midshipman Recreational Facilities," LOG 64, no. 3 (Dec. 1974): 31; Robert McNitt, "Uncle Charlie," Shipmate 51, no. 5 (June 1988): 8; James Loewen, "The Shrouded History of College Campuses," Chronicle of Higher Education, 28 Jan. 2000, B6; Calvert, The Naval Profession, 99–102; Lovell, Neither Athens Nor Sparta?, 182, 291; Sweetman and Cutler, The U.S. Naval Academy, 172, 236–37, 255, 259.

20 Hanson Baldwin, "The Academies: Old Tools, New Methods," NYT Magazine, 16 Apr. 1961, 32; James Loewen, "The Shrouded History of College Campuses," Chronicle of Higher Education, 28 Jan. 2000, B6; Fleming, Annapolis Autumn, 26–27; Keegan, Fields of Battle, 141; Lovell, Neither Athens Nor Sparta?, 34, 248–49, 276.

21 Ruby Duvall, "The Perpetuation of History and Traditions at the U.S. Naval Academy

Today," *USNIP* 64, no. 5 (May 1938): 669–77; Ruby Duvall, "The Naval Academy Cemetery on 'Strawberry Hill,'" *USNIP* 72, no. 4 (Apr. 1946): 74–77.

22 Ruby Duvall, "The Perpetuation of History and Traditions at the U.S. Naval Academy Today," *USNIP* 64, no. 5 (May 1938): 677; Richard West Jr., "The Superintendents of the Naval Academy," *USNIP* 71, no. 7 (July 1945): 809; Harry Baldridge, "Naval Academy Museum—the First 100 Years," *USNIP* 72, no. 4 (Apr. 1946): 78–92.

23 EI with Gary Roughead, Annapolis, Md., 7 Jan. 1999; A. G. Esch to Richard Dorso, 14 Jan. 1956, SR4, Folder "A7-4/1-1: Television Series," 6; "Bancroft Hall," USNAW (<www.usna.edu/pao/virtual/map/bancroft/html>, 21 May 1999); "Something to Think About," *LOG* 40, no. 14 (13 Apr. 1951): 16; 1951 BOV, 12; Frank Rigler, "Some Thoughts on the Naming of Buildings," *Shipmate* 31, no. 4 (Apr. 1968): 3–4.

24 Ruby Duvall, "The Perpetuation of History and Traditions at the U.S. Naval Academy Today," *USNIP* 64, no. 5 (May 1938): 669–77; Louis Bolander, "The Naval Academy in Five Wars," *USNIP* 72, no. 4 (Apr. 1946): 35–45; Stewart, *The Brigade in Review*, 64–65.

25 Ruby Duvall, "The Perpetuation of History and Traditions at the U.S. Naval Academy Today," *USNIP* 64, no. 5 (May 1938): 669–77; "Secretary's Notes: 'The Masts of The Maine,'" *USNIP* 69, no. 2 (Feb. 1943): 306; Louis Bolander, "A Hundred Years of the Naval Academy," *USNIP* 72, no. 4 (Apr. 1946): 146; J. K. Poole, "The Young Men's Monument," *LOG* 45, no. 5 (18 Nov. 1955): 12; Pam Warnken, "Unique Memorial: Tripoli Gets Facelift," *Trident*, 7 July 2000,: 1, 10.

26 Charles Buchanan, "Naval Academy Traditions," speech before the Naval Academy Women's Club, 7 Oct. 1952, 7, CR, Box 1, "Miscellaneous Speeches Presented by Commandants, 1952–1960," Folder 5; 1978 LB, 10; "The Founding of the Naval Academy by Bancroft and Buchanan," *USNIP* 61, no. 10 (Oct. 1935): 1366; "Donald Duck," *LOG* 30 (4 Apr. 1941): 11; E. C. Matheson, "Tecumseh," *LOG* 41, no. 2 (12 Oct. 1951): 8–9; Cover, *LOG* 43, no. 9 (5 Feb. 1954); "On The Cover," *LOG* 43, no. 9 (5 Feb. 1954): 3; "A Way of Life: From Past to Present," *LOG* 45 (1956): 11; Russ Henderson, "A Grave Image," *LOG* 47, no. 3 (18 Oct. 1957): 8–9; Don Woodman, "A West Point Cow in Tecumseh's Court," *LOG* 50, no. 15 (28 Apr. 1961): 28; J. Scott Burd, "The Ultimate Over-The-Wall," *Shipmate* 56, no. 10 (Dec. 1993): 21–22, 25; Fleming, *Annapolis Autumn*, 18–19; Keegan, *Fields of Battle*, 141; Stewart, *The Brigade in Review*, 64–65.

27 Charles Buchanan, "Naval Academy Traditions," speech before the Naval Academy Women's Club, 7 Oct. 1952, 7, CR, Box 1, "Miscellaneous Speeches presented by Commandants, 1952–1960," Folder 5; E. C. Waller to E. Carlton Guillot Jr., 24 June 1982, SR2, Sec. 12770/1, Folder "1982"; 1983 LB, 60, 164–65; 1998 LB, 31; "The Charge of 1000: The History and Traditions of the Herndon Monument Climb," USNAW (<www.usna.edu/pao/facts/herndon/html>, 21 May 1999); Cover, *LOG* 41, no. 7 (30 May 1952); "Remember?," *LOG* 58, no. 14 (18 Apr. 1969): 33; Angus Philips, "'Hat Trick' Caps Long Year at Academy," *WP*, 21 May 1983, B3; "Memorandum about Herndon taking place on Japanese Monument," *LOG* 81, no. 1 (Sept. 1991): 13; "T-Minus Herndon," *EC*, 9 May 1992, 1; Roy Smith, "The Herndon Monument Club," *Shipmate* 57, no. 4 (May 1994): 14; Roy Smith, "The Mail Boat," *Shipmate* 58,

no. 5 (Oct. 1995); Martha Thorn, "Class of 2002 Climbs Toward Youngster Year," *Trident*, 21 May 1999, 1; "Commissioning Week 2000," *Trident*, 19 May 2000, 10; Martha Thorn, "Herndon Climb Predictions Right On target," *Trident*, 26 May 2000, 1; Martha Thorn, "Monument Gets Greased, Scaled, Cleaned," *Trident*, 26 May 2000, 13; Stewart, *The Brigade in Review*, 102–3.

28 Pierre Nora, "Between Memory and History: Les Lieux de Memoire," *Representations* 26 (Spring 1989): 8, 19, 23–24; Steele, *A Sense of Place*, x, 11–12, 30, 71, 93–95, 101, 106, 120, 202–3.

29 PI, Interviewees #18, 40; *Reminiscences of Vice Admiral Charles L. Melson*, 275; USNA Notice 5050, 3 July 1963, SR2 Sec. 5800/1, Folder "1 Jan 1968–31 Dec 1968"; "U.S. Naval Academy, Annapolis, Maryland," National Historic Landmark files, NPS/ NRHP; Lebby, "Professional Socialization of the Naval Officer," 74; John Meroney, "Is The Naval Academy Off Course?," *American Enterprise* 10, no. 4 (July/Aug. 1999): 47; Fleming, *Annapolis Autumn*, 12–17; Lovell, *Neither Athens Nor Sparta?*, 3–4, 276.

30 The following discussion of mission statements is based on *Reminiscences of Draper L. Kauffman*, 666; *Reminiscences of Vice Admiral Charles L. Melson*, 11, 290; "Superintendent's Instruction on Naval Academy Organization and Management Manual, 1973," 6 Apr. 1973, CR, Sec. 5400/2, Folder "1973"; James Calvert to J. H. Webb, 14 Nov. 1987, SR3, 1987, Box 12009–13950, Folder "1531/ON"; List of Mission Statements, undated, SR5, Box 4; Earl Thompson, "The Naval Academy as an Undergraduate College," *USNIP* 74, no. 3 (Mar. 1948): 271; Hanson Baldwin, "The Academies: Old Ideals, New Methods," *NYT*, 16 Apr. 1961, 33; "Salty Sam," *LOG* 70 (Oct. 1980): 20; Calvert, *The Naval Profession*, 102–3, 112; Meade, ed., *Reef Points 1997–1998*, 22; Timberg, *The Nightingale's Song*, 401.

31 List of Mission Statements, undated, SR5, Box 4.

32 Ibid.

33 The following discussion of the federal oversight over USNA is based on PI, Interviewee #177; *Reminiscences of Rear Admiral Robert W. McNitt*, 616–17; "The U.S. Service Academies and Their Task Environment," in Lovell, *Neither Athens Nor Sparta?*, 213, 232–40.

34 The following discussion of the relation between USNA and the Navy is based on Interview with William P. Lawrence, USNIOH, 1039; *Reminiscences of Rear Admiral Julian T. Burke Jr.*, 337–38; *Reminiscences of Rear Admiral Draper L. Kauffman*, 678, 821–24; *Reminiscences of Vice Admiral William P. Mack*, 642; *Reminiscences of Vice Admiral Charles L. Melson*, 132; *Reminiscences of Vice Admiral Charles S. Minter Jr.*, 483, 485; *Reminiscences of Vice Admiral William R. Smedberg III*, 502, 504–6; "Superintendent's Instruction on Naval Academy Organization and Management Manual, 1973," 6 Apr. 1973, CR, Sec. 5400/2, Folder "1973"; Chief of Naval Operations, "Memorandum for Deputy Chief of Naval Operations for Manpower, Director of Naval Education and Training, and Superintendent, Naval Academy," 3 Nov. 1975, SR2, Sec. NC/1531, Folder "1977"; William Bonwit to Kinnaird McKee, undated, CR, Sec. 5211/2, Folder "1976"; Robert Shapiro to Joseph Shields, 25 Aug. 1989, SR3, 1989, Box 1000– 1531/2, Folder "1531/1"; Fred Frederici Jr., "Study of the United States Naval Academy," MFCP #1130, 1957, 13; "Change of Command Setup Urged for Naval Acad-

emy," NYT, 27 Dec. 1973, 29; "Changes in the Making: A Note to the Brigade," LOG 65 (Feb. 1976): 4; Lovell, *Neither Athens Nor Sparta?*, 242–43.

35   1968 BOV, 1.

36   *Reminiscences of Rear Admiral Robert W. McNitt*, 405–6; V. L. Hill Jr. to Barry Goldwater, 6 Sept. 1988, SR3, 1988, Box 5214–5420, Folder "5420/1"; 1968 BOV, 1; "Annapolis Told to List Reforms," NYT, 2 May 1966, 40.

37   TI with H. Ross Perot, Dallas, Tex., 11 Dec. 2000; R. E. Heise to Capt. Keith, 19 Sept. 1950, ARF "History: Accreditation/Degree Awarding/General Information"; "Historical Sketch," undated, ARF "History: Accreditation/Degree Awarding/General Information"; William Miller to USNA Listserve, 7 May 1999, HMG; J. R. Harstreiter, "The Naval Academy Curriculum: From Professionalism to Present Day Modern Education," MFCP #675, 1966, 2; "A Way of Life: From Past to Present," LOG 45 (1956): 11; Ben Franklin, "Annapolis Chided on Grade Quotas," NYT, 1 May 1966, 1; "Annapolis Told to List Reforms," NYT, 2 May 1966, 40; Lovell, *Neither Athens Nor Sparta?*, 232–33; Sheppard, "An Analysis of Curriculum Changes at the United States Naval Academy," 7.

38   Military Secretary of the Board of Visitors to Midshipman Food Services Officer, 20 Aug. 1982, CR, Sec. 5400/4, Folder "1982"; Barry Goldwater to R. F. Marryott, 28 June 1988, SR3, 1988, Box 5214–5420, Folder "5420/1"; 1968 BOV, 1; V. L. Hill Jr. to Barry Goldwater, 6 Sept. 1988, SR3, 1988, Box 5214–5420, Folder "5420/1"; 1968 BOV, 1.

39   *Reminiscences of Rear Admiral Robert W. McNitt*, 405–6; *Reminiscences of Vice Admiral William R. Smedberg III*, 574; 1942 BOV, 5; 1948 BOV, 7; 1968 BOV, 1; Robert McNamara, "Memorandum for the President," 5 Sept. 1966, Fact Sheet, LBJ, Folder "ND 15-8: U.S. Naval Academy, 1965–1967"; Barry Goldwater to R. F. Marryott, 28 June 1988, SR3, 1988, Box 5214–5420, Folder "5420/1"; V. L. Hill Jr. to Barry Goldwater, 6 Sept. 1988, SR3, 1988, Box 5214–5420, Folder "5420/1"; "Report of the Committee on Women's Issues, U.S. Naval Academy Board of Visitors," 9 Oct. 1990, SR5, Box 4; V. L. Hill Jr., "Memorandum for the Chief of Naval Operations," 8 Jan. 1991, SR3, 1991, Box 5238–5700, Folder "5420/3"; "The Higher Standard: Assessing the United States Naval Academy, Report of the Special Committee to the Board of Visitors, U.S. Naval Academy," June 1997; John Williams, "Book Review: 'The Higher Standard: Assessing the United States Naval Academy,'" USNIP 123, no. 8 (Aug. 1997): 78–79; Heise, *The Brass Factories*, 173.

40   The following discussion of superintendents is based on *Reminiscences of Rear Admiral John F. Davidson*, 423; *Reminiscences of Rear Admiral Draper L. Kauffman*, 679; *Reminiscences of Vice Admiral Charles L. Melson*, 246; *Reminiscences of Vice Admiral Charles S. Minter Jr.*, 555; Robert McNamara, "Memorandum for the President," 5 Sept. 1966, Fact Sheet, LBJ, Folder "ND-158: U.S. Naval Academy, 1965–1967"; Draper Kauffman to Gary Filosa, 9 Feb. 1966, SR2, Sec. ON/1531, Folder "1962–1967"; Richard West Jr., "The Superintendents of the Naval Academy," USNIP 71, no. 7 (July 1945): 806; Ben Franklin, "Annapolis Chided on Grade Quotas," NYT, 1 May 1966, 1; John Williams, "Book Review: 'The Higher Standard: Assessing the U.S. Naval Academy,'" USNIP 123, no. 8 (Aug. 1997): 79; John Ryan, "Constancy of Effort and Raising the Bar of

Excellence," *Shipmate* 68, no. 10 (Dec. 1998): 4, 6–7; Lovell, *Neither Athens Nor Sparta?*, 192–93, 205–7, 221, 251; Sheppard, "An Analysis of Curriculum Changes at the United States Naval Academy," 339; Sweetman and Cutler, *The U.S. Naval Academy*, 270–71.

41 Lovell, *Neither Athens Nor Sparta?*, 196; Fleming, *Annapolis Autumn*, 183–84.

42 *Reminiscences of Vice Admiral Charles L. Melson*, 239; *Reminiscences of Vice Admiral William R. Smedberg, III*, 419, 539–40; William Smedberg, "Superintendent's Talk to the Faculty," Annapolis, Md., 4 Sept. 1956, SC, William Renwick Smedberg Papers, Box 1; Drew Middleton, "Service Academies Strive to Stay in Step with the Times," NYT, 20 Feb. 1971, 54; Lovell, *Neither Athens Nor Sparta?*, 184–88.

43 James Calvert, USNA Instruction 5060.1, 18 May 1970, ARF "Distinguished Lecture Series: Forrestal Lecture"; USNA Command History IV, 1972–1973, Vol. I, 66; Robert Love Jr., "Fighting a Global War, 1941–1945," in Hagan, ed., *In Peace and War*, 269; Dean Allard, "An Era of Transition, 1945–1953," in Hagan, ed., *In Peace and War*, 293.

44 TI, Interviewee #67; *Reminiscences of Rear Admiral Julian T. Burke Jr.*, 378–79; *Reminiscences of Rear Admiral John F. Davidson*, 284, 365; *Reminiscences of Rear Admiral Draper L. Kauffman*, 829; *Reminiscences of Rear Admiral Robert W. McNitt*, 375; *Reminiscences of Vice Admiral Charles L. Melson*, 239; *Reminiscences of Vice Admiral William R. Smedberg, III*, 396.

45 *Reminiscences of Vice Admiral Charles S. Minter Jr.*, 527–28; Roger Staubach, "Naval Academy Memories," *Naval History* 9, no. 5 (Sept./Oct. 1995): 15.

46 Charles Larson to Eugene Farrell, 3 Oct. 1994, SR3, 1994, Sec. 1000–1531, Folder "1531"; Charles Larson to John Shepherd, 2 Nov. 1994, SR3, 1994, Sec. 5100–5700, Folder "5700"; Charles Larson, Letter to the Editor, NYT, 19 Aug. 1996, SR3, 1996, Sec. 5700–5720, Folder "5700"; "Goals: Academic Year, 1984–1985," undated, CR, Sec. 5400/4, Folder "1984"; Charles Larson, "The Next 150 Years Begin," USNIP 122, no. 9 (Sept. 1996): 65–69; Fleming, *Annapolis Autumn*, 180–82.

47 The following discussion of the USNA bureaucratic structure is based on Interview with William P. Lawrence, USNIOH, 1022; *Reminiscences of Rear Admiral Robert W. McNitt*, 541–42; *Reminiscences of Vice Admiral Charles L. Melson*, 131; *Reminiscences of Vice Admiral William R. Smedberg III*, 563; USNA Organizational Flowchart, 1952, SR1, Box 1, "General Correspondence, Administration, USNA Organization, 1923–1959," Folder 8; "Historical Sketch of the Severn River Naval Command," 1958, ARF "History: History of the Severn River Naval Command"; USNA Organizational Flowchart, 6 Mar. 1970, SR1, Box 1, "General Correspondence, Administration, USNA Organization, 1923–1959," Folder 8; USNA Organizational Flowchart, 1973, CR, Sec. 5400/2, Folder "1973"; USNA Organizational Flowchart, 1978, CR, Sec. 5400/2, Folder "1979"; USNA Organizational Flowchart, 1998, USNA Public Affairs Office; USNA Organizational Flowchart, 1998, USNA Public Affairs Office; "The Man at the Helm," LOG 45 (1956): 2–3; Lovell, *Neither Athens Nor Sparta?*, 245, 269–70.

48 The following discussion of admissions is based on *Reminiscences of Rear Admiral Robert W. McNitt*, 554–55; USNA Catalog, 2000–2001, 19–20, 49; "United States Naval Academy: A Guide for Candidates and Counselors," 2000, HMG; "Midshipmen Pay and Benefits," USNAW (<www.usna.edu/admissions/benefits.htm>,

2 Feb. 2000); "U.S. Colleges and Universities Report Record Numbers of Applicants This Year; Service Academies Experience Falling Numbers of Applicants," *All Things Considered* on National Public Radio, 29 June 2000; David Brown, "Congress Approves Raises for Midshipmen," *EC*, 23 Nov. 1998, 4; Calvert, *The Naval Profession*, 229, 234–35; Lovell, *Neither Athens Nor Sparta?*, 248.

49   The following discussion of nominations is based on *Reminiscences of Rear Admiral John F. Davidson*, 419; *Reminiscences of Rear Admiral Robert W. McNitt*, 545–47, 582–84, 599, 606–7; Interview with William P. Lawrence, USNIOH, 986–87; 1941 BOV, 9; 1959 BOV, 2; 1967 BOV, 5; USNA Catalog, 2000–2001, 21–23; "United States Naval Academy: A Guide for Candidates and Counselors," 2000, HMG; Foreign Midshipmen at the U.S. Naval Academy, 11 June 1951, SR1, Box 5, "Brigade of Midshipmen: Intrabrigade Competition, Minority Midshipmen, 1897–1959," Folder 8; R. T. S. Keith to Robert Smith, SR1, Box 5, 15 Aug. 1951, "General Correspondence, Midshipmen: Policy and Administration: Statistics and Policy Regarding Visits, 1927–1964," Folder 1; A. G. Esch to Richard Dorso, 14 Jan. 1956, SR4, Folder "A7-4/1-1: Television Series," 4; William Smedberg, "Superintendent's Talk to the Faculty," Annapolis, Md., 4 Sept. 1956, 9, SC, William Renwick Smedberg Papers, Box 1; Wayne Hoof to Superintendent, 4 June 1967, ARF "Graduation and June Week: Anchor Man"; John Chafee to Spiro Agnew, 30 Apr. 1970, CR, Sec. 5710, Folder "1970"; Edward Hidalgo, "Memorandum for Deputy Assistant Secretary of Defense," 23 June 1973, enclosure 4, SR2, Sec. 5800/1, Folder "1978"; C. N. Mitchell to Superintendent, 16 July 1974, SR2, Sec. 5800/1, Folder "1974"; William Mack to Assistant Secretary of the Navy, 3 Jan. 1975, SR2, Sec. 5800/1, Folder "1974"; C. N. Mitchell to Superintendent, 3 Jan. 1975, SR2, Sec. 5800/1, Folder "1975"; R. E. Bowman, "Memorandum for the Record," 15 Nov. 1983, SR2, Sec. 5800/1, Folder "1983"; James Cheevers, "USNA: The Modern Era, Part IV," *Shipmate* 58, no. 5 (Oct. 1995): 37; Scott Harper, "The Legacy," *EC*, 13 Nov. 1988, 1, 15; Calvert, *The Naval Profession*, 231–33, 238–39; Fleming, *Annapolis Autumn*, 236, 241; Stewart, *The Brigade In Review*, x.

50   The following discussion of the organization of USNA admissions is based on PI, Interviewee #94; *Reminiscences of Rear Admiral Robert W. McNitt*, 556–57, 632–33; USNA Catalog, 2000–2001, 163; Charles Larson to Commander, Navy Recruiting Command, 22 Aug. 1994, SR3, 1994, Sec. 1000–1531, Folder "1531."

51   The following discussion of the Blue and Gold program is based on *Reminiscences of Rear Admiral Robert W. McNitt*, 550, 559, 595; *Blue and Gold Newsletter*, July 1971, Vol. 3, No. 7, ARF "Midshipmen: Minority Recruiting"; William Mack to Henry Ramirez, 20 Apr. 1973, SR2, Sec. 5800/1, Folder "1973"; Virgil Hill Jr. to Blue and Gold Officers, 31 Aug. 1990, SR3, 1996, Sec. 1000–1531, Folder "1531/1"; USNA Catalog, 2000–2001, 33–37; "Superintendent's Report to Board of Trustees Meeting," *Shipmate* 26, no. 1 (Jan. 1963): 16; Smallwood, *The Naval Academy Candidate Book*, 86–88.

52   *Reminiscences of Rear Admiral Robert W. McNitt*, 595; *Reminiscences of Vice Admiral Charles L. Melson*, 302; William Smedberg III to Distribution List, 8 Nov. 1957, SR1, Box 5, "Midshipmen: Activities: Miscellaneous Activities, 1922–1959," Folder 12; Commandant Notice 5720, 27 Jan. 1977, CR, Sec. 5720/3, Folder "1975"; Hanson Bald-

win, "Annapolis Aweigh," *NYT*, 8 Apr. 1957, 6; Banana Oil Henderson and Jimmy Boy Williams, "Operation Propaganda," *LOG* 47, no. 7 (13 Dec. 1957): 32, 34; James Cheevers, "USNA: The Modern Era, Part IV," *Shipmate* 58, no. 5 (Oct. 1995): 35; 1956 BOV, 13; 1967 BOV, 21.

53 PI, Interviewees #5, 29, 79, 164, 184, 210; EI, Interviewee #164; *Reminiscences of Rear Admiral Robert W. McNitt*, 592; "United States Naval Academy: A Guide for Candidates and Counselors," 2000, HMG.

54 PI, Interviewee #49; *Reminiscences of Vice Admiral William P. Mack*, 793–95; USNA Catalog, 2000–2001, 30–31; "United States Naval Academy: A Guide for Candidates and Counselors," 2000, HMG; "U.S. Colleges and Universities Report Record Number of Applications This Year; Service Academies Experience Falling Number of Applicants," *All Things Considered* on National Public Radio, 29 June 2000; Martha Thorn, "Realistic Navy Training Catches Teens' Attention," *Trident*, 23 June 2000, 1; Martha Thorn, "Summer Seminar Settles College Debate," *Trident*, 23 June 2000, 10.

55 *Reminiscences of Rear Admiral Robert W. McNitt*, 591.

56 PI, Interviewees #5, 10, 29, 49, 79, 164, 184.

57 The following discussion of the Admissions Board is based on PI with Robert McNitt, Annapolis, Md., 7 Apr. 2000; PI, Interviewees #5, 29, 34, 88, 129, 132, 146, 164, 184, 211; EI, Interviewee #184; John Ryan, Speech to Guidance Counselors, 21 Mar. 2000, USNA; *Reminiscences of Rear Admiral Robert W. McNitt*, 550, 554, 580–81, 596; Fleming, *Annapolis Autumn*, 230–41, 245, 247–54.

58 The following discussion of candidate evaluation is based on PI with Robert McNitt, Annapolis, Md., 7 Apr. 2000; *Reminiscences of Rear Admiral Draper L. Kauffman*, 802; *Reminiscences of Rear Admiral Robert W. McNitt*, 398, 546, 549–50, 552, 554–55, 562–64, 576, 578, 580, 617, 624; *Reminiscences of Vice Admiral Charles L. Melson*, 281–84; Speech by R. T. S. Keith to Cosmos Club, Washington, D.C., 1953, ARF "History: Talk by CAPT R. T. S. Keith," 8; C. L. Melson to Naval Academy Parents, 26 Feb. 1958, SR1, Box 1, "General Correspondence: Special Occasions, June Week, 1889–1963," Folder 6; Charles Melson to Robert Carney, 1 Sept. 1959, SR1, Box 5, "General Correspondence, Midshipmen: Statistics and Policy Regarding Visits, 1927–1964," Folder 2; 1959 BOV, 2; 1944 BOV, 7; 1945 BOV, 10; 1951 BOV, 8–9; 1952 BOV, 10; 1953 BOV, 11; 1954 BOV, 19; 1957 BOV, 19–20; 1958 BOV, 13; Richard West Jr., "The Superintendents of the Naval Academy," *USNIP* 71, no. 7 (July 1945): 804; C. L. Melson, "The Superintendent Reports," *Shipmate* 22, no. 3 (Mar. 1959): 14; Wayne Hughes Jr., "New Directions in Naval Academy Education," *USNIP* 86, no. 5 (May 1960): 44; "Message from Superintendent Kauffman," *LOG* 56, no. 1 (30 Sept. 1966): 5; Robert McNitt, "Challenge and Change, 1959–1968," *Shipmate* 35, no. 4 (Apr. 1972): 3; Charles Larson, "The Next 150 Years Begin," *USNIP* 122, no. 9 (Sept. 1996): 69; "U.S. Colleges and Universities Report Record Numbers of Applicants This Year; Service Academies Experience Falling Numbers of Applicants," *All Things Considered* on National Public Radio, 29 June 2000; Calvert, *The Naval Profession*, 120–21; Fleming, *Annapolis Autumn*, 234.

59 The following discussion of NAPS is based on *Reminiscences of Rear Admiral Robert W. McNitt*, 553, 596; USNA Catalog, 2000–2001, 31; "History of NAPS/NAPC," Apr.

1990, SC, Eugene Shine Papers; "Naval Prep School Moved," NYT, 10 May 1951, 2; Chief of Naval Education and Training to Chief of Navy Technical Training, 5 June 1974, SR2, Sec. NC1500, Folder "1974"; Kinnaird McKee to Admiral Shear, 30 Mar. 1976, SR2, Sec. NC1500, Folder "1976"; Charles Butler to Clinton Blankenship, 21 Nov. 1996, SR3, 1996, Sec. 1000–1531, Folder "1531"; Eli Vinock, "Secretary of the Navy Appointments: A Report," 10–12, SC, Eugene Shine Papers; William Mack and H. F. Rommel, "NAPS Comes of Age," Shipmate 76, no. 10 (Oct. 1950): 1107–13; Calvert, The Naval Profession, 133, 238; Fleming, Annapolis Autumn, 235.

60   PI, Interviewee #185; EI, Interviewee #164; Reminiscences of Rear Admiral Draper L. Kauffman, 828; Reminiscences of Vice Admiral William P. Mack, 747, 756–58; Reminiscences of Rear Admiral Robert W. McNitt, 384–87, 581–82; Interview with William P. Lawrence, USNIOH, 989; USNA Catalog, 2000–2001, 31; "Naval Academy Class of 2003 Profile," USNAW (<www.usna.edu/admissions/admprof.htm>, 3 Feb. 2001); Charles Melson to F. E. M. Whiting, 28 Apr. 1959, SR1, Box 1, "General Correspondence: Athletics, Athletic Policy, and Administration: Naval Academy Athletic Association, 1924–1969," Folder 13; F. E. M. Whiting to Charles Melson, 7 May 1959, SR1, Box 1, "General Correspondence: Athletics, Athletic Policy, and Administration: Naval Academy Athletic Association, 1924–1969," Folder 13; J. O. Coppedge to Superintendent, 17 Nov. 1972, SR2, Sec. NC1500, Folder "1972"; Charles Larson to Elliot Loughlin, 28 Jan. 1985, SR3, 1985, Sec. 1530–1710/34, Folder "1531/1"; Undersecretary of Defense, "Memorandum on Service Academy Preparatory Schools," 15 June 1994, SR3, 1994, Sec. 1000–1531, Folder "1531"; W. F. Fitzgerald Jr., "The Alumni Foundation and the Preparatory School Program," Shipmate 21, no. 4 (Apr. 1958): 2; Elliot Loughlin, "The U.S. Naval Academy Foundation, Inc.," Shipmate 43, no. 1 (Jan./Feb. 1980): 6; "Private Support of the Naval Academy," Shipmate 54, no. 7 (Sept. 1991): 16–17; Calvert, The Naval Profession, 237–38.

61   Reminiscences of Rear Admiral Robert W. McNitt, 555–56.

62   Reminiscences of Rear Admiral John F. Davidson, 264; Reminiscences of Vice Admiral William R. Smedberg III, 506; Speech by R. T. S. Keith to Cosmos Club, Washington, D.C., 1953, ARF, Folder "History: Talk by CAPT R. T. S. Keith," 19; "Talk by Vice Admiral William R. Smedberg, III, USN, to the Naval Academy Alumni Association, Lawyer's Club, NYC," 12 Nov. 1962, 1, SC, William Renwick Smedberg Papers, Box 1; E. E. Mallick, "Memorandum for the Superintendent," 12 June 1969, ARF "Faculty: Civilian/Military Faculty Mix at USNA"; W. W. Jeffries to Deputy for Management, 14 Feb. 1974, ARF "Faculty: Civilian/Military Faculty Mix at USNA"; E. B. Potter, "U.S. Military/Civilian Faculty," undated, ARF "Faculty: Civilian/Military Faculty Mix at USNA"; 1941 BOV, 14; 1942 BOV, 15–22; 1953 BOV, 4; 1958 BOV, 15; Earl Thomson, "The Naval Academy as an Undergraduate College," USNIP 74, no. 3 (Mar. 1948): 282; Wayne Hughes Jr., "New Directions in Naval Academy Education," USNIP 86, no. 5 (May 1960): 44; Ben Franklin, "Grades Inflated for Mids," NYT, 10 Apr. 1966, 1; Calvert, The Naval Profession, 109; Lovell, Neither Athens Nor Sparta?, 174, 254; Sheppard, "An Analysis of Curriculum Changes at the United States Naval Academy," 137, 349–50, 395.

63 Lebby, "Professional Socialization of the Naval Officer," 80–81; Lovell, *Neither Athens Nor Sparta?*, 182.

64 Charles Larson to Sharon Stoll, 18 June 1996, SR3, 1996, Sec. 1531, Folder "1531."

65 EI, Interviewee #5; *Reminiscences of Rear Admiral John F. Davidson*, 281, 293, 356–58; *Reminiscences of Rear Admiral Draper L. Kauffman*, 669–70, 683–702, 733, 750; *Reminiscences of Rear Admiral Robert W. McNitt*, 383, 402; *Reminiscences of Vice Admiral Charles S. Minter Jr.*, 562–65; *Reminiscences of Vice Admiral William R. Smedberg III*, 509; 1957 BOV, 22; Draper Kauffman to Faculty, 6 May 1966, SR2, Sec. ON/1531, Folder "1962–1967"; James Calvert to J. H. Webb, 14 Nov. 1987, SR3, 1987, Sec. 12009–13950, Folder "1531/ON"; V. L. Hill Jr., "Memorandum for the Chief of Naval Operations," 8 Jan. 1991, SR3, 1991, Sec. 5238–5700, Folder "5420/3"; T. C. Lynch to Assistant Secretary of the Navy for Manpower and Reserve Affairs, 10 Sept. 1991, SR3, 1991, Sec. 5238–5700, Folder "5420"; Ben Franklin, "Annapolis Chided on Grade Quotas," NYT, 1 May 1966, 1; "Annapolis Told to List Reforms," NYT, 2 May 1966, 40; Ben Franklin, "Rift at Annapolis Remains After Mediators Leave," NYT, 20 Nov. 1966, 77; "Service Academies," *Time*, 22 Apr. 1966, 30; J. H. Nevins Jr., "The Naval Academy and Its Curriculum," *Shipmate* 31, no. 3 (Mar. 1968): 10; Robert McNitt, "Challenge and Change, 1959–1968," *Shipmate* 35, no. 4 (Apr. 1972): 5; "Facts on Naval Academy Commissioning Week Traditions," *Trident*, 10 May 1996, 11; Royall Whitaker to R. F. Marryott, 4 Aug. 1988, SR3, 1998, Sec. 5214–5420, Folder "5420"; Fleming, *Annapolis Autumn*, 186–94; Lovell, *Neither Athens Nor Sparta?*, 56, 165, 168–72, 181–82, 185–87, 254; Sheppard, "An Analysis of Curriculum Changes at the United States Naval Academy," 368.

66 PI, Interviewee #177; EI, Interviewee #87; *Reminiscences of Rear Admiral Julian T. Burke Jr.*, 371; *Reminiscences of Rear Admiral Draper L. Kauffman*, 270, 669, 705, 733; *Reminiscences of Vice Admiral William P. Mack*, 654; *Reminiscences of Rear Admiral Robert W. McNitt*, 369, 373–74; *Reminiscences of Vice Admiral Charles S. Minter Jr.*, 560; *Reminiscences of Vice Admiral William R. Smedberg III*, 420; 1946 BOV, 7; 1948 BOV, 4; 1954 BOV, 3; 1955 BOV, 4; 1957 BOV, 23; J. R. Harstreiter, "The Naval Academy Curriculum: From Professionalism to Present Day Modern Education," MFCP #675, 1966, 4; Robert McNamara, "Memorandum for the President," Fact Sheet, 2, 5 Sept. 1966, LBJ, Folder "ND-15-8: U.S. Naval Academy, 1965–1967"; Kinnaird McKee to R. A. Ekelund, 24 Feb. 1977, SR2, Sec. NC/1531, Folder "1977"; "The Superintendents of the Naval Academy," USNIP 71, no. 7 (July 1945): 808; "Message from Superintendent Kauffman," LOG 56, no. 1 (30 Sept. 1966): 5; Calvert, *The Naval Profession*, 109; Heise, *The Brass Factories*, 111–23; Lebby, "Professional Socialization of the Naval Officer," 84; Lovell, *Neither Athens Nor Sparta?*, 8, 55, 162, 164–66, 209–10, 217–18, 253–54, 291; Sheppard, "An Analysis of Curriculum Changes at the United States Naval Academy," 374.

67 PI, Interviewee #177; EI, Interviewee #5; *Reminiscences of Rear Admiral Robert W. McNitt*, 568; Kinnaird McKee to H. Ross Perot, 8 Mar. 1977, SR2, Sec. NC/1531, Folder "1977"; Charles Larson to Elliott Loughlin, 28 Jan. 1985, SR3, 1985, Sec. 1530–1710/34, Folder "1531/1"; "Remarks by Admiral John R. Ryan, USN, Superinten-

dent, United States Naval Academy, given to the Naval Academy Alumni Association President's Circle, September 11, 1998," 1, USNAW (<www.usna.edu/pao/speeches/speechjr4.htm>, 21 May 1999); "Remarks by Admiral John R. Ryan, USN, Superintendent, United States Naval Academy, given at the Naval Academy Class of 1944 Reunion, October 2, 1998," USNAW (<www.usna.edu/pao/speeches/speechjr1.htm>, 21 May 1999); "Remarks by Admiral John R. Ryan, USN, Superintendent, United States Naval Academy, given to the Pennsylvania Parents Club, February 1999," 2, USNAW (<www.usna.edu/pao/speeches/speechjr8.htm>, 21 May 1999); Chris Price, "Permanent Military Professors, Proven Assets to the Navy," *Trident*, 11 Sept. 1998, 3; Susan Hensen, "Permanent Military Professors Sought," *Trident*, 8 Jan. 1999, 5; John Ryan, "The State of the Academy," *Shipmate* 62, no. 2 (Mar. 1999); Robert Niewoneu, "Senior Fleet Officers Take Classroom Command," *Shipmate* 62, no. 10 (Dec. 1999): 27; Melissa Marks, "Academy Faculty Go to Sea," *Trident*, 24 Mar. 2000, 11.

68 PI with Robert McNitt, Annapolis, Md., 7 Apr. 2000; 1948 BOV, 11.

69 John Ryan, Speech to Guidance Counselors, 21 Mar. 2000, USNA; Fleming, *Annapolis Autumn*, 248. On the origins and early meaning of the term "extra instruction," see Karsten, *The Naval Aristocracy*, 37.

70 *Reminiscences of Rear Admiral Julian T. Burke Jr.*, 350–51; *Reminiscences of Rear Admiral Robert W. McNitt*, 372, 397; J. R. Harstreiter, "The Naval Academy Curriculum: From Professionalism to Present Day Modern Education," MFCP #675, 1966, 3; Wayne Hughes Jr., "New Directions in Naval Academy Education," USNIP 86, no. 5 (May 1960): 41, 43; J. H. Nevins Jr., "The Naval Academy and Its Curriculum," *Shipmate* 31, no. 3 (Mar. 1968): 8; "Annapolis Honors Educator," NYT, 25 Apr. 1971, 67; Lovell, *Neither Athens Nor Sparta?*, 162; Sheppard, "An Analysis of Curriculum Changes at the United States Naval Academy," 8, 239.

71 PI, Interviewee #177; 1955 BOV, 5; 1957 BOV, 16; R. A. Gurcyznski, "Leadership and Law," 18 Jan. 1994, ARF "History: Department Histories, 150th Anniversary"; Rae Jean Goodman, "Economics," 2 May 1995, ARF "History: Department Histories, 150th Anniversary"; Richard West Jr., "The Superintendents of the Naval Academy," USNIP 71, no. 7 (July 1945): 808; Calvert, *The Naval Profession*, 106; Forney, *The Midshipman Culture and Educational Reform*, 272; Lovell, *Neither Athens Nor Sparta?*, 10; McCain and Salter, *Faith of My Fathers*, 119; Sheppard, "An Analysis of Curriculum Changes at the United States Naval Academy," 8, 204.

72 Interview with Wesley Brown, USNIOH, 155, 160; Interview with William P. Lawrence, USNIOH, 53–56; *Reminiscences of Rear Admiral Julian T. Burke Jr.*, 349; *Reminiscences of Vice Admiral Charles L. Melson*, 145, 256; *Reminiscences of Vice Admiral Charles S. Minter Jr.*, 19; "Changes at Academy Are Debated," WP, 17 Dec. 1987, Md. Sec. 19; "Changes and Challenges for Naval Academy," NYT, 25 Dec. 1987, 38; Sheppard, "An Analysis of Curriculum Changes at the United States Naval Academy," 380.

73 *Reminiscences of Vice Admiral William R. Smedberg III*, 541–42.

74 James Calvert to J. H. Webb, 14 Nov. 1987, SR3, 1987, Sec. 12009–13950, Folder "1531/ON"; 1953 BOV, 4; 1959 BOV, 8; John Hayes, "With a Round Turn," *Shipmate* 22, no. 8 (Aug. 1959); Wayne Hughes Jr., "New Directions in Naval Academy Educa-

tion," USNIP 86, no. 5 (May 1960): 45; Ben Franklin, "Rift at Academy Remains After Mediators Leave," NYT, 20 Nov. 1966, 77; Neil Henry, "Rickover's Nuclear Navy," WP, 16 June 1981, A1; Richard Halloran, "Military Academies Are Becoming Even Tougher on Body and Mind," NYT, 23 May 1988, Sec. 4, 4; Stacy Danzuso, "Academy Ranks High in Student Survey," EC, 8 Aug. 2000, B1; Sheppard, "An Analysis of Curriculum Changes at the United States Naval Academy," 267, 274.

75 The following discussion of Folsom's findings is based on PI, Interviewee #177; Sheppard, "An Analysis of Curriculum Changes at the United States Naval Academy," 223, 237, 245, 250, 257.

76 PI with Robert McNitt, Annapolis, Md., 7 Apr. 2000; *Reminiscences of Rear Admiral Robert W. McNitt*, 368, 538–39, 540, 621; "Superintendent's Talk to the Faculty," 4 Sept. 1956, 27, SC, William Renwick Smedberg Papers, Box 1; Forney, *The Midshipman Culture and Educational Reform*, 38–39, 94–95, 114–15, 179, 265; Lovell, *Neither Athens Nor Sparta?*, 173–74, 182, 206–10, 214–15, 253, 274–75; Sheppard, "An Analysis of Curriculum Changes at the United States Naval Academy," 13–14, 182–83, 250–51, 262, 348, 381, 382, 414–15.

77 *Reminiscences of Rear Admiral Robert W. McNitt*, 376; J. R. Harstreiter, "The Naval Academy Curriculum: From Professionalism to Present Day Modern Education," MFCP #675, 1966, 2–3; Sheppard, "An Analysis of Curriculum Changes at the United States Naval Academy," 225, 293.

78 *Reminiscences of Rear Admiral Draper L. Kauffman*, 709, 718, 719; *Reminiscences of Rear Admiral Robert W. McNitt*, 372, 376; 1959 BOV, 8; "Presentation by Vice Admiral William R. Smedberg, IV, USN, CNP, Before the Naval Academy Alumni Association, Roosevelt Hotel, New York City," 18 Mar. 1960, 2, SC, William Renwick Smedberg Papers, Box 1; W. W. Jeffries, "Development of the Validation, Electives, and Majors Program at the U.S. Naval Academy," 20 Mar. 1963, ARF "Curriculum: Development of the Validation, Electives, and Majors Program at the U.S. Naval Academy"; J. R. Harstreiter, "The Naval Academy Curriculum: From Professionalism to Present Day Modern Education," MFCP #675, 1966, 3, 6–7; J. H. Nevins Jr., "The Naval Academy and Its Curriculum," *Shipmate* 31, no. 3 (Mar. 1968): 8.

79 *Reminiscences of Rear Admiral Draper L. Kauffman*, 708–10; J. R. Harstreiter, "The Naval Academy Curriculum: From Professionalism to Present Day Modern Education," MFCP #675, 1966, 5–11; Charles Melson, "The Superintendent Speaks," *Shipmate* 23, no. 6/7 (June/July 1960): 20; John Davidson, "The Superintendent Speaks," *Shipmate* 25, no. 3/4 (Mar./Apr. 1962): 13; H. O. Werner, "Breakthrough at the U.S. Naval Academy," USNIP 89, no. 10 (Oct. 1963): 58.

80 Lovell, *Neither Athens Nor Sparta?*, 269.

81 *Reminiscences of Rear Admiral John F. Davidson*, 362–63.

82 The following discussion of the civilian dean and A. Bernard Drought is based on PI with Robert McNitt, Annapolis, Md., 7 Apr. 2000; *Reminiscences of Rear Admiral John F. Davidson*, 356–58; *Reminiscences of Rear Admiral Draper L. Kauffman*, 662–65; *Reminiscences of Rear Admiral Robert W. McNitt*, 368–69, 372–73, 380–83, 397–98, 631–32; *Reminiscences of Vice Admiral Charles S. Minter Jr.*, 512, 558; "Weakening the Naval Academy," NYT, 23 June 1962, 22; Jack Raymond, "Annapolis Gets First Academic

Dean, A Civilian," NYT, 14 June 1963; Jerry O'Leary Jr., "The Naval Academy Sets New Course," *Navy: The Magazine of Sea Power* 7, no. 8 (Aug. 1964): 6–8; J. H. Nevins Jr., "The Naval Academy and Its Curriculum," *Shipmate* 31, no. 3 (Mar. 1968): 8; Robert McNitt, "Challenge and Change, 1959–1968," *Shipmate* 35, no. 4 (Apr. 1972): 4; Lebby, "Professional Socialization of the Naval Officer," 81; Lovell, *Neither Athens Nor Sparta?*, 158–64, 166–69, 203–4; Sheppard, "An Analysis of Curriculum Changes at the United States Naval Academy," 9, 288.

83 The following discussion of the restructuring of the Academic Division is based on *Reminiscences of Vice Admiral Charles L. Melson*, 256–57, 263; *Reminiscences of Vice Admiral Charles S. Minter Jr.*, 522, 554, 562–64; *Reminiscences of Rear Admiral Robert W. McNitt*, 377–78, 397, 628–29; W. W. Jeffries, "Development of the Validation, Electives, and Majors Program at the U.S. Naval Academy," 20 Mar. 1963, ARF "Curriculum: Development of the Validation, Electives, and Majors Program at the U.S. Naval Academy"; "Chemistry," undated, ARF "History: Department Histories, 150th Anniversary"; 1959 BOV, 7; Wayne Hughes Jr., "New Directions in Naval Academy Education," USNIP 86, no. 5 (May 1960): 42; Robert McNitt, "Challenge and Change, 1959–1968," *Shipmate* 35, no. 4 (Apr. 1972): 3–4; Lovell, *Neither Athens Nor Sparta?*, 166–67.

84 W. W. Jeffries, "Development of the Validation, Electives, and Majors Program at the U.S. Naval Academy," 20 Mar. 1963, ARF "Curriculum: Development of the Validation, Electives, and Majors Program at the U.S. Naval Academy"; Lebby, "Professional Socialization of the Naval Officer," 79.

85 PI, Interviewees #101, 177; *Reminiscences of Rear Admiral Draper L. Kauffman*, 714, 728, 833; *Reminiscences of Rear Admiral Robert W. McNitt*, 400; *Reminiscences of Vice Admiral Charles S. Minter Jr.*, 517–22; Stu Eizenstat and Beth Abromowitz to James Carter, 29 Sept. 1977, SR2, Sec. NC/1531, Folder "1977"; Rae Jean Goodman, "Economics," ARF "History: Department Histories, 150th Anniversary"; Superintendent to Academic Department Heads, 8 Jan. 1964, Appendix D in J. R. Harstreiter, "The Naval Academy Curriculum: From Professionalism to Present Day Modern Education," MFCP #675, 1966; James Calvert, "Thoughts Upon Conclusion of a Four Year Tour," *Shipmate* 35, no. 4 (Apr. 1972): 8; "Changes at Academy are Debated," WP, 17 Dec. 1987, Md. section 19; "Changes and Challenges for Naval Academy," NYT, 25 Dec. 1987, 28; Andrew Crawford, "The Major Decision," *Character Quarterly* 4, no. 3 (Spring 2000): 4; Calvert, *The Naval Profession*, 107; Sheppard, "An Analysis of Curriculum Changes at the United States Naval Academy," 9, 294.

86 Calvert, *The Naval Profession*, 107–9; Sheppard, "An Analysis of Curriculum Changes at the United States Naval Academy," 229–30.

87 James Calvert, "Superintendent's Memorandum No. 7," 21 Mar. 1972, CR, Sec. 5400/19, Folder "1972"; Lebby, "Professional Socialization of the Naval Officer," 76; Lovell, *Neither Athens Nor Sparta?*, 7, 186–87.

88 Sheppard, "An Analysis of Curriculum Changes at the United States Naval Academy," 15–16.

89 *Reminiscences of Rear Admiral Draper L. Kauffman*, 714; *Reminiscences of Rear Admiral Robert W. McNitt*, 538; Charles Larson to Charles Bishop, 29 Apr. 1996, SR3, 1996, Sec. 1531,

Folder "1531"; Majors of Classes of 1969, 1970, and 1971, undated, ARF "Midshipmen, Majors, Classes 1969–1971"; 1971 LB, 207–8, 216–19; James Calvert, "Thoughts Upon Conclusion of a Four Year Tour," *Shipmate* 35, no. 4 (Apr. 1972): 8; Andrew Crawford, "The Major Decision," *Character Quarterly* 4, no. 3 (Spring 2000): 4; Lovell, *Neither Athens Nor Sparta?*, 182; Sheppard, "An Analysis of Curriculum Changes at the United States Naval Academy," 323–25, 328–30.

90 James Calvert, "Superintendent's Memorandum No. 7," 21 Mar. 1972, CR, Sec. 5400/19, Folder "1972"; D. A. Ellison, "Editorial," LOG 59, no. 5 (30 Jan. 1970): 7; 1971 LB, 207–8; Forney, *The Midshipman Culture and Educational Reform*, 220, 249, 272.

91 PI, Interviewee #177; *Reminiscences of Vice Admiral William P. Mack*, 664; Interview with William P. Lawrence, USNIOH, 991–92, 999; Kinnaird McKee to James Watkins, 16 Mar. 1977, SR2, Sec. ON/1531, Folder "1962–1967"; Stu Eizenstat and Beth Abromowitz to James Carter, 29 Sept. 1977, SR2, Sec. NC/1531, Folder "1977"; Academic Dean to A. R. Potvin, 19 Dec. 1979, SR2, Sec. NC/1531, Folder "1979"; E. C. Waller to Lando Zelch Jr., 31 Mar. 1982, SR2, Sec. 5900/1, Folder "1982"; R. A. Gurczynski, "Leadership and Law," 18 Jan. 1994, ARF "History: Department Histories, 150th Anniversary"; Charles Larson to Charles Bishop, 29 Apr. 1996, SR3, 1996, Sec. 1531, Folder "1531"; 1971 LB, 216–19; ACADEANINST 1531.72, "The Majors Program: Class of 2000," 1 Oct. 1997, iv, HMG; "Academic Majors," USNAW (<www.usna. edu/admissions/majors.htm>, 3 Feb. 2000); "Remarks by Admiral John R. Ryan, USN, Superintendent, United States Naval Academy, given to the Pennsylvania Parents Club, February 1999," 2, USNAW (<www.usna.edu/pao/speeches/speechjr8. htm>, 21 May 1999); Lovell, *Neither Athens Nor Sparta?*, 7; Sheppard, "An Analysis of Curriculum Changes at the United States Naval Academy," 331–33; Stewart, *The Brigade in Review*, 39.

92 *Reminiscences of Vice Admiral William R. Smedberg*, 540; William Smedberg, "Superintendent's Talk to the Faculty," Annapolis, Md., 4 Sept. 1956, 9, SC, William Renwick Smedberg Papers, Box 1; 1957 BOV, 19; William Smedberg to Chief of Naval Personnel, 27 Sept. 1956, SR1, Box 4, "General Correspondence: Midshipmen: Policy and Administration," Folder 14; USNAINST 1531.4, 27 Sept. 1956, ARF "Midshipmen: Superintendents'/Commandants'/Deans' Lists"; USNAINST 1531.16 FCH-1, 24 Feb. 1972, ARF "Midshipmen: Superintendents'/Commandants'/Deans' Lists."

93 *Reminiscences of Rear Admiral Draper L. Kauffman*, 721; Martha Thorn, "Mids Juggle Courses at Academy, Graduate School," *Trident*, 30 Apr. 1999, 13; "Voluntary Graduate Education Program," USNAW (<www.usna.edu/admissions/acprogs.htm>, 3 Feb. 2000); Sheppard, "An Analysis of Curriculum Changes at the United States Naval Academy," 368; Stewart, *The Brigade in Review*, 39.

94 The following discussion of increased course offerings and the Trident Scholars Program is based on PI with Robert McNitt, Annapolis, Md., 7 Apr. 2000; EI, Interviewees #177, 178; *Reminiscences of Rear Admiral Draper L. Kauffman*, 723–24; *Reminiscences of Rear Admiral Robert W. McNitt*, 381–82; *Reminiscences of Vice Admiral William R. Smedberg III*, 510; A. G. Esch to Richard Dorso, 14 Jan. 1956, SR4, Folder "A7-4/1-1: Television Series," 10; USNA Notice 1500, 25 Apr. 1963, ARF "Midshipmen: Trident Scholars"; "Trident Scholar Program," 1984, ARF "Midshipmen: Tri-

dent Scholars"; J. E. Shade to Brigade of Midshipmen, 12 Apr. 1999, HMG; "Trident Scholars," USNAW (<www.usna.edu/admissions/acadprogs.htm>, 3 Feb. 2000); Robert McNitt, "Uncle Charlie," *Shipmate* 51, no. 5 (June 1988): 8; Robert McNitt, "Challenge and Change: The Naval Academy, 1959–1968," *Shipmate* 35, no. 4 (Apr. 1972): 6; John Bodnar, "USNA Performance and Career Fleet Performance," 7 June 1996, unpublished statistics, HMG; John Bodnar, "Trident Scholars: On the Road to Admiral or to CIVLANT," undated, unpublished article, HMG; Lebby, "Professional Socialization of the Naval Officer," 81; Lovell, *Neither Athens Nor Sparta?*, 167–68, 184; Sheppard, "An Analysis of Curriculum Changes at the United States Naval Academy," 287; Stewart, *The Brigade in Review*, 39.

95 *Reminiscences of Rear Admiral Draper L. Kauffman*, 753, 759; *Reminiscences of Rear Admiral Robert W. McNitt*, 408; "Rear Admiral Kauffman's Remarks to the Board of Visitors," 4 Nov. 1965, LBJ, Folder "ND 15-8: U.S. Naval Academy, 1965–1967"; Robert McNamara, "Memorandum for the President," 5 Sept. 1966, Fact Sheet, 2, LBJ, Folder "ND 15-8: U.S. Naval Academy, 1965–1967"; James Calvert to Parents, 30 Dec. 1969, CR, Box "Commandant of Midshipmen: Instructions, Notices, Miscellaneous Correspondence," Folder "Miscellaneous, 1968–1976"; Brian Fors, "Library," undated, ARF "History: Department Histories, 150th Anniversary"; 1959 BOV, 23–24; Tim Heeley, "E Pluribus Unum . . . Nimitz Library," *LOG* 63, no. 2 (26 Oct. 1973): 14–16; Calvert, *The Naval Profession*, 110; Lovell, *Neither Athens Nor Sparta?*, 8, 183, 291.

96 John Kelley to Commandant, 15 Dec. 1983, CR, Sec. 5420/1, Folder "1983"; Superintendent to Deputy Chief of Naval Operations, 18 Aug. 1989, SR3, 1989, Sec. 1000–1531/2, Folder "1531/1"; Superintendent to Chief of Naval Operations, 2 Nov. 1990, SR3, 1990, Sec. 1531/1–1710/5, Folder "1531/1."

97 PI with William Miller, Annapolis, Md., 22 Feb. 1999; *Reminiscences of Vice Admiral William P. Mack*, 658–62, 728; *Reminiscences of Vice Admiral Charles S. Minter Jr.*, 531–45; *Reminiscences of Vice Admiral William R. Smedberg III*, 726–27; Gary Ballard to Superintendent, 7 Aug. 1968, SR2, Sec. 12770/1, Folder "1968–1969"; John Hayes, "With a Round Turn," *Shipmate* 22, no. 8 (Aug. 1959); "Rickover Assails the Navy System," NYT, 19 June 1961, 10; C. Yates McDaniel, "Rickover Rakes Navy, Would Abolish Academy," WP, 19 June 1961, 1; "McNamara Chides Rickover on Views," NYT, 24 June 1961, 10; "Weakening the Naval Academy," NYT, 23 June 1962, 22; Evert Clark, "Arms Cost Stress Scored by Rickover," NYT, 9 June 1967, 1; "Rickover Assails Pentagon on Information Flow," NYT, 16 July 1968, 4; George Wilson, "Rickover Delivers Speech Critical of Present U.S. Navy Organization," WP, 31 Aug. 1974, A2; "Changes at Academy are Debated," WP, 17 Dec. 1987, Md. sec. 19; "Changes and Challenge for Naval Academy," NYT, 25 Dec. 1987, 28; Polmar and Allen, *Rickover*, 305, 307, 310–12, 480.

98 The following discussion of the commandant is based on PI with Charles Buchanan, Annapolis, Md., 17 Nov. 1999; PI with Leon Edney, Annapolis, Md., 16 May 1999; PI with Donald K. Forbes, Manassas, Va., 24 Apr. 1998; PI with Samuel Locklear, Annapolis, Md., 6 Apr. 2000; PI with James Winnefeld, Annapolis, Md., 23 Feb. 1999; PI, Interviewee #182; *Reminiscences of Rear Admiral Julian T. Burke Jr.*, 337, 341; *Reminiscences of Rear Admiral Robert W. McNitt*, 411–13; *Reminiscences of Vice Admiral*

Charles L. Melson, 148–50; *Reminiscences of Vice Admiral Charles S. Minter Jr.*, 442–43; 1959 BOV, 7; Robert McNamara, "Memorandum for the President," 5 Sept. 1966, Fact Sheet, 2, LBJ, Folder "ND 15-8"; Leon Edney to Brigade Officers, 23 Sept. 1981, CR, Sec. 5400/5, Folder "1981"; USNA Organizational Flowchart, 1998, USNA Public Affairs Office; List of Commandants of Midshipmen, undated, USNA Archives; Charles Melson, "The Superintendent Reports," *Shipmate* 22, no. 4 (Apr. 1959): 18; Jim Stavridis, "New Dant Discusses Goals," *LOG* 63, no. 1 (5 Oct. 1973): 18–19; Lovell, *Neither Athens Nor Sparta?*, 199. In 2002, Colonel John Allen became the first Marine to serve as commandant.

99   The following discussion of commandants' varying leadership styles is based on PI with Leon Edney, Annapolis, Md., 16 May 1999; TI with Robert Coogan, San Diego, Calif., 14 Nov. 1999; PI, Interviewees #7, 10, 24, 30, 36, 40, 41, 42, 58, 78, 79, 87, 121, 139, 179, 180, 182, 185; *Reminiscences of Rear Admiral Robert W. McNitt*, 366; 1970 LB, 162, 190–91, 372–73, 801; 1971 LB, 39; Bill Smith, "Editorial," *LOG*, 20 Feb. 1970, 4; David Kanab, "A Few Inches From The Yard," *Shipmate* 42, no. 1 (Jan./Feb. 1979): 33; "The Bancroft Horror Picture Show, Part 1," *LOG* 71, no. 2 (Oct. 1981): 5–10; "The Bancroft Horror Picture Show, Part 2," *LOG* 71, no. 3 (Nov. 1981): 22–27; "The Bancroft Horror Picture Show, Part 3," *LOG* 71, no. 5 (Jan. 1982): 28–33; "Good Morning, Navy!," *LOG* 72, no. 7 (Mar. 1983): 8.

100 Officer in Charge, Midshipmen's Store to Commandant, 17 Sept. 1956, ARF "Midshipmen: Welfare Fund"; Staff JAG Officer to Postmaster, United States Postal Service, 20 Oct. 1972, ARF "Midshipmen: Welfare Fund"; P. M. Callaghan, Report on Food Preparation, 2 Nov. 1981, ARF "Midshipmen: Food Preparation"; PAO Announcement 4472, undated, ARF "Midshipmen: Food Preparation"; Richard Langton, "Heroes of King Hall," *USNIP* 121, no. 10 (Oct. 1995): 51.

101 *Reminiscences of Rear Admiral John F. Davidson*, 42; William Smedberg, "Speech Delivered to First Class, and Class Officers, Plus Other Classes Over Bancroft Hall Radio," Annapolis, Md., 12 Apr. 1956, 7, SC, William Renwick Smedberg Papers, Box 1; Barton Strong, "A History of the Marine Barracks, Annapolis, Maryland," MFCP #1586, 1964, 1, 8, 11; 1948 BOV, 13; 1970 LB, 48; John Greenwood, "The Corps' Old School Tie," *USNIP* 101, no. 11 (Nov. 1975): 51; Merrill Bartlett, "Annapolis Marines," *USNIP* 118, no. 4 (Apr. 1982): 94; Fleming, *Sex, Art, and Audience*, 5–6, 8–9, 15; Mary Ryan, "The American Parade: Representations of Nineteenth-Century Social Order," in Hunt, ed., *The New Cultural History*, 132–53; Stewart, *The Brigade in Review*, 72.

102 EI, Interviewee #22; *Reminiscences of Rear Admiral John F. Davidson*, 13; *Reminiscences of Rear Admiral Draper L. Kauffman*, 741; *Reminiscences of Vice Admiral Charles L. Melson*, 296; USNA Catalog, 2000–2001, 125–30; Joe Califano, "Memorandum for the President," 10 June 1968, Attachment 2, LBJ, White House Central Files, Subject File "ND 15-8: U.S. Naval Academy, 1968," Box 190; Clark Clifford, "Memorandum for the President," 23 July 1968, 1, Attachment 2, LBJ, White House Central Files, Subject File "ND 15-8: U.S. Naval Academy, 1968," Box 190; James Calvert to Parents of the Class of 1970, 29 Aug. 1969, 1, SR2, Sec. RG, Folder "1958–1977"; James Calvert to Parents, 21 May 1972, CR, Sec. 5400/19, Folder "1972"; COMDTMIDN Instruction

1531.14A, 8 Jan. 1975, CR, Sec. 5420/4, Folder "1975"; Kinnaird McKee to Chief of Naval Operations, 6 Oct. 1977, SR5, Box 4; "Gold Team Plan for an Integrated Professional Development Program at the U.S. Naval Academy," Feb. 1979, CR, Sec. 5213/1, Folder "1979"; E. C. Waller to Daniel Ogden, 6 June 1983, SR2, Sec. ON/1531, Folder "1983"; Charles Larson to Charles Krulak, 18 Apr. 1996, SR3, 1996, Sec. 1531, Folder "1531"; Charles Larson to Michelle Behrens, 8 Oct. 1996, SR3, 1996, Sec. 1531, Folder "1531"; Brigade Training Officer to Brigade, 3 Nov. 2000, HMG; R. A. Gurczynski, "Leadership and Law," undated, ARF "History: Department Histories"; "Remarks by Admiral Charles R. Larson, USN, Superintendent, United States Naval Academy, before the San Diego Alumni Assembly, 6 September 1997," USNAW (<www.nadn.navy.mil/pao/speech03.html>, 21 May 1999); Douglas Cray, "Knowledge Industry Trains Guns on Annapolis," NYT, 15 Oct. 1967, Bus. sec. 1; "No Chapel for Middies," EC, 6 Jan. 1972, 1; William Lawrence, "Superintendent's Report," Shipmate 42, no. 8 (Oct. 1979): 17–20; Stephen Chadwick, "The Commandant Speaks," Shipmate 48, no. 10 (Dec. 1985): 15; Bernard Trainor, "Officers Fear Backlash from Iran/Contra Affair," NYT, 10 Mar. 1987: 24; Scott Harper, "Mids Must Be Trained First, Grill Plebes Later," EC, 22 Aug. 1991, 1; "Salty Sam," LOG 83, no. 1 (Aug. 1993): 8; Lauren Majchizak, "A Few Inches From the Yard," Shipmate 62, no. 3 (Apr. 1999): 30–31; Rob Cain, "Some Mids Cruise Under Foreign Flags, Distant Horizons," Trident, 26 May 2000, 8; Stephen Woolverton, "Mids' Summer Cruises Are Not a Vacation," Trident, 26 May 2000, 8; Stephanie Milo, "Yard Patrol Craft Summer Cruises Under Way," Trident, 23 June 2000, 11; Stephanie Sealy, "Mids Live Enlisted Life at Sea This Summer," Trident, 23 June 2000, 4.

103 Reminiscences of Vice Admiral William P. Mack, 706–8; COMDTMIDN Notice 1531, 5 Jan. 1973, ARF "Midshipmen: Mandatory Chapel, 1970–1973"; Max Morris to Joy Wood, 10 Jan. 1973, CR, Sec. 1730, Folder "1973"; Superintendent's Report to Board of Visitors, undated, CR, Sec. 5420/4, Folder "1973"; Charles Larson to Eugene Farrell, 3 Oct. 1994, SR3, 1994, Sec. 1000–1531, Folder "1531"; Charles Larson to Ralph Gilbert, 13 Dec. 1995, SR3, 1995, Sec. 1000–1531, Folder "1531"; Charles Larson to Editor of the New York Times, 19 Aug. 1996, SR3, 1996, Sec. 5700–5720, Folder "5700"; Charles Larson, "Service Academies: Critical to Our Future," USNIP 121, no. 10 (Oct. 1995): 35; Michael Janofsky, "Academy Head Defends Ethics of Midshipmen," NYT, 18 Apr. 1996, B8.

104 PI, Interviewees #9, 166; Reminiscences of Rear Admiral Julian T. Burke Jr., 352; Reminiscences of Rear Admiral Robert W. McNitt, 562; Reminiscences of Vice Admiral William R. Smedberg III, 763; Oral History Transcript, Henry John Rotrige, 42, 84–85; Interview with William P. Lawrence, USNIOH, 916; Interview with Pamela Wacek Svendsen, USNIOH, OHFFG, 26; "Minority Midshipmen Study Group Report to the Superintendent, 12 Nov. 1996, SR3, 1996, Sec. 1000–1531, Folder "1531"; "U.S. Naval Academy Letter of the Superintendent to Parents and Guardians of Midshipmen," July 1953, SC Folder "USNA: Midshipmen"; A. G. Esch to Vincent Lonergan, 17 Jan. 1956, SR4, Folder "A7-4/1-1: Television Series"; John O'Connor to Superintendent and Commandant, 20 Oct. 1972, CR, Sec. 1730, Folder "1972"; Sarah Robert,

"Extracurricula: Midshipmen Organizations and Activities," USNIP 71, no. 4 (Apr. 1945): 385; "Chaplain's Corner," LOG 52, no. 3 (19 Oct. 1962): 9.

105 PI with Ed Peery, Annapolis, Md., 4 Nov. 1999; "Naval Academy Athletics," USNAW (<www.usna.edu/admissions/athletes.htm>, 3 Feb. 2000); USNA Catalog, 2000–2001, 138.

106 PI, Interviewee #84.

107 PI with Dave Smalley, Annapolis, Md., 18 Feb. 2000; PI with James Calvert, St. Michaels, Md., 4 May 2000; PI, Interviewee #88; Reminiscences of Vice Admiral Charles L. Melson, 306; Reminiscences of Vice Admiral Charles S. Minter Jr., 509–10; Physical Education Notice 5400, 5 Jan. 1993, ARF "Athletics: NAAA"; 1940 BOV, 9; 1942 BOV, 8–9; 1955 BOV, 7; 1952 BOV, 12–13; Hanson Baldwin, "84% of Athletes Reported Screened and Assisted," NYT, 15 June 1952, 1; "Private Support of the Naval Academy," Shipmate 54, no. 7 (Sept. 1991): 16–17; Jack Falla, NCAA, 16, 23, 167, 174, 210–12.

108 "Sports at Navy," LOG 45 (1956): 12; Calvert, The Naval Profession, 110–11; Stewart, The Brigade in Review, 48–59.

109 USNA Catalog, 2000–2001, 138. Women's sports include basketball, crew, cross country, soccer, swimming, indoor track, outdoor track, and volleyball. Men's sports include baseball, basketball, heavyweight crew, lightweight crew, cross country, football, lightweight football, golf, gymnastics, lacrosse, soccer, squash, swimming, tennis, indoor track, outdoor track, water polo, and wrestling. The three co-ed sports are rifle, intercollegiate sailing, and offshore sailing.

110 Winfield Scott to Ronald Marryott, 31 Mar. 1987, SR3, 1987, Sec. 1531/1–1710/2, Folder "1710/1"; USNA Catalog, 2000–2001, 135–36; James Cheevers, "USNA: The Modern Era, Part IV," Shipmate 58, no. 5 (Oct. 1995): 35; Calvert, The Naval Profession, 101–2; Stewart, The Brigade in Review, 48.

111 Admiral James Calvert Coaches Award Plaque and Vice Admiral William P. Lawrence Sword for Personal Excellence in Women's Athletics Plaque, Lejeune Hall, USNA, Annapolis, Md.

112 Wayne Fong to Brigade of Midshipmen, 6 Dec. 1999, HMG; George Stephan, "Stage Lighting at the Naval Academy: A History of the Midshipmen's Juice Gang," MFCP #1497, 1965, 13; 1971 LB, 237, 238; Jean Ebbert, "Women Midshipmen: A Report on the First Six Months," Shipmate 40, no. 2 (Mar. 1977): 17.

113 PI, Interviewees #6, 35, 47, 82, 88; Interview with William P. Lawrence, USNIOH, 129; Leon Edney to Brigade of Midshipmen, Oct. 1981, CR, Sec. 5400/5, Folder "1981"; M. E. Chang, "Climate Assessment of the U.S. Naval Academy," 11 June 1990, 3, SR5, Box 4; "Truman Orders Inquiry Into Cadet Football," NYT, 10 Aug. 1951, 8; "Navy's Eleven Loses Class-By-Itself Status," NYT, 8 June 1958, Sec. 5, 3; Mark Christenson, "A Few Inches From the Yard," Shipmate 56, no. 8 (Oct. 1993): 23.

114 PI, Interviewees #31, 35, 36, 83, 84, 88, 92, 96; Reminiscences of Rear Admiral Draper L. Kauffman, 37; Jack Flanagan, "The LOG Salutes Coach Ed Peery," LOG 58, no. 2 (11 Oct. 1968): 29; Tim Strabbing, "Coach Peery: Impacting Midshipmen for Decades," Character Quarterly 3, no. 5 (Commissioning Week 1999): 3.

115   PI, Interviewees #34, 84, 88, 96; Lovell, *Neither Athens Nor Sparta?*, 258.

116   PI, Interviewees #6, 17, 24, 31, 34, 36, 40, 47, 70, 79, 82, 83, 84, 85, 88, 90, 96, 105,
       108, 110, 114, 127, 150, 152, 156, 159, 167, 175, 212; EI, Interviewee #74; Inter-
       view with Tina-Marie D'Ercole, USNIOH, OHFFG, 30; Interview with Crystal Lewis,
       USNIOH, OHFFG, 26; Lovell, *Neither Athens Nor Sparta?*, 256.

117   The following discussion of the USNA St. John's Croquet Series is based on *Reminis-
       cences of Rear Admiral Draper L. Kauffman*, 31; 1983 LB, 156; "Robinson Leads Navy
       Basketball, St. John's Croquet," *LOG* 84, no. 1 (Sept. 1998): 29; Chris Price, "Mids
       Take On Johnnies," *Trident*, 30 Apr. 1999, 1; Gary Mihoces, "Navy, St. John's Cross
       Mallets," *USA Today*, 1 May 2000, 3C.

118   EI with Dave Smalley, Annapolis, Md., 15 May 2000; Bruce Watson, "It's More Than
       Just A Game," *Smithsonian* (Nov. 1999): 142–59; "Historic Contest Hits 100 Mark,"
       Trident, 3 Dec. 1999, 1; John Feinstein, "The Spirit of Army-Navy," *Shipmate* 62, no. 10
       (Dec. 1999): 38; Lovell, *Neither Athens Nor Sparta?*, 257–58; Stewart, *The Brigade in
       Review*, 58.

119   B. M. Bryant to W. F. Boone, 23 Nov. 1955, SR1, Box "General Correspondence,
       Athletics: Army-Navy Football: Motion Pictures, Correspondence on Change of
       Sites, Games in General, Correspondence, 1927–1959," Folder 4; W. F. Boone to
       B. M. Bryant, 25 Nov. 1955, SR1, Box "General Correspondence, Athletics: Army-
       Navy Football: Motion Pictures, Correspondence on Change of Sites, Games in
       General, Correspondence, 1927–1959," Folder 4; Assistant Midshipmen Food Ser-
       vice Officer to Midshipmen Food Service Officer, 1 Dec. 1978, SR2, Sec. 5830, Folder
       "1978"; Paul Englemayer, "The Annapolis Mess: It's No Fun Feeding Future Admi-
       rals," *Wall Street Journal*, 14 Dec. 1983, 12.

120   Cory Boruck to Brigade of Midshipmen, 7 Dec. 1999, HMG; "Abe Says 'Beat Army'
       '86 USNA," *LOG* 76, no. 3 (Nov. 1986): 8–9; Thomas Boswell, "Army and Navy Play a
       Different Game," *WP*, 3 Dec. 1987, B1; Molly Sinclair, "Police Aren't Laughing at
       Midshipmen's Pranks," *WP*, 3 Dec. 1988, B5.

121   *Reminiscences of Rear Admiral Julian T. Burke Jr.*, 361–63; Commandant of Cadets and
       Commandant of Midshipmen, "Memorandum of Agreement," 24 July 1992, ARF
       "Athletics: Army-Navy Football"; "Navy Kid Napped By Point Corpsmen," *EC*,
       23 Nov. 1953; Bruce Watson, "It's More Than Just A Game," *Smithsonian* (Nov. 1999):
       158–59; Wertsch, *Military Brats*, 311–12.

122   Colin Powell to Thomas Lynch, 23 Aug. 1993, SR3, 1993, Sec. 5340–5700, Folder
       "5700."

123   Martha Thorn, "Army, Navy Jockeys in Supreme Football Rivalry," *Trident*, 3 Dec.
       1999, 5.

124   Brigade Size Statistics, ARF "Midshipmen: Brigade Strength, 1863–1972"; 1949 LB;
       1959 LB; 1969 LB; 1979 LB; 1989 LB; 1999 LB; COMDT Notice 1000, 24 Jan. 1996, ARF
       "Midshipmen: Change of Company"; "United States Naval Academy Minority Attri-
       tion Summary By Classes, 1980–2003," 30 Sept. 1999, USNA Registrar's Office;
       1999 USNA Alumni Register.

125   The following discussion of the Brigade organization is based on *Reminiscences of
       Rear Admiral Draper L. Kauffman*, 1788–89; *Reminiscences of Vice Admiral Charles S. Minter*

Jr., 438, 442–43; A. G. Esch to Richard Dorso, 14 Jan. 1956, SR4, Folder "A7-4/1-1: Television Series"; M. E. Chang, "Climate Assessment of the U.S. Naval Academy," 11 June 1990, 1, SR5, Box 4; COMDT Notice 1000, 24 Jan. 1996, ARF "Midshipmen: Change of Company"; "Brigade Life," USNAW (<www.usna.edu/admissions/brig life.htm>, 3 Feb. 2000); R. B. Pirie to Louis Stockstill, undated, SR 1, Box "General Correspondence, Office of the Commandant," Folder 11; "Questions and Answers Alumni Assembly 1985," *Shipmate* 49, no. 1 (Jan./Feb. 1986): 29; Stewart, *The Brigade in Review*, 34.

126 The following discussion of Company Officers is based on *Reminiscences of Rear Admiral Julian T. Burke Jr.*, 337–38; *Reminiscences of Rear Admiral Draper L. Kauffman*, 789; *Reminiscences of Rear Admiral Robert W. McNitt*, 561–62; Interview with William P. Lawrence, USNIOH, 959; 1971 LB, 32; Arthur Rimback, "Prediction of Officer Potential of Midshipmen of the United States Naval Academy," MFCP #1530, 1961, 1–4; COMDTMIDN Instruction 1531.14A, 8 Jan. 1975, CR, Sec. 5420/4, Folder "1975"; Director of Professional Development, "Memorandum for the Record," 30 Sept. 1977, SR5, Box 4; Leon Endey to Superintendent, 27 Apr. 1981, CR, Sec. 5400/5, Folder "1981"; Leon Edney to Executive Assistant to Superintendent, 17 Aug. 1982, CR, Sec. 5400/19, Folder "1982"; Charles Larson, "Goals for Academic Year 1984–1985," undated, CR, Sec. 5400/4, Folder "1984"; "Remarks by Admiral Charles R. Larson, USN, Superintendent, United States Naval Academy, before San Diego Alumni Assembly, 6 September 1997," 4, USNAW (<www.nadn.navy.mil/pao/speech03.html>, 5 Nov. 1997); Charles Larson, "The Next 150 Years Begin," *USNIP* 122, no. 9 (Sept. 1996): 67; John Ryan, "The State of the Academy," *Shipmate* 62, no. 2 (Mar. 1999).

127 Charles Larson to Doug Menikhelm, 11 May 1995, SR3, 1995, Sec. 1531–1710, Folder "1531"; "Remarks by Admiral Charles R. Larson, USN, Superintendent, United States Naval Academy, before San Diego Alumni Assembly, 3 September 1997," 4, USNAW (<www.nadn.navy.mil/pao/speech03.html>, 5 Nov. 1999).

128 William Smedberg, "Speech Delivered to First Class, All Class Officers, Plus Other Classes Over Bancroft Hall Radio," 12 Oct. 1956, 5, SC, William Renwick Smedberg Papers, Box 1; Director of Professional Development to Dean of Admissions, 29 Nov. 1976, CR, Sec. 5211/2, Folder "1976"; Leon Edney to Brigade Officers, 23 Sept. 1981, CR, Sec. 5400/5, Folder "1981"; "Interview with Commandant Leslie Palmer: 20 Questions," *LOG* 73, no. 7 (Mar. 1984): 48; COMDTMIDNINST 1602.12, 4 Oct. 1986, ARF "Midshipmen: Brigade Striper Organization and Selection Procedures."

129 The following discussion of companies is based on EI, Interviewee #8; *Reminiscences of Rear Admiral Draper L. Kauffman*, 769–70; A. G. Esch to Richard Dorso, 14 Jan. 1956, SR4, Folder "A7-4/1-1: Television Series," 6; Dirk Debbink, Brigade Commander Instruction 11103.1, 29 Nov. 1976, ARF "Midshipmen: Dining-In"; "Brigade Routine," USNAW (<www.usna.edu/admissions/briglife.htm>, 3 Feb. 2000); 1957 BOV, 19; 1979 LB, 4; Hanson Baldwin, "Annapolis Aweigh," NYT, 8 Apr. 1957, 6; Gene Fluckey, "Inside the Main Gate," *Shipmate* 20, no. 10 (Oct. 1957): 14; Daniel Goldenberg, "A Few Inches From the Yard," *Shipmate* 54, no. 5 (June 1991): 29; "Facts on Naval Academy Commissioning Week Traditions," *Trident*, 10 May 1996,

11; Lauren Majchronk, "A Few Inches From the Yard," *Shipmate* 61, no. 10 (Dec. 1998): 32; "Marching Through 153 Years of History," *Trident*, 21 May 1999, 3; Lovell, *Neither Athens Nor Sparta?*, 256; Stewart, *The Brigade in Review*, 62, 78.

130 On wall decorations in Bancroft Hall, see Fleming, *Annapolis Autumn*, 19.

131 Daniel Goldenberg, "A Few Inches From the Yard," *Shipmate* 54, no. 5 (June 1991): 29.

132 William Smedberg III to Superintendent, 5 Mar. 1949, SR1, Box 4, "General Correspondence, Midshipmen, Policy, and Administration," Folder 6; J. L. Holloway to Secretary of the Academic Board, 15 June 1949, SR1, Box 4, "General Correspondence, Midshipmen, Policy, and Administration," Folder 6; J. Lloyd Abbot Jr., "The Plebe Sponsor Program," *Shipmate* 22, no. 4 (Apr. 1959): 20.

133 William Smedberg III to Head, Department of Electrical Engineering, 12 Sept. 1950, SR1, Box 4, "General Correspondence, Midshipmen, Policy, and Administration," Folder 14.

134 J. L. Holloway to Secretary of the Academic Board, 15 June 1949, SR1, Box 4, "General Correspondence, Midshipmen, Policy, and Administration," Folder 6; M. Sunderland to Secretary of the Academic Board, 20 Sept. 1950, SR1, Box 4, "General Correspondence, Midshipmen, Policy, and Administration," Folder 14; W. H. Price to Secretary of the Academic Board, 22 Sept. 1950, SR1, Box 4, "General Correspondence, Midshipmen, Policy, and Administration," Folder 14; William Smedberg, "Superintendent's Talk to the Faculty," 4 Sept. 1956, 3, SC, William Renwick Smedberg Papers, Box 1; C. S. Seabring to Secretary of the Academic Board, undated, SR1, Box 4, "General Correspondence, Midshipmen, Policy, and Administration," Folder 14; J. Lloyd Abbot Jr., "The Plebe Sponsor Program," *Shipmate* 22, no. 4 (Apr. 1959): 20.

135 William Smedberg III to Commandant, 4 May 1956, SR1, Box 4, "General Correspondence, Midshipmen, Policy, and Administration," Folder 14; "Superintendent's Address to the Class of 1960," 15 Aug. 1956, 10–12, SC, William Renwick Smedberg Papers, Box 1; William Smedberg, "Superintendent's Talk to the Faculty," 4 Sept. 1956, 3, SC, William Renwick Smedberg Papers, Box 1; "Superintendent's Talk to the First Class," 9 Sept. 1957, 12, SC, William Renwick Smedberg Papers, Box 1; Superintendent to 4/C, 28 Apr. 1958, SR1, Box 4, "General Correspondence, Midshipmen, Policy, and Administration," Folder 14; DOC to Commandant, 23 May 1959, SR1, Box 4, "General Correspondence, Midshipmen, Policy, and Administration," Folder 14; 1957 BOV, 19; Hanson Baldwin, "Annapolis Aweigh," NYT, 8 Apr. 1957, 6; J. Lloyd Abbot Jr., "The Plebe Sponsor Program," *Shipmate* 22, no. 4 (Apr. 1959): 20.

136 PI, Interviewees #3, 7, 8, 9, 10, 24, 31, 34, 36, 45, 89, 105, 156, 165, 176, 212, 213; EI, Interviewee #74, 143; "Complaint/Grievance Procedures at the U.S. Naval Academy," undated, SR5, Binder 5; Charles Bolden, "Speech for Black History Month to Black Midshipmen Study Group," Annapolis, Md., 9 Feb. 1999; David Kanab, "A Few Inches From The Yard," *Shipmate* 41, no. 3 (Apr. 1978); "Sponsor Program Helps Families Parent A Plebe," *Trident*, 24 Mar. 2000.

137 "Sponsor Program Helps Families Parent A Plebe," *Trident*, 24 Mar. 2000.

138 Harry Hill to Parents, 24 July 1950, SR1, Box 1, "General Correspondence, Special Occasions, Parents Open House Weekend, 1950–1959," Folder 1; Morgan Barrett to Harry Hill, 15 Sept. 1950, SR1, Box 1, "General Correspondence, Special Occasions, Parents Open House Weekend, 1950–1959," Folder 1; James Calvert to Parents, 30 Dec. 1969, CR, Sec. "Commandant of Midshipmen: Instructions, Notices, Miscellaneous Correspondence," Box 6; Max Morris to Class of 1977, 13 July 1973, CR, Sec. 1730, Folder "1973"; William Mack to Parents, 13 Dec. 1974, CR, Sec. 5211, Folder "1973"; 1951 BOV, 12; James Calvert, "A Letter from the Superintendent," LOG 58, no. 1 (27 Sept. 1968): 5; James Cheevers, "USNA: Modern Era, Part IV," Shipmate 58, no. 5 (Oct. 1995): 35.

139 Joan Mack, "History of Parents' Clubs," Shipmate 57, no. 4 (May 1994): 28.

140 EI with Dick Goodwin, Lake Oswego, OR, 18 Oct. 1998, 13 Jan. 1999, 17 May 1999; Robert McNitt, "Memorandum for the Record," 7 Mar. 1978, CR, Sec. 5213/1, Folder "1978"; Shipped from Oregon: Newsletter of the United States Naval Academy Parents' Club of Oregon, Fall 1998, HMG; "Connections: United States Naval Academy Parents' Club of Oregon Handbook," 1999, HMG; U.S. Naval Academy Parents' Club of Oregon Agenda, 13 June 1999, HMG.

141 Reminiscences of Rear Admiral Robert W. McNitt, 629.

142 PI, Interviewee #145; Superintendent to Chief of Naval Operations, 18 Aug. 1989, SR3, 1989, Sec. 1000–1531/2, Folder "1531/1"; Leon Edney to Virgil Hill, 20 July 1990, SR3, 1990, Sec. 5314–5700/2, Folder "5700"; Charles Larson, "Goals for Academic Year 1984–1985," 11, undated, CR, Sec. 5400/4, Folder "1984"; "Remarks by Admiral John R. Ryan, USN, Superintendent, United States Naval Academy, given to the Pennsylvania Parents' Club, 3 February 1999," 4, USNAW (<www.nadn.navy.mil/pao/speech03.html>, 21 May 1999); Mahlon Tisdale, "The Naval Academy Today and Its Mission," USNIP 49, no. 3 (Mar. 1923): 463; Lebby, "Professional Socialization of the Naval Officer," 85.

143 A. G. Esch to Richard Dorso, 14 Jan. 1956, SR4, Folder "A7-4/1-1: Television Series," 6, 7; Photograph of midshipmen visiting Fleet Admiral Chester Nimitz, LOG 54, no. 6 (12 Dec. 1964): 10; Chester Nimitz, Letter to the Editor, LOG 59, no. 9 (10 Apr. 1970): 7–8; Pat McKim, "On the Beach: Interview with '23's Arleigh Burke," LOG 64, no. 3 (29 Nov. 1974): 24–25.

144 PI, Interviewee #36; E. C. Waller to Daniel Ogden, 6 June 1983, SR2, Sec. ON1531, Folder "1983"; Neil Henry, "Absorbing the Navy Mystique," WP, 14 June 1981, A1; "Remarks of Adm. Jeremy M. Boorda, USN, at U.S. Naval Academy Change of Command," Shipmate 57, no. 7 (Sept. 1994): 13.

145 Jean Ross, "Class of '50 to Give '00 Golden Send Off," Trident, 19 May 2000, 1.

146 Interview with Vice Admiral William P. Lawrence, USNIOH, 1037–38; Charles Larson to Elliott Loughlin, 28 Jan. 1985, SR3, 1985, Boc 1530–1710/34, Folder "1531/1"; Robert Baldwin, "The Campaign for the Naval Academy: What Is The Plan?," Shipmate 51, no. 7 (Sept. 1988): 6; Ronald Marryott, "The Campaign for the Naval Academy: Why Do We Need It?," Shipmate 51, no. 7 (Sept. 1988): 7–8; "Private Support of the Naval Academy," Shipmate 54, no. 7 (Sept. 1991): 16–17; Lovell, Neither Athens Nor Sparta?, 227–28.

147 Sleight, *Sixteen Hundred Men*, 147–48.

148 The following discussion of alumni complaints is based on EI, Interviewees #25, 33; *Reminiscences of Rear Admiral Draper L. Kauffman*, 28; *Reminiscences of Vice Admiral Charles S. Minter Jr.*, 432; Bradford McDonald, "A Few Inches From The Yard," *Shipmate* 40, no. 4 (May 1977): 39; "Changes and a Challenge for Naval Academy," *NYT*, 25 Dec. 1987, 28; "Superintendent's Call: Interview with Admiral John Ryan," *Shipmate* 62, no. 3 (Apr. 1999): 17; "The Firsts and Lasts of the Class of 1999," *LOG* 84, no. 5 (May 1999): 55; Lovell, *Neither Athens Nor Sparta?*, 177, 228–29.

149 *Reminiscences of Vice Admiral William P. Mack*, 658–62, 728; *Reminiscences of Rear Admiral Robert W. McNitt*, 408–10, 567–70; *Reminiscences of Vice Admiral Charles S. Minter Jr.*, 450–52, 531–46; *Reminiscences of Vice Admiral William R. Smedberg III*, 726–27; John Hayes, "With A Round Turn," *Shipmate* 22, no. 8 (Aug. 1959); "Rickover Assails the Navy System," *NYT*, 19 June 1961, 10; C. Yates McDaniel, "Rickover Rakes Navy, Would Abolish Academy," *WP*, 19 June 1961, 1; "McNamara Chides Rickover on Views," *NYT*, 24 June 1961, 10; "Weakening the Naval Academy," *NYT*, 23 June 1962, 22; Evert Clark, "Arms Cost Stress Scored by Rickover," *NYT*, 9 June 1967, 2; "Rickover Assails Pentagon on Info Flow," *NYT*, 16 July 1968, 4; "Rickover Criticizes Annapolis System," *WP*, 16 July 1968, 4; "Rickover on USNA," *LOG* 63, no. 8 (26 Apr. 1974): 10–11; George Wilson, "Rickover Delivers Speech Critical of Present U.S. Navy Organization," *WP*, 31 Aug. 1974, A2; Lovell, *Neither Athens Nor Sparta?*, 159–64, 168, 210, 229–30, 235, 241–42; Polmar and Allen, *Rickover*, 305–11, 480.

150 The following discussion of events on I-Day is based on EI with Sean Doyle, Annapolis, Md., 19 Jan. 1999; Leon Edney to Secretary of the Board of Visitors, 21 July 1982, CR, Sec. 5422/4, Folder "1982"; John Bodnar, "Changes in Reef Points Slang," 7 June 1996, HMG; Ron Zapata, "U.S. Naval Academy Welcomes New Students," Associated Press, 30 June 2000, USNAAW (<www.usna.com/news_pubs/news/viewniewsdate.asp?date-7/05/2000>, 5 July 2000); Sarah Robert, "Extracurricula: Midshipmen Organizations and Activities," *USNIP* 71, no. 4 (Apr. 1945): 394; Vince Schumaker, "The Book of the Year," *LOG* 53, no. 4 (15 Nov. 1963): 22; 1971 LB, 235; Paul Costello, "A Few Inches From the Yard," *Shipmate* 48, no. 10 (Dec. 1985): 31; Disher, *First Class*, 1, 9, 14–19, 21–22; Lovell, *Neither Athens Nor Sparta?*, 176; Meade, ed., *Reef Points 1997–1998*, 25–27; Stewart, *The Brigade in Review*, 3, 6, 11; Timberg, *The Nightingale's Song*, 25.

151 The following discussion of finding rooms in Bancroft Hall is based on PI, Interviewees #23, 31, 40, 47, 49, 79, 88, 90, 110, 142; Interview with Sandy Daniels, USNIOH, OHFFG, 10; Disher, *First Class*, 23–24; Drew, ed., *Letters from Annapolis*, 175–76.

152 M. E. Chang, "Climate Assessment of the U.S. Naval Academy," 11 June 1990, 2, SR5, Box 4; Charles Larson to Eugene Farrell, 5 Oct. 1994, SR3, 1994, Sec. 1000–1531, Folder "1531"; "Plebe Summer," USNAW (<www.usna.edu/admissions/summers.htm>, 3 Feb. 2000); "The Next 150 Years Begin," *USNIP* 122, no. 9 (Sept. 1996): 67; Martha Thorn, "Officer Challenges Plebes: Stay Through Summer for Full Impact of Program," *Trident*, 30 June 2000, 3; McCain and Salter, *Faith of My Fathers*, 118; Stewart, *The Brigade in Review*, 13–29.

153 Stewart, *The Brigade in Review*, 13.

154 "Faculty and Academic Advising," USNAW (<www.usna.edu/pao/virtual/academic/faculty.html>, 21 May 1999).

155 PI, Interviewees #9, 22, 142, 152; Lovell, *Neither Athens Nor Sparta?*, 264; McCain and Salter, *Faith of My Fathers*, 119–20; Timberg *The Nightingale's Song*, 24–27, 415.

156 "Seagoing Slang: A Line on Bancroft Lingo," 1922, ARF "Midshipmen: Slang"; Charles Buchanan, "Naval Academy Traditions," speech before the Naval Academy Women's Club, 7 Oct. 1952, 6, CR, Box 1, "Miscellaneous Speeches Presented by Commandants, 1952–1960," Folder 5; Michael Parker, ed., "Good Gouge: An Investigation Into the Origins of Naval Academy Slang," HE 111 Class Project, 1982; John Bodnar, "Changes in Reef Points Slang," 7 June 1996, HMG; 1998 LB, 26, 28, 31, 33, 34, 37, 39, 41, 42, 46, 48, 50, 54, 58, 64, 66, 74; Carroll Alden, "The Changing Naval Academy: A Retrospect of 25 Years," USNIP 55, no. 6 (June 1929): 500; Sarah Robert, "Extracurricula: Midshipmen Organizations and Activities," USNIP 71, no. 4 (Apr. 1945): 390; "A Way of Life," *LOG*, vol. 45, Class of 1956 Public Distribution Issue, 11; Don Woodman, "A West Point Cow in Tecumseh's Court," *LOG* 50, no. 15 (28 Apr. 1961): 18–19; Timberg, *The Nightingale's Song*, 25–26.

157 The following discussion of plebe summer is based on PI, Interviewees #3, 6, 9, 10, 15, 17, 22, 23, 24, 31, 35, 40, 41, 47, 49, 70, 77, 82, 85, 88, 90, 105, 110, 127, 129, 142, 150, 152, 156, 171, 175, 177, 180, 185, 190; EI, Interviewees #74, 76, 198; *Reminiscences of Rear Admiral Julian T. Burke Jr.*, 338–39; *Reminiscences of Vice Admiral William R. Smedberg III*, 558; Interview with Pamela Wacek Svendsen, USNIOH, OHFFG, 6; J. M. Boorda, "Report of the Informal Review Board on the Honor Concept and Conduct System at the U.S. Naval Academy," 2, 10 Aug. 1990, ARF "Midshipmen: Honor"; Plebe Summer Resignation Percentages by Gender, Classes of 1990–1996, undated, SR5, Box 4; Calvert, *The Naval Profession*, 104, 115–16, 119; Lebby, "Professional Socialization of the Naval Officer," 14, 39.

158 The following discussion of Brigade Reform Day is based on PI, Interviewees #3, 10, 31, 47, 49, 156, 180; Timberg *The Nightingale's Song*, 27.

159 William Smedberg, "Superintendent's Address to Class of 1960," 16 Aug. 1956, 9–10, SC, William Renwick Smedberg Papers, Box 1.

160 The following discussion of plebe year requirements is based on PI, Interviewee #31; Harry Hill to Thomas Card, 31 Mar. 1952, SR1, Box 1, "General Correspondence, Office of the Commandant," Folder 13; E. C. Waller, Candidate Guidance Brochure, undated, 9, HMG; "U.S. Colleges and Universities Report Record Numbers of Applicants This Year; Service Academies Experience Falling Numbers of Applicant," *All Things Considered* on National Public Radio, 29 June 2000; "Brigade Routine," USNAW (<www.usna.edu/admissions/briglife.htm>, 3 Feb. 2000); J. Lloyd Abbot Jr., "The Naval Academy of Today and Its Mission," USNIP 86, no. 9 (Sept. 1960): 35; Stewart, *The Brigade in Review*, 25, 28, 62.

161 *Reminiscences of Vice Admiral William P. Mack*, 8; W. F. Boone to M. R. Greer, 10 Jan. 1956, SR1, Box 5, "General Correspondence: Midshipmen: Policy and Administration: Statistics and Policy Regarding Visits, 1927–1964," Folder 2; Calvert, *The Naval Profession*, 116–17; Lovell, *Neither Athens Nor Sparta?*, 264.

162 McCain and Salter, *Faith of My Fathers*, 121.

163 Drew, ed., *Letters From Annapolis*, 203; Stewart, *The Brigade in Review*, 16, 44.

164 William Smedberg, "Talk by Vice Admiral William R. Smedberg III, USN, Chief of Naval Personnel, Before the Naval Academy Class of 1962," 19 Sept. 1961, 2, SC, William Renwick Smedberg Papers, Box 1.

165 *Reminiscences of Rear Admiral Draper L. Kauffman*, 793–98; John Worden to E. J. Horton, 3 May 1874, ARF "Midshipmen: Hazing"; H. A. Hobert to Superintendent, 16 Nov. 1894, ARF "Midshipmen: Hazing"; Midshipman H. B. Jarrett, Non-Hazing Contract, 1920, ARF "Midshipmen: Hazing"; R. A. French to Marcy Dupre, 19 Dec. 1958, ARF "Midshipmen: Hazing"; Barrett Smith, "Hazing, Honor, and the Early Twentieth Century Naval Academy," USNA History Honors Thesis, Spring 2000, HMG; Richard West Jr., "The Superintendents of the Naval Academy," *USNIP* 71, no. 7 (July 1945): 803; Karsten, *The Naval Aristocracy*, 38; Sweetman and Cutler, *The U.S. Naval Academy*, 50, 67, 104, 124, 155–56, 159–60, 171, 172, 180.

166 TI, Interviewee #58; 1950 BOV, 15; Harry Hill to Thomas Card, 31 Mar. 1952, SR1, Box 1, "General Correspondence, Office of the Commandant," Folder 13; Joe Califano to Lyndon Johnson, 13 Apr. 1966, LBJ, Folder "ND-158: U.S. Naval Academy, 1965–1967"; "Memorandum for the Assistant Secretary of Defense for Manpower and Reserve Affairs," 23 Jan. 1975, SR5, Box 4; "Memorandum for the Record," 16 Apr. 1975, CR, Sec. 5213/1, Folder "1975"; M. E. Chang, "Climate Assessment of the U.S. Naval Academy," 11 June 1990, 5, SR5, Box 4; "Conduct System and Administration of Discipline at the U.S. Naval Academy," 27 June 1990, 5; U.S. General Accounting Office, "Testimony Before the Subcommittee on Manpower and Personnel, Committee on Armed Services, U.S. Senate, Status Report on Reviews of Student Treatment, Department of Defense Service Academies," 2 June 1992, 2; Ben Franklin, "Annapolis Chided on Grade Quotas," NYT, 1 May 1966, 1; Draper Kauffman, "Message from Superintendent Kauffman," LOG 56, no. 1 (30 Sept. 1966): 1; Thomas Sher, "A Word From Today," *Shipmate* 33, no. 8 (Sept./Oct. 1970): 19; Neil Henry, "Absorbing the New Mystique," WP, 14 June 1981, A1; Neil Henry, "Rickover's Nuclear Navy: Making Men Into Machines," WP, 16 June 1981, A1; "The SUPE's Perspective: A Conversation with Rear Admiral Virgil L. Hill Jr.," *Shipmate* 53, no. 6 (July/Aug. 1990): 9–10.

167 William Smedberg, "Superintendent's Talk to the First Class (1958)," 5 Sept. 1957, 8, SC, William Renwick Smedberg Papers, Box 1; William Smedberg, "Talk by Vice Admiral William R. Smedberg III, USN, Chief of Naval Personnel, Before the Naval Academy Class of 1962," 19 Sept. 1961, 2, SC, William Renwick Smedberg Papers, Box 1; James Winnefeld, "Memorandum for the Dean of Admissions," 21 July 1976, CR, Sec. 5600, Folder "1976"; Lebby, "Professional Socialization of the Naval Officer," 68; Lovell, *Neither Athens Nor Sparta?*, 263–66.

168 *Reminiscences of Rear Admiral Draper L. Kauffman*, 797–98; James Calvert to Arleigh Burke, 22 Aug. 1969, SR2, Sec. ON/1531, Folder "1968–1969"; James Calvert to Parents of the Members of the Class of 1970, 29 Aug. 1969, 1, SR2, Sec. RG, Folder "1958–1977"; Charles Larson, "Goals for Academic Year 1984–1985," CR, Sec. 5400/4, Folder "1984"; Charles Larson to Robert Schram, 2 Jan. 1996, SR3, 1996,

Box 1531–1851, Folder "1531"; "Remarks by Admiral John R. Ryan, USN, Superintendent, United States Naval Academy, given to the Naval Academy Alumni Association President's Circle, 11 Sept. 1998," 3, USNAW (<www.usna.edu/pao/speeches/speechjr4.htm>, 21 May 1999); David Ellison, "Looking Out," *LOG* 59, no. 2 (17 Oct. 1969): 8; Drew Middleton, "Service Academies Strive to Stay In Step With The Times," *NYT*, 20 Feb. 1971, 54; "Changes at Academy are Debated," *WP*, 17 Dec. 1987, Md. sec. 19; "Changes and Challenges for Naval Academy," *NYT*, 25 Dec. 1987, 28; "The Supe's Perspective: A Conversation with Rear Admiral Virgil L. Hill Jr.," *Shipmate* 53, no. 6 (July/Aug. 1990): 9–10; John Ryan, "Constancy of Purpose and Raising the Bar of Excellence," *Shipmate* 61, no. 10 (Dec. 1998): 6; Heise, *The Brass Factories*, 101–8; Lebby, "Professional Socialization of the Naval Officer," 69–70; Lovell, *Neither Athens Nor Sparta?*, 172–74.

169   William Smedberg to Everett Dirksen, 9 Nov. 1957, SR1, Box 2, "Aptitude for Service; Conduct," Folder 11.

170   PI, Interviewees #40, 79; *Reminiscences of Rear Admiral Draper L. Kauffman*, 796; Jack Everett, "An Exacting Plebe Year Is Necessary," MFCP #462, 1964, 22; R. B. Minton to H. Allen Smith, 5 Feb. 1969, SR2, Sec. 5215/2, Folder "1968–1969"; Photograph of plebe sleeping in room, *LOG* 38, no. 8 (21 Jan. 1949): 10; Ben Franklin, "Rift At Academy Remains After Mediators Leave," *NYT*, 20 Nov. 1966, 77; "Plebe Restriction Eased," *NYT*, 21 Aug. 1969, 15; Doug Brown, "New Brigade Commander Thinks Reform," *WP*, 26 Dec. 1974, C10; David Kanab, "A Few Inches From The Yard," *Shipmate* 42, no. 1 (Jan./Feb. 1979): 33; Mark Christensen, "A Few Inches From The Yard," *Shipmate* 56, no. 8 (Oct. 1993): 23; Ellen Uzelac, "Reveille, Taps, are Revived at Academy," unidentified article, SCF "U.S. Naval Academy: Midshipmen: Customs and Traditions"; Drew, ed., *Letters From Annapolis*, 200, 204; Heise, *The Brass Factories*, 95, 98–104, 107; Lovell, *Neither Athens Nor Sparta?*, 176–77.

171   The following discussion of plebe difficulties and relations with upperclassmen is based on PI, Interviewees #2, 31, 35, 47, 49, 77, 83, 105; EI, Interviewee #9; D. K. Forbes to T. R. M. Emery, 17 Sept. 1973, CR, Sec. 5211, Folder "1973"; Charles Bolden, "Speech for Black History Month to Black Midshipmen Study Group," Annapolis, Md., 9 Feb. 1999; "Salty Sam," *LOG* 61, no. 1 (24 Oct. 1971): 11; Drew, ed., *Letters From Annapolis*, 178; Stewart, *The Brigade in Review*, 28; Webb, *A Sense of Honor*, passim.

172   The following discussion of bold plebes' actions is based on PI, Interviewees #2, 3, 9, 10, 11, 45, 49, 80, 112, 129, 134; EI, Interviewee #9; Charles Buchanan, "Outline of Talk on Naval Academy Traditions to the Naval Academy Women's Club," 7 Oct. 1952, CR, Sec. "Miscellaneous Speeches by Commandants," Folder 13; 1970 LB, 323; 1971 LB, 23; 1978 LB, 162–63; 1995 LB, 41; Cartoon of "The Wildman," *LOG* 40, no. 5 (17 Nov. 1950): 43; "Plebe Poll Question," *LOG Splinter* 1, no. 10 (23 Feb. 1951): 3; Jay Lawrence, "100th Night," *LOG* 57, no. 9 (16 Feb. 1968): 9–10; Daniel Goldenberg, "A Few Inches From The Yard," *Shipmate* 54, no. 10 (Dec. 1991): 21–22; *The Plebeian*, various issues, SR1, Box 4, "Midshipmen Activities: Miscellaneous Activities, 1922–1959," Folder 11; "Sob Sunday," unidentified article, ARF "History: Sob Sunday"; Drew, ed., *Letters From Annapolis*, 182, 207, 209.

173   The following discussion of youngster year is based on PI, Interviewee #47; EI, Interviewee #22; Interview with Maureen Foley, USNIOH, OHFFG, 22; James Calvert to the Parents of the Class of 1970, 29 Aug. 1969, 1, SR2, Sec. RG, Folder "1958–1977"; James Calvert to Parents, 30 Dec. 1969, CR, Sec. "Commandant of Midshipmen: Instructions, Notices, Miscellaneous Correspondence," Folder "1968–1976"; Kinnaird McKee to Chief of Naval Operations, 6 Oct. 1977, SR5, Box 4; Charles Larson to Charles Krulak, 18 Apr. 1996, SR3, 1996, Box 1531, Folder "1531"; 1946 BOV, 12; 1954 BOV, 20; 1955 BOV, 13; USNA Catalog, 2000–2001, 138; "Remarks by Admiral Charles R. Larson, USN, Superintendent, United States Naval Academy, before San Diego Alumni Assembly, 6 September 1997," 4, USNAW (<www.nadn.navy.mil/pao/speech03.html>, 5 Nov. 1997); Angus Phillips, "'Hat Trick' Caps Long Year at Academy," WP, 21 May 1983, B3; Stephanie Woolverton, "Mids' Cruises Are Not Vacations," Trident, 26 May 2000, 8; Stephanie Milo, "Yard Patrol Craft Summer Cruise Under Way," Trident, 23 June 2000, 11; Martha Thorn, "Damage Control Is Sea Power," Trident, 23 June 2000, 3; Martha Thorn, "No Longer Plebes, Youngsters Lead The Way," Trident, 23 June 2000, 3; Calvert, The Naval Profession, 117–18; Lovell, Neither Athens Nor Sparta?, 176; Stewart, The Brigade in Review, 89.

174   The following discussion of the difficulties of youngster year is based on PI, Interviewees #3, 6, 7, 9, 10, 15, 17, 22, 24, 35, 41, 47, 82, 83, 85, 88, 90, 108, 110, 127, 129, 132, 142, 152, 156, 158, 171; EI, Interviewees #74, 198; Reminiscences of Rear Admiral Draper L. Kauffman, 15; Reminiscences of Vice Admiral William P. Mack, 82; Reminiscences of Rear Admiral Robert W. McNitt, 600–601; John Padgett III, "Back When I Was A Plebe . . . ," Shipmate 56, no. 9 (Nov. 1993): 8; Calvert, The Naval Profession, 236–37; Stewart, The Brigade in Review, 34; Timberg, The Nightingale's Song, 28.

175   The following discussion of "secondclass summer" is based on PI, Interviewees #27, 45, 83, 90, 91, 108, 114, 142; 1952 BOV, 13; 1956 BOV, 27; U.S. Naval Academy Catalog, 2000–2001, 65; Calvert, The Naval Profession, 118; Stewart, The Brigade in Review, 92.

176   E. C. Waller, Candidate Guidance Brochure, undated, 10, HMG.

177   Reminiscences of Rear Admiral Julian T. Burke Jr., 380–81; Charles Arnold to Frank Knox, 5 Sept. 1942, ARF "Midshipmen: Service Academy Exchange Program"; Commandant to Superintendent, 23 Sept. 1942, ARF "Midshipmen: Service Academy Exchange Program"; Press Release, 18 Apr. 1946, ARF "Midshipmen: Service Academy Exchange Program"; Hugo Johnson to C. R. Burke, 8 May 1946, ARF "Midshipmen: Service Academy Exchange Program"; Armed Forces Policy Council Meeting Agenda, 16 Nov. 1949, SR1, Box 5, "Midshipmen Activities: Service Academies Exchange Program, 1942–1959," Folder 2; John Parry to John LeVien, 2 Mar. 1951, ARF "Midshipmen: Service Academy Exchange Program"; George Dorsey to John Parry, 15 May 1951, SR1, Box 5, "Midshipmen Activities: Service Academies Exchange Program, 1942–1959," Folder 2; Superintendent to Chief of Naval Operations, 9 Jan. 1952, SR1, Box 5, "Midshipmen Activities: Service Academies Exchange Program, 1942–1959," Folder 2; J. F. McLendon to W. F. Boone, 16 Dec. 1955, SR1, Box 5, "Midshipmen Activities: Service Academies Exchange Program, 1942–1959," Folder 3; W. F. Boone to J. F. McLendon, 4 Jan. 1956, SR1, Box 5, "Midshipmen Activities:

Service Academies Exchange Program, 1942–1959," Folder 3; Garrison Davidson to C. L. Melson, 6 Aug. 1958, ARF "Midshipmen: Service Academy Exchange Program"; Frank Andrews and John Lindbeck to Superintendent, 19 Jan. 1959, SR1, Box 5, "Midshipmen Activities: Service Academies Exchange Program, 1942–1959," Folder 3; 1946 BOV, 7; 1948 BOV, 5; 1952 BOV, 11; 1953 BOV, 12; 1954 BOV, 20; Kalman Siegel, "Midshipmen Land at West Point for First Interacademy Training," NYT, 30 July 1949, 1, 6.

178 PI, Interviewees #7, 17, 37, 82, 110, 142; W. P. Mack to A. B. Engel, 18 Sept. 1972, ARF "Midshipmen: Service Academy Exchange Program"; John Thompson to W. P. Mack, 5 Jan. 1973, ARF "Midshipmen: Service Academy Exchange Program"; COMDTMIDN Notice 1531, 13 Aug. 1975, ARF "Midshipmen: Service Academy Exchange Program"; Joint Letter of the Commandants of the Corps of Cadets and Brigades of Midshipmen, 9 Apr. 1979, ARF "Midshipmen: Service Academy Exchange Program"; PAO Announcement on Service Academy Exchange Program, 1990, ARF "Midshipmen: Service Academy Exchange Program"; Jean Ross, "Cadets Blend With Mids Behind Enemy Lines," Trident, 3 Dec. 1999, 3.

179 Reminiscences of Vice Admiral William P. Mack, 802.

180 Louis Bolander to J. G. Roenigk, 15 May 1933, SCF "United States Naval Academy: Midshipmen: Customs and Traditions"; Marcy Dupre III to Alice Chance, 2 Oct. 1956, ARF "Midshipmen: Class Rings and Policy Regarding"; "Memorandum for Cdr. Ewing Concerning Naval Academy Ring Dance," 18 Jan. 1962, ARF "Graduation and June Week: Ring Dance"; W. C. Kelley to YNCS Mochell, 17 Mar. 1970, ARF "Graduation and June Week: Ring Dance"; Carroll Alden, "The Changing Naval Academy: A Retrospect of 25 Years," USNIP 55, no. 6 (June 1929): 449; Wade DeWeese, "The Nineteenth Anniversary Class Ring Celebration," USNIP 62, no. 4 (Apr. 1936): 515.

181 Charles Buchanan, Commandant's Brigade Order #5-54, 3 Feb. 1954, ARF "Midshipmen: Class Rings and Policy Regarding"; C. G. Grojean to Superintendent, 17 Mar. 1954, ARF "Midshipmen: Class Rings and Policy Regarding"; Commandant to Superintendent, 23 Mar. 1954, SR1, Box 2, "General Correspondence: Midshipmen, Activities, Miscellaneous Activities," Folder 6; Commandant to Superintendent, 24 Sept. 1954, ARF "Midshipmen: Class Rings and Policy Regarding"; Commandant to Superintendent, 25 Sept. 1954, SR1, Box 2, "General Correspondence: Midshipmen, Activities, Miscellaneous Activities," Folder 6; A. G. Esch to Mary Stewart, 4 May 1955, SR1, Box 2, "General Correspondence: Midshipmen, Activities, Miscellaneous Activities," Folder 6; Marcy Dupre III to Alice Chance, 2 Oct. 1956, ARF "Midshipmen: Class Rings and Policy Regarding"; Wade DeWeese to Elizabeth Anderson, 8 Aug. 1957, ARF "Graduation and June Week: Ring Dance"; "U.S. Naval Academy Alumni Association Guide to Class Crests, 1846–1981," 1981, ARF "Midshipmen: Class Crests"; 1971 LB, 230; "Facts on Commissioning Week Traditions," Trident, 10 May 1996, 11.

182 The following discussion of 1/C Year is based on Reminiscences of Rear Admiral Robert W. McNitt, 410–11; USNA Catalog, 2000–2001, 65; Mike Nassr, "The Annapolis Air Force," Shipmate 62, no. 8 (Oct. 1999): 6–9; Calvert, The Naval Profession, 117–18;

Lovell, *Neither Athens Nor Sparta?*, 176; McCain and Salter, *Faith of My Fathers*, 125, 135–41; Stewart, *The Brigade in Review*, 47, 79–83, 96.

183   The following discussion of Rickover interviews is based on *Reminiscences of Rear Admiral Julian T. Burke Jr.*, 358; *Reminiscences of Rear Admiral Robert W. McNitt*, 410–11; *Reminiscences of Vice Admiral Charles S. Minter Jr.*, 531–37, 542–45; Interview with William P. Lawrence, USNIOH, 966–71; "Nuclear Power Interview," cartoon, *LOG* 59, no. 3 (21 Nov. 1969): 28; "Salty Sam," *LOG* 66 (Oct. 1976): 6; "The Admiral Rickover Interview," *LOG* 66 (Mar. 1977): 9; Beth Leadbetter, "A Few Inches From The Yard," *Shipmate* 43, no. 4 (May 1980): 38; Neil Henry, "Rickover's Nuclear Navy: Making Men Into Machines," *WP*, 16 June 1981, A1; Richard Gribble, "My 38 Minutes With Admiral Rickover," *Shipmate* 51, no. 1 (June 1987): 25–26; John Crawford, "Passing Rickover's Muster," *Naval History* 6, no. 2 (Spring 1992): 35–38; Mike Nassr, "The Annapolis Air Force," *Shipmate* 62, no. 8 (Oct. 1999): 6–9; Lovell, *Neither Athens Nor Sparta?*, 160.

184   *Reminiscences of Rear Admiral Robert W. McNitt*, 627–28; Calvert, *The Naval Profession*, 113; USNA Command History IV, 1972–1973, vol. I, 63–64; Lovell, *Neither Athens Nor Sparta?*, 177–78, 247.

185   *Reminiscences of Rear Admiral Julian T. Burke Jr.*, 343, 357; *Reminiscences of Vice Admiral William P. Mack*, 691, 703; *Reminiscences of Vice Admiral Charles S. Minter Jr.*, 462–63; *Reminiscences of Vice Admiral William R. Smedberg III*, 405, 542–45; 1971 LB, 229; Leon Edney to Secretary of the Board of Visitors, 21 July 1982, CR, Sec. 5420/4, Folder "1982"; J. M. Boorda to Frank Kelso, 10 Aug. 1990, SR5, Binder 5; Christina Ianzito to Thomas Lynch, 7 July 1994, SR3, 1994, Box 1000–1531, Folder "1531"; Charles Larson to Alan Foster, 12 Dec. 1996, SR3, 1996, Box 1000–1531, Folder "1531"; Midshipman Bushnell, "The United States Naval Academy Honor Concept," 18 Mar. 1998, HMG; "The Naval Academy Honor Concept," *Shipmate* 30, no. 6 (June/July 1967): 24; "The Honor Concept of the Brigade of Midshipmen," *Shipmate* 31, no. 2 (Feb. 1968): 2–3, 12, 13; Robert Thomas Jr., "Annapolis and Air Force Disagree On Honor Code," *NYT*, 3 June 1976, 40; Jean Ebbert, "Honor Code for a Taut Ship," *WP*, 18 Feb. 1978, A17; "Remarks by Admiral Charles R. Larson, USN, Superintendent, United States Naval Academy, before the San Diego Alumni Assembly, 6 September 1997," 5, USNAW (<www.nadn.navy.mil/pao/speech03.htm>, 5 Nov. 1997); "Remarks by Admiral John R. Ryan, USN, Superintendent, United States Naval Academy, given to the Pennsylvania Parents' Club, 3 February 1999," 2, USNAW (<www.nadn.navy.mil/pao/speech03.html>, 21 May. 1999); "Remarks by Admiral John R. Ryan, USN, Superintendent, United States Naval Academy, given to the Naval Academy Alumni Association President's Circle, 11 September 1998," 2, USNAW (<www.usna.edu/pao/speeches/speechjr4.htm>, 21 May 1999); Calvert, *The Naval Profession*, 113–14.

186   Jean Ebbert, "Honor Code for a Taut Ship," *WP*, 18 Feb. 1978, A17.

187   On the cheating scandal, see "Cheating Inquiry At Naval Academy," *NYT*, 10 Feb. 1993, 18; Eric Schmitt, "Naval Academy Pushing Inquiry About Cheating," *NYT*, 16 Sept. 1993; Eric Schmitt, "An Inquiry Finds 125 Cheated On Naval Academy Exam," *NYT*, 13 Jan. 1994; Eric Schmitt, "Expulsions Urged In Navy Cheating Case,"

NYT, 1 Apr. 1994. On Lynch's and Larson's actions, see PI, Interviewee #18; "Report of the Honor Review Committee to the Secretary of the Navy on Honor at the U.S. Naval Academy," 22 Dec. 1993, ARF "Studies and Reports: Midshipmen/Graduates"; Thomas Lynch, "Superintendent's Letter," *Shipmate* 57, no. 4 (May 1994): 2–3; Charles Larson to Eugene Farrell, 3 Oct. 1994, SR3, 1994, Box 1000–1531, Folder "1531"; Charles Larson to John Shepherd, 2 Nov. 1994, SR3, 1994, Box 5100–5700, Folder "5700."

188   *Reminiscences of Vice Admiral Charles S. Minter Jr.*, 575; *Reminiscences of Vice Admiral William R. Smedberg III*, 564; "Marriage Bans," 30 June 1950, ARF "Midshipmen: Marriage"; William Smedberg, "Superintendent's Talk to the First Class (1957)," 26 Sept. 1956, 14–15, SC, William Renwick Smedberg Papers, Box 1; William Smedberg, "Superintendent's Talk to the Faculty," 4 Sept. 1957, 5–10, SC, William Renwick Smedberg Papers, Box 1; William Smedberg, "Superintendent's Talk to the First Class (1958)," 5 Sept. 1957, 8, SC, William Renwick Smedberg Papers, Box 1; William Smedberg to Carl Vinson, May 1958, SR1, Box 2, "Aptitude for Service; Conduct," Folder 4; James Calvert to Parents of the Members of the Class of 1970, 29 Aug. 1969, 2, SR2, Sec. RG, Folder "1958–1977"; Max Morris to Brigade, 28 Nov. 1972, CR, Sec. 5400/5, Folder "1972"; "Proposed Changes to the Conduct Instruction," 2 Dec. 1975, SR5, Box 3, Folder "Policies, Regulations—Admission of Women, 1975–1976"; "Commandant's Memorandum," 9 Mar. 1976, SR5, Box 4; Leon Edney to Secretary of the Board of Visitors, 21 July 1982, CR, Sec. 5420/4, Folder "1982"; Thomas Jurkowsky to Roger Henderson, 6 Dec. 1985, SR3, 1995, Box 5216–5700, Folder "5700"; "6000 Series Offenses," undated, SR5, Binder 5; "Statement on Alcoholic Beverage Regulation Change," undated, ARF "Midshipmen: Alcohol Beverages, Regulation Change"; "A Way of Life: From Past to Present," LOG, vol. 45, Class of 1956 Public Distribution Issue, 11; C. W. Nimitz, Letter to the Editor, LOG 59, no. 9 (10 Apr. 1970): 7–8; Brad Foster, "Analyzing the New Naval Academy," LOG 60, no. 2 (9 Oct. 1970): 2; "Salty Sam," LOG 66 (May 1977): 13; David Kanab, "A Few Inches From the Yard," *Shipmate* 42, no. 1 (Jan./Feb. 1978): 33; Arthur Brisbane, "Naval Academy's Harsh Attrition," WP, 19 May 1984, A1; Stephen Chadwick, "The Commandant Speaks," *Shipmate* 48, no. 10 (Dec. 1985): 16; Daniel Barchi, "A Few Inches From The Yard," *Shipmate* 54, no. 2 (Mar. 1991): 28; Drew, ed., *Letters From Annapolis*, 197; Stewart, *The Brigade in Review*, 33, 36.

189   EI, Interviewee #3; *Reminiscences of Rear Admiral Draper L. Kauffman*, 764–65; *Reminiscences of Vice Admiral Charles S. Minter Jr.*, 450–52, 574; Interview with William P. Lawrence, USNIOH, 79–80; J. L. Holloway to Cecil Cue, 31 Jan. 1949, SR1, Box 1, "General Correspondence, Office of the Commandant," Folder 10; Charles Buchanan, "Outline of Talk on Naval Academy Traditions to the Naval Academy Women's Club," 7 Oct. 1952, CR, Sec. "Miscellaneous Speeches by Commandants," Folder 13; Charles Buchanan, "Speech to the First Class," 19 Jan. 1953, CR, Box "Miscellaneous Speeches Presented by Commandants, 1952–1960," Folder 12; Kinnaird McKee to R. P. Huston, 20 Oct. 1976, CR, Sec. 5211/2, Folder "1976"; Leon Edney to Superintendent, 27 Apr. 1981, CR, Sec. 5400/5, Folder "1981"; Charles Larson to Robert Schram, 2 Jan. 1996, SR3, 1996, Box 1531–1851, Folder "1531";

1970 LB, 162, 372; 1971 LB, 39; 1983 LB, 80–83; "Remarks by Admiral John R. Ryan, USN, Superintendent, United States Naval Academy, given to the Naval Academy Alumni Association Presidents Circle, 11 September 1998," 4, USNAW (<www.usna.edu/pao/speeches/speech.jr4.htm>, 5 Nov. 1998); "U.S. Colleges and Universities Report Record Numbers of Applications This Year; Service Academies Experience Falling Number of Applicants," *All Things Considered* on National Public Radio, 29 June 2000, USNAAW (<www.usna.com/news_pubs/news/viewnewsdate.asp?date=7/05/2000>, 5 July 2000); Richard West Jr., "The Superintendents of the Naval Academy," USNIP 71, no. 7 (July 1945): 803–4; Hanson Baldwin, "The Academies: Old Ideals, New Methods," NYT, 16 Apr. 1961, 32; Brad Foster, "Analyzing the New Naval Academy," LOG 60, no. 2 (9 Oct. 1970): 2; Drew Middleton, "Service Academies Strive to Stay In Step with the Times," NYT, 20 Feb. 1971, 54; "Interview with Commandant Leslie Palmer: Twenty Questions," LOG 73, no. 7 (Mar. 1984): 35; Stephen Chadwick, "The Commandant Speaks," *Shipmate* 48, no. 10 (Dec. 1985): 16; "Crackdown at Naval Academy," NYT, 25 Apr. 1996, B10; John Williams, "U.S. Naval Academy: Stewardship and Direction," USNIP 123, no. 5 (May 1997): 71; Amy Argentsinger, "Tough Rules Get Tougher at Naval Academy," WP, 18 Sept. 1998, B3; Drew, ed., *Letters From Annapolis*, 185; Fleming, *Annapolis Autumn*, 154–55; Stewart, *The Brigade in Review*, 84–85.

190 John Williams, "U.S. Naval Academy: Stewardship and Direction," USNIP 123, no. 5 (May 1997): 71.

191 Saundra Saper, "Woman At The Top Of The Naval Academy Has That Extra Bit Of Determination," WP, 19 May 1984, A10; William Brown, "Midshipman Sample," *Shipmate* 54, no. 5 (June 1991): 15; McCain and Salter, *Faith of My Fathers*, 129–34, 144–48; Timberg, *The Nightingale's Song*, 33–34.

192 Calvert, *The Naval Profession*, 122; Lovell, *Neither Athens Nor Sparta?*, 266–68; Stewart, *The Brigade In Review*, ix.

193 Timberg, *The Nightingale's Song*, 23.

194 1952 BOV, 11; Charles Larson to Charles Bishop, 29 Apr. 1996, SR3, 1996, Box 1531, Folder "1531."

195 E. C. Waller, Candidate Guidance Brochure, undated, 9–10; 1971 LB, 131, 229–39; USNA Catalog, 2000–2001, 46; "LOG Interview: Captain Max Morris," LOG 61, no. 1 (29 Oct. 1971): 20; Stewart, *The Brigade in Review*, 69.

196 PI, Interviewees #87, 159; Superintendent to Arleigh Burke, May 1959, SR1, Box 3, "Midshipmen: Activities: Forensics, Publications, Singing, 1923–1959," Folder 13; "U.S. Naval Academy Glee Club on the Mike Douglas Show," circa 1967, ERC; "Brigade Activities," 1971 LB, 237; Public Affairs Office Release #0029-91, Feb. 1991, ARF "Midshipmen: Naval Academy Gospel Choir."

197 M. H. Blum to R. K. Lewis, 22 Apr. 1974, CR, Sec. 2070, Folder "1974"; Leon Edney to W. S. Busik, 16 Feb. 1982, CR, Sec. 2070, Folder "1982"; Paul Limbacher to Activities Officer, 24 Mar. 1982, CR, Sec. 2070, Folder "1982"; Keith Mahosky to USNA Alumni Association, undated, Sec. 2070, Folder "1982"; 1971 LB, 239; 1979 LB, 617; Paul Klinedinst, "The Mids' Radio Station Moves Ahead," LOG 45, no. 2 (7 Oct. 1955): 16; Jack Meckler, "WENV: Radio Navy," LOG 49, no. 12 (18 Mar. 1960):

12–13; Christopher Graves, "A Few Inches From the Yard," *Shipmate* 55, no. 10 (Dec. 1992): 23–24.

198 The following discussion of the LOG is based on *Reminiscences of Rear Admiral Julian T. Burke Jr.*, 336; 1958 LB, 145; "Salty Sam Sez," LOG 20 (21 Oct. 1932): 7; "Salty Sam," LOG 23, no. 13 (8 Mar. 1935): 12; "Salty Sam," LOG 23, no. 17 (24 May 1935): 18; "Salty Sam," LOG 24, no. 13 (1 May 1936): 17; "Salty Sam," LOG 32, no. 1 (2 Oct. 1942): 21; Charles Buchanan, "To the Brigade," LOG 44, no. 2 (8 Oct. 1954): 9; Leon Edney, "Message to The LOG from Commandant Edney," LOG 72, no. 8B (Apr. 1983): 7; "Salty Sam," LOG 83, no. 1 (1993): 8; "Salty Sam," LOG 84, no. 2 (Winter 1995): 20; "Salty Sam '99 Rides Again!," LOG 84, no. 3 (Dark Ages 1999): 18; *The LOG Splinter* 1, no. 1 (29 Sept. 1950); LOG online, <www.thelog.westhost.com>.

199 The following discussion of the Eighth Wing Players is based on PI, Interviewees #9, 40, 44, 45, 79, 85, 114; 1983 LB, 132; "Have You Seen This Man?," LOG 72, no. 2 (Oct. 1982): 5; Christopher Graves, "A Few Inches From the Yard," *Shipmate* 55, no. 10 (Dec. 1992): 23–24.

200 *Reminiscences of Rear Admiral Draper L. Kauffman*, 748; Stephen Chadwick, "The Commandant Speaks," *Shipmate* 48, no. 10 (Dec. 1985): 14; Fleming, *Annapolis Autumn*, 4.

201 E. C. Waller to E. Carlton Guillot Jr., 24 June 1982, SR2, Sec. 12770/1, Folder "1982"; 1970 LB, 16; 1983 LB, 60; "Seniors For Only One More Day" (photograph), NYT, 28 May 1980, 1; Gene Bisbee, "Academy Launches Largest Class; An Old Tradition Lives," EC, 25 May 1983, 12; Photo of 1/C Jumping into Lejeune Pool, BS, 27 May 1992, D2; Photo of 1/C Jumping into Spa Creek, BS, 31 May 1995, 28.

202 Movietone News, MGM, and Paramount News showed newsreels of USNA graduation ceremonies in theaters across the nation between 1951 and 1967; see newsreel collections, MPSVC.

203 "Middies Cleared, Get Commissions," NYT, 12 June 1954, 8.

204 "1999 Commissioning Week Schedule," *Trident*, 21 May 1999, 12; "Commissioning Week 2000," *Trident*, 19 May 2000, 10–11; Fleming, *Annapolis Autumn*, 5.

205 "830 Receive Degrees From Naval Academy," NYT, 4 June 1970, 35; "Laird at Academy," NYT, 1 July 1972, 32; "President Warns Policy of Defense Bars Interfering," NYT, 6 June 1974, 1; Eric Schmitt, "Schwarzkopf Praises Navy, and Teamwork, for Gulf Role," NYT, 30 May 1991, B8; Timberg, *The Nightingale's Song*, 48.

206 Wayne Hoof to Superintendent, 9 June 1967, ARF "Graduation and June Week: Anchor Man"; Dean of Admissions to Albert Jenks, 9 June 1975, ARF "Graduation and June Week: Anchor Man"; COMDTMIDNNOTE 5060, 14 May 1976, ARF "Graduation and June Week: Anchor Man"; John Kelley to Superintendent, 14 June 1979, ARF "Graduation and June Week: Anchor Man"; Deputy Chairman of Objectives Review Board to Chairman of Objectives Review Board, 10 July 1979, ARF "Graduation and June Week: Anchor Man"; Joseph McGettigan to Commandant, 14 Apr. 1980, ARF "Graduation and June Week: Anchor Man"; Commandant to Registrar, 15 June 1981, ARF "Graduation and June Week: Anchor Man"; "List of Anchormen Since 1854," undated, ARF "Graduation and June Week: Anchor Man"; "List of Anchormen Since 1930," undated, ARF "Graduation and June Week: Anchor Man"; Fleming, *Annapolis Autumn*, 7.

207 N. G. Rodes, "Now, When I Was A Mid," *LOG Splinter* 3, no. 13 (3 Apr. 1953), SCF "USNA Midshipmen: Customs and Traditions"; Leon Edney to Nancy Parmett, undated, ARF "Graduation and June Week: Historical Facts"; Charles Miner to Jean Evans, undated, ARF "Graduation and June Week: Historical Facts"; Fleming, *Annapolis Autumn*, 8–9.

208 David Sullivan, "A History of the Lucky Bag, 1894–1959," MFCP #1210, 1959; Jim McIsaac to Class of 1977 Classmates, Dec. 1976, CR, Sec. 5600/4, Folder "1973–1979"; "What's In A Name," *Shipmate* 22, no. 11 (Nov. 1958): 7.

Chapter Two

1 The following discussion of the 1955 Sugar Bowl is based on EI with Dave Smalley, Annapolis, Md., 15 May 2000; EI with Mike Nassr, Roswell, Ga., 13 Mar. 2004; *Reminiscences of Vice Admiral Charles S. Minter Jr.*, 294; Television Schedule, NYT, 1 Jan. 1955, 22; Allison Danzion, "Navy Beats Mississippi, 21–0; Duke Routs Nebraska; Ohio State Tops USC, 20–7; Georgia Tech Over Wisconsin, 14–6," NYT, 2 Jan. 1955, Sec. 5, 1; Claassen and Boda, *Ronald Encyclopedia of Football*, 273, 275, 676; Anthony Di Marco, *The Big Bowl Football Guide*, 58–59; Eilerston, *Major College Football Results*, 175; Sweetman and Cutler, *The U.S. Naval Academy*, 210.

2 The following discussion of Boone and 1950s conditions is based on *Reminiscences of Rear Admiral John F. Davidson*, 263; 1956 BOV, 13; Walter Boone to Overton Brooks, 25 Jan. 1956, SR1, Box 5, "General Correspondence, Midshipmen, Policy, and Administration," Folder 2; "Attrition Rates by Classes," 22 Oct. 1954, SR1, Box 5, "General Correspondence, Midshipmen, Policy, and Administration," Folder 2; Commandant Notice 5720, 27 Jan. 1977, CR, Folder 5720/3, 1975; Roy Smith, "Mail Bag," *Shipmate* 58, no. 5 (Oct. 1995): 35.

3 The following discussion of interest in attending USNA is based on EI with Dave Smalley, Annapolis, Md., 15 May 2000; EI, Interviewee #88; *Reminiscences of Vice Admiral Charles S. Minter Jr.*, 294; Hugo Johnson to C. R. Burke, 8 May 1946, ARF "Midshipmen: Service Academy Exchange Program"; George Dorsey to John Parry, 15 May 1951, SR1, Box "Midshipmen Activities: Service Academies Exchange Program, 1942–1959," Folder 2; Metro-Goldwyn-Mayer, Movie Tone News, and Paramount News editions featuring Naval Academy activities between the 1940s and late 1960s, MPSVC; Hanson Baldwin, "Annapolis Aweigh," NYT, 8 Apr. 1957, 6; Calvert, *The Naval Profession*, 99.

4 The films include *Hero of Submarine D2*, 1916; *Madam Spy*, 1918; *The Midshipman*, 1925; *West Point*, 1928; *Annapolis*, 1928; *Salute*, 1929; *The Flying Fleet*, 1929; *Shipmates*, 1931; *Midshipman Jack*, 1933; *Annapolis Farewell*, 1935; *Shipmates Forever*, 1935; *Hold-Em Navy*, 1937; *Navy Blue and Gold*, 1937; *Annapolis Salute*, 1937; *Touchdown Army*, 1938; *Pride of the Navy*, 1939; *The Splinter Fleet*, 1939; *Naval Academy*, 1941; *Hello Annapolis*, 1942; *Minesweeper*, 1943. See Larry Clemens, "List of Films Featuring USNA," ERC; Lawrence Suid, *Sailing on the Silver Screen*.

5 The following discussion of Op Info is based on *Reminiscences of Vice Admiral Charles L. Melson*, 312; 1955 BOV, 5; William Smedberg III to Distribution List, 8 Nov. 1957,

SR1, Box 4, "Midshipmen Activities: Miscellaneous Activities, 1922–1959," Folder 12; R. C. McFarlane to H. H. Bell, 12 Jan. 1959, SR1, Box 4, "Midshipmen: Activities: Miscellaneous Activities, 1922–1959," Folder 1; 1956 BOV, 13; Banana Oil Henderson and Jimmy Boy Williams, "Operation Propaganda," LOG 47, no. 7 (13 Dec. 1957): 32, 34; Jim Poole, "He Leads Us All," LOG 47, no. 8 (24 Jan. 1958): 6; Robert Timberg, The Nightingale's Song, 47, 59.

6 The following discussion of visual technology and An Annapolis Story is based on EI with Sherman Alexander, St. Petersburg, Fla., 16 Oct. 2001; 1956 BOV, 13; Barnouw, A History of Broadcasting, vol. 3, 244; Falla, NCAA, 101; Schaller, Scharff, and Schulzinger, Coming of Age, 325–27; Suid, Sailing on the Silver Screen, 9, 34, 110–12.

7 The following discussion of ZIV's activities is based on EI with Marcy Dupre, Pensacola, Fla., 24 Jan. 2000; EI with Sherman Alexander, St. Petersburg, Fla., 25 Apr. 2001; 1956 BOV, 13; 1957 BOV, 20; "Memorandum of Agreement," 9 Dec. 1955, 1, SR4, Folder "A7-4/1-1: Television Series"; Chief of Information to Chief, Pictorial Branch, OPI/OSD, 16 Dec. 1955, SR4, Folder "A7-4/1-1: Television Series"; Walter Boone to Jack Dorso, 28 Dec. 1955, SR4, Folder "A7-4/1-1: Television Series"; A. G. Esch to Richard Dorso, 14 Jan. 1956, SR4, Folder "A7-4/1-1: Television Series"; Eugene Nicolait Jr. to Public Information officer, 8 Jan. 1957, SR4, Folder "A7-4/1-1: Television Series"; Men of Annapolis Still Photo Collection, UA Series 7.6 ZIV Stills, WCFTR; Sherman Alexander, "Men of Annapolis: The Television Series," Shipmate 62, no. 9 (Nov. 1999): 12, 13; Barnouw, A History of Broadcasting, vol. 3, 83–84; Rouse, "A History of the F. W. Ziv Radio and Television Syndication Companies, 1930–1960," 212–14.

8 The following discussion of the development of story lines is based on EI with Marcy Dupre, Pensacola, Fla., 24 Jan. 2000; PI with Charles Larson, Annapolis, Md., 22 June 2000; A. G. Esch to Richard Dorso, 14 Jan. 1956, SR4, Folder "A7-4/1-1: Television Series," 1; "Logging," The LOG, vol. 45, Special Issue, 1955, 5; "Men of Annapolis," Shipmate 21, no. 4 (Apr. 1958): 4; Sherman Alexander, "Men of Annapolis: The Television Series," Shipmate 62, no. 9 (Nov. 1999): 2–5, 12, 13.

9 The following discussion of story lines is based on EI with Marcy Dupre, Pensacola, Fla., 24 Jan. 2000; "Counter Flood," MOA Episode 1, 1956, WCFTR; "Mail Call," MOA Episode 3, 1956, ERC; "All American," MOA Episode 4, 1956, WCFTR; "Miss Fire," MOA Episode 7, 1956, WCFTR; "Ship's Log," MOA Episode 10, 1956, WCFTR; "The Star," MOA Episode 13, 1956, WCFTR; "Underfire," MOA Episode 19, 1957, WCFTR; "The Clash," MOA Episode 22, 1957, WCFTR; "Sea v. Air," MOA Episode 25, 1957, WCFTR; "Hot Steam," MOA Episode 28, 1957, WCFTR; "Breakaway," MOA Episode 31, 1957, WCFTR; "The Jinx," MOA Episode 34, 1957, WCFTR; "Color Competition," MOA Episode 37, 1957, WCFTR; "Rescue at Sea," MOA Episode 39, 1957.

10 The following discussion of story lines from Esch's report is based on A. G. Esch to Richard Dorso, 14 Jan. 1956, SR4, Folder "A7-4/1-1: Television Series," 6–11; "Mail Call," MOA Episode 3, 1956, ERC; "Blinding Light," MOA Episode 8, 1956, ERC; "The Challenge," MOA Episode 16, 1956, WCFTR; "Hot Steam," MOA Episode 28, 1957, WCFTR.

11 Rouse, "A History of the F. W. Ziv Radio and Television Syndication Companies," 212–14; Sherman Alexander, "Men of Annapolis: The Television Series," *Shipmate* 62, no. 9 (Nov. 1999): 12.

12 John Sinn to William Smedberg, 11 May 1956, SR4, Folder "A7-4/1-1: Television Series."

13 A. G. Esch to Vincent Lonergan, 19 Jan. 1956, SR4, Folder "A7-4/1-1: Television Series"; Public Information Office Memo, 4 Sept. 1956, SR4, Folder "A7-4/1-1: Television Series"; Superintendent to Head, Pictorial Branch, Secretary of Defense; 26 Sept. 1956, SR4, Folder "A7-4/1-1: Television Series"; *Men of Annapolis* Still Photo Collection, UA Series 7.6 ZIV Stills, WCFTR.

14 Cartoon, *LOG* 46, no. 9 (8 Feb. 1957): 4.

15 W. D. McCord, Memo for files, 31 May 1956, SR4, Folder "A7-4/1-1: Television Series."

16 The following discussion of reaction to *Men of Annapolis* is based on W. D. McCord, Memo for files, 31 May 1956, SR4, Folder "A7-4/1-1: Television Series"; William Smedberg to Richard Dorso, 7 June 1956, SR4, Folder "A7-4/1-1: Television Series"; "Counter Flood," MOA Episode 1, 1956, WCFTR; "Annapolis Loses Its Social Hub as Hotel, a Landmark, Closes," NYT, 4 July 1965, 26.

17 The following discussion of the drunken actors incident is based on Timothy Keating to A. T. Anderson, 21 Oct. 1956, SR4, Folder "A7-4/1-1: Television Series"; William Smedberg to John Sinn, 2 Nov. 1956, SR4, Folder "A7-4/1-1: Television Series."

18 EI with Jim Farley, Washington, D.C., 14 Apr. 2001; "Men of Annapolis" Still Photo Collection, UA Series 7.6 ZIV Stills, WCFTR; Sherman Alexander, "Men of Annapolis: The Television Series," *Shipmate* 62, no. 9 (Nov. 1999): 13–14.

19 EI with Marcy Dupre, Pensacola, Fla., 24 Jan. 2000.

20 Public Information Officer Memo for Television Station Managers, undated, SR1, Box 4, "Midshipmen Activities," Folder 12.

21 Marcy Dupre to Harold Smeling Jr., 14 Nov. 1958, SR4, Folder "A7-4/1-1: Television Series"; Hanson Baldwin, "Annapolis Aweigh," NYT, 8 Apr. 1957, 6.

22 PI, Interviewee #177; Marcy Dupre to Harold Semling Jr., 14 Nov. 1958, SR4, Folder "A7-4/1-1: Television Series"; 1957 BOV Report, 6.

23 The following discussion of assessments of *Men of Annapolis* is based on J. D. Oliver to Executive Officer, 26 July 1957, SR4, Folder "A7-4/1-1: Television Series"; Commandant to Flag Secretary, 29 July 1957, SR4, Folder "A7-4/1-1: Television Series"; 3rd Battalion survey on *Men of Annapolis*, undated, SR4, Folder "A7-4/1-1: Television Series."

24 The following discussion of debates on continuing *Men of Annapolis* is based on EI with Sherman Alexander, St. Petersburg, Fla., 25 Apr. 2001; John Ryan, Speech to Guidance Counselors, 21 Mar. 2000, USNA; "The Runaway," MOA Episode 35, 1957, WCFTR; "Rescue at Sea," MOA Episode 39, 1957, WCFTR; William Smedberg to Chief of Naval Information, 26 Aug. 1957, SR4, Folder "A7-4/1-1: Television Series"; Richard Dorso to William Smedberg, 29 Aug. 1957, SR4, Folder "A7-4/1-1: Television Series"; "Resume of the 39 Stories Produced by the ZIV Television Pro-

grams, Inc., Reflecting the Consensus of Opinion of the Naval Academy," undated, SR4, Folder "A7-4/1-1: Television Series"; Sherman Alexander, "Men of Annapolis: The Television Series," *Shipmate* 62, no. 9 (Nov. 1999): 12–13, 15; Barnouw, *A History of Broadcasting*, vol. 3, 65; Rouse, "A History of the F. W. Ziv Radio and Television Syndication Companies," 214.

25 Secretary of the Navy, Certificate of Recognition, 25 Sept. 1957, *Men of Annapolis* Still Photo Collection, UA Series 7.6 ZIV Stills, WCFTR.

26 The following discussion of continuing media appearances is based on *Reminiscences of Vice Admiral William R. Smedberg III*, 507–8; Thomas Carr to J. L. Holloway, 24 Dec. 1947, SR4, Folder "Radio Broadcast Station, Annapolis QV"; J. L. Holloway to Charles Roeder, 2 July 1948, SR4, Folder "Radio Broadcast Station, Annapolis QV"; W. G. Cooper to H. H. Caldwell, 15 Nov. 1949, SR1, Box 4, "Midshipman Activities: Miscellaneous Activities, 1922–1959," Folder 14; "Navy News Release," USNA Release #78, 6 Nov. 1950, SR1, Box 4, "Midshipman Activities: Miscellaneous Activities, 1922–1959," Folder 14; Superintendent to Arleigh Burke, draft, May 1959, SR1, Box 4, "Midshipman Activities: Miscellaneous Activities, 1922–1959," Folder 13; Charles Melson, "The Superintendent Reports," *Shipmate* 22, no. 12 (Dec. 1959): 10; Jack Meckler, "WRNV: Radio Navy," *LOG* 49, no. 12 (18 Mar. 1960): 12–13; Barnouw, *A History of Broadcasting*, vol. 2, 303; Barnouw, *A History of Broadcasting*, vol. 3, 3; Eilerston, *Major College Football Results*, 159.

27 The following discussion of *Five Steps to the Brigade* and *Ring of Valor* is based on *Ring of Valor*, 1960, ERC; J. A. Lark to Superintendent, 22 Jan. 1960, SR2, Sec. 5720/1, Folder "1960–1965"; W. R. Smedberg to Superintendent, 3 Mar. 1960, SR2, Sec. 5720/1, Folder "1960–1965"; "Ring of Valor" shooting schedule, 15–20 May 1960, SR2, Sec. 5720/1, Folder "1960–1965"; USNA Notice 5728, May 1960, SR2, Sec. 5720/1, Folder "1960–1965"; Charles Minter to Robert Taylor, 1 Feb. 1965, SR2, Sec. 5720/1, Folder "1960–1965"; Charles Melson to Chief of Naval Personnel, undated, SR2, Sec. 5720/1, Folder "1960–1965"; Chief of Naval Personnel to Superintendent, 1960, SR2, Sec. 5720/1, Folder "1960–1965."

28 The following discussion of the Blue and Gold program is based on EI with Mike Nassr, Roswell, Ga., 13 Mar. 2004; Interview with William Lawrence, unpublished manuscript, USNIOH, 1990, 989; PI, Interviewees #7, 35, 105; 2000–2001 USNA Catalog, 33–37; William Mack to Henry Ramirez, 20 Apr. 1973, SR2, Sec. 5800/1, Folder "1973"; "Superintendent's Report to the Board of Trustees Meeting," *Shipmate* 26, no. 9 (Sept./Oct. 1963): 16; Bob Donaldson, "Rip Miller," *LOG* 53, no. 3 (31 Oct. 1963): 22–23.

29 J. L. Holloway to John Dady, 19 Apr. 1948, SR1, Box 4, "General Correspondence: Midshipmen: Policy and Administration," Folder 19.

30 "History of Negro Midshipmen or Negro Candidates for Midshipmen," 21 Sept. 1944, ARF "Midshipmen: Black Midshipmen."

31 Chin Kim and Bok Lim Kin, "Asian Immigrants in American Law: A Look at the Past and the Challenge That Remains," in McClain, ed., *Asian Indians, Filipinos, Other Asian Communities, and the Law*, 326–28; Milton Milch, "Visas and Petitions," in Sellin, ed., *Proceedings of the New York University Conference on Practice and Procedure Under the Immigra-*

tion and Nationality Act, 7; Schaller, Scharff, and Schulzinger, Coming of Age, 290–91, 343–44; Urofsky, A March of Liberty, 763–79.

32 The Academy appears to have categorized members of Asian ethnic groups as "Mongolian" and "Malayan" in a random manner which somewhat resembles 1943 categories of the Immigration and Naturalization Service. See "Summary of Non-White Appointments to the U.S. Naval Academy," undated, ARF "Midshipmen: Black Midshipmen"; Charles Gordon, "The Racial Barrier to American Citizenship," in Gordon, ed., Asian Indians, Filipinos, Other Asian Communities, and the Law, 299. Peter Karsten has demonstrated that USNA textbooks, as early as 1862, were using racial terminology; see Kartsen, The Naval Aristocracy, 35.

33 Skerry, Counting on the Census?, 31, 45, 58, 200.

34 Dinnerstein and Reimers, Ethnic Americans, 13–14, 41–44.

35 "Hispanics in America's Defense," Department of Defense, Office of the Deputy Assistant Secretary of Defense for Military Manpower and Personnel Policy, 1989, ARF "Midshipmen: Minority Groups," 181; Skerry, Counting on the Census?, 31.

36 EI, Interviewees #93, 222; "Foreign Midshipmen at the U.S. Naval Academy," 11 June 1951, SR1, Box 5, "Brigade of Midshipmen: Intra-Brigade Competition, Minority Midshipmen, 1897–1959," Folder 8; 1959 LB; 1931 LB.

37 1963 Cruise, 40.

38 The following discussion of American Indian midshipmen is based on John Dady to James Holloway, 3 Mar. 1948, SR1, Box 4, "General Correspondence: Midshipmen: Policy and Administration," Folder 19; J. L. Holloway to John Dady, 19 Apr. 1948, SR1, Box 4, "General Correspondence: Midshipmen: Policy and Administration," Folder 19; William Smedberg, "Superintendent's Talk to the Faculty," 4 Sept. 1956, 9, SC, William Renwick Smedberg Papers, Box 1; R. E. Heise to C. R. Berquist, 17 Apr. 1959, SR1, Box 5, "General Correspondence, Midshipmen, Policy and Administration: Statistics and Policy Regarding Visits, 1927–1964," Folder 3; "Summary of Non-White Appointments to the U.S. Naval Academy," undated, ARF "Midshipmen: Black Midshipmen"; Louis Bolander, "Names of Naval Academy Graduates Who Have Some Degree of Indian Blood," undated, SR1, Box 4, "General Correspondence: Midshipmen: Policy and Administration," Folder 19.

39 1918 LB, 56; "Native American Heritage Month," Commandant of Midshipmen Plan of the Day, 16 Nov. 1998, 2, HMG; "National American Indian Heritage Month," Commandant of Midshipmen Plan of the Day, 26 Oct. 1999, 2; U.S. Navy Naval Vessel Register (<http://www.nvr.navy.mil/nvrships/ffg11.htm>, 18 July 2001).

40 EI, Interviewee #106.

41 Tom Trueblood to Gary LaValley, List of USNA Oklahoma Appointments, 30 Mar. 2000, HMG; 1895–1965 LB entries of midshipmen with Oklahoma nominations; 1913 LB, 114, 140; 1914 LB, 60; 1916 LB, 192; 1918 LB, 63; 1919 LB, 187; 1920 LB, 114, 174, 249; 1921 LB, 472; 1922 LB, 137, 217; 1924 LB, 79, 261; 1925 LB, 39; 1927 LB, 166; 1928 LB, 117; 1929 LB, 308; 1932 LB, 208; 1933 LB, 199; 1934 LB, 99; 1937 LB, 185; 1939 LB, 108, 256; 1940 LB, 316, 321, 333; 1944 LB, 293; 1946 LB, 259; 1947 LB, 138; 1948B LB, 315; 1950 LB, 473; 1953 LB, 210, 268; 1954 LB, 382; 1962 LB, 456; 1963 LB, 335.

42 1922 LB, 60; 1927 LB, 166; 1931 LB, 186; 1952 LB, 245; 1978 LB, 181.

43 Holm, *Strong Hearts, Wounded Souls*, 88–90.

44 Tom Trueblood to Gary LaValley, List of USNA Alaska Appointments, 4 Apr. 2000, HMG; 1915–65 LB entries of midshipmen with Alaska nominations; Steve Harvey, "A Girl at Annapolis," *New Haven Register*, 24 Jan. 1972, in SR2, Sec. 12770/1, Folder "1970."

45 EI, Interviewee #205; 1934 LB; *The Golden Lucky Bag: Class of 1934*, 97; Tom Trueblood to Gary LaValley, List of USNA Hawaii Appointments, 5 July 2000, HMG.

46 "Summary of Non-White Appointments to the U.S. Naval Academy," undated, ARF "Midshipmen: Black Midshipmen"; 1948B LB, 317; 1959 LB, 94, 328; 1959 *Cruise*, 43.

47 EI, Interviewee #51; 1934 LB; *The Golden Lucky Bag: Class of 1934*, 97.

48 The following discussion of Japanese citizens at USNA is based on P. H. Cooper to *Cassier's Magazine*, 24 Sept. 1897, SR1, Box 5, "Brigade of Midshipmen: Intra-Brigade Competition, Minority Midshipmen, 1897–1959," Folder 8; Chester Wood to Sidney Dillon, 30 Sept. 1940, SR1, Box 5, "Brigade of Midshipmen: Intra-Brigade Competition, Minority Midshipmen, 1897–1959," Folder 8; Louis Bolander, Manuscript on Japanese Midshipmen, 7 Dec. 1941, SR1, Box 5, "Brigade of Midshipmen: Intra-Brigade Competition, Minority Midshipmen, 1897–1959," Folder 10; Louis Bolander to Cdr. Zondorak, 7 Dec. 1941, ARF "Midshipmen: Japanese Midshipmen"; R. E. Heise to C. R. Berquist, 17 Apr. 1959, SR1, Box 5, "General Correspondence: Midshipmen, Policy, and Administration: Statistics and Policy Regarding Visitors, 1927–1964," Folder 3; Dave Evans, "List of Japanese Students at the U.S. Naval Academy, 1869–1906," 1986, ARF "Midshipmen: Japanese Midshipmen"; J. M. Ellicott, "Japanese Students at the U.S. Naval Academy," USNIP 73, no. 3 (Mar. 1947): 303, 307; Sweetman and Cutler, *The U.S. Naval Academy*, 102, 156, 158.

49 The following discussion of Filipino citizens at USNA is based on A. G. Esch to Richard Dorso, 14 Jan. 1956, SR4, Folder "A7-4/1-1: Television Series," 11; R. E. Heise to C. R. Berquist, 17 Apr. 1959, SR1, Box 5, "General Correspondence: Midshipmen, Policy, and Administration: Statistics and Policy Regarding Visitors, 1927–1964," Folder 3; "List of Filipino Students Admitted to the U.S. Naval Academy as Midshipmen," undated, ARF "Midshipmen: Minority Groups"; Blitz, *The Contested State*, 31, 49–52.

50 TI with Gloria Steinem, New York, N.Y., 4 Dec. 2000; John Bodnar, "How Long Does It Take to Change a Culture?: Integration at the U.S. Naval Academy," *Armed Forces and Society* 25, no. 2 (Winter 1999): 292; Reimers, *Still The Golden Door*, 29.

51 The following discussion of Yoshihara is based on EI with Takeshi Yoshihara, Aiea, Hawaii, 25 Sept. 1999; Tom Trueblood to Gary LaValley, List of USNA Hawaii Appointments, 5 July 2000, HMG; "Summary of Non-White Appointments to the U.S. Naval Academy," undated, ARF "Midshipmen: Black Midshipmen"; "Annapolis Swears In First Nisei," NYT, 13 July 1949, 22; Heather Harlan, "In Command of His Ship," *Asian Week*, 18 June 1998, 9; Niiya, ed., *Japanese American History*, 226, 233.

52 Harry Lindauer, "List of Jewish Midshipmen," undated, ARF "Jewish Midshipmen, Classes of 1868–1950."

53 PI, Interviewee #73; Seymour Einstein, "Pride Without Prejudice," undated manuscript for *Shipmate*, ARF "Midshipmen: Jewish Midshipmen, Classes of 1868–1950";

M. E. Roberts to Commandant, 17 Sept. 1975, CR, Folder 1730, 1974–75; Kinnaird McKee to John J. O'Connor, 8 Dec. 1975, CR, Folder 1730, 1974–75; Francis Jacques, "Rabbi Trains Academy Staff," EC, 25 Feb. 1987, B4; Janie Mines, "The Jewish Chapel," *Shipmate* 58, no. 1 (Jan./Feb. 1995): 28; James Cheevers, "U.S. Naval Academy: Modern Era, Part IV," *Shipmate* 58, no. 5 (Oct. 1995): 37.

54 Harry Lindauer, "List of Jewish Midshipmen," undated, ARF "Jewish Midshipmen, Classes of 1868–1950"; A. G. Esch to Richard Dorso, 14 Jan. 1956, SR4, Folder "A7-4/1-1: Television Series," 12; 1979 LB, 606; Robert Crown Sailing Center, USNAW (<www.usna.edu/PAO/virtual/map/Rcrown.html>, 21 Feb. 2002); Lovell, *Neither Athens Nor Sparta?*, 32.

55 Dinnerstein, *Antisemitism in America*, viii, ix–xxviii, 3–104.

56 The following discussion of Rickover is based on PI, Interviewee #42; TI, Interviewee #58; Harry Lindauer, "List of Jewish Midshipmen," undated, ARF "Jewish Midshipmen, Classes of 1868–1950"; Reuben Woodall to Eugene Shine, 12 July 1998, SC, Eugene Shine Papers; Polmar and Allen, *Rickover*, 59.

57 The following discussion of Kaplan's experiences is based on EI, Interviewee #214; 1922 LB, unnumbered page; Plaque Honoring Jerauld Olmsted, northeast wall of Deck 2, Dahlgren Hall, USNA; J. L. Olmsted, "Statement in Regard to My Conduct as Editor of the 1922 Lucky Bag," 28 May 1922, SC, Eugene Shine Papers; Vernon Tate to W. Stewart Peery, 22 Sept. 1958, ARF "Midshipmen: Leonard Kaplan, Class of '22"; Eli Vinock to Eugene Shine, 21 Nov. 1991, SC, Eugene Shine Papers; Eugene Shine to Eli Vinock, 2 Dec. 1991, 2, SC, Eugene Shine Papers; Eli Vinock to Henry Cooke, 2 Dec. 1991, SC, Eugene Shine Papers; Eli Vinock to Eugene Shine, 21 Dec. 1991, ARF "Midshipmen: Leonard Kaplan, Class of '22"; "The Silence," EC, 19 Mar. 1910, SCF Folder "USNA: Midshipmen Customs and Traditions"; "A Dark Page Out of Naval Academy History," *Annapolitan Magazine*, Nov. 1989, 48.

58 J. L. Olmsted, "Statement in Regard to My Conduct as Editor of the 1922 Lucky Bag," 28 May 1922, SC, Eugene Shine Papers.

59 PI, Interviewees #89, 165, 176; John Bodnar, "How Long Does It Take to Change a Culture?: Integration at the U.S. Naval Academy," *Armed Forces and Society* 25, no. 2 (Winter 1999): 290–91; Brown, *The Other Annapolis*, 14; Dalfiume, *Desegregation of the Armed Forces*, 22, 26, 29–30, 53–56, 101–2; Evans, *A Sailor's Log*, 156; Schneller, *Breaking the Color Barrier*, ix.

60 The following discussion of Conyers is based on Assorted Ledger 8 pages, Navy Department Bureau of Navigation, ARF "Midshipmen: Black Midshipmen"; "History of Negro Midshipmen or Negro Candidates for Midshipmen," undated, SR1, Box "Brigade of Midshipmen: Intrabrigade Competition, Minority Midshipmen, 1897–1959," Folder 8; R. L. Field, "The Black Midshipmen at the U.S. Naval Academy," USNIP 99, no. 4 (Apr. 1973): 28–29; Penny Vahsen, "Blacks in White Hats," USNIP 113, no. 4 (Apr. 1987): 66; Alonzo McClennan Statement, in Willard Gatewood, "Alonzo Clifton McClennan: Black Midshipman from South Carolina, 1873–1874," *South Carolina Historical Magazine* 89, no. 1 (Jan. 1988): 33; Evans, *A Sailor's Log*, 156–57; Lamson, *The Glorious Failure*, 112–13, 148; Nalty, *Strength for the Fight*, 81; Schneller, *Breaking the Color Barrier*, 8–27.

61 The following discussion of McClennan is based on Alonzo McClennan Statement, in Willard Gatewood, "Alonzo Clifton McClennan: Black Midshipman from South Carolina, 1873–1874," *South Carolina Historical Magazine* 89, no. 1 (Jan. 1988): 31–36; Assorted Ledger 8 pages, Navy Department Bureau of Navigation, ARF "Midshipmen: Black Midshipmen"; Bruce Chapman to Felix Johnson, undated, SRI Box "Brigade of Midshipmen: Intrabrigade Competition, Minority Midshipmen, 1897–1959"; Kenneth Mann, "Richard Harvey Cain, Congressman, Minister, and Champion for Civil Rights," *Negro History Bulletin* 35, no. 3 (Mar. 1972): 64–65; R. L. Field, "The Black Midshipmen at the U.S. Naval Academy," USNIP 99, no. 4 (Apr. 1973): 30; Penny Vahsen, "Blacks in White Hats," USNIP 113, no. 4 (Apr. 1987): 66; Willard Gatewood, "Alonzo Clifton McClennan: Black Midshipman from South Carolina, 1873–1874," *South Carolina Historical Magazine* 89, no. 1 (Jan. 1988): 25–39; Nalty, *Strength for the Fight*, 81–82; Schneller, *Breaking the Color Barrier*, 28–34.

62 The following discussion of Baker is based on Assorted Ledger 8 pages, Navy Department Bureau of Navigation, ARF "Midshipmen: Black Midshipmen"; R. L. Field, "The Black Midshipmen at the U.S. Naval Academy," USNIP 99, no. 4 (Apr. 1973): 30; Penny Vahsen, "Blacks in White Hats," USNIP 113, no. 4 (Apr. 1987): 66; *Biographical Dictionary of the American Congress*, 624; Nalty, *Strength for the Fight*, 81, 82; Schneller, *Breaking the Color Barrier*, 34–41.

63 Charles Buchanan, "Naval Academy Traditions," speech to Naval Academy Women's Club, Annapolis, Md., 7 Oct. 1952, 3, CR, Box "Miscellaneous Speeches Presented by Commandants, 1952–1960," Folder 13; "A New Mascot for Navy: Young Goat Mounts Throne Left By Old Bill," unidentified newspaper article, SCF "Mascots."

64 Felix Johnson to Roberta Holmes, 9 Dec. 1942, SRI, Box "Brigade of Midshipmen: Intrabrigade Competition, Minority Midshipmen, 1897–1959," Folder 8.

65 "History of Negro Midshipmen or Negro Candidates for Midshipmen," undated, SRI, Box "Brigade of Midshipmen: Intrabrigade Competition, Minority Midshipmen, 1897–1959," Folder 8; "Joseph Gavagan, Justice, Dies," NYT, 19 Oct. 1968, 37; R. L. Field, "The Black Midshipmen at the U.S. Naval Academy," USNIP 99, no. 4 (Apr. 1973): 30; *Biographical Directory of the American Congress*, 1081, 1531, 1809, 2044; Alexander, *Homelands and Waterways*, 463; Martis, *The Historical Atlas of the United States Congressional Districts*, 54, 131, 163, 169; Nalty, *Strength for the Fight*, 82; Schneller, *Breaking the Color Barrier*, 60–80.

66 Anderson and Pickering, *Confronting the Color Line*, 47–52; Mullen, *Popular Fronts*, 8–9; St. Drake and Clayton, *Black Metropolis*, 349, 353, 369.

67 The following discussion of Johnson is based on *Reminiscences of Vice Admiral William P. Mack*, 35–36; William Wilson to Franklin Roosevelt, 11 Apr. 1938, SRI, Box "Brigade of Midshipmen: Intrabrigade Competition, Minority Midshipmen, 1897–1959," Folder 8; "History of Negro Midshipmen or Negro Candidates for Midshipmen," undated, SRI, Box "Brigade of Midshipmen: Intrabrigade Competition, Minority Midshipmen, 1897–1959," Folder 8; "Charge Plot to Get Middy," *The Afro-American*, 27 Feb. 1937, SRI, Box "Brigade of Midshipmen: Intrabrigade Competition, Minority Midshipmen, 1897–1959," Folder 9A; "Annapolis: Negro Midship-

man Finds Race Trouble at Academy," *Newsweek*, 27 Feb. 1937, 12; R. L. Field, "The Black Midshipmen at the U.S. Naval Academy," *USNIP* 99, no. 4 (Apr. 1973): 31; Bruce Hayden, "Letter to the Editor," *USNIP* 99, no. 8 (Aug. 1973): 98; Penny Vahsen, "Blacks in White Hats," *USNIP* 113, no. 4 (Apr. 1987): 66; John Bodnar, "How Long Does It Take to Change a Culture?: Integration at the U.S. Naval Academy," *Armed Forces and Society* 25, no. 2 (Winter 1999): 291; Schneller, *Breaking the Color Barrier*, 81–110.

68 Norman Meyer, quoted in Paul Stillwell, ed., *The Golden Thirteen*, 194.

69 The following discussion of Trivers is based on Unpublished Interview with Wesley Brown, USNIOH, 1986, 73; Edward Strong to Claude Swanson, 10 July 1937, SR1, Box "Brigade of Midshipmen: Intrabrigade Competition, Minority Midshipmen, 1897–1959," Folder 8; M. F. Draemel to Superintendent, 28 Apr. 1938, SR1, Box "Brigade of Midshipmen: Intrabrigade Competition, Minority Midshipmen, 1897–1959," Folder 8; "History of Negro Midshipmen or Negro Candidates for Midshipmen," undated, SR1, Box "Brigade of Midshipmen: Intrabrigade Competition, Minority Midshipmen, 1897–1959," Folder 8; Penny Vahsen, "Blacks in White Hats," *USNIP* 113, no. 4 (Apr. 1987): 66; Wesley Brown, "As I Recall the Road to the Naval Academy," *USNIP* 113, no. 4 (Apr. 1987): 76; Schneller, *Breaking the Color Barrier*, 111–21.

70 M. F. Draemel to Superintendent, 28 Apr. 1938, SR1, Box "Brigade of Midshipmen: Intrabrigade Competition, Minority Midshipmen, 1897–1959," Folder 8.

71 Chief of Bureau of Investigation to Superintendent, 17 July 1937, SR1, Box "Brigade of Midshipmen: Intrabrigade Competition, Minority Midshipmen, 1897–1959," Folder 8.

72 "History of Negro Midshipmen or Negro Candidates for Midshipmen," undated, SR1, Box "Brigade of Midshipmen: Intrabrigade Competition, Minority Midshipmen, 1897–1959," Folder 8; *Biographical Directory of the American Congress*, 1201; Kemper, *Decade of Fear*, 4–5, 12: Martis, *The Historical Atlas of the United States Congressional Districts*, 169.

73 The following discussion of segregated Annapolis is based on PI, Interviewees #89, 165, 173, 176; *Reminiscences of Vice Admiral Charles S. Minter Jr.*, 510–11; "Annapolis Loses Its Social Hub as Hotel, a Landmark, Closes," *NYT*, 4 July 1965, A26; John Bodnar, "How Long Does It Take to Change a Culture?: Integration at the U.S. Naval Academy," *Armed Forces and Society* 25, no. 2 (Winter 1999): 292; Brown, *The Other Annapolis*, 32–35, 44, 137; Calcott, *Maryland and America*, 147–51; Nalty, *Strength for the Fight*, 210–11; Stillwell, ed., *The Golden Thirteen*, 201; Warren, *Then Again*, 134, 183, 197.

74 The following discussion of Brown and Powell is based on PI with Ben Holt, Wyckoff, N.J., 18 June 2000; Unpublished Interview with Wesley Brown, USNIOH, 1986, 73, 81, 82, 90, 143; "Memo for Mr. Duvall," 22 Oct. 1945, SR1, Box "Brigade of Midshipmen: Intrabrigade Competition, Minority Midshipmen, 1897–1959," Folder 8; *Biographical Directory of the American Congress*, 919, 1682; *The Historical Atlas of the United States Congressional Districts*, 177; Robert Schneller, "Breaking the Color Barrier: Wesley Brown and Racial Integration at the U.S. Naval Academy, 1945–1949," speech at Marine Corps Historical Center, Washington, D.C., 18 Feb. 1997, 7,

10, ARF "Midshipmen: Black Midshipmen"; Wesley Brown, "The First Negro Graduate of Annapolis Tells His Story," *Saturday Evening Post*, 25 June 1949, 111; Wesley Brown, "As I Recall the Road to the Naval Academy," *USNIP* 113, no. 4 (Apr. 1987): 71; Penny Vahsen, "Blacks in White Hats," *USNIP* 113, no. 4 (Apr. 1987): 66; James Schneider, " 'Negroes Will Be Tested!'—FDR," *Naval History* 7, no. 1 (Spring 1993): 11–15; John Bodnar, "How Long Does It Take to Change a Culture?: Integration at the U.S. Naval Academy," *Armed Forces and Society* 25, no. 2 (Winter 1999): 294; Dalfiume, *Desegregation of the Armed Forces*, 180; Isserman and Kazin, *America Divided*, 41; MacGregor, *Integration of the Armed Forces*, 58–122, 309–14; MacGregor and Nalty, *Blacks in the United States Armed Forces*, vol. 12, 89; Powell, *Adam by Adam*, 78; Schneller, "Breaking the Color Barrier," 163–65, 176–79, ARF "Midshipmen: Black Midshipmen"; Sherry, *In The Shadow of War*, 144–46; Stillwell, ed., *The Golden Thirteen*, xxi, 269; Young, *Minorities and the Military*, 210–20.

75 The following discussion of Brown's approach to being a midshipman is based on Unpublished Interview with Wesley Brown, USNIOH, 1986, 106, 110, 112, 125–29, 131–33, 135–39, 150–53, 191–92, 206–7, 330; Unpublished Interview with William Lawrence, USNIOH, 1990, 130, 244; "The First Negro Graduate of Annapolis Tells His Story," *Saturday Evening Post*, 25 June 1949, 112; Colleen Reddick, "First Black Academy Graduate Goes Back to Sea," *Shipmate* 45, no. 6 (July/Aug. 1982): 37; Penny Vahsen, "Blacks in White Hats," *USNIP* 113, no. 4 (Apr. 1987): 66; Robert Schneller, "Breaking the Color Barrier: Wesley Brown and Racial Integration at the U.S. Naval Academy, 1945–1949," speech at Marine Corps Historical Center, Washington, D.C., 18 Feb. 1997, 15–19; Schneller, *Breaking the Color Barrier*, 185–89, 192, 194, 206–23, 225, 228, 232–33, 236–37, 253.

76 The following discussion of Brown's support network is based on PI, Interviewees #89, 165, 176; Unpublished Interview with Wesley Brown, USNIOH, 1986, 92–95, 146, 192–93, 202, 255–56, 271–73; 1949 LB, 63; Aubrey Fitch to Howard Chapnick, 11 Oct. 1946, SR1, Box 5, "Brigade of Midshipmen: Intrabrigade Competition, Minority Midshipmen, 1897–1959," Folder 8; Robert Schneller, "Breaking the Color Barrier: Wesley Brown and Racial Integration at the U.S. Naval Academy, 1945–1949," speech at Marine Corps Historical Center, Washington, D.C., 18 Feb. 1997, 22–23; H. C. Cooper to Editor, *Our World*, 12 Jan. 1949, SR1, Box 1, "Commandant of Midshipmen," Folder 5; "First Negro to Get Annapolis Scroll," *NYT*, 27 May 1949, 23; Bill Brinkley, "Annapolis Fair, First Negro Ever Graduated There Says," *WP*, 27 May 1949, A1; Colleen Reddick, "First Black Academy Graduate Goes Back to Sea," *Shipmate* 45, no. 6 (July/Aug. 1982): 37; Penny Vahsen, "Blacks in White Hats," *USNIP* 113, no. 4 (Apr. 1987): 66; Haygood, *King of the Cats*, 412; MacGregor, *Integration of the Armed Forces*, 414; Powell, *Adam by Adam*, 78–79; Schneller, "Breaking the Color Barrier," 205–6, 215–34, ARF "Midshipmen: Black Midshipmen."

77 Unpublished Interview with Wesley Brown, USNIOH, 1986, 192–93. The practice of plebes sitting with no chair was called sitting "shoved out."

78 Powell, *Adam by Adam*, 78–79; Haygood, *King of the Cats*, 412.

79 *Reminiscences of Rear Admiral John F. Davidson*, 285, 419.

80   Unpublished Interview with Wesley Brown, USNIOH, 1986, 239, 249; 1959 LB; "Foreign Midshipmen at USNA," 11 July 1951, SR1, Box "Brigade of Midshipmen: Intrabrigade Competition, Minority Midshipmen, 1897–1959," Folder 8; Hugh Elsbree to C. R. Berquist, 6 Apr. 1959, SRI, Box "General Correspondence, Midshipmen, Policy, and Administration: Statistics and Policy Regarding Visits, 1927–1964," Folder 3; R. E. Heise to C. R. Berquist, 17 Apr. 1959, SRI, Box "General Correspondence, Midshipmen, Policy, and Administration: Statistics and Policy Regarding Visits, 1927–1964," Folder 3; "Summary of Non-White Appointments to USNA, through Class of 1963," undated, ARF "Midshipmen: Black Midshipmen"; "Summary of Non-White Appointees to USNA, through Class of 1963," undated, SRI, Box "Brigade of Midshipmen: Intrabrigade Competition, Minority Midshipmen, 1897–1959," Folder 8; "Son of Harlem School Bias Foe Wins Appointment to Annapolis," NYT, 3 June 1962, 118; Penny Vahsen, "Blacks in White Hats," USNIP 113, no. 4 (Apr. 1987): 66; John Bodnar, "USNA Performance and Career Fleet Performance," 7 June 1996, HMG, 15.

81   1959 LB; Hugh Elsbree to C. R. Berquist, 6 Apr. 1959, SRI, Box "General Correspondence, Midshipmen, Policy, and Administration: Statistics and Policy Regarding Visits, 1927–1964," Folder 3; R. E. Heise to C. R. Berquist, 17 Apr. 1959, SRI, Box "General Correspondence, Midshipmen, Policy, and Administration: Statistics and Policy Regarding Visits, 1927–1964," Folder 3; "Summary of Non-White Appointees to USNA, through Class of 1963," undated, SRI, Box "Brigade of Midshipmen: Intrabrigade Competition, Minority Midshipmen, 1897–1959," Folder 8.

82   "The Clean Up Crew," unknown publication, 1956, SRI, Box "General Correspondence, Office of the Commandant, Executive Department, Civilian Employees, Requirements and Correspondence, 1951–1959," Folder 6; "The Bancroft-Hoffman," LOG 54, no. 6 (12 Dec. 1964): 21.

83   William Smedberg, "Superintendent's Talk to the Faculty," 4 Sept. 1956, 9, SC, William Renwick Smedberg Papers, Box 1.

84   "EID," unidentified letter, 14 Jan. 1958, SRI, Box 5, "Brigade of Midshipmen: Intra-Brigade Competition, Minority Midshipmen, 1897–1959," Folder 9; Photographs of basketball game against Temple University, LOG 46, no. 9 (8 Feb. 1957): 22–23; Charles Martin to Gary LaValley, 14 Aug. 1998, ARF "Midshipmen: Black Midshipmen"; John Bodnar, "How Long Does It Take to Change a Culture?: Integration at the U.S. Naval Academy," Armed Forces and Society 25, no. 2 (Winter 1999): 292; Dalfiume, Desegregation of the Armed Forces, 30.

85   The following discussion of Smedberg's actions is based on Reminiscences of Vice Admiral William R. Smedberg III, 656, 744–45.

86   Kenneth Gobel, Richard Hillsberg, and Barry Cohen to Charles Melson, 27 Oct. 1959, SRI, Box 5, "Brigade of Midshipmen: Intra-Brigade Competition, Minority Midshipmen, 1897–1959."

87   The previous two quotes are from Mack Johnson to Kenneth Gobel, undated, SRI, Box 5, "Brigade of Midshipmen: Intra-Brigade Competition, Minority Midshipmen, 1897–1959," Folder 9.

Chapter Three

1 The following discussion of the Kennedys' actions is based on TI with Clifford
Alexander Jr., Washington, D.C., 2 Aug. 2002; *Reminiscences of Rear Admiral Julian T.
Burke Jr.*, 363–64; *Reminiscences of Vice Admiral Charles S. Minter Jr.*, 631–33; Heymann,
RFK, 278–79; Hilty, *Robert Kennedy*, 308, 315–16, 340, 402–4; Hunter-Gault, *In
My Place*, 207–11, 250–51; Navasky, *Kennedy Justice*, 96–99, 132–40, 204–6, 227–
30, 240–52; Schlesinger, *Robert Kennedy and His Times*, 293–94; Thomas, *Robert Kennedy*, 127.

2 The following discussion of Alexander's and White's actions is based on *Reminiscences of Rear Admiral Draper L. Kauffman*, 808; "EID," unidentified letter, 14 Jan.
1958, SR1, Box 5, "Brigade of Midshipmen: Intra-Brigade Competition, Minority
Midshipmen, 1897–1959," Folder 9; Clifford Alexander Jr. to Lee White, 21 July
1965, LBJ, Office Files of White House Aides, Lee White, Folder "Civil Rights—
Miscellaneous 1965"; Lee White to Clifford Alexander, 24 July 1965, LBJ, Office Files
of White House Aides, Lee White, Folder "Civil Rights—Miscellaneous 1965"; Lee
White to The President, 30 July 1965, LBJ, Office Files of White House Aides, Lee
White, Folder "Civil Rights—Miscellaneous 1965"; "Negro Cadet Total Rises at
Academies," AP wire, undated, LBJ, Office Files of White House Aides, Lee White,
Folder "Civil Rights—Miscellaneous 1965"; "Negro Cadet Total Rises At Academies," AP wire, undated, LBJ, Office Files of White House Aides, Lee White, Folder
"Civil Rights—Miscellaneous 1965."

3 Lyndon Johnson, "Memorandum for the Secretary of the Navy," undated, LBJ, Office
Files of White House Aides, Lee White, Folder "Civil Rights—Miscellaneous 1965";
Lyndon Johnson, "Memorandum for the Secretary of the Navy," undated, LBJ, White
House Central Files Subject File, ND 15-8, 1968, Box 190.

4 The following discussion of Wilkins's activities in the White House is based on TI
with Clifford Alexander Jr., Washington, D.C., 2 Aug. 2002; "Johnson Orders Study
on Academy Negroes," NYT, 4 Aug. 1965, 19; "Wilkins Says Too Few Negroes in
Academy," EC, 4 Aug. 1965, 1; Michael Beschloss, ed., *Reaching For Glory*, 161, 163,
225, 281, 387, 389; Kearns, *Lyndon Johnson and the American Dream*, 183–84; Lawson,
"Mixing Moderation With Militancy: Lyndon Johnson and African-American Leadership," in Divine, ed., *The Johnson Years*, vol. 3, 83–85; Wilkins and Mathews,
Standing Fast, 243, 298, 311.

5 The following discussion of Nitze's actions is based on TI with Clifford Alexander
Jr., Washington, D.C., 2 Aug. 2002; Paul Nitze, "Memorandum for the President,"
5 Aug. 1965, LBJ, Office Files of White House Aides, Lee White, Folder "Civil
Rights—Miscellaneous 1965"; Unknown White House official to Lee White, 18 Aug.
1965, LBJ, Office Files of White House Aides, Lee White, Folder "Civil Rights—
Miscellaneous 1965"; Lyndon Johnson to Paul Nitze, 24 Aug. 1965, LBJ, Office Files
of White House Aides, Lee White, Folder "Civil Rights—Miscellaneous 1965"; R. L.
Field, "The Black Midshipmen at the U.S. Naval Academy," USNIP 99, no. 4 (Apr.
1973): 33.

6   Robert Caro, "Lyndon B. Johnson: The Race for Power," in Wilson, ed., *Power and the Presidency*, 71–74; Dallek, *Flawed Giant*, 7, 224–26, 329; Isserman and Kazin, *America Divided*, 140; Kearns, *Lyndon Johnson and the American Dream*, 230–32; Lawson, "Mixing Moderation with Militancy: Lyndon Johnson and the African-American Leadership," in Divine, ed., *The Johnson Years*, vol. 3, 83–84, 106; MacGregor, *Integration of the Armed Forces*, 586–91; Wilkins and Mathews, *Standing Fast*, 311.

7   *Reminiscences of Rear Admiral Draper L. Kauffman*, 808–10.

8   "Naval Academy Is Getting Its First Negro Professor," NYT, 20 Jan. 1966, 69; Martha Thorn, "Chemistry, A Catalyst to Fit the Times," *Trident*, 11 Sept. 1998, 5; Mary Felter, "Former Academy Professor Honored for Life's Work," EC, 23 Oct. 1999, 1; "Chemistry," undated, ARF "History: Department Histories, 150th Anniversary," 6, 9.

9   *Reminiscences of Rear Admiral Draper L. Kauffman*, 815.

10 The following discussion of developments during Minter and Kauffman's administrations is based on *Reminiscences of Rear Admiral Draper L. Kauffman*, 764, 781–82, 803–7; 1967 BOV, 20; "Rear Admiral Kauffman's Remarks to the Board of Visitors," 4 Nov. 1965, LBJ, White House Central Files Subject File, ND 15-8, 1965–1967, Box 190; "Rear Admiral Kauffman's Remarks to the Board of Visitors," Apr. 1967, LBJ, White House Central Files Subject File, ND 15-8, 1965–1967, Box 190; Herring, *America's Longest War*, 147; Lovell, *Neither Athens Nor Sparta?*, 178; Schulzinger, *A Time For War*, 226–42; John Bodnar, "How Long Does It Take to Change a Culture?: Integration at the U.S. Naval Academy," *Armed Forces and Society* 25, no. 2 (Winter 1999): 301; R. L. Field, "The Black Midshipmen at the U.S. Naval Academy," USNIP 99, no. 4 (Apr. 1973): 34; Penny Vahsen, "Blacks in White Hats," USNIP 113, no. 4 (Apr. 1987): 67; USNA Advertising Insert, NYT, 24 Oct. 1965.

11 The following discussion of *Ring of Valor* is based on *Ring of Valor*, 1966, ERC; C. S. Minter to Robert Taylor, 1 Feb. 1965, SR2, Sec. 5720/1, Folder "1960–1965"; "Ring of Valor Shooting Schedule," May 1965, SR2, Sec. 5720/1, Folder "1960–1965."

12 The following discussion of *Mark* is based on *Mark*, 1966, ERC; John Butler to John Davidson, 27 July 1961, SR2, Sec. 5720/1, Folder "1960–1965."

13 "Rear Admiral Kauffman's Remarks to the Board of Visitors," Apr. 1967, LBJ, White House Central Files Subject File, ND 15-8, 1965–1967, Box 190.

14 The following discussion of Kauffman is based on *Reminiscences of Rear Admiral Draper L. Kauffman*, 812; *Reminiscences of Vice Admiral William R. Smedberg III*, 745; Board of Visitors Statement to the President, 4 Nov. 1965, 5–6, LBJ, White House Central Files Subject File, ND 15-8, 1965–1967, Box 190; *Blue and Gold Newsletter*, vol. 2, no. 10, Oct. 1970, ARF "Midshipmen: Minority Recruiting"; Dalfiume, *Desegregation of the Armed Forces*, 22, 26; MacGregor, *Integration of the Armed Forces*, 58; Nalty, *Strength for the Fight*, 84–86; Stillwell, ed., *The Golden Thirteen*, 252–53.

15 The following discussion of Kauffman's actions is based on PI, Interviewee #88; *Reminiscences Draper L. Kauffman*, 813–16; "Rear Admiral Kauffman's Remarks to the Board of Visitors," 4 Nov. 1965, LBJ, White House Central Files Subject File, ND 15-8, 1965–1967, Box 190; Board of Visitors Statement to the President, 4 Nov. 1965, 5, LBJ, White House Central Files Subject File, ND 15-8, 1965–1967, Box 190; Superintendent's Statement to the Board of Visitors, Apr. 1967, LBJ, White House Central

Files Subject File, ND 15-8, 1965–1967, Box 190; Charles Baird to the President, 26 Dec. 1967, LBJ, White House Central Files Subject File, ND 15-8, 1968, Box 190; John Bodnar, "How Long Does It Take to Change a Culture?: Integration at the U.S. Naval Academy," *Armed Forces and Society* 25, no. 2 (Winter 1999): 300; R. L. Field, "The Black Midshipmen at the U.S. Naval Academy," USNIP 99, no. 4 (Apr. 1973): 34; Issacs, *All The Moves*, 210–11. Texas Western is now University of Texas–El Paso.

16 The following discussion of the results of Kauffman's actions is based on *Reminiscences of Rear Admiral Draper L. Kauffman*, 810, 817; Paul Nitze to the President, 29 Jan. 1966, LBJ, White House Central Files Subject File, ND 15-8, 1965–1967, Box 190; Board of Visitors Remarks on Minority Group Candidates, Jan. 1966, LBJ, White House Central Files Subject File, ND 15-8, 1965–1967, Box 190; Joe Califano to the President, 13 Apr. 1966, LBJ, White House Central Files Subject File, ND 15-8, 1965–1967, Box 190; Board of Visitors Statement to the President, 1 May 1966, 21–22, LBJ, White House Central Files Subject File, ND 15-8, 1965–1967, Box 190; Robert McNamara to the President, 5 Sept. 1966, LBJ, White House Central Files Subject File, ND 15-8, 1965–1967, Box 190; 1967 BOV, 20–21; Charles Baird to the President, 22 Dec. 1967, LBJ, White House Central Files Subject File, ND 15-8, 1968, Box 190; John Steadman to James Cross, 28 Dec. 1967, LBJ, White House Central Files Subject File, ND 15-8, 1968, Box 190; James Cross to the President, 12 Jan. 1968, LBJ, White House Central Files Subject File, ND 15-8, 1968, Box 190; Joe Califano to the President, 22 July 1967, LBJ, White House Central Files Subject File, ND 15-8, 1965–1967, Box 190; Fact Sheet on Board of Visitors Report, 5 May 1968, LBJ, White House Central Files Subject File, ND 15-8, 1968, Box 190; Board of Visitors to the President, 5 May 1968, LBJ, White House Central Files Subject File, ND 15-8, 1968, Box 190; "Negro Gains at Naval Academy Cited," EC, 14 Jan. 1968, 2; "Minorities for Annapolis," NYT, 30 May 1971, 22; R. L. Field, "The Black Midshipmen at the U.S. Naval Academy," USNIP 99, no. 4 (Apr. 1973): 34; John Bodnar, "USNA Performance and Career Fleet Performance," 7 June 1996, HMG, 15.

17 The following discussion of Calvert's ideas and recollections is based on PI with James Calvert, St. Michaels, Md., 4 May 2000; Clark Clifford to the President, 23 July 1968, LBJ, White House Central Files Subject File, ND 15-8, 1968, Box 190; James Calvert to James Tyree Jr., 3 Sept. 1968, SR2, Sec. ON/1531, Folder "1962–1967"; "Negroes Urged to Apply to Military Academies," NYT, 25 Dec. 1968, 25.

18 The following discussion of Calvert's actions is based on PI, Interviewee #89; EI, Interviewee #164; *Reminiscences of Rear Admiral Robert W. McNitt*, 543; Robert McNitt to Superintendent, 27 Aug. 1976, SR5, Box 1, Folder "Admission of Women, 1975–1976"; Superintendent's Statement to the Board of Visitors, Apr. 1967, 20, LBJ, White House Central Files Subject File, ND 15-8, 1965–1967, Box 190; *Blue and Gold Newsletter*, vol. 2, no. 10, Oct. 1970, ARF "Midshipmen: Minority Recruiting"; *Blue and Gold Newsletter*, vol. 3, no. 7, July 1971, ARF "Midshipmen: Minority Recruiting"; USNA Command History IV, 1972–1973, vol. I, 87; John Bodnar, "How Long Does It Take to Change a Culture?: Integration at the U.S. Naval Academy," *Armed Forces and Society* 25, no. 2 (Winter 1999): 301; James Cheevers, "USNA: Modern Era, Part IV," *Shipmate* 58, no. 5 (Oct. 1995): 37; Melissa McNitt, "Interview With Kenneth John-

son," *USNIP* 113, no. 4 (Apr. 1987): 68; Penny Vahsen, "Blacks in White Hats," *USNIP* 113, no. 4 (Apr. 1987): 66–68; Fleming, *Annapolis Autumn*, 235; Lovell, *Neither Athens Nor Sparta?*, 178; Nalty, *Strength for the Fight*, 310–12; Stillwell, ed., *The Golden Thirteen*, 271; Zumwalt, *On Watch*, 217–60.

19 The following discussion of BOOST is based on PI, Interviewee #155; EI, Interviewees #130, 164, 197; Chief of Naval Personnel to Commanding Officer, Naval Academy Preparatory School, 19 Dec. 1968, SR2, Sec. NC/1500, Folder "1968"; Commanding Officer, Naval Training Center, Bainbridge, to Chief of Naval Personnel, 24 Feb. 1969, SR2, Sec. NC/1500, Folder "1969"; Commanding Officer, Service School Command, Naval Training Center, San Diego, to Superintendent, 13 Apr. 1972, SR2, Sec. NC/1500, Folder "1972"; Commander, Naval Education and Training, to Commander, Naval Technical Training, 5 June 1974, SR2, Sec. NC/1500, Folder "1974"; Dean of Admissions to Superintendent, 10 Apr. 1979, SR2, Sec. NC/1500, Folder "1979"; Superintendent Notice 5700, 20 Dec. 1989, SR3, 1989, Box 5297–5700/1–19, Folder "5700"; Superintendent to Chief of Naval Operations, 2 Nov. 1990, SR3, 1990, Box 1531/1–1710/5, Folder "1531/1"; R. L. Field, "The Black Midshipmen at the U.S. Naval Academy," *USNIP* 99, no. 4 (Apr. 1973): 35; Andrew Karalis, "Fleet Smart Sailors," *All Hands*, July 1991, 10–13; Penny Vahsen, "Blacks in White Hats," *USNIP* 113, no. 4 (Apr. 1987): 67; Northrup et al., *Black and Minority Participation*, 157–58.

20 Advertisement for Robert Werntz's Naval Academy Preparatory School, 1897 LB; Donald Thomas, "Bobby Werntz's 'War College,'" *Shipmate* 55, no. 6 (June 1992): 18.

21 *Reminiscences of Rear Admiral Draper L. Kauffman*, 828; *Reminiscences of Vice Admiral William P. Mack*, 747, 756–58; John Ryan, Speech to Guidance Counselors, 21 Mar. 2000, USNA; F. E. M. Whiting to Charles Melson, 7 May 1959, SR1, Box 1, "General Correspondence: Athletics, Athletic Policy, and Administration: Naval Academy Athletic Association, 1924–1969," Folder 13; J. O. Coppedge to Superintendent, 17 Nov. 1972, SR2, Sec. NC1500, Folder "1972"; Charles Larson to Elliot Loughlin, 28 Jan. 1985, SR3, 1985, Sec. 1530–1710/34, Folder "1531/1"; Interview with Vice Admiral William P. Lawrence, USNIOH, 989; Undersecretary of Defense, "Memorandum on Service Academy Preparatory Schools," 15 June 1994, SR3, 1994, Sec. 1000–1531, Folder "1531"; 1969 BOV, 2; W. F. Fitzgerald Jr., "The Alumni Foundation and the Preparatory School Program," *Shipmate* 21, no. 4 (Apr. 1958): 2; Elliot Loughlin, "The U.S. Naval Academy Foundation, Inc.," *Shipmate* 43, no. 1 (Jan./Feb. 1980): 6; "Private Support of the Naval Academy," *Shipmate* 54, no. 7, 16–17; Lovell, *Neither Athens Nor Sparta?*, 258.

22 John Bodnar, "How Long Does It Take to Change a Culture?: Integration at the U.S. Naval Academy," *Armed Forces and Society* 25, no. 2 (Winter 1999): 296–97.

23 Ruth Wilson, "Statement from the American Civil Liberties Union Concerning Segregation and Discrimination in the U.S. Navy, Submitted to the Department of the Navy," June 1955, in MacGregor and Nalty, *Blacks in the United States Armed Forces*, vol. 12, 306.

24 MacGregor, *Integration of the Armed Forces*, 246.

25 The following discussion of the history of NAPS is based on PI, Interviewee #79; *Reminiscences of Rear Admiral Draper L. Kauffman*, 821–24; *Reminiscences of Vice Admiral William P. Mack*, 186; *Reminiscences of Vice Admiral Charles L. Melson*, 26–28; *Reminiscences of Rear Admiral Robert W. McNitt*, 601–2, 614; 1947 BOV, 6; 1965 BOV, 5; 1967 BOV, 6; Chief of Naval Personnel to Superintendent, 22 Apr. 1968, SR2, Sec. NC1500, Folder "1968"; Superintendent to Chief of Naval Personnel, 14 May 1968, SR2, Sec. NC1500, Folder "1968"; Commanding Officer, NAPS, to Superintendent, 12 Feb. 1969, SR2, Sec. NC1500, Folder "1969"; James Calvert to Fred Becker, 25 Aug. 1969, SR2, Sec. ON/1531, Folder "1968–1969"; "NAPS: Gateway to Annapolis," brochure, undated, SR2, Sec. NC1500, Folder "1969"; "Naval Academy Athletic Association Summary of Policy Procedure and Instruction for the Recruiting of Student-Athletes, 1968–1969," undated, 1, SR1, Box 1, "Superintendent, General Correspondence, Athletics, Athletic Policy, and Administration, Naval Academy Athletic Association, 1924–1969," Folder 9; Ray Davis to James Calvert, 27 Jan. 1972, CR, Folder 5400/19, 1972; Chief, Naval Education and Training to Chief, Naval Technical Training, 5 June 1974, SR2, Sec. NC1500, Folder "1974"; D. L. Prince, English Department Evaluation, 1974, SR2, Sec. NC1500, Folder "1974"; Chief, Naval Technical Training to Chief, Naval Education and Training, 18 Aug. 1975, SR2, Sec. NC1500, Folder "1975"; Kinnaird McKee to H. E. Shear, 30 Mar. 1976, SR2, Sec. NC1500, Folder "1976"; Kinnaird McKee to James Wilson, 1 Apr. 1976, SR2, Sec. NC1500, Folder "1976"; NAPS Organizational Flowchart, 1976, SR2, Sec. NC1500, File "1976"; Bureau of Naval Personnel to Vice Chief of Naval Operations, 20 Aug. 1977, SR2, Sec. NC1500, Folder "1977"; Robert McNitt, "Memorandum for the Record," 13 Oct. 1977, CR, Folder 5213/1, 1977; "History of Enlisted Men to USNA," Apr. 1990, SC, Eugene Shine Papers; "History of NAPS/NAPC," Apr. 1990, SC, Eugene Shine Papers; Robert McNitt to Eli Vinock, 19 Sept. 1991, SC, Eugene Shine Papers; Thomas Lynch to Ronald Matchley, 26 Oct. 1993, SR3, 1993, Sec. 5340–5700, Folder "5700"; "Naval Prep School Moved," *NYT*, 10 May 1951; Harold Baumberger and W. J. Brown, "The Admiral Strikers," *Shipmate* 21, no. 10 (Oct. 1958): 10; Cartoon, *LOG* 59, no. 6 (20 Feb. 1970): 18; Thomas Lynch, "NAPS and the Naval Academy—Partners in Success," *Trident*, Oct. 1993, ARF "Midshipmen: Enlisted Men Entering USNA." The Navy offered NAPC in Bainbridge, Md., Newport, R.I., Norfolk, Va., San Francisco, Calif., and San Diego, Calif. NAPS has been located in Newport, R.I. (1915–22), Norfolk, Va. (1922–42), Bainbridge, Md. (1943–47), Newport (1947–51), Bainbridge (1951–74), and Newport (1974–present).

26 Kinnaird McKee to H. E. Shear, 30 Mar. 1976, SR2, Sec. NC1500, Folder "1976."

27 The following discussion of the organization of NAPS is based on PI, Interviewees #46, 48, 98, 155; *Reminiscences of Rear Admiral Robert W. McNitt*, 615; *Reminiscences of Vice Admiral Charles L. Melson*, 28; 1967 Cruise; 1972 Cruise; 1973 Cruise; Superintendent to Chief of Naval Personnel, 24 June 1966, SR2, Sec. NC1500, Folder "1960–1966"; Chief, Naval Technical Training to Chief, Naval Education and Training, 18 Aug. 1975, SR2, Sec. NC1500, Folder "1975"; NAPS Diagram, "Memorandum on Academic Preparatory School Study," 21 Oct. 1976, SR2, Sec. NC1500; Howard Kay to Kinnaird McKee, 6 Sept. 1977, SR2, Sec. NC1500, Folder "1977"; Officer in Charge,

NAPS Detail, to Commandant, 19 Aug. 1980, CR, Folder 5213/1, 1980; "First Black is Named Navy Varsity Coach," *WP*, 24 Mar. 1972, D3.

28 The following discussion of NAPS and minorities is based on PI, Interviewees #34, 36, 48; EI, Interviewee #197; Interview with Vice Admiral William P. Lawrence, USNIOH, 990; *Reminiscences of Rear Admiral Robert W. McNitt*, 614; 1964–70 *Cruise*; Commanding Officer, Naval Training Center, Bainbridge, to Chief of Naval Personnel, 24 Feb. 1969, SR2, Sec. NC1500, Folder "1969"; Superintendent to Chief of Naval Education and Training, 27 Sept. 1973, SR2, Sec. NC1500, Folder "1974"; Howard Kay to Robert McNitt, 11 Feb. 1976, SR2, Sec. NC1500, Folder "1976"; Kinnaird McKee to H. E. Shear, 30 Mar. 1976, SR2, Sec. NC1500, Folder "1968"; EI, Interviewee #197; Superintendent to Chief of Naval Operations, SR3, 1990, Sec. 1531/1–1710/5, Folder "1531/1"; Superintendent to Chief of Naval Operations, 4 Nov. 1993, SR3, 1993, Sec. "Originator Codes 5–30," Folder "28"; Eli Vinock, "Secretary of the Navy Appointments: A Report," undated, SC, Eugene Shine Papers; Bob Womer, "LOG's Guide to Mids in the Yard," *LOG* 70, no. 3 (Nov. 1980): 39; Thomas Lynch, "NAPS and the Naval Academy—Partners in Success," *Trident*, undated, ARF "Midshipmen: Enlisted Men Entering NAPS"; John Ryan, "SUPT's Call," *Shipmate* 62, no. 6 (July–Aug. 1999): 3–5.

29 *Reminiscences of Vice Admiral William P. Mack*, 673; USNA Command History IV, 1972–1973, vol. I, 130.

30 PI, Interviewee #124; Zumwalt, *On Watch*, 168, 201; Z-Gram 66, "Equal Rights and Opportunities for Women," USNHCW (<www.history.navy.mil/faqs/faq93–66.htm>, 15 June 2000); Max Morris to class of 1973, 7 Nov. 1972, CR, Folder 5400/5, 1972; Max Morris to Brigade, 20 Nov. 1972, CR, Folder 5400/5, 1972.

31 C. Mark Brinkley, "Commandant Chapman Ushered in Racial Equality," *Marine Corps Times*, 24 Jan. 2000, 11.

32 Earl Caldwell, "Navy Determined to Recruit Blacks," *NYT*, 12 Mar. 1973, 16.

33 The following discussion of Mack's actions is based on PI, Interviewee #182; *Reminiscences of Vice Admiral William P. Mack*, 681, 793–95; *Reminiscences of Rear Admiral Robert W. McNitt*, 590–91, 593; U.S. Naval Academy Catalog, 1972–1973; John Bodnar, "Blacks/Women: Number of Incoming Plebes," Aug. 1996, HMG; Dean of Admissions to Commandant, 4 Oct. 1972, CR, Folder 5720/1, 1973; William Mack to Commander, U.S. Navy Recruiting Command, 11 Feb. 1975; William Mack to David Bagley, 18 Feb. 1975, SR2, Sec. 5727/3, Folder "1973"; U.S. Navy Minority Recruiting Communications Pilot Plan for Navy ROTC and the U.S. Naval Academy, 16 Apr. 1975, SR2, SR2, Sex. 5727/3, Folder "1973"; R. B. McClinton to William Mack, 15 Aug. 1975, SR2, Sec. ON/1531, Folder "1975"; "U.S. Colleges and Universities Report Record Numbers of Applicants This Year; Service Academies Experience Falling Numbers of Applicants," *All Things Considered* on National Public Radio, 29 June 2000; Northrup et al., *Black and Minority Participation*, 70–71.

34 Barry Shambach to Parents, 6 Apr. 1968, in Drew, ed., *Letters From Annapolis*, 211; Franklin and Moss Jr., *From Slavery to Freedom*, 518; Fraser 1968, 189–90; Isserman and Kazin, *America Divided*, 226–28, 231; Zinn, *A People's History of the United States*, 453–54.

35 Hanson Baldwin, "The Academies: Old Ideals, New Methods," *New York Times Magazine*, 16 Apr. 1961, 32; "Annapolis Loses Its Social Hub as Hotel, a Landmark, Closes," NYT, 4 July 1965, 3; Jody Klemerud, " 'Tea Fight' at Annapolis Introduces Plebes to Social Life," NYT, 6 May 1969, 42.

36 Jody Klemerud, " 'Tea Fight' at Annapolis Introduces Plebes to Social Life," NYT, 6 May 1969, 42.

37 James Calvert to Deputy Assistant Secretary of Defense, 6 May 1969, SR2, Sec. 12770/1, Folder "1968–1969."

38 Superintendent to Thomas Mull, 6 Dec. 1971, SR2, Sec. 5830, Folder "1970–1971."

39 The following discussion of Calvert's actions is based on USNA Command History III, 1971–1972, vol. I, 77; USNA Command History IV, 1972–1973, vol. I, 133; Gregory Mann to C. F. Rauch Jr., 16 Feb. 1972, CR, Folder 5211, 1972; William Mack to Parents, Families, and Friends, 7 Dec. 1973, CR, Folder 5400/19, 1973; V. H. Krulak to William Mack, 29 Apr. 1974, CR, Folder 5420/4, 1974; Ronald Stanton, "Open Letter From the Human Relations Council," LOG 61, no. 4 (18 Feb. 1972): 14; "Academy Lists Black History," NYT, 15 Mar. 1972, B5; "First Black Is Named Navy Varsity Coach," NYT, 24 Mar. 1972, D3; Doulas Watson, "Julian Bond Cites Civil Rights Losses," WP, 27 Nov. 1972, A15; "Rickover on USNA," LOG 63, no. 8 (26 Apr. 1974): 10–11.

40 The following discussion of racial changes is based on EI with Mike Nassr, Roswell, Ga., 13 Mar. 2004; *Reminiscences of Rear Admiral Draper L. Kauffman*, 818–21; Max Morris to class of 1973, 7 Nov. 1972, CR, Folder 5400/5, 1972; D. K. Forbes to class of 1974, 23 Oct. 1973, CR, Folder 5400/5, 1973–1976; John Bodnar, "Changes in Reef Points Slang," 7 June 1996, HMG; John Bodnar, "How Long Does It Take to Change a Culture?: Integration at the U.S. Naval Academy," *Armed Forces and Society* 25, no. 2 (Winter 1999): 296.

41 The following discussion of the persistence of racism is based on TI, Interviewees #65, 68, 130; EI, Interviewee #130; Penny Vahsen, "Blacks in White Hats," USNIP 113, no. 4 (Apr. 1987): 66.

42 EI, Interviewee #130.

43 The following discussion of racial progress is based on TI, Interviewee #65; "The Bancroft-Hoffman," cartoon, LOG 54, no. 6 (12 Dec. 1964): 21; D. A. Ellison, "The Outriggers [sic] New Look," LOG 57, no. 6 (15 Dec. 1967): 12–13; Eileen Baltimore (photograph), LOG 58, no. 14 (18 Apr. 1969): 44; C. E. Riley, "Do You Know Him," LOG 58, no. 14 (9 May 1969): 11; Cleveland Cooper Pictorial, LOG 64, no. 6 (31 Mar. 1975): 13–17; Penny Vahsen, "Blacks in White Hats," USNIP 113, no. 4 (Apr. 1987): 69; Rochelle Riley, "Cultural Club Gives Black Midshipmen an Anchor," WP, 12 Dec. 1988, D1.

44 The following discussion of continuing recruiting policies is based on 1977–78 USNA Catalog, 24; "United States Naval Academy Minority Outlook," USNA Admissions Office, 2000, HMG; Robert McNitt to Superintendent, 27 Aug. 1976, SR5, Box 1, Folder "Admission of Women, 1975–1976"; Superintendent's Notice 5600, 22 Aug. 1979, CR, Folder 5720/1, 1979; Ismael Ortiz Jr. to Director of Candidate Guidance, 11 Feb. 1981, CR, Folder 5720/3, 1981; Robert Largo to Special Assistant

to the Secretary of the Navy for Minority Affairs, 14 Oct. 1981, CR, Folder 5720/3, 1981; Director of Candidate Guidance to Superintendent, 23 May 1990, SR3, 1990, Sec. 1000–1531/1, Folder "1531/1"; V. L. Hill Jr. to Blue and Gold Officers, 31 Aug 1990, SR3, 1990, Sec. 1000–1531/1, Folder "1531/1"; "U.S. Colleges and Universities Report Record Numbers of Applicants This Year; Service Academies Experience Falling Numbers of Applicants," *All Things Considered* on National Public Radio, 29 June 2000; James Ferron, "Service Academies See Rise in Quality of Applicants," NYT, 12 Apr. 1984, B1; Richard Halloran, "Military Academies Are Becoming Even Tougher on Body and Mind," NYT, 22 May 1988, Sec. 4, 4; Lovell, *Neither Athens Nor Sparta?*, 6.

45 The following discussion of NAPS is based on PI, Interviewees #46, 48, 83, 90, 98, 218; EI, Interviewees #33, 197; Interview with Vice Admiral William P. Lawrence, USNIOH, 990; 1986–96 *Cruise*; Superintendent to Chief of Naval Operations, 2 Nov. 1990, SR3, 1990, Sec. 1531/1–1710/5, Folder "1531/1"; Superintendent to Chief of Naval Operations, 4 Nov. 1993, SR3, 1993, Sec. Originator Codes 5–30, Folder "28"; "Justification: NAPS," undated, SR2, Sec. NC/1531, Folder "1977"; Charles Larson to Thomas Townsend, 23 May 1996, SR3, 1996, Sec. 5700–5720, Folder "5700"; John Ryan, Speech to Guidance Counselors, 21 Mar. 2000, USNA; John Ryan, "Constancy of Purpose and Raising the Bar of Excellence," *Shipmate* 61, no. 10 (Dec. 1998): 4; John Ryan, "SUPT's Call," *Shipmate* 62, no. 6 (July–Aug. 1999): 3–5; Skerry, *Counting on the Census?*, 58, 200.

46 "U.S. Colleges and Universities Report Record Numbers of Applicants This Year; Service Academies Experience Falling Numbers of Applicants," *All Things Considered* on National Public Radio, 29 June 2000.

47 Bruce Watson, "It's More Than Just A Game," *Smithsonian* (Nov. 1999): 142–59; "Historic Contest Hits 100 Mark," *Trident*, 3 Dec. 1999, 1; Martha Thorn, "Army, Navy Jockeys in Supreme Football Rivalry," *Trident*, 3 Dec. 1999, 5; John Feinstein, "The Spirit of Army-Navy," *Shipmate* 62, no. 10 (Dec. 1999): 38.

48 EI, Interviewee #87; "Salty Sam," LOG 77, no. 6 (Mar. 1988): 9. Other television series including characters who were described as USNA graduates include *Hawaii 5-0* and *Homicide: Life On The Street.*

49 EI, Interviewee #174; Suid, *Sailing on the Silver Screen*, 227–36, 240–41, 243, 249, 255–56; "Academy Applications Increase By 10 Percent," WP, 6 Jan. 1987, B2; James Cheevers, "USNA: Modern Era, Part IV," *Shipmate* 58, no. 5 (Oct. 1995): 38.

50 John Ryan, Speech to Guidance Counselors, 21 Mar. 2000, USNA.

51 Jimmy Buffett, "We Are The People Our Parents Warned Us About," *One Particular Harbor* (musical recording), 1983.

52 The following discussion of minority statistics is based on EI, Interviewee #164; D. W. Davis, Brief on Minority Accessions Plan, 16 Aug. 1989, SR3, 1989, Sec. 1000–1531/1, Folder "1531/1"; 1966–81, 1983–92, and 1994–96 *Cruise*; Appendix A.

53 The following discussion of minority statistics is based on Superintendent to Chief of Naval Operations, 4 Nov. 1993, SR3, 1993, Sec. Originator Codes 5–30, Folder "28"; Northrup et al., *Black and Minority Participation*, 133; Appendix B; Appendix C.

54 The following discussion of comparative minority statistics is based on EI, Inter-

viewee #106; Ross, *Success Factors of Young African-American Males*, 9–11; Smith, *The Challenge of Diversity*, 18, 23, 47–48.

55 Smith, *The Challenge of Diversity*, 23.

56 The following discussion of the Superintendent's panel is based on "Report to the Superintendent on the Study of Minority Midshipmen," 1989, cited in Minority Midshipmen Study Group, "Report to the Superintendent on the Status of Minorities in the Brigade of Midshipmen," 1996, 1, 6, ARF "USNA: Studies and Reports"; Superintendent to Chief of Naval Operations, 18 Aug. 1989, SR3, 1989, Sec. 1000–1531/2, Folder "1531/1."

57 The following discussion of the GAO report is based on U.S. General Accounting Office, "Testimony Before the Subcommittee on Manpower and Personnel, Committee on Armed Services, U.S. Senate, Status Report on Reviews of Student Treatment, Department of Defense Service Academies," 2 June 1992, 3–4, SR5, Box 4.

58 The following discussion of the MMSG is based on Minority Midshipmen Study Group, "Report to the Superintendent on the Status of Minorities in the Brigade of Midshipmen," 1996, 4–6, 8, 12, 17, 24–25, ARF "USNA: Studies and Reports"; Ronald Marryott to Minority Midshipmen Study Group, 1 Aug. 1988, SR3, 1988, Sec. 5214–5420, Folder "5420"; Smith, *The Challenge of Diversity*, 56.

59 The following discussion of the BOV report is based on USNA Board of Visitors, "The Higher Standard: Assessing the United States Naval Academy," 1997, 29. On low academic performance among minorities more recently, see Fleming, *Annapolis Autumn*, 244.

60 The following discussion of racism is based on PI, Interviewees #78, 158; 1978 LB, vol. 2, 10; 1979 LB, 83; 1980 LB, 370, 423, 429, 453; "Teamwork . . . The Key To Success," 1977, 2, SR5, Box 4; F. R. Donovan to Commandant, 25 Sept. 1980, SR5, Box 4; "Sexual Harassment," undated, SR5, Binder 5; Molly Moore, "Admiral Scuttles Academy's 'Playmid,'" *WP*, 13 Apr. 1981; Brian Ray, "The Commandant's Considerations: An Interview with Captain Locklear," *Character Quarterly* 4, no. 3 (Spring 2000): 3; Derrick Bell, "The Real Costs of Discrimination," in Franklin and McNeil, eds., *African Americans and the Living Constitution*, 183–92.

61 The following discussion of midshipmen's experiences is based on PI, Interviewees #5, 7, 19, 41, 47, 83, 89, 90, 141, 165, 176, 216; Penny Vahsen, "Blacks in White Hats," *USNIP* 113, no. 4 (Apr. 1987): 69–70.

62 The following discussion of coping mechanisms is based on PI, Interviewees #7, 9, 19, 31, 45, 47, 85, 89, 90, 159, 216; CI, Interviewee #7; Interview with Vice Admiral William P. Lawrence, USNIOH, 979–80; "Naval Academy Gospel Choir," Public Affairs Release #0029-91, Feb. 1991, ARF "Midshipmen: Naval Academy Gospel Choir"; 2000–2001 USNA Catalog, 46; Penny Vahsen, "Blacks in White Hats," *USNIP* 113, no. 4 (Apr. 1987): 69–70; Rochelle Riley, "Cultural Club Gives Black Midshipmen an Anchor," *WP*, 12 Dec. 1988, D1; Stillwell, ed., *The Golden Thirteen*, 276–77.

63 The following discussion of minority recruiting programs is based on PI, Interviewees #3, 10, 49, 94, 164, 216; EI, Interviewee #76; Ismael Ortiz Jr. to Director of Candidate Guidance, 11 Feb. 1981, CR, Folder 5720/3, 1981; Superintendent to

Deputy Chief of Naval Operations, 18 Aug. 1989, SR3, 1989, Sec. 1000–1531/2, Folder "1531/1"; John Ryan, Speech to Guidance Counselors, 21 Mar. 2000, USNA; "All Hands," *Shipmate* 61, no. 8 (Oct. 1998): 23; Cozy Bailey Jr., "Academy Alumni and Mids Want to Make a Difference," *Trident*, 11 Dec. 1998, 3; "U.S. Colleges and Universities Report Record Numbers of Applicants This Year; Service Academies Experience Falling Numbers of Applicants," *All Things Considered* on National Public Radio, 29 June 2000; "Minority Alumni Profiles," USNAW (<www.usna.edu/admissions/ student1.htm>, 23 June 2000).

64   PI, Interviewees #94, 164.

65   Melissa McNitt, "Interview With Kenneth Johnson," USNIP 113, no. 4 (Apr. 1987): 68.

66   PI, Interviewees #36, 103, 182; EI, Interviewee #197.

67   TI, Interviewee #215.

68   PI with Charles Larson, Annapolis, Md., 22 June 2000; Thomas Lynch to Edward Meyers, 30 July 1992, SR3, 1992, Sec. 1000–1531, Folder "1531."

69   Chief of Naval Operations, "Memorandum on Minority Representation in Service Academies," 26 July 1976, SR2, Sec. 5800/1, Folder "1976."

70   David Hughes, "Black Mid Leader Closer to Dream," EC, 12 Apr. 1976, 6; "Notes On People," NYT, 27 May 1976, 41; Penny Vahsen, "Blacks in White Hats," USNIP 113, no. 4 (Apr. 1987): 68; Richard Halloran, "Military Academies Are Becoming Even Tougher On Body And Mind," NYT, 22 May 1988, Sec. 4, 4.

71   Winfield Scott to Ronald Marryott, 31 Mar. 1987, SR3, 1987, Sec. 1710/1, Folder "1710/1"; "Robinson Leaves Navy Basketball for St. John's Croquet," LOG 84, no. 1 (Sept. 1998): 29; "Minority Alumni Profiles," USNAW (<www.usna.edu/admissions/ student1.htm>, 23 June 2000). Robinson, who was NCAA basketball player's player of the year in 1987, is popularly known as "The Admiral" and had a remarkable professional career with the San Antonio Spurs.

72   Interview with William P. Lawrence, USNIOH, 979–80; Kinnaird McKee to Deputy Undersecretary of the Navy, 17 Nov. 1977, SR2, Sec. NC/1531, Folder "1977"; Wiley Hall, "New Chaplain at the Naval Academy," BS, 5 Oct. 1976; "All Hands," *Shipmate* 53, no. 4 (May 1990): 10.

73   Interview with Vice Admiral William P. Lawrence, USNIOH, 24; Forrestal Lecture Brochures, ARF "Distinguished Visitors: Forrestal Lecture Series"; "Native American Heritage Month," Commandant of Midshipmen Plan of the Day, 17 Nov. 1998, HMG; "1999 National American Indian Heritage Month," Commandant of Midshipmen Plan of the Day, 27 Oct. 1999, HMG; "Native American Heritage Month 1999," Commandant of Midshipmen Plan of the Day, 19 Nov. 1999, HMG; "African American History Month," Commandant of Midshipmen Plan of the Day, 2 Feb. 2000, HMG; Martha Thorn, "Celebrating Accomplishments During Black Heritage Month," *Trident*, 5 Feb. 1999, 3; Martha Thorn, Interview with Jacqueline Brytt, *Trident*, 3 Mar. 2000, 8; Jean Ross and Martha Thorn, "Cultural Diversity . . . The Strength of Our Great Nation," *Trident*, 3 Mar. 2000, 8; "Asian Pacific American Heritage Month Creates Sharing, Celebration in Annapolis," *Trident*, 26 May 2000, 7.

74   PI, Interviewees #89, 165, 176; Kunte Kinte/Alex Haley Memorial Statue and Plaque,

Annapolis City Dock, Dedicated 9 Dec. 1999; Brown, *A Century of Separate But Equal*; Calcott, *Maryland and America*, 147, 150–51.

75 PI, Interviewee #153.

76 PI, Interviewees #5, 18, 26, 37, 42, 47, 48, 79, 87, 88, 89, 93, 98, 106, 110, 132, 155, 158, 164, 165, 166, 169, 176, 210, 217; EI, Interviewees #51, 164, 183; Charles Bolden, Address Before the Midshipmen Black Studies Group, USNA, Annapolis, Md., 9 Feb. 1999; Cozy Bailey Jr., "Academy Alumni and Mids Want to Make a Difference," *Trident*, 11 Dec. 1998, 3; Martha Thorn, Interview with Jacqueline Brytt, *Trident*, 3 Mar. 2000, 8; Smith, *The Challenge of Diversity*, 56.

77 Charles Larson to Charles Bishop, 29 Apr. 1996, SR3, 1996, Sec. 1531, Folder "1531"; BOV, "The Higher Standard: Assessing the United States Naval Academy," 1997, 30; John Hope Franklin, *The Color Line*, 75.

78 Dave Vetter, quoted in "All Hands," *Shipmate* 61, no. 8 (Oct. 1998): 44.

Chapter Four

1 King and King, *The United States Naval Academy Chapel*, 11.

2 John O'Connor to Superintendent, 23 Mar. 1973, CR, Sec. 1730, Folder "1973."

3 Alexander and Solomon, *College and University Law*, 410–23; Kaplin and Lee, *The Law of Higher Education*, 371–74.

4 Eliot, *Notes Toward the Definition of Culture*, 15; Kammen, *Mystic Chords of Memory*, 195, 204; Marty, *Modern American Protestantism and Its World*, ix–xii.

5 The following discussion of USNA chapel regulations is based on USNA Command History IV, 1972–1973, vol. I, 61; King and King, *The United States Naval Academy Chapel*, 3, 4, 8; "The Chapel of the United States Naval Academy," 1969, SCF Folder "USNA: Chapel, Buildings, and Grounds," 15; "Compulsory Chapel—Beginning of," ARF "Midshipmen: Mandatory Chapel, 1970–1973," 2–4.

6 King and King, *The Naval Academy Chapel*, 3.

7 Superintendent's Memo for Files, 23 Dec. 1946, SR1, Box 2, Folder "Religion: Correspondence on Compulsory Chapel Attendance, 1937–1958."

8 PI, Interviewee #73; Seymour Einstein, "Pride Without Prejudice," manuscript for *Shipmate*, ARF "Midshipmen: Jewish Midshipmen, Classes of 1868–1950"; Harry Lindauer, "L'Chaim to the U.S. Naval Academy," ARF "Midshipmen: Jewish Midshipmen," 20; King and King, *The Naval Academy Chapel*, 5; Oral History Transcript, Henry John Rotrige, 42.

9 Testimony of Robert Drinan, 9 Feb. 1970, AvL1, *Anderson v. Laird*, 70 Civ. A. No. 169–70, 316 F. Supp. 1081, Testimony Book 1, 62–65.

10 "Plaintiffs' Memorandum of Law," 2 June 1970, 21, AvL1, vol. 2.

11 David Bazelon, "Opinion," *Anderson v. Laird*, 151 U.S. App. D. C. 112; 466 F.2d 283, 3, AvL2, vol. 1.

12 Palmer, *The Vinson Court Era*, 1, 7.

13 Pritchett, *Civil Liberties and the Vinson Court*, 10.

14 Superintendent's Memo for Files, 23 Dec. 1946, SR1, Box 2, Folder "Religion: Correspondence on Compulsory Chapel Attendance, 1937–1958."

15 *Everson v. Board of Education*, 330 U.S. at 15–16.

16 Aubrey Fitch to ACLU, 23 Dec. 1946, SR1, Box 2, Folder "Religion: Correspondence on Compulsory Chapel Attendance, 1937–1958."

17 *Illinois ex rel. McCollum v. Board of Education*, 333 U.S. at 212; *Illinois ex rel. McCollum v. Board of Education*, 333 U.S. 203; Redlich, Schwartz, and Attaniso, *Constitutional Law*, 1450; "Complaint," 20 Jan. 1970, 5, AvLI, vol. I.

18 *Illinois ex rel. McCollum v. Board of Education*, 333 U.S. at 254–55.

19 Frank Hughes to R. G. Leedy, 31 Mar. 1951, SR1, Box 2, Folder "Religion: Correspondence on Compulsory Chapel Attendance, 1937–1958."

20 W. F. Boone to Herbert Levy, 15 Apr. 1955, SR1, Box 2, Folder "Religion: Correspondence on Compulsory Chapel Attendance, 1937–1958."

21 *Zorach v. Clauson*, 343 U.S. at 314.

22 Clarence Randall to D. King, 17 Feb. 1956, SR1, Box 2, Folder "Religion: Correspondence on Compulsory Chapel Attendance, 1937–1958."

23 William Smedberg to Nancy Sherman, 10 Apr. 1956, SR1, Box 2, Folder "Religion: Correspondence on Compulsory Chapel Attendance, 1937–1958."

24 Curtis Crawford to William Smedberg, 29 Aug. 1957, SR1, Box 2, Folder "Religion: Correspondence on Compulsory Chapel Attendance, 1937–1958."

25 *Reminiscences of Vice Admiral William R. Smedberg III*, 513.

26 "United States Military Academy Cadet Chapel Services Statement of Policy," 23 Dec. 1957, LTP.

27 Curtis Crawford to Charles Melson, 8 Sept. 1958, SR1, Box 2, Folder "Religion: Correspondence on Compulsory Chapel Attendance, 1937–1958."

28 "Annapolis Policy Hit," NYT, 11 Sept. 1958, 25.

29 Pollack, *Earl Warren*, 186–90, 210–11.

30 *Dixon v. Alabama State Board of Education*, 294 F.2d 150; *Braunfield v. Brown*, 366 U.S. 421; *Engle v. Vitale*, 370 U.S. 421; *Abington School District v. Schempp*, 374 U.S. 208; Kaplin and Lee, *The Law of Higher Education*, 371; Alexander and Solomon, *College and University Law*, 412.

31 *Reminiscences of Vice Admiral Charles S. Minter*, 497.

32 *Reminiscences of Roland W. Faulk*, 385–97; A. S. Heyward Jr. to Commandant, 11th Naval District, 4 Apr. 1963, William Smedberg to Secretary of the Navy, 5 August 1963, both in *Reminiscences of Roland W. Faulk*, 397.

33 R. Tenney Johnson, "Memorandum for the Secretary of the Army," 13 Mar. 1964, LTP, 6.

34 "Duty to Pray," *Newsweek* 63, no. 8 (24 Feb. 1964): 62–63.

35 R. Tenney Johnson, "Memorandum for the Secretary of the Army," 13 Mar. 1964, LTP, 3–7.

36 Paul Ignatius to Assistant Secretary of Defense for Manpower, 19 Mar. 1964, LTP, 2.

37 *Reminiscences of Rear Admiral Robert W. McNitt*, 407–8; *Reminiscences of Vice Admiral Charles S. Minter Jr.*, 481–82; Sweetman and Cutler, *The U.S. Naval Academy*, 218.

38 *Reminiscences of Rear Admiral Robert W. McNitt*, 371–72, 407–8; *Reminiscences of Vice Admiral Charles S. Minter Jr.*, 481–82; "Academy Expansion Stirs Annapolis Ire," NYT, 11 Mar. 1962, 3.

39 *Reminiscences of Rear Admiral Robert W. McNitt*, 408; Frank Rigler, "Some Thoughts on the Naming of Buildings," *Shipmate* 31, no. 4 (Apr. 1968): 4; Robert W. McNitt, "Uncle Charlie," *Shipmate* 51, no. 5 (June 1988): 8.

40 Robert W. McNitt, "Uncle Charlie," *Shipmate* 51, no. 5 (June 1988): 8.

41 *Reminiscences of Vice Admiral Charles S. Minter*, 481.

42 The Naval Academy named the south tower after William Chauvenet, one of the Academy's first civilian instructors. Then-superintendent Draper Kauffman named the north tower for Albert Michelson, an 1873 graduate who won the Nobel Prize for being the first person to measure the wavelength of light, which he did as part of experiments he conducted at the exact spot of the building later named for him. See *Reminiscences of Rear Admiral Draper L. Kauffman*, 750; A. G. Esch to Jack Dorso, 14 Jan. 1956, SR4 Folder "Television Series," 12; 1979 LB, 606; 2000 LB, 100; Potter, ed., *Sea Power*, 112.

43 D. C. Gilley, "Sob Sunday," *Trident*, June Week 1947, 18–19.

44 EI, Interviewee #192; "John Phillips of 'The Mamas and the Papas' Dies in California," Agence France Presse press release, 19 Mar. 2001.

45 "Dodo Revisited," LOG 57, no. 3 (3 Nov. 1967): 24–25. See also "Remember?," LOG 58, no. 14 (18 Apr. 1969): 33; Judy Holckan, "Dodo, The Brigade Dog," LOG 59, no. 3 (21 Nov. 1969): 25; "Rumor Has It," LOG 60, no. 10, 6; Steve Kimball, "Dodo Remembered," LOG 76, no. 3 (Nov. 1986): 11–13.

46 *Reminiscences of Rear Admiral Draper L. Kauffman*, 29; "Monopoly" spoof, LOG 55, no. 8 (14 Jan. 1966): 20–21; "The Wizard of Midd," LOG 56, no. 9 (3 Mar. 1967): 10; Heise, *The Brass Factories*, 100–101.

47 *Reminiscences of Rear Admiral Draper L. Kauffman*, 853–54.

48 R. Tenney Johnson, "Memorandum for the Secretary of the Army," 13 Mar. 1964, LTP, 3.

49 Wertsch, *Military Brats*, 173–76.

50 The following discussion of the activities of Leslie, Swick, Truscott, and Vaught at West Point is based on PI with Lucian Truscott IV and David Vaught, Los Angeles, Calif., 9 Sept. 2000; EI with David Vaught, Naperville, Ill., 16 Oct. 1999; TI with Lucian Truscott IV, Los Angeles, Calif., 19 Feb. 2001; Lucian Truscott IV and David Vaught, "Chapel Case Chronology," 1972, LTP, 1, 4, 7, 10–11; Leslie and Truscott, "The Hotbed Sheet," Sept. 1968, LTP, 1–2; Lucian Truscott IV and David Vaught, "Notes from Meeting with Col. Ross, 29 Oct. 1968," LTP, 1–3; Testimony of Michael Anderson, AvL1, 10 Feb. 1970, Testimony Book 1, 203; Testimony of Robert Leslie, AvL1, vol. 7, 359–69; Testimony of David Vaught, 10 Feb. 1970, AvL1, Testimony Book 1, 159–63, 171, 175, 185–86.

51 1969 *Howitzer*, 62–63.

52 Lucian Truscott IV to Treasurer, Corps of Cadets, 5 Sept. 1968, LTP.

53 Lucian Truscott IV to Treasurer, U.S. Military Academy, 10 Sept. 1968, LTP; Lucian Truscott IV to Commandant of Cadets, 10 Sept. 1968, LTP; Lucian Truscott IV to Treasurer through Commandant of Cadets, 10 Sept. 1968, LTP.

54 PI with Lucian Truscott IV and David Vaught, Los Angeles, Calif., 9 Sept. 2000; Leslie Testimony, 29 Apr. 1970, AvL1, vol. 7, 369; Vaught Testimony, 10 Feb. 1970, AvL1,

Testimony Book 1, 185–86; Lucian Truscott IV and David Vaught, "Notes from Meeting with Col. Ross, 29 Oct. 1968," LTP, 1–3.

55 Lucian Truscott IV, "Truscott IG Complaint," undated, LTP, 3.

56 David Vaught, "Action Request," 21 Nov. 1968, AvLı, vol. 2.

57 W. E. Brinker to David Vaught, 30 Dec. 1968, AvLı, vol. 2, Plaintiff's Exhibits; Vaught Testimony, 10 Feb. 1970, AvLı, Testimony Book 1, 171.

58 Ironically, the Army later investigated Koster for his involvement in covering up events at My Lai in Vietnam; see Bilton and Sim, *Four Hours in My Lai*, 177–78, 184–88, 195, 237, 287, 299–304, 307, 310, 326–28, 353.

59 The following discussion of Travis's actions is based on Testimony of Thomas Travis, 12 Feb. 1970, AvLı, Testimony Book 2, 400–401, 410–11.

60 *Eleventh Annual Conference of Superintendents of the Academies of the Armed Forces Record of Proceedings*, 32.

61 Thomas Travis to Commandant, 21 Nov. 1969, AvLı, vol. 2.

62 Commandant Notice 5450.3, 18 July 1969, AvLı, vol. 2.

63 Thomas Travis to Brigade Communications Organization, 21 Nov. 1969, AvLı, vol. 2.

64 Handwritten note signed "Mike," on Thomas Travis to Brigade Communications Organization, 21 Nov. 1969, AvLı, vol. 2.

65 Testimony of Lawrence Speiser, 9 Feb. 1970, AvLı, Testimony Book 1, 51.

66 Testimony of David Osborn, 10 Feb. 1970, AvLı, Testimony Book 1, 255–58.

67 Robert McComas to Richard Creighton, 4 Dec. 1969, AvLı, vol. 2.

68 The following discussion of Enna's situation is based on Affidavit of Nicholas Enna, 7 Jan. 1970, AvLı, vol. 1; Report of Conduct, Midshipman Nicholas Enna, 19 Jan. 1969, AvLı, vol. 1.

69 The following discussion of Speiser's actions is based on Roger Kelly to Lawrence Speiser, 15 Dec. 1969, AvLı, vol. 1; Lawrence Speiser to Editor, *The Beacon*, 30 Dec. 1969, AvLı, vol. 2; Affidavit of Lawrence Speiser, 19 Jan. 1970, AvLı, vol. 1, 50; Speiser Testimony, 9 Feb. 1970, AvLı, Testimony Book 1, 50, 55; D. A. Ellison, "Editorial," *LOG* 59, no. 7 (13 Mar. 1970): 4.

70 The following discussion of Travis's actions is based on Richard Creighton to Thomas Travis, 4 Jan. 1970, AvLı, vol. 2; Robert Coogan to Thomas Travis, 12 Jan. 1970, AvLı, vol. 2; Thomas Travis to Commandant, 14 Jan. 1970, AvLı, vol. 2; Travis Testimony, 12 Feb 1970, AvLı, Testimony Book 2, 413, 421, 428.

71 The following discussion of Anderson's and Morriss's actions is based on EI with Michael Anderson, Red Wing, Minn., 10 Oct. 2000, 11 Oct. 2000, 28 Feb. 2001; Testimony of Michael Anderson, AvLı, 10 Feb. 1970, Testimony Book 1, 198; Testimony of James Simms, 12 Feb. 1970, AvLı, Testimony Book 2, 459–60; Testimony of Richard Tallman, 12 Feb. 1970, AvLı, Testimony Book 2, 483.

72 EI with Michael Anderson, Red Wing, Minn., 11 Oct. 2000.

73 The following discussion of Cooper, Gossett, Hopper, and Osborn is based on Osborn Testimony, 10 Feb. 1970, AvLı, Testimony Book 1, 258, 264–70; Testimony of James Simms, 12 Feb. 1970, AvLı, Testimony Book 2, 459–60; Testimony of Paul Jones, 12 Feb. 1970, AvLı, Testimony Book 2, 472–75. Osborn mentions that two

other midshipmen, named Graveley and Harper, who participated in this meeting, but class rolls in the U.S. Naval Academy Alumni Association Register of Alumni do not include Graveley, and the identity of Harper is unclear. Currey and Enna were in USNA's 10th Company; Cooper, Bradley, Gossett, and Osborn were in USNA's 23rd Company.

74   The forms read "I, the undersigned, hereby authorize the ACLU to provide counsel for me in filing suit to challenge the compulsory chapel or chapel attendance requirement of the U.S. _____ Academy. I understand there is no cost, there will be attorney-client relations, [and that] signing may have an adverse effect on my future career as an officer"; see "Authorization Statement," AvLi, vol. 2.

75   Testimony of Michael Anderson, 9 Feb. 1970, AvLi, Testimony Book 1, 199; Testimony of Paul Jones, 12 Feb. 1970, AvLi, Testimony Book 2, 472; Affidavit of Lawrence Speiser, 22 Jan. 1970, AvLi, vol. 1.

76   "Seven at Service Academies Sue to End Chapel Requirement," NYT, 25 Jan. 1970, 72.

77   Lawrence Speiser to Lucian Truscott and David Vaught, 26 Feb. 1970, LTP, 2; Order of Judge Howard Corcoran, 29 Apr. 1970, AvLi, vol. 1. Naval Academy and Military Academy regulations stipulated that all midshipmen and cadets would attend chapel services on Sundays. Air Force Academy regulations, however, were different. Freshmen and sophomores were required to attend the Protestant, Jewish, or Catholic chapel services at the Academy. Juniors could opt to attend church services in houses of worship in Colorado Springs, and seniors were not required to attend any services at all. West Point, unlike the other two academies, did not permit cadets to attend church services outside of the academy. See "Points and Authorities in Support of Motion for Temporary Restraining Order," 22 Jan. 1970, 2, AvLi, vol. 1.

78   "Complaint," 20 Jan. 1970, 6, AvLi, vol. 1. The First Amendment of the Constitution reads, in part, that "Congress shall make no law respecting an establishment of religion or prohibiting the free exercise thereof." Article VI, Section 3, of the Constitution states, "No religious Test shall ever be required as a Qualification to any Office or public Trust under the United States."

79   "Complaint," 20 Jan. 1970, 6, AvLi, vol. 1.

80   *Everson v. Board of Education*, 330 U.S. 15; *Zorach v. Clauson*, 343 U.S. 314; *Braunfield v. Brown*, 366 U.S. 421; *Engle v. Vitale*, 370 U.S. 421.

81   *Cantwell v. Connecticut*, 296 U.S. 303.

82   *United States v. Ballard*, 322 U.S. 87.

83   The following discussion of Calvert's testimony is based on Affidavit of James Calvert, 4 Feb. 1970, 2–3, AvLi, vol. 1.

84   The following discussion of Mack's involvement is based on *Reminiscences of Vice Admiral William P. Mack*, 810.

85   Jack Anderson, "Compulsory Religion," WP, 8 Mar. 1970, AvL2, vol. 1.

86   "Opposition to Plaintiffs' Motion for Preliminary Injuction and Suggestion of Lack of Subject Matter Jurisdiction Made Pursuant to Rule 12(h)(3) of the Federal Rules of Civil Procedure," 6 Feb. 1970, 11, 28, AvLi, vol. 1.

87 EI with Michael Anderson, Red Wing, Minn., 3 Dec. 2000.

88 Anonymous Letter to the Editor, *Playboy*, Feb. 1970, ARF "Midshipmen: Mandatory Chapel 1970–1973."

89 The following discussion of Graham's sermon at USNA is based on Testimony of Rear Admiral James Calvert, 10 Feb. 1970, AvL1, Testimony Book 1, 141; Jim Carter, "Dr. Billy Graham," LOG 59, no. 6 (20 Feb. 1970): 31–32; Cartoon of Billy Graham, LOG 59, no. 6 (20 Feb. 1970): 38; Robert Timberg, "Curtailing Academy Worship Part of Plan, Graham Says," EC, 9 Feb. 1970; "LOG opposes Plaintiffs," EC, 28 Apr. 1970. Graham had preached at USNA earlier in the 1960s; see *Reminiscences of Rear Admiral Julian T. Burke*, 366–67.

90 "Letter from a Believer and a Nonbeliever," LOG 59, no. 9 (19 Apr. 1970): 8.

91 The following discussion of Calvert's testimony is based on Testimony of Rear Admiral James Calvert, 9 Feb. 1970, AvL1, Testimony Book 1, 13.

92 Testimony of Rev. Glenn Jones, 9 Feb. 1970, AvL1, Testimony Book 1, 4–37; Testimony of Fr. Robert Drinan, 9 Feb. 1970, AvL1, Testimony Book 1, 62–65; Testimony of Rev. Earl Brill, 9 Feb. 1970, AvL1, Testimony Book 1, 81–85; Testimony of Rabbi Eugene Lipman, 9 Feb. 1970, AvL1, Testimony Book 1, 97; Testimony of Dean Kelley, 29 Apr. 1970, AvL1, vol. 7, 330–37; "Motion for Leave to File Brief Amica Curiae on Behalf of the American Jewish Congress et al," 2 Nov. 1970, AvL2, vol. 1.

93 The following discussion of Calvert's testimony is based on Testimony of Rear Admiral James Calvert, 10 Feb. 1970, AvL1, Testimony Book 1, 114.

94 "Suit Asks Academies To End Must Attendance At Chapel," *Navy Times*, 11 Mar. 1970, ARF "Midshipmen: Mandatory Chapel, 1970–1973"; Carroll Alden, "The Changing Naval Academy: A Retrospect of 25 Years," USNIP 55, no. 6 (June 1929): 500.

95 "Opposition to Plaintiffs' Motion for Preliminary Injunction and Suggestion of Lack of Subject Matter Jurisdiction Made Pursuant to Rule 12(h)(3) of the Federal Rules of Civil Procedure," 6 Feb. 1970, 8, AvL1, vol. 1.

96 Travis Testimony, 12 Feb. 1970, AvL1, Testimony Book 2, 415, 421.

97 The following discussion of Kaplan and Speiser's actions is based on EI with Michael Anderson, Red Wing, Minn., 12 Oct. 2000; PI with Warren Kaplan, Washington, D.C., 29 Mar. 2000; PI with Lucian Truscott IV and David Vaught, Los Angeles, Calif., 9 Sept. 2000; EI with David Vaught, Naperville, Ill., 16 Oct. 1999; Lucian Truscott IV and David Vaught, "Chapel Case Chronology," 1972, LTP, 24–25; Testimony of David Vaught, 10 Feb. 1970, AvL1, Testimony Book 1, 157–93.

98 Testimony of Michael Anderson, 9 Feb. 1970, AvL1, Testimony Book 1, 198.

99 Testimony of David Osborn, 10 Feb. 1970, AvL1, Testimony Book 1, 253–57; Testimony of Thomas Travis, 12 Feb. 1970, AvL1, Testimony Book 2, 401–18.

100 Testimony of David Osborn, 10 Feb. 1970, AvL1, Testimony Book 1, 258–59. Uniform Code of Military Justice, Section 11 Miscellaneous Provisions, Article 138 Complaints of Wrongs, states that "any member of the armed forces who believes himself wronged by his commanding officer, and who, upon due application to that commanding officer, is refused redress, may complain to any superior commissioned officer, who shall forward the complaint to the office exercising court-

martial jurisdiction over the officer against whom it is made. The officer exercising general court-martial jurisdiction shall examine into the complaint and take proper measures for redressing the wrong complained of; and he shall, as soon as possible, send to the Secretary concerned a true statement of that complaint, with the proceedings therein."

101 Testimony of James Calvert, 11 Feb. 1970, AvL1, Testimony Book 2, 306. USNA Regulations, Part 0603 UCMJ, state that "although subject to punishment under UCMJ, midshipmen are normally not charged under the Code except for the most grave offenses"; see USNA Regulations, AvL1, vol. 2.

102 Testimony of Lawrence Speiser, 9 Feb. 1970, AvL1, Testimony Book 1, 57; Order of Judge Corcoran, 9 Mar. 1970, 1–2, AvL1, vol. 1.

103 PI with Warren Kaplan, Washington, D.C., 29 Mar. 2000.

104 EI with Michael Anderson, Red Wing, Minn., 12 Oct. 2000.

105 PI with Warren Kaplan, Washington, D.C., 29 Mar. 2000.

106 EI with David Vaught, Naperville, Ill., 16 Oct. 1999.

107 Testimony of James Calvert, 11 Feb. 1970, AvL1, Testimony Book 2, 344–50.

108 Testimony of Thomas Travis, 12 Feb. 1970, AvL1, Testimony Book 2, 429.

109 The previous two quotes are from EI with Michael Anderson, Red Wing, Minn., 12 Oct. 2000.

110 "Brown Defends Services," EC, 22 Jan. 1970, ARF "Midshipmen: Mandatory Chapel, 1970–1973."

111 Order of Judge Corcoran, 10 Apr. 1970, AvL1, vol. 1; Robert Timberg, "Agreement Made in Chapel Case," EC, 3 Apr. 1970.

112 The following discussion of midshipmen's reactions to the plaintiffs is based on EI, Interviewee #199; D. A. Ellison, "Editorial," LOG 59, no. 5 (30 Jan. 1970): 7; "The Chapel Seven," cartoon, LOG 59, no. 7 (13 Mar. 1970): 31; Steven Wohler, quoted in "LOG Opposes Plaintiffs," EC, 28 Apr. 1970.

113 "Hearing on Preliminary Injunction," 27 Apr. 1970, AvL1, Testimony Book 2, 15.

114 EI, Interviewee #199; "Hearing on Preliminary Injunction," 29 Apr. 1970, AvL1, vol. 7, 329.

115 The following discussion of Applecrist is based on Testimony of Ray Applecrist, 27 Apr. 1970, AvL1, Testimony Book 3, 276–80; "Motion of the General Commission of Chaplains and Armed Forces Personnel for Leave to File Brief Amicus Curiae in Support of Appellants," 21 Oct. 1970, AvL2, vol. 1.

116 The following discussion of Moorer's testimony is based on Testimony of Thomas Moorer, 27 Apr. 1970, AvL1, Testimony Book 2, 191–92, 205–8, 242–43; Testimony of Thomas Moorer, 27 Apr. 1970, AvL1, Testimony Book 3, 269.

117 The following discussion of Kelley's testimony is based on PI with Warren Kaplan, Washington, D.C., 29 Mar. 2000; Testimony of Roger Kelley, 27 Apr. 1970, AvL1, Testimony Book 2, 35, 38, 87–90; "Defense Official Defends Compulsory Chapel at Academies," WP, 28 Apr. 1970, C3.

118 Testimony of Roger Kelley, 27 Apr. 1970, AvL1, Testimony Book 2, 88–89.

119 The following discussion of Leslie and Van Atta is based on EI with David Vaught, Naperville, Ill., 16 Oct. 1999; Lucian Truscott IV and David Vaught, "Chapel Case

Chronology," 1972, LTP, 29, 30–31; Leslie Testimony, 29 Apr. 1970, AvL1, vol. 7, 359–74, 385, 407; Fred Van Atta, "Was God Killed By The System?," 1 May 1968, entered as Plaintiff's Exhibit, 20 May 1970, AvL1, vol. 2.

120 The following discussion of Kaplan and Speiser's Memorandum of Law is based on Warren Kaplan and Lawrence Speiser, "Plaintiffs' Memorandum of Law," 2 June 1970, 11–12, 16, 18–19, 34, 36–37, 41, 54, AvL1, vol. 2.

121 "Hearing on Preliminary Injunction," 25 June 1970, AvL1, vol. 8, 446, 449.

122 "Motion to Dismiss This Action as to Midshipman Plaintiffs," 10 July 1970, 1–2, AvL1, vol. 2.

123 The following discussion of Corcoran's opinion is based on Howard Corcoran, "Opinion and Order," 31 July 1970, 3, 5–6, 8, 11–12, 18, 21–24, AvL1, vol. 2.

124 PI with Warren Kaplan, Washington, D.C., 29 Mar. 2000.

125 Warren Kaplan and Lawrence Speiser to Howard Corcoran, "Notice of Appeal," 7 Aug. 1970, AvL1, vol. 2.

126 Richard Nixon to James Calvert, 25 Aug. 1970, ARF "Midshipmen: Mandatory Chapel."

127 James Calvert to Richard Nixon, 29 Aug. 1970, SR2 Sec. ON/1531, Folder "1970."

128 The following discussion of potential White House involvement in *Anderson v. Laird* is based on TI with Lucian Truscott, Los Angeles, Calif., 19 Feb. 2001; PI, Interviewee #103; Robert Timberg, "The Chapel Case: Did White House Lend Support?," EC, undated, ARF "Midshipmen: Mandatory Chapel 1970–1973"; James Hughes to William Knowlton, 2 Sept. 1970, LTP.

129 *Anderson v. Laird*, 151 U.S. App. D. C. 112; 466 F.2d 283, AvL2, vol. 1; Warren Kaplan to David Bazelon, 25 May 1972, AvL2, vol. 1.

130 1971 LB, 232.

131 Warren Kaplan to David Bazelon, 25 May 1972, AvL2, vol. 1.

132 "Laird at Annapolis," NYT, 8 June 1972, 32.

133 The following discussion of Bazelon's decision is based on David Bazelon, "Opinion," *Anderson v. Laird*, 151 U.S. App. D. C. 112; 466 F.2d 283, 6, 17–18, 28–29, AvL2, vol. 1.

134 *Torasco v. Watkins*, 367 U.S. 488; *Engle v. Vitale*, 370 U.S. 421; *Abington School District v. Schempp*, 374 U.S. 208.

135 David Bazelon, "Opinion," *Anderson v. Laird*, 151 U.S. App. D. C. 112; 466 F.2d 283, 28–29, AvL2, vol. 1.

136 The following discussion of Leventhal's opinion is based on Harold Leventhal, "Concurring Opinion," *Anderson v. Laird*, 151 U.S. App. D. C. 112; 466 F.2d 283, 29–30, 46–47, AvL2, vol. 1.

137 The following discussion of MacKinnon's dissent is based on George MacKinnon, "Dissenting Opinion," *Anderson v. Laird*, 151 U.S. App. D. C. 112; 466 F.2d 283, 48–50, 53, AvL2, vol. 1.

138 The following discussion of attempts to get the case heard in the Supreme Court is based on John Malley, Amicus Curiae Brief to the Supreme Court of the United States, 27 Oct. 1972, 6, SR2, Sec 5900/1, Folder "1972"; John Malley to William

Mack, 3 Nov. 1972, SR2, Sec 5900/1, Folder "1972"; Frank Young, "Ruling on Chapel Upheld by Court," EC, 19 Dec. 1972, 1.

139 Notification of the United States Supreme Court, in re: Melvin Laird v. Michael Anderson (Case # 72-653), 18 Dec. 1972, AvL2, vol. 1; USNA Command History IV, 1972–1973, vol. I, 61.

140 "Prayer by the Numbers," editorial, NYT, 24 Dec. 1972, Sec. IV, 8.

141 Melvin Laird to Secretaries of the Army, Navy, and Air Force, 2 Jan. 1973, ARF "Midshipmen: Mandatory Chapel 1970–1973."

142 Anonymous Midshipman, "Letter to the Editor," Playboy, Jan. 1973, ARF "Midshipmen: Mandatory Chapel."

143 Howard Corcoran, "Order," 8 Jan. 1973, AvL2, vol. 1; USNA Command History IV, 1972–1973, vol. I, 61.

144 The following discussion of Mack's actions and reactions is based on Reminiscences of Vice Admiral William P. Mack, 811; William P. Mack, Memo for Brigade, Faculty, and Staff, 5 Jan. 1973, CR Sec. 1730, Folder "1973"; USNA Command History IV, 1972–1973, vol. I, 61–62; "No Chapel for Middies," EC, 6 Jan. 1973, 1.

145 The following discussion of USNA's immediate alterations in chapel policies is based on Reminiscences of Vice Admiral William P. Mack, 811; Travis Testimony, 12 Feb. 1970, 415, AvL1, Testimony Book 2; Max Morris, Commandant Notice 1531, 5 Jan. 1973, CR, Sec. 1730, Folder "1973"; William Mack to Clarence Long, 12 Jan. 1973, SR2, Sec. 5800/1, Folder "1973"; Robert Timberg, "Naval Academy Catalog Lists Chapel Alternatives," EC, 25 Apr. 1970; Frank Young, "Ruling on Chapel Upheld by Court," EC, 19 Dec. 1972, 1.

146 William Mack to Clarence Long, 12 Jan. 1973, SR2, Sec. 5800/1, Folder "1973."

147 EI with Michael Anderson, Red Wing, Minn., 17 Oct. 2000.

148 Michael Anderson to Secretaries of the Army, Air Force, and Navy, and the Superintendents of the Military Academy, Naval Academy, and Air Force Academies, 11 Jan. 1973, SR2, Sec. 5800/1, Folder "1973."

149 John O'Connor to Commandant, 9 Jan. 1973, CR, Sec. 1730, Folder "1973"; Brigade of Midshipmen Statistics, ARF "Midshipmen: Brigade Strength." John J. O'Connor later became the chief of the Navy Chaplain Corps, and then cardinal of the Catholic Diocese of New York.

150 Reminiscences of Vice Admiral William P. Mack, 812; Michael Elliott, "First Catholic Head Chaplain at Annapolis," Catholic Review, 2 Feb. 1973, SCF Folder "Chaplains."

151 Max Morris, Commandant Notice 1531, 5 Jan. 1973, CR, Sec. 1730, Folder "1973"; Frank Young, "Middies Still Go to Church," EC, 1 Feb. 1973.

152 John O'Connor to Superintendent, 23 Mar. 1973, CR, Sec. 1730, Folder "1973"; Frank Young, "Middies Still Go to Church," EC, 1 Feb. 1973.

153 Reminiscences of Vice Admiral William P. Mack, 811, 813.

154 1973 LB, 709. The rack is military slang for "bed."

155 The following discussion of O'Connor's activities is based on Oral History Transcript of Samuel Sobel, 46; John O'Connor to Superintendent, 27 Mar. 1973, CR, Sec. 1730, Folder "1973"; Kinnaird McKee to John O'Connor, 17 Sept. 1975, CR, Sec 1730,

Folder "1974–1975"; James Cheevers, "USNA: Modern Era, Part IV," *Shipmate* 58, no. 5 (Oct. 1995): 37.

156 The following discussion of the course is based on PI, Interviewee #185; *Reminiscences of Vice Admiral William P. Mack*, 675, 678, 706, 708, 714–15; William Mack, "Sunday Morning Activities," Superintendent's Report to the Board of Visitors, 1973, CR, Sec. 5420/4, Folder "1973"; Charles Sheppard, "An Analysis of Curriculum Changes at the United States Naval Academy," 343–44.

157 The following discussion of Lawrence's actions is based on William Lawrence, "Superintendent's Report," *Shipmate* 42, no. 8 (Oct. 1979): 19.

158 The following discussion of incidents in the 1990s is based on Virgil Hill to James Exon, 11 June 1990, SR3, Box 1990, Folder "5700"; "Electrical Engineering Exam Compromise Chronology," 1992, ARF "Midshipmen: Electrical Engineering Exam Compromise," 1–2; Martin Weil and Lisa Leff, "Naval Academy Relieves Head of Department," WP, 25 Feb. 1990, D5; "The SUPE's Perspective: A Conversation with Rear Admiral Virgil Hill," *Shipmate* 53, no. 6 (July–Aug. 1990): 8.

159 The following discussion of Armitage and Larson is based on PI with Charles Larson, Annapolis, Md., 22 June 2000; EI, Interviewee #87; Richard Armitage, chair, "Report of the Honor Review Committee to the Secretary of the Navy on Honor at the U.S. Naval Academy," 22 Dec. 1993, ARF "Studies and Reports: Midshipmen and Graduates"; "Honor Concept," unidentified, SR5, "Naval Academy Action Items (Women at USNA), Background and Status Reports and Responses"; Charles Larson, "Service Academies: Critical to Our Future," *USNIP* 121, no. 10 (Oct. 1995): 34–36; Eric Schmitt, "Expulsions Urged in Navy Cheating Case," NYT, 1 Apr. 1994, 12; Catherine Manegold, "Soul Searching by Class of '94 at Annapolis," NYT, 3 Apr. 1994, 1, 14.

160 The following discussion of *Anderson v. Laird*'s impact at West Point is based on CI with Patrick Finnegan, West Point, N.Y., 5 Jan. 2001; EI, Interviewee #50; David Brown, "The Abolishment of Compulsory Chapel Attendance at West Point and Its Impact on Moral/Ethical Development at USMA: An Historical Appraisal," Paper for LD 720 course, December 1993, U.S. Military Academy Archives.

161 *Reminiscences of Vice Admiral William R. Smedberg III*, 415.

162 *Reminiscences of Rear Admiral John F. Davidson*, 409.

163 *Reminiscences of Vice Admiral Charles S. Minter Jr.*, 497–98.

164 *Reminiscences of Rear Admiral Draper L. Kauffman*, 853, 855.

165 The previous two quotes are from *Reminiscences of Vice Admiral William P. Mack*, 814.

166 The previous three quotes are from PI with James Calvert, St. Michael's, Md., 4 May 2000. In January 2002, a federal judge indicated that the mealtime grace tradition at the Virginia Military Institute was a violation of the constitutional separation of church and state. Because the Naval Academy is the only service academy that currently has such a mealtime grace, the VMI case seemed like it might have some impact at Annapolis. However, the Supreme Court decided not to hear the case in 2004, leaving VMI, and presumably the Naval Academy, to continue their mealtime prayers. See Ariel Sobyer, "Court Case Could Affect Naval Academy Prayer; VMI Cadets Challenge Required Meal Grace," BS, 20 Mar. 2002, 14.

Chapter Five

1   Disher, *First Class*, 351.

2   EI with Lucian Truscott IV, Los Angeles, Calif., 17 May 2000.

3   EI with David Vaught, Naperville, Ill., 16 Oct. 1999.

4   1983 LB, 62; Virginia Dondy, "Plaintiff's Statement of Genuine Issue," 15 May 1974, 11–16, WvS2, File 1; Kathleen Durning, "Women at The Naval Academy: An Attitude Survey," *Armed Forces and Society* 4, no. 4 (Summer 1978): 570; Ebbert and Hall, *Crossed Currents*, 221–22; Kerber, *No Constitutional Right To Be Ladies*, 223, 246–47, 250–52, 278–81.

5   Louis Bolander to Industrial Relations Officer, 30 Mar. 1948, SCF Folder "USNA-Employees," 3; Photograph of Superintendent's Staff, 1920s, USNA Archives Photograph Collection, "Faculty and Staff: Staff Groups."

6   James Calvert, *The Naval Profession*, 119–20; Edward Beach, "Foreword," in Ebbert and Hall, *Crossed Currents*, ix. Midshipmen first used the term "drag" to describe their dates in the late 1890s; see Michael Parker, ed., "Good Gouge: An Investigation into the Origins of Naval Academy Slang," HE 111 course class project, USNA, 1982, 7. "Drag" first appeared in *Reef Points*, the Naval Academy's plebe manual, in 1933; see John Bodnar, "Changes in Reef Points Slang," 7 June 1996, 7, HMG.

7   1896 LB, 45, 123.

8   Notes on Naval Academy Museum Exhibition, "The Navy Girl," 1 Dec. 1971–15 Dec. 1972, ARF "Midshipmen: Navy Girls, 1900–1925"; Gillon Jr., ed., *The Gibson Girl and Her America*; Warshaw, ed., *The Gibson Girl*. Similar images appeared in other editions of the *Lucky Bag*, most notably: 1900 LB, 50, 79, 115, 188; and 1922 LB, 6, 6 overleaf.

9   Charles Buchanan, "Naval Academy Traditions," speech before the Naval Academy Women's Club, 7 Oct. 1952, 7, CR, Box 1, "Miscellaneous Speeches presented by Commandants, 1952–1960," Folder 5.

10 "About the Naval Academy's Women's Club," USNAW, (<www.usna.edu/womens club/nawcabout.html>, 24 June 2001).

11 William Smedberg, "Superintendent's Talk to the Faculty," 3 Sept. 1957, 1, SC, William Renwick Smedberg Papers, Box 1.

12 The following discussion of the 1930 prank is based on *Reminiscences of Francis D. Foley*, 60–64; "Girls Regret Prank That Ousted Middies," NYT, 27 July 1930, 19; "17 Middies Punished for Girl Escapade," NYT, 20 July 1930, 2; "Midshipmen Who Took Girls to Academy Mess to Be Ousted," NYT, 25 July 1930, 1; "Asks Clemency for Middies Who Took Girls to Academy," NYT, 5 Dec. 1930, 1; "Adams Asks Congress to Bar Annapolis Case," NYT, 7 Jan. 1931, 11; "Mrs. Owen Defends Ousted Midshipmen," NYT, 16 Jan. 1931, 16; *Biographical Dictionary of the American Congress*, 1037, 1618, 1813, 2008.

13 Slaff, *The Navy Drag's Handbook*; Van Slyck, *Free To All*, xxvii, 17, 155–57.

14 The following discussion of enlisted women at USNA during World War II is based on "First Woman to Teach at Academy was WAVE Instructor on Link Trainer," *Maryland Gazette*, undated, ARF "Faculty: Women"; Ebbert and Hall, *Crossed Currents*, 30–34, 38–41, 100.

15 "Drag of the Week," *LOG*, 18 Mar. 1949, 11.

16 The following discussion of Genevieve Waselewski is based on Genevieve Waselewski to USNA, 4 Aug. 1949, SR1, Box "General Correspondence: Midshipmen: Policy and Administration," Folder "1936–1949"; R. G. Leedy to Genevieve Waselewski, 5 Aug. 1949, SR1, Box "General Correspondence: Midshipmen: Policy and Administration," Folder "1936–1949."

17 R. Raymond, "All's Well That Ends Wells," *LOG* 41, no. 10 (15 Feb. 52); Cartoon, *LOG* 45, no. 1 (23 Sept. 1955): 23.

18 "If Navy Were Coed," *LOG* 44, no. 12 (18 Mar. 1955): 6–8.

19 The following discussion of Bonalsky is based on "Radcliffe, Indeed—Girl Aims to Enter Annapolis," *NYT*, 24 Oct. 1956, 37; "Girl Wants To Be A Midshipman," *WP*, 24 Oct. 1956, A11; "Batten All Hatches! Navy Prepares to Repel Girl Applying for Academy," *NYT*, 31 Oct. 1956, 27.

20 Evans, *Personal Politics*, 3–6, 15–19, 122; Halberstam, *The Fifties*, 592–98; Davidson and Lytle, *After the Fact*, 312–24.

21 The following discussion of the 1958 prank is based on *Reminiscences of Rear Admiral Robert W. McNitt*, 379–80; "Girl At Annapolis Poses for Middie," *NYT*, 27 Nov. 58, 1, 32; "Girl, 17, Sneaked Into Naval Academy Dorm, Breaks 113-Year Old Tradition," *WP*, 27 Nov. 1958, 1; "Pitcher Takes Oath Despite Suit," *EC*, 28 Nov. 1958, 3; "Midshipmen Punished," *NYT*, 28 Nov. 1958, 10; Robert Pierpont to Commandant, 28 Nov. 1958, SR1, Box 2, Folder "Conduct/General Correspondence, 1933–1959"; Bailey, *From Front Porch to Backseat*, 56; Timberg, *The Nightingale's Song*, 60.

22 Robert Pierpont to Commandant, 28 Nov. 1958, SR1, Box 2, Folder "Conduct/General Correspondence, 1933–1959."

23 Bailey, *From Front Porch to Backseat*, 57–76; Halberstam, *The Fifties*, 570–76; Isserman and Kazin, *America Divided*, 151.

24 Centerfold, *LOG* 47, no. 13 (4 Apr. 1958): 16–17.

25 "Guided Tour," *LOG* 47, no. 17 (30 May 1958): 14–15; Cover, *LOG* 49, no. 7 (18 Dec. 1959).

26 "We Do Have Our Tradition," *LOG* 53, no. 1 (27 Sept. 1963): 28; "Chronology," 1970 *LB*, 273.

27 "The Bancroft-Hoffman," *LOG* 54, no. 6 (12 Dec. 1964): 21.

28 "Company Cuties," *LOG* 55, no. 1 (24 Sept. 1965): 20–21; Advertisement for Peerless Clothing Company, Back Cover, *LOG* 55, no. 10 (25 Feb. 1966).

29 "What Sort of Man Reads LOG," *LOG* 56, no. 3 (28 Oct. 1966): 11; "Gifts for Middies," *LOG* 56, no. 5 (Dec. 1966): 28–29.

30 "Midshipman Advisor," *LOG* 57, no. 7 (19 Jan. 1968): 12; "Drag of the Week," *LOG* 57, no. 12 (5 Apr. 1968): 14–15.

31 Cover, *LOG* 58, no. 14 (18 Apr. 1969); Photograph of Eileen Baltimore, *LOG* 58, no. 14 (18 Apr. 1969): 44.

32 Photographs of Julie Biggs, *LOG* 59, no. 7 (13 Mar. 1970): 27–30.

33 Changes 9 to U.S. N. A. Regulations 1964, Part II, 21 Aug. 1969, SR2, Sec. 5215/2, Folder "Published Documents, Correspondence, 1968–1969."

34 PI, Interviewees #40, 77; Fleming, *Annapolis Autumn*, 22.

35 Gay Ann Cornell, "The U.S. Coed Naval Academy of 1980," *LOG* 49, no. 9 (Feb. 1960): 9–11.

36 James Cheevers, "U.S. Naval Academy: Modern Era, Part IV," *Shipmate* 58, no. 5 (Oct. 1995): 37.

37 The following discussion of Brimmer and Javits is based on Jacob Javits to John Chafee, 22 Sept. 1971, SR2, Sec. 5800/1, Folder "Jan.–Jun. 1974"; Richard Madden, "Javits Seeks to Enroll First Girl in the Naval Academy," NYT, 27 Nov. 1971, 23; "Shaping Up for Naval Academy," NYT, 25 Jan. 1972, 28; Ebbert and Hall, *Crossed Currents*, 221; Frantzich, *Citizen Democracy*, 106–7; Holm, *Women in the Military*, 305; Lance Janda, " 'A Simple Matter of Equality': The Admission of Women at West Point," in DeGroot and Peniston-Bird, eds., *A Soldier and a Woman*, 315; Javits and Steinberg, *Javits*, 110, 242 (photograph); Valeo, *Mike Mansfield*, 269–70.

38 32 CFR 710.12 (a), USC Title X, Secs. 5031, 6958.

39 Douglas Pate, Memo, 24 Sept. 1971, SR2, Sec. 5800/1, Folder "Jan.–Jun. 1974."

40 EI with Jean Ebbert, Alexandria, Va., 21 Nov. 1998; DeCew, "The Combat Exclusion and the Role of Women in the Military," in DiQuinzio and Young, eds., *Feminist Ethics and Social Policy*, 77–92; Wayne Dillingham, "Women Prisoners of War: Justification for Combat Exclusion Rules?," *Naval Law Review*, vol. 13, 1990, 202–3; Ebbert and Hall, *Crossed Currents*, ix–x, 123–24, 139, 155, 242–45, 273, 290–94, 313–14; Marilyn Gordon and Mary Jo Ludvigson, "The Combat Exclusion for Women Aviators: A Constitutional Analysis," *Naval Law Review*, vol. 13, 1990, 180–83; Kerber, *No Constitutional Right To Be Ladies*, 261–64, 283; Ortner, *Making Gender*, 11–12; Rotundo, *American Manhood*, 232–34, 285–91; Paul Roush, "The Exclusionists and Their Message," *Naval Law Review*, vol. 13, 1990, 163–70; Jonathan Salkoff, "Changing Attitudes Toward Devotion and Duty in Western Literature," Trident Scholar Project, USNA, 1990; Stiehm, *Bring Me Men and Women*, 288–301. For an excellent description of combat conditions, see Moore, *We Were Soldiers Once . . . And Young.*

41 Enloe, *Does Khaki Become You?*, 7. See also Fleming, *Annapolis Autumn*, 137–38.

42 Douglas Pate, Memo, 24 Sept. 1971, SR2, Sec. 5800/1, Folder "Jan.–Jun. 1974."

43 On warrior traditions, see Keegan, *Fields of Battle*, 295; Holm, *Strong Hearts, Wounded Souls*, 26–65.

44 The following discussion of Javits's and McDonald's activities is based on Jacob Javits to John Chafee, 7 Oct. 1971, SR2, Sec. 5800/1, Folder "Jan.–Jun. 1974"; James Johnson to Jacob Javits, 11 Jan. 1972, SR2, Sec. 5800/1, Folder "Jan.–Jun. 1974"; E. C. Waller to Lando Zelch Jr., 31 Mar. 1982, SR2, Section 5800/1, Folder "1979"; Richard Madden, "Javits Seeks to Enroll First Girl in the Naval Academy," NYT, 27 Nov. 1971, 23; "Women for Naval Academy?," WP, 19 Jan. 1972, B12; "Annapolis Test Case," NYT, 20 Jan. 1972, 54; Steve Harvey, "A Girl at Annapolis," *New Haven Register*, 24 Jan. 1972, SR2 Sec. 12770/1, Folder "1970"; "Shaping Up for Naval Academy," NYT, 25 Jan. 1972, 28; Frank Young, "Javits Nominates Girl for Academy," EC, 25 Jan. 1972, 1; "Naval Academy Choirs," 1971 LB, 232; "Homecoming Queens," 1971 LB, 263; Ebbert and Hall, *Crossed Currents*, 221; Frantzich, *Citizen Democracy*, 106–8.

45 John Chafee to Laraine Laudati, 14 Dec. 1971, SR2, Sec. 12770/1, Folder "1970."

46 *Reminiscences of Rear Admiral Robert W. McNitt*, 611; John Chafee to Jacob Javits, 10 Feb.

1972, SR2, Sec. 5800/1, Folder "1972"; Ronald Campbell to Charles Mosher, 15 Mar. 1972, SR2, Sec. 5800/1, Folder "1974"; Ronald Campbell to Virginia Dondy, 20 Aug. 1973, SR2, Sec. 5800/1, Folder "1973"; "Navy to Keep Its Academy All-Male," NYT, 9 Feb. 1972, 43; Ebbert and Hall, *Crossed Currents*, 220; Holm, *Women in the Military*, 306; Stiehm, *Bring Me Men and Women*, 11.

47   Holm, *Women in the Military*, 309.

48   G. William Whitehurst to John Chafee, 4 Apr. 1972, SR2, Sec. 5800/1, Folder "1974"; Carmen Neuberger, "Women Entering the United States Naval Academy Environment, Their Expectations, and Likely Fit," undated, 1, SR5, Box 4; John Lawlor, Letter to the Editor, NYT, 12 Feb. 1977, 20; Barone, Ujifusa, and Matthews, *The Almanac of American Politics*, 876; Brumberg, *The Body Politic*, photograph 60, 198; Dowling, *The Frailty Myth*, 151–55; Ebbert and Hall, *Crossed Currents*, 178; Evans, *Personal Politics*, 217; Festle, *Playing Nice*, 111–13; Gelb and Palley, *Women and Public Policy*, 103–7; Kaplin and Lee, *The Law of Higher Education*, 385–86; Sherry, *In The Shadow Of War*, 368, 372–74; Stiehm, *Bring Me Men and Women*, 11.

49   Jacob Javits, "Concurrent Resolution Relating to the Denial of Admission to Any Military Service Academy of the United States Solely on the Ground of Sex," 92nd Congress, 2nd Session, Senate Concurrent Resolution 71, 28 Mar. 1972, SR2, Sec. 5800/1, Folder "1974."

50   Barone, Ujifusa, and Matthews, *The Almanac of American Politics*, 389; Stiehm, *Bring Me Men and Women*, 11, 13; Zumwalt, *On Watch*, 245.

51   The following discussion of Steinem's and Pitman Hughes's Forrestal Lecture is based on TI with Gloria Steinem, New York, N.Y., 4 Dec. 2000; PI with James Calvert, St. Michael's, Md., 4 May 2000; EI, Interviewee #129; Forrestal Lecture Program, Gloria Steinem and Dorothy Pitman Hughes, 4 May 1972, ARF "Distinguished Visitors: Forrestal Lecture Series"; Gloria Steinem, "Forrestal Lecture," 4 May 1972, USNA Archives; Dorothy Pitman Hughes, "Forrestal Lecture," 4 May 1972, USNA Archives; Lovell, *Neither Athens Nor Sparta?*, 4.

52   The previous three quotes from Gloria Steinem, "Forrestal Lecture," 4 May 1972, USNA Archives.

53   The following discussion of Zumwalt's actions is based on Zumwalt, *On Watch*, 172–96, 261–65; "Z And Me," 1970 LB, 58–60; "Zumwalt Wants 'Chicken Regs' Out," LOG 60, no. 7 (19 Feb. 1971): 12–14; Jay Johnson, quoted in "Tribute to Admiral Zumwalt," ERC, 2000; Z-Gram 116, "Equal Rights and Opportunities for Women," USNHCW, (<www.history.navy.mil/faqs/faq93–116.htm>, 15 June 2000); PI, Interviewee #124; Kathleen Durning, "Women at The Naval Academy: An Attitude Survey," *Armed Forces and Society* 4, no. 4 (Summer 1978): 570; Ebbert and Hall, *Crossed Currents*, 181–83; Susan Godson, *Serving Proudly*, 225–26; Isserman and Kazin, *America Divided*, 122–24; Lovell, *Neither Athens Nor Sparta?*, 222.

54   The following discussion of female faculty is based on USNA Command History IV, 1972–1973, vol. I, 40; 1972 *Cruise*, 20; Peter Ruehl, "Academy's First Woman Teacher," EC, 30 Sept. 1972; Martha Thorn, "Professor Succeeds in String of Firsts," *Trident*, 22 Oct. 1993, 9; Rae Jean Goodman, History of Economics Department, 1995,

3, ARF "History: Departmental Histories, 150th Anniversary"; James Cheevers, "U.S. Naval Academy: Modern Era, Part IV," *Shipmate* 58, no. 5 (Oct. 1995): 37.

55 Jacob Javits to John Warner, 18 Sept. 1972, SR2, Sec. 5800/1, Folder "1972."

56 Dan Edelstein, "Letter to the Editor," *LOG* 61, no. 8 (31 May 1972): 4.

57 Photograph of Superintendent and Mrs. James Calvert, *LOG* 61, no. 8 (31 May 1972): 1.

58 Jeanne Bauer and Gail Storms to Elmo Zumwalt, 19 Dec. 1972, SR2, Sec. 5800/1, Folder "1973."

59 William Mack to Jeanne Bauer and Gail Storms, 17 Jan. 1973, SR2, Sec. 5800/1, Folder "1973."

60 Ronald Campbell to Jerome Waldie, 17 Feb. 1973, SR2, Sec. 5800/1, Folder "1974"; Elmo Zumwalt to Jerome Waldie, 31 Mar. 1973, WvS1, Folder 2.

61 James Burke to Ronald Campbell, 13 Mar. 1973, SR2, Sec. 5800/1, Folder "1974."

62 Elmo Zumwalt to James Burke, 31 Mar. 1973, SR2, Sec. 5800/1, Folder "1974."

63 John Warner to William Proxmire, 23 Mar. 1973, SR2, Sec. 5800/1, Folder "1974"; Ronald Campbell to James Corman, 17 July 1973, SR2, Sec. 5800/1, Folder "1973"; William Mack to Patricia Schroeder, 24 Sept. 1973, SR2, Sec. 5800/1, Folder "1973."

64 William Mack to Patricia Schroeder, 24 Sept. 1973, SR2, Sec. 5800/1, Folder "1973."

65 "Women for Naval Academy?," *WP*, 19 Jan. 1972, B12.

66 The following discussion of Edwards's and Waldie's actions is based on *Edwards v. Schlesinger, Waldie v. Schlesinger*, 377 F. Supp. 1092 (1974); *Edwards v. Schlesinger, Waldie v. Schlesinger*, 377 F. Supp. 1091; Virginia Dondy, "Plaintiffs' Interrogatories to Defendants," 19 Nov. 1973, 21, WvS1, Folder 2; Virginia Dondy, "Complaint for Declaratory Judgment, Injunction, and Damages," 19 Nov. 1973, 2, 6, WvS1, Folder 2; Ronald Campbell to Cora Lee [*sic*] Cross, 1 Feb. 1973, cited in Virginia Dondy, "Plaintiff's Statement of Genuine Issue," 15 May 1974, 2, WvS2, File 1; Ronald Campbell to Jerome Waldie, 17 Feb. 1973, SR2, Sec. 5800/1, Folder "1974"; Joyce Shafer to Commandant, 2 Oct. 1973, CR, Folder 5211, 1974; "Women Sue Service Academies," *WP*, 27 Sept. 1973, A34; "Academies Sued to Admit Women," unidentified article, CR, Folder 5211, 1974.

67 *Edwards v. Schlesinger, Waldie v. Schlesinger*, 377 F. Supp. 1091–92.

68 Earl Silbert, "Memorandum of Points and Authorities in Support of Defendants' Motion to Dismiss or in the Alternative Summary Judgment," 26 Apr. 1974, 13, WvS2, File 1.

69 W. G. Fisher Jr. to Joyce Shafer, 15 Oct. 1973, CR, Folder 5211, 1973.

70 Harold Titus Jr., "Answers," 20 Dec. 1973, 1–3, WvS1, Folder 2.

71 W. G. Fisher Jr. to Joyce Shafer, 15 Oct. 1973, CR, Folder 5211, 1973; Holm, *Women in the Military*, 306.

72 Stiehm, *Bring Me Men and Women*, 12–14.

73 William Brehm to Deputy Secretary of the Navy, 4 Jan. 1974, SR2, Sec. 5800/1, Folder "1973"; "Senate Backs Women in Military Academies," *NYT*, 21 Dec. 1973, 36; Stiehm, *Bring Me Men and Women*, 14; Valeo, *Mike Mansfield*, 268–71, 276.

74 Sherry, *In The Shadow of War*, 367–68; Lance Janda, "'A Simple Matter of Equality':

The Admission of Women at West Point," in DeGroot and Peniston-Bird, eds., *A Soldier and a Woman*, 311.

75 R. Shep Melnick, "The Courts, Congress, and Programmatic Rights," in Harris and Milkis, eds., *Remaking American Politics*, 193–94.

76 The following discussion of Mack's actions is based on *Reminiscences of Vice Admiral William P. Mack*, 716; William Mack to Parents, Families, and Friends, 7 Dec. 1973, CR, Folder 5400/19, 1973; "Female Applicants for Class of 1978," 21 Jan. 1974, SR2, Sec. 5800/1, Folder "1974"; Earl Silbert to Thomas Martin and Virginia Dondy, 5 Apr. 1974, WvS2, File 2; William Mack to Chief of Naval Personnel, 30 Apr. 1974, SR2, Sec. 5800/1, Folder "1974"; Virginia Dondy, "Plaintiff's Statement of Genuine Issue," 15 May 1974, 3, WvS2, File 1.

77 The following discussion of Mack's viewpoints is based on *Reminiscences of Vice Admiral William P. Mack*, 716–17; "Affidavit of Vice Admiral William P. Mack, Superintendent, for *Don Edwards v. James Schlesinger*, U.S. District Court, 1825–73," 8–10, SR2, Sec. 5800/1, Folder "1974."

78 The following discussion of Dondy's arguments is based on Jerome Waldie, "Affidavit in Support of Motion in Opposition to Defendants' Motion for Enlargement of Time in which to Answer," 29 Nov. 1973, WvS1, Folder 2; William Brehm to Deputy Secretary of the Navy, 4 Jan. 1974, SR2, Sec. 5800/1, Folder "1973"; "Female Applicants for Class of 1978," 21 Jan. 1974, SR2, Sec. 5800/1, Folder "1974"; Virginia Dondy, "Plaintiff's Statement of Genuine Issue," 15 May 1974, 2–3, 6–8, 11–16, 44, 46, WvS2, File 1; "Women Gain Backer," NYT, 12 June 1974, 31.

79 Karlyn Barker, "House Panel Is Told Law Bars Women at Service Schools," NYT, 13 June 1974, A38.

80 The previous three quotes are from *Reminiscences of Vice Admiral William P. Mack*, 718, 721.

81 Virginia Dondy, "Complaint for Declaratory Judgment, Injunction, and Damages," 19 Nov. 1973, WvS1, Folder 2; Virginia Dondy, "Plaintiff's Statement of Genuine Issue," 15 May 1974, WvS2, File 1.

82 The following discussion of Gasch's decisions is based on Oliver Gasch, "Transcript of Proceedings," 14 June 1974, 15, WvS1, Folder 1; Oliver Gasch, "Order on the Merits," 14 June 1974, WvS2, Folder 2; *Edwards v. Schlesinger, Waldie v. Schlesinger*, 377 F. Supp. 1097–99; *Reminiscences of Vice Admiral William P. Mack*, 716–17; Timothy Robinson, "Military Sex Rule is Upheld," WP, 20 June 1974, A22.

83 Young, *Minorities and the Military*, 225–35.

84 William Mack to Secretary of the Navy, 11 July 1974, SR2, Sec. 5212/2, Folder "1974"; Ebbert and Hall, *Crossed Currents*, 192; Stiehm, *Bring Me Men and Women*, 289–90.

85 De Pauw, *Battle Cries and Lullabies*, 275.

86 William Mack to Secretary of the Navy, 11 July 1974, SR2, Sec. 5212/2, Folder "1974."

87 Bruce Davidson to Superintendent, 9 July 1974, SR2, Sec. 5212/2, Folder "1974"; D. K. Forbes to Superintendent, 8 July 1974, SR2, Sec. 5212/2, Folder "1974."

88 David Bagley to Chief of Naval Personnel, 1 Oct. 1974, SR2, Sec. 5800/1, Folder "1974."

89 "Air Force, Naval Academies Urged to Admit Women," NYT, 3 Nov. 1974, 28.

90   The following discussion of Wright's findings is based on *Edwards v. Schlesinger, Waldie v. Schlesinger,* 509 F.2d. 508–11 (1974).

91   "Air Force, Naval Academies Are Urged to Admit Women," *NYT,* 3 Nov. 1974, 28.

92   Deputy Chief of Staff, Manpower to Assistant Secretary of Defense, Manpower and Reserve Affairs, 17 Jan. 1975, SR5, Box 4; "Memorandum for the Assistant Secretary of Defense for Manpower and Reserve Affairs," 23 Jan. 1975, SR5, Box 4.

93   Stiehm, *Bring Me Men and Women,* 15.

94   "Memo for the Record in re: Rep. Stratton's Press Conference on the General Accounting Office Report on Service Academies," 16 Apr. 1975, CR, Folder 5213/1, 1975.

95   Cross, *Samuel Stratton,* 37–44, 60, 85, 138, 141.

96   The following discussion of NOW's activities is based on CI with Karen DeCrow, Jamesville, N.Y., 3 Feb. 2001; *Reminiscences of Vice Admiral William P. Mack,* 716–17; "NOW Will Discuss Women at the Academy," *EC,* 24 Sept. 1975, 17; Carabillo, Meuli, and Csida, *Feminist Chronicles,* 69, 73; Lance Janda, " 'A Simple Matter of Equality': The Admission of Women at West Point," in DeGroot and Peniston-Bird, eds., *A Soldier and a Woman,* 316.

97   *Reminiscences of Vice Admiral William P. Mack,* 719.

98   OPNAV Instruction 1531 #3, 19 Apr. 1975, SR5, Box 4.

99   William Mack to Chief of Naval Operations, 13 May 1975, SR5, Box 1, Folder "Admission of Women, 1975–1976," and SR2, Sec. 5800/1, Folder "1975."

100   List of Mission Statements, undated, SR5, Assorted Loose Papers.

101   32 CFR 710.12 (a), USC Title X, Secs. 5031, 6958.

102   PI with Donald Forbes, Manassas, Va., 7 Aug. 1998; Deputy Chief of Staff, Manpower to Assistant Secretary of Defense, Manpower and Reserve Affairs, 17 Jan. 1975, SR5, Box 4; "Memorandum for the Assistant Secretary of Defense for Manpower and Reserve Affairs," 23 Jan. 1975, SR5, Box 4; Richard Lyons, "House Votes $32 Billion for Weapons," *WP,* 21 May 1975, A1.

103   Holm, *Women in the Military,* 309.

104   David Maxfield, "Women in Academies," *Congressional Quarterly,* 24 May 1975, 1079.

105   "House Rejects a 70,000 Cut in Overseas Training," *NYT,* 21 May 1975, 15; Richard Lyons, "House Votes $32 Billion for Weapons," *WP,* 21 May 1975, A1.

106   CI, Interviewee #28; Stiehm, *Bring Me Men and Women,* 42.

107   CI with Jean Ebbert, Alexandria, Va., 21 Feb. 2002.

108   The previous two quotes are from "Notes on People," *NYT,* 23 May 1975, 34.

109   EI, Interviewee #25.

110   The following discussion of midshipmen's opinions is based on Tom Conkley, *EC,* 22 May 1975, 1.

111   The following discussion of congressional actions is based on Linda Charlton, "Bill to Open Military Academies to Women is Passed by Senate," *NYT,* 7 June 1975, 22; Spencer Rich, "$25 Billion Voted for Arms in 1976," *WP,* 7 June 1975, A1; Doug Struck, "Back Room Deal Eased Women Into the Academies," *EC,* 7 June 1975, 1, 10; John Finney, "Conferees Back Arms Fund Rise," *NYT,* 26 July 1975, 1; Ebbert and Hall, *Crossed Currents,* 222; Lovell, *Neither Athens Nor Sparta?,* 293.

112   D. K. Forbes, Memo for Distribution, 13 Feb. 1976, SR5, Box 2, Folder "General Internal Management Correspondence, 1975–1976"; Kinnaird McKee to Brigade of Midshipmen, 17 Feb. 1976, SR2, Sec. 5727/3, Folder "1976"; Kinnaird McKee to Faculty and Staff, 17 Feb. 1976, SR5, Box 4.

113   R. K. Lewis Jr. to Commandant, 5 Aug. 1975, SR5, Binder 2.

114   Commandant Memorandum, 6 Aug. 1975, 6, SR5, Box 1, Folder "Admission of Women, 1975–1976."

115   Robert McNitt to Director, Professional Development, 8 May 1979, SR5, Box 4; Ebbert and Hall, *Crossed Currents*, 222; Holm, *Women in the Military*, 311; *Reminiscences of Rear Admiral Robert W. McNitt*, 548–49, 612.

116   Falla, *NCAA*, 164, 167–69, 174, 182, 210–12.

117   Commandant Memorandum, 6 Aug. 1975, 6, SR5, Box 1, Folder "Admission of Women, 1975–1976," 5–6; "Naval Academy Class of 1980 Will Be Fully Integrated," *USNIP* 102, no. 4 (Apr. 1976): 117.

118   N. J. Saltz, "Memo for the Record," 8 Aug. 1975, SR5, Box 1, Folder "Admission of Women, 1975–1976"; Kinnaird McKee to James Watkins, 8 Aug. 1975, SR2, Sec. 5800/1, Folder "1975."

119   Kinnaird McKee to Glenn Beall, 12 Aug. 1975, SR2, Sec. 5800/1, Folder "1975."

120   Kinnaird McKee to Chief of Naval Operations, 29 Aug. 1975, SR2, Sec. 5800/1, Folder "1975."

121   Chief of Naval Operations to Superintendent, 12 Aug. 1975, SR2, Sec. 5800/1, Folder "1975"; D'Ann Campbell and Francine D'Amico, "Lessons on Gender Integration from the Military Academies," in D'Amico and Weinstein, eds., *Gender Camouflage*, 74.

122   Senior Medical Officer to Commandant, 19 Aug. 1975, SR5, Box 4; Joseph McCullen Jr., "Memorandum for Assistant Secretary of Defense on Pregnancy Policy for U.S. Naval Academy Women Midshipmen," 5 Aug. 1976, SR2, Sec. 5800/1, Folder "1976."

123   Public Affairs Plan on Admission of Women, Aug. 1975, SR2, Sec. 5800/1, Folder "1975."

124   EI with Judith Stiehm, Santa Monica, Calif., 14 June 2000.

125   The following discussion of summer training and women on Navy vessels is based on 1942 BOV Report, 6; 1951 BOV Report, 13; 1952 BOV Report, 13; 1953 BOV Report, 12; 1954 BOV Report, 20; 1955 BOV Report, 20; 1956 BOV Report, 27; 1959 BOV Report, 20–21; James Calvert to Parents, 30 Dec. 1969, CR, Box "Commandant of Midshipmen: Instructions, Notices, and Miscellaneous Correspondence," Folder 8; 1971 Lucky Bag, 39; N. J. Saltz, "Memo for the Record," 8 Aug. 1975, SR5, Box 1, Folder "Admission of Women, 1975–1976"; D. K. Forbes to Admiral Trost, 19 Aug. 1975, SR5, Box 1, Folder "Career Planning/Professional Training Issue"; Kinnaird McKee to Brigade of Midshipmen, 17 Feb. 1976, SR2, Sec. 5727/3, Folder "1976"; Edward Meade Jr. to Members of the Secretary of the Navy's Advisory Board on Education and Training, 15 June 1976, CR, Folder 5213/1, 1976; "Report of the Secretary of the Navy's Advisory Board on Education in Training on the Impact of Changing Roles of Women in the Navy," undated, SR5, Binder 1; "Naval Academy

Class of 1980 Will Be Fully Integrated," USNIP 102, no. 4 (Apr. 1976): 117; Ebbert and Hall, Crossed Currents, 3–18, 99, 242; Holm, Women in the Military, 311; Sweetman and Cutler, The U.S. Naval Academy, 42, 45–47, 55, 67–74, 90, 95, 103, 133, 164–65, 195.

126   Mack and Connell, Naval Ceremonies, Customs, and Traditions, 292–93.

127   The following discussion of the Interservice Academies' Conference is based on EI with Jean Ebbert, Alexandria, Va., 21 Nov. 1998; Schedule for Interservice Academies' Conference on the Admission of Women, 8–9 Sept. 1975, SR5, Box 4; W. J. Holland to Superintendent, 15 Sept. 1975, SR5, Box 1, Folder "Candidate Guidance 1975, No. 1"; "Women at the Service Academies: Notes for Superintendents' Conference," undated, SR5, Box 3, Folder "Policies, Regulations—Admission of Women, 1975–1976"; "Naval Academy Class of 1980 Will Be Fully Integrated," USNIP 102, no. 4 (Apr. 1976): 117; Sherry, In The Shadow Of War, 368; Stiehm, Bring Me Men and Women, 71, 144–45.

128   The following discussion of Merchant Marine and Coast Guard Academies' experiences is based on W. J. Holland to Superintendent, 15 Sept. 1975, SR5, Box 1, Folder "Candidate Guidance 1975, No. 1," and SR5, Box 3, Folder "Policies, Regulations—Admission of Women, 1975–1976"; John Wagner, "Report on Interservice Academy Conference," 20 Oct. 1975, SR5, Box 1, Folder "Candidate Guidance 1975, No. 1"; Donald Cline, "Memorandum for the Record," undated, SR5, Box 1, Folder "Candidate Guidance 1975, No. 1"; Stiehm, Bring Me Men and Women, 145.

129   Donald Cline, "Memorandum for the Record," undated, SR5, Box 1, Folder "Candidate Guidance 1975, No. 1."

130   D. K. Forbes, "Program Actions and Milestones for Women at the U.S. Naval Academy," various dates, SR5, Box 4; D. K. Forbes, "Memorandum for Distribution," 13 Feb. 1976, SR5, Box 2, Folder "General Internal Management Correspondence, 1975–1976"; D. K. Forbes to Staff Judge Advocate, 18 Feb. 1976, SR5, Box 4; Commandant to Superintendent, undated, SR5, Box 2, Folder "General Internal Management Correspondence, 1975–1976"; "Training Information and Education: General Plan on Target Identification," undated, SR5, Binder 1.

131   Richard Evans to Public Works Officer, 14 Oct. 1974, SR5, Box 1, Folder "Berthing of Women, 1975–1976, No. 2"; J. O. Coppedge to Dean of Admissions, 29 Sept. 1975, SR5, Box 1, Folder "Athletics/Physical Education"; Military Construction Project Data Form, 29 Sept. 1975, SR5, Box 4; Superintendent to Assistant Secretary of the Navy, Installations and Logistics, 7 Oct. 1975, SR5, Box 4; "Memorandum for the Assistant Chief of Naval Personnel for Personnel Planning and Programming," 9 Oct. 1975, SR2, Sec. 5800/1, Folder "1975"; E. A. McManus to Commandant, 22 Mar. 1976, SR5, Box 2, Folder "Costs for Augmentation of Women"; J. W. Blanchard Jr. to Commandant, 24 Mar. 1976, SR5, Box 2, Folder "Costs for Augmentation of Women"; "Plan for Admission of Women to U.S. Naval Academy," undated, 11, SR5, Box 4; Jeanette Smyth, "With Coed Cadets, It's All Academic," WP, 29 Nov. 1975, B5.

132   R. H. Schmidt to R. W. McNitt, 7 Oct. 1975, SR2, Sec. NC 1500, Folder "1975."

133   Reminiscences of Rear Admiral Robert W. McNitt, 600; "Plan for Selection and Appointment of Women to the Naval Academy, Revised Alternate Plan No. 1," 29 Aug. 1975,

SR2, Sec. 5800/1, Folder "1975"; C. N. Mitchell, "Memorandum for Director, Office of Defense Education," 7 Oct. 1975, SR5, Box 1, Folder "Admission of Women, 1975–1976"; Robert McNitt to Director, Professional Development, 8 May 1979, SR5, Box 4.

134 Kinnaird McKee to Chief of Naval Personnel, 1 Oct. 1975, SR2, Sec. 5800/1, Folder "1975."

135 "Public Law 94-106," SR5, Box 4; *Reminiscences of Rear Admiral Robert W. McNitt*, 611; D. K. Forbes to Capt. Holland, 9 Oct. 1975, SR5, Box 2, Folder "General Internal Management Correspondence, 1975–1976"; "Two Defense Bills Totaling $34.6 Billion Signed by Ford," *NYT*, 9 Oct. 1975, 44; Doug Struck, "Academy Required to Admit Women," *WP*, 9 Oct. 1975, 1.

136 Kinnaird McKee to Brigade of Midshipmen, 17 Feb. 1976, SR2, Sec. 5727/3, Folder "1976."

137 "Statement by Superintendent When President Signed Authorization Bill Admitting Women to the Service Academies," 9 Oct. 1975, SR2, Sec. 5800/1, Folder "1975"; Public Affairs News Release, 9 Oct. 1975, SR2, Sec. 5800/1, Folder "1975"; W. J. Holland Jr., "Report on Issues to Consider for the Integration of Women," 18 Jan. 1976, SR5, Box 4; "Principal Personnel Involved In Planning and Preparation for Admission of Women Midshipmen," undated, SR5, Box 2, Folder "DACOWITS, 1976, 1981."

138 PI, Interviewee #158; "Minutes of the Meeting of the Midshipmen's Planning Review Group for Women at the U.S. Naval Academy," 5 Dec. 1975, SR5, Binder 1; Holm, *Women in the Military*, 311.

139 The results of the midshipmen's study are unknown. Charles Campbell, "Midshipwomen??? Never!," *LOG* 65 (Oct. 1975): 22.

140 "Navy School Seeks Women," *NYT*, 19 Oct. 1975, 30.

141 D. K. Forbes to Capt. Holland, 9 Oct. 1975, SR5, Box 2, Folder "General Internal Management Correspondence, 1975–1976." USNA officials gave midshipmen written notice in February 1976; see Kinnaird McKee to Brigade of Midshipmen, 17 Feb. 1976, SR2, Sec. 5727/3, Folder "1976."

142 PI, Interviewee #158.

143 W. J. Holland Jr. to Commandant, 20 Oct. 1975, SR5, Binder 1.

144 Charles Campbell, "Midshipwomen??? Never!," *LOG* 65 (Oct. 1975): 22.

145 Pat McKinn, "LOG Report: Women at the Naval Academy—For Male Eyes Only," *LOG* 65 (Oct. 1975): 34–35; "Notes from LOG Meeting," Oct. 1975, SR5, Box 2, Folder "General Internal Management Correspondence, 1975–1976."

146 "LOG Interview: George C. Scott," *LOG* 65 (Oct. 1975): 8.

147 Richard Ustick, "U.S. Naval Academy Experience: Women Midshipmen," 28 June 1978, 15, SR5, Box 4; Report of Midshipman Edgar Ballasteros, undated, SR5, Box 2, Folder "General Internal Management Correspondence, 1975–1976"; Gregory Jenkins to LCDR Daly, undated, SR5, Box 2, Folder "General Internal Management Correspondence, 1975–1976"; "Opinions and Attitudes Toward Women as Midshipmen for 13th, 14th, 15th, 16th, 17th, and 18th Companies," undated, SR5, Box 2, Folder "General Internal Management Correspondence, 1975–1976"; "Naval Acad-

emy Class of 1980 Will Be Fully Integrated," *USNIP* 102, no. 4 (Apr. 1976): 117; Dowling, *The Frailty Myth*, 153–54.

148 Elaine Malone, Charles Cochran, and Paul Roush, "Gender and Moral Reasoning: Empirical Study of the Relationship Between Gender, Attitudinal/Behavioral Indicators, and Moral Reasoning: A Cross Sectional Analysis of the Midshipmen at the United States Naval Academy," *Minerva* 15, no. 3/4 (Fall/Winter 1997): 84–86.

149 The previous two quotes from Lucinda Joy Peach, "Gender Ideology in the Ethics of Women in Combat," in Stiehm, ed., *It's Our Military Too!*, 161–62.

150 Interview with Tina Mare D'Ercole, USNION, OHFFG, 12.

151 The following discussion of male midshipmen's reactions is based on Gregory Jenkins to LCDR Daly, undated, SR5, Box 2, Folder "General Internal Management Correspondence, 1975–1976"; Report of Midshipman Edgar Ballasteros, undated, SR5, Box 2, Folder "General Internal Management Correspondence, 1975–1976"; Report of Midshipman T. J. Frey, undated, SR5, Box 2, Folder "General Internal Management Correspondence, 1975–1976"; "Opinions and Attitudes Toward Women as Midshipmen for 13th, 14th, 15th, 16th, 17th, and 18th Companies," undated, SR5, Box 2, Folder "General Internal Management Correspondence, 1975–1976."

152 D. K. Forbes to Superintendent, 2 June 1976, SR5, Box 4; J. M. Brown to Capt. Holland, undated, SR5, Box 2, Folder "General Internal Management Correspondence, 1975–1976"; "Preparation for Women at the U.S. Naval Academy: Information and Education Programs," Dec. 1975, SR5, Box 4.

153 "Admission of Women to the U.S. Naval Academy, Public Affairs, Internal Plan," undated, SR5, Box 2, Folder "General Internal Management Correspondence, 1975–1976"; "Training Information and Education: General Plan on Target Information," undated, SR5, Binder 1.

154 Edward Meade Jr. to Members of the Secretary of the Navy's Advisory Board on Education and Training, 15 June 1976, CR, Folder 5213/1, 1976; "Report of the Secretary of the Navy's Advisory Board on Education in Training on the Impact of Changing Roles of Women in the Navy," undated, SR5, Binder 1.

155 Clippings of articles from *Public Management* and *The Counseling Psychologist*, SR5, Box 4; Eugen Galluscio to Richard Ustick, 7 Jan. 1977, SR5, Box 4; Richard Ustick to Commandant, 17 Jan. 1977, SR5, Box 4.

156 W. J. Holland Jr. to Commandant, undated, SR5, Box 2, Folder "General Internal Management Correspondence, 1975–1976."

157 TI with Edith Seashore, Columbia, Md., 19 July 2000; William Mack to Mrs. David Leland, 10 Dec. 1975, SR2, Sec. 5727/3, Folder "1973"; James Winnefeld to Superintendent, 13 Oct. 1976, CR, Sec. 5420/4, Folder "1976"; Richard Ustick to Mike Stankosky, 30 Nov. 1977, SR5, Box 4; Superintendent to U.S. Defense Attache, Oslo, Norway, 13 Apr. 1979, SR5, Box 4.

158 Kinnaird McKee to Delphone Telles, 14 Sept. 1976, SR5, Folder "DACOWITS, 1976, 1981"; "Capt. Holland's Briefing to DACOWITS," 17 Nov. 1976, SR5, Folder "DACOWITS, 1976, 1981"; Commandant to L. J. Gionet Jr., 18 Nov. 1976, SR5, Folder "DACOWITS, 1976, 1981"; "Memorandum for the Record," 8 Dec. 1976,

SR5, Folder "DACOWITS, 1976, 1981"; F. T. Gieseman to Director, 19 Oct. 1979, SR5, Box 4; Ebbert and Hall, *Crossed Currents*, 143–44; Enloe, *Does Khaki Become You?*, xviii.

159   W. J. Holland to Commandant, 12 Feb. 1976, SR5, Box 2, Folder "General Internal Management Correspondence, 1975–1976"; Richard Ustick, "Memorandum for Deputy Commandant," 3 Mar. 1977, SR5, Box 4; Director of Professional Development, "Memorandum for Distribution," 19 Apr. 1978, SR5, Box 4; F. T. Geisemann, "Memorandum," 13 Sept. 1979, SR5, Box 4; Superintendent to Chief of Naval Operations, 27 July 1981, SR5, Box 2, Folder "DACOWITS, 1976, 1981."

160   *Reminiscences of Rear Admiral Robert W. McNitt*, 600, 612; Secretary of the Navy to Superintendent, 12 Dec. 1975, SR2, Sec. 5800/1, Folder "1975"; Kinnaird McKee to Brigade of Midshipmen, 17 Feb. 1976, SR2, Sec. 5727/3, Folder "1976"; "Women Officer Accessions by Major Source," SR5, Binder 2; "600 Girls Ask Navy About Bid to Academy," WP, 15 Nov. 1975, A16; "Naval Academy Class of 1980 Will Be Fully Integrated," USNIP 102, no. 4 (Apr. 1976): 117.

161   By 1978, all companies had women. Kinnaird McKee to Brigade of Midshipmen, 17 Feb. 1976, SR2, Sec. 5727/3, Folder "1976"; William Holland Jr. to Kenneth Stecklein, 28 Mar. 1976, CR, Folder 5211/2, 1976; John Brown, "Mother Bancroft's Daughters Arrive," LOG 65 (Dec. 1975): 9; Director of Professional Development, "Memorandum for the Record," 30 Sept. 1977, SR5, Box 4; R. O. Worthington to Commandant, 14 June 1978, SR5, Box 4.

162   William Holland Jr. to Kenneth Stecklein, 28 Mar. 1976, CR, Folder 5211/2, 1976; Commandant Memorandum for Superintendent, 30 Oct. 1975, SR5, Box 1, Folder "Admissions of Women, 1975–1976"; "Berthing," undated, SR5, Binder 1.

163   P. E. Treagy Jr., "Memorandum for Director, Professional Development," 5 Apr. 1977, SR5, Box 4; "Organizational/Living Arrangements," SR5, Box 1, Folder "Berthing of Women, 1975–1976, No. 1"; "Berthing," undated, SR5, Binder 1; Fleming, *Annapolis Autumn*, 185.

164   22nd Company Officer to 4th Battalion Officer, 21 Jan. 1977, SR5, Box 4; James Winnefeld, "Memorandum for Distribution," 24 June 1977, SR5, Box 4; Superintendent to Chief of Naval Operations, 27 July 1981, SR5, Box 2, Folder "DACOWITS, 1976, 1981."

165   "Proposed Changes to Conduct Instruction," 2 Dec. 1975, SR5, Box 3, Folder "Policies, Regulations—Admission of Women, 1975–1976"; W. J. Holland, "Report on Issues to Consider for Integration of Women," 18 Jan. 1976, SR5, Box 4.

166   John Brown, "Mother Bancroft's Daughters Arrive," LOG 65 (Dec. 1975): 9; "Preparation for Women at the U.S. Naval Academy: Information and Education Programs," Dec. 1975, SR5, Box 4; J. M. Brown to W. J. Holland, undated, SR5, Box 2, Folder "General Internal Management Correspondence, 1975–1976."

167   K. W. Drew to W. J. Holland, 23 Sec. 1975, SR5, Box 1, Folder "Career Planning/Professional Training Issue"; Jeanette Smyth, "With Coeds, It's All Academic," WP, 29 Nov. 1975, B5.

168   Bert Barnes, "Military Colleges Wooing Women for Class of '80," WP, 22 Dec. 1975, A8.

169 "Women at Annapolis: Addendum to the United States Naval Academy Catalog, 1975–1976," 1975; Robert McNitt to Director, Professional Development, 8 May 1979, SR5, Box 4.

170 Lovell, *Neither Athens Nor Sparta?*, 180–81.

Chapter Six

1 The following discussion of women at NAPS is based on PI with Janice Buxbaum, Springfield, Va., 9 Feb. 2000; PI, Interviewee #109; "Naps First Women In Nimitz," 1976 *Cruise*, 19; R. H. Schmidt to Robert McNitt, 7 Oct. 1975, SR2, Sec. NC1500, Folder "1975"; "Annapolis Prep to Get Women," *WP*, 17 Oct. 1975, A3; "Radio Feed to AFRTS," 16 Nov. 1975, SR2, Sec. 5800/1, Folder "1975"; H. N. Kay to Kinnaird McKee, 25 Nov. 1975, SR2, Sec. 5800/1, Folder "1975"; "Now Hear This: New Wave for Annapolis," NYT, 14 Mar. 1976, Sec. 21, 2.

2 Montel Williams graduated from USNA in1980.

3 M. F. Roberts to Commandant, 14 Jan. 1976, SR5, Box 1, Folder "Admissions of Women, 1975–1976"; Kinnaird McKee to Brigade of Midshipmen, 17 Feb. 1976, SR2, Sec. 5727/3, Folder "1976"; Kinnaird McKee to Faculty and Staff, 17 Feb. 1976, SR5, Box 4.

4 June Krunholz, "Air Force Academy, Going Coed, Ponders Pockets and Calories," *Wall Street Journal*, 18 Feb. 1976, 1, in SR5, Box 2, Folder "Internal Information Releases."

5 Commandant to Superintendent, 26 Apr. 1976, SR5, Box 4.

6 PI with James Winnefeld, Annapolis, Md., 23 Feb. 1999; W. J. Holland, "Report on Issues to Consider for Integration of Women," 18 Jan. 1976, SR5, Box 4; D. K. Forbes to Superintendent, 2 June 1976, SR5, Box 4.

7 D. K. Forbes, "Changes to Midshipmen Regulations, Conduct Instructions, and Aptitude Instructions Required to Accommodate Women Entering the U.S. Naval Academy," 9 Mar. 1976, 2, 5, 6, ARF "Midshipmen: Uniforms."

8 W. J. Holland, "Report on Issues to Consider for Integration of Women," 18 Jan. 1976, SR5, Box 4.

9 Elizabeth Hillman, "Uniform Identities," 17–18.

10 W. J. Holland, "Report on Issues to Consider for Integration of Women," 18 Jan. 1976, SR5, Box 4; "Naval Academy Class of 1980 Will Be Fully Integrated," USNIP 102, no. 4 (Apr. 1976): 117; D. K. Forbes to Commandant, 2 June 1976, SR5, Box 4.

11 Elizabeth Hillman, "Uniform Identities," 17–18.

12 Elizabeth Hillman, "Dressed to Kill? The Paradox of Women in Military Uniforms," in Katzenstein and Reppy, eds., *Beyond Zero Tolerance*, 71.

13 The following discussion of athletic requirements is based on PI, Interviewee #84; W. J. Holland Jr., "Report on Issues to Consider for the Integration of Women," 18 Jan. 1976, SR5, Box 4; Capt. Blanchard, "Memorandum on Physical Education Deviations," 9 Feb. 1976, SR5, Box 1, Folder "Athletics/Physical Education"; Capt. Blanchard, "Plebe Summer Physical Education Test Standards," 9 Feb. 1976, SR5, Box 4; Commandant Instruction 1531.15B, 12 Feb. 1979, SR5, Box 4; Kinnaird

McKee to Brigade of Midshipmen, 17 Feb. 1976, SR2, Sec. 5727/3, Folder "1976"; "Naval Academy Class of 1980 Will Be Fully Integrated," USNIP 102, no. 4 (Apr. 1976): 117; Edward Meade Jr. to Members of the Secretary of the Navy's Advisory Board on Education and Training, 15 June 1976, CR, Folder 5213/1, 1976; "Progress Report on Women, 6 July–17 December 1976," 6, SR5, Box 4; Superintendent to U.S. Defense Attache, Oslo, Norway, 13 Apr. 1979, SR5, Box 4; Robert McNitt to Director, Professional Development, 8 May 1979, SR5, Box 4.

14 Kinnaird McKee, "Naval Academy Policy on Paternity/Maternity (Article 0423), Passed by Chief of Naval Operations," Apr. 1976, SR2, Sec. 5800/1, Folder "1976."

15 D. K. Forbes to Cdr. Drew, undated, SR5, Binder 2.

16 M. F. Roberts to Commandant, 14 Jan. 1976, SR5, Box 1, Folder "Admissions of Women, 1975–1976."

17 Ibid.

18 The following discussion of female officers is based on W. J. Holland to Superintendent, 15 Sept. 1975, SR5, Box 1, Folder "Candidate Guidance, 1975, No. 1"; W. J. Holland, "Report on Issues to Consider for Integration of Women," 18 Jan. 1976, SR5, Box 4; LCdr. Canfield to Capt. Holland, 1 Mar. 1976, SR5, Box 3, Folder "Preparation for Women to Naval Academy, 1975"; D. K. Forbes to Barbara Vittitoe, 20 May 1976, SR5, Box 4; D. K. Forbes to Superintendent, 2 June 1976, SR5, Box 4; Commandant to Superintendent, 8 June 1976, SR5, Binder 1; Kinnaird McKee to John Finneran, 23 Sept. 1976, SR5, Folder "DACOWITS, 1976, 1981"; Kinnaird McKee to Deputy Undersecretary of the Navy, 17 Nov. 1977, in SR2, Sec. NC/1531, Folder "1977."

19 The following discussion of Lt. Susan Stevens is based on LCdr. Daly to Capt. Holland, 9 Dec. 1975, SR5, Box 2, Folder "General Internal Management Correspondence, 1975–1976"; John Brown, "An Interview with LT Susan Stephens [sic] Concerning Women at the Naval Academy," 9 Mar. 1976, SR5, Box 2, Folder "Internal Information Releases"; "An Interview with LT Susan Stevens," LOG 65 (Mar. 1976): 4, 8; Kinnaird McKee to John Finneran, 23 Sept. 1976, SR5, Folder "DACOWITS, 1976, 1981."

20 Robert McNitt to Superintendent, 25 Feb. 1976, SR5, Box 1, Folder "Admission of Women, 1975–1976."

21 "First Seven Women Named to the Naval Academy," NYT, 19 Mar. 1976, 12.

22 PI with Robert McNitt, Annapolis, Md., 7 Apr. 2000; Interview with Pamela Wacek Svendsen, USNIOH, OHFFG, 5; Class of 1980 Profile, ARF "Midshipmen: Class Profiles."

23 Reminiscences of Rear Admiral Robert W. McNitt, 603; Robert McNitt to Director, Professional Development, 8 May 1979, SR5, Box 4; Edward Hidalgo, "Memorandum for Deputy Assistant Secretary of Defense," 23 June 1978, SR2, Sec. 5800/1, Folder "1978"; Holm, Women in the Military, 311.

24 EI with Jean Ebbert, Alexandria, Va., 21 Nov. 1998.

25 Recounted in Interview with Crystal Lewis, USNIOH, OHFFG, 5.

26 The following discussion of women's motivations to attend USNA is based on PI with Elizabeth Sternaman, Annapolis, Md., 21 Dec. 1999; PI, Interviewees #32, 152;

Interview with Sandy Daniels, USNIOH, OHFFG, 3; Interview with Tina-Marie D'Ercole, USNIOH, OHFFG, 1; Interview with Maureen Foley, USNIOH, OHFFG, 1, 2; Interview with Crystal Lewis, USNIOH, OHFFG, 1–2, 23; Interview with Barbette Henry Lowndes, USNIOH, OHFFG, 4; Richard Ustick, "U.S. Naval Academy Experience: Women Midshipmen," 28 June 1978, 7; Superintendent to U.S. Defense Attache, Oslo, Norway, 13 Apr. 1979, SR5, Box 4; Roland Brandquist, "Women at the Academy: Are They Measuring Up?," Shipmate 43, no. 1 (Jan./Feb. 1980): 18; Class of 1980 Profile, ARF "Midshipmen: Class Profiles"; Saundra Saperstein, "Woman at the Top of Naval Academy Class Has That Extra Bit of Determination," WP, 19 May 1984, A10; Disher, First Class, 5, 12, 19, 94, 177–78, 206–7, 236, 304–5, 312.

27 D'Ann Campbell and Francine D'Amico incorrectly contend that it was not until the classes of 1983 and 1984 that women began to attend service academies for a reason other than to be pioneers and "prove something"; see Campbell and D'Amico, "Lessons on Gender Integration from the Military Academies," in D'Amico and Weinstein, eds., Gender Camouflage, 74. On women as pioneers, see Robert Morris, "A Plebe Looks at Women Plebes," Shipmate 39, no. 9 (Nov. 1976): 39; Jean Ebbert, "Women Midshipmen: A Report on the First Six Months," Shipmate 40, no. 2 (Mar. 1977): 18; Edith Seashore to William Ustick, 30 May 1977, SR5, Box 4; William Lawrence, "Superintendent's Report," Shipmate 42, no. 8 (Oct. 1979): 18; Biography of Tina-Marie D'Ercole, 1980 LB, 368.

28 R. E. Tygstad, "Doonesbanana," LOG 65, no. 9 (May 1976).

29 R. E. Tygstad, "Doonesbanana," LOG 65, no. 10 (June 1976).

30 PI with Donald K. Forbes, Manassas, Va., 7 Aug. 1998; PI with Robert McNitt, Annapolis, Md., 7 Apr. 2000.

31 TI with Edith Seashore, Columbia, Md., 19 July 2000.

32 Superintendent's Notice 1110, 17 Dec. 1975, SR5, Box 1, Folder "Admissions of Women, 1975–1976"; "Admission of Women to the U.S. Naval Academy: Public Affairs External Plan," undated, SR5, Binder 1; "Important Notice to Candidates Who Are Authorized to Report to the U.S. Naval Academy for Admission as Midshipmen," July 1976, SR5, Box 4.

33 PI with Robert McNitt, Annapolis, Md., 7 Apr. 2000.

34 The following discussion of the class of 1980's Induction Day is based on PI with James Winnefeld, Annapolis, Md., 23 Feb. 1999; PI with Robert McNitt, Annapolis, Md., 7 Apr. 2000; EI with Sharon Disher, Annapolis, Md., 18 Nov. 2001; PI, Interviewees #3, 9, 10, 23, 31, 40, 47, 49, 109, 110, 158, 180, 182; Interview with Maureen Foley, USNIOH, OHFFG, 5; Interview with Crystal Lewis, USNIOH, OHFFG, 5, 8; Interview with Barbette Henry Lowndes, USNIOH, OHFFG, 71; Disher, First Class, 9–30; Ebbert and Hall, Crossed Currents, 222–23; "Review of Press Coverage, 1976," undated, SR5, Box 2, Folder "DACOWITS"; "Public Affairs Aspects of Women at the U.S. Naval Academy," undated, SR5, Binder 2; "Public Affairs Aspects of Women at the U.S. Naval Academy," undated, SR5, Binder 2; "Progress Report on Women, 18 December 1976–25 January 1978," undated, SR5, Box 4; Jean Ebbert, "Women Midshipmen: A Report on the First Six Months," Shipmate 40, no. 2 (Mar. 1977): 13; Beth Leadbetter, "A Few Inches From the Yard," Shipmate 42, no. 6 (July/Aug. 1979): 36.

35　The following discussion of women's initial experiences is based on PI with Elizabeth Sternaman, Annapolis, Md., 21 Dec. 1999; Interview with Sandy Daniels, USNIOH, OHFFG, 10; PI, Interviewees #31, 47, 88, 110; Interview with Maureen Foley, USNIOH, OHFFG, 4, 6; Interview with Barbette Henry Lowndes, USNIOH, OHFFG, 6–7, 59–60; Commandant to Superintendent, 25 Aug. 1977, SR5, Box 4; Class of 1980 Profile, ARF "Midshipmen: Class Profiles"; Disher, *First Class*, 16, 20, 23–24; Robert Morris, "A Plebe Looks at Women Plebes," *Shipmate* 39, no. 6 (Nov. 1976): 39; Beth Leadbetter, "A Few Inches From the Yard," *Shipmate* 42, no. 6 (July/Aug. 1979): 36; Roland Brandquist, "Women at the Academy: Are They Measuring Up?," *Shipmate* 43, no. 1 (Jan./Feb. 1980): 18.

36　The following discussion of Janie Mines is based on PI, Interviewee #37; Interview with Tina Mare D'Ercole, USNIOH, OHFFG, 50–51; Interview with Barbette Henry Lowndes, USNIOH, OHFFG, 9–10; Janie Mines, "The Jewish Chapel," *Shipmate* 58, no. 1 (Jan./Feb. 1995): 28; Disher, *First Class*, 35; Public Affairs Notice 0036, 16 Feb. 1990, ARF "Graduates: Black Graduates."

37　Janie Mines, "The Jewish Chapel," *Shipmate* 58, no. 1 (Jan./Feb. 1995): 28.

38　Interview with Sandy Daniels, USNIOH, OHFFG, 12; Disher, *First Class*, 20–21.

39　Edward Meade Jr. to Members, Secretary of the Navy's Advisory Board on Education and Training, 15 Jan. 1976, CR, Folder 5213/1, Folder "1976"; William Holland, Hygiene Lecture for Plebe Summer, 16 Feb. 1976, SR5, Box 1, Folder "Awareness Training, 1976–1978"; Interview with Sandy Daniels, USNIOH, OHFFG, 16; Disher, *First Class*, 37–38.

40　Interview with Sandy Daniels, USNIOH, OHFFG, 17. Such fears arose from the mass marketing of tampons, which began in 1936; see Brumberg, *The Body Politic*, 160–65.

41　Jean Ebbert, "Women Midshipmen: A Report on the First Six Months," *Shipmate* 40, no. 2 (Mar. 1977): 15; Disher, *First Class*, 38, 44, 45, 51, 52, 58.

42　PI, Interviewee #109; Photographs of Lt. Susan Stevens demonstrating female midshipmen's uniforms, SR5, Box 3, Folder "Uniforms"; Interview with Crystal Lewis, USNIOH, OHFFG, 16; Interview with Pamela Wacek Svendsen, USNIOH, OHFFG, 13; Disher, *First Class*, 3, 35–37; Sweetman and Cutler, *The U.S. Naval Academy*, 241.

43　22nd Company Officer to 4th Battalion Officer, 21 Jan. 1977, SR5, Box 4; Elizabeth Hillman, "Dressed to Kill? The Paradox of Women in Military Uniforms," in Katzenstein and Reppy, eds., *Beyond Zero Tolerance*, 69, 71–72.

44　"Background for Commandant on Items of Interest for Mrs. Telles," 2 Oct. 1976, SR5, Binder 1; Disher, *First Class*, 66–67; Jean Ebbert, "Women Midshipmen: A Report on the First Six Months," *Shipmate* 40, no. 2 (Mar. 1977): 15.

45　Hillman, "Uniform Identities," 21; "Background for Commandant on Items of Interest for Mrs. Telles," 2 Oct. 1976, SR5, Binder 1.

46　Interview with Crystal Lewis, USNIOH, OHFFG, 51.

47　Hillman, "Uniform Identities," 22.

48　James Winnefeld to Superintendent, 13 Oct. 1976, CR, Folder 5240/4, 1976.

49　Interview with Barbette Henry Lowndes, USNIOH, OHFFG, 48–49.

50　Ibid., 10.

51　The following discussion of the "mutiny" is based on PI with Janice Buxbaum,

Springfield, Va., 9 Feb. 2000; PI, Interviewees #32, 37, 152; Richard Ustick to Commandant, 14 June 1977, SR5, Box 4; Disher, *First Class*, 300; Ebbert and Hall, *Crossed Currents*, 223; Interview with Barbette Henry Lowndes, USNIOH, OHFFG, 11–12; Tina-Marie D'Ercole, *Reflections*, 11.

52 James Winnefeld to Superintendent, 13 Oct. 1976, CR, Sec. 5420/4, Folder "1976"; "Women at Four Service Academies Viewed as Equal to Men," *NYT*, 11 Sept. 1976, 52. Attrition rates for the class of 1980 were 27 percent overall and 32 percent for women; see USNA Admissions Office, "United States Naval Academy History of Incoming Class Composition" 1999, HMG.

53 Joan Lunden, Interview with Melissa Harrington, *Good Morning New York* (television program), 12 June 1980, ARF "Midshipmen: Women Midshipmen Clippings and Releases."

54 Interview with Maureen Foley, USNIOH, OHFFG, 12.

55 PI, Interviewee #37.

56 Interview with Barbette Henry Lowndes, USNIOH, OHFFG, 48–49; Disher, *First Class*, 98, 99, 100, 106, 107, 116, 157, 159, 162, 185, 188, 204; 22nd Company Officer to 4th Battalion Officer, 21 Jan. 1977, SR5, Box 4; Roland Brandquist, "Women at the Academy: Are They Measuring Up?," *Shipmate* 43, no. 1 (Jan./Feb. 1980): 18; Durning, "Women at the Academy: An Attitude Survey," *Armed Forces and Society* 4, no. 4 (Summer 1978): 584.

57 Interview with Crystal Lewis, USNIOH, OHFFG, 10; Director of Professional Development, "Memorandum for the Record," 30 Sept. 1977, SR5, Box 4; Superintendent to U.S. Defense Attache, Oslo, Norway, 13 Apr. 1979, SR5, Box 4.

58 Interview with Pamela Wacek Svendsen, USNIOH, OHFFG, 16.

59 J. M. Brown to Capt. Holland, undated, SR5, Box 2, Folder "General Internal Management Correspondence, 1975–1976"; "Overview: Entry of Women Into the U.S. Naval Academy," SR5, Binder 1.

60 PI, Interviewee #37; 22nd Company Officer to 4th Battalion Officer, 21 Jan. 1977, SR5, Box 4; Roland Brandquist, "Women at the Academy: Are They Measuring Up?," *Shipmate* 43, no. 1 (Jan./Feb. 1980): 18; Durning, "Women at the Academy: An Attitude Survey," *Armed Forces and Society* 4, no. 4 (Summer 1978): 584.

61 PI, Interviewee #37; Interview with Crystal Lewis, USNIOH, OHFFG, 11; Disher, *First Class*, 160; Director of Professional Development to Commandant, 11 Dec. 1978, SR5, Box 4.

62 PI, Interviewee #37; Interview with Tina Marie D'Ercole, USNIOH, OHFFG, 9–11; Interview with Maureen Foley, USNIOH, OHFFG, 7–9; Interview with Barbette Henry Lowndes, USNIOH, OHFFG, 9; Kathy Slevin to William Lawrence, 24 Jan. 1981, SR2, Sec. ON/1531, Folder "1981"; Disher, *First Class*, 160–62, 169, 266, 273–74, 302, 341–42, 345, 353, 355–56; Comic strip, *LOG* 66 (Feb. 1977): 9; Roland Brandquist, "Women at the Academy: Are They Measuring Up?," *Shipmate* 43, no. 1 (Jan./Feb. 1980): 15–18.

63 Carmen Neuberger to Robert McNitt, 10 Nov. 1976, CR, Sec. 5213/1, Folder "1976"; Sherry, *In The Shadow Of War*, 368; Holm, *Women in the Military*, 311.

64 Kinnaird McKee to Deputy Undersecretary of the Navy, 17 Nov. 1977, in SR2, Sec.

NC/1531, Folder "1977," and SR5, Box 4. The twenty-eight women represented 8 percent of the teaching staff. Female officers had been a regular part of USNA's faculty since 1973; see "Acceptance and Training of Women Within the Deputate of Military Instruction," undated, SR5, Box 4.

65 Interview with Tina-Marie D'Ercole, USNIOH, OHFFG, 19; PI, Interviewee #37; Interview with Maureen Foley, USNIOH, OHFFG, 9.

66 Director of Professional Development to Commandant, 11 Dec. 1978, SR5, Box 4; Superintendent to Chief of Naval Operations, 27 July 1981, SR5, Box 2, Folder "DACOWITS, 1976, 1981."

67 Interview with Maureen Foley, USNIOH, OHFFG, 10; Interview with Pamela Wacek Svendsen, USNIOH, OHFFG, 15.

68 PI, Interviewee #32.

69 Interview with Maureen Foley, USNIOH, OHFFG, 10.

70 Disher, First Class, 39, 51, 58, 81, 84, 107, 139, 140, 164, 173, 174, 175, 177, 186, 209–10, 224, 229, 235, 241, 304, 321–23, 324, 345–46; Ebbert and Hall, Crossed Currents, 223.

71 PI, Interviewees #37, 109; Interview with Barbette Henry Lowndes, USNIOH, OHFFG, 35.

72 John Bodnar, "Blacks v. Women: Number of Incoming Plebes, 1960–1999," 1996, HMG; Class Profiles, ARF "Midshipmen: Class Profiles."

73 PI, Interviewee #109.

74 Interview with Pamela Wacek Svendsen, USNIOH, OHFFG, 20–21; Disher, First Class, 177; Director of Professional Development to Commandant, 11 Dec. 1978, SR5, Box 4; Patrick Harrison and Beth Leadbetter, "Comparisons of Men and Women at the U.S. Naval Academy: Outcomes and Processes in their Development," undated, SR5, Box 4; Superintendent to Chief of Naval Operations, 27 July 1981, SR5, Box 2, Folder "DACOWITS, 1976, 1981."

75 Interview with Maureen Foley, USNIOH, OHFFG, 18.

76 TI with Edith Seashore, Columbia, Md., 19 July 2000; Richard Ustick to G. W. Horsley Jr., 6 June 1979, SR5, Box 4.

77 Durning quoted in Julie Gill and Daniel Bozung, "Male Midshipmen Attitudes Toward Women, 1976–1996," paper presented at "Leadership in a Gender Diverse Military: Women at the Nation's Service Academies—The Twenty Year Mark" conference, New London, Conn., 20–23 Mar. 1997, 4.

78 TI with Edith Seashore, Columbia, Md., 19 July 2000; Interview with Maureen Foley, USNIOH, OHFFG, 14; Richard Ustick, "U.S. Naval Academy Experience: Women Midshipmen," 28 June 1978, 18.

79 PI with Janice Buxbaum, Springfield, Va., 9 Feb. 2000; Durning, "Women at the Academy: An Attitude Survey," Armed Forces and Society 4, no. 4 (Summer 1978): 584.

80 Interview with Pamela Wacek Svendsen, USNIOH, OHFFG, 41; Robert Bomboy and James Rowland, "Women at Annapolis: Full Speed Ahead," Waterloo Sunday Courier, 4 Sept. 1977, 5, in SR5, Box 4.

81 Interview with Pamela Wacek Svendsen, USNIOH, OHFFG, 41.

82 PI with Janice Buxbaum, Springfield, Va., 9 Feb. 2000.

83 Interview with Sandy Daniels, USNIOH, OHFFG, 90.

84 Director of Professional Development to Commandant, 11 Dec. 1978, SR5, Box 4; Richard Ustick to G. W. Horsley Jr., 6 June 1979, SR5, Box 4.

85 Interview with Tina-Marie D'Ercole, USNIOH, OHFFG, 15.

86 PI, Interviewee #84.

87 Interview with Tina-Marie D'Ercole, USNIOH, OHFFG, 30; Disher, First Class, 109, 143, 159–60, 171–72, 177; Jean Ebbert, "Women Midshipmen: A Report on the First Six Months," Shipmate, 17; Director of Professional Development, "Memorandum for the Record," 30 Sept. 1977, SR5, Box 4; "Progress Report on Women, 18 December 1976–25 January 1978," undated, SR5, Box 4; Director of Professional Development to Commandant, 11 Dec. 1978, SR5, Box 4; Superintendent to U.S. Defense Attache, Oslo, Norway, 13 Apr. 1979, SR5, Box 4; James Winnefeld to Superintendent, 13 Oct. 1976, CR, Sec. 5420/4, Folder "1976"; Durning, Women at the Naval Academy, quoted in Superintendent to Chief of Naval Operations, 27 July 1981, SR5, Box 2, Folder "DACOWITS, 1976, 1981"; Ebbert and Hall, Crossed Currents, 223.

88 PI with Dave Smalley, Annapolis, Md., 11 Apr. 2000.

89 PI, Interviewee #40; Interview with Crystal Lewis, USNIOH, OHFFG, 12, 26; Interview with Barbette Henry Lowndes, USNIOH, OHFFG, 69.

90 PI, Interviewee #96.

91 Interview with Crystal Lewis, USNIOH, OHFFG, 10.

92 The following discussion of dating is based on PI, Interviewee #20; Interview with Maureen Foley, USNIOH, OHFFG, 18; Interview with Crystal Lewis, USNIOH, OHFFG, 41–47; Interview with Barbette Henry Lowndes, USNIOH, OHFFG, 37, 80; Patrick Harrison and Beth Leadbetter, "Comparisons of Men and Women at the U.S. Naval Academy: Outcomes and Processes in their Development," undated, SR5, Box 4.

93 W. J. Holland Jr., "Report on Issues to Consider for the Integration of Women," 18 Jan. 1976, SR5, Box 4.

94 Ibid.

95 James Winnefeld to Superintendent, 18 Apr. 1977, SR5, Box 4; Interview with Barbette Henry Lowndes, USNIOH, OHFFG, 38.

96 J. R. Donovan to R. L. Hazard, 6 Aug. 1979, SR5, Box 2, Folder "Annual Awareness Counseling Briefings, 1978–1979"; Superintendent to U.S. Defense Attache, Oslo, Norway, 13 Apr. 1979, SR5, Box 4; Richard Ustick, "U.S. Naval Academy Experience: Women Midshipmen," 28 June 1978, 7, 18.

97 Enloe, Does Khaki Become You?, 4–5; Enloe, Maneuvers, 34.

98 Director of Professional Development to Commandant, 11 Dec. 1978, SR5, Box 4; Patrick Harrison and Beth Leadbetter, "Comparisons of Men and Women at the U.S. Naval Academy: Outcomes and Processes in their Development," undated, SR5, Box 4; James Webb, "Women Can't Fight," Washingtonian, Nov. 1979, 275; Timberg, The Nightingale's Song, 260.

99 PI, Interviewees #20, 37, 40.

100   Interview with William P. Lawrence, USNIOH, 1004–6; Interview with Crystal Lewis, USNIOH, OHFFG, 24; Disher, *First Class*, 273–75, 278; Timberg, *The Nightingale's Song*, 260.

101   PI, Interviewees #20, 37, 40; Disher, *First Class*, 305–6; Timberg, *The Nightingale's Song*, 260.

102   Paul Roush, "A Tangled Webb the Navy Can't Afford," in Katzenstein and Reppy, eds., *Beyond Zero Tolerance*, 87–88; Disher, *First Class*, 217–19, 305–6, 318–20.

103   Interview with William P. Lawrence, USNIOH, 923–27; "Naval Academy Dismisses Charge of Rape," NYT, 24 Dec. 1978, 12; Gene Bisbee, "Academy Drops Rape Charges Against Middie," EC, 26 Dec. 1978, 1.

104   Director of Professional Development to Commandant, 20 July 1979, SR5, Box 2, Folder "Annual Awareness Counseling Briefings, 1978–1979."

105   The following discussion of women as cheerleaders is based on PI with James Winnefeld, Annapolis, Md., 23 Feb. 1999; PI, Interviewee #37; Donald Forbes to Superintendent, 2 June 1976, SR5, Box 4; Disher, *First Class*, 70, 104–5, 108, 131, 165.

106   The following discussion of women's determination is based on Interview with Sandy Daniels, USNIOH, OHFFG, 18; Interview with Crystal Lewis, USNIOH, OHFFG, 25, 78; Interview with Pamela Wacek Svendsen, USNIOH, OHFFG, 6.

107   Interview with Tina-Marie D'Ercole, USNIOH, OHFFG, 14.

108   The following discussion of the class of 1980 Herndon Ceremony is based on Interview with Barbette Henry Lowndes, USNIOH, OHFFG, 23–24; Angus Phillips, " 'Hat Trick' Caps Long Year at Academy," WP, 31 May 1983, B3; Tina-Marie D'Ercole, *Reflections*, 9; Disher, *First Class*, 187–89, 191–94.

109   Interview with Maureen Foley, USNIOH, OHFFG, 37.

110   James Winnefeld, quoted in Jean Ebbert, "Women Midshipmen: A Report on the First Six Months," USNIP 40, no. 7, 18.

111   The following discussion of the class of 1980 YP Cruise is based on Interview with Maureen Foley, USNIOH, OHFFG, 22–24; Interview with Crystal Lewis, USNIOH, OHFFG, 27; Interview with Barbette Henry Lowndes, USNIOH, OHFFG, 42–43; Interview with Pamela Wacek Svendsen, USNIOH, OHFFG, 27; Superintendent to Chief of Naval Operations, 22 Dec. 1976, SR5, Box 4; 22nd Company Officer to 4th Battalion Officer, 21 Jan. 1977, SR5, Box 4; Deputy Director of Naval Education and Training to Deputy Chief of Naval Operations for Manpower, 25 Feb. 1977, SR5, Box 3, Folder "Summer Training, 1975–1976"; Director, Professional Development to Superintendent, 10 Mar. 1977, SR5, Box 4; Director of Professional Development, "Memorandum for the Record," 30 Sept. 1977, SR5, Box 4; Deputy Assistant Chief for Personnel Planning and Programming, "Memorandum for Distribution," 7 Nov. 1977, SR2, Sec. NC/1531, Folder "1977"; "Unclassified Announcements," Dec. 1977, SR5, Box 4; W. R. Drukker to Director of Professional Development, 26 Apr. 1978, SR5, Box 4; Superintendent to U.S. Defense Attache, Oslo, Norway, 13 Apr. 1979, SR5, Box 4; Superintendent to Chief of Naval Operations, 27 July 1981, SR5, Box 2, Folder "DACOWITS, 1976, 1981"; Disher, *First Class*, 181, 201–9, 238; Ebbert and Hall, *Crossed Currents*, 223.

112   Interview with Maureen Foley, USNIOH, OHFFG, 23.

113 Ibid., 19; Interview with Barbette Henry Lowndes, USNIOH, OHFFG, 24.

114 Interview with Sandy Daniels, USNIOH, OHFFG, 29; PI, Interviewees #7, 18, 22, 23, 33, 34, 35, 36, 40, 41, 77, 79, 83, 85, 110, 141, 166, 171, 192.

115 The previous two quotes are from Interview with Pamela Wacek Svendsen, USNIOH, OHFFG, 6.

116 The following discussion of the cheerleaders' experiences is based on CI, Interviewee #28; PI, Interviewee #37; Disher, First Class, 219–24, 304.

117 The following discussion of the relations between women in the classes of 1980 and 1981 is based on TI with Edith Seashore, Columbia, Md., 19 July 2000; PI, Interviewees #37, 109; Interview with Sandy Daniels, USNIOH, OHFFG, 94; Interview with Maureen Foley, USNIOH, OHFFG, 39; Interview with Barbette Henry Lowndes, USNIOH, OHFFG, 25–26, 36–37; Interview with Pamela Wacek Svendsen, USNIOH, OHFFG, 36–37; J. C. Knapp, "Memorandum for the Record," 2 Nov. 1976, SR5, Box 2, Folder "DACOWITS, 1976–1981"; Edith Seashore to Richard Ustick, 30 May 1977, SR5, Box 4; Robert Bomboy and James Rowland, "Women at Annapolis: Full Speed Ahead," Waterloo Sunday Courier, 4 Sept. 1977, 5, in SR5, Box 4; Richard Ustick, "Current Assessment of the Assimilation of Women Into the Brigade of Midshipmen," 29 Mar. 1979, SR5, Box 4; Class of 1981 Profile, ARF "Midshipmen Class Profiles"; "Attitude Survey for the Class of 1981," undated, SR5, Box 4; Disher, First Class, 213.

118 Interview with Maureen Foley, USNIOH, OHFFG, 39.

119 The following discussion of men's actions against women is based on PI, Interviewee #152; Interview with Barbette Henry Lowndes, USNIOH, OHFFG, 25–26, 30–33; Interview with William P. Lawrence, USNIOH, 942, 947; Director of Professional Development to Commandant, 11 Dec. 1978, SR5, Box 4; "Salty Sam," LOG 69 (Oct. 1979): 16; "Salty Sam," LOG 69 (May 1980): 34; Chip Brown, "Making Merry in Annapolis," WP, 25 May 1980, C1; Patrick Harrison and Beth Leadbetter, "Comparisons of Men and Women at the U.S. Naval Academy: Outcomes and Processes in their Development," undated, SR5, Box 4; D'Ercole, Reflections, 6–7; Disher, First Class, 177–78, 187, 222, 243, 270–71, 275–76, 303; Ebbert and Hall, Crossed Currents, 223.

120 Interview with Maureen Foley, USNIOH, OHFFG, 6; Interview with Pamela Wacek Svendsen, USNIOH, OHFFG, 8.

121 Kathy Slevin to William Lawrence, 24 Jan. 1981, SR2, Sec. ON/1531, Folder "1981"; D'Ercole, Reflections, 7, 10; Interview with William P. Lawrence, USNIOH, 942, 947; Disher, First Class, 234, 303; Interview with Barbette Henry Lowndes, USNIOH, OHFFG, 26–28.

122 Sam Tangredi, "Class History," 1978 LB, vol. 1, 19; "Salty Sam," LOG 66 (Oct. 1976): 6; "Salty Sam," LOG 66 (Nov. 1976): 9; "Salty Sam," LOG 69 (Feb. 1977): 6; Russ Penniman, "Interview With John Wayne," LOG 66 (Feb. 1977): 11; "Salty Sam," LOG 66 (Mar. 1977): 7; "Law of the Month, Derived from the First Law of Thermodynamics," LOG 66 (Mar. 1977): 9; "Salty Sam," LOG 69 (Mar. 1980): 28–29; Time magazine cover spoof, LOG 69 (Apr. 1980): 13; Disher, First Class, 180.

123 PI, Interviewee #32, 125; EI, Interviewee #129; Disher, First Class, 181; Lovell, Neither Athens Nor Sparta?, 180.

124 Interview with Barbette Henry Lowndes, USNIOH, OHFFG, 99; J. C. Knapp, "Memorandum for the Record," 2 Nov. 1976, SR5, Box 2, Folder "DACOWITS, 1976–1981"; "Salty Sam," *LOG* 66 (Nov. 1976): 9; Wendy Lawrence to Company Officers, 24 Nov. 1980, SR5, Box 4; Kathy Slevin to William Lawrence, 24 Jan. 1981, SR2, Sec. ON/1531, Folder "1981"; Disher, *First Class*, 306, 346; Felicity Barringer, "Four Inquiries Cite Naval Academy for Rife Sexism," NYT, 10 Oct. 1990, 12; Fleming, *Annapolis Autumn*, 105–6.

125 The following discussion of women's weight issues is based on 22nd Company Officer to 4th Battalion Officer, 21 Jan. 1977, SR5, Box 4; "Salty Sam," *LOG* 66 (Mar. 1977): 7; Edith Seashore, "Talking Paper: Women Midshipmen Interviews," Mar. 1977, SR5, Box 4; Richard Ustick, "U.S. Naval Academy Experience: Women Midshipmen," 28 June 1978, 18; "King Hall Questions and Answers," undated, ARF "Midshipmen: Food Preparation"; Patrick Harrison and Beth Leadbetter, "Comparisons of Men and Women at the U.S. Naval Academy: Outcomes and Processes in their Development," undated, SR5, Box 4; "King Hall Questions and Answers," undated, ARF "Midshipmen: Food Preparation"; D'Ercole, *Reflections*, 9–10; Disher, *First Class*, 17, 36–38, 60, 92, 124, 149, 159–60, 164, 180–81, 234–35, 267, 271, 275, 277, 307, 337, 343.

126 J. C. Knapp, "Memorandum for the Record," 2 Nov. 1976, SR5, Box 2, Folder "DACOWITS, 1976–1981"; Edith Seashore to Richard Ustick, 30 May 1977, SR5, Box 4.

127 EI with Cheryl Spohnholtz, Alexandria, Va., 21 July 2000; D'Ercole, *Reflections*, 10.

128 The previous two quotes from Interview with Pamela Wacek Svendsen, USNIOH, OHFFG, 25–26.

129 TI with Edith Seashore, Columbia, Md., 19 July 2000; J. C. Knapp, "Memorandum for the Record," 2 Nov. 1976, SR5, Box 2, Folder "DACOWITS, 1976–1981"; 22nd Company Officer to 4th Battalion Officer, 21 Jan. 1977, SR5, Box 4.

130 Interview with Maureen Foley, USNIOH, OHFFG, 11; Interview with Tina-Marie D'Ercole, USNIOH, OHFFG, 27–28.

131 Ebbert and Hall, *Crossed Currents*, 223.

132 The following discussion of female officers is based on PI with James Winnefeld, Annapolis, Md., 23 Feb. 1999; PI, Interviewee #109; Interview with Sandy Daniels, USNIOH, OHFFG, 30–37; Interview with Crystal Lewis, USNIOH, OHFFG, 16; Interview with Barbette Henry Lowndes, USNIOH, OHFFG, 56–57; Interview with Pamela Wacek Svendsen, USNIOH, OHFFG, 13; Kinnaird McKee to Deputy Undersecretary of the Navy, 17 Nov. 1977, in SR2, Sec. NC/1531, Folder "1977"; Director of Professional Development to Commandant, 11 Dec. 1978, SR5, Box 4; Disher, *First Class*, 24–38.

133 The following discussion of male officers is based on PI with James Winnefeld, Annapolis, Md., 23 Feb. 1999; PI, Interviewee #37; Interview with Barbette Henry Lowndes, USNIOH, OHFFG, 27–29; Edith Seashore to Richard Ustick, 30 May 1977, SR5, Box 4; Director of Professional Development to Commandant, 11 Dec. 1978, SR5, Box 4.

134 W. J. Holland Jr., "Report on Issues to Consider for the Integration of Women," 18 Jan. 1976, SR5, Box 4; Disher, *First Class*, 169–71.

135 The following discussion of Lawrence's actions is based on TI with Edith Seashore, Columbia, Md., 19 July 2000; PI, Interviewees #37, 109; Interview with Maureen Foley, USNIOH, OHFFG, 18; Interview with William P. Lawrence, USNIOH, 942–43, 978–79, 1243; Superintendent to U.S. Defense Attache, Oslo, Norway, 13 Apr. 1979, SR5, Box 4; Richard Ustick to Women of 1980, 1981, and 1982, 27 Apr. 1979, SR5, Box 4; Superintendent to Chief of Naval Operations, 27 July 1981, SR5, Box 2, Folder "DACOWITS, 1976, 1981"; Disher, *First Class*, 39, 51, 58, 81, 84, 107, 139, 140, 164, 173, 174, 175, 177, 186, 209–10, 224, 229, 235, 241, 304, 321–23, 324, 345–46.

136 The following discussion of Lawrence's attitudes on women's sports is based on Interview with William P. Lawrence, USNIOH, 1031–35; Carmen Neuberger to Robert McNitt, 10 Nov. 1976, CR, Sec. 5213/1, Folder "1976"; Richard Ustick to Commandant, 14 June 1977, SR5, Box 4; Superintendent to U.S. Defense Attache, Oslo, Norway, 13 Apr. 1979, SR5, Box 4; Kathy Slevin to William Lawrence, 24 Jan. 1981, SR2, Sec. ON/1531, Folder "1981"; "Vice Admiral William P. Lawrence Sword for Personal Excellence in Women's Athletics," plaque, Lejeune Hall, USNA, Annapolis, Md.; Jean Ebbert, "Women Midshipmen: A Report on the First Six Months," *Shipmate* 40, no. 7 (Mar. 1977): 17; Patrick Harrison and Beth Leadbetter, "Comparisons of Men and Women at the U.S. Naval Academy: Outcomes and Processes in their Development," undated, SR5, Box 4.

137 Interview with William P. Lawrence, USNIOH, 1032.

138 William Lawrence to Frank Wigelius, undated, SR2, Sec. 12770/1, Folder "1980."

139 The following discussion of women's rooms and roommates is based on PI with James Winnefeld, Annapolis, Md., 23 Feb. 1999; TI with Edith Seashore, Columbia, Md., 19 July 2000; Interview with Barbette Henry Lowndes, USNIOH, OHFFG, 54; Richard Ustick to Commandant, 3 Sept. 1976, SR5, Box 1, Folder "Berthing of Women, 1975–1976, No. 2"; J. C. Knapp, "Memorandum for the Record," 2 Nov. 1976, SR5, Box 2, Folder "DACOWITS, 1976–1981"; 2/C Brigade Commander to 1/C Brigade Commander, 6 Dec. 1976, SR5, Box 1, Folder "Berthing of Women, 1975–1976, No. 2"; 22nd Company Officer to 4th Battalion Officer, 21 Jan. 1977, SR5, Box 4; Director of Professional Development, "Memorandum for the Record," 30 Sept. 1977, SR5, Box 4; Robert McNitt to Commandant, 20 Nov. 1977, SR5, Box 4; Patrick Harrison to Director of Professional Development, 10 Feb. 1978, SR5, Box 4; Director of Professional Development to Commandant, 6 June 1978, in SR5, Box 2, Folder "Annual Awareness Counseling Briefings, 1978–1979," and SR5, Box 4; Director of Professional Development to Commandant, 11 Dec. 1978, SR5, Box 4; "Progress Report on Women, 18 December 1976–25 January 1978," undated, SR5, Box 4; Staff JAG to Major Stankosky, 17 May 1978, SR5, Box 4; Patrick Harrison and Beth Leadbetter, "Comparisons of Men and Women at the U.S. Naval Academy: Outcomes and Processes in their Development," undated, SR5, Box 4; Jean Ebbert, "Women Midshipmen: A Report on the First Six Months," *Shipmate* 40, no. 7 (Mar. 1977): 13.

140 The following discussion of women's relationships with other women is based on
PI, Interviewees #32, 109; Interview with Sandy Daniels, USNIOH, OHFFG, 7; In-
terview with Maureen Foley, USNIOH, OHFFG, 50; Interview with Crystal Lewis,
USNIOH, OHFFG, 52–53; Interview with Barbette Henry Lowndes, USNIOH,
OHFFG, 11–12, 36; Interview with Pamela Wacek Svendsen, USNIOH, OHFFG, 22;
"Progress Report on Women, 18 December 1976–25 January 1978," undated, SR5,
Box 4; Patrick Harrison and Beth Leadbetter, "Comparisons of Men and Women at
the U.S. Naval Academy: Outcomes and Processes in their Development," undated,
SR5, Box 4; D'Ercole, *Reflections*, 10–11.

141 The following discussion of summer training is based on Kinnaird McKee to Deputy
Undersecretary of the Navy, 17 Nov. 1977, in SR2, Sec. NC/1531, Folder "1977," and
SR5, Box 4; W. R. Drukker, "Analysis of Legal Implications of Assigning Female
Naval and/or Non-Navy U.S. Military Officers as OICs of U.S. Naval Academy Yard
Patrol (YP) Vessels for LANTPATRAMID and NS 300 Training," 28 May 1978, SR5,
Box 4; J. D. Stewart to Richard Ustick, 29 Sept. 1978, SR5, Box 4; Richard Ustick to
Commandant, 2 Oct. 1978, SR5, Box 4; James Poole to William Lawrence, 28 Oct.
1979, SR5, Box 4; Richard Ustick to Commandant, 18 Dec. 1978, SR5, Box 4; Chief
of Naval Operations, "Memorandum for U.S. Naval Academy," Dec. 1978, SR5, Box
4; Richard Ustick to Commandant, 13 Mar. 1979, SR5, Box 3, Folder "Summer
Training, 1975–1976"; William Lawrence to Lando Zech Jr., 4 June 1979, SR5, Box 4;
Richard Ustick to Superintendent, 11 July 1979, SR5, Box 4; J. R. Lund to N. F.
Gustin, 19 Sept. 1979, SR5, Box 4; Patricia Garrison to F. R. Donovan, 10 Dec. 1979,
SR5, Box 4; J. R. Hogg, "Memorandum," 4 Jan. 1980, SR5, Box 4; Susan Canfield to
Editor, *Navy Times*, 7 Apr. 1977, SR5, Box 4; William Lawrence, "Superintendent's
Report," *Shipmate* 42, no. 8 (Oct. 1979): 18.

142 D'Ercole, *Reflections*, 9.

143 Beth Leadbetter, "A Few Inches From the Yard," *Shipmate* 42, no. 6 (July/Aug. 1979):
36–37.

144 The following discussion of the class of 1980's Ring Dance is based on PI, Interviewee #109; Interview with Crystal Lewis, USNIOH, OHFFG, 46, 66–67; Interview
with Barbette Henry Lowndes, USNIOH, OHFFG, 20–22, 39, 76; Director of Professional Development to Commandant, 11 Dec. 1978, SR5, Box 4; "Women Midshipmen Update," Mar. 1979, SR5, Box 4; Kathy Slevin to William Lawrence, 24 Jan.
1981, SR2, Sec. ON/1531, Folder "1981"; Superintendent to Chief of Naval Operations, 27 July 1981, SR5, Box 2, Folder "DACOWITS, 1976, 1981"; Disher, *First Class*,
62–63, 73, 116, 130, 153, 236–37, 343; Robert Morris, "A Plebe Looks at Women
Plebes," *Shipmate* 39 (Nov. 1976): 39; Roland Brandquist, "Women at the Academy:
Are They Measuring Up?," *Shipmate* 43, no. 1 (Jan./Feb. 1980): 18.

145 The following discussion of the class of 1979 is based on PI with James Winnefeld,
Annapolis, Md., 23 Feb. 1999; PI, Interviewees #40, 152; Interview with William P.
Lawrence, USNIOH, 948–49; Grant Thornton to Commandant, 15 May 1978, CR,
Folder 5600/4; Lucky Bag Officer Representative to Commandant, 19 May 1978, CR,
Folder 5600/4; Patrick Harrison and Beth Leadbetter, "Comparisons of Men and

Women at the U.S. Naval Academy: Outcomes and Processes in their Development," undated, SR5, Box 4; U.S. Naval Academy Alumni Association, "U.S. Naval Academy: Classes and Crests, 1846–1981," ARF "Midshipmen: Class Crests"; 1979 LB, 54; Jean Ebbert, "Women Midshipmen: A Report on the First Six Months," *Shipmate* 40, no. 2 (Mar. 1977): 16; Disher, *First Class*, 205; Ebbert and Hall, *Crossed Currents*, 221; Holm, *Women in the Military*, 311; Timberg, *The Nightingale's Song*, 259–60.

146 Interview with William P. Lawrence, USNIOH, 949. This statement is likely a reflection of the senior experiences of the class of 1952, which will be described in Chapter Eight.

147 Grant Thornton, "Editor's Statement," 1979 LB, 1–9, 26, 621.

148 The following discussion of the Hayward's Forrestal Lecture is based on EI with Cheryl Spohnholtz, Alexandria, Va., 31 July 2000; EI, Interviewee #120; Thomas Hayward, "Forrestal Lecture," 29 Oct. 1979, Archives, USNA, Annapolis, Md.; Forrestal Lecture programs, ARF "Distinguished Lecture Series: Forrestal Lecture"; W. J. Holland Jr., "Report on Issues to Consider for the Integration of Women," 18 Jan. 1976, SR5, Box 4; "110X Woman Career Development," Sept. 1978, SR5, Box 4; Director of Professional Development to Commandant, 11 Dec. 1978, SR5, Box 4; "Career Planning for Women Officers," undated, SR5, Box 1, Folder "Career Planning/Professional Training Issue"; "Letter from Peggy's Mom," USNAW (<http://www.usna.edu/JBHO/sea_stories/letter_from_peggy's_mom.htm>, 9 Jan. 2001).

149 The following discussion of Webb is based on Interview with Maureen Foley, USNIOH, OHFFG, 33; Interview with Crystal Lewis, USNIOH, OHFFG, 57; Interview with William P. Lawrence, USNIOH, 950–51; Paul Roush, "A Tangled Webb the Navy Can't Afford," in Katzenstein and Reppy, eds., *Beyond Zero Tolerance*, 82–99; Timberg, *The Nightingales' Song*, 258–62.

150 The following discussion of "Women Can't Fight" is based on James Webb, "Women Can't Fight," *Washingtonian*, Nov. 1979, 144–48, 273, 275–78, 282; Edward Meade Jr. to Members of the Secretary of the Navy's Advisory Board on Education and Training, 15 June 1976, CR, Sec. 5213/1, Folder "1976"; Paul Roush, "A Tangled Webb the Navy Can't Afford," in Katzenstein and Reppy, eds., *Beyond Zero Tolerance*, 82–84, 89–91; Timberg, *The Nightingale's Song*, 259–61.

151 The following discussion of reactions to "Women Can't Fight" is based on PI, Interviewees #2, 37; Interview with Sandy Daniels, USNIOH, OHFFG, 68–70; Interview with Tina-Marie D'Ercole, USNIOH, OHFFG, 20–21; Interview with Maureen Foley, USNIOH, OHFFG, 32–33; Interview with Crystal Lewis, USNIOH, OHFFG, 57; Interview with Barbette Henry Lowndes, USNIOH, OHFFG, 90; Interview with Pamela Wacek Svendsen, USNIOH, OHFFG, 18; Kathy Slevin to William Lawrence, 24 Jan. 1981, SR2, Sec. ON/1531, Folder "1981"; D'Ercole, *Reflections*, 17; Disher, *First Class*, 307–10, 320, 324–26, 331, 338; Paul Roush, "A Tangled Webb the Navy Can't Afford," in Katzenstein and Reppy, eds., *Beyond Zero Tolerance*, 88.

152 I am grateful to Catherine Clinton for raising this point.

153 The following discussion of Lawrence's response to "Women Can't Fight" is based

on Interview with William P. Lawrence, USNIOH, 951–53; Interview with Maureen Foley, USNIOH, OHFFG, 16–17, 42; Interview with Barbette Henry Lowndes, USNIOH, OHFFG, 26–27; William Lawrence to John Limpert, 16 Nov. 1979, SR5, Box 4; Timberg, *The Nightingale's Song*, 262.

154 The following discussion of women's leadership is based on Interview with Barbette Henry Lowndes, USNIOH, OHFFG, 25–26; *Reminiscences of Vice Admiral Charles S. Minter Jr.*, 443; Richard Ustick, "Current Assessment of the Assimilation of Women Into the Brigade of Midshipmen," 29 Mar. 1979, SR5, Box 4; Superintendent to U.S. Defense Attache, Oslo, Norway, 13 Apr. 1979, SR5, Box 4; J. R. Donovan to R. L. Hazard, 6 Aug. 1979, SR5, Box 2, Folder "Annual Awareness Counseling Briefings, 1978–1979"; Mary Ellen Hanley to Elizabeth Belzer, 2 Oct. 1979, CR, Sec. 5420/4, Folder "1979"; Ebbert and Hall, *Crossed Currents*, 224–25; Superintendent to Chief of Naval Operations, 27 July 1981, SR5, Box 2, Folder "DACOWITS, 1976, 1981"; Patrick Harrison and Beth Leadbetter, "Comparisons of Men and Women at the U.S. Naval Academy: Outcomes and Processes in their Development," undated, SR5, Box 4; "Leadership Performance of Women at the U.S. Naval Academy," undated, SR5, Box 1, Folder "Awareness Training, 1976–1978"; William Lawrence, "Superintendent's Report," *Shipmate* 42, no. 8 (Oct. 1979): 18. See also Roland Brandquist, "Women at the Academy: Are They Measuring Up?," *Shipmate* 43, no. 1 (Jan./Feb. 1980): 17; Ebbert and Hall, *Crossed Currents*, 224–25.

155 The following discussion of pre-graduation media reports is based on *Reminiscences of Vice Admiral William R. Smedberg III*, 559–60; E. B. Smedberg to Superintendent, 21 June 1978, SR5, Box 4; Superintendent to U.S. Defense Attache, Oslo, Norway, 13 Apr. 1979, SR5, Box 4; Patrick Harrison and Beth Leadbetter, "Comparisons of Men and Women at the U.S. Naval Academy: Outcomes and Processes in their Development," undated, SR5, Box 4; William Lawrence, "Superintendent's Report," *Shipmate* 42, no. 8 (Oct. 1979): 18; James Ferron, "First Battle Over, Women Leave Academies for Careers in Military," NYT, 25 May 1980, 1, 42; "Pioneers," EC, 27 May 1980, 1, 16; Chip Brown, "Women Midshipmen Begin New Era," WP, 29 May 1980, A28; Paul Roush, "A Tangled Webb the Navy Can't Afford," in Katzenstein and Reppy, eds., *Beyond Zero Tolerance*, 86.

156 The following discussion of the 1980 graduation is based on PI with Interviewees #20, 32, 100, 125; Interview with Crystal Lewis, USNIOH, OHFFG, 71; Interview with Pamela Wacek Svendsen, USNIOH, OHFFG, 19–20; Superintendent to BUPERS, 31 Mar. 1996, SR3, 1996, Box 1531, Folder 1531; Photograph of Midshipmen in Reflecting Pool, EC, 28 May 1980, 12; Gene Bisbee, "Navy Graduates First Women," EC, 28 May 1980, 12; "Seniors for Only One More Day," NYT, 28 May 1980, 1; Chip Brown, "Women Midshipmen Begin New Era," WP, 29 May 1980, A28; James Ferron, "Service Academies Hail First Female Graduates," NYT, 29 May 1980, 18; Gene Bisbee, "Navy Graduates First Women," EC, 28 May 1980, 12; Durning, "Women at the Naval Academy," 585; Disher, *First Class*, 346–58; Timberg, *The Nightingale's Song*, 260.

157 Chip Brown, "Women Midshipmen Begin New Era," WP, 29 May 1980, A28.

Chapter Seven

1   William Lawrence to Kathy Slevin, 1981, SR2, Sec. ON/1531, Folder "1981."

2   Superintendent to U.S. Defense Attache, Oslo, Norway, 13 Apr. 1979, SR5, Box 4; Richard Ustick to G. W. Horsley Jr., 15 June 1979, SR5, Box 4; Holm, *Women in the Military*, 311.

3   Richard Ustick to G. W. Horsley Jr., 15 June 1979, SR5, Box 4.

4   Beth Leadbetter, "A Few Inches From the Yard," *Shipmate* 42, no. 6 (July/Aug. 1979): 36–37.

5   The previous two quotes are from Wendy Lawrence to Company Officers, 24 Nov. 1980, SR5, Box 4.

6   F. R. Donovan to Commandant, 25 Sept. 1980, SR5, Box 4.

7   PI with Leon Edney, Annapolis, Md., 16 May 1999.

8   "Expulsion From Annapolis In Sex Case Upheld," NYT, 31 Jan. 1981, 8.

9   Kimberly Bibik to John Lenehan, 19 Aug. 1981, CR, Sec. 5600/2, Folder "1981"; Gerald Lahr to Kimberly Bibik, 25 Aug. 1981, CR, Sec. 5600/2, Folder "1981"; Superintendent to Kimberly Bibik, 3 Sept. 1981, CR, Sec. 5600/2, Folder "1981."

10 Commandant to Superintendent, 27 Apr. 1981, CR, Sec. 5400/5, Folder "1981."

11 Interview with William P. Lawrence, USNIOH, 942.

12 Guenter-Schlesinger, "Persistence of Sexual Harassment," in Katzenstein and Reppy, eds., *Beyond Zero Tolerance*, 206.

13 The following discussion of Leon Edney's steps is based upon PI with Leon Edney, Annapolis, Md., 27 May 1999; Director of Professional Development to Commandant, 11 Dec. 1978, SR5, Box 4; Leon Edney to Kaye Quinn, 14 Jan. 1982, CR, Sec. 1531/1, Folder "1982"; Commandant to Secretary of the Board of Visitors, 21 July 1982, CR, Sec. 5420/4, Folder "1982."

14 Charles Larson to James Webb, 8 Feb. 1984, SR2, Sec. 5721, Folder "1984"; Interview with Maureen Foley, USNIOH, OHFFG, 48.

15 "Navy Board to Review Dismissal of Woman," NYT, 13 Apr. 1984, 36; "Midshipman Excused from Tower Jump," NYT, 14 Apr. 1984, 12.

16 Kaye Thompson, "First Pregnant Middie Leaves the Academy; May Reapply Later," WP, 25 Apr. 1984, B1.

17 The following discussion of Kristin Holdereid is based on "Woman Tops the Class at the Naval Academy," NYT, 17 May 1984, 20; Sandra Saperstein, "Woman at Top of Naval Academy Class Has That Extra Bit of Determination," WP, 19 May 1984, A10; Arthur Brisbane, "Naval Academy's Harsh Attraction," WP, 19 May 1984, A1; Photograph of Kristin Holdereid, NYT, 24 May 1984, 1; James Cheevers, "U.S. Naval Academy: Modern Era, Part IV," *Shipmate* 58, no. 5, 38; Ebbert and Hall, *Crossed Currents*, 225.

18 "Interview with Commandant Leslie Palmer: 20 Questions," *LOG* 73 (Mar. 1984): 48.

19 Charles Larson, "Goals for Academic Year 1984–1985," CR, Sec. 5400/4, Folder "1984."

20 Leslie Palmer to Pat Crigler, 12 Oct. 1984, CR, Sec. 5400/4, Folder "1984."

21 Robert McNitt to Commandant, 6 Mar. 1985, SR3, 1985, Box 1530–1710/34, Folder "1531/1."

22 Commandant to Superintendent, 15 Mar. 1985, SR3, 1985, Box 1530–1710/34, Folder "1531/1."

23 The previous two quotes are from Stephen Chadwick, "The Commandant Speaks," *Shipmate* 48, no. 10 (Dec. 1985): 16.

24 Centerfold photograph, *LOG* 76, no. 6 (Feb. 1987): 28–29; "Salty Sam," *LOG* 76, no. 3, 9.

25 Mary Evert to Ronald Marryott, 9 Mar. 1987, SR3, 1987, Box 1531/1–1710/2, Folder "1710."

26 Superintendent to Mary Evert, 1 Apr. 1987, SR3, 1987, Box 1531/1–1710/2, Folder "1710."

27 Effie Coffman, "Navy Nominee Defends Views on Mids-Pros," *EC*, 1, 7.

28 John Cushman Jr., "Navy Nominee Has Reservations on Role of Women at Academy," *NYT*, 7 Apr. 1987, 33.

29 "Senate OK's Webb for Navy Post," *EC*, 7 Apr. 1987, 1.

30 Interview with Sandy Daniels, USNIOH, OHFFG, 68–70; Interview with Tina-Marie D'Ercole, USNIOH, OHFFG, 38.

31 Timberg, *The Nightingale's Song*, 398.

32 Women Midshipmen Study Group, "The Integration of Women in the Brigade of Midshipmen," Nov. 1987, i, SR5, Box 4; Women Midshipmen Study Group Subcommittee, USNA Board of Visitors, "The Assimilation of Women in the Brigade of Midshipmen," Apr. 1991, 2, SR5, Binder 7; Ebbert and Hall, *Crossed Currents*, 224.

33 "Integration of Women in the Brigade: Interview with Rear Admiral R. F. Marryott, Superintendent," *Shipmate* 51, no. 5 (June 1988): 15.

34 The following discussion of the 1987 WMSG report is based on Women Midshipmen Study Group, "The Integration of Women in the Brigade of Midshipmen," Nov. 1987, ii–iv, viii, 69–78, 85, 88–89, 95–96, SR5, Box 4.

35 Dowling, *The Frailty Myth*, 82–83.

36 Women Midshipmen Study Group, "Report to the Superintendent on the Integration of Women in the Brigade of Midshipmen," 1 July 1990, 64–78, SR5, Binder 5; "Navy Advised to Seek Women with Math, Sports Interests," *WP*, 31 Mar. 1988, Maryland Section, 1.

37 Leon Edney to Ronald Marryott, 24 Mar. 1988, SR3, 1988, Box 1000–1531/1, Folder "1531/1."

38 "Integration of Women in the Brigade: Interview with Rear Admiral R. F. Marryott, Superintendent," *Shipmate* 51, no. 5 (June 1988): 16.

39 "Company Cuties," *LOG* 77, no. 6 (Mar. 1988): 48.

40 "What Female Mids Hate," *LOG* 77, no. 6 (Mar. 1988): 35.

41 "Not a Game Any More," *EC*, 14 Oct. 1988, A1.

42 The following discussion of the March 1989 *LOG*, subsequently published in *Playboy* magazine, is based on Scott Harper, "Superintendent Scuttles Mids' 'Swimsuit Issue,'" *EC*, 12 Apr. 1989, 1, 12; Molly Moore, "Admiral Scuttles Naval Academy's 'Playmid,'" *WP*, 13 Apr. 1989, in ARF "Midshipmen: 'Playmid' Log Magazine";

Caleb Laning to Virgil Hill Jr., 18 Apr. 1989, SR3, 1989, Box 12306–13950, Folder "1531/ON"; Scott Harper, "Navy Probes Theft of Taboo Magazines," EC, 19 Apr. 1989, 1, 12; Arlene Foreshew to Virgil Hill Jr., 23 Apr. 1989, SR3, 1989, Box 12306–13950, Folder "1531/ON"; Scott Harper, "Academy Ends Probe of Magazine Theft," EC, 9 June 1989, 1; Scott Harper, "Playmid is Still Making Waves," EC, 24 July 1989, 1; Virgil Hill Jr., "Letter to the Editor," EC, 30 July 1989; "1989 Best and Worst of Annapolis: Most Sought-After Publication," Annapolitan, July 1989, 45; Elizabeth Donovan, "Squelched 'Playmid' to be Revealed in 'Playboy,'" Navy Times, 14 Aug. 1989, 9; "Playboy Forum: Top-Secret Classified for Your Eyes Only: Naval Cadets Learn a Lesson in Censorship," Playboy, Sept. 1989, 46–47, PMA; Jim Burmeister, "LOG Notes," LOG 79, no. 1 (Sept. 1989): 1; Virgil Hill Jr., "Letter to the Editor, Playboy," LOG 79, no. 1 (Sept. 1989): 3; PI, Interviewee #129.

43   The following discussion of the Gwen Dreyer incident is based on "Taunted, Woman Quits Academy," NYT, 14 May 1990, B9; Felicity Barringer, "Harassment of Woman Shakes Naval Academy," NYT, 20 May 1990, 22; Garry Trudeau, "Dress White Blues," NYT, 1 June 1990, 29; Virgil Hill Jr. to James Exon, 11 June 1990, SR3, 1990, Box 5314–5700/2, Folder "5700"; Virgil Hill Jr. to Carol Holland, 28 June 1990, SR3, 1990, Box 1000–1531/1, Folder "1531/1"; Virgil Hill Jr. to Mary Boergers, 28 June 1990, SR3, 1990, Box 5314–5700/2, Folder "5700"; "The SUPE's Perspective: A Conversation with Rear Admiral Virgil L. Hill Jr.," Shipmate 53, no. 6 (July–Aug. 1990): 8; "Report of the Committee on Women's Issues, U.S. Naval Academy Board of Visitors," 9 Oct. 1990, 15, SR5, Box 4; Felicity Barringer, "Four Inquiries Cite Naval Academy for Rife Sexism," NYT, 10 Oct. 1990, 12; Daniel Barchi, "A Few Inches From the Yard," Shipmate 53, no. 8 (Oct. 1990): 28; James Cannon to President of the United States, 28 Dec. 1990, SR5, Binder 7; "Women at the Naval Academy," 15 Jan. 1991, SR5, Binder 7; Campbell and D'Amico, "Lessons on Gender Integration from the Military Academies," in D'Amico and Weinstein, eds., Gender Camouflage, 75; Ebbert and Hall, Crossed Currents, 226; Godson, Serving Proudly, 257.

44   Phyllis Witcher to Virgil Hill Jr., 30 Jan. 1990, SR3, 1990, Box 5314–5700/2, Folder "5700."

45   The previous two quotes are from Michael Boorda, Transcript of Speech to Midshipmen, USNA, Annapolis, Md., 19 Oct. 1990, 6, SR5, Box 4.

46   M. E. Chang, "Climate Assessment of the U.S. Naval Academy," 7–9, SR5, Box 4; J. M. Boorda, "Report of the Informal Review Board of the Honor and Conduct System," 10 Aug. 1990, 7–23, SR5, Binder 5.

47   J. L. Johnson, "Memorandum for Head, Education Programs Branch," 30 Oct. 1990, SR5, Binder 3.

48   The following discussion of Bowman's comments is based on William Bowman to Superintendent, 24 May 1990, SR3, 1990, Box 5314–5700/2, Folder "5700."

49   The following discussion of the BOV's findings is based on "Report of the Committee on Women's Issues, U.S. Naval Academy Board of Visitors," 9 Oct. 1990, 11, 12, 16, 19–25, SR5, Box 4.

50   Transcript of U.S. Naval Academy Board of Visitors Press Conference, 9 Oct. 1990, SR5, Binder 5.

51 The following discussion of the 1990 WMSG report is based on Women Midshipmen Study Group, "Report to the Superintendent on the Assimilation of Women in the Brigade of Midshipmen," 1 July 1990, 2–3, 23, 24, 29, 38–39, 62, SR5, Binder 5.

52 The following discussion of Julianne Gallina is based on Scott Harper, "YES, Ma'am!," EC, 27 Apr. 1991, 1; "Woman to Lead Midshipmen," NYT, 28 Apr. 1991, 27; Randi Henderson, "Leader of the Pack," BS, 2 Dec. 1991, 1, 6, 7; Juliane Gallina, "A Woman's Perspective," USNA Admissions pamphlet, undated, ARF "Midshipmen: Women Midshipmen Clippings and Releases"; Ebbert and Hall, Crossed Currents, 227, 298–311.

53 Juliane Gallina, "A Woman's Perspective," USNA Admissions pamphlet, undated, ARF "Midshipmen: Women Midshipmen Clippings and Releases."

54 The following discussion of women's recollections is based on EI, Interviewees #143, 198; PI, Interviewees #6, 85, 156, 171; Cummings, Hornet's Nest, 9, 16, 53; Campbell and D'Amico, "Lessons on Gender Integration From Military Academies," in D'Amico and Weinstein, Gender Camouflage, 69–70, 73.

55 Women Midshipmen Study Group Subcommittee, USNA Board of Visitors, "The Assimilation of Women in the Brigade of Midshipmen," Apr. 1991, 21, SR5, Binder 7; Dean of Academics, "Memorandum for Distribution," 22 Aug. 1991, SR3, 1991, Box 5238–5700, Folder "5420."

56 Thomas Lynch to Mary Kay Turner, 18 July 1992, SR3, 1992, Box 1000–1531, Folder "1531."

57 The following discussion of the GAO report is based on U.S. General Accounting Office, "Testimony Before the Subcommittee on Manpower and Personnel, Committee on Armed Services, U.S. Senate, Status Report on Reviews of Student Treatment, Department of Defense Service Academies," 2 June 1992, 2–5, SR5, Box 4.

58 The following discussion of Carol Burke is based on Burke, "Dames at Sea," New Republic, 17/24 Aug. 1992, 16, 18, 20; Burke, "Pernicious Cohesion," in Stiehm, ed., It's Our Military Too!, 205–18.

59 Thomas Lynch, "Letter to the Editor, New Republic," 6 Aug. 1992, SR5, Binder 2.

60 Angela Callahan, "Lynch: Academy On Course Despite Cheating Scandal," EC, 26 Feb. 1993, 1.

61 "Cheating Inquiry at Naval Academy," NYT, 10 Feb. 1993, 18; Eric Schmitt, "An Inquiry Finds 125 Cheated on a Naval Academy Exam," NYT, 13 Jan. 1994, 1; Brent Filbert, "Failing the Article 31 UCMJ Test: The Role of the Navy Inspector General in the Investigation of the Naval Academy Cheating Scandal," Naval Law Review, vol. 42, 1995, 1–34.

62 The previous three quotes are from Christopher Graves, "A Few Inches From The Yard," Shipmate 56, no. 2 (Mar. 1993): 13.

63 Ebbert and Hall, Crossed Currents, 227, 297–314; D'Ercole, "Combat Exclusion . . . Repealed!," 23–38; Cummings, Hornet's Nest, 145–46; William Lawrence, "Capitol Hill," Shipmate 54, no. 8 (Oct. 1991): 28; William Lawrence, "Capitol Hill, Et Cetera," Shipmate 57, no. 2 (Mar. 1994): 29.

64 The following discussion of the Cowards and Smith's activities is based on PI with

Asbury Coward IV, Annapolis, Md., 4 Nov. 1999; PI with Croom Coward, Annapolis, Md., 4 Nov. 1999; EI with Lynne Smith, Tulsa, Okla., 30 Oct. 1999.

65   PI with Charles Larson, Annapolis, Md., 22 June 2000.

66   Richard Armitage, chair, "Report of the Honor Review Committee to the Secretary of the Navy on Honor at the U.S. Naval Academy," 22 Dec. 1993, 1, ARF "Studies and Reports: Midshipmen and Graduates."

67   Charles Larson, "The Next 150 Years Begin," USNIP 122, no. 9 (Sept. 1996): 66–67.

68   Public Affairs News Release on Pregnancy and Parenthood, 21 Aug. 1995, ARF "Midshipmen: Pregnancy and Parenthood"; Ebbert and Hall, *Crossed Currents*, 225.

69   Charles Larson to Maurice Rindskopf, 20 Feb. 1996, SR3, 1996, Box 5700–5720, Folder "5700."

70   EI, Interviewee #147.

71   Charles Larson, "Guidelines for All Hands to Live By," SR3, 1996, Box 1531, Folder "1531."

72   "Midshipmen Are Indicted in Scheme to Steal and Resell Autos," NYT, 12 Apr. 1996, 15.

73   Michael Janofsky, "Academy Head Defends Ethics of Midshipmen," NYT, 18 Apr. 1996, B8.

74   Charles Larson, "The Next 150 Years Begin," USNIP 122, no. 9 (Sept. 1996): 68.

75   The following discussion of the Gill-Bozung report is based on Julie Gill and Daniel Bozung, "Male Midshipmen Attitudes Toward Women, 1976–1996," paper presented at "Leadership in a Gender Diverse Military: Women at the Nation's Service Academies—The Twenty Year Mark" conference, New London, Conn., 20–23 Mar. 1997, 10–15.

76   Ibid., 15.

77   Carmen Neuberger initially proposed this concept; see Superintendent to Chief of Naval Operations, 27 July 1981, SR5, Box 2, Folder "DACOWITS, 1976, 1981."

78   Felicity Barringer, "Four Inquiries Cite Naval Academy for Rife Sexism," NYT, 10 Oct. 1990, 12; Transcript of U.S. Naval Academy Board of Visitors Press Conference, 9 Oct. 1990, SR5, Binder 5; Kathleen Durning to Richard Ustick, 20 July 1977, SR5, Box 4.

79   PI, Interviewees #3, 10, 49, 180.

80   PI, Interviewees #2, 4, 9, 35, 45, 77.

81   PI, Interviewee #32.

82   EI, Interviewee #219.

83   The following discussion of women in the classes of 1997–2002 is based upon PI, Interviewees #1, 7, 9, 17, 24, 40, 45, 82, 88, 96, 105, 108, 128, 146; EI, Interviewees #74, 87, 167; CI, Interviewee #107; Helen Purkitt and Gale Mattox, "Bridging Gaps: Reflections of Two Civilian Professors at the U.S. Naval Academy," in D'Amico and Weinstein, eds., *Gender Camouflage*, 156.

84   For a comparative perspective on female college students' bonds, see Lefkowitz-Horowitz, *Alma Mater*, 5.

84   EI, Interviewee #167.

86   EI, Interviewee #87.

87   The term is common enough at USNA that it came up in many interviews and conversations with recent midshipmen, officers, and faculty: PI, Interviewees #2, 3, 4, 8, 9, 10, 11, 18, 22, 27, 31, 35, 36, 40, 41, 45, 47, 49, 70, 77, 78, 79, 81, 87, 91, 112, 114, 127, 134, 142, 152, 169, 180, 207.

88   Alton Stewart Jr., "Learn to Accept Women at the Naval Academy," USNIP 124, no. 6 (June 1998): 42, 44.

89   The following discussion of the class of 2000 Ring Dance is based upon PI, Interviewees #1, 9, 18, 24, 31, 34, 45, 85, 108, 112, 128, 136; EI, Interviewee #7.

90   The following discussion of events during Locklear's term as commandant is based on PI with Samuel Locklear, Annapolis, Md., 6 Apr. 2000; EI with Bradford McDonald, Annapolis, Md., 15 Nov. 1999; EI with Bradford McDonald, Annapolis, Md., 7 Dec. 1999; PI, Interviewees #28, 40, 78, 85, 171; EI, Interviewee #78; EI with Mary Jo Sweeney, Norfolk, Va., 28 Oct. 1999; Brian Ray, "The Commandant's Considerations: An Interview with Captain Locklear," *Character Quarterly* 4, no. 3 (Spring 2000): 3. On perceptions of females having sex at USNA, see Fleming, *Annapolis Autumn*, 137.

91   "Letter from the Editor," LOG 82, no. 1 (Jan. 1997): 2; "Interview with Dep Dant Capt. Farrell," LOG 82, no. 2 (Mar. 1997): 6; "Last Note from the Editor," LOG 82, no. 3 (May 1997): 2.

92   See, in particular, "T.H.E.Y. Are Here," LOG 84, no. 1 (Sept. 1998): 18–19; "Midshipman Regulations Manual Revision," LOG 84, no. 1 (Sept. 1998): 24–26; "What Sort of Mid Reads The LOG?," LOG 84, no. 3 (Jan. 1999): back cover; "Case No. 2001: The Case of the Dead Dogs," LOG 84, no. 4 (Feb. 1999): 36–39; "Capt. Evil, USN: Part II: Lt. Col. Accuz-U, USMC," LOG 84, no. 5 (May 1999): 16–19; "Pass In Review," LOG 85, no. 1 (Sept. 1999): 10–11; "Do You Suffer from CDS?," LOG 85, no. 1 (Sept. 1999): 13; Centerfold, LOG 85, no. 1 (Oct. 1999): 16–17; "J. O. Data Sheet, 2nd Company Officer," LOG 85, no. 2 (Dec. 1999): 15.

93   The LOG issue would have been vol. 85, no. 3. The LOG shortly thereafter went online, at <www.thelog.westhost.com>, with a new set of editors, and produced several issues before ceasing operations in December 2001.

94   The following discussion of women's accomplishments is based, partly, on Purkitt and Mattox, "Bridging Gaps," in D'Amico and Weinstein, eds., *Gender Camouflage*, 152, 155, 160–61.

95   PI, Interviewees #32, 37, 156; EI, Interviewee #74, 143; Disher, *First Class*, 360–62; Interview with Barbette Henry Lowndes, USNIOH, OHFFG, 101; Interview with Crystal Lewis, USNIOH, OHFFG, 72; Ebbert and Hall, *Crossed Currents*, 226.

96   EI, Interviewee #28.

97   Tami Terella, "Sisters Lend Support to Midshipmen Legacy," *Trident*, 22 May 1992, 1; Karen Myers, "Mississippi Family Returns to Yard, Attends Third Daughter's Graduation," *Trident*, 19 May 2000, 3; Ebbert and Hall, *Crossed Currents*, 226.

98   Campbell and D'Amico, "Lessons on Gender Integration from the Military Acade-

mies," in D'Amico and Weinstein, eds., *Gender Camouflage*, 68. See Statistical Appendix.

99 EI, Interviewee #7.

100 The Joy Bright Hancock Club had its origin as the Women's Professional Association, begun in 1988 after the 1987 Women Midshipmen Study Group recommended its creation; see Women Midshipmen Study Group, "Report to the Superintendent on the Integration of Women in the Brigade of Midshipmen," 1 July 1990, 2. The club became more active in 1999 and now supports professional, service, and social activities for female midshipmen; see PI, Interviewee #37; Joy Bright Hancock Club, USNAW (<www.usna.edu/JBHO>, 7 July 2000).

101 PI, Interviewees #40, 79, 108.

102 PI with Shannon French, Annapolis, Md., 13 Apr. 2000; Gene Andersen, ed., *Leadership*, 513–49.

103 PI, Interviewees #1, 3, 5, 6, 7, 9, 10, 18, 20, 25, 26, 28, 32, 33, 34, 36, 37, 39, 40, 44, 45, 47, 67, 77, 82, 85, 87, 95, 96, 105, 109, 128, 132, 158, 169, 189, 206; EI, Interviewee #189; Fleming, *Annapolis Autumn*, 138–39, 143, 271–72.

104 Fleming, *Annapolis Autumn*, 147.

105 PI, Interviewees #3, 7, 9, 40, 45; Campbell and D'Amico, "Lessons on Gender Integration," in D'Amico and Weinstein, eds., *Gender Camouflage*, 69.

106 PI, Interviewees #1, 2, 3, 5, 6, 7, 8, 9, 10, 11, 18, 22, 26, 27, 31, 36, 40, 41, 45, 49, 77, 78, 79, 85, 105, 112, 171, 180; Amy Argetsinger, "Academy Plumbs Its Depths: Latest Review's Goal is More Civility Among Midshipmen," *WP*, 19 July 2000, B1, B9.

107 See, for example, Class of 1979 Class Notes, *Shipmate* 65, no. 1 (Jan./Feb. 2002): 127.

108 A review and discussion of the book appeared in a USNA publication; see Joyce Randle, "First in Courage," *Character Quarterly* 3, no. 1 (Graduation 1998): 6–7.

109 PI, Interviewees #20, 37; EI, Interviewees #32, 109, 119; Godson, *Serving Proudly*, 284.

110 EI, Interviewees #6, 26, 37. The study was the Rondeau Cultural Assessment, 2000.

111 PI, Interviewees #32, 169; EI, Interviewee #37.

112 PI with Leon Edney, Annapolis, Md., 16 May 1999; TI with H. Ross Perot, Dallas, Tex., 11 Dec. 2000.

113 EI, Interviewee #95.

114 *Reminiscences of Vice Admiral William R. Smedberg III*, 559–60, 773.

115 PI with James Calvert, St. Michael's, Md., 4 May 2000.

116 Campbell and D'Amico, "Lessons on Gender Integration from the Military Academies," in D'Amico and Weinstein, eds., *Gender Camouflage*, 75.

Chapter Eight

1 The following discussion on H. Ross Perot's senior paper is based upon TI with H. Ross Perot, Dallas, Tex., 11 Dec. 2000; H. Ross Perot, "The History of Honor at the United States Naval Academy From Its Founding Up to the Establishment of Our Present Honor Committee," 1953, ARF "Midshipmen: Honor Concept: Perot"; L. F.

Safford to H. Ross Perot, 10 Feb. 1953, ARF "Midshipmen: Honor Concept: Perot"; "All Hands," *Shipmate* 60, no. 3 (Apr. 1997): 22; "Honor, the Brigade, and Midshipmen," Permanent Exhibit, Smoke Hall, Bancroft Hall, USNA, Panel 1.

2 Albert McCarthy to H. Ross Perot, 17 Feb. 1953, ARF "Midshipmen: Honor Concept: Perot."

3 Charles Moore to H. Ross Perot, 5 Feb. 1953, ARF "Midshipmen: Honor Concept: Perot."

4 Christopher Graves, "A Few Inches From the Yard," *Shipmate* 55, no. 10 (Dec. 1992): 23–24. I am grateful to Admiral Thomas Marfiak who suggested the term "effervescence" to describe the midshipmen's activities included in this chapter.

5 The following discussion of the creation of the Honor Concept is based upon "A Report from Midshipman Perot to the Commandant of Midshipmen, C. A. Buchanan, to Acquaint Him with the Class Honor Committee and the Brigade Executive Committee," 1953, 1–4, 8–9, 10–12, 31, ARF "Midshipmen: Honor Concept: Perot"; H. Ross Perot, "The History of Honor at the United States Naval Academy From Its Founding Up to the Establishment of Our Present Honor Committee," 1953, 4, 12–13, 15, ARF "Midshipmen: Honor Concept: Perot"; Harry Hill to H. Ross Perot, 11 Feb. 1953, ARF "Midshipmen: Honor Concept: Perot"; William Lawrence to Executive Officer, Bancroft Hall, 23 Aug. 1951, ARF "Midshipmen: Honor"; Harry Hill to Allan Reich, 16 Oct. 1951, ARF "Midshipmen: Honor"; "Final Notes for Honor Committee Booklet," undated, 2–15, 27–29, ARF "Midshipmen: Honor Concept: Perot"; Jean Ebbert, "Honor Code for a Taut Ship," *WP*, 18 Feb. 1978, A17; Unpublished Interview with William Lawrence, USNIOH, 70–75, 77, 983–84; Bob Rau and Anne Marie Drew, "The Concept of Honor at USNA: A Historical Summary, Part II: 1921–1985," *Shipmate* 60, no. 9 (Nov. 1997): 12–14; TI with H. Ross Perot, Dallas, Tex., 11 Dec. 2000; Barrett Smith, "Hazing, Honor, and the Early Twentieth Century Naval Academy" (History Honors Thesis, U.S. Naval Academy, 2000), 18–19, HMG; "Honor, The Brigade, and Midshipmen," Permanent Exhibit, Smoke Hall, Bancroft Hall, USNA, Panel 2.

6 TI with H. Ross Perot, Dallas, Tex., 11 Dec. 2000.

7 *Reminiscences of Rear Admiral John F. Davidson*, 43.

8 William Lawrence to Executive Officer, Bancroft Hall, 23 Aug. 1951, ARF "Midshipmen: Honor."

9 Harry Hill to H. Ross Perot, 11 Feb. 1953, ARF "Midshipmen: Honor Concept: Perot." In 1985, Commandant Stephen Chadwick suggested a third root; he wrote that "the formal process of accepting honor as a system did not begin until 1945 when Captain S. H. Ingersoll, then Commandant, testified before Congress on the Title X U.S. Code. This code authorized the service academies to discharge cadets and midshipmen for moral failing. From these hearings, the modern honor concept began to evolve." See Stephen Chadwick, "The Commandant Speaks," *Shipmate* 48, no. 10 (Dec. 1985): 14. However, this event does not appear to have led to any specific action at the Academy.

10 This basic statement stems from 1933 USNA regulations; see H. Ross Perot, "The History of Honor at the United States Naval Academy From Its Founding Up to the

Establishment of Our Present Honor Committee," 1953, 2, 12–13, ARF "Midshipmen: Honor Concept: Perot." However, this specific terminology dates from 1977; see Stephen Chadwick, "The Commandant Speaks," *Shipmate* 48, no. 10 (Dec. 1985): 14; Unpublished Interview with William Lawrence, USNIOH, 77.

11   Robert Thomas Jr., "Annapolis and Air Force Disagree on Honor Code," NYT, 3 June 1976, 40; William Lawrence, "SUPT's Report," *Shipmate* 42, no. 8 (Oct. 1979): 19; *Reminiscences of Vice Admiral Charles S. Minter Jr.*, 462–63; Stephen Chadwick, "The Commandant Speaks," *Shipmate* 48, no. 10 (Dec. 1985): 14.

12   William Lawrence to Executive Officer, Bancroft Hall, 23 Aug. 1951, ARF "Midshipmen: Honor."

13   Unpublished Interview with William Lawrence, USNIOH, 71, 983; Jean Ebbert, "Honor Code for a Taut Ship," *WP*, 18 Feb. 1978, A17.

14   Unpublished Interview with William Lawrence, USNIOH, 984.

15   "The Naval Academy Honor Concept," *Shipmate* 30, no. 6 (June/July 1967): 24.

16   William Smedberg to Brigade of Midshipmen, June 1958, SR1, Box 3, Folder "Publications/The Log, 1938–1959"; James Calvert, "A Program for the Best—Find Them," *Shipmate* 33, no. 1 (Jan. 1970): 4.

17   The West Point court case in question is *Dunmar v. Ailes*, 348F 2d. 51 (1965), and a second West Point case, *Hagopian v. Knowlton*, 470F 2d. 201 (2d Cir 1972), brought similar scrutiny; see D. K. Forbes to Deputy Assistant Secretary of Defense for Education, 13 Mar. 1974, SR2, Sec. 5800/1, Folder "1974."

18   "The Honor Concept of the Brigade of Midshipmen," *Shipmate* 31, no. 2 (Feb. 1968): 13; "Statement of Rear Admiral Kinnaird McKee, Superintendent, U.S. Naval Academy, Before the Manpower and Personnel Subcommittee of the Committee on Armed Services, U.S. Senate, Concerning the Honor Codes of the Service Academies," 22 June 1976, ARF "Midshipmen: Honor"; "Academy Pleased With New System," *EC*, 15 Feb. 1968, 1; Robert McNitt, "Challenge and Change: The Naval Academy, 1959–1968," *Shipmate* 35, no. 4 (Apr. 1972): 5–6; Virgil Hill to Chief of Naval Operations, 29 Nov. 1990, 2–5, SR5, Binder 3.

19   See, for example, Charles Larson, "Goals for Academic Year 1984–1985," undated, CR, Sec. 5400/4, Folder "1984."

20   On the 1974 navigation examination cheating case and study of the Honor Concept, see Bill Richards, "Scandal Uncovers Doubt On Academy's Honor Code," *WP*, 1 June 1974, C1. See also Fleming, *Annapolis Autumn*, 158, 179.

21   U.S. Naval Academy Board of Visitors, "Report of the Committee on Women's Issues," 9 Oct. 1990, SR5, Box 4; Virgil Hill to Chief of Naval Operations, 29 Nov. 1990, 4–5, SR5, Binder 3.

22   J. M. Boorda, "Report of the Informal Review Board of the Honor Concept and Conduct System," 10 Aug. 1995, 7, SR5, Binder 5; M. E. Chang, "Climate Assessment of the U.S. Naval Academy," 11 June 1990, SR5, Box 4.

23   Christina Ianzito to Thomas Lynch, 7 July 1994, SR3, Box 1994, Folder "1531"; "Report of the Honor Review Committee to the Secretary of the Navy on Honor at the U.S. Naval Academy," 22 Dec. 1993, ARF "Studies and Reports: Midshipmen/Graduates"; Charles Larson, "The Next 150 Years Begin," USNIP 122, no. 9, 65–69.

24 1971 LB, 229; "Introducing the New Honor Staff," *Character Quarterly* 3, no. 1 (Graduation 1998): 4–5.

25 Stephen Chadwick, "The Commandant Speaks," *Shipmate* 48, no. 10 (Dec. 1985): 14.

26 Charles Larson to Bart Fordham Jr., 31 May 1996, SR3, Box 1996, Folder "5700."

27 PI, Interviewee #45.

28 PI, Interviewee #18; Leo Mehalic, "Class of 1999 Reaffirms Commitment to Honor, Country," *Trident*, 18 Aug. 1995, 1; "Honor, the Brigade, and Midshipmen," Permanent Exhibit, Smoke Hall, Bancroft Hall, USNA; Charles Larson to Bart Fordham Jr., 31 May 1996, SR3, Box 1996, Folder "5700"; Charles Larson to Robin Meyer, 7 June 1996, SR3, Box 1996, Folder "1531"; Charles Larson, "The Next 150 Years Begin," *USNIP* 122, no. 9, 65–69; "Remarks by Admiral John R. Ryan, USN, Superintendent, United States Naval Academy, Given to the Naval Academy Alumni Association President's Circle," 11 Sept. 1998, 2, USNAW (<www.usna.edu/pao/speeches/speechJR4.htm>, 21 May 1999). The Smoke Hall display was the creation of midshipman Erin Goralnik, class of 1995; see "Building Honor," EC, 6 May 1997, 1.

29 The following discussion of the 1952 June Week Parade is based on PI, Interviewees #116, 121; "A June Week Highlight" (photograph), EC, 6 June 1952, 1; "Spectators Have Field Day As Shoes, Handkerchiefs, Gloves Are Discarded By Graduates," EC, 6 June 1952, 1; R. S. Wentworth Jr. to Superintendent, 9 June 1952, SR1, Box 2, Folder "Activities/Comments and Evaluations of June Week, 1932–1953"; C. E. Trescott to Superintendent, 13 June 1952, SR1, Box 2, Folder "Activities/Comments and Evaluations of June Week, 1932–1953"; J. S. Weiler to Superintendent, 13 June 1952, SR1, Box 2, Folder "Activities/Comments and Evaluation of June Week, 1932–1953"; C. A Buchanan to Superintendent, 25 June 1952, SR1, Box 1, Folder "Activities/Comments and Evaluations of June Week, 1932–1953."

30 Unpublished Interview with William Lawrence, USNIOH, 79–80.

31 "United States Naval Academy Program of Events for June Week 1952," CR, Box 3, "Commandant of Midshipman Instructions and Notices, 1959–1971," Folder 12; "Schedule of Events for the Month of June 1952: Events at the Naval Academy," CR, Box 3, "Commandant of Midshipman Instructions and Notices, 1959–1971," Folder 12; R. S. Wentworth Jr. to Superintendent, 9 June 1952, SR1, Box 1, Folder "Activities/Comments and Evaluations of June Week, 1932–1953."

32 The previous two quotes are from EI, Interviewees #116, 121.

33 "Rear Admiral Charles A. Buchanan's Talk to the First Class, 1953," 27 May 1953, CR, Box 1, "Miscellaneous Speeches Presented by Commandants, 1952–1960," Folder 15. The red lanterns were meant to symbolize "taking up the end," as did cabooses at the end of trains.

34 EI, Interviewee #121.

35 "Spectators Have Field Day As Shoes, Handkerchiefs, Gloves Are Discarded By Graduates," EC, 6 June 1952, 1.

36 USNA June Week events were a typical subject for cinematic news reel productions, and both Navy and independent film crews were on hand to record the 1952 Color Parade; see "Spectators Have Field Day As Shoes, Handkerchiefs, Gloves Are Discarded By Graduates," EC, 6 June 1952, 1. However, in spite of the existence of

Metro/Goldwyn/Mayer News, Movietone News, and Paramount News reels of the graduation activities for years before and after 1952, news reels of the 1952 June Week activities could not be located at MPSVC. It is unclear whether the Navy permitted the 1952 events to be distributed to those news services, but Admiral Hill thanked the Naval Photographic Center for filming the June Week events; see Superintendent to Commanding Officer, Naval Photographic Center, Naval Air Station, Anacostia, 13 June 1952, SR1, Box 2, Folder "Special Occasions: June Week, 1946–1957." It does appear, however, that the USNA administration was successful in quashing the newspaper coverage of the incident; the only newspaper in which the 1952 Color Parade appeared was the *Annapolis Capital*.

37 "769 Midshipmen Commissioned In Three Services," EC, 6 June 1952, 1; William Fechteler, "A Formula for Success," USNIP 78, no. 10 (Oct. 1952): 1122.

38 Lemuel Shepherd to Harry Hill, 7 May 1952, SR1, Box 3, Folder "Graduation/ Invitations to Speakers and Participants, Correspondence, 1951–1953"; Lawrence Kuler to H. W. Hill, 9 May 1952, SR1, Box 3, Folder "Graduation/Invitations to Speakers and Participants, Correspondence, 1951–1953."

39 R. S. Wentworth Jr. to Superintendent, 9 June 1952, SR1, Box 2, Folder "Activities/ Comments and Evaluations of June Week, 1932–1953"; C. E. Trescott to Superintendent, 13 June 1952, SR1, Box 2, Folder "Activities/Comments and Evaluations of June Week, 1932–1953."

40 J. S. Weiler to Superintendent, 13 June 1952, SR1, Box 2, Folder "Activities/Comments and Evaluations of June Week, 1932–1953"; M. F. Ranirez de Arellano to Superintendent, 16 June 1952, SR1, Box 2, Folder "Activities/Comments and Evaluations of June Week, 1932–1953"; C. A. Buchanan to Superintendent, 25 June 1952, SR1, Box 2, Folder "Activities/Comments and Evaluations of June Week, 1932–1953."

41 PI, Interviewee #79; "Commandant's Talk To First Class, Class of 1953, Beginning of Academic Year 1952–1953," 8 Sept. 1952, CR, Box 1, "Miscellaneous Speeches Presented by Commandants, 1952–1960," Folder 10; J. P. Sagaser, "Midshipmen Share Bond With USNA '52," *Trident*, 10 Nov. 1995, SCF "U.S. Naval Academy Class of 1952."

42 "Rear Admiral Charles A. Buchanan's Talk to the First Class, 1953," 27 May 1953, CR, Box 1, "Miscellaneous Speeches Presented by Commandants, 1952–1960," Folder 15; R. S. Wentworth to Superintendent, 8 June 1953, SR1, Box 2, Folder "Activities/Comments and Evaluation of June Week, 1932–1953"; W. Hague to G. H. Rohill, 31 May 1953, SR1, Box 1, Folder "Activities and Correspondence, 1951–1956"; "Rear Admiral Charles A. Buchanan's Talk to the First Class, 1954," 8 Sept. 1953, CR, Box 1, "Miscellaneous Speeches Presented by Commandants, 1952–1960," Folder 15.

43 "Rear Admiral Charles A. Buchanan's Talk to the First Class, 1954," 8 Sept. 1953, CR, Box 1, "Miscellaneous Speeches Presented by Commandants, 1952–1960," Folder 15.

44 "Captain R. T. S. Keith, Commandant, Talk to the First Class ('55)," 15 Sept. 1954, CR, Box 1, "Miscellaneous Speeches Presented by Commandants, 1952–1960," Folder 15.

45 William Smedberg, "Speech Delivered To First Class Officers, All Class Officers, Plus Other Classes Over Bancroft Hall Radio On 12 April '56," 12 Apr. 1956, SC, William Renwick Smedberg Papers, Box 1.

46 EI, Interviewee #116.

47 J. P. Sagaser, "Midshipmen Share Bond With USNA '52," *Trident*, 10 Nov. 1995, in SCF "U.S. Naval Academy: Class of 1952."

48 EI, Interviewee #121.

49 EI, Interviewee #116.

50 TI, Interviewee #25.

51 A. G. Esch to Richard Dorso, 14 Jan. 1956, 11, SR4, Folder "Television Series A7-4/1-1."

52 McCain and Salter, *Faith of My Fathers*, 144–48, 150–51.

53 *Reminiscences of Rear Admiral John F. Davidson*, 406. Being "unsat in juice" means the midshipmen were not successful in their electrical engineering course.

54 For historical perspectives on student activism in the 1960s, see Conde, ed., *Student Activism*, 1–16; Fraser, 1968, 1–3.

55 Bourne, *Jimmy Carter*, 48–49.

56 Lovell, *Neither Athens Nor Sparta?*, 209–10, 222, 267–68, 276.

57 PI with Bradley Nemeth, San Diego, Calif., 4 June 1999; PI with Michael Oliver, San Diego, Calif., 4 June 1999; PI with Rick Rubel, Annapolis, Md., 9 May 2000; Isserman and Kazin, *America Divided*, 150–52.

58 The following discussion of the "sit-in" is based upon PI with Bradley Nemeth, San Diego, Calif., 4 June 1999; PI with Mike Oliver, San Diego, Calif., 4 June 1999; EI with Nicholas Visco, Springfield, Va., 19 May 1999.

59 1971 LB, 28. The exact nature of the "Coed Pep Rally" is unknown, but Bradley Nemeth and Michael Oliver recalled that it involved some type of misconduct.

60 EI with Nicholas Visco, Springfield, Va., 19 May 1999.

61 PI with Bradley Nemeth, San Diego, Calif., 4 June 1999; PI with Michael Oliver, San Diego, Calif., 4 June 1999.

62 The previous three quotes are from PI with Michael Oliver, San Diego, Calif., 4 June 1999.

63 PI with Bradley Nemeth, San Diego, Calif., 4 June 1999; PI with Michael Oliver, San Diego, Calif., 4 June 1999; EI with Nicholas Visco, Springfield, Va., 19 May 1999.

64 PI with Bradley Nemeth, San Diego, Calif., 4 June 1999.

65 TI with Robert Coogan, San Diego, Calif., 20 Dec. 1999; 1970 LB, 372; TI with Bradley Nemeth, San Diego, Calif., 22 Dec. 1999.

66 TI with Robert Coogan, San Diego, Calif., 20 Dec. 1999.

67 James Calvert, "A Program For The Best—Find Them," *Shipmate* 33, no. 1 (Jan. 1970): 4–5.

68 TI with Robert Coogan, San Diego, Calif., 20 Dec. 1999; 1970 LB, 162, 190–91, 372; 1971 LB, 39.

69 1970 LB, 801.

70 The following discussion of events surrounding the LOG is based upon PI with James Calvert, St. Michaels, Md., 4 May 2000; TI with Robert Coogan, San Diego,

Calif., 14 Nov. 1999; TI with Kevin Mulkern, San Diego, Calif., 8 Dec. 2000; EI with Kevin Mulkern, San Diego, Calif., 26 June 2000; EI with Daniel Ellison, Helena, Mont., 28 Feb. 2004; Robert Timberg, "Log Flap: Major Loses Post at Academy; High U.S. Officials Irked," EC, 16 July 1970, 1, 2; C. Mason White, "Midshipman Magazine Aide Says Politics Caused Firing," BS, 17 July 1970; Robert Timberg, "Log Flap: Coffee Klatch Talk Has Reverberations on Capitol Hill," EC, 17 July 1970, 1, 2; Robert Timberg, "Magazine Editor Is Transferred," EC, 18 July 1970, 1; Thomas Hasler, "Relevance and the Navy: Will Log Take a New Track?," BS, 23 July 1970, D6.

71 James Calvert, "A Letter From The Superintendent," LOG 58, no. 1 (27 Sept. 1968): 5.

72 Brad Harbin, "Letter to the Editor," LOG 59, no. 2 (17 Oct. 1969): 7.

73 Mike Trent, "Mids'Eye View of Woodstock," LOG 59, no. 1 (3 Oct. 1969): 48.

74 D. A. Ellison, "Editorial," LOG 59, no. 5 (30 Jan. 1970): 7.

75 Items from LOG 59, no. 4 (19 Dec. 1969), include cover art; " 'Woodstock'—A Screen Celebration to the Aquarian Age," 10, 13; "Another Answer To An Old Question," 13; M. I. D., "A Reason To Believe," 12–13; "'Tis The Season To Be Jolly" (cartoon), 21; "Yes, Ma'am, That's Two Please" (cartoon), 19; "Super Mid" (cartoon), 26–27.

76 Smith, *Declaration of Conscience*, 426; Sherman, *No Place For A Woman*, 58, 90–93, 208; Valeo, *Mike Mansfield*, 269–70; Wallace, *Politics of Conscience*, xiv, 59–64, 178–79; Zumwalt, *On Watch*, 125.

77 On M. E. Marshall, see *Reminiscences of Rear Admiral Julian T. Burke Jr.*, 369.

78 PI with James Calvert, St. Michaels, Md., 4 May 2000.

79 Mark Gardner, "The Log's New Officer Representative—Major Albans," LOG 59, no. 5 (30 Jan. 1970): 29, 30; Clark Reynolds to Margaret Chase Smith, 12 Aug. 1970, MCS, Folder "Armed Services Committee, Marine Corps Personnel Records, Constantine Albans"; Biography of Constantine Albans, MCS, Folder "Armed Services Committee, Marine Corps Personnel Records, Constantine Albans."

80 Robert Timberg, "Magazine Editor Is Transferred," EC, 18 July 1970, 1.

81 TI with Robert Coogan, San Diego, Calif., 14 Nov. 1999.

82 Mark Gardner, "The Log's New Officer Representative—Major Albans," LOG 59, no. 5 (30 Jan. 1970): 30.

83 Items from LOG 59, no. 5 (19 Jan. 1970), include Stephen Sisa, "In Defense of Tradition: A Letter to the Editor," 9–10; Daniel Ellison, "Response to Sisa," 10.

84 Robert Timberg, "Log Flap: Major Loses Post at Academy; High U.S. Officials Irked," EC, 16 July 1970, 2.

85 Items from LOG 59, no. 6 (20 Feb. 1970), include Bill Smith, "Editorial," 4; "The 64,000 Banana Question," 16; Midshipman Gardner, "After This, Who's To Say Chapel Shouldn't Be Mandatory" (cartoon), 38; "And He'll Make A Great Marine When He Graduates, Too" (cartoon), 18.

86 Although the archives of the Margaret Chase Smith Library contain a copy of the March 1970 LOG, I suggest this because there is no correspondence to indicate otherwise; see LOG 59, no. 7 (13 Mar. 1970), MCS, Folder "Armed Services Committee, Military Installations, United States Naval Academy, 'LOG' Controversy."

87 Items from LOG 59, no. 7 (13 Mar. 1970), include photograph spread of Julie Briggs, 27–30; "Worth 10,000 Words" (photograph spread), 37; Daniel Ellison, "Editorial,"

4; "Salty Sam," 19; "The Chapel Seven" (cartoon), 31; W. G. Smith, "Cartoon Mocking Margaret Chase Smith," 31.

88 TI with Kevin Mulkern, San Diego, Calif., 8 Dec. 2000.

89 The previous four quotes are from Robert Timberg, "Log Flap: Coffee Klatch Talk Has Reverberations on Capitol Hill," EC, 17 July 1970, 1, 2.

90 Clark Reynolds to Margaret Chase Smith, 12 Aug. 1970, MCS, Folder "Armed Services Committee, Marine Corps Personnel Records, Constantine Albans"; Margaret Chase Smith to Clark Reynolds, 19 Aug. 1970, MCS, Folder "Armed Services Committee, Marine Corps Personnel Records, Constantine Albans."

91 Robert Timberg, "Log Flap: Coffee Klatch Talk Has Reverberations on Capitol Hill," EC, 17 July 1970, 2.

92 Ibid.

93 1970 LB, 372.

94 Robert Timberg, "Log Flap: Major Loses Post at Academy; High U.S. Officials Irked," EC, 16 July 1970, 2.

95 Dan Ellison, "Editorial," LOG 59, no. 10 (1 May 1970): 4.

96 PI, Interviewees #78, 158; EI, Interviewee #147.

97 Commandant of Midshipman Instruction 1650.10, "Senator Margaret Chase Smith Leadership Excellence Award," 30 June 2000, HMG.

98 The following discussion of wigs is based on Nan Robertson, "Wigs—Long Hair On Short—Brings Solace to GIs," NYT, 4 Mar. 1970, 49; John Woodfield, "Midshipmen Flip Their Wigs Over Short Hair," WP, 7 Mar. 1970, B4; "Wanda's Wigs, Inc." (cartoon), LOG 59, no. 4 (13 Mar. 1970): 32–33.

99 Nan Robertson, "Wigs—Long Hair On Short—Brings Solace to GIs," NYT, 4 Mar. 1970, 49.

100 John Woodfield, "Midshipmen Flip Their Wigs Over Short Hair," WP, 7 Mar. 1970, B4; D. A. Ellison, "Editorial," LOG 59, no. 7 (13 Mar. 1970): 4.

101 EI with Bradley Nemeth, San Diego, Calif., 30 Sept. 2002; EI with Michael Oliver, San Diego, Calif., 28 Sept. 2002; "Igor's Gifts For Mids," LOG 58, no. 6 (20 Dec. 1968): 24; Daniel Ellison, "70's Top Headlines," LOG 59, no. 7 (13 Mar. 1970): 56.

102 "Wanda's Wigs, Inc." (cartoon), LOG 59, no. 4 (13 Mar. 1970): 32–33; 1971 LB, 39; 1970 LB, 273.

103 James Calvert to Arleigh Burke, 31 Mar. 1970, SR2, Sec. ON/1531, Folder "1970."

104 The following discussion of POW issues at USNA is based on PI with Rick Rubel, Annapolis, Md., 9 May 2000; PI, Interviewee #129; TI with H. Ross Perot, Dallas, Tex., 11 Dec. 2000; EI with Joe Glover, Dallas, Tex., 21 Apr. 2000; EI, Interviewees #25, 129; "'72 Mounts POW Letter Writing Campaign," LOG 60, no. 4 (20 Nov. 1970): 22; Paul Montgomery, "POW Camp Raiders Honored At The Half In Army-Navy Game," NYT, 29 Nov. 1970, 1; Joe Glover, "POW Campaign in Bancroft Hall," Shipmate 34, no. 7 (July/Aug. 1971): 9; Frank Gibson, "Man On Top—Joe Glover," LOG 61, no. 1 (29 Oct. 1971): 16–17; 1971 LB, 158–62; 1972 LB, 681.

105 "History of the 1960s," 1983 LB, 60.

106 Unpublished Interview with William Lawrence, USNIOH, 741–839.

107 Stockdale and Stockdale, In Love And War.

108 "Annapolis Bans War Foes," *NYT*, 7 Oct. 1970, 23. That policy did not last long. In 1972, Gloria Steinem and Julian Bond, two outspoken opponents of the Vietnam War, addressed the Brigade as Forrestal Lecturers.

109 The previous two quotes are from PI with Rick Rubel, Annapolis, Md., 9 May 2000.

110 Photographs of the return of Wendell Rivers, James Bell, and Edward Davis to USNA, *LOG* 68, no. 8 (25 Apr. 1973): 14–15.

111 EI with James Bell, Alexandria, Va., 10 June 2000.

112 James Calvert to Parents, 21 May 1972, CR, Sec. 5400/19, Folder "1972."

113 Henry Thompson Jr. to Superintendent, 28 July 1978, CR, Sec. 5211/2, Folder "1978"; J. J. Shanley Jr. to Henry Thompson Jr., 22 Sept. 1978, CR, Sec. 5211/2, Folder "1978."

114 1971 LB, 121; "Remember?," *LOG* 58, no. 14 (18 Apr. 1969): 34.

115 1970 LB, 120.

116 Max Morris to Company Officers, 5 Dec. 1972, CR, Sec. 5400/5, Folder "1972"; D. K. Forbes to T. R. M. Emery, 17 Sept. 1973, CR, Sec. 5211, Folder "1973"; 1998 LB, 54; Christopher Graves, "A Few Inches From The Yard," *Shipmate* 56, no. 3 (Apr. 1993): 25; Barry Shambach, quoted in Drew, ed., *Letters From Annapolis*, 205; Timberg, *The Nightingale's Song*, 23. Cannonballs are prepared by coring apples and filling them with cinnamon sugar, rolling them in dough, baking them at 425 degrees for 25 minutes, and then covering them with butter, sugar, and vanilla.

117 Michael Parker, ed., "Good Gouge: An Introduction Into the Origins of Naval Academy Slang," Class Project, HE-111, USNA, Fall 1982, 18; 1998 LB, 48; Susan Herendeen, "Bancroft Hall," EC, 10 May 1998, A1.

118 PI, Interviewees #3, 10, 49, 117, 129; Michael Parker, ed., "Good Gouge: An Introduction Into the Origins of Naval Academy Slang," Class Project, HE-111, USNA, Fall 1982, 18; Joseph Herlihy, "A Few Inches From The Yard," *Shipmate* 52, no. 9 (Nov. 1989): 30.

119 1978 LB, 22.

120 *Reminiscences of Rear Admiral Robert W. McNitt*, 629–30.

121 Bradley Peniston, "The Highest Honor," EC, undated, SCF "U.S. Naval Academy: Midshipmen."

122 "Naval Academy Midshipmen Action Group Plans Upcoming Events," Public Affairs Office Release, 22 Mar. 1991, 3, ARF "Midshipmen: Midshipmen Action Group"; Patricia Barrows, "Mids . . . You Can Count On 'Em," *Trident*, 5 May 2000, 9.

123 EI with Blake Bush, Santa Clara, Calif., 5 June 2000.

124 "Midshipmen Action Group," USNAW (<www.usna.edu/mag>, 24 Oct. 2002).

125 Isserman and Kazin, *America Divided*, 302.

126 Lekfowitz-Horowitz, *Campus Life*, xi.

127 Pam Warnken, "Dant To Command Norfolk Battle Group," *Trident*, 10 Dec. 1999, 1.

Conclusion

1 *Reminiscences of Rear Admiral John F. Davidson*, 363.

2 James Calvert to Parents, 21 May 1972, CR, Sec. 5400/19, Folder "1972."

3 "Edited Remarks as Delivered by The Honorable Richard Danzig, Secretary of the Navy, Forrestal Lecture Series, U.S. Naval Academy, Annapolis, Maryland, 17 April 2000," USNW (<www.chinfo.navy.mil/navpalib/people/secnav/speeches/forrestal 0417.html>, 30 June 2000), 9. For commentary on homosexuality and homoeroticism at USNA, see Fleming, *Annapolis Autumn*, 131, 147–50, 272.

4 John Bodnar, "How Long Does It Take to Change a Culture?: Integration at the U.S. Naval Academy," *Armed Forces and Society* 25, no. 2 (Winter 1999): 290.

5 Wendy Lawrence, Address before the Combined Service Academy Study Group, USNA, Annapolis, Md., 19 Oct. 1999.

6 Charles Bolden, Address before the Black Midshipmen Study Group, USNA, Annapolis, Md., 9 Feb. 1999.

7 Hugh Thompson, Address before Midshipmen Enrolled in Ethics Courses, USNA, Annapolis, Md., 8 Apr. 1999.

8 *Reminiscences of Vice Admiral William P. Mack*, 814.

9 "Leadership laboratory" is a common term that members of the Academy community utilize to describe USNA's role in educating midshipmen and then allowing them to develop their leadership skills.

Bibliography

Archival Sources

Annapolis, Maryland
    United States Naval Academy, Nimitz Library, Archives
        Archives Reference Files
        Board of Visitors Reports
        National Archives and Records Administration, U.S. Naval Academy Records
        Records of the Commandant
        Records of the Superintendent
    United States Naval Academy, Nimitz Library, Electronic Resources Center Collections
    United States Naval Academy, Nimitz Library, Special Collections
        Eugene Shine Papers
        The Log Splinter Collection
        Midshipman First Class Papers
        Special Collections Reference Files
        U.S. Navy Chaplain Corps Oral History Program Collection
        William Renwick Smedberg Papers
    United States Naval Institute, Oral History Collections
        Oral Histories with the First Female Graduates of the U.S. Naval Academy
            Collection
        Published Oral History Collection
        Unpublished Oral History Collection
Austin, Texas
    Lyndon B. Johnson Presidential Library
        Lyndon B. Johnson Presidential Papers
Chicago, Illinois
    Playboy Enterprises, Incorporated
        Playboy Magazine Archives
College Park, Maryland
    National Archives and Records Administration
        Motion Picture, Sound, and Video Collection
Los Angeles, California
    Lucian K. Truscott IV Papers, Personal Collection

Madison, Wisconsin
   Wisconsin Historical Society/University of Wisconsin
      Wisconsin Center for Film and Theater Research
         Film and Archival Collections
Newport, Rhode Island
   United States Naval Academy Preparatory School, Collection of Yearbooks
Skowhegan, Maine
   Margaret Chase Smith Library
      Margaret Chase Smith Papers
Suitland, Maryland
   National Archives and Records Administration, Washington National Records Center
      United States Court of Appeals for the District of Columbia Records
         Anderson v. Laird Papers
         Waldie v. Schlesinger Papers
      United States District Court for the District of Columbia Records
         Anderson v. Laird Papers
         Waldie v. Schlesinger Papers
Tucson, Arizona
   H. Michael Gelfand Papers, Personal Collection
Washington, D.C.
   National Park Service
      National Register of Historic Places Records
   U.S. Marine Corps Historical Center, Washington Navy Yard
      Reference Files
   U.S. Naval Historical Center, Washington Navy Yard
      Reference Files
West Point, New York
   United States Military Academy Library, Special Collections
      Special Collections Vertical Files

Interviews by the Author

Please see the Note on Sources for further information about interviews.

Anonymous Interviews
Non-Anonymous Interviews
   Clifford Alexander Jr., Washington, D.C.
   Sherman Alexander, St. Petersburg, Florida
   Michael Anderson, Red Wing, Minnesota
   Steven Arendt, Newport, Rhode Island
   James Bell, Alexandria, Virginia
   Richard Black, Newport, Rhode Island, and Annapolis, Maryland
   Philip Brown, Annapolis, Maryland
   Rachel Brown, Annapolis, Maryland

Charles Buchanan, Annapolis, Maryland
Julian Burke, Alexandria, Virginia
Blake Bush, Santa Clara, California
Janice Buxbaum, Springfield, Virginia
James Calvert, St. Michaels, Maryland
Rick Clothier, Annapolis, Maryland
Robert Coogan, San Diego, California
Asbury Coward IV, Annapolis, Maryland
Croom Coward, Annapolis, Maryland
Karen DeCrow, Jamesville, New York
Tina Marie D'Ercole, Alexandria, Virginia
Sharon Disher, Annapolis, Maryland
Sean Doyle, Annapolis, Maryland
Marcy Dupre, Pensacola, Florida
Jean Ebbert, Alexandria, Virginia
Leon Edney, Annapolis, Maryland, and Coronado, California
Seymour Einstein, Tucson, Arizona
Jim Farley, Washington, D.C.
Patrick Finnegan, West Point, New York
Donald K. Forbes, Manassas, Virginia
Shannon French, Annapolis, Maryland
Joe Glover, Dallas, Texas
Dick Goodwin, Lake Oswego, Oregon
Ben Holt, Wyckoff, New Jersey
Warren Kaplan, Washington, D.C.
Randolph King, Annapolis, Maryland
Charles Larson, Annapolis, Maryland
Samuel Locklear, Annapolis, Maryland
Bradford McDonald, Annapolis, Maryland
John McMaster, Tucson, Arizona
Robert McNitt, Annapolis, Maryland
William Miller, Annapolis, Maryland
Donald Montgomery, Annapolis, Maryland
Kevin Mulkern, San Diego, California
Mike Nassr, Roswell, Georgia
Bradley Nemeth, San Diego, California
Michael Oliver, San Diego, California
Ed Peery, Annapolis, Maryland
H. Ross Perot, Dallas, Texas
Gary Roughead, Annapolis, Maryland
W. Rick Rubel, Annapolis, Maryland
Leonard Sapera, Athens, Georgia
Edith Seashore, Columbia, Maryland
Dave Smalley, Annapolis, Maryland

William Smedberg IV, Ponte Vedra Beach, Florida
Lynne Smith, Tulsa, Oklahoma
Cheryl Spohnholtz, Alexandria, Virginia
Gloria Steinem, New York, New York
Elizabeth Sternaman, Annapolis, Maryland
Judith Stiehm, Santa Monica, California
Mary Jo Sweeney, Norfolk, Virginia, and Annapolis, Maryland
Lucian Truscott IV, Los Angeles, California
David Vaught, Naperville, Illinois, and Los Angeles, California
Nicholas Visco, Springfield, Virginia
James Winnefeld, Annapolis, Maryland
Takeshi Yoshihara, Aiea, Hawaii

Magazines, Journals, and Newspapers

The Afro-American
American Architect and Building News
American Enterprise
Annapolitan Magazine
Armed Forces and Society
Asian Week
Baltimore Sun
Catholic Review
Character Quarterly
Chronicle of Higher Education
Congressional Quarterly
Evening Capital
Indiana Magazine of History
Journal of Military History
The LOG
The LOG Splinter
Maryland Gazette
Military Affairs
Minerva
Naval History
Naval Law Review
Navy: The Magazine of Sea Power
Navy Times
Negro History Bulletin
New Haven Register
New Republic
Newsweek
New York Times
New York Times Magazine

Playboy
Representations
Saturday Evening Post
Scientific American
Shipmate
Smithsonian
South Carolina Historical Magazine
Trident
United States Naval Institute Proceedings
USA Today
Wall Street Journal
Washingtonian Magazine
Washington Post
Waterloo Sunday Courier
Yard Talk

Books

Alexander, Adele Logan. *Homelands and Waterways: The American Journey of the Bond Family, 1846–1926*. New York: Pantheon Books, 1999.

Alexander, Kern, and Erwin Solomon. *College and University Law*. Charlottesville, Va.: Michie Co., 1972.

Allen, William. *George Washington: A Collection*. Indianapolis: Liberty Classics, 1988.

The Anchor Watch. The Annual of the U.S. Naval Reserve (Officers) Force. Annapolis: U.S. Naval Academy, 1918.

Andersen, Gene, ed. *Leadership: Theory and Application*. Needham Heights, Mass.: Simon and Schuster, 1999.

Anderson, Alan, and George Pickering. *Confronting the Color Line: The Broken Promise of the Civil Rights Movement in Chicago*. Athens: University of Georgia Press, 1986.

Appleby, Joyce, Lynn Hunt, and Margaret Jacob. *Telling The Truth About History*. New York: Norton, 1994.

Bacon, Mardges. *Ernest Flagg: Beaux Arts Architect and Urban Reformer*. New York: Architectural History Foundation, 1986.

Bailey, Beth. *From Front Porch to Backseat: Courtship in Twentieth-Century America*. Baltimore: Johns Hopkins University Press, 1988.

Barnouw, Eric. *A History of Broadcasting in the United States*. Vol. 2, *The Golden Web, 1933 to 1953*. New York: Oxford University Press, 1968.

———. *A History of Broadcasting in the United States*. Vol. 3, *The Image Empire, From 1953*. New York: Oxford University Press, 1970.

Barone, Michael, Grant Ujifusa, and Douglas Matthews. *The Almanac of American Politics: The Senators, The Representatives—Their Records, States, and Districts, 1974*. Boston: Gambit, 1974.

Bearden, Bill, ed. *The Bluejackets' Manual*. 21st ed. Annapolis: U.S. Naval Institute Press, 1990.

Beschloss, Michael, ed. *Reaching For Glory: Lyndon Johnson's Secret White House Tapes, 1964–1965*. New York: Simon and Shuster, 2001.

Bilton, Michael, and Kevin Sim. *Four Hours in My Lai*. New York: Penguin, 1993.

Biographical Directory of the American Congress, 1774–1996. Alexandria, Va.: C. Q. Staff Directories, 1997.

Blitz, Amy. *The Contested State: American Foreign Policy and Regime Change in the Philippines*. Lanham, Md.: Rowman and Littlefield, 2000.

Bourne, Peter. *Jimmy Carter: A Comprehensive Biography from Plains to Post-Presidency*. New York: Scribners, 1997.

Brown, Philip. *A Century of Separate but Equal in Anne Arundel County*. New York: Vantage, 1988.

———. *The Other Annapolis: 1900–1950*. Annapolis: Annapolis Publishing Co., 1994.

Brumberg, Joan. *The Body Politic: An Intimate History of American Girls*. New York: Random House, 1997.

Calcott, George. *Maryland and America: 1940–1980*. Baltimore: Johns Hopkins University Press, 1985.

Calvert, James. *The Naval Profession*. New York: McGraw-Hill, 1971.

Carabillo, Toni, Judith Meuli, and June Bundy Csida. *Feminist Chronicles: 1953–1993*. Los Angeles: Women's Graphics, 1993.

Carroll, Ward. *Punk's War*. Annapolis: U.S. Naval Institute Press, 2001.

Claassen, Harold, and Steve Boda Jr. *Ronald Encyclopedia of Football*. New York: Ronald Press Co., 1961.

Coffman, Edward. *The Old Army: A Portrait of the American Army in Peacetime, 1784–1898*. New York: Oxford University Press, 1986.

Crackel, Theodore. *West Point: A Bicentennial History*. Lawrence: University Press of Kansas, 2002.

Cremin, Lawrence. *American Education: The Colonial Experience, 1607–1783*. New York: Harper and Row, 1970.

———. *American Education: The Metropolitan Experience, 1876–1980*. New York: Harper and Row, 1988.

———. *American Education: The National Experience, 1783–1876*. New York: Harper and Row, 1980.

Cross, Wilbur. *Samuel Stratton: A Story of Political Gumption*. New York: James H. Heineman, 1964.

The Cruise. The Annual of the Naval Academy Preparatory School. Bainbridge, Md., and Newport, R.I.: Naval Academy Preparatory School, various years.

Cummings, Missy. *Hornet's Nest: The Experiences of One of the Navy's First Female Fighter Pilots*. San Jose, Calif.: Writer's Showcase, 1999.

Cunningham, Noble, Jr. *In Pursuit of Reason: The Life of Thomas Jefferson*. Baton Rouge: Louisiana State University Press, 1987.

Dalfiume, Richard. *Desegregation of the Armed Forces: Fighting on Two Fronts, 1939–1953*. Columbia: University of Missouri Press, 1969.

Dallek, Robert. *Flawed Giant: Lyndon Johnson and His Times, 1961–1973*. New York: Oxford University Press, 1998.

D'Amico, Francine, and Laurie Weinstein, eds. *Gender Camouflage: Women and the U.S. Military*. New York: New York University Press, 1999.

Davidson, James, and Mark Lytle. *After the Fact: The Art of Historical Detection*. 4th ed. Vol. 2. Boston: McGraw Hill, 2000.

De Conde, Alexander. *Student Activism: Town and Gown in Historical Perspective*. New York: C. Scribner's Sons, 1971.

De Groot, Gerard, and Corinna Peniston-Bird, eds. *A Soldier and a Woman: Sexual Integration in the Military*. Harlow, U.K.: Longman, 2000.

De Pauw, Linda Grant. *Battle Cries and Lullabies: Women in War from Prehistory to the Present*. Norman: University of Oklahoma Press, 1998.

D'Ercole, Tina Marie. *Reflections: A Short Synopsis*. Burke, Va.: published by author, 1997.

Di Marco, Anthony. *The Big Bowl Football Guide*. New York: Putnam, 1976.

Dinnerstein, Leonard. *Antisemitism in America*. New York: Oxford University Press, 1994.

Dinnerstein, Leonard, and David Reimers. *Ethnic Americans: A History of Immigration*. 4th ed. New York: Columbia University Press, 1999.

Di Quinzio, Patrice, and Iris Marion Young, eds. *Feminist Ethics and Social Policy*. Bloomington: Indiana University Press, 1997.

Disher, Sharon Hanley. *First Class: Women Join the Ranks at the Naval Academy*. Annapolis: U.S. Naval Institute Press, 1998.

Divine, Robert, ed. *The Johnson Years*. Vol. 3, *LBJ At Home and Abroad*. Lawrence: University Press of Kansas, 1994.

Dober, Richard. *Campus Planning*. New York: Reinhold Publishing Co., 1963.

Dowling, Colette. *The Frailty Myth: Redefining the Physical Potential of Women and Girls*. New York: Random House, 2000.

Drake, St. Clair, and Horace Clayton, *Black Metropolis: A Study of Negro Life in a Northern City*. Rev. ed. Chicago: University of Chicago Press, 1993.

Drew, Anne Marie, ed. *Letters from Annapolis: Midshipmen Write Home, 1848–1969*. Annapolis: U.S. Naval Institute Press, 1998.

Durning, Kathleen. *Women at the Naval Academy: The First Year of Integration*. San Diego: Navy Personnel Research and Development Center, 1978.

Earle, Ralph. *Life at the U.S. Naval Academy*. New York: Putnam, 1917.

Ebbert, Jean, and Marie-Beth Hall. *Crossed Currents: Navy Women in a Century of Change*. 3rd ed. Washington, D.C.: Brassey's, 1999.

Eilerston, Douglas. *Major College Football Results, 1957–1981*. Kinston, N.C.: Opus Associates, 1982.

Eliot, T. S. *Notes Toward the Definition of Culture*. London: Faber and Faber, 1948.

Enloe, Cynthia. *Does Khaki Become You?: The Militarization of Women's Lives*. London: Pandora Press, 1988.

——. *Ethnic Soldiers: State Security and Divided Societies*. Athens: University of Georgia Press, 1990.

——. *Maneuvers: The International Politics of Militarizing Women's Lives*. Berkeley: University of California Press, 2000.

Evans, Robley. *A Sailor's Log: Recollections of Forty Years of Naval Life*. New York: D. Appleton and Co., 1901.

Evans, Sara. *Personal Politics: The Roots of Women's Liberation in the Civil Rights Movement and the New Left.* New York: Vintage Books, 1979.

Falla, Jack. *NCAA, The Voice of College Sports: A Diamond Anniversary History, 1906–1981.* Mission, Kans.: National Collegiate Athletic Association, 1981.

Festle, Mary Jo. *Playing Nice: Politics and Apologies in Women's Sports.* New York: Columbia University Press, 1996.

Fleming, Bruce. *Annapolis Autumn: Life, Death, and Literature at the U.S. Naval Academy.* New York: New Press, 2005.

——. *Sex, Art, and Audience: Dance Essays.* New York: Peter Lang, 2000.

Forney, Todd. *The Midshipman Culture and Educational Reform: The U.S. Naval Academy, 1946–1976.* Newark, Del.: University of Delaware Press, 2004.

Foucault, Michel. *Discipline and Punish: The Birth of the Prison.* New York: Vintage Books, 1979.

Franklin, John Hope. *The Color Line: Legacy for the Twenty-First Century.* Columbia: University of Missouri Press, 1993.

Franklin, John Hope, and Genna Rae McNeil, eds. *African Americans and the Living Constitution.* Washington, D.C.: Smithsonian Institution Press, 1995.

Franklin, John Hope, and Alfred Moss Jr. *From Slavery to Freedom: A History of African Americans.* New York: Knopf, 1994.

Frantzich, Stephen. *Citizen Democracy: Political Activists in a Cynical Age.* Lanham, Md.: Rowman and Littlefield, 1999.

Fraser, Ronald. *1968: A Student Generation In Revolt.* New York: Pantheon, 1988.

French, Shannon. *The Code of the Warrior: Exploring Warrior Values Past and Present.* Lanham, Md.: Rowman & Littlefied, 2003.

Gelb, Joyce, and Marian Palley. *Women and Public Policy: Reassessing Gender Politics.* Charlottesville: University of Virginia Press, 1996.

George, James. *The U.S. Navy in the 1990s: Alternatives for Action.* Annapolis: U.S. Naval Institute Press, 1992.

Giamatti, A. Bartlett. *Reflections on Our University.* Athens: University of Georgia Ferdinand Phinizy Lectures, 1985.

——. *The University and the Public Interest.* New York: Atheneum, 1981.

Gillon, Edmund, Jr., ed. *The Gibson Girl and Her America: The Best Drawings of Charles Dana Gibson.* New York: Dover Publications, 1969.

Godson, Susan. *Serving Proudly: A History of Women in the U.S. Navy.* Annapolis: U.S. Naval Institute Press, 2001.

The Golden Lucky Bag: Class of 1934. Annapolis: U.S. Naval Academy, 1984.

Gould, Alberta. *Lady of the Senate: A Life of Margaret Chase Smith.* Mt. Desert, Maine: Windswept House Publishers, 1995.

Gregory, James. *American Exodus: The Dust Bowl Migration and Okie Culture in California.* New York: Oxford University Press, 1989.

Hagan, Kenneth. *This People's Navy: The Making of American Sea Power.* New York: Free Press, 1991.

——, ed. *In Peace and War: Interpretations of American Naval History, 1775–1984.* 2nd ed. Westport, Conn.: Greenwood Press, 1984.

Halberstam, David. *The Fifties*. New York: Villard, 1993.

Hamlin, Talbot. *Benjamin Henry Latrobe*. New York: Oxford University Press, 1955.

Harris, Richard, and Sidney Milkis, eds. *Remaking American Politics*. Boulder, Colo.: Westview Press, 1989.

Hartmann, Frederick. *Naval Renaissance: The U.S. Navy in the 1980s*. Annapolis: U.S. Naval Institute Press, 1990.

Hattendorf, John, B. Mitchell Simpson III, and John Wadleigh. *Sailors and Scholars: The Centennial History of the U.S. Naval War College*. Newport, R.I.: Naval War College Press, 1984.

Haygood, Wil. *King of the Cats: The Life and Times of Adam Clayton Powell Jr.* Boston: Houghton-Mifflin Co., 1993.

Heise, J. Arthur. *The Brass Factories: A Frank Appraisal of West Point, Annapolis, and the Air Force Academy*. Washington, D.C.: Public Affairs Press, 1969.

Herring, George. *America's Longest War: The United States and Vietnam, 1950–1975*. 3rd ed. New York: Knopf, 1986.

Heymann, C. David. *RFK: A Candid Biography of Robert F. Kennedy*. New York: Dutton, 1998.

Hilty, James. *Robert Kennedy: Brother Protector*. Philadelphia: Temple University Press, 1997.

Hobsbawm, Eric, and Terence Ranger. *The Invention of Tradition*. Cambridge: Cambridge University Press, 1992.

Holm, Jeanne. *Women in the Military: An Unfinished Revolution*. Rev. ed. Novato, Calif.: Presidio Press, 1992.

Holm, Tom. *Strong Hearts, Wounded Souls: Native American Veterans of the Vietnam War*. Austin: University of Texas Press, 1996.

The Howitzer of Cadets. The Annual of the United States Military Academy. West Point: U.S. Military Academy, various years.

Hunt, Lynn, ed. *The New Cultural History*. Berkeley: University of California Press, 1989.

Hunter-Gault, Charlayne. *In My Place*. New York: Farrar, Straus, and Giroux, 1992.

Isaacs, Neil. *All The Moves: A History of College Basketball*. New York: Harper Colophon, 1984.

Isserman, Maurice, and Michael Kazin. *America Divided: The Civil War of the 1960s*. New York: Oxford University Press, 2000.

Javits, Jacob, and Rafael Steinberg. *Javits: The Autobiography of a Public Man*. Boston: Houghton-Mifflin, 1981.

Joyner, Charles. *Drums and Shadows: Survival Studies Among the Georgia Coastal Negroes*. Athens: University of Georgia Press, 1986.

Kammen, Michael. *Mystic Chords of Memory: The Transformation of Tradition in American Culture*. New York: Vintage, 1993.

Kaplin, William, and Barbara Lee. *The Law of Higher Education: A Comprehensive Guide to Legal Implications of Administrative Decision Making*. San Francisco: Jossey-Bass Publishers, 1995.

Karsten, Peter. *The Naval Aristocracy: The Golden Age of Annapolis and the Emergence of Modern American Navalism*. New York: Free Press, 1972.

Katzenstein, Mary, and Judith Reppy, eds. *Beyond Zero Tolerance: Discrimination in Military Culture*. Lanham, Md.: Rowman and Littlefield, 1999.

Kearns, Doris. *Lyndon Johnson and the American Dream*. New York: Harper and Row, 1976.

Keegan, John. *Fields of Battle: The Wars for North America*. New York: Vintage, 1997.

Kemper, Donald. *Decade of Fear: Senator Hennings and Civil Liberties*. Columbia: University of Missouri Press, 1965.

Kerber, Linda. *No Constitutional Right to Be Ladies: Women and the Obligations of Citizenship*. New York: Hill and Wang, 1998.

King, Margaret, and Randolph King. *The United States Naval Academy Chapel: ". . . For Those in Peril on the Sea."* Annapolis: U.S. Naval Academy Alumni Association, 1994.

King, Randolph. *The United States Naval Academy, 1845–1995: Chronology, Bibliography, and Sources of Information*. Arnold, Md.: Randolph King, 1995.

Kohn, Richard. *Eagle and Sword: The Federalists and the Creation of the Military Establishment in America, 1783–1802*. New York: Free Press, 1975.

Lamson, Peggy. *The Glorious Failure: Black Congressman Robert Brown Elliott and the Reconstruction in South Carolina*. New York: W. W. Norton, 1973.

Lefkowitz-Horowitz, Helen. *Campus Life: Undergraduate Cultures from the End of the Nineteenth Century to the Present*. New York: Alfred A. Knopf, 1987.

Levine, Lawrence. *Black Culture and Black Consciousness: Afro-American Folk Thought from Slavery to Freedom*. New York: Oxford University Press, 1977.

Lipsky, David. *Absolutely American: Four Years at West Point*. Boston: Houghton Mifflin, 2003.

Lovell, John. *Neither Athens Nor Sparta?: The American Service Academies in Transition*. Bloomington: Indiana University Press, 1979.

The Lucky Bag. The Annual of the Brigade of Midshipmen. Annapolis: U.S. Naval Academy, various years.

MacGregor, Morris, Jr. *Integration of the Armed Forces, 1940–1965*. Washington, D.C.: Military History, U.S. Army, 1981.

MacGregor, Morris, Jr., and Bernard Nalty. *Blacks in the U.S. Armed Forces: Basic Documents*. Wilmington, Del.: Scholarly Resources, 1977.

Mack, William, and Royal Connell. *Naval Ceremonies, Customs, and Traditions*. 5th ed. Annapolis: U.S. Naval Institute Press, 1980.

Maclean, Norman. *A River Runs Through It and Other Stories*. Chicago: University of Chicago Press, 2001.

Mahan, Alfred Thayer. *The Influence of Sea Power Upon History, 1660–1783*. Boston: Little, Brown, and Co., 1914.

Martis, Kenneth. *The Historical Atlas of the United States Congressional Districts, 1789–1983*. New York: Free Press, 1982.

Marty, Martin. *Modern American Protestantism and Its World*. Vol. 3, *Civil Religion, Church and State*. New York: K. G. Saur, 1992.

Mayer, David. *The Constitutional Thought of Thomas Jefferson*. Charlottesville: University of Virginia Press, 1994.

McCain, John, and Mark Salter. *Faith of My Fathers: A Family Memoir*. New York: Perennial, 1999.

McClain, Charles, ed. *Asian Indians, Filipinos, Other Asian Communities, and the Law*. New York: Garland, 1994.

Meade, Mark, ed. *Reef Points 1997–1998: The Annual Handbook of the Brigade of Midshipmen.*
Annapolis: U.S. Naval Academy, 1997.

Moore, Harold. *We Were Soldiers Once . . . And Young: Ia Drang—The Battle That Changed The
War In Vietnam.* New York: Random House, 1992.

Mullen, Bill. *Popular Fronts: Chicago and African-American Cultural Politics, 1935–1946.*
Urbana: University of Illinois Press, 1999.

Meyer, Leisa. *Creating GI Jane: Sexuality and Power in the Women's Army Air Corps During World
War II.* New York: Columbia University Press, 1996.

Nalty, Bernard. *Strength for the Fight: A History of Black Americans in the Military.* New York:
Free Press, 1986.

Navasky, Victor. *Kennedy Justice.* New York: Atheneum, 1971.

Nelson, Dennis. *The Integration of the Negro into the U.S. Navy.* Washington, D.C.: Office of
Naval Personnel, 1947.

Niiya, Brian, ed. *Japanese American History: An A–Z Reference from 1868 to the Present.* New
York: Facts on File, 1993.

Northrup, Herbert, et al. *Black and Minority Participation in the All-Volunteer Navy and Marine
Corps.* Philadelphia: University of Pennsylvania, 1979.

Oral History Transcript, R. A. Henry John Rotrige, CHC, USN (Ret.). Washington, D.C.: Oral
History Program, Chaplain Corps, U.S. Navy, 1983.

Oral History Transcript, Capt. Samuel Sobel, CHC, USN (Ret.). Washington, D.C.: Oral History
Program, Chaplains Corps, U.S. Navy, 1980.

Oral History Transcript, John D. Zimmerman, CHC, USN (Ret.). Washington, D.C.: Oral History
Program, Chaplains Corps, U.S. Navy, 1981.

Ortner, Sherry. *Making Gender: The Politics and Erotics of Culture.* Boston: Beacon Press, 1996.

Palmer, Jan. *The Vinson Court Era: The Supreme Court's Conference Votes; Data and Analysis.* New
York: AMS Press, 1990.

Pollack, Jack. *Earl Warren, the Judge Who Changed America.* Englewood Cliffs, N.J.: Prentice-
Hall, 1979.

Polmar, Norman, and Thomas B. Allen. *Rickover.* New York: Simon and Schuster, 1982.

Potter, E. B., ed. *Sea Power: A Naval History.* Annapolis: Naval Institute Press, 1981.

Powell, Adam Clayton, Jr. *Adam by Adam: The Autobiography of Adam Clayton Powell Jr.* New
York: Dial Press, 1971.

Poyer, David. *The Return of Philo T. McGiffin.* Annapolis: U.S. Naval Institute Press, 1997.

Pratt, Robert. *The Color of Their Skin: Education and Race in Richmond, Virginia, 1954–1989.*
Charlottesville: University Press of Virginia, 1992.

Pritchett, C. Herman. *Civil Liberties and the Vinson Court.* Chicago: University of Chicago
Press, 1954.

Prucha, Francis Paul. *The Great Father: The United States Government and the American Indians.*
Lincoln: University of Nebraska Press, 1993.

Puleston, W. D. *Mahan: The Life and Work of Captain Alfred Thayer Mahan, U.S.N.* New Haven:
Yale University Press, 1939.

Redlich, Norman, Bernard Schwartz, and John Attaniso. *Constitutional Law.* 2d ed. New
York: Matthew Bender and Co., 1989.

Reimers, David. *Still the Golden Door: The Third World Comes To America.* New York: Columbia University Press, 1985.

Reminiscences of Rear Admiral Julian T. Burke Jr., USN (Ret.). Annapolis: U.S. Naval Institute, 2003.

Reminiscences of Rear Admiral John F. Davidson, USN (Ret.). Annapolis: U.S. Naval Institute, 1986.

Reminiscences of Captain Roland W. Faulk, CHC, U.S. Navy (Ret.). Annapolis: U.S. Naval Institute, 1975.

Reminiscences of Rear Admiral Francis D. Foley, USN (Ret.). Annapolis: U.S. Naval Institute, 1988.

Reminiscences of Rear Admiral Draper L. Kauffman, USN (Ret.). Annapolis: U.S. Naval Institute, 1982.

Reminiscences of Vice Admiral William P. Mack, USN (Ret.). Annapolis: U.S. Naval Institute, 1980.

Reminiscences of Rear Admiral Robert W. McNitt, USN (Ret.). Annapolis: U.S. Naval Institute, 2002.

Reminiscences of Vice Admiral Charles L. Melson, USN (Ret.). Annapolis: U.S. Naval Institute, 1974.

Reminiscences of Vice Admiral Charles S. Minter Jr., USN (Ret.). Annapolis: U.S. Naval Institute, 1981.

Reminiscences of Vice Admiral William R. Smedberg III, USN (Ret.). Annapolis: U.S. Naval Institute, 1979.

Rosaldo, Renato. *Ilongot Headhunting, 1883–1974: A Study in Society and History.* Stanford, Calif.: Stanford University Press, 1980.

Ross, Marilyn. *Success Factors of Young African-American Males at Historically Black Colleges.* Westport, Conn.: Bergin and Garvey, 1998.

Rotundo, E. Anthony. *American Manhood: Transformations in Masculinity from the Revolution to the Modern Era.* New York: Basic Books, 1993.

Sahlins, Marshall. *Culture and Practical Reason.* Chicago: University of Chicago Press, 1976.

———. *How "Natives" Think: About Captain Cook, for Example.* Chicago: University of Chicago Press, 1995.

———. *Islands of History.* Chicago: University of Chicago Press, 1985.

Scanlon, Jennifer. *Significant Contemporary American Feminists: A Biographical Sourcebook.* Westport, Conn.: Greenwood Press, 1999.

Schaller, Michael, Virginia Scharff, and Robert Schulzinger. *Coming of Age: America in the Twentieth Century.* Boston: Houghton Mifflin, 1998.

Schlesinger, Arthur, Jr. *Robert Kennedy and His Times.* Boston: Houghton Mifflin, 1978.

Schneller, Robert, Jr. *Breaking the Color Barrier: The U.S. Naval Academy's First Black Midshipmen and the Struggle for Racial Equality.* New York: New York University Press, 2005.

Schorr, Gene, and Pete Dawkins. *100 Years of Army-Navy Football.* New York: Henry Holt, 1989.

Sellin, Harry, ed. *Proceedings of the New York University Conference on Practice and Procedure Under* the *Immigration and Nationality Act (McCarran-Walter Act)*. New York: New York University Press, 1954.

Sherman, Janann. *No Place For a Woman: A Life of Senator Margaret Chase Smith.* New Brunswick, N.J.: Rutgers University Press, 2000.

Sherry, Michael. *In The Shadow of War: The United States Since The 1930s.* New Haven, Conn.: Yale University Press, 1995.

Shesol, Jeff. *Mutual Contempt: Lyndon Johnson, Robert Kennedy, and the Feud That Defined a Decade.* New York: Norton, 1997.

Skerry, Peter. *Counting on the Census?: Race, Group Identity, and the Evasion of Politics.* Washington, D.C.: Brookings Institution Press, 2000.

Slaff, Allan. *The Navy Drag's Handbook.* 3rd ed. Annapolis: U.S. Naval Academy, 1944.

Sleight, Robert. *Sixteen Hundred Men: A Personal Remembrance, USNA, 1932–1936.* White Stone, Va.: Brandylane Publishers, 1998.

Smallwood, William. *The Naval Academy Candidate Book: How to Prepare, How to Get In, How to Survive.* Buhl, Idaho: Beacon Books, 1997.

Smith, Daryl. *The Challenge of Diversity: Involvement or Alienation in the Academy?* Washington, D.C.: George Washington University, 1989.

Smith, Margaret Chase. *Declaration of Conscience.* Garden City, N.Y.: Doubleday, 1972.

Steele, Fritz. *The Sense Of Place.* Boston: CBI, 1981.

Stegner, Wallace. *The Sound of Mountain Water: The Changing American West.* New York: Penguin, 1997.

Stewart, Robert. *The Brigade in Review: A Year at the U.S. Naval Academy.* Annapolis: U.S. Naval Institute Press, 1993.

Stiehm, Judith. *Bring Me Men and Women: Mandated Change at the U.S. Air Force Academy.* Berkeley: University of California Press, 1981.

———. *It's Our Military, Too!: Women and the U.S. Military.* Philadelphia: Temple University Press, 1996.

Stillwell, Paul, ed. *The Golden Thirteen: Recollections of the First Black Naval Officers.* Annapolis: U.S. Naval Institute Press, 1993.

Stockdale, James, and Sybil Stockdale. *In Love and War: The Story of a Family's Ordeal and Sacrifice During the Vietnam Years.* Annapolis: Naval Institute Press, 1990.

Suid, Lawrence. *Sailing on the Silver Screen: Hollywood and the U.S. Navy.* Annapolis: U.S. Naval Institute Press, 1996.

Susman, Warren. *Culture As History: The Transformation of American Society in the Twentieth Century.* New York: Pantheon Books, 1984.

Sweetman, Jack, and Thomas Cutler. *The U.S. Naval Academy: An Illustrated History.* 2nd ed. Annapolis: U.S. Naval Institute Press, 1995.

Thomas, Evan. *Robert Kennedy: His Life.* New York: Simon and Shuster, 2000.

Timberg, Robert, *The Nightingale's Song.* New York: Touchstone, 1995.

United States Naval Academy Alumni Association Register of Alumni, Graduates, and Former Naval Cadets and Midshipmen. Annapolis: United States Naval Academy Alumni Association, 1999.

United States Naval Academy North Severn Master Plan. Alexandria, Va.: Onyx Group, 1996.

University of Georgia Master Plan. Athens: University of Georgia Department of University Architects, 1999.

Urofsky, Melvin. *A March of Liberty: A Constitutional History of the United States*. New York: Alfred A. Knopf, 1988.

Valeo, Francis. *Mike Mansfield, Majority Leader: A Different Kind of Senate, 1961–1976*. Armonk, N.Y.: M. E. Sharpe, 1999.

Van Slyck, Abigail. *Free To All: Carnegie Libraries And American Culture, 1880–1920*. Chicago: University of Chicago Press, 1995.

Wallace, Patricia Ward. *Politics of Conscience: A Biography of Margaret Chase Smith*. Westport, Conn.: Praeger, 1995.

Warren, Mame. *Then Again . . . : Annapolis, 1900–1965*. Annapolis: Time Exposures, 1990.

Warshaw, Steven, ed. *The Gibson Girl: Drawings of Charles Dana Gibson*. Berkeley, Calif.: Diablo Press, 1968.

Webb, James. *A Sense of Honor*. Annapolis: U.S. Naval Institute Press, 1995.

Wertsch, Mary Edwards. *Military Brats: Legacies of Childhood Inside the Fortress*. New York: Harmony Books, 1991.

Wilkins, Roy, and Tom Mathews. *Standing Fast: The Autobiography of Roy Wilkins*. New York: Viking Press, 1982.

Wilson, August. *Fences: A Play*. New York: New American Library, 1986.

Wilson, Robert, ed. *Power and the Presidency*. New York: Public Affairs, 1999.

Young, Warren. *Minorities and the Military: A Cross-National Study in World Perspective*. Westport, Conn.: Greenwood Press, 1982.

Zinn, Howard. *A People's History of the United States, 1492–Present*. New York: Harper Perennial, 1995.

Zumwalt, Elmo, Jr. *On Watch: A Memoir*. New York: Quadrangle, 1976.

Theses, Dissertations, Trident Projects, and Honors Papers

Cantello, Albert. "An Investigation of Personality Changes Resulting from Participation in Varsity Intercollegiate Athletics at the U.S. Naval Academy." M.A. thesis, Bowie State College, 1974.

D'Ercole, Tina-Marie. "Combat Exclusion . . . Repealed!" M.A. thesis, Industrial College of the Armed Forces, National Defense University, 1998.

Hillman, Elizabeth Lutes. "Uniform Identities: Women, Gender, and Images at the United States Service Academies." M.A. thesis, University of Pennsylvania, 1994.

Lebby, David. "Professional Socialization of the Naval Officer: The Effect of Plebe Year at the U.S. Naval Academy." Ph.D. dissertation, University of Pennsylvania, 1970.

Neuberger, Carmen. "A Comparative Study of Environmental Expectations of Female v. Male Midshipmen Entering the United States Naval Academy." Ph.D. dissertation, American University, 1977.

Rouse, Morleen. "A History of the F. W. Ziv Radio and Television Syndication Companies, 1930–1960." Ph.D. dissertation, University of Michigan, 1976.

Salkoff, Jonatahan. "Changing Attitudes Toward Devotion and Duty in Western Literature." Trident Scholar Project, U.S. Naval Academy, 1990.

Sheppard, Charles. "An Analysis of Curriculum Changes at the United States Naval Academy During the Period 1959 through 1974." Ph.D. dissertation, George Washington University, 1974.

Smith, Barrett. "Hazing, Honor, and the Early Twentieth Century Naval Academy." History Honors Thesis, U.S. Naval Academy, 2000.

Index

Lindquist, Beth, 161
Lipsky, David, xxiii, 224
Locklear, Samuel, 19, 74, 184, 186–87, 238
"Lock-step" curriculum, 16–18, 192
LOG (USNA publication), xxii, 20, 34, 38,
    41, 55, 69, 70, 74, 84, 90, 98, 111, 113–
    14, 118, 130–31, 138–39, 140, 152, 164–
    66, 171–72, 173, 176, 181, 186, 201–8,
    205, 218, 222–23, 338 (n. 93)
Lovell, John, xxii, 12, 126, 133, 224
Lowndes, Barbette Henry, 161
Luce, Stephen, 3
Luce Hall, 9
Lucky Bag (USNA yearbook), 35, 47, 49–
    50, 74–75, 102, 105–106, 110, 157, 199,
    201, 207, 222
Lynch, Thomas, 22, 33, 77, 178–80, 238
Lyndon B. Johnson Presidential Library,
    223

MacArthur, Douglas, 126
Macdonough Hall, 244 (n. 15)
MacGregor, Marcus, 227
Mack, William, 11, 51, 65–67, 92–93, 104–
    7, 118–23, 125, 217, 226, 238
Mackenzie, Alexander, 2
MacKinnon, George, 102–4
Magnum P.I. (TV series), 71
Mahan, Alfred Thayer, 3–4
Mahan Hall, 7, 41, 244, n.15
Maine, USS, Foremast, 9
Mamas and Papas, 84
Mansfield, Mike, 120, 227
Marching and formations, 3, 16–17, 20,
    23, 33–34, 56, 80, 82, 110, 112, 142, 161,
    195, 202, 218
Marcy, Samuel, 3
Margaret Chase Smith Foundation, 206
Margaret Chase Smith Library, 223
Marix, Adolph, 48
Mark (film), 59–60
Marquette University, 17
Marryott, Ronald, 74, 166–67, 171, 175–
    76, 238

Marshall, M. E., 202
Maryland State House, 5
Masaoka, Michael, 48
Mascots, 22, 51, 84
Masculinity, xxii, 109, 117, 131, 133, 136,
    188, 228–29
Massie, Samuel, 59
Mathews, Tom, 227
Matsumura, Junzo, 48
Maury Hall, 7, 244 (n. 15)
McCain, John, xiii–xiv, 28, 198–99, 225
McCarran-Walter Act, 46
McCarthyism, xxii, 34
McCauley, William, 238
McClennan, Alonzo, 50–51
McComas, Robert, 89, 94
McDonald, Bradford, 186
McDonald, Jack, 116
McFarlane, Robert, 38–39
McKee, Kinnaird, 18, 30, 64–65, 106, 126–
    27, 129, 133, 136–37, 154, 238
McManus, Stephanie, 77
McNamara, Robert, 10, 58
McNitt, Robert, xviii, 14, 17, 19, 46, 83–84,
    129, 138–39, 141, 155, 166, 226
Meals. See King Hall, mess hall, and meals
Mealtime prayers, xxiii, 130, 306 (n. 166)
Medal of Honor recipients, 9, 13
Media Coverage of USNA, xvi, xxi, 10, 11,
    38, 55, 57–58, 60, 65–68, 72, 82–83,
    93, 110–12, 118, 126, 128–29, 139–41,
    144, 147, 152, 157, 159–60, 162, 164–65,
    174–76, 179–81, 195–96, 209, 342
    (n. 36)
Medical staff and assistance, 12, 127, 164,
    176, 179
Melnick, R. Shep, 120
Melson, Charles, 9, 14, 18, 45, 82, 226, 238
Memorial Hall, 7, 9, 26
Men of Annapolis (TV series), xx, 39–45, 42,
    222–23, 225
Mess Hall. See King Hall, mess hall, and
    meals
Metcalf, Lee, 206